More information about this series at https://link.springer.com/bookseries/7899

Communications in Computer and Information Science   **1755**

Miguel Botto-Tobar ·
Marcelo Zambrano Vizuete ·
Sergio Montes León · Pablo Torres-Carrión ·
Benjamin Durakovic (Eds.)

Applied Technologies

4th International Conference, ICAT 2022
Quito, Ecuador, November 23–25, 2022
Revised Selected Papers, Part I

 Springer

Editors
Miguel Botto-Tobar 🆔
Eindhoven University of Technology
Eindhoven, The Netherlands

Marcelo Zambrano Vizuete 🆔
Universidad Técnica del Norte
Ibarra, Ecuador

Sergio Montes León 🆔
Universidad Rey Juan Carlos
Madrid, Spain

Pablo Torres-Carrión 🆔
Universidad Técnica Particular de Loja
Loja, Ecuador

Benjamin Durakovic 🆔
International University of Sarajevo
Sarajevo, Bosnia and Herzegovina

ISSN 1865-0929   ISSN 1865-0937 (electronic)
Communications in Computer and Information Science
ISBN 978-3-031-24984-6   ISBN 978-3-031-24985-3 (eBook)
https://doi.org/10.1007/978-3-031-24985-3

This Springer imprint is published by the registered company Springer Nature Switzerland AG
The registered company address is: Gewerbestrasse 11, 6330 Cham, Switzerland

Preface

The Universidad de las Fuerzas Armadas ESPE in its 100th anniversary organized the International XVII Congress on Science and Technology and co-hosted the 4th International Conference on Applied Technologies (ICAT) in the main campus in Quito, Ecuador during November 23–25, 2022 and was organized in collaboration with GDEON. The ICAT series aims to bring together top researchers and practitioners working in different domains in the field of computer science to exchange their expertise and to discuss the perspectives of development and collaboration. The content of this volume is related to the following subjects:

- Communication
- e-Learning
- Intelligent Systems
- Machine Vision
- Security
- Technology Trends

ICAT 2022 received 415 submissions written in English by 1245 authors coming from 12 different countries. All these papers were peer-reviewed by the ICAT 2022 Program Committee consisting of 185 high-quality researchers. To ensure a high-quality and thoughtful review process, we assigned each paper at least three reviewers. Based on the peer reviews, 114 full papers were accepted, resulting in an 27% acceptance rate, which was within our goal of less than 40%.

We would like to express our sincere gratitude to the invited speakers for their inspirational talks, to the authors for submitting their work to this conference, and to the reviewers for sharing their experience during the selection process.

November 2022

Miguel Botto-Tobar
Marcelo Zambrano Vizuete
Sergio Montes León
Pablo Torres-Carrión
Benjamin Durakovic

Organization

General Chair

Miguel Botto-Tobar — Eindhoven University of Technology, The Netherlands

Program Committee Chairs

Miguel Botto-Tobar — Eindhoven University of Technology, The Netherlands
Marcelo Zambrano Vizuete — Universidad Técnica del Norte, Ecuador
Sergio Montes León — Universidad Rey Juan Carlos, Spain
Pablo Torres-Carrión — Universidad Técnica Particular de Loja, Ecuador
Benjamin Durakovic — International University of Sarajevo, Bosnia and Herzegovina

Organizing Chairs

Miguel Botto-Tobar — Eindhoven University of Technology, The Netherlands
Marcelo Zambrano Vizuete — Universidad Técnica del Norte, Ecuador
Sergio Montes León — Universidad Rey Juan Carlos, Spain
Pablo Torres-Carrión — Universidad Técnica Particular de Loja, Ecuador
Benjamin Durakovic — International University of Sarajevo, Bosnia and Herzegovina

Steering Committee

Miguel Botto-Tobar — Eindhoven University of Technology, The Netherlands
Angela Díaz Cadena — Universitat de Valencia, Spain

Program Committee

Andrea Bonci — Marche Polytechnic University, Italy
Ahmed Lateef Khalaf — Al-Mamoun University College, Iraq
Aiko Yamashita — Oslo Metropolitan University, Norway
Alejandro Donaire — Queensland University of Technology, Australia

Alejandro Ramos Nolazco	Instituto Tecnólogico y de Estudios Superiores Monterrey, Mexico
Alex Cazañas	The University of Queensland, Australia
Alex Santamaria Philco	Universitat Politècnica de València, Spain
Alfonso Guijarro Rodriguez	University of Guayaquil, Ecuador
Allan Avendaño Sudario	Escuela Superior Politécnica del Litoral (ESPOL), Ecuador
Alexandra González Eras	Universidad Politécnica de Madrid, Spain
Ana Núñez Ávila	Universitat Politècnica de València, Spain
Ana Zambrano	Escuela Politécnica Nacional (EPN), Ecuador
Andres Carrera Rivera	University of Melbourne, Australia
Andres Cueva Costales	University of Melbourne, Australia
Andrés Robles Durazno	Edinburgh Napier University, UK
Andrés Vargas Gonzalez	Syracuse University, USA
Angel Cuenca Ortega	Universitat Politècnica de València, Spain
Ángela Díaz Cadena	Universitat de València, Spain
Angelo Trotta	University of Bologna, Italy
Antonio Gómez Exposito	University of Sevilla, Spain
Aras Can Onal	Tobb University Economics and Technology, Turkey
Arian Bahrami	University of Tehran, Iran
Benoît Macq	Université catholique de Louvain, Belgium
Benjamin Durakovic	International University of Sarajevo, Bosnia and Herzegovina
Bernhard Hitpass	Universidad Federico Santa María, Chile
Bin Lin	Università della Svizzera italiana (USI), Switzerland
Carlos Saavedra	Escuela Superior Politécnica del Litoral (ESPOL), Ecuador
Catriona Kennedy	University of Manchester, UK
César Ayabaca Sarria	Escuela Politécnica Nacional (EPN), Ecuador
Cesar Azurdia Meza	University of Chile, Chile
Christian León Paliz	Université de Neuchâtel, Switzerland
Chrysovalantou Ziogou	Chemical Process and Energy Resources Institute, Greece
Cristian Zambrano Vega	Universidad de Málaga, Spain, and Universidad Técnica Estatal de Quevedo, Ecuador
Cristiano Premebida	Loughborough University, ISR-UC, UK
Daniel Magües Martinez	Universidad Autónoma de Madrid, Spain
Danilo Jaramillo Hurtado	Universidad Politécnica de Madrid, Spain
Darío Piccirilli	Universidad Nacional de La Plata, Argentina
Darsana Josyula	Bowie State University, USA
David Benavides Cuevas	Universidad de Sevilla, Spain

Marcelo Zambrano Vizuete	Universidad Técnica del Norte, Ecuador
María José Escalante Guevara	University of Michigan, USA
María Reátegui Rojas	University of Quebec, Canada
Mariela Tapia-Leon	University of Guayaquil, Ecuador
Marija Seder	University of Zagreb, Croatia
Marisa Daniela Panizzi	Universidad Tecnológica Nacional – Regional Buenos Aires, Argentina
Marius Giergiel	KRiM AGH, Poland
Markus Schuckert	Hong Kong Polytechnic University, Hong Kong, China
Matus Pleva	Technical University of Kosice, Slovakia
Mauricio Verano Merino	Technische Universiteit Eindhoven, The Netherlands
Mayken Espinoza-Andaluz	Escuela Superior Politécnica del Litoral (ESPOL), Ecuador
Miguel Botto-Tobar	Eindhoven University of Technology, The Netherlands
Miguel Fornell	Escuela Superior Politécnica del Litoral (ESPOL), Ecuador
Miguel Gonzalez Cagigal	Universidad de Sevilla, Spain
Miguel Murillo	Universidad Autónoma de Baja California, Mexico
Miguel Zuñiga Prieto	Universidad de Cuenca, Ecuador
Mohamed Kamel	Military Technical College, Egypt
Mohammad Al-Mashhadani	Al-Maarif University College, Iraq
Mohammad Amin	Illinois Institute of Technology, USA
Monica Baquerizo Anastacio	Universidad de Guayaquil, Ecuador
Muneeb Ul Hassan	Swinburne University of Technology, Australia
Nam Yang	Technische Universiteit Eindhoven, The Netherlands
Nathalie Mitton	Inria, France
Nayeth Solórzano Alcívar	Escuela Superior Politécnica del Litoral (ESPOL), Ecuador and Griffith University, Australia
Noor Zaman	King Faisal University, Saudi Arabia
Omar S. Gómez	Escuela Superior Politécnica del Chimborazo (ESPOCH), Ecuador
Óscar León Granizo	Universidad de Guayaquil, Ecuador
Oswaldo Lopez Santos	Universidad de Ibagué, Colombia
Pablo Lupera	Escuela Politécnica Nacional, Ecuador
Pablo Ordoñez Ordoñez	Universidad Politécnica de Madrid, Spain
Pablo Palacios	Universidad de Chile, Chile
Pablo Torres-Carrión	Universidad Técnica Particular de Loja (UTPL), Ecuador

Patricia Ludeña González	Universidad Técnica Particular de Loja (UTPL), Ecuador
Paulo Batista	CIDEHUS.UÉ-Interdisciplinary Center for History, Cultures, and Societies of the University of Évora, Portugal
Paulo Chiliguano	Queen Mary University of London, UK
Pedro Neto	University of Coimbra, Portugal
Praveen Damacharla	Purdue University Northwest, USA
Priscila Cedillo	Universidad de Cuenca, Ecuador
Radu-Emil Precup	Politehnica University of Timisoara, Romania
Ramin Yousefi	Islamic Azad University, Iran
René Guamán Quinche	Universidad de los Paises Vascos, Spain
Ricardo Martins	University of Coimbra, Portugal
Richard Ramirez Anormaliza	Universitat Politècnica de Catalunya, Spain
Richard Rivera	IMDEA Software Institute, Spain
Richard Stern	Carnegie Mellon University, USA
Rijo Jackson Tom	SRM University, India
Roberto Murphy	University of Colorado Denver, USA
Roberto Sabatini	RMIT University, Australia
Rodolfo Alfredo Bertone	Universidad Nacional de La Plata, Argentina
Rodrigo Barba	Universidad Técnica Particular de Loja (UTPL), Ecuador
Rodrigo Saraguro Bravo	Universitat Politècnica de València, Spain
Ronald Barriga Díaz	Universidad de Guayaquil, Ecuador
Ronnie Guerra	Pontificia Universidad Católica del Perú, Perú
Ruben Rumipamba-Zambrano	Universitat Politecnica de Catalanya, Spain
Saeed Rafee Nekoo	Universidad de Sevilla, Spain
Saleh Mobayen	University of Zanjan, Iran
Samiha Fadloun	Université de Montpellier, France
Sergio Montes León	Universidad de las Fuerzas Armadas (ESPE), Ecuador
Stefanos Gritzalis	University of the Aegean, Greece
Syed Manzoor Qasim	King Abdulaziz City for Science and Technology, Saudi Arabia
Tatiana Mayorga	Universidad de las Fuerzas Armadas (ESPE), Ecuador
Tenreiro Machado	Polytechnic of Porto, Portugal
Thomas Sjögren	Swedish Defence Research Agency (FOI), Sweden
Tiago Curi	Federal University of Santa Catarina, Brazil
Tony T. Luo	A*STAR, Singapore
Trung Duong	Queen's University Belfast, UK
Vanessa Jurado Vite	Universidad Politécnica Salesiana, Ecuador

Waldo Orellana	Universitat de València, Spain
Washington Velasquez Vargas	Universidad Politécnica de Madrid, Spain
Wayne Staats	Sandia National Labs, USA
Willian Zamora	Universidad Laíca Eloy Alfaro de Manabí, Ecuador
Yessenia Cabrera Maldonado	University of Cuenca, Ecuador
Yerferson Torres Berru	Universidad de Salamanca, Spain and Instituto Tecnológico Loja, Ecuador
Zhanyu Ma	Beijing University of Posts and Telecommunications, China

Organizing Institutions

Sponsoring Institutions

Collaborators

Contents – Part I

Machine Vision

Security

Technology Trends

Contents – Part II

Electronics

Knowledge Exploration in Life Sciences

Contents – Part III

Communications

Hybrid Solar-Radiofrequency Energy Harvesting System for Fifth Generation 5G Terminals

Carlos Gordón[1](✉) , Danny Merino[1] , Myriam Cumbajín[2] ,
and Carlos Peñafiel[3]

[1] GITED Research Group, Facultad de Ingeniería en Sistemas, Electrónica e Industrial,
Universidad Técnica de Ambato, UTA, 180207 Ambato, Ecuador
{cd.gordon,dmerino2235}@uta.edu.ec

[2] SISAu Research Center, Facultad de Ingeniería, Industria y Producción, Universidad
Tecnológica Indoamérica, UTI, 180103 Ambato, Ecuador
myriamcumbajin@uti.edu.ec

[3] Facultad de Ingeniería, Universidad Nacional de Chimborazo, UNACH, 060108 Riobamba,
Ecuador
carlospenafiel@unach.edu.ec

Abstract. This paper describes in detail the design and implementation process of a Hybrid Solar-Radiofrequency Energy Harvesting System for Fifth Generation 5G Terminals, in order to take advantage of the energies present in the environment and convert them into electrical energy, the system has two voltage outputs, 9 V and 5 V, that will serve as a power source for different applications. The methodology used consists of 4 stages in which the design, simulation, fabrication and characterization of the stages that conform the system are shown. Operational tests showed that the system works as indicated, during the day the system can fully charge a 9 V battery at 250 mA in approximately 3 h, while the total energy collected during a full night was 560 mV. The voltage outputs vary between 8.86 V and 5.04 V respectively when the battery is charging and 9.11 V and 5.16 V respectively when the battery is fully charged. This work is intended to lay a foundation for future research on hybrid energy harvesting systems.

Keywords: Energy harvesting · 5G terminals · Hybrid system · Solar · Radiofrequency

1 Introduction

In recent years, the use of clean energy has been gradually increasing, due to the need to reduce carbon emissions and pollution generated by traditional energy sources [1], different studies have focused on the generation of energy from renewable sources [2] and that do not imply a significant impact on the environment, such as solar energy and wind energy [3], which are currently being used for large-scale applications such as supplying electricity to cities or industries [4]. The technology known as Energy Harvesting is born from this premise, where the possibility of harnessing the energy present in the environment and transforming it into electrical energy, capable of powering low-consumption electronic devices such as wireless sensors, cell phones, IoT terminals, among others [5, 6]. Lately, several investigations focused on energy harvesting have been developed as shown in the articles: "A Survey on Recent Energy Harvesting Mechanisms", where the authors present a study about electromagnetic, electrostatic and piezoelectric energy harvesting [7] and "Recent advances and future prospects in energy harvesting technologies", which describes the development of materials, procedures and challenges presented by Energy Harvesting technologies [8].

The use of radiofrequency as a source for energy harvesting has been of great interest because signals such as radio, television, cell phone, Wi-Fi, satellite, among others, remain present in the environment all the time [9]. However, the energy collected by this type of system is low, usually in the millivolt range as shown in: "Logarithmic antennas for electromagnetic energy harvesting applications" [10]; "Portable Electromagnetic Energy Harvesting System" [11]; and "Radio frequency energy harvesting circuits design for the applications of low power electronics" [12].

A type of energy harvesting system that presents good results is the one that takes advantage of solar energy, the voltage collected by this type of system is higher compared to Radio Frequency, as shown in "An Efficient Solar Energy Harvesting System for Wireless Sensor Nodes" [13], However, these results vary according to the hours of the day, and during the night the energy harvesting is null. It is for this reason that we propose the design and implementation of an energy harvesting system that combines the advantages of radio frequency and solar systems to create an efficient hybrid system that is capable of continuously powering fifth generation 5G IoT devices. The methodology used for the development of the system is divided into 4 stages: the first one describes the design process of the elements that make up the system; the second one shows the simulations performed; the third describes the manufacturing method that was used; Finally, in the fourth stage, the methods used to take measurements are detailed.

2   Methodology

The methods used for the design, simulation, fabrication and characterization of each stage of the system are described below.

2.1   Design

The block diagram of the hybrid system is shown in Fig. 1. The solar panels convert solar energy into electrical energy which enters the Step-up converter that is responsible for raising it to the battery charger that delivers the voltage to the 9V battery until it is fully charged, then disconnects, the antenna captures the radio frequency waves present in the environment, the voltage multiplier rectifies and raises the voltage captured, This stage connects to the battery charger, the voltage selector stage works as a switch to keep the output voltage constant by switching between the Step-up converter voltage and the battery, finally the voltage divider stage reduces the 9 V output to 5 V which can be used for different applications.

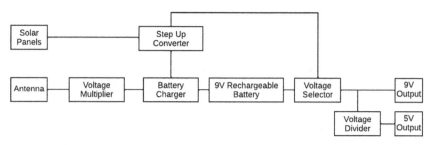

Fig. 1. Block diagram of proposed hybrid energy harvesting system.

Antenna

Of the several types of existing antennas for energy harvesting, the most used are the patch or microstrip type, likewise within this type of antennas there are a variety of geometries such as: square, rectangular, circular, elliptical, triangular, among others [14].

For the system, the design of a slotted patch antenna is proposed, and the resonance frequency is taken as $F_r = 2.4\,\text{GHz}$, the substrate material is FR4 glass fiber, which has a dielectric constant $\varepsilon_r = 4.3$ and a thickness $h = 1.465\,\text{mm}$. The following equations were used for the mathematical calculation.

Patch width

$$W = \frac{c}{2F_r} * \sqrt{\frac{2}{\varepsilon_r + 1}} \tag{1}$$

$$W = 3.839\,\text{cm}$$

Effective dielectric constant

$$\varepsilon_{\text{reff}} = \frac{\varepsilon_r + 1}{2} + \frac{\varepsilon_r - 1}{2} * \left[1 + 12\frac{h}{W}\right]^{-\frac{1}{2}} \tag{2}$$

$$\varepsilon_{\text{reff}} = 4.128$$

Patch length

$$\Delta L = (h)0.412 * \frac{(\varepsilon_{\text{reff}} + 0.3) * \left(\frac{W}{h} + 0.264\right)}{(\varepsilon_{\text{reff}} - 0.258) * \left(\frac{W}{h} + 0.8\right)} \tag{3}$$

$$\Delta L = 0.07637$$

$$L = \frac{c}{2(F_r)(\sqrt{\varepsilon_{\text{reff}}})} - 2(\Delta L) \tag{4}$$

$$L = 2.923\,\text{cm}$$

where W = patch width, c = speed of light $(3 \times 10^8 \text{m/s})$, F_r = Resonant frequency, ε_r = Dielectric constant of the substrate, $\varepsilon_{\text{reff}}$ = Effective dielectric constant of the patch, h = substrate thickness, and L = Patch length [14].

Solar Panels

For this stage we chose to use 4 identical solar panels, each one delivers a voltage of 2.4 V and a current of 80 mA when working at its maximum capacity, because the system must have the necessary current to power fifth generation 5G devices and also to charge the battery, a mixed Series-Parallel configuration was made, which is shown in Fig. 2. For the connection of the solar panels the calculations were made with Eqs. 5 and 6.

$$V_T = V_{panel1} + V_{panel2} = V_{panel3} + V_{panel4} \tag{5}$$

where V_T = Total voltage that will have the array of solar panels, because the panels are identical the voltage obtained by adding V_{panel1} and V_{panel2} is the same by adding V_{panel3} and V_{panel4} and as the voltage of two sources in parallel is maintained, this will be the output voltage of the array of panels $V_T = 4.8V$.

$$I_T = I_{serie1} + I_{serie2} \tag{6}$$

where I_T = Total current of the array, because when connecting two sources in series the current is maintained, the I_{serie1} is equal to the panel current in this case 80 mA, thus, the $I_T = 160$ mA.

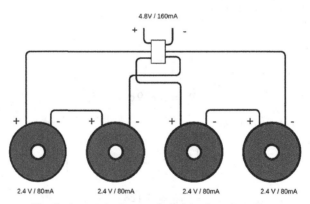

Fig. 2. Array of solar panels in mixed configuration.

Voltage Multiplier

For this stage, the design of a Cockcroft-Walton 5-stage voltage multiplier using 100 uF electrolytic capacitors and HSMS286C Schottky diodes is proposed because it presents better results for this type of applications than other diodes such as BAT43 or 1N5819, as shown in "Conditioning System for an Electromagnetic Energy Collection Device" [15], in addition to its low consumption of approximately 30 mV and fast response at high frequencies. Figure 3 shows the multiplier designed in Proteus software.

Step-Up Converter

The MT3608 Step-up converter was used for this stage due to its features such as: input voltage from 2 V to 24 V, adjustable output voltage up to 28 V, integrated current limiter,

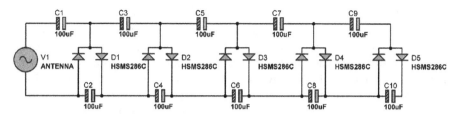

Fig. 3. Cockcroft-Walton 5 stage voltage multiplier designed.

low current consumption, efficiency up to 97% and small size, making it perfect for use in low power applications. The circuit design was based on the basic application circuit suggested in the datasheet. Thus, the circuit shown in Fig. 4 was obtained.

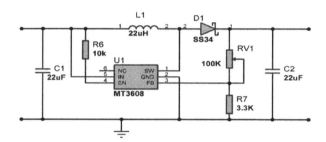

Fig. 4. Step-up converter designed.

Battery Charger

For the battery charger circuit, a simple configuration was chosen using a 5 V relay, 2 Schottky 1N5819W diodes, 1 S8050 transistor and 1K precision potentiometer. The battery is connected to the normally closed pin of the relay, once the battery voltage reaches its maximum charge the relay is activated sending the charge voltage to the normally open pin, with the potentiometer the maximum charge voltage that the battery will reach can be varied. Figure 5 shows the battery charger circuit designed in Proteus.

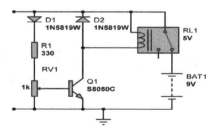

Fig. 5. Battery charger circuit designed.

Voltage Selector
This stage was designed so that the output voltage of the system is constant, and the battery is used only, when necessary, thus extending the life of the battery. A P-channel Mosfet transistor is used as a switch, 10K resistor and a Schottky diode. The designed circuit is shown in Fig. 6. In this way, whenever there is a positive voltage at the Mosfet gate, the Mosfet will remain open and the output voltage will be the one coming from the Step-up converter, while if the Step-up converter voltage drops, the Pull-Down resistor grounds the Mosfet gate, so it will close allowing the battery voltage to pass through, the Schottky diode serves as protection.

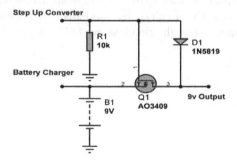

Fig. 6. Voltage selector circuit designed.

Voltage Divider
To also have an output of 5 V for applications that require lower supply voltage, a voltage divider circuit is made using two resistors, for the calculation of their values Eq. 5 is used where V_o = output voltage and V_{in} = input voltage. A value of $R_1 = 1K$ is used and the input voltage $V_{in} = 9V$, with this data can be replaced in Eq. 5 and clear R_2 to calculate its value.

$$V_o = V_{in} * \frac{R_2}{R_1 + R_2} \tag{7}$$

$$R_2 = 1.25K$$

Circuit Diagram
Once the design of each stage of the system was completed and to optimize dimensions, it was decided to unify the stages of Step-up converter, Battery Charger, Voltage Selector and Voltage Divider, in a single circuit, thus obtaining the circuit shown in Fig. 7.

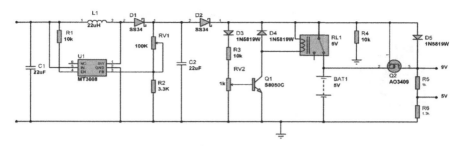

Fig. 7. Diagram of the combined circuits.

2.2 Simulation

Antenna
To perform the simulation of the patch antenna, the CST STUDIO SUITE 2019 software is used since it allows the design, analysis, and optimization of electromagnetic systems with a high precision, it also has the necessary simulation tools to determine the results required for the study.

Slots
As shown in the article "Design and Analysis of Slotted Microstrip Patch Antenna, A review" [16] adding slots to the patch antenna geometry affects various antenna properties such as gain, radiation pattern, directivity and return loss, depending on the shape, number, and dimensions of the slots. Another benefit is harmonic suppression as described in "A 2.45 GHz Harmonic Suppression Rectangular Patch Antenna with Circular Polarization for Wireless Power Transfer Application" [17].

With this information as a basis, tests were carried out with different types of slots until reaching the design shown in Fig. 8(a), as the upper corners were also rounded, with this design it was possible to reduce the frequency of the second harmonic up to 2.43 GHz to -16.2 dB, also taking as a reference a resonance threshold of -10 dB, the antenna would work from 2.29 GHz up to 2.46 GHz. Figure 8(b), shows a comparison between the results obtained at the beginning (red line) and once the slots were inserted (green line).

Solar Panels
For the simulation of the solar panels, the MatLab-Simulink software is used, with the PV ARRAY component a mixed array of panels can be simulated, the characteristic data of the panels is entered. The results obtained were: 4.8V and 160 mA, these results are shown in Fig. 9.

2.3 Fabrication

Antenna
For the fabrication of the antenna the ironing method is used, for this the design made in

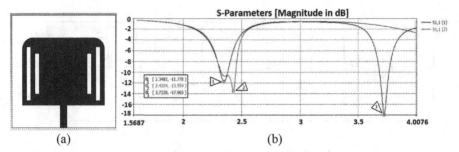

(a)   (b)

Fig. 8. a) Designed 2.43 GHz slotted patch antenna, b) Comparison between the patch antenna without slots (red line) and with slots (green line). (Color figure online)

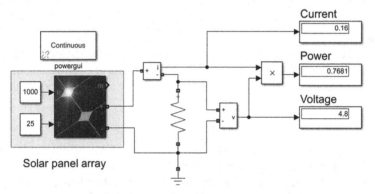

Fig. 9. Mixed solar panel array simulation in MatLab.

CST Studio Suite was exported to a DXF file to later transform it to a PNG image file, to finally print the design and fabricate it in FR4 substrate. Figure 10 shows the result of the antenna fabrication. Finally, a 50-Ω RP-SMA male connector is soldered.

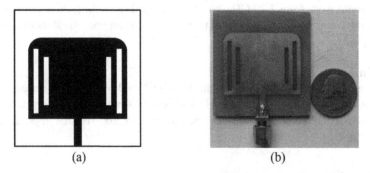

(a)   (b)

Fig. 10. (a) Designed antenna, (b) Manufactured antenna.

Circuits Fabrication

Once the circuits have been designed in Proteus, the PCB Wizard tool is used to design the PCB Layout of each one, due to the size of the elements used, it has been necessary to use precision tools for SMD soldering. Figure 11 shows the PCB Layout designed and the manufacturing result for the circuits of the designed system.

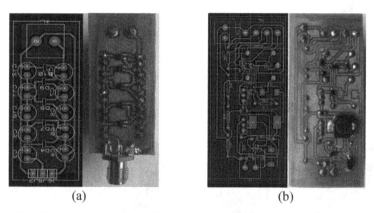

(a)   (b)

Fig. 11. PCB layout and fabricated a) voltage multiplier circuit, b) complete system.

2.4 Characterization

Antenna

To analyze the parameters of the manufactured slotted patch antenna, the NanoVNA V2 vector network analyzer is used, in which the parameter S11, S22 and antenna impedance are measured. The analyzer must be calibrated before use. Figure 12 shows the result obtained by the analyzer, the resonance frequency of the antenna is 2.429 GHz at − 15.71 dB, with frequencies between 2.395 GHz and 2.461 GHz being below −10 dB and an impedance of 50 ohms at 2.431 GHz.

Solar Panel

The voltage and current delivered by the mixed array of solar panels were measured using a multimeter. The tests were performed at 12:05 pm with a completely clear sky, and a measured voltage of 4.51 V and a current of 160.4 mA were obtained. Figure 13 shows results of practical measurements.

Voltage Multiplier

To conduct the measurement of the voltage multiplier circuit, it must be connected to the antenna. For this reason, an SMA connector is soldered to connect the antenna and the multiplier. In this case, for reasons of availability, a male SMA connector was used and a SMA female to RP-SMA male adapter. The measurements were made next to a Huawei Wi-Fi router. Figure 14 shows the measurement that resulted in a maximum voltage of 597 mV.

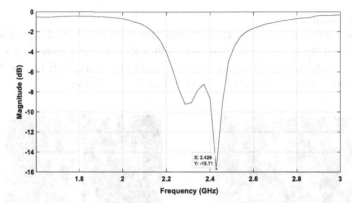

Fig. 12. Graph of parameter S11 measured from the manufactured antenna.

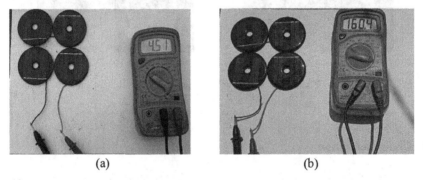

(a)   (b)

Fig. 13. Measurements taken from the solar mixed panel array: a) measured voltage, b) measured current.

Fig. 14. Voltage measured at the output of the 5-stage voltage multiplier.

Step-up Converter

Using a multimeter, the operation of the designed Step-up converter is verified, finding that the circuit starts to work from 1.8 V. As shown in Fig. 15, the circuit reaches a maximum output voltage of 29.5 V when 2 V is supplied to its input. From here on, no changes will be registered in the output of the circuit despite increasing the input voltage.

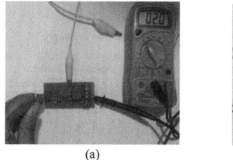

| (a) | (b) |

Fig. 15. a) input voltage, b) Step-up converter output voltage.

Implemented System

Once the operation of each of the circuits that make up the system has been verified, they are connected to each other according to the block diagram shown in Fig. 1. The complete system is shown in Fig. 16. During the day, the greatest amount of energy will be obtained from the solar panels, while, at night, the antenna will be the one that provides the voltage to the circuit.

| (a) | (b) |

Fig. 16. Hybrid Solar-Radiofrequency Energy Harvesting System for Fifth Generation 5G Terminals. a) Solar Panels, b) Antenna, circuits, and battery.

3 Analysis of Results

Once the operation of each of the stages was verified, energy storage tests were conducted using a 9V battery at 250 mA and a 1000 uF Capacitor at 50V, in three different environments: next to a Wi-Fi router, in the garden of a house located in the urban area and in the gardens of the Technical University of Ambato (UTA). In Table 1. The results of the measurements of the voltage captured by the antenna are shown, as can be seen the antenna collected more voltage when placing it near a 2.4 GHz radiation source such as the Wi-Fi Router.

Table 1. Energy Harvested by the Antenna in a 9V rechargeable battery.

Ambient	Delivered Voltage (V)	Initial Voltage (V)	Voltage Harvested in Minutes (V)			Voltage Harvested (V)
			30	60	90	
Wi-Fi Router	0.597	8.51	8.58	8.62	8.66	0.150
Urban area	0.0421	8.3	8.31	8.32	8.33	0.030
Garden of UTA	0.0642	8.37	8.39	42	8.43	0.060

Tests were conducted with the solar panels, the measurements were taken on a sunny day and a cloudy day, in this way it can be determined how the weather influences the amount of energy stored in each time. As shown in Table 2, the voltage level of the panels on a sunny day as on a cloudy day does not present a significant difference, however, on a sunny day the total voltage collected is much higher because the current delivered by the panels is directly proportional to the amount of light that hits them, so the battery is charged more quickly in this case the battery collected 1.22V in 90.

Table 2. Energy Harvested by Solar Panels in a 9V rechargeable battery.

Ambient	Delivered Voltage (V)	Delivered Current (V)	Initial Voltage (V)	Voltage Harvested in Minutes (V)			Total Voltage Harvested (V)
				30	60	90	
Sunny Day	9.55	159.6	8.03	9.06	9.18	9.25	1.22
Cloudy Day	9.52	38.4	7.97	8.56	9.02	9.14	1.17

Table 3 shows the results of the measurements taken with the complete system, these tests were performed in an urban area for both a sunny and a cloudy day and during the night. It can be seen how the total energy collected during the day is very similar to the results of Table 2, obtained with the solar panels, while for the night the total voltage collected in a period of 90 min reached 110 mV, additionally the total energy collected in a period of 11 h from 7pm to 6am was measured obtaining a voltage of 560mV. It was also proven that during the day the system can fully charge a 9 V at 250 mA battery in around 180 min regardless of whether the day is cloudy or sunny.

Table 3. Energy harvested by the complete system.

Ambient Urban Area	Delivered Voltage (V)	Delivered Current (V)	Initial Voltage (V)	Voltage Harvested in Minutes (V)			Total Voltage Harvested (V)
				30	60	90	
Sunny Day	9.58	153.7	7.79	8.69	8.84	9.03	1.24
Cloudy Day	9.46	36.9	8.08	8.70	8.89	9.16	1.08
Night	0.135	0.0008	7.73	7.75	7.79	7.84	0.11

Finally, the battery charger stage was calibrated to automatically disconnect when the battery voltage reaches 9.25V, thus protecting the battery from overcharges that could reduce its lifetime. In addition, it was found that when the solar panels did not reach the 2V required for the operation of the Step-up Converter, the output voltage automatically switches to the battery voltage, this transition is done almost immediately due to the speed of the Mosfet used for the voltage selector stage, so that the devices that are connected to the system will not notice it.

Measurements of the voltage outputs were taken, proving that when the system is charging the battery the voltage at the 9V output is 8.86V while at the 5V output it is 5.04V, while once the battery is fully charged the voltage at the outputs is 9.11V and 5.16V respectively, these results can be seen in Fig. 17.

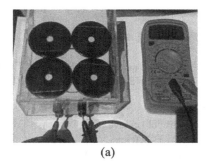 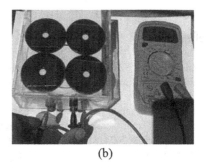

(a)   (b)

Fig. 17. a) voltage measured at system 9V output, b) voltage measured at system 5V output.

The system has been designed for 5G devices, due to the requirements for the execution of the research project "Captación de Energía Limpia de Baja Potencia para Alimentación de Dispositivos de Quinta Generación (5G)", which is being carried out. However, it can be used for other types of devices such as cell phones, if the energy required is not greater than that delivered by the system, 9V and 160 mA approximately.

4 Conclusions

In this paper, the design, simulation, fabrication and characterization of each of the stages of a hybrid solar-radiofrequency energy harvesting system for fifth generation 5G terminals has been conducted. Through measurements and tests, it was verified that the proposed system works as designed, maintaining voltages of 8.86 V and 5.04 V at its outputs when the battery is charging and 9.11V and 5.16V when the battery stops charging. Charging times may vary depending on weather conditions, time of day and the distance of the system from an RF source, but it has been found that during the day the battery can be fully charged in approximately 3 h. The energy collected by the antenna does not reach the 2 V required for the step-up converter, so it has been chosen to connect it directly to the battery charging stage, this will be useful during the nights as according to the results obtained it could collect around 560 mV. The system can be used to power low power devices such as wireless sensors or terminals based on 5G technology, it can also be calibrated for use with batteries of different voltages, using the two precision potentiometers located on the main PCB, with the first one the output voltage of the Step-up converter is regulated, while the second is used to indicate the voltage of the relay to be activated to stop charging the battery.

Acknowledgments. The authors thank the Technical University of Ambato and the "Dirección de Investigación y Desarrollo" (DIDE) for their support in carrying out this research, in the execution of the project "Captación de Energía Limpia de Baja Potencia para Alimentación de Dispositivos de Quinta Generación (5G)", approved by resolution "Nro. UTA-CONIN-2022-0015-R". Project code: SFFISEI 07.

References

1. Li, Y., Chiu, Y.H., Lin, T.Y.: Research on new and traditional energy sources in OECD countries. Int. J. Environ. Res. Public Health **16**(7), 1122 (2019). https://doi.org/10.3390/ije rph16071122
2. Blazu, R., Blachut, J., Ciepiela, A., Labuz, R., Papiez, R.: Renewable energy sources vs. an air quality improvement in urbanized areas – the metropolitan area of kraków case. Front. Energy Res. **9**(767418), 1–11 (2021). https://doi.org/10.3389/fenrg.2021.767418
3. Asantewaa, P., Asumadu-Sarkodie, S.: A review of renewable energy sources, sustainability issues and climate change mitigation. Cogent Eng. **3**(1), 1–14 (2016). https://doi.org/10.1080/23311916.2016.1167990
4. Perea, M., Escobedo, Q., Perea, A.: Renewable energy in Urban Areas: worldwide research trends. Energies **11**(3), 1–19 (2018). https://doi.org/10.3390/en11030577
5. Tony, A., Hiryanto, L.: A review on energy harvesting and storage for rechargeable wireless sensor networks. IOP Conference Series: Materials Science and Engineering. 508, 1-11 (2019)
6. Pop, A., Pop, P., Tihomir, L., Barz, C.: Research about harvesting energy devices and storage method. Open conference systems, innovative ideas in science 4(2), pp. 102–120 (2015)
7. Abdul-Rahman, K., Mohammad, S.: A survey on recent energy harvesting mechanisms. In: IEEE Canadian Conference on Electrical and Computer Engineering (CCECE), pp. 1–5 (2016). https://doi.org/10.1109/CCECE.2016.7726698
8. Akinaga, H.: Recent advances and future prospects in energy harvesting technologies. Jpn. J. Appl. Phys. **59**(110201), 1–10 (2020)

9. Hassani, S., Hassani, H., Boutammachte, N.: Overview on 5G radio frequency energy harvesting. Adv. Sci. Technol. Eng. Syst. J. **4**(4), 328–346 (2019). https://doi.org/10.25046/aj0 40442

10. Gordón, C., Freire, E., Brito, G., Salazar, F.: Logarithmic antennas for electromagnetic energy harvesting applications. In: Botto-Tobar, M., Zambrano Vizuete, M., Diaz Cadena, A., Vizuete, A.Z. (eds.) Latest Advances in Electrical Engineering, and Electronics. Lecture Notes in Electrical Engineering, vol 933. Springer, Cham (2022). https://doi.org/10.1007/ 978-3-031-08942-8_17

11. Cuji, J., Mendoza, L., Brito, G., Gordón, C.: Portable electromagnetic energy harvesting system. In: Chauvin, M.I.A., Botto-Tobar, M., Díaz Cadena, A., Montes León, S. (eds.) CSECity. LNNS, vol. 379, pp. 81–91. Springer, Cham (2022). https://doi.org/10.1007/978-3-030-94262-5_8

12. Banerjee, J., Banerjee, S.: Radio frequency energy harvesting circuits design for the applications of low power electronics. Int. J. Electron. Lett. **10**(12), (2021) https://doi.org/10.1080/ 21681724.2020.1870719

13. Sharma, H., Haque, A., Jaffery, Z.: An efficient solar energy harvesting system for wireless sensor nodes. In: 2nd IEEE International Conference on Power Electronics, Intelligent Control and Energy Systems (ICPEICES), pp. 461–464 (2018). https://doi.org/10.1109/ICPEICES. 2018.8897434

14. Balanis, C.: Antenna Theory Analysis and Design, 2nd edn. Jhon Wiley & Sons, Inc., Ney York (2017)

15. Balarezo, D., Gordón, C., Cuji, J., Salazar, F.: Conditioning System for an Electromagnetic Energy Collection Device. In: Garcia, M.V., Fernández-Peña, F., Gordón-Gallegos, C. (eds) Advances and Applications in Computer Science, Electronics, and Industrial Engineering. CSEI 2021. Lecture Notes in Networks and Systems, vol 433. Springer, Cham (2022). https:// doi.org/10.1007/978-3-030-97719-1_13

16. Thangjam, R., Bhattacharyya, K.: Design and analysis of slotted microstrip patch antenna. A review. J. Telecommun. Study **4**(2), 1–17 (2018)

17. Nurzaimah, Z., Zahriladha, Z., Maisarah, A., Mawarni, M.: A 2.45 GHz harmonic suppression rectangular patch antenna with circular polarization for wireless power transfer application. IETE J. Res. **64**(3), 310–316 (2018). https://doi.org/10.1080/03772063.2017.1355751

Smart Antenna Array for Optimal Electromagnetic Energy Capture

Myriam Cumbajín[1] (ID), Patricio Sánchez[1] (ID), Ernesto Escobar[2] (ID), and Carlos Gordón[2(✉)] (ID)

[1] SISAu Research Center, Facultad de Ingeniería, Industria y Producción, Universidad Tecnológica Indoamérica, UTI, 180103 Ambato, Ecuador
{myriamcumbajin,patriciosanchez}@uti.edu.ec

[2] GITED Research Group, Facultad de Ingeniería en Sistemas, Electrónica e Industrial, Universidad Técnica de Ambato, UTA, 180207 Ambato, Ecuador
cd.gordon@uta.edu.ec

Abstract. Smart antennas are currently one of the most exploited fields in terms of wireless networks, allowing high data transmission capacities, this is achieved by focusing the radiation on the desired direction and adjusting to the environment and conditions in which communications are developed. Smart antennas employ a set of radiating and emitting and combining elements organized in the form of arrangements connected at a common point to guarantee the required power, the signals from these elements are combined to form a moving beam pattern that follows a pattern determined by the user or designer. The consumption of energy within communication systems is considered a big problem and a challenge when carrying out implementations in media where the storage or recharging of the end terminals is complicated by their location, this trend grows with the presence of the Internet of the IoT things, where it is directly dependent on the construction of a large wireless network that allows everything to be interconnected, for this reason there are investigations in the 2.4 and 5.8 GHz bands and represents future work for the 5th Generation (5G) cell phone. The great possibility of collecting electromagnetic energy from densely populated urban areas becomes a great renewable source of power for communication devices for both existing Wi-Fi technology and new technologies such as the 5G network.

Keywords: Antenna array · Energy capture · Smart antennas

1 Introduction

Antenna arrays are a combination of multiple elements that through a combiner device can maximize the power obtained from the environment in an automated way to adjust to the direction of the signal emitted by different radiation points [1], the array is capable to couple to the different ranges of the spectrum for which they were designed in the present case from 1.8 to 2.6 GHz [2].

The design of the array in the first instance was considered using patch-type antennas and was based on an empirical model connected through a transmission line that, given its results [3], did not generate the necessary power levels to meet the objective of the study, having previous work carried out using Log-Periodic antennas [4], they are addressed in an optimization and improvement method to guarantee a more efficient energy collection [5].

Many of the simulation results for the proposed arrays indicate a very narrow bandwidth, so they are discarded as they were implemented in the special FR4 material for high frequencies [6].

Unlike other studies, the proposed design must be able to adapt to possible miniaturization due to limited space in terminal equipment, as well as the use of couplers that facilitate the integration of new frequencies, adapting to technological changes [7].

The antennas that are usually used to form the array are the planar ones with microstrip technology [8], but due to their composition and geometry [9], they can have great directivity [10], but a limited bandwidth [11], so to build it in array formation, a lot is required [12]. In addition to its low power capture, the antennas proposed for this design are based on the Log-Periodic antenna [13].

Given the public health problems worldwide, the determining factor such as field work makes this research even more challenging for all the actors involved in it, so it was tried to approach the reality of current normality and adjust as best as possible to a future improvement in design and analysis.

2 Methodology

The process used for the design, simulation, manufacturing, and characterization of the proposed smart antenna array is detailed below.

2.1 Design

The design of the Wilkinson combiner is detailed, which is the simplest within the set of RF combiners and dividers [14]. The design is seen in Fig. 1.

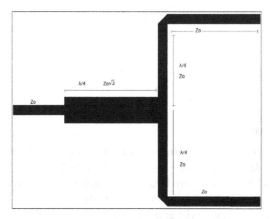

Fig. 1. Wilkinson Combiner-Splitter.

As a first step, calculate the width of the transmission line at λ/4 with a frequency of 2.4 GHz [15]:

$$\lambda/4 = L1 \tag{1}$$

$$L1Zo = 31.25 \text{ mm} \tag{2}$$

$$Zo = 50\,\Omega \tag{3}$$

$$Z1 = Z0 * \sqrt{2} \tag{4}$$

$$Z1 = 70 \text{ Oh} \tag{5}$$

For the transmission line was used the web https://www.emtalk.com with calculation at 50 Ω with a frequency of 2.4 GHz. Figure 2 shows the calculations.

Microstrip Line Calculator

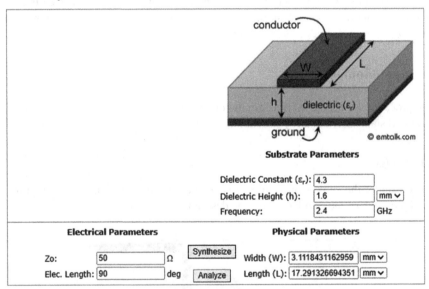

Fig. 2. Transmission Line Calculations in Software.

2.2 Antenna Arrays

Continuing with the design of the proposed Log-Periodic antenna array, now the best frequencies will be determined where one of the 2 arrays to be implemented resonates between the 3G and WIFI operating frequencies, in this case the antenna that is proposed to be designed is in frequencies from 1.8 GHz to 2.4 GHz [16], therefore, the dimensions of the dipole that works at the frequency of 1.8 GHz are established, once these dimensions were obtained [17], the rest of the required elements were calculated.

2.3 Design

Transmission line, considering the substrate to be used and the impedance Substratum: FR4: a 50Ω.

$$\varepsilon = 4.3 \tag{6}$$

$$h = 1.6 \tag{7}$$

$$t = 0.035 \tag{8}$$

For the power and transmission line of the first dipole which in this case will be the same distance through the web https://www.emtalk.com, we perform the calculation at 50 Ω with a frequency of 1.8 GHz [18], so we obtain:

The calculation of the length of the first dipole was carried out based on the lower operating frequency than 1.8 GHz, which corresponds to the 3G cellular frequency [19], using the CST Studio software, the value is varied between λ/2 y λ/4 to achieve the optimal value of the dipole, that is why, we have:

$$fl = 1.8 \text{ GHz} \tag{9}$$

$$\lambda = 0.17 \text{ m}\lambda \tag{10}$$

$$2/ = 8.5 \text{ cm} \tag{11}$$

$$\lambda4/ = 4.25 \text{ cm} \tag{12}$$

With the results of the simulation, it is concluded that the length of the first dipole must be L1 = 60 mm for it to resonate at the frequency of 1 800 MHz. With the length and width of the first dipole, additional calculations are made, such as the number of elements and their separations [20], however, for the width of the elements it will be 3.11 mm as the optimal measure to guarantee the bandwidth required for the investigation:

A gain of 8 dB was taken to establish a value for the scale factor $\tau = 0.88$ and spacing $\sigma = 0.161$; [27] $B = 2.6/1.8$ $\alpha = \tan - 1[1 - \tau4\sigma]$ $\alpha = 0.18$ $Bar = 1.1 + 7.7 (1 - \tau2)$ cotα pole

$$Bar = 1.696 \tag{13}$$

$$Bs = BBar = 1.696 * 1.44 \tag{14}$$

$$Bs = 2.443 \tag{15}$$

$$N = 1 + (ln(Bs)ln(1\tau/)) \tag{16}$$

$$N = 1 + (ln(2.443)ln(1/0.88)) \tag{17}$$

$$N = 1 + (0.890.13) \tag{18}$$

$$N = 7.84 \tag{19}$$

To reduce the size of the array, the value of 7 elements that make up the Log-Periodic antenna is taken [21, 22].

The separation of the first dipole from the next is given by:

$$SN = 12(LN - LN - 1)\cot\alpha(12) \tag{20}$$

$$L2 = \tau * L1 = 52.8 \text{ mm} \tag{21}$$

$$S2 = 19.78 \text{ mm} \tag{22}$$

With these values, the other dipoles are calculated with their respective separations [23], which are detailed in Table 1.

Table 1. Calculation results for Log-Periodic antenna design

N° Dipole	Longitude (mm)	Separation (mm)	Width (mm)
1	60,00	19,79	3,11
2	52,80	17,41	3,11
3	46,46	15,32	3,11
4	40,89	13,48	3,11
5	35,98	11,86	3,11
6	31,66	10,44	3,11
7	27,86	31,92*	3,11

* Distance corresponds between the smallest dipole and the feed point towards the energy collector [10].

2.4 Simulation

The simulation results for subsequent manufacturing are shown below with the results of Table 3, the Antenna is designed in CST Microwave Studio [24, 25], and Fig. 3 shows the design in the software.

Figure 4 indicates the parameter S11 whose value represents the power reflected in port 1 compared to the power applied to the same port.

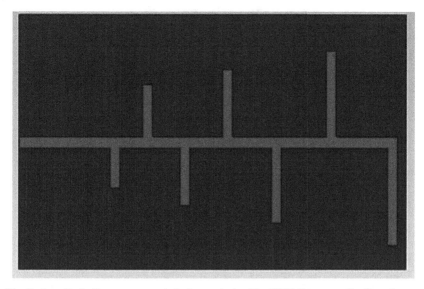

Fig. 3. Log-Periodic antenna array design optimized in CST Microwave Studio software.

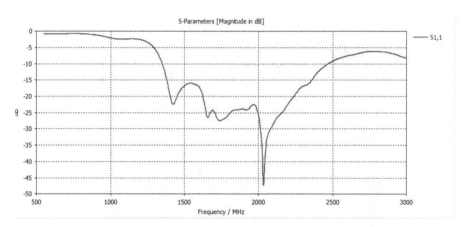

Fig. 4. Simulation result, Parameter S11 Log-Periodic Antenna.

2.5 Manufacturing

With the results obtained in the simulation, we proceed with the implementation of the antenna array and the Wilkinson combiner for its subsequent characterization.

As a first step, the Wilkinson combiner is printed and the SMA connectors are placed, as depicted in Fig. 5.

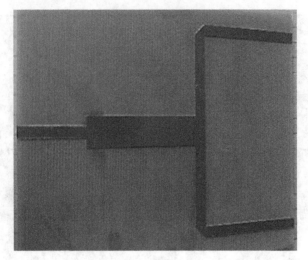

Fig. 5. Combinator Wilkinson Fabricate.

Subsequently, the 2 arrays of Log-Periodic antennas were manufactured as sketched in Fig. 6.

Fig. 6. Log Antenna arrays -periodic manufactured.

As a last step, the energy collector circuit is coupled for the subsequent measurement of the captured voltage. Then, Fig. 7 sketches the smart antenna array.

Fig. 7. Log-periodic antenna arrays made with combiner.

2.6 Characterization

With the results of the simulated and manufactured Wilkinson combiner, a comparison was made in Table 2. Figure 8 shows the setup implemented for the characterization of the smart antenna array.

Table 2. Comparison to 2.4 GHz Simulated Vs Implemented Combiner (dB)

Simulator	Implemented
− 4 dB	− 8 dB

Results Analysis

Analysis of Log-Periodic Antenna Results

In the practical measurement of the individual Log-Periodic antenna array it is determined that the implemented antenna has a bandwidth considerably higher than simulated and can be used for the collection of electromagnetic energy in the range of 1.6 GHz to 2.8 GHz [26, 27], without considering, that in the design frequencies between 1.8 - 2.6 GHz were established, the resonance frequencies of the antenna are summarized in Table 3 with their respective bandwidths, analyzing those for meters S11 according to the results obtained in practice.

In a comparison with the simulation and what was obtained in practice, the operating bandwidth of the antenna is decreased, since in the simulated the operating frequency ranged from 1.6 GHz to 2.8 GHz with a resonance peak of -33dB in the frequency of 2.2 GHz, however, in practice the resonance value obtained by measuring the parameter S11 is equal to -33dB but with a bandwidth from 1.8 GHZ to 2.6 GHz, so it is considered that for higher frequencies the implemented antenna collects a greater amount of electromagnetic energy.

Fig. 8. Smart Antenna Arrays implemented and connected to the NanoVNA.

Table 3. Log-periodic antenna measurement

Initial frequency (GHz)	End frequency (GHz)	Bandwidth (GHz)
1,6	2,8	1,2

Table 4 below shows the actual measurements of the antenna array together with the combiner:

Table 4. Antenna array measurement together with the combiner

Initial frequency (GHz)	End frequency (GHz)	Bandwidth (GHz)
1,750	1,950	0,2
1,975	2,1	0,13
2,150	2,250	0,1
2,3	2,5	0,2
2,6	2,9	0,3

Figure 9 shows the Log-Periodic antenna of 7 elements optimized in this research together with the electromagnetic energy harvesting circuit designed by Eng. Darío Balarezo, and in the Table 5 shows the comparison of research results.

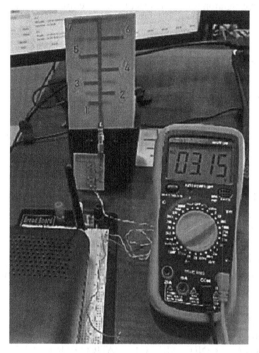

Fig. 9. Smart antenna array connected to the 2-stage circuit.

Table 5. Comparison of Results Electromagnetic Energy Harvesting Log-Periodic Antenna Eng. Félix Reinoso vs Log-Periodic Antennas current research

Stage	Time	Collected voltage investigation felix Reinoso [1]	Collected voltage current investigation
2	30 min	1,437 VDC	3,15 VDC

The results obtained by the array of Log-Periodic antennas together with the electromagnetic energy harvester and the coupling to the servo motor that varies the angle of orientation of the antenna to optimize the energy capture, the WIFI Network used is indicated in Fig. 9 and in Table 6 the measurements are shown below:

3 Conclusions

In the present research work, an array of intelligent antennas was implemented for the optimal capture of energy through a 2-stage electromagnetic energy harvesting circuit,

Table 6. Comparison of Results Electromagnetic Energy Harvesting of the Array of Log-Periodic Antennas current research vs Log-Periodic antenna of Felix Reinoso[1].

Stage	Time	Collected voltage investigation ing. Felix Reinoso [1]	Angle with respect to the router	Collected voltage current investigation	Angle with respect to the router
2	30 min	1,437 VDC	N/A	9,04 VDC	40°
2	30 min	1,437 VDC	N/A	5,52 VDC	0°
2	30 min	1,437 VDC	N/A	2,66 VDC	90°
2	30 min	1,437 VDC	N/A	4,91 VDC	180°

the frequency at which the antenna array works is at 1.6 and 2.8 GHz, so you can take advantage of the different cellular networks, as well as WIFI networks for the efficient capture of RF energy for subsequent storage. The optimization of the Log-periodic antenna improved the characteristics of the same, both in individual size and in electromagnetic energy harvesting, so that, when using the CST Software for this purpose it is clearly shown that the simulations and the values obtained are fundamental for a correct manufacture. The array of Log-Periodic Antennas together with the combiner increased the usable bandwidth of up to 300 MHz for resonant frequency, this improves the capture of electromagnetic energy by setting the frequencies that are present in the environment, for subsequent storage.

Acknowledgments. The authors thank the invaluable contribution of the Technological University Indoamerica, for his support in conducting the research project "ESTUDIO DE ALGO-RITMOS HIBRIDOS DE APRENDIZAJE AUTOMATICO PARA LA PREDICCION DE GEN-ERACIÓN DE ENERGÍAS RENOVABLES", Project Code: 281.230.2022. Also, the authors thank the Technical University of Ambato and the "Dirección de Investigación y Desarrollo" (DIDE) for their support in conducting this research, in the execution of the project "Captación de Energía Limpia de Baja Potencia para Alimentación de Dispositivos de Quinta Generación (5G)", approved by resolution "Nro. UTA-CONIN-2022-0015-R". Project code: SFFISEI 07.

References

1. Reinoso, F.: Optimization of antennas for electromagnetic energy harvesting systems, p. 94 (2022)
2. Anguera, J.: Theory of Antennas, p. 336
3. Fernández, A.: Design and characterization of an array of antennas in flat technology in the 8 GHz band with circular polarization, p. 114
4. Isbell, D.: Log periodic dipole arrays. IRE Trans. Antennas Propag **8**(3), 260–267 (1960)
5. Baladines, C: Antenna Theory
6. Ing. Walter.: Polytechnic University of Valencia. 18(1) (2014)
7. Rubiano, C., Castaneda, F.: Design, Optimization and Construction of a Wilkinson Divider, p. 6
8. Balarezo, A.: Optimization of the conditioning system for an electromagnetic energy harvesting device, p. 86

9. Martinez, J., Medina, A., Bonilla, C., Villegas, J., Aldaz, J.: Radio frequency energy harvesting system making use of 180° hybrid couplers and multiple antennas to improve the DC output voltage. IEEE Lat. Am. Trans. **18**(3), 604–612 (2020)
10. Schemmel, D., Nayeri, P.: A smart wireless energy harvesting system with adaptive beamforming and power management. In: 2017 IEEE International Symposium on Antennas and Propagation & USNC/URSI National Radio Science Meeting, pp. 1085–1086 (2017)
11. Mavaddat, A., Armaki, S., Erfanian, A.: Millimeter-wave energy harvesting using 4×4 microstrip patch antenna array. IEEE Antennas Wirel. Propag. Lett. **14**, 515–518 (2015)
12. Castillo, A.: Antennas for UHF Band Energy Harvesting Applications, p. 69
13. Olan, K.: Design, Modeling, and Characterization of Microstrip Antenna Arrays for Internet of Things Applications
14. Dakulagi, V., Bakhar, M.: Advances in smart antenna systems for wireless communication. Wireless Pers. Commun. **110**(2), 931–957 (2019). https://doi.org/10.1007/s11277-019-067 64-6
15. Campanella, H., Comas, A., Alba, Y.: Smart antennas with application in SDMA, p. 7
16. Kausar, A., Mehrpouyan, H., Sellathurai, M., Qian, R., Kausar. R.: Energy efficient switched parasitic array antenna for 5G networks and IoT. In: 2016 Loughborough Antennas & Propagation Conference (LAPC), pp. 1–5 (2016)
17. Zhang, J., Huang, Y., Cao, P.: Harvesting RF energy with rectenna arrays. In: 2012 6th European Conference on Antennas and Propagation (EUCAP), pp. 365–367 (2012)
18. Balanis, C.: Antenna Theory: Analysis and Design, 4th edn. John Wiley & Sons, New Jersey (2016)
19. Guney, K., Sarikaya, N.: Resonant frequency calculation for circular microstrip antennas with a dielectric cover using adaptive network-based fuzzy inference system optimized by various algorithms. Progress Electromagnetics Res. **72**, 279–306 (2007)
20. Chia, M.: Design of Linear Grouping of Microstrip Patches for Wifi Applications (802 11a-N), p. 125
21. DuHamel, R., Isbell, D.: Broadband logarithmically periodic antenna structures, 1958 IRE International Convention Record. 1958 IRE International Convention Record, pp. 119–128 (1957)
22. Avila, E.: Design, Modeling, Manufacturing, and Measurement of Printed Antennas for Wireless Communications, p. 259
23. Carrel, R.: The Design of W-Periodic Dipole Antennas. 1958 IRE International Convention Record, pp. 61–75 (1961)
24. Shibu, S., Arjun, D., Rao, S., Satish, A., Navaneeth, M.: Automatic antenna reorientation system for affordable marine internet service. In: 2018 IEEE International Conference on Computational Intelligence and Computing Research (ICCIC), pp. 1–4 (2018)
25. Villar, R.: Design, Construction, and Testing of a Bidirectional Amplifier for WiFi at 2.4 GHz, p. 22
26. Perez, L., Sendoya, D., Vera, C., Bernal, E., Campaña, S.: Finite element method for characterizing microstrip antennas with different substrate for high temperature sensors. Publications E Investig. **11**(2), 47–55 (2017)
27. Pozar, D.: Microwave Engineering, 4th ed. Wiley (2011)

e-Learning

Virtual Training Module for the Production of Rubber Adhesives Through the Production of Cyclopentenol

Edwin P. Lema$^{(\boxtimes)}$ ⓘ, Brayan A. García ⓘ, Cesar A. Naranjo ⓘ,
and Víctor H. Andaluz ⓘ

Universidad de Las Fuerzas Armadas ESPE, Sangolquí, Ecuador
{eplema1,bagarcia6,canaranjo,vhandaluz1}@espe.edu.ec

Abstract. This article developed a didactic module that presents the evolution of the process of a Perfectly Agitated Reactor to obtain Cyclopentenol, which is used for the production of rubber adhesives. For this process was implemented controllers such as: Numerical Methods, Fuzzy and MPC. The mathematical model of the process as well as the control algorithms are implemented on the Raspberry Pi board which is embedded in the module. The module has connectivity with a computer in which it has a virtual environment that resembles an industrial process which was developed in Unity 3D, the same environment is interactive and immersive for anyone interested in the area of control and virtualization. The virtual environment simulates the process through animations allowing to visualize a process as if it were real showing elements such as: SCADA systems for the control room, industrial instrumentation in the process lines, catastrophic events when an error occurs, sounds of an industrial environment, etc. Finally, the evaluation of each of the controllers implemented in the process was verified.

Keywords: CSTR reactor · Advanced controllers · Virtual reality · Didactic module

1 Introduction

Chemical, food, manufacturing, etc. industries have implemented process automation through the use of various technologies with the objective of controlling a large number of variables involved in a process and in turn limiting human intervention in the processes [1, 2]. The implementation of process automation allows higher productivity and better product quality, decreases the cost of the production process and ensures the safety of operators and equipment in critical and hazardous areas of the industry [3, 4]. Industry 4.0 has climbed to the top of industrial process automation where productive systems are interconnected with the digital society through the use of technologies such as: artificial intelligence, big data, robotics, cloud communication, internet of things, internet of everything, internet of everything, cybersecurity, Wireless industrial automation, industrial networks, nanotechnology, network virtualization, augmented reality and virtual reality [5, 6].

M. Botto-Tobar et al. (Eds.): ICAT 2022, CCIS 1755, pp. 33–45, 2023.
https://doi.org/10.1007/978-3-031-24985-3_3

The industry for process automation has relied on different mathematical software that allow implementing different control strategies in industrial processes among them there are free software (Open Source) such as Arduino, Python [7], C++, C#, Scilab and commercial software Ros, Matlab [8], Maple [9], Labview [10] such software provide the ability to combine symbolic, numerical and graphical calculation. Due to the excessive costs in the implementation of controllers in a real process, the alternative of using 3D graphic engines such as Unity, Un-real Engine, RPG Maker, Godot, the last mentioned software allows the simulation of industrial environments in an immersive way [11, 12].

Augmented reality and virtual reality are immersive technologies that have made inroads in the automotive, food, chemical and medical industries, whose objective is the virtualization of immersive industrial processes, achieving interaction with the process layout, machinery, instrumentation, operating elements, signaling and control. Immersive technologies make it possible to observe the performance of the process and in turn enable personnel to acquire monitoring and manipulation skills and abilities for their subsequent performance in a real plant or process [13]. To develop the virtualization of industrial processes there are currently several ways, as described in [14], in which it uses different forms of modeling and software, which causes greater emphasis to the development of 3D Virtual Reality (VR) environments. VRs are a great tool for training skills as, for example, in the area of the food industry the work presented by [13] presents a VR training system of a pasteurization plant with equipment, structures and other instrumentation. In the manufacturing domain it shows the virtualization of a leather tanning process which is immersive and able to train operators [15]. In the automotive field [16] shows a VR system which is low-cost to simulate vehicle prototypes quickly. The examples are countless as the field of research is advancing daily.

As described above, this work proposes the development of a physical training module for the implementation of different advanced control strategies for the production of cyclopentenol to be used in the production of rubber adhesives. A didactic module was developed which is composed of a control unit (raspberry pi card) which incorporates the advanced control shakers (MPC, Fuzzy and Numerical Methods) and an HMI (led screen) to visualize the performance of the controllers in real time; it is also proposed to develop a 3D virtual environment of the mentioned process using Unity software, which must be interactive and immersive for the user, while incorporating the mathematical model of the process to provide the realism of the animations and the behavior of the process. Finally, experimental tests are carried out with the developed prototype in order to check the usability and performance of the virtual training module of a CSTR reactor for the production of cyclopentenol used for the production of rubber adhesives.

This article consists of Seven Sections, the Sect. 1 contains the Introduction, whereas Sect. 2 describes the training module, the structure of which is governed by the design of the training module. Section 3 consists of the development of the virtual environment, In the Sect. 4, the mathematical model of a perfectly stirred reactor is described in detail. The Sect. 5 consists of the design of advanced controllers (MPC, Fuzzy and Numerical Methods), Sect. 6 details the results obtained through the evolution of the controllers where the user chooses the control algorithm to visualize and analyze the results, finally, the conclusions of the work carried out are described in the Sect. 7.

2 Methodology

Virtual Reality (VR) has provided a great help in the field of research and education in recent years because one of the qualities is to provide experimental data and provide training environments very close to a real industrial system. For the development of the 3D virtualization of the processes, techniques such as modeling, controller design, implementation in a didactic module and inclusion of a virtual environment for the experimentation process are used.

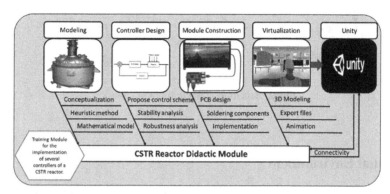

Fig. 1. Methodology for a CSTR reactor training and visualization module.

The scheme shown in Fig. 1 consists of four main stages, which must be consecutive: *(i) Mathematical Modeling* is obtained in order to mathematically represent the process performed by a CSTR reactor for the production of cyclopentenol used as part of the production of rubber adhesives. Therefore, a MIMO mathematical model is considered that represents the characteristics taking into account the inputs as cyclopentadiene flow and temperature flow and as outputs as cyclopentenol flow and internal temperature of the reactor jacket; *(ii) Controller Design*, in the case of this research, advanced control algorithms will be implemented, such as: numerical methods, Fuzzy and finally MPC, considering that it is a MIMO system; *(iii) Construction of the Module* which consists of hardware and software with the HIL (Hardware in the Loop) technique, which allows emulating the behavior of the CSTR reactor, for which a raspberry pi is implemented where the mathematical model of the plant is located, it also has a screen considered an HMI which allows us to observe the behavior of the controllers and the system; *(iiii) Virtualization* of a perfectly agitated reactor together with the elements of the virtual environment are designed in CAD software, based on their real shapes in order to obtain a process with a high degree of realism, we export the files compatible with Unity 3D software; Finally, tests of the training module are performed by applying communication with the virtual environment in order to apply the use of VR (Virtual Reality) in the teaching-learning methodology as an alternative for testing new proposals for advanced control algorithms.

Figure 2 details the schematic of a training system for cyclopentenol production, which consists of a physical module that operates independently. In the module there is a control unit (Raspberry Pi card) in which the mathematical model is implemented as the control algorithms allowing to observe on an LCD screen the performance of the implemented controllers. The prototype has the option to communicate with a computer that contains a virtual environment allowing interaction with the virtualized process. The virtual environment will receive the process variable data sent from the module.

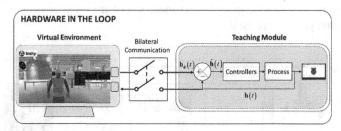

Fig. 2. Diagram of the training module.

3   Virtual Environment

To design the virtual environment of the process, the following procedures were developed as shown in Fig. 3. The industrial environment is based on a real process to be followed in order to perform the virtualization, CAD software is used to create a 3D drawing of the model. Subsequently the 3D model is exported with the sketchup software which allows compatibility with Unity where the different animations are made. In the Unity software it allows the insertion of an avatar, which performs a tour of the entire process environment guided by the user.

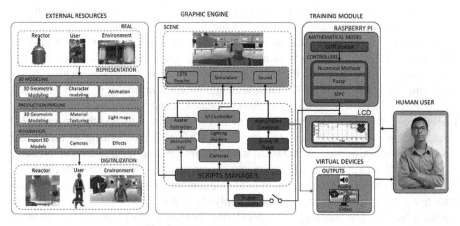

Fig. 3. Virtualization of the process.

4 Modeling of the Process

When automation of industrial processes is performed, mathematical modeling is necessary, which is directly involved in the development of advanced control algorithms. This Section describes the process of a reactor that through temperature-driven reactions allows an input component to undergo a chemical change in order to obtain a product with different properties.

The mathematical model of the CSTR reactor is composed of a stirring system which maintains a continuous motion that performs a constant movement inside the reactor, which allows stirring to produce several reactions in series and in parallel described by the Diels-Alder principle which allow the production of cyclopentenol by chemical intervention of cyclopentadiene [11]. Figure 4 describes the process of a perfectly stirred reactor, by means of the inputs and outputs the mathematical model was obtained, which is composed of an internal tank which is covered by an external structure with an intermediate vacuum between the two structures through which the heat flow Q enters to transmit the temperature to the inside of the reactor T_k, to obtain the cyclopentenol concentrate, several chemical reactions are provoked inside the reactor by the variation of the inlet flow C_{ao} and the temperature.

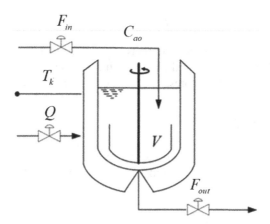

Fig. 4. Process of a CSTR reactor

For the product of the Cyclopentadiene balance input, the following equation is considered:

$$\frac{dC_A}{dt} = \frac{F}{V}(C_{A0} - C_A) - k_1 C_A - k_3 C_A^2 \tag{1}$$

To obtain the desired product, the Ciclopentenol balance is obtained:

$$\frac{dC_B}{dt} = -\frac{F}{V}C_B + k_1 C_A - k_2 C_B \tag{2}$$

To determine the temperature of the system, the temperature mass balance is obtained:

$$\frac{dT}{dt} = \frac{1}{\rho C_\rho}\left[k_1 C_A(-\Delta H_{RAB}) + k_2 C_B(-\Delta H_{RBC}) + k_3 C_A^2(-\Delta H_{RAD})\right]$$
$$+ \frac{F}{V}(T_0 - T) + \frac{k_w A_R}{\rho C_\rho V}(T_k - T)$$

(3)

The parameters of the reaction rates k_1, k_2 and k_3 depend on the temperature by means of the Arrhenius law. The above equations of the process were based on the work [11]. By placing (1), (2) and (3) into state variables gives the following equation:

$$\begin{bmatrix} \dot{C}_B \\ \dot{T} \end{bmatrix} = \begin{bmatrix} -C_B & 0 \\ T_0 - T & \frac{K_w A_R}{C_\rho \rho V} \end{bmatrix} \begin{bmatrix} F_{in} \\ Q \end{bmatrix} + \begin{bmatrix} P_{C_B} \\ P_T \end{bmatrix}$$

(4)

where, cyclopentenol is defined as C_B; T is the reactor temperature; K_w is the heat transfer coefficient; A_R is the surface area of the reactor; C_ρ is the heating capacity; ρ is the constant density of the liquid and V is the reactor volume. Equation (4) can be compactly described as

$$\dot{h} = Hv + P$$

(5)

where **v** defines the control actions (variations of: cyclopentadiene flow and heat flow); **P** are the disturbances that exist in the process; $\dot{h}$ represents the rate of change of the process output; **H** is the matrix representing the behavior inside the reactor.

5 Controllers Design

In this Section advanced controllers such as: Fuzzy, MPC and Numerical Methods were implemented which can be selected in order to evaluate the process behavior as detailed in the diagram in Fig. 5

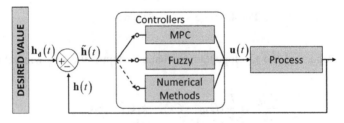

Fig. 5. General scheme of proposed controllers

where: h_d are desired values such as (ciclopentenol flow and reactor temperature); **h** are real values of the process; $\tilde{h}$ are errors that enter the controllers and finally **u** are the control actions (cyclopentadiene flow and heat flow).

5.1 Control of Numerical Methods

To obtain cyclopentenol by means of a control based on numerical methods, the variables of temperature flow and cyclopentadiene concentration flow are considered. The process is represented by a matrix structure in which theorems and axioms of linear algebra are applied.

Discretizing (4) through Euler's method we have:

$$\mathbf{h}(k+1) = t_s(\mathbf{H}(k)\mathbf{v}(k) + \mathbf{P}(k)) + \mathbf{h}(k) \tag{6}$$

where t_s represents the proposed sampling time according to the Nyquist theorem and k is discrete time for which its evolution in an instant of time is $k+1$.

By implementing the Markov Chain, it is possible to establish the evolution of the variables to be controlled after they have undergone a sampling period as shown below: $\mathbf{h}(k+1) = \mathbf{h_d}(k+1) - \mathbf{W}[\mathbf{h_d}(k) - \mathbf{h}(k)]$. From here, the control law can be defined on the basis of [17]:

$$\mathbf{v_c}(k) = \frac{1}{t_s}\mathbf{H}^{-1}[\mathbf{h_d}(k+1) - \mathbf{W}[\mathbf{h_d}(k) - \mathbf{h}(k)] - \mathbf{h}(k)] - \mathbf{P}(k) \tag{7}$$

in (7), defined as $\tilde{\mathbf{h}} = \mathbf{h_d} - \mathbf{h}$; $\mathbf{h_d} = [C_{bd}\ T_d]^T$ and finally the diagonal gain matrix is defined as $\mathbf{W} \in R^{2x2}$ which weights the control errors of the process and contains values between zero and one, when the gain matrix takes values close to zero the system behaves stably and if they take values close to one the behavior is unstable.

5.2 Control of Fuzzy

To control temperature and ciclopentenol flow with fuzzy logic, the following linguistic variables were considered $\tilde{\mathbf{h}}(t)$ and $\mathbf{u}(t)$. The 7 control rules are used where the input flows will respond according to the error that enters the controller.

With the help of the inference method, the membership function is obtained:

$$\mu_{\mathbf{B'_i}}(\mathbf{u}(t)) = \vee_{\tilde{\mathbf{h}}(t)}\left[\mu_{\mathbf{A'_i}}\left(\tilde{\mathbf{h}}(t)\right) \wedge \mu_{\mathbf{R'_i}}\left(\tilde{\mathbf{h}}(t), \mathbf{u}(t)\right)\right] \tag{8}$$

considering that $\mathbf{A}'$ is a singleton set, the following expression is obtained:

$$\mu_{\mathbf{B'_i}}(\mathbf{u}(t)) = \mu_{\mathbf{A'_i}}\left(\tilde{\mathbf{h}}_0(t)\right) \wedge \mu_{\mathbf{B'_i}}(\mathbf{u}(t)) \tag{9}$$

where $\mathbf{A_i}$ is a linguistic term for the input to the controller known as the error; $\mathbf{B_i}$ is the ligustic term obtained at the output of the controller; $\wedge\mu_{\mathbf{R'_i}}$ the minimum value of the ratio of the Cartesian product of the membership function of the input is considered and output is considered.; $\vee_{\tilde{\mathbf{h}}(t)}$ refers to the maximum values of temperature and cyclpentenol error occurring in the Reactor, and finally $\tilde{\mathbf{h}}_0(t)$ the first small value that takes the value of the membership known as a merging value of the antecedent of the input to the controller.

5.3 Control MPC

The MPC controller is applicable for multi-input and multi-output processes (MIMO), which seeks to minimize the cyclopentenol error and temperature error. Therefore, it can be said that it seeks to minimize the abrupt control actions of temperature flow and cyclopentadiene concentration flow, therefore the simultaneous control of two process variables is performed to determine the control actions as shown in the following equation:

$$J(k) = \sum_{i=N_w}^{N_p} \delta(k) \left\| \hat{\mathbf{h}}(k+i|k) - \mathbf{h_d}(k+i|k) \right\|_{\mathbf{D}}^2 + \sum_{i=0}^{N_C-1} \lambda(k) \|\Delta\mathbf{u}(k+i-1)\|_{\mathbf{F}}^2 \quad (10)$$

Subject to:

$$\Delta\mathbf{u}_{min} \leq \Delta\mathbf{u} \leq \Delta\mathbf{u}_{max} \quad (11)$$

$$\mathbf{h}_{min} \leq \mathbf{h} \leq \mathbf{h}_{max} \quad (12)$$

where N_w y N_p is defined as the start of the prediction horizon and the number of samples of the prediction horizon respectively; N_c as the control horizon, which must always be shorter than the prediction horizon; $\hat{\mathbf{h}}$ are the predicted outputs of cyclopentenol flow and reactor temperature.

For process optimization, there are control action constraints such as cyclopetadiene concentrate flow and temperature flow defined as $\Delta\mathbf{u}$. The same is true for the maximum and minimum limits of the process outputs represented by $\mathbf{h}$. The constants δ and λ correspond to the weight of the error and the weight of the variations of the control actions respectively.

6 Experimental Results

This Section defines the operation of the training module in conjunction with the virtualized process where the user can interact and analyze the evolution of the various control algorithms proposed for the production of cyclopentenol by means of a perfectly stirred reactor.

6.1 Module Construction

The didactic training module is composed of a Raspberry Pi card as a control unit and has a display for visualizing the performance of the controllers. The module is powered by a portable power source in this case is a Lipo battery and has protections against over current, also has an Xbee card which allows wireless communication with the virtual environment. Figure 6 shows the electrical diagram of the didactic module.

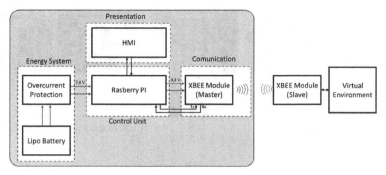

Fig. 6. Training module electrical schematic

Once the electrical connections of the elements and the programming in the control unit have been made, several tests can be performed. Figure 7 shows the results of the tests performed on the module in conjunction with the virtual environment, where the evolution of the controller in the module's HMI and its communication with the virtual environment can be seen.

Fig. 7. Operation of the training module

6.2 Virtual Environment

In order to allow the user to analyze the performance and recognize the Cyclopentenol production process, a virtual environment was developed (see Fig. 8), which represents the production of this concentrate, the user can navigate represented by an avatar that can move throughout the industrial process: exploring and visualizing the existing industrial instrumentation in the process line, SCADA system that allows modifying the desired values and in turn provides real-time information on the variables to be controlled. The virtual environment contains safety and caution signs throughout the cyclopentenol production area making it an immersive environment.

a)   CSTR Reactor   b)   Control and monitoring screen

c)   Process in critical state.

Fig. 8. Virtualized process industrial environment

After the product obtained from the process will be sent to a packaging process in industrial tanks which will be sent for further manufacturing spindle in solvents and rubber adhesives as shown in Fig. 9.

Fig. 9. Packaging area of cyclopentenol concéntrate.

6.3   Controllers Performance

The implemented controllers have a correct operation so that when evolving the process variables reach the desired value in the course of time, due to this the control errors approach the value of zero in each of the variations of the desired value.

The performance of the controllers is similar between them, but when varying the set point of concentrate B (cyclopentenol), there are differences due to the existence of over impulses when implementing the MPC and Fuzzy controllers. The percentage of overshoot of the MPC controller is higher with respect to the overshoot of the Fuzzy controller as opposed to the Numerical Methods controller which has no overshoot. As for the performance of the controllers in the temperature variable, there is no evident difference between them, it should be noted that the production of cyclopentenol depends directly on the temperature flow as can be seen in Fig. 10.

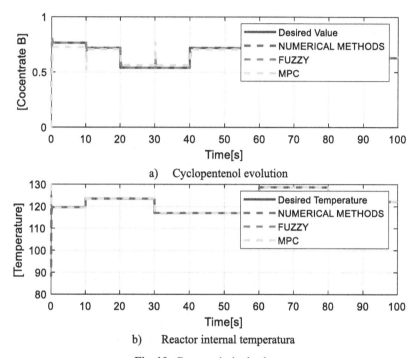

a)   Cyclopentenol evolution

b)   Reactor internal temperatura

Fig. 10. Process desired values.

The Numerical Methods based control actions have abrupt changes in the control actions for both the input flow (cyclopentadiene) and temperature flow, unlike the control actions of the MPC and Fuzzy controllers whose changes are of smaller magnitude so they are suitable for the final control elements as indicated in Fig. 11.

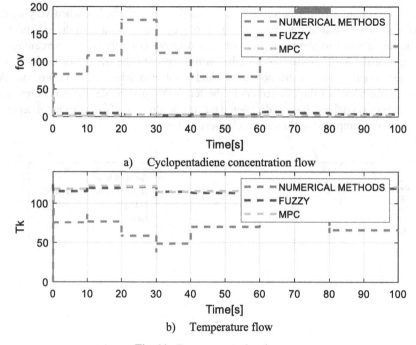

Fig. 11. Process control actions.

7   Conclusions

In this work we presented the didactic module for the user interaction where it will be possible to visualize the performance of the proposed control algorithms for process, through a communication channel is connected to a VR of an industrial process, which interacts in parallel with the didactic module. The virtual environment is focused on a chemical industry where CSTR reactors and process instrumentation are managed. To create the virtual environment, different techniques were implemented, one of which is to obtain the mathematical representation of the reactor and then advanced control algorithms were developed, such as: Numerical Methods, Fuzzy and MPC. When these algorithms were implemented, satisfactory performance was achieved, given that the desired values of the cyclopentenol concentrate flow and the internal temperature of the reactor were reached, while the control errors tended to stabilize at values close to zero.

Acknowledgment. The authors would like to thank the Universidad de las Fuerzas Armadas ESPE, the Coorporación Ecuatoriana para el Desarrollo de la Investigación y Academia CEDIA for their contribution in inonovation, through the CEPRA projects, especially the project CEPRA-XIV-2020-08-RVA "Tecnologías Inmersivas Multi-Usuario Orientadas a Sistemas Sinérgicos de Enseñanza-Aprendizaje" and also the ARSI research group for the support for the development of this work.

References

1. Alcocer Quinteros, P., Calero Zurita, M., Cedeño Zambrano, N., Lapo Manchay, E.: Automation of industrial processes. J. Bus. Entrepreneurial Stud. **4**(2), 123–131 (2020)
2. Suárez Concepción, F., Piñero Aguilar, R., Prieto Moreno, A., Alfonso Cordovíl, A., Carbó Castro, J.C., Llanes Santiago, O.: Methodology for the automation of technological processes in the Cuban pharmaceutical industry. SciELO **43**(1), 2–4 (2022)
3. Mejia Neira, Á., Jabba, D., Carrillo Caballero, G., Caicedo Ortiz, J.: The Influence of Software Engineering in Industrial Automation Processes. SciELO **30**(5), 2 (2019)
4. Núñez Alvarez, J.R., Benitez Pina, I.F., Rodriguez Martínez, A., Perez, D., De Oliveira, D.L.: Tools for the implementation of a SCADA system in a desalination process. IEEE **17**(11), 3 (2019)
5. Barona López, G., Velasteguí, L.E.: Automatización de procesos industriales mediante Industria 4.0. Alfapublicaciones **3**(3.1), 2–3 (2021)
6. Yebenes Serrano, J., Zorrilla, M.: A data governance framework for industry 4.0. IEEE **19**(12), 4–6 (2021)
7. Alcalá Fdez, J., Alonso, J., Castiello, C., Mencar, C., Soto-Hidalgo, J.: Py4JFML: a python wrapper for using the IEEE Std 1855-2016 through JFML. IEEE Xplore **9**(3), 3–4 (2019)
8. Sásig, E., et al.: Una implementación en el software Matlab para el diseño de controladores no lineales basada en álgebra lineal para procesos de tanques cuádruples. Springer **746**, 5 (2018)
9. Eyrikh, N., Markova, N., Zhunusakunova, A., Bazhenov, R., Matveeva, E., Gorbunova, T.: Using computer algebra system maple for teaching the basics of the finite element method. IEEE, pp. 616–620 (2021)
10. Salim, Ohri, J.: Correction to: Performance Study of LabVIEW Modelled PV Panel and Its Hardware Implementation. Springer, vol. 123, p. 2775 (2022)
11. Amores, D.D., et al.: Virtual control of a perfectly stirred reactor for cyclopentene production. In: De Paolis, L.T., Arpaia, P., Bourdot, P. (eds.) AVR 2021. LNCS, vol. 12980, pp. 680–689. Springer, Cham (2021). https://doi.org/10.1007/978-3-030-87595-4_49
12. Quevedo, W., et al.: Virtual reality system for training in automotive mechanics. Springer **9768**, 2–3 (2017)
13. Porras, A.P., Solis, C.R., Andaluz, V.H., Sánchez, J.S., Naranjo, C.A.: Virtual training system for an industrial pasteurization process. In: De Paolis, L.T., Bourdot, P. (eds.) AVR 2019. LNCS, vol. 11614, pp. 430–441. Springer, Cham (2019). https://doi.org/10.1007/978-3-030-25999-0_35
14. Shubo, W., Jian, C., Zichao, Z., Guangqi, W., Yu, T., Yongjun, Z.: Construction of a virtual reality platform for UAV deep learning. IEEE, pp. 3912–3916 (2017)
15. Andaluz, V.H., et al.: Training of tannery processes through virtual reality. In: De Paolis, L.T., Bourdot, P., Mongelli, A. (eds.) AVR 2017. LNCS, vol. 10324, pp. 75–93. Springer, Cham (2017). https://doi.org/10.1007/978-3-319-60922-5_6
16. Schroeter, R., Gerber, M.: A low-cost VR-based automated driving simulator for rapid auto-motive UI prototyping. In: Adjunct Proceedings of the 10th International Conference on Automotive User Interfaces and Interactive Vehicular Applications, pp. 248–251 (2018)
17. Ortiz, J., Palacios Navarro, G., Andaluz, V., Recalde, L.: Three-dimensional unified motion control of a robotic standing wheelchair for rehabilitation purposes. SENSOR **21**(9), 3057 (2021)

Virtual Training Module for the Extraction of Essential Oils Using a Distillation Column

Carmen L. Benalcázar[✉], Byron E. Chacón, and Víctor H. Andaluz

Universidad de las Fuerzas Armadas ESPE, Sangolquí, Ecuador
{clbenalcazar,bechacon,vhandaluz1}@espe.edu.ec

Abstract. The present project considers the development of a training system for a distillation column used for essential oil extraction processes based on the Hardware-in-the-Loop technique. The mathematical model is of the multivariable MIMO type obtained through the heuristic method considering the perturbations. According to the mathematical model obtained from the plant, it is implemented advanced nonlinear control algorithms that consider PID, FUZZY and MPC techniques. This allows the performance of the proposed controllers to be analyzed by means of the response time. With this information, the stability and robustness of the implemented algorithms are analyzed to evaluate the response of each process and possible errors. The system has an interactive and immersive virtual environment through a 3D graphic engine (Unity). The communication is bilateral in real time so that the process can be controlled and monitored. The implemented HMI interface is multifunctional as it can simulate the process in case the real plant is not available. The mathematical model resides in the virtual environment and the control is realized directly from MATLAB; with the real process, it would work as a graphical interface that allows showing the obtained results from the hardware.

Keywords: Training systems · Hardware-in-the-Loop · Distillation column · Control algorithm · HMI interface

1 Introduction

Industry 4.0 emerged in Germany in 2011, used to implement high-tech strategies that integrate advanced control systems with ICT to enable communication between the people, products and complex systems that make up an industry [1], considering the technologies that are integrated in the so-called CPS (Cyber Physical Systems), changes are generated in engineering systems and higher education [2], at the same time this allows the development of embedded systems, their connectivity and interaction of the physical world with the virtual world, providing integration of objects, information and people, which improves the production and use of goods and services, this being its main advantage; in addition, by associating various technologies, data can be stored in clouds, generating shared information, giving access to all authorized personnel in the industry [3]. The main technologies involved in Industry 4.0 are: *(i) Big data and data cloud:* manages opportunities for the improvement of future factories, manufacturing processes

© The Author(s), under exclusive license to Springer Nature Switzerland AG 2023
M. Botto-Tobar et al. (Eds.): ICAT 2022, CCIS 1755, pp. 46–60, 2023.
https://doi.org/10.1007/978-3-031-24985-3_4

and enable the factory to provide new products and services [4]; (ii) *IoT or Internet of Things:* has applications to support industrial networks; it also performs intelligent monitoring and control through sensors, smart meters and smart mobile devices; (iii) *Smart manufacturing processes:* include dynamic, efficient processes, automated and real-time process communication for the management and control of a highly dynamic IoT-enabled environment; *(iv) Robotics:* they acquire innovative skills with capabilities to work without a human supervisor, including working to automate and coordinate a range of logistics processes and production tasks; *(v) Virtual Reality (VR):* Recreates spaces and situations in a virtual and interactive way, allows training industrial systems so that the user knows what he has to do in a real situation [5].

Virtual reality allows the virtualization of a process or scenario. Its objective is to provide the user comfort with a sense of immersion and interactivity to capture their attention [6]. It has diverse applications: support in design, industrial, education and commercial activities. The systems that use this digital tool have a very detailed perspective since it is possible to visualize structures and installations that are difficult to access, in addition to facilitating the design and appreciation of a realistic environment [7]. For industry and education, virtual systems can be effective and useful induction modules. Virtual environments seek to implement collaborative spaces that facilitate users to acquire skills and familiarize themselves with activities that will be carried out in real life [8]. In turn, these processes integrate actual parameters and units, which are of importance for new users of the facilities [9]. Virtual environments allow us to visualize the behavior of the control algorithms implemented in the simulations, which helps us to safely identify errors and monitor the functionality of the systems [10].

Advanced control algorithms allow to take control of a certain process, they can be implemented in embedded cards, computer software or with logic gates, the algorithms used are in open and closed loop with or without disturbances [11]. They can be simulated in free and commercial software, some of the control algorithms at industrial level are; *i) PID:* they are algorithms used with three variables: proportional, derivative and integral, hence their acronym [12], *ii) FUZZY:* for its implementation, lines of code are generated establishing rules or conditions to be fulfilled [13], *iii) MPC:* It is a predictive type controller in which a prediction horizon is generated, it is programmed by code or block diagram [14]. For the project, the three controllers are implemented in MATLAB software, then the behavior of each of them is analyzed according to the expected results. The training systems use this methodology to simulate industrial processes [15]. For the project, the three controllers are implemented in MATLAB software, then the behavior of each of them is analyzed according to the expected results. The training systems use these algorithms to simulate industrial processes in real time. The method used to evaluate them is the Hardware-in-the-Loop technique since the HIL implementation includes the use of the Unity 3D graphic engine used for the development of the virtual environment [16].

The COVID 19 pandemic caused the suspension of on-site classes, so that students of technical careers did not have access to laboratories for practice, so a didactic training system is built for a distillation column for essential oil extraction processes through the Hardware-in-the-Loop (HIL) technique. The present work consists of the construction of a didactic module that includes hardware and software through the HIL technique, which allows to emulate the dynamic behavior of the distillation column, for which a control unit (Raspberry Pi) is implemented in which the mathematical model SISO is located, which was obtained through the heuristic method and determines the characteristics and restrictions of the industrial process, in addition to considering the disturbances of the plant in closed loop, the model will be validated with data obtained in scientific bases. The control algorithms implemented in closed loop are: PID, FUZZY and MPC, the behavior of each process and errors will be evaluated. With the information obtained, the stability and robustness of the implemented algorithms will be analyzed to evaluate the behavior of each process and possible errors. For the HMI interface, an interactive and immersive virtual environment is considered through a 3D graphic engine (Unity), with real-time bilateral communication between Unity 3D and MATLAB to monitor and control the process. In addition, to facilitate connectivity, a switch is implemented to select whether the connection is via ethernet cable or wireless; the virtual environment will be executable on other Android devices so that all students can easily access it.

The following document consists of six sections. Section 1. Introduction to the topic to be covered, Sect. 2. Describes the essential oil extraction process, mathematical model and applications. Section3. Describes the development of the virtual environment in Unity 3D software according to the industrial process, Sect. 4. Implements and analyzes the implemented control algorithms PID, FUZZY and MPC, Sect. 5. Presents the results obtained from the simulation and an analysis. Finally, Sect. 6 contains the conclusions of the project.

2   Extraction of Essential Oils

This section describes the SISO mathematical model of the essential oil distillation column plant to be used, which is obtained using the heuristic method and taking into account the perturbations, to then virtualize its behavior in the Unity 3D graphic engine. The following characteristics were established for the selection of the plant, in order to obtain the equations that describe the process.

2.1   Process Description

It is an industrial-type process (see Fig. 1) in which water is heated in a boiler to produce superheated steam, which is transported through a pipeline to the vessel, the steam helps to release the essential oil molecules from the plant by increasing the temperature and pressure. The oil molecules released from the plant are then mixed with the steam. This mixture rises through the hydro distiller and reaches the condenser, which allows the mixture to cool and change to liquid phase. Finally, the liquid mixture reaches the Florentine, where the oil and water are separated. This water is known as hydrolat or hydrosol and is valuable in various industries.

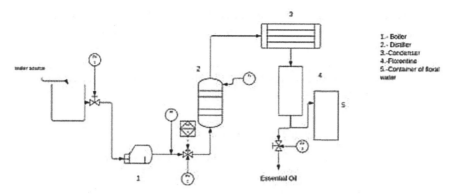

Fig. 1. P&ID diagram of the essential oil extraction process.

To determine the model of the essential oil extraction column, the following parameters are taken into account: The extraction system is isothermal and isobaric type, the number of leaves to be used in grams, the leaves should be similar in structure and preservation. The vapor phase inside the distillation vessel must have a perfect mixture, with a constant flow rate [17]. The accumulation of oil in the vapor phase is precise and thus facilitates the pure extraction of the oil. All the oil inside the trichomes is extracted during the process. The system consists of four phases: oil inside the trichome, condensed water, free oil outside the trichome and vapor phase. The essential oil is considered as a mixture of 1 or several components. The compound oil within the trichomes matches the distilled essential oil collected throughout the process. The composition is determined by GC/MS, gas chromatography (through) and mass spectrometry. Condensed water and essential oil are completely immiscible. The steam stream fed to the distillation vessel is free of impurities, that is to say that the oil is as pure as possible within the established times, for this process it is suggested between 0 to 30 min, since after that, burnt oil is obtained [18].

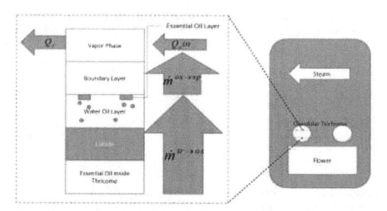

Fig. 2. Stages for the production of essential oils.

The mathematical model for the plant considers three stages (see Fig. 2) in the process of obtaining essential oils: *(i)* thermal oil whey obtained from the glandular trichomes, *(ii)* vapor-liquid equilibrium at the interface, taking into account the individual oil components, and *(iii)* oil mass transfer in the vapor phase [19].

Table 1 below shows the parameters under which each of the dynamic equations representing the mathematical model are evaluated.

Table 1. Initial plant conditions.

Acronym	Description	Used value
W	Leaf mass	2175 [gr]
K_{tr}	Kinetic constant of exudation	0.072 min^{-1}
C_1	Oil mass concentration equilibrium	0.001 [gr/cm^3]
h	Average thickness of oil spots	0,0115 [cm]
ρ_{eo}	Density of the essential oil liquid	1 [gr/cm^3]
$x_1(0)$	Initial oil mass fraction within trichomes	0.07[gr/gr]
$x_2(0)$	Initial mass of oil in the aqueous layer	0 gr
$x_3(0)$	Initial oil mass collected	0 gr

The following is a description of each of the stages for obtaining essential oils, taking into account the dynamics of the plant:

Stage 1. Thermal oil serum obtained from the glandular trichomes, to obtain it we use the following expression (1):

$$m^{tr \to os} = \frac{d(GW)}{dt} = K_{tr}GW \tag{1}$$

Stage 2. Equilibrium between vapor and liquid at the interface, taking into account the individual components of the oil, to determine this equilibrium we rely on the following expression (2):

$$\frac{dM^{os}}{dt} = K_{tr}GW - \frac{K_g M^{os}}{h\rho_{eo}}(C_1 - C) \tag{2}$$

Stage 3. Mass transfer of oil in vapor phase, as shown in (3).

$$\frac{dM^{sd}}{dt} = m^{os \to vp} = QC \tag{3}$$

These equations for the simulation of the different control algorithms implemented are represented in state spaces for which the variables change as follows: manipulated input ($x = u$), mass of oil inside the trichomes per mass of leaves [gr/gr]($x_1 = G$) oil mass in the aqueous layer [gr]($x_2 = M^{os}$), oil mass collected $\left(x_3 = M^{sd}\right)$ [20].

The state vector (x) and the manipulated input (u) are defined as follows (4):

$$x = [x_1, x_2, x_3]^T = \left[G, M^{os}, M^{sd}\right]^T, u = Q \tag{4}$$

The following expressions (5), (6) and (7) represent the dynamics of the three stages of the oil extraction process in state spaces, for which the following change of variables is used $Q = u$ the same that represents the volumetric flow of the steam [cm^3/min]

System input is represented by u and the output is $x_3 = \sum_{i=0}^{n} x_{i3}$

$$\dot{x}_1 = -K_{tr}Wx_1 \tag{5}$$

$$\dot{x}_2 = K_{tr}Wx_1 - \frac{K_gC_1x_2}{h\rho_{eo}}\left[1 - \left(\frac{K_gx_2}{\mu h\rho_{eo} + K_gx_2}\right)\right] \tag{6}$$

$$\dot{x}_3 = \frac{K_g\mu C_1x_2}{(\mu h\rho_{eo} + K_gx_2)} \tag{7}$$

From the equations described above all are constant parameters except for K_g which is the mass transfer coefficient, which varies as a function of the vapor volumetric flow rate Q. According to the close relationship between these two variables and the experimental data obtained, the following expression is approximated, taking into account that the relationship is valid for flow rates that have as maximum and minimum values $21100 < Q < 100000\left[cm^3/\min\right]$, a constant steam flow is assumed $Q = u\left[cm^3/\min\right]$ [21]

$$K_g = 470.000(Q - 74400) + 31.4 \tag{8}$$

Once the equations of the mathematical model and each one of the parameters are established, each one of them is entered into the MATLAB software to validate the selected model. The graph below (see Fig. 3) shows the results obtained from the mathematical model implemented where (a) mass of leaves; (b) aqueous phase; (c) oil collected; (d) yield in percentage.

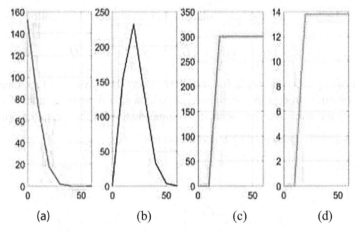

(a)   (b)   (c)   (d)

Fig. 3. Behavior of the mathematical model (a) mass of leaves; (b) aqueous phase; (c) oil collected; (d) yield in percentage.

3 Virtual Environment

For the teaching-learning process, virtual environments are oriented to simulate processes or scenes as in real life, to allow the person to interact with the simulation as if he/she were in the real environment. The objective of the training systems is to improve the implemented techniques and methods of the simulated processes, for their application in work or educational activities [22]. The implemented training system consists of a virtual environment designed in Unity 3D software in which the graphs obtained from each of the implemented control techniques (PID, FUZZY and MPC) will be shown. In addition, the environment allows the user to visualize the stages of the process as if they were in the industrial plant [23]. The virtual environment will additionally be executable on Android devices.

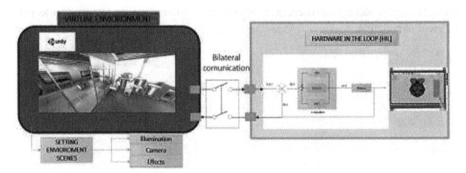

Fig. 4. Virtualization of the process.

The virtual environment for its development is based on the scheme presented in Fig. 4, which has the following phases: *(i) External resources:* includes all the components that are immersed in the virtual environment, which can be organized into two groups: (a) The simulation of the user who is represented by an Avatar and uses the simulator as a person would in real life; (b) the virtualized industrial oil extraction plant in which the different advanced control algorithms are implemented so that the behavior of the mathematical model can be controlled and verified. *(ii)* For the development process of the *virtual environment* in Unity 3D is organized in two groups: (a) Virtualized plant: this scenario has each of the processes followed to extract the essential oil, a control room where the graphs obtained from each controller (PID, FUZZY and MPC) are displayed, and an operator (Avatar) that simulates the user. It is worth mentioning that the communication between MATLAB and Unity 3D; (b) programming scripts are used to develop virtual environments, so for plant virtualization several scripts are used to simulate plant characteristics considering plant disturbances. The virtual input libraries are managed through scripts making communication and interaction in the system possible. Other scripts are used for virtual scenery, lighting and user interface. All scripts together make the simulated virtual environment interactive and immersive. *(iii) the controller* which allows the implementation of advanced control algorithms to evaluate and monitor plant behavior. The scheme implemented is based on a cascade system, using wireless communication to link the controller and the MATLAB software, as well as bilateral communication between the didactic module and the virtual environment, taking into account disturbances. Finally, we have *(iv) the human operator* whose function is to modify the simulation parameters and provide the disturbance data by means of the valve placed in the virtual environment and the module.

4   Control Algorithms

This section presents the proposed control algorithms for the essential oil extraction process, which are of nonlinear type. PID, FUZZY and MPC techniques have been considered to be implemented, this scheme (See Fig. 5) shows the design in two main stages according to the requirements of the system to be implemented: *(i)* In this stage MATLAB software is used to simulate the controllers based on the mathematical model of the plant; *(ii)* The second stage refers to virtual reality, for which the Unity 3D simulator is used in which the mathematical models that simulate the behavior of the industrial plant are placed. This system is designed so that the user can change the controller to be used and enter the value of the perturbation, also the process can be visualized on an Android device, which provides convenience to users and has a bidirectional communication [24].

Where: $x3_d$ are desired values (grams of essential oil harvested), $x3$ are actual process values, $\tilde{h}$ are errors entering the controllers, and finally u are the control actions.

4.1   PID Control

A classic control is the PID whose control algorithm consists of three basic methods, proportional (P), integral (I) and derivative (D), the most used are the basic algorithms P, PI or PID [18].

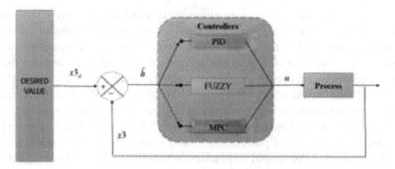

Fig. 5. General scheme of proposed controllers.

For the mathematical representation of a PID controller in discrete time, three control actions described in Eq. (9) are taken into account:

$$u(t) = k_c e(t) + \frac{k_c}{\tau_i} \int_0^1 e(t)dt + k_c \tau_d \frac{de(t)}{dt} \tag{9}$$

The error of the PID controller is defined by the difference of the Set Point, ($x3d$), and the process variable ($x3$), as shown in expression (10) in discrete time.

$$e(k) = x3_d - x3 \tag{10}$$

4.2 Fuzzy Control

Fuzzy logic aims to identify whether something or someone is part of a given set [23]. The steam entrainment essential oil distillation column has an input x = u which represents the volumetric flow; and an output which represents the collected essential oil x3, for the development of the Output Membership Functions (FMS) at the ends are placed trapezoids and in the center triangles, the operating range of the optimal oil output is [0–30] minutes which is the time taken by the extraction process and is constituted by the following sets: HM (high mass), MM (medium), LM (low). For the Inlet Membership Function (IMF) in a similar way as for the volumetric flow rate as for the volumetric flow whose range is 21100<u<10000 [cm^3/min], trapezoids are placed at the ends and central triangles, the operating range for the volumetric flow and is constituted by the following sets VS (very slow), M (medium), VF (very fast). For the development of this controller, a total of seven rules were established taking into account the inputs and outputs of the process.

4.3 MPC Control

The MPC controller applied to a SISO steam entrainment essential oil extraction system seeks to minimize the volumetric flow error. Therefore, it can be said that it seeks to minimize the abrupt control actions of the volumetric flow that affect the concentration of floral water and essential oil during steam entrainment, so the control of the process variable Q is performed to determine the control actions as shown in the following equation

$$J(k) = \sum_{i=N_w}^{N_p} \delta(k) \left\| \hat{h}(k+i|K) - h_d(k+i|k) \right\|_D^2 + \sum_{i=0}^{N_C-1} \lambda(k) \|\Delta u(k+i-1)\|_D^2 \quad (11)$$

Governed by the following boundaries

$$\Delta u_{\min} \leq \Delta u \leq \Delta u_{\max} \quad (12)$$

$$h_{\min} \leq h \leq h_{\max} \quad (13)$$

There are control action constraints such as volumetric steam flow as Δ_u. The same is true for the maximum and minimum limits of the process outputs represented by h. The constants and correspond to the weight of the error and the weight of the control action variations, respectively.

Where N_w, N_p and N_c are the start of the prediction horizon, the number of samples of the prediction horizon and the control horizon respectively; the control horizon must always be shorter than the prediction horizon; $\hat{h}$ are the predicted outputs of the collected oil mass. In addition, $\delta(k)$ and $\lambda(k)$ are constant values and thus $J(k)$ can be expressed as a function that depends only on future control actions. To implement the predictive control model, MPC, it is necessary to represent the equations in state spaces as shown in the expressions (5), (6) and (7).

5 Analysis and Results

This section presents the training system developed in each of its stages: the control algorithms implemented in the Raspberry Pi and in the MATLAB software. The virtual environment that shows the processes to obtain the essential oil, the valve that will allow us to enter the perturbations. In addition, the results obtained can be displayed on a screen in the didactic module and at the same time in the virtual environment in the control room.

5.1 Implemented Module

In Fig. 6 shows the electrical schematic implemented in the didactic module, which consists of the following components: *(i) Control unit:* a Raspberry pi 4 model b is used, for the power supply the power is transformed from 120/220 V to 5V in direct current; *(ii) Input:* the control unit has inputs for peripherals (keyboard, mouse, among others) and analog inputs; in our case we use this input to simulate disturbances in the plant. *(iii) Output Peripherals:* for the implemented module we have a 7" screen compatible with Raspberry pi and a monitor. The communication is bilateral between the module components, also the embedded card is the one that stores the advanced controllers for the simulation.

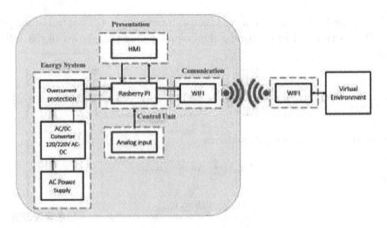

Fig. 6. Electrical block diagram

Fig. 7. Training module operation

5.2 Virtual Environment

The designed interface is developed in Unity 3D software (See Fig. 7a), for its development several scripts were taken as a basis for the simulation environment to be interactive and immersive. The design consists of a control station in which six screens can be displayed, two of them present the graphs of the variables of the mathematical model and the reaction of the traditional PID controller (See Fig. 7b), for the FUZZY and MPC control algorithm the same visualization method is used (model and control algorithm). The avatar shown in the environment can move around the plant simulating being the operator of the system, it is also responsible for interacting with the interface to give the appearance of entering the values required by the plant to operate and the values of the disturbances. It is also possible to visualize within the simulation each of the stages that must be followed to extract the essential oil.

(a)   (b)

Fig. 8. (a) Process control room, (b) SCADA monitoring and virtualized plant.

5.3 Implemented Control Schemes

The PID, Fuzzy and MPC control algorithms were implemented for the distillation column, which, when the process variables evolve in a given time, reach the desired value, therefore the control error value in the implemented controllers approaches zero. The implemented controllers have a correct operation since when the process variables evolve they reach the desired value in a certain course of time, due to this the control errors approach the value of zero in each of the variations made. In (Fig. 9) the implemented PID, FUZZY and MPC controls represent the response obtained from the plant as a function of the *(i) error*: the one that tends to zero asymptotically in the three controllers. *(ii) Control value*: in this graph it can be seen that when there is an overshoot, the controllers

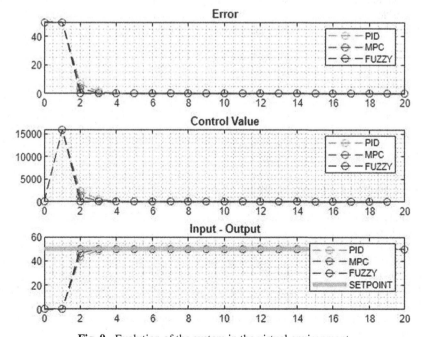

Fig. 9. Evolution of the system in the virtual environment.

perform an optimal process control since their performance is similar, the controller from which the best response is obtained is the FUZZY. *(iii) Inputs and outputs:* the three implemented controllers reach the desired values in the Set Point, being the PID control the slowest for the implemented process. It should be noted that our process is slow, so a range of 0 to 20 min is taken. Finally, after analyzing each of the responses obtained from the controllers, it can be said that the FUZZY controller is the optimal one for our process.

6 Conclusions

The design and construction of the virtual training module through the Hardware-in-the-Loop technique allows students to access the industrial practices in a realistic and friendly virtual environment, as it can simulate the process in case of not having the real plant as is the case of the process of extraction of essential oils by steam entrainment; the mathematical model runs in MATLAB online and communicates with the Unity platform, the Raspberry Pi card that acts as a control unit is responsible for running the MATLAB file online; Through this file it is possible to run and evaluate the response of each PID controller, FUZZY and MPC with respect to the plant allowing the user to act through the built-in HMI allowing the display of 2d screens with the responses of the algorithms applied in this project; having a Raspberry card can be connected to other attachments such as two potentiometers that act as analog elements and through them you can enter setpoint values and disturbances locally.

Acknowledgment. This article shows the results of the Degree Project of the Master's Programme in "Maestría en Electrónica y Automatización con Mención en Redes Industriales" of the Postgraduate Centre of the Universidad de las Fuerzas Armadas ESPE.

References

1. Zambrano, J.I., Bermeo, D.A., Naranjo, C.A., Andaluz, V.H.: Multi-user virtual system for training of the production and bottling process of soft drinks. In: 2020 15th Iberian Conference on Information Systems and Technologies (CISTI), June 2020, pp. 1–7. https://doi.org/10.23919/CISTI49556.2020.9141140
2. Thames, L.: Industry 4.0: an overview of key benefits, technologies, and challenges. http://link.springer.com/https://doi.org/10.1007/978-3-319-50660-9_1
3. Dalenogare, G.B., Santos, L., Benitez: The expected contribution of Industry 4.0 technologies for industrial performance. Artículo Rev. Sist. Exp. Septiembzre (2018). https://doi.org/10.1016/j.ijpe.2018.08.019
4. Ortiz, J.S., et al.: Teaching-learning process through VR applied to automotive engineering. In: ACM International Conference Proceeding Ser., pp. 36–40, December 2017. https://doi.org/10.1145/3175536.3175580
5. Quevedo, W.X., et al.: Assistance system for rehabilitation and valuation of motor skills. Lect. Notes Comput. Sci. (including Subser. Lect. Notes Artif. Intell. Lect. Notes Bioinformatics), vol. 10325. LNCS, pp. 166–174 (2017). https://doi.org/10.1007/978-3-319-60928-7_14/COVER

6. Wang, S., Chen, J., Zhang, Z., Wang, G., Tan, Y., Zheng, Y.: Construction of a virtual reality platform for UAV deep learning. In: 2017 Chinese Automation Congress (CAC), October 2017, pp. 3912–3916. https://doi.org/10.1109/CAC.2017.8243463

7. de Paiva Guimarães, M., Dias, D.R.C., Mota, J.H., Gnecco, B.B., Durelli, V.H.S., Trevelin, L.C.: Immersive and interactive virtual reality applications based on 3D web browsers. Multimed. Tools Appl. **77**(1), 347–361 (2016). https://doi.org/10.1007/s11042-016-4256-7

8. Velosa, J.D., Cobo, L., Castillo, F., Castillo, C.: Methodological proposal for use of virtual reality VR and augmented reality AR in the formation of professional skills in industrial maintenance and industrial safety. Lect. Notes Networks Syst. **22**, 987–1000 (2018). https://doi.org/10.1007/978-3-319-64352-6_92/COVER

9. Porras, A.P., Solis, C.R., Andaluz, V.H., Sánchez, J.S., Naranjo, C.A.: Virtual Training System for an Industrial Pasteurization Process, pp. 430–441 (2019)

10. Lv, Z., Chen, D., Lou, R., Song, H.: Industrial security solution for virtual reality. IEEE Internet Things J. **8**(8), 6273–6281 (2021). https://doi.org/10.1109/JIOT.2020.3004469

11. Yuan, D., Wang, Y.: Data driven model-free adaptive control method for quadrotor formation trajectory tracking based on RISE and ISMC algorithm. Sensors **21**(4), 1289 (2021). https://doi.org/10.3390/s21041289

12. Carvajal, C.P., Solís, L.A., Tapia, J.A., Andaluz, V.H.: SCADA/HMI Systems for Learning Processes of Advanced Control Algorithms, pp. 77–85 (2018)

13. Meng, F., Liu, S., Liu, K.: Design of an optimal fractional order pid for constant tension control system. IEEE Access **8**, 58933–58939 (2020). https://doi.org/10.1109/ACCESS.2020.2983059

14. Varela-Aldas, J., Andaluz, V.H., Chicaiza, F.A.: Modelling and control of a mobile manipulator for trajectory tracking. In: 2018 International Conference on Information Systems and Computer Science (INCISCOS), November 2018, pp. 69–74. https://doi.org/10.1109/INCISCOS.2018.00018

15. Lozada, G.F., Pruna, J.K., Naranjo, C.A., Andaluz, V.H.: Level process control with different tank configurations: hardware-in-the-loop technique, pp. 587–605 (2022)

16. Jorque, B.S., Mollocana, J.D., Ortiz, J.S., Andaluz, V.H.: Mobile Manipulator Robot Control Through Virtual Hardware in the Loop, 80–91 (2021)

17. Lainez-Cerón, E., Ramírez-Corona, N., López-Malo, A., Franco-Vega, A.: An overview of mathematical modeling for conventional and intensified processes for extracting essential oils," Chem. Eng. Process. - Process Intensif. **178**, 109032 (2022). https://doi.org/10.1016/J.CEP.2022.109032

18. Valderrama, F., Ruiz, F.: An optimal control approach to steam distillation of essential oils from aromatic plants. Comput. Chem. Eng. **117**, 25–31 (2018). https://doi.org/10.1016/j.compchemeng.2018.05.009

19. Cerpa, M.G., Mato, R.B., José Cocero, M.: Modeling steam distillation of essential oils: application to lavandin super oil. AIChE J. **54**(4), 909–917 (2008). https://doi.org/10.1002/aic.11438

20. Andaluz, V.H., Castillo-Carrión, D., Miranda, R.J., Alulema, J.C.: Virtual Reality Applied to Industrial Processes, pp. 59–74 (2017)

21. Ortiz, J.S., Palacios-Navarro, G., Andaluz, V.H., Guevara, B.S.: Virtual Reality- based framework to simulate control algorithms for robotic assistance and rehabilitation tasks through a standing wheelchair. Sensors **21**(15), 5083 (2021). https://doi.org/10.3390/s21155083

22. Pruna, E., Andaluz, V.H., Proano, L.E., Carvajal, C.P., Escobar, I., Pilatasig, M.: Construction and analysis of PID, fuzzy and predictive controllers in flow system. In: 2016 IEEE International Conference on Automatica (ICA-ACCA), October 2016, pp. 1–7. https://doi.org/10.1109/ICA-ACCA.2016.7778493

23. Othman, M.H., et al.: Genetic algorithm-optimized adaptive network fuzzy inference system-based vsg controller for sustainable operation of distribution system. Sustainability **14**(17), 10798 (2022). https://doi.org/10.3390/su141710798
24. Flores-Bungacho, F., Guerrero, J., Llanos, J., Ortiz-Villalba, D., Navas, A., Velasco, P.: Development and application of a virtual reality biphasic separator as a learning system for industrial process control. Electronics **11**(4), 636, (2022). https://doi.org/10.3390/electronics11040636

Teaching Digital Competences in University Professors: A Meta-analysis and Systematic Literature Review in Web of Science

Andrés Cisneros-Barahona[1]([⊠]) (ID), Luis Marqués Molías[2] (ID),
Gonzalo Samaniego Erazo[1] (ID), María Isabel Uvidia-Fassler[1] (ID),
Gabriela De la Cruz-Fernández[1] (ID), and Wilson Castro-Ortiz[1] (ID)

[1] Universidad Nacional de Chimborazo, Riobamba 060150, Ecuador
ascisneros@unach.edu.ec
[2] Universitat Rovira I Virgili, 43007 Tarragona, Spain

Abstract. This article aims to analyze the scientific production from the Web of Science (WoS) database, associated to teaching digital competence (TDC) in universities. Based on the PRISMA methodology, the following research variables were taken into consideration: 1. Countries in which researches are carried out; 2. Researchers interested in the topic; 3. Methodological designs used in the investigations; 4. Objectives stated in the studies and 5. Main findings or contributions. The research was delimited through ERIC thesaurus or its approximations, 187 scientific publications were located. It is evident that, at the European level, especially in Spain, there is a significant number of authors who concentrate their interest in the subject, at the Latin American level there are isolated efforts and limited policies to develop digital teaching skills, so the status of study is germinal; research approaches are predominantly quantitative. It is discovered that the ambiguity caused by the complexity of conceptualization of the subject limits the possibility of establishing satisfactory protocols in the generation of training plans; through the research analyzed a significant gap is identified in some of the dimensions based on the different frames of reference. The research is established as the starting point for a similar analysis in other scientific databases, and it is noticed the need to define and develop TDC reference frameworks oriented to hybrid, online or distance study modalities.

Keywords: Systematic literature review · Higher education · Teachers' education · ICT · Digital literacy · Teaching digital competence

1 Introduction

Competence is the comprehensive action that allows the human being to identify, interpret, argue, and solve problems of a context in an appropriate and ethical manner, integrating understanding how to be, how to do, and how to know [1]. Likewise, it is the ability to analyze, reason and communicate effectively as problems are presented[2], solved and interpreted in a variety of settings and are manifested in actions such as behaviors or choices that can be measured and observed [3].

© The Author(s), under exclusive license to Springer Nature Switzerland AG 2023
M. Botto-Tobar et al. (Eds.): ICAT 2022, CCIS 1755, pp. 61–74, 2023.
https://doi.org/10.1007/978-3-031-24985-3_5

Digital competence encompasses the combination of knowledge, attitudes, abilities and capabilities [4–6], whose purpose is the usage of digital tools in a responsible, safe and critical manner [7–9].

In this context, teaching digital competence refers to the critical and safe application of information society technologies for communication, work and leisure [8], and comprise abilities, knowledge and attitudes of professors to improve student learning, through the design and transformation of practices within the classroom, thus enriching the teaching occupation [10]. Similarly, [11], state that those characterize the current professional teaching profile in higher education.

Due to the pandemic and other factors, in recent years it has become essential to implement educational processes in virtuality, because of that there are questions about the levels of digital skills of teachers and students [12]; thus, in order that students achieve planned learning efficiently, university professors must improve their skills, while it is expected that members of society in general receive formal digital literacy as well [13], however, in many cases, less value is given to tasks related to the design of teaching activities, creation of material with digital resources, monitoring and communication with the student, compared to the work generated by publications of scientific articles [14].

Undoubtedly, digital competence is an emerging issue in the 21st century [15], although different frameworks are visualized, most focus on the pre-university level or adult training, the most researched topic areas have been teacher training, language teaching, hospital care, tourism or information technology [16], and digital technologies practice in university education that concentrates on student's learning instead of teachers' teaching [17], so the current challenge is to get teachers and future teachers to reflect, investigate and understand from the daily presence of information and communication technologies (ICT) in trainers' job [18], so the training gap in relation to this topic is evident in the university environment [19–21]. Also, the study of important findings show the role that the teacher performs to handle the learning process and to encourage students about the acquisition of digital competences [22].

This research addresses a systematic literature review (SLR) in the Web of Science (WoS), about digital competences in higher education teaching, to obtain a clear and complete vision in this line of research; for which the following primary research questions are raised: 1. Which are the countries where researches related to the subject are developed?; 2. What researchers worldwide are interested on the subject?; 3. What methodological designs are used in these investigations?; 4. What objectives are intended to be achieved through the investigations?; and 5. Which are the main findings or contributions?. To give rigor to the systematic review process, additional or secondary research questions related to the meta-analysis of the scientific productions located in the search were established: a. ¿In what years there is a larger number of publications? b. ¿What is the origin of these works? c. ¿Which authors concentrate the production of this topic? d. ¿From which countries do the investigations come? e. ¿What kind of documents are these investigations based on? f. ¿What areas of research do these documents focus on? g. ¿What is the predominant language? h. ¿What are the most cited works? and i. ¿What entities are funding research in this field?.

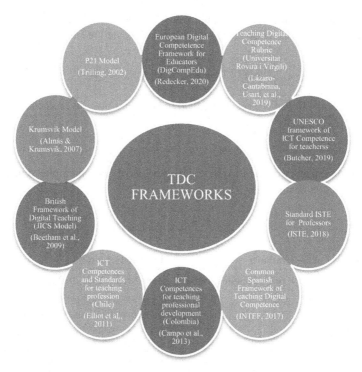

Fig. 1. Teaching digital competence frameworks [23–32].

2 Method

This research was a systematic literature review (SLR), with a meta-analysis [34], based on the quality indicators of PRISMA Declaratory [35]; these analyzes improve the quality of the methods and results of the publications [38, 39].

The objective was to analyze the scientific production with the greatest impact from the Web of Science (WoS) database, about teaching digital competence in universities, the following primary research variables were taken into consideration [38]: 1. Countries in which the investigations are carried out; 2. Researchers interested in the investigated topic; 3. Methodological designs used; 4. Objectives to be achieved through the investigations and 5. Main findings or contributions; with the meta-analysis application, additional variables were established in order to strengthen the systematic review process, as follows: a. In what years there is a larger number of publications? b. What is the origin of these works? c. In which authors the production of this theme is concentrated? d. From which countries do the investigations come? e. What kind of documents these investigations are based on? f. What areas of research do these documents focus on? g. What is the predominant language? h. What are the most cited works? and i. What entities are funding research in this field? The review was carried out in a sequential and rigorous manner, delimiting the research through ERIC thesaurus or its approximations, trying to have a standardized and controlled language [39–42], descriptors were selected, by using the operator "and" in the search, according to Table 1: "digital competences" as the main aspect, "higher education", "university teachers" and "teaching", to define the context of the investigation; the search was performed in English.

Table 1. Database search procedure WoS

Descriptors	Digital competences; Higher education; University teachers; Teaching
Operator	And

Inclusion criteria were defined for each of the variables contemplated in the research for data selection (Table 2).

Table 2. Inclusion criteria

Number of variable	Variable	Inclusion Criteria
1	Year of publication	Year 2012 – Year 2022 (august)
2	Origin	They are selected from the fact that three or more investigations converge in the same resource (magazine, book, etc.)
3	Authors	Investigations must be possessed, at least, three references about the topic
4	Countries	Investigations must be possessed, at least, three references about the topic
5	Documentary typology	All references are taken account
6	Investigation area	Investigations must be possessed, at least, three references about the topic
7	Languages	All references are taken account
8	Most cited publications	Investigations must be possessed, at least, six references about the topic
9	Financing Entities	Investigations must be possessed, at least, two references about the topic

3   Results

It was identified 187 indexed articles in the Web of Science (WoS) database for the meta-analysis process, after a complete observation, 40 references were selected to answer the main research questions.

3.1   Meta-analysis Results

Variable a: Analysis of the Scientific Productions Obtained According to the Year of Publication. Based on the inclusion criterion previously defined, the search was carried out from 2012, including august 2022, that means the ten prior years to the investigation (Table 3).

Table 3. Amount of scientific productions per year.

Year of publication	Number of scientific productions	% de 187
2021	31	16,58%
2020	38	20,32%
2019	39	**20,86%**
2018	21	11,23%
2017	18	9,63%
2016	10	5,35%
2015	12	6,42%
2014	6	3,21%
2013	4	2,14%
2012	8	4,28%
Total	187	100,00%

Variable b: Analysis of the Scientific Productions Obtained According to their Origin Table 4 shows the titles of the sources of the scientific publications on the subject matter. Table 4 can be seen in the attached web link (https://bit.ly/unach-edu-ec).

Variable c: Analysis of the Scientific Productions Obtained According to the Authors To know who are the most relevant authors that investigate about teaching digital competences in higher education (Table 5), it was stablished at least three scientific productions as inclusion criterion.

Variable d: Analysis of the Scientific Productions Obtained According to the Country Where it Originates. The concentration of the number of scientific productions by country, according to the topic raised in this research, is presented in Table 6.

Table 6 can be seen in the attached web link (https://bit.ly/unach-edu-ec).

Variable e: Analysis of the Scientific Productions Obtained According to the Type of Document. All types of existing documents have been considered in the search, this means, articles, book chapters, reviews, conferences, etc., as shown in Table 7.

Variable f: Analysis of the Scientific Productions Obtained According to the Research Area. Table 8 reveals the research areas of publications, according to the search defined based on the inclusion criteria, which consider at least three scientific productions.

Table 5. Amount of scientific productions per author.

Authors	Number of scientific productions	% de 187
Ainoutdinova I	3	**1,60%**
Artal-Sevil JS	3	**1,60%**
Barroso-Osuna J	3	**1,60%**
Blagoveshchenskaya A	3	**1,60%**
Cabero-Almenara J	3	**1,60%**
Dmitrieva E	3	**1,60%**
Esteve-Mon, Francesc M	3	**1,60%**
Gisbert-Cervera, Mercè	3	**1,60%**
Guillen-Gamez FD	3	**1,60%**
Nurutdinova A	3	**1,60%**
Palacios-Rodríguez A	3	**1,60%**
Other	154	83,35%
Total	187	100,00%

Table 7. Amount of scientific productions as the category of document.

Type of document	Number of scientific productions	% de 187
Articles	112	**59,89%**
Books	1	0,53%
Early access	4	2,14%
Meetings	79	42,25%
Other	3	1,60%
Review Articles	3	1,60%

Variable g: Analysis of the Scientific Productions Obtained According to the Language of the Publication. All scientific writing has been considered, without establishing exclusion criteria based on language for this research (Table 9).

Variable h: Analysis of the Scientific Productions Extracted based on Citations. The most recognized scientific productions about digital competencies of university teachers are specified in Table 10 (Number of scientific productions based on citations).

Table 10 can be seen in the attached web link (https://bit.ly/unach-edu-ec).

Variable i: Analysis of the Scientific Productions Obtained According to the Financing Entities. It can be seen in Table 11, the worldwide entities with metadata in the search: educational, governmental, public, and private, that finance the study of the topic of this investigation.

Table 8. Amount of scientific productions according to the research area.

Research area	Number of scientific productions	% de 187
Educational Research	158	**84,49%**
Computer Science	10	5,35%
Psychology	10	5,35%
Social Science	7	3,74%
Communication	6	3,21%
Environment and Ecology	6	3,21%
Health Science Services	6	3,21%
Business and Economy	5	2,67%
Information Science and Library	4	2,14%
Occupational Health	4	2,14%
Geography	3	1,60%
Science, technologies, and other areas	3	1,60%

Table 9. Amount of scientific productions according to the language of the publication.

Languages	Number of scientific productions	% de 187
English	126	**67,38%**
Spanish	53	28,34%
Russian	3	1,60%
German	2	1,07%
Korean	2	1,07%
Latvian	1	0,53%
Total	187	100,00%

3.2 Primary Research Results

To answer the research questions, it was elaborated the Primary Research Results Matrix in Table 12 (Research Results), which contains the country where investigations have been developed, the research design raised in the works, which authors have participated in the research, what is the main objective of these productions and their main findings. Table 12 can be seen in the attached web link (https://bit.ly/3ToEHqW).

4 Discussion

It can be appreciated that 57.75% of the scientific production is concentrated on 2019, 2020 and 2021, with a total of 108 scientific products. Rejecting the year 2021, in 2019

Table 11. Amount of scientific productions based on financing entities.

Financing entities	Number of scientific productions	% de 187
Zaragoza University	3	1,60%
European Comission	2	1,07%
Finland Ministry of Education and Culture	2	1,07%
María Paula Alonso de Ruiz Martínez Foundation	2	1,07%
Rudn University	2	1,07%

a higher number of products is observed comparing to the remaining years, with a total of thirty-nine productions, which make up 20.86% of the total. It can be considered that the 2021 will surely be the year with the greatest scientific production, because until October it has thirty-one scientific productions, equivalent to 16.58% of the total. Less development around the proposed theme is found in 2013, with a total of four scientific productions, which represent 2.14% of the total search; on average, about 19 works are produced per year related to digital competences in university teachers. Since 2017, it is evident a growth in the publication of scientific works related to the subject.

Eighteen titles of publications are included, which host one hundred and twelve scientific productions, this is equivalent to 59.89% of the production located in the proposed search, the origin that presents a greater number of productions is Edulearn Proceedings, with a total of twenty two works, that is, 11.76% of the total. It can be seen that 50.80% of the production of the inclusion group corresponds to ninety-five works of relevance from congresses and conferences: Edulearn Proceedings, Iceri Proceedings and Inted Proceedings and seventeen articles published in five indexed journals: Virtual Campuses, Elearning and Software for Education, Edmetic, International Journal of Environmental Research and Public Health and Latinamerican Journal of Educative Technology (Revista Latinoamericana de Tecnología Educativa RELATEC), which are equivalent to 9.09% of the inquiry. A significant number of origins that have not met the requirement of having at least three scientific products are not included in the analysis, among which we can mention: Open Classroom (Aula Abierta), Education Sciences, Information Technologies and Learning Tools, Pixel Bit Education and Media Journal (Revista de Medios y Educación), Teachers Magazine of Curriculum and Teacher Training, Psychology, Knowledge and Society, Conrado Magazine, Interuniversity Magazine of Teacher Training Rifop, Sustainability, Technology Knowledge And Learning, among others. It is relevant to note that most of these titles allow publications in the English language.

The locations where scientific productions have been developed are concentrated in nineteen countries that encompass one hundred and eighty-four works, equivalent to 98.40% of the total: Spain; Russia; Italy; Finland; Ecuador; Germany; Chili; Colombia; Mexico; Portugal; Romania; Brazil; Hungary; Peru; Czech Republic; France; Norway;

Sweden; Ukraine; an Ibero-American and European interest is appreciated, emphasizing, once again, Spain, with eighty-nine scientific productions equivalent to 47.59%; Russia stands out with thirteen scientific productions equivalent to 0.95%; countries are excluded from the analysis, based on Table 2, for instance: Latvia, the United States and the United Kingdom.

The search reveals articles, communications/lectures (meetings), early access articles (only in the main collection of Web of Science, [43]), review articles and books; predominating the category of articles, with a total of one hundred and twelve works, equivalent to 59.89% of all products; the importance and validity of the object of study of the research is revealed by viewing seventy-nine communications or presentations, which represent 42.25% of the totality; a relevant work corresponding to the books category is estimated, which represents 0.53%.

According to the scope of publication, the predominant research area is educational research, with a total of one hundred fifty-eight works, equivalent to 84.49% of the total; scientific productions in areas such as: computer science, psychology, social sciences, communication, environment and ecology, health science services, business, economics, among others, can be observed on a smaller scale.

From the metadata obtained through the Web of Science based on the defined search, only it has been obtained information of fifty-six scientific productions, equivalent to 29.95% related to the entities that finance the research; it can be considered that in general, the entities dedicated to financing the study of the subject in question come from the European Continent, essentially Spain has a significant number of entities that have invested resources to address the subject.

In the publication titles that house the most referenced scientific productions, a prevalence of the English language and with European origin is observed. With sixty-two citations, the most referenced work is published by the first quartile indexed journal "International Journal of Educational Technology in Higher Education", of Dutch origin [44]; it is consider valuable scientific productions such as [45], published in Salamanca University journal "Education in the Knowledge Society" and [23] in the Spain journal Comunicar".

A total of fifty-three articles in Spanish are observed, representing 28.34% of the totality of localized works; however, the research variable origin of the publication titles shows a total of one hundred twenty-six articles in the English language, which represent 67.38% in general.

There are eleven authors, who have at least three works, and are equivalent to 17.60% of the total scientific production located: Ainoutdinova I.; Artal-Sevil JS; Barroso-Osuna J.; Blagoveshchenskaya A.; Cabero-Almenara J.; Dmitrieva E.; Esteve-Mon Francesc; Gisbert-Cervera Mercè; Guillen-Gamez F.D.; Nurutdinova and Palacios-Rodriguez A.; most belong to universities of Spanish origin and from Russian Federation; authors such as: Artalsevil JS; Cuevas-Cervero A.; De Rossi M; Duta N; Gomez MCS.; Gómez-Hernández JA.; Gutierrez-Castillo JJ.; Kauppinen S.; Lahti J.; Leone V.; Llorente AMP.; Luojus S.; Marine VI; Martin-Cuadrado A M.; Mayorga-Fernández MJ.; Merchant C.; Muukkonen H.; Ship EP.; Perez E.; Perez KVP.; Perez-Sanchez L.; Restiglian E.; Rivilla AM; Romero M.; Ruiz-Cabezas A.; Salts D; Zhao Y.; among others, are excluded from the analysis for not meeting the criteria mentioned.

The design of the investigations located through the search descriptors mostly follows quantitative methodologies, with 50% of the totality; the mixed research method is used in 27.77% of the works, and the qualitative method characterizes 22.23% of the references; a fact that is consistent with the interest of researchers related to the subject, since they concentrate their efforts fundamentally on studies related to the design, validation and/or application of evaluation rubrics of teaching digital competences in various contexts and under the premise of analysis of numerous quantitative variables that are related to the dimensions that are part of the various current reference frameworks or that are developed for this purpose. Other aspects that arouse the dedication of authors are related to the analysis and comparison of digital teaching competences levels in higher education through the use of technological resources and tools; inquiries aimed at determining teaching profiles related to digital competences can also be seen, emphasizing variables such as gender, age, initial training, professional training, among others. Moreover, efforts to clarify the evident conceptualization problem of teaching digital competences can be observed, mostly through systematic literature reviews.

Because many institutions for teachers intend to create and evaluate teachers' capabilities in teaching practice [46–48], inquiries about TDC contribute to improving the understanding of the teaching-learning processes, based on the study of the improvement of abilities and skills of the university academic members and the initial and continuous training processes that are implemented.

Results of this study highlight the need for efficient training, establishing teachers' profiles with specific parameters based on clearly determined groups through the variables object of study of several investigations, strengthening the pedagogical dimension, which is described with lower levels of achievement [49–52], therefore, it is necessary to develop potentialities from digital tools to teach/learn and generate digitally competent students. Within this study, it is proposed to develop research whose scope considers the inclusion of educational data mining techniques[47, 53–60]; in order to be able to establish, for example, if the evaluations of the competences based on the frameworks described, established well-defined levels of responsibilities and professional recognition [61]. It is recommended to implement a similar analysis in other scientific databases, which allows responding to the difficulties detected by defining and developing TDC reference frameworks in universities with online or distance modalities.

5 Conclusions

There is a considerable bias since 2019 around the growth of works related to the subject, which could be because of the effects produced in the educational field the Covid 19 pandemic, the same one that instituted a greater relevance in the proposed research topic. Unlike other studies that show greater scientific production in other years [62].

It could be evident a strong relationship between the nationality of the authors and the countries where most of investigations originate with the language in which they are published (Spanish Language); however, the research variable origin of publication titles represents the opposite through the predominance of the English language for scientific works.

Through the definition of the descriptors, without considering the inclusion criteria, that means before 2012, a qualitative production related to the matter object of study from Anglo-Saxon countries can be noticed specially in aspects associated to the conceptualization of digital competences and its application.

Despite the fact that it is a widely extended concept in the European educational field (Spain with the highest incidence), there is no a single way of understanding digital competence. In studies deployed from the old continent to the Latin American context, the application of TDC evaluation rubrics can be seen in several countries (Chile, Ecuador, Peru, Uruguay, among others), where it has been necessary a prior validation of instruments from the terminology used, a fact that confirms that it is essential to make the understanding of the subject more flexible, by considering the transversality of the concept and assimilating that digital competences are multifunctional, therefore, they encompass all the necessary competences for an appropriate development in the actual society.

Although some Latin American governments (Chile, Colombia, Uruguay) have looked at the study of teaching digital competences with some interest, very little has been developed regarding to the implementation of educational policies in the university context; its study is on the initial stage and most of the efforts are carried out in an isolated manner through regional or local institutions or universities. Likewise, very few efforts are observed of national governments to establish reference frameworks that guide action protocols in training teaching staff.

Through the various studies carried out around the world, important gaps can be seen in the various dimensions of TDC, however, teacher profiles have not been determined in a disaggregated manner based on the variables object of study (gender, age, initial training, professional training, etc.), in order to determine if there are common problems between various populations that could be addressed through strategic training plans previously implemented in other latitudes.

References

1. Perrenoud, P.: BUILDING COMPETENCES - IS IT TO TURN AWAY FROM KNOWL-EDGE? Revista de Docencia Universitaria. 274 (2008)
2. María Jesús Gallego Arrufat, Vanesa Gámiz Sánchez, E.G.S.: Vista del futuro docente ante las conformación y comunicación para enseñar. Edutec. Revista Electrónica de Tecnologia Educativa (2010)
3. OCDE: La definición y selección de competencias clave (2005)
4. Rangel, A.: Propuesta De Un Perfil Digital Teaching Skills : a Profile. Pixel-Bit. Revista de Medios y Educación, 235–248 (2015)
5. Vivar, D.M.: Ramón Cózar Gutiérrez y Mª del Valle de Moya Martínez (coords.) (2013) Las TIC en el aula desde un enfoque multidisciplinar. Aplicaciones practices. Barcelona: Octaedro. ENSAYOS. Revista de la Facultad de Educación de Albacete. **29**, 181–182 (2014). https://doi.org/10.18239/ensayos.v29i2.645
6. Zepeda, H., Méndez, M.E., Galván, H.: Evaluación de la Competencia Digital en Profesores de Educación Superior de la Costa Norte de Jalisco. Revista Iberoamericana de producción académica y gestión educativa. 6 (2019)
7. Ferrari, A.: Digital Competence in Practice: An Analysis of Frameworks. Joint Research Centre of the European Commission, 91 (2013). https://doi.org/10.2791/82116
8. Cisneros-Barahona, A., Marqués Molías, L., Samaniego Erazo, N., Uvidia Fassler, M., Castro-Ortiz, W., Rosas-Chávez, P.: Digital competence of university teachers. An overview of the state of the art. HUMAN REVIEW. International Humanities Review / Revista Internacional de Humanidades. 11, 1–25 (2022). https://doi.org/10.37467/revhuman.v11.4355

9. Cisneros-Barahona, A., Marqués Molías, L., Samaniego Erazo, G., Uvidia-Fassler, M., de la Cruz-Fernández, G., Castro-Ortiz, W.: Teaching Digital Competence in Higher Education. A Comprehensive Scientific Mapping Analysis with Rstudio BT - Doctoral Symposium on Information and Communication Technologies. Presented at the (2022)
10. Grande-De-Prado, M., Cañón-Rodríguez, R., Cantón-Mayo, I.: Competencia digital y tratamiento de la información en futuros maestros de Primaria. Educatio Siglo XXI. **34**, 101 (2016). https://doi.org/10.6018/j/275961
11. Hall, R., Atkins, L., Fraser, J.: Defining a self-evaluation digital literacy framework for secondary educators: the DigiLit Leicester project. Res. Learn. Technol. **22**, 1–17 (2014)
12. Cateriano-Chavez, T.J., Rodríguez-Rios, M.L., Patiño-Abrego, E.L., Araujo-Castillo, R.L., Villalba-Condori, K.O.: Digital skills, methodology and evaluation in teacher trainers I Competencias digitales, metodología y evaluación en formadores de docentes. Campus Virtuales. **10**, 153–162 (2021)
13. Cuadrado, A.M.M., Sánchez, L.P., de la Torre, M.J.: Teachers digital competences in Digcomp-based university environments. Educar em Revista. **36**, 1–21 (2020). https://doi.org/10.1590/0104-4060.75866
14. Alejaldre L., Á.E.: Digital teaching competence of the university professor 3.0 I La competencia digital docente del profesor universitario 3.0. Caracteres. **8**, 205–236 (2019)
15. Mattila, A.: The future educator skills in the digitization era: effects of technological development on higher education. In: Proceedings - 2015 5th International Conference on e-Learning, ECONF 2015. 358, pp. 212–215 (2016). https://doi.org/10.1109/ECONF.2015.18
16. Sánchez-Caballé, A., Gisbert-Cervera, M., Esteve-Mon, F.: The digital competence of university students: a systematic literature review. Aloma: Revista de Psicologia, Ciències de l'Educació i de l'Esport. **38**, 63–74 (2020). https://doi.org/10.51698/aloma.2020.38.1.63-74
17. Esteve-Chavez, F.M., Llopis-Nebot, M.A., Adell-Segura, J.: Digital teaching competence of university teachers: a systematic review of the literature. IEEE Revista Iberoamericana de Tecnologias del Aprendizaje. **15**, 399–406 (2020). https://doi.org/10.1109/RITA.2020.303 3225
18. Guri-Rosenblit, S.: E-teaching in higher education: an essential prerequisite for e-learning. J. New Approach. Educ. Res. **7**, 93–97 (2018). https://doi.org/10.7821/naer.2018.7.298
19. Gallardo, E., Marqués, L., Gisbert-Cervera, M.: Importance of Ict Competences Within the Framework of. Edutec. Revista Electrónica de Tecnologia Educativa. **36**, 1–15 (2011)
20. Angulo, J., García, R.I., Torres, C.A., Pizá, R.I., Ortíz, E.R.: Nivel de Logro de Competencias Tecnológicas del Profesorado Universitario. Int. Multilingual J. Contemporary Res. **3**, 67–80 (2015). https://doi.org/10.15640/imjcr.v3n1a8
21. Juan Gutiérrez, J.C.: A Case study self-percepcion digital competence of the university student in Bachelor's degrees in the Pre-School Teacher Education and Primary. 2 (2016)
22. Fernandez-Diaz, M., Robles-Moral, F.J., Ayuso-Fernández, G.E.: Una propuesta para trabajar la competencia digital docente a través de Instagram y el Pensamiento Visual: el estudio de la sostenibilidad. Revista Latinoamericana de Tecnología Educativa - RELATEC. **20**, 87–102 (2021). https://doi.org/10.17398/1695-288X.20.1.87
23. Pérez-Mateo-Segura, M., Romero-Carbonell, M., Romeu-Fontanillas, T.: Collaborative construction of a project as a methodology for acquiring digital competences. Comunicar. **21**, 15–24 (2014). https://doi.org/10.3916/C42-2014-01
24. Trilling, B.: 21st Century Student Outcomes (2002)
25. Almås, A.G., Krumsvik, R.: Digitally literate teachers in leading edge schools in Norway. J. In-Service Educ. **33**, 479–497 (2007). https://doi.org/10.1080/13674580701687864
26. Beetham, H., McGill, L., Littlejohn, A.: Thriving in the 21st century: the report of the LLiDA project (Learning Literacies for the Digital Age): Competency frameworks A JISC funded study, pp. 1–24 (2009)

27. Elliot, J., Gorichon, S., Irigoin, M., Maurizi, M.: Competencias y Estándares TIC para la Profesión Docente (2011)
28. Campo, F., Segovia, R., Martínez, P., Rendón, H., Calderón, G.: Competencias TIC para el desarrollo profesional docente (2013)
29. INTEF: Marco Común de Competencia Digital Docente (2017)
30. ISTE: Crosswalk: Future Ready Librarians Framework and ISTE Standards for Educators. (2008)
31. Butcher, N.: Marco de competencias docentes en materia de TIC UNESCO (2019)
32. Lázaro-Cantabrana, J.L., Usart, M., Cervera, M.G.: Assessing teacher digital competence: the construction of an instrument for measuring the knowledge of pre-service teachers. J. New Approac. Educ. Res. **8**, 73–78 (2019). https://doi.org/10.7821/naer.2019.1.370
33. Redecker, C.: Marco Europeo para la Competencia Digital de los Educadores: DigCompEdu (2020)
34. Cardona Arias, J.A., Higuita Gutiérrez, L.F., Ríos Osorio, L.A.: Revisiones sistemáticas de la literatura científica: La investigación teórica como principio para el desarrollo de la ciencia básica y aplicada (2016). https://doi.org/10.16925/9789587600377
35. Urrutia, G., Bonfill, X.: PRISMA declaration: a proposal to improve the publication oy systematic reviews and meta-analyses (2010)
36. Gálvez, P.G.: Training on research and articles discussed. Enferm Intensiva. **30**, 33–37 (2019). https://doi.org/10.1016/j.enfi.2019.01.001
37. Panic, N., Leoncini, E., de Belvis, G., Ricciardi, W., Boccia, S.: Evaluation of the endorsement of the preferred reporting items for systematic reviews and meta-analysis (PRISMA) statement on the quality of published systematic review and meta-analyses. PLoS One **8** (2013). https://doi.org/10.1371/journal.pone.0083138
38. Rodríguez-García, A.-M., Raso Sánchez, F., Ruiz-Palmero, J.: Competencia digital, educación superior y formación del profesorado: un estudio de meta-análisis en la web of science. Pixel-Bit, Revista de Medios y Educación, 65–82 (2019). https://doi.org/10.12795/pixelbit. 2019.i54.04
39. Fernández Quijada, D.: El uso de tesauros para el análisis temático de la producción científica: apuntes metodológicos desde una experiencia práctica. BiD. Textos Universitaris de Biblioteconomia i Documentacio. **29**(9) (2012). https://doi.org/10.1344/BiD2012.29.15
40. Montoya, C.A.: Descripción del tesauro del Sistema tesauro de información de la literatura colombiana. Redalyc. **32**, 123–146 (2010)
41. Martínez Tamayo, A.M., Mendes, P.V.: Diseño y desarrollo de tesauros. (2015)
42. Blanco, S.A., Martín Álvarez, R.: Tesauros: ¡menuda palabrota! No todo es clínica. Actualización en Medicina de Familia. **15**, 509–515 (2019)
43. Analytics, C.: Colección principal de Web of Science Ayuda. https://images.webofknowledge. com/WOKRS535R111/help/es_LA/WOS/hs_document_type.html. Accessed 10 Nov 2021
44. Bond, M., Marín, V.I., Dolch, C., Bedenlier, S., Zawacki-Richter, O.: Digital transformation in German higher education: student and teacher perceptions and usage of digital media. Int. J. Educ. Technol. High. Educ. 15(1), 1–20 (2018). https://doi.org/10.1186/s41239-018-0130-1
45. García-Peñalvo, F.J., Corell, A., Abella-García, V., Grande, M.: Online assessment in higher education in the time of COVID-19. Educ. Knowl. Soc. **21**, 26 (2020). https://doi.org/10. 14201/eks.23013
46. Marqués-Molías, L., Esteve-González, V., Holgado-Garcia, J., Cela-Ranilla, J., Sánchez-Caballé, A.: Student perceptions of ePortfolio as competence assessment during the practical training period for early childhood and primary school teaching. In: Proceedings of the European Conference on e-Learning, ECEL. 2016-Janua, pp. 777–781 (2016)
47. Uvidia-Fassler, M., Cisneros-Barahona, A., Viñan-Carrera, J.: Minería de Datos de la Evaluación Integral del Desempeño Académico de la Unidad de Nivelación. Descubre, pp. 44–54 (2017)

48. Silva, J., Morales, M.-J., Lázaro-Cantabrana, J.-L., Gisbert, M., Miranda, P., Rivoir, A., Onetto, A.: Digital teaching competence in initial training: case studies from Chile and Uruguay. Educ Policy Anal Arch. **27**, 93 (2019). https://doi.org/10.14507/epaa.27.3822
49. Ojeda, P.B.A., Aguilar, M.F.G., Zeran, E.S.: Formación Inicial Docente (FID) y Tecnologías de la Información y Comunicación (TIC) en la Universidad de Magallanes - Patagonia Chilena. Digital Education Review, 135–146 (2016)
50. Lago Martínez, S., Méndez, A., Gendler, M.: Contribuciones al estudio de procesos de apropiación de tecnologías (2017)
51. Ayale-Pérez, T., Joo-Nagata, J.: The digital culture of students of pedagogy specialising in the humanities in Santiago de Chile. Comput Educ. **133**, 1–12 (2019). https://doi.org/10.1016/j.compedu.2019.01.002
52. Silva Quiroz, J., Miranda Arredondo, P.: Presencia de la competencia digital docente en los programas de formación inicial en universidades públicas chilenas. Revista de Estudios y Experiencias en Educación. **19**, 149–165 (2020). https://doi.org/10.21703/rexe.20201941s ilva9
53. B.Aher, S., L.M.R.J, L.: Mining association rule in classified data for course recommender system in E-Learning. Int. J. Comput. Appl. **39**, 1–7 (2012). https://doi.org/10.5120/4829-7086
54. Chatti, M.A., Dyckhoff, A.L., Schroeder, U., Thüs, H.: A reference model for learning analytics Mohamed Amine Chatti *, Anna Lea Dyckhoff. Int. J. Technol. Enhanced Learn. **4**, 318–331 (2012)
55. Uvidia-Fassler, M.I., Cisneros Barahona, A.S., Ávila-Pesántez, D.F., Rodríguez Flores, I.E.: Moving towards a methodology employing knowledge discovery in databases to assist in decision making regarding academic placement and student admissions for universities. In: Botto-Tobar, M., Esparza-Cruz, N., León-Acurio, J., Crespo-Torres, N., Beltrán-Mora, M. (eds.) CITT 2017. CCIS, vol. 798, pp. 215–229. Springer, Cham (2018). https://doi.org/10.1007/978-3-319-72727-1_16
56. Uvidia-Fassler, M.I., Cisneros Barahona, A.S., Dumancela Nina, G.J., Samaniego Erazo, G.N., Villacrés Cevallos, E.P.: Application of knowledge discovery in data bases analysis to predict the academic performance of university students based on their admissions test. In: Botto-Tobar, M., León-Acurio, J., Díaz Cadena, A., Montiel Díaz, P. (eds.) ICAETT 2019. AISC, vol. 1066, pp. 485–497. Springer, Cham (2020). https://doi.org/10.1007/978-3-030-32022-5_45
57. Cisneros Barahona, A.S., Uvidia Fassler, M.I., Samaniego Erazo, G.N., Dumancela Nina, G.J., Casignia Vásconez, B.A.: Complementary admission processes implemented by ecuadorian public universities promote equal opportunities in access: an analysis through knowledge discovery in databases. In: Botto-Tobar, M., Zamora, W., Larrea Plúa, J., Bazurto Roldan, J., Santamaría Philco, A. (eds.) ICCIS 2020. AISC, vol. 1273, pp. 208–222. Springer, Cham (2021). https://doi.org/10.1007/978-3-030-59194-6_18
58. Uvidia M., C.A.: Análisis de data mining para la toma de decisiones en la unidad de nivelación y admisión a nivel universitario. In: IV Workshop de ciencia innovacion tecnologia y saberes. Unach, p. 2017 (2017)
59. Uvidia, M., Cisneros Barahona, A.: Análisis de data mining para la toma de decisiones en la unidad de nivelación y admisión a nivel universitario. (2017)
60. Ferguson, R.: Learning analytics: drivers, developments and challenges. Int. J. Technol. Enhanced Learn. **4**, 304–317 (2012). https://doi.org/10.1504/IJTEL.2012.051816
61. Fortuño M., Cervera M, Molías L., R.N.: Competency evaluation. Revista de enfermería (2009)
62. Cisneros-Barahona, A., Marqués Molías, L., Samaniego Erazo, G., Uvidia-Fassler, M., de la Cruz-Fernández, G., Castro-Ortiz, W.: Teaching Digital Competence in Higher Education. A Comprehensive Scientific Mapping Analysis with Rstudio. Presented at the (2022). https://doi.org/10.1007/978-3-031-18347-8_2

Evaluation of the Kahoot Tool as an Applied Assessment in Physical Education Learning

Gustavo Buele-Guerrero and Pablo Torres-Carrión[(⊠)] [iD]

Universidad Técnica Particular de Loja, Loja 1101608, Ecuador
{gfbuele,pvtorres}@utpl.edu.ec

Abstract. Technology and gamification strategies have influenced and modified the teaching-learning methods through various educational tools that allow motivating, arousing interest and complementing the training of students, however, it is essential to analyze the use of these as new assessment tools to obtain formative results. Therefore, the proposed objective is to analyze the valuation of Kahoot as an evaluation tool in the subject of Physical Education, for which the perception of 77 high school students of the tenth year of EGB and their teacher has been evaluated; the intervention is carried out in 6 classes with different topics of study. The results were positive because they help to strengthen learning, memorize concepts, self-evaluate knowledge and generate great interest, in conclusion, they consider Kahoot as an effective tool for the evaluation of the teaching process of the subject.

Keywords: Education · Gamification · Physical education · Kahoot

1 Introduction

The natural predisposition of human beings towards competition and play, and learning strategies based on play, favor student interaction, motivate the development of academic activities and improve academic results [1], even in environments of gestural interaction, in people with learning limitations, as in the case of people with Down Syndrome, significant improvements have been achieved [2, 3]. The assessment process has always been a challenge for the entire educational system, and technology has been a great ally. Making use of game strategies and technological tools, as tools and strategies to improve the evaluation process in the COVID-19 era, is the context from which this research work is proposed.

1.1 The Problem and Context

The educational system worldwide had to face great challenges in the face of the health pandemic of COVID-19, leading educational strategies and policies towards the virtual modality, being the curricular readjustment a great challenge, particularly for those subjects that have a practical nature such as physical education [4]. In [5], the support capabilities and response levels of online education platforms during COVID-19 are explored, and corresponding measures are proposed to improve the performance of these platforms, being the most used: MOOCm TIM, Chaoxing, ZoomCloud, WeChat Work, Tencent Meeting and DingTalk; regarding the User Experience results of these platforms, Zoom has been the one with the best score.

The learning assessment process has been a major challenge during the COVID-19 pandemic. Previous studies have focused on the levels of teacher motivation and student engagement from the educator's perspective, as a complementary strategy to the use of communication technologies [6]; In [7], researchers prove that WhatsApp application can support online learning evaluation activities even though the implementation process is not optimal. In [8], an online instructional process is proposed, in which teachers implemented Google's Jamboard collaborative whiteboard as a tool to develop collaborative activities and evaluate learning outcomes; the results show that the use of virtual workspaces helps students to develop their collaborative skills. Thus, there is an abundance of research that demonstrates the feasibility of using digital tools for learning assessment.

Regarding the evaluation in areas related to physical activity and health, in [9] they state that sport and other subjects related to physical activity, have practical elements that in pandemic have experienced complications to provide continuity, and answer questions such as how to teach? where to teach? and propose transformative changes in what sport management academicians teach. In the case of physical education, the main problem is that physical skills and activities are complicated to transmit through a screen and often require close supervision and even physical contact to ensure that the exercise is executed correctly.

1.2 Aspectos Teóricos Relevantes

In this work, the **assessment of learning** is the main theoretical-scientific area under study, with emphasis on the use of technologies and game strategies. According to [10] the traditional evaluation is characterized by multiple choice, true or false, ordering, evaluative judgment, in addition the evaluator presents by means of a score the student's knowledge and the evaluation is under the teacher's decision. While the alternative evaluation is carried out through debates, portfolios, experiments, judgment based on observation and professional judgment, it is an individual evaluation with respect to the student's own learning, allowing them to participate in their own evaluation. Table 1 shows the procedures to assess learning according to the approaches proposed by Mateo [10].

Table 1. Evaluation procedures

Traditional assessment procedures	
Objective tests Clear and precise questions that demand from the student an answer limited to a choice among a series of alternatives. The following is a description of the wording of the questions or items	
Single choice items	The question is preceded by a set of answers among which only one is true, and others (the distractors) are false
Multiple choice items	You must choose several answers that are true among different alternatives
Best answer selection items	All are true and you must determine which is the best
Incorrect answer selection items	The student who marks the answer that is not correct. The distractors correspond precisely to correct answers
Common base items	The same information is used to generate, around it, different sets of questions
Ordering items	The student reads a series of concepts that appear out of order, which must be ordered according to a criterion that has been previously established
Graph identification and map location items	A graph or a map is presented and the student must carry out the identification or localization exercise
True or false items	The student's response requires a separate decision regarding the correctness or incorrectness of statements
Matching items	They consist of two lists, one of premises and one of answers, and clear instructions for matching the two lists
Scientific-mathematical problem items	Quantitative relations, presents a problem that one must try to represent only what one wants to test
Alternative evaluation procedures	
Portfolio	Compilation of the student's work, collected over time, which provides evidence of the student's knowledge
Project Development	Period of time the student must perform a complex activity, with a specific objective, communication skills, team or individual work are evaluated

(*continued*)

Table 1. (*continued*)

Traditional assessment procedures	
Mixed evaluation procedures	
Free written tests	It refers to the presentation of the questions and the orientation of the type of answer expected
Oral free examinations	Free test consisting of a dialogue between one or more examiners and an examinee, in order to test the student's mastery of certain knowledge and skills

Regarding Gamification, Zichermann and Cunningham [11] mention that it can be understood as the use of elements in game systems to create experiences and can be applied in different fields, such as: politics, finance, health, education, etc. González et al. [12] divides gamification into three parts: a) game elements, are those universal elements that most games possess such as strategies, points, avatars, etc.; b) development techniques: It is mainly based on the design of the games, and the construction mechanics behind them; c) the context, which refers to the non-game area where the different gamification strategies are developed. Gamification thanks to its mechanics and tools, generates fun for learning, stimulate the brain and this is extrapolable to theoretical learning; According to Werbach and Hunter [13] there are six fundamental steps to be able to gamify something, which have been adapted to the educational context, these are:

1. Define the objectives of the subject, as well as its competencies.
2. Predefine the behaviors of the human factors present (students and teachers).
3. To place and label the players (to predefine behaviors and performances).
4. Devise activity loops.
5. Make it fun.
6. Implement the tools that are ideal for each moment

In this theoretical context, this study is proposed, which promotes the evaluation of learning by applying game techniques and strategies.

1.3 Related Work

A systematic literature search was conducted following Torres-Carrión's method [14], proposing as the main concept the evaluation of learning in sports and physical culture; as filters, documents referring to the use of the technological tool Kahoot were considered and limited to the years 2020 and 2021, which were the years of pandemic, in which it was necessary to apply technological evaluation tools in virtual mode. As a final result, six documents are obtained, which are detailed in Table 2.

Table 2. Studies in which the Kahoot! tool is valued in the educational field.

Title	Author	Year	Method
Effectiveness of Kahoot on high school students' physics exam scores: a case study in Vietnam	[15]	2021	Quantitative evaluation
Assessing Kahoot's Impact on EFL Students' Learning Outcomes	[16]	2020	Mixed method
The Effectiveness of Using Kahoot! Application as An Evaluation Tool in Arabic Vocabulary Learning at Madrasah Ibtidaiyah	[17]	2021	Quasi-experimental method using T-test and ANOVA test
Evaluation of Kahoot! use in presential and virtual higher education	[18]	2020	Quantitative method
Kahoot! EFL instructors' implementation experiences and their impact on students' vocabulary knowledge	[19]	2020	Quasi-experimental mixed-method design
Effectiveness of Kahoot on high school students' physics exam scores: a case study in Vietnam	[20]	2020	Pre-test and Post-test

1.4 About This Document

The objective of this study is to analyze and evaluate the use of the Kahoot tool in the evaluation process through student and teacher feedback. As a research methodology, a descriptive methodology with a qualitative and quantitative approach is applied, for which an educational strategy of gamification with the Kahoot tool is designed; 77 students of tenth grade of General Basic Education (EGB) participate in the didactic intervention, who participate in online gamified evaluations; at the same time, observation by the teacher is carried out to analyze and describe the intervention. Finally, a survey is applied to evaluate the use of the Kahoot tool in the evaluation.

To facilitate the reading of the document, the IMRaD structure is used: Introduction, Method, Results and Discussions. In the Introduction section, the problem of teaching Physical Education and sports, as well as related works, has been explicitly stated. The next section explains the tools and materials used, as well as the research method, including the evaluation tests. Section three contains the relevant results of the study and the final part identifies the main conclusions.

2 Materials and Method

The general objective is *to evaluate the Kahoot tool as an applied evaluation in the learning of Physical Education,* for which the following research questions have been proposed: a) Does Kahoot as an evaluation tool contribute to the measurement of aptitudes and skills in the teaching-learning process? b) What is the students' perception of the use of the Kahoot tool in the teaching-learning evaluation process of Physical Education? which are evaluated on the basis of the following hypothesis:

(h0) Kahoot as a didactic evaluation tool to improve aptitudes and skills related to the subject of Physical Education.

2.1 Materials

The measurement instrument used to evaluate the Kahoot tool is based on the Likert scale and is proposed by the authors Hernández, Belmonte (2020), which is adapted and modified for research purposes. The scale includes 17 items divided into three sections: first assessment of educational skills provided by Kahoot in the evaluation process, second assessment of the use of Kahoot in Physical Education in relation to other subjects, third general assessment of the Kahoot tool in the evaluation process, it consists of 5 response options distributed as follows: Strongly disagree (1), disagree (2), neither agree nor disagree (3), agree (4), strongly agree (5). Likewise, the reliability of the instrument was assessed through Cronbach's Alpha, obtaining a very high value of 0.96. The instrument is applied online through Google forms.

To obtain the measurement and numerical score of the evaluations applied to the students, reports in Excel format are generated and downloaded from the Kahoot tool. In the report the following can be reviewed: correct and incorrect answers, number of participants, response time for each question, best score, with this data it is possible to analyze and make a comparison on the extent to which the learning objectives were met.

2.2 Method

A descriptive methodology with a mixed approach was applied [21]. Neuretier's method [20], adapted to the proposed research purposes, was used to carry out the didactic intervention.

As shown in Fig. 1, in the planning phase we work on the didactic design for the six classes that make up the academic unit. In this phase we follow the specifications established and requested by the Ministry of Education. Activities are planned for the three moments of the class: anticipation (5 min.), knowledge construction (15 min.) and finalization (10 min.), which includes the assessment; additionally, we work on graphic resources for interaction that are placed on slides to be presented to the students. In the second phase, the specific elements of the evaluation are designed, knowing that these must then be adapted to the Kahoot tool, so the items are limited to closed questions; six evaluations are designed, one for each class. In the third phase, which consists of the didactic and practical application of the elaborated pla-nification, the gamified tests are applied in Kahoot, the data is exported in a spreadsheet and the corresponding analysis is carried out. This phase is carried out virtually, due to the restrictions of the pandemic; for the interaction we use the zoom tool, which all the students master, as it has been the way of working for more than a year.

This is a descriptive, non-inferential study, applied to a small sample of students, following the group case study methodology proposed by Stake [22]. Thus, tenth grade students from three different classrooms of the "Unidad Educativa Paltas" participated, with a total of 76 children (f = 42), with an average age of 14.3 years old.

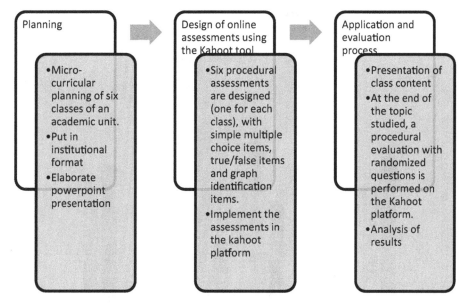

Fig. 1. Macro research process

In order to obtain descriptive data, the participant observation instrument proposed by Richard and Lockhart [23] is used. The observation process takes place between the observed and the observer, where the observer is personified by the researcher who plans the study and keeps the record of each of the observation sections [24]. The observation is carried out in relation to the context of learning and motivation of the students with respect to the activities recorded from the perspective of the teacher.

3   Results and Discussions

3.1   Assessment Process

The results shown in Fig. 2 reflect the percentages of the reports downloaded from the Kahoot tool in the physical education evaluations; It can be seen that there is no greater percentage difference between correct and incorrect questions, however, the curve of correct answers, with the exception of class 3 and class 4, tends to rise.

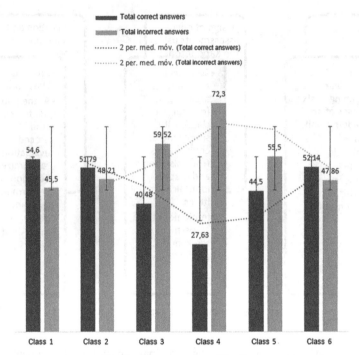

Fig. 2. Summary of qualifications

3.2 Educational Skills

Of the skills and aptitudes evaluated, analysis and reflection, along with comprehension and self-learning, are the ones that have been developed by the students in the highest percentage. These data coincide with those obtained in related gamification studies, such as [19] in English, in [3] writing learning with people with cognitive disabilities and [17] in vocabulary learning (Fig. 3).

Kahoot served as a motivational tool in class, as shown by the result, with 36.4% of the students totally agreeing and 40% agreeing that using Kahoot makes the subject more motivating; this is due to the fact that Kahoot is a playful and didactic tool that avoids the monotony of learning. Kahoot facilitates the organization of study, and there is evidence that it is ideal to include as a study tool, facilitating the organization of content.

The results demonstrate the importance of the Kahoot tool as a gamification methodology in the subject. The same results coincide with what was proposed by Neureiter, Klieser, Neumayer, Winkeilmann, Urbás and Kiesslich [20] who consider that Kahoot generates greater motivation and commitment in students for the acquisition of new knowledge, in addition to improving motivation and promoting relevant learning experiences for students. Finally, Saleh Alharthi [16], demonstrated that the use of Kahoot as an assessment tool in English language teaching proved to be effective in the acquisition of language skills and vocabulary, thus corroborating that the integration of technology enriches learning and that students value Kahoot as an important tool in the educational process.

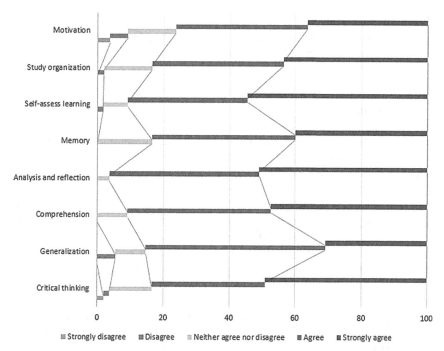

Fig. 3. Educational skills and aptitudes

3.3 Participant Observation

In order to analyze the intervention of the Kahoot tool in the evaluation process, participant observation and data recording were carried out. The Kahoot application serves as an evaluation tool in the subject of Physical Education, applying the gamified evaluation method. The Kahoot application is easily received by the participants, who respond to the items and are motivated as the scores move. It is an effective and fundamental tool, because through the game it allows the teacher to evaluate the progress and knowledge of the students; the planned tests are answered promptly by the students, increasing their attention on the screen and analyzing it quickly and efficiently.

The tool enhances the interaction between teacher and students, because it allows active participation, avoids distractions and includes those students who have learning difficulties; in addition, it generates digital skills in the student due to its easy adaptation, while facilitating the acquisition of knowledge, memorizing, correcting errors with immediate feedback and autonomy by taking responsibility for the answers that measure their knowledge.

In spite of having been a positive tool in the Physical Education class, some difficulties were also found in its application, such as connection problems that did not allow some students to easily complete the tests, they did not have adequate technological equipment that would allow them to develop the activity, some presented attention problems because they had family members with health difficulties.

Finally, it is important to state that the tool in the area of Physical Education generates interest through competition, motivates and encourages students to become more actively involved in the development of the class and facilitates the teacher to teach theoretical contents in a more fun way.

4 Conclusions

- Kahoot, as a new motivational and playful experience, allows students to understand and correct concepts, think quickly, be attentive and exercise memorization, as well as receive immediate feedback to analyze where they have failed. These aspects make students accept it positively as another element of the classroom.
- Kahoot is a useful and innovative tool to be used in the subject of Physical Education or sciences related to sports. It encourages students to consider the development of critical thinking, synthesis capabilities of the theoretical content, for a better understanding, facilitating the acquisition of new concepts. It is considered as a viable didactic resource to comply with the learning evaluation process, providing skills and educational aptitudes, providing feedback on learning and motivating permanent improvement.
- Regarding the perception that students have about the use of Kahoot in Physical Education and its relationship with other subjects, it has been positively evaluated, in contrast to teaching practices where it is not applied; for him it is a motivating and attractive factor, which serves to improve and implement educational strategies of gamification in the subject, making it a playful and didactic tool, which does not fall into monotony, and allows the student to perform his own self-evaluation.
- Gamification through the use of Kahoot is closely related to physical activity, because its mechanism helps in three aspects such as: overcoming levels through points, giving badges for achievement and sharing leaderboards, where the student (player) verifies his position in relation to others, and contributes to a real experience that is lived in the subject in person, although the classes are conducted virtually.
- Regarding the general assessment of the Kahoot tool applied to evaluation, and in response to the proposed hypothesis, scientific evidence of the improvements it promotes in learning has been presented. More than 75% of the students who made up this group, agree and completely agree, in the broad development of skills and aptitudes in Physical Education; they agree that they would like to maintain the use of Kahoot in the subject, since it has been possible to incorporate the game in online teaching, achieving the purpose of being an ideal tool for the evaluation and acquisition of new learning.

References

1. Dindar, M., Ren, L., Järvenoja, H.: An experimental study on the effects of gamified cooperation and competition on English vocabulary learning (2021)
2. Torres-Carrión, P. V., et al.: Improving cognitive visual-motor abilities in individuals with down syndrome. Sensors **19**, 3984 (2019). https://doi.org/10.3390/S19183984

3. Torres-Carrión, P.: Evaluación de Estrategias de Aprendizaje con HCI Kinect en alumnos con Síndrome de Down (2017). http://e-spacio.uned.es/fez/view/tesisuned:ED_Pg_CyEED-Pvtorres
4. Rapanta, C., Botturi, L., Goodyear, P., Guàrdia, L., Koole, M.: Balancing technology, pedagogy and the new normal: post-pandemic challenges for higher education. Postdigital Science and Education **3**(3), 715–742 (2021). https://doi.org/10.1007/s42438-021-00249-1
5. Chen, T., Peng, L., Jing, B., Wu, C., Yang, J., Cong, G.: The impact of the COVID-19 pandemic on user experience with online education Platforms in China (2020). https://doi.org/10.3390/su12187329
6. Kumar, V., Verma, A.: An exploratory assessment of the educational practices during COVID-19. Qual. Assur. Educ. **29**, 373–392 (2021). https://doi.org/10.1108/QAE-12-2020-0170
7. Yahya, F., Hermansyah, H., Mardhia, D., Sahidu, H., Gunawan, G.: The use of whatsapp application in learning evaluation activities during Covid-19 pandemic. In: Proceedings of the 2nd Annual Conference on Education and Social Science (ACCESS 2020), pp. 371–374. Atlantis Press, Mataram (2021). https://doi.org/10.2991/assehr.k.210525.111
8. Castillo-Cuesta, L., Ochoa-Cueva, C., Cabrera-Solano, P.: Virtual workspaces for enhancing collaborative work in EFL learning: a case study in higher education. Int. J. Emerg. Technol. Learn. **17**, 4–18 (2022)
9. Weese, W.J., El-Khoury, M., Brown, G., Weese, W.Z.: The future is now: preparing sport management graduates in times of disruption and change. Front. Sport. Act. Living. **4** (2022). https://doi.org/10.3389/fspor.2022.813504
10. Mateo Andrés, J.: Medición y evaluación educativa. Editorial La Muralla S.A., Madrid, España (2008)
11. Zichermann, G., Cunningham, C.: Gamification by Desing: Implementing games Mechanics in Web and Mobile Apps Cambridge. O´Reilly Media, MA (2011)
12. González-González, C., Blanco-Izquierdo, F.: Designing social videogames for educational uses. Comput. Educ. **58**, 250–262 (2012). Doi:https://doi.org/10.1016/j.compedu.2011.08.014
13. Werbach, K., Hunter, D.: Gamificación: revoluciona tu negocio con las técnicas de los juegos. Pearson Educación (2014)
14. Torres-Carrión, P., González-González, C., Aciar, S., Rodríguez-Morales, G.: Methodology for systematic literature review applied to engineering and education. In: EDUCON2018 – IEEE Global Engineering Education Conference. IEEE Xplore Digital Library, Santa Cruz de Tenerife - España (2018). https://doi.org/10.1109/EDUCON.2018.8363388
15. Anh, T.T.N., Duy, N.N., Nguyen, N.T.: Effectiveness of kahoot on high school students' physics exam scores: a case study in Vietnam. J. Leg. Ethical Regul. Issues. **24**, 1–12 (2021)
16. Alharthi, S.: Assessing kahoot's impact on EFL students' learning outcomes. TESOL Int. J. **15**, 31–64 (2020)
17. Fiani, I.N., Ahsanuddin, M., Morhi, R.: The effectiveness of using kahoot! application as an evaluation tool in arabic vocabulary learning at madrasah ibtidaiyah. Izdihar J. Arab. Lang. Teaching, Linguist. Lit. **4**, 243–256 (2021)
18. Hernández-Ramos, J.P., Belmonte, M.L.: Evaluación del empleo de Kahoot! en la enseñanza superior presencial y no presencial. Educ. Knowl. Soc. **21**, 13 (2020)
19. Reynolds, E.D., Taylor, B.: Kahoot!: EFL instructors' implementation experiences and impacts on students' vocabulary knowledge. Comput. Lang. Learn. Electron. J. **21**, 70–92 (2020)
20. Neureiter, D., Klieser, E., Neumayer, B., Winkelmann, P., Urbas, R., Kiesslich, T.: Feasibility of Kahoot! as a real-time assessment tool in (histo-) pathology classroom teaching. Adv. Med. Educ. Pract. **11**, 695 (2020)
21. Hernández Sampieri, R., Méndez Valencia, S., Mendoza Torres, C., Cuevas Romo, A.: Fundamentos de investigación. McGraw-Hill/Interamericana, México (2017)

22. Stake, R.E., Easley, J.A., Anastasiou, C.J.: Case studies in science education. Center for Instructional Research and Curriculum Evaluation, University of … (1978)
23. Richards, J.C., Lockhart, C.: Estrategias de reflexión sobre la enseñanza de idiomas. Cambridge University Press, Cambridge (1998)
24. Anguera Argilaga, M.T.: Observación en la escuela: aplicaciones. Edicions Universitat Barcelona, Barcelona (1999)

Intelligent Systems

Enhanced Books Recommendation Using Clustering Techniques and Knowledge Graphs

Priscila Valdiviezo-Diaz$^{(\boxtimes)}$ ⓘ and Janneth Chicaiza ⓘ

Departamento de Ciencias de la Computación y Electrónica,
Universidad Técnica Particular de Loja, Loja, Ecuador
{pmvaldiviezo,jachicaiza}@utpl.edu.ec

Abstract. Nowadays, there is an increased interest in recommender systems in different fields, since they allow personalizing the delivery of content according to the needs and preferences of each user. This paper proposes a recommendation approach that suggests books according to their metadata and explicit feedback given by users to them. First, we reuse a public dataset of books and use k-means to identify different groups of books based on their information. Second, we analyze the variation between these groups to predict the rating that a specific user would give a book. Third, we use the collaborative filtering technique to represent books, using the information of the user's rating and the group of the book to be recommended. Finally, users will receive an enhanced explainable response, i.e. a list of books with relevant metadata, i.e., the output could be helpful for users to understand the delivered recommendations. The original book's metadata was enriched using information available on DBPedia, a well-known RDF-based Knowledge Graph fed from Wikipedia. Results include experiments of clustering and prediction techniques because our approach considers the information of the user's ratings and the available information of the books to the recommendation, facilitating the understanding of the outputs.This approach achieves a good performance using Precision, Recall, and F-measure to measure the quality of the recommendations, and MAE to measure the prediction's accuracy.

Keywords: Books · Collaborative filtering · K-means · Knowledge graph · Recommender system

1 Introduction

Every day, users employ search engines to find resources such as books, articles, products, services, software, and people. Many of these resources also are accessible in specialized data sources such as institutional web pages, document repositories, and databases. However, it is not easy for users with specific needs to search and find relevant resources due to the large number of online resources and data sources distributed all over the web. To alleviate this situation, recommender systems are one of the most popular applications provided by the industry.

In many contexts, the Recommender Systems (RS) are helpful to address the problem of delivering relevant material to users. RS can leverage the information available on resources and users to find similar resources according to the topic of interest and the user's profile. For example, integrating RS in e-learning environments enables students to enrich their learning process with online resources, reducing the time for selecting the right resources. In e-commerce, RS help customers find products to purchase.

RS are tools capable of filtering relevant information according to the needs and data of a specific user. For a target user, these systems identify the preferences, interests, and opinions of other users with similar interests or preferences as him/her. Different information filtering techniques are used for recommendation, including collaborative filtering, content-based, demographic, knowledge-based, and hybrid approaches. In this article, we focus on studying the first filtering strategy, which is, Collaborative Filtering (CF).

CF is the most popular technique for recommending appropriate items to a user. It uses a rating matrix that represents the user's tastes for an item in the past; that is, it uses the available ratings given by similar users. To discover suitable information for a target user, CF-based recommender systems can be designed by following two approaches [1]: (a) Memory-Based, which generally uses the K-Nearest Neighbor (KNN) algorithm to predict the rating of users using similarity measures (for example, Cosine, Pearson, Jaccard); these models are simple to implement, and the results are easy to understand [2]. (b) Model-Based, which uses a model to predict the rating of the registered users. Some examples of these models are those based on matrix factorization methods [3], bayesian models [4], clustering [5], and knowledge graphs [6]. The matrix factorization methods present good performance but the main problem with these methods is that may be very difficult to understand and explain the recommendations [7].

In addition to the lack of explanation of traditional RS, there are other associated problems such as scalability, data sparsity, and cold-start [2]. To address these issues, mainly the cold-start (new item), that is when no users of the system have rated the new item yet, this paper proposes a recommendation approach that suggests books according to explicit feedback (also called ratings) given by users and metadata of the books.

1.1   Related Work

Recommendation systems have been successfully implemented in domains such as e-commerce [8], e-learning [9], tourism [10], social networks [11] and health [12]. Likewise, interest in RS has increased due to information overload since they are at the forefront of personalizing content, adapting its delivery to the needs and preferences of each user.

In this section, we review proposals related to the use of CF and the k-means algorithm in recommendation systems. Later, we introduce the use of knowledge graphs in this kind of application.

CF-Based Recommender Systems Using K-means Clustering Algorithm. In the educational field, there are some researches where k-means had been used to cluster learners or items. According to [13], RS could have a key role to build virtual communities of similar interest. In this context, we highlight three proposals: (1) [14] propose a system that recommends suitable courses to learners based on their learning history and past performance. (2) [15] face the problem of low user satisfaction and long response time in traditional online English education platforms. Here, clustering is used to cluster the learners and a CF algorithm selects a set of relevant course materials for learners according to their English level. (3) [13] carried out a comparative study between K-Nearest Neighbors and K-means; the comparison is made to identify the most efficient algorithm in terms of prediction and accuracy.

In another field, e-commerce, for the recommendation of movies, we found three proposals: (1) [16] designed a recommender system that uses the concept of typicality to improve accuracy and predict ratings of the user based on ratings of neighbours. (2) Another similar proposal is presented by [17] that is based on user and item clustering to recommend movies for an active user. (3) [18] analyze two similarity measures: KL Divergence and Euclidean distance; the results show that CF using Euclidean distance metrics for similarity measure performs well than the KL divergence.

To alleviate the sparsity and the new user problem, in [19] presents a CF-based system in which users are clustered based on their *personality traits*. In the proposed method, users with similar personalities are placed in the same cluster using the k-means algorithm.

According to the analysis of the presented works, we can conclude that the k-means clustering algorithm has been used to group users, and thus deal with the cold-start problem of the new user. In the case of [13], K-means turns out to be better than KNN, and in [16] it turns out to be better than Topic Modelling. Furthermore, according to [15] user satisfaction is significant and the response times of the proposed system are acceptable. Unlike these works, our proposal uses K-means to deal with the cold-start problem of the new item, which means that the recommendation system will be prepared to offer recommendations when new books are added to the base.

Use of Knowledge Graphs in Recommendation. A Knowledge Graph (KG) contains pieces of knowledge that describe the entities of a domain, their attributes, and semantic relations between them [20].

According to [21], Artificial Intelligence will drive the next industrial technology revolution, and KGs comprise the main foundation of this revolution. Last years, knowledge graphs have been increasingly applied not only in academia but also in several industries [22].

The growing interest in KGs is because data structures organized as graphs facilitate the integration and querying of data from different sources. In addition, a graph allows describing complex relationships between data and reduces the chances of information-meaning problems occurring. These features facilitate the implementation of applications such as search engines, recommenders, question/answering systems, chatbots, and others.

Regarding recommendation, in a previous work [6], we found that features of a KG can be leveraged by a recommender system to overcome the problems faced by collaborative and content-based filtering approaches. Mainly, when there are no data about users or items, a knowledge-based RS can take advantage of domain knowledge and data available in open RDF-based KGs.

In this work, we use data available in DBPedia for the final stage of the recommendation, that is, to generate sets of items including key information that help the user to make a better decision.

1.2 Main Contributions

We reuse an online dataset of books, and to understand its structure, we carry out a dataset analysis to identify relationships between features and detect anomalies in the data. Next, we use unsupervised learning to analyze the related metadata to the books so that the preferences of a target user can be predicted according to books that other similar users have rated. Then, a model-based CF approach is used through a method of matrix factorization based on clustering for the prediction of books.

Also, to help users understand the output generated by a recommender system, the latest generations of RS include the use of Knowledge Graphs. Using knowledge of a given domain or cross-domain, and using structures of related entities as a graph, the system could make recommendations with some domain knowledge and tell the user why such items are recommended [6]. In this paper, in addition to proposing a CF-based recommendation approach, we try to take advantage of the data from the RDF-based graph named DBPedia which is fed from Wikipedia content. Specifically, in our proposal, we use the graph data to enrich the books' metadata to be recommended and generate outputs with the necessary information so that the user can take action as soon as the recommendations are received.

The paper is structured as follows: Sect. 2 includes materials and methods; Sect. 3 encloses the results of the experiments; and Sect. 4 shows the conclusions of this paper.

2   Material and Methods

In this section, we present two subsections: the data preparation realized for the experiments and the recommendation proposed approach. Programming and experiments were performed using the R language.

2.1 Data Preparation

For the experiments, we use two sources of data: (1) A dataset[1] available in the Kaggle repository that contains users' ratings for books and books' metadata; and (2) DBPedia[2] which is a repository that contains structured and machine-readable descriptions of millions of entities such as people, organizations, books, etc. The first dataset named *goodbooks-10k* was used for generating the recommendation model, and the second dataset was used to enrich the first one and explain the recommendation outputs.

Data for Recommendations. The dataset *goodbooks-10k* is made up of five CSV files with 981,756 ratings provided by 53,424 users on 10,000 books. From the original dataset, we use three files: ratings.csv, books.csv, tags.csv. The first file contains all users' ratings of the books, the second file contains 23 variables with information on the books such as the book identifier, best book identifier, the number of editions for a given work, author, publication year, ISBN, language, title, image URL, and details about the rating. Finally, tags.csv contains the tags users have assigned to that books.

From dataset analysis, we find that users tend to give positive ratings to books. Most of the ratings are in the 3–5 range, while very few ratings are in the 1–2 range. Furthermore, the largest number of books corresponds to the years of publication from 2000–2016. Next, we proceeded to perform a processing of our data set in which:

- Some variables that do not provide relevant information about books were removed from the file books.csv
- Duplicate ratings were removed.
- Users who rated fewer than 5 books were removed.
- 25% users were selected from the original dataset for experiments setting.
- Genres attribute is calculated by grouping similar tags.

Once the data processing has been carried out, a final data set is obtained. Table 1 shows the information of the final data set used for generating the recommendations.

Table 1. Descriptive information of the final data set

Entity	Count
#Users	8,902
#Books	9,497
#Ratings	231,119
Scale	5-stars
#Book attributes	13

---

[1] https://www.kaggle.com/zygmunt/goodbooks-10k.
[2] https://www.dbpedia.org.

Data for Improving Explanations. To enrich descriptions of books, we annotate the original data using the Tagme API[3]. From the books' titles, the API finds candidates between the Wikipedia pages that match the title. After a semi-supervised process of checking, we find the equivalent Wikipedia pages for 4,548 books which represents one in two resources that make up the population. Next, from this corpus, we select 3,129 books that are part of the books set that was used for generating the recommendations. The metadata of these books was used to enrich the explanation of the recommendations given to the user.

From the set of verified pages, we implement queries using the SPARQL language and the DBPedia Endpoint to extract additional data from each book such as: abstract, type of work (book, novel, series, collection, etc.), publisher, author's page, country and external links where the user can find detailed information about books and its authors.

Data collected from DBPedia is used at the final stage of the recommender system to provide users with organized and dynamic information about the books that can be interesting for them.

2.2   Recommendation Approach Based on Books Clustering

In the proposed approach, the neighbour of an item is found based on the application of K-means. Unlike traditional approaches which use similarity measures based on memory for computing the neighbours of an item, in this case, we compute with a clustering algorithm, which makes it more efficient to generate a more similar neighbourhood set to the target item.

Three phases are part of this approach: (1) book clustering (2) rating prediction, and (3) book recommendation and visualization.

Books Clustering. To generate the books clusters according to their characteristics we used the K-means algorithm. The first step is to find the optimal number of clusters. We determine the optimal number of clusters using the elbow method [23], obtaining as result 4 clusters as the most optimal. The next step is to cluster each book based on its similarity using the K-means algorithm. Books with the most common characteristics are grouped into the same cluster. We evaluated the grouping using silhouette score [24], with which we obtained a value of 0.613.

From the cluster analysis, we can highlight the following:

– 23% of the books are in Cluster 1, whose year of publication is mostly in the range 2006–2009. Most of the books correspond to the genre: fantasy, historical-fiction and science-fiction. This group contains books with few qualifications followed by cluster 4. This means that the number of users' ratings on those books is small.

---

[3] https://sobigdata.d4science.org/web/tagme/tagme-help.

– In Cluster 2, about 5% of the books are grouped, most of which correspond to the year 2006. The genre of book that stands out the most in this group is fantasy followed by historical-fiction. These books have the highest ratings compared to other groups. However, although it is the smallest cluster, it is the group that has the books that have received the most ratings from users, that is, this group focuses on the most rated books.

– 61% of the books are in cluster 3, the largest number of books of this group correspond to the years 2003–2016, this group also contains the older texts. A considerable amount of books is related to genres: fantasy, mystery, horror, and memoir. In this group are the less frequently rated books.

– 11% of books belong to cluster 4, most of which correspond to the year 1999–2002, the genre of book that stands out the most in this group is fantasy and science-fiction, Moreover is the group with the lowest ratings.

Rating Prediction. We proceed to make the predictions of the ratings of the books that have not been seen by users using the CF technique, for we generate a predicted rating matrix using the Probabilistic Matrix Factorization (PMF) [25] method. We selected this method because it provides good prediction and recommendation results, as well as a higher scalability [26]. PMF factorizes the rating matrix into two matrices that represent the users and items in a latent factor space of dimensionality k [27], in our case, k value will be the optimal number of clusters.

The prediction of rating is computed by the dot product between user feature vectors and book feature vectors that belong to a specific cluster. Therefore, for the predictions, all books of the dataset are not considered but only the books of the cluster where the target book is located.

The predicted rating that the user u will give to the book belonging to a given cluster ic is computed as shown in the following equation:

$$\hat{r}(u, ic) = p_u \cdot q_{ic}^T \tag{1}$$

where: p_u is the latent user vector, and q_{ic} is the latent items vector of a given cluster.

Table 2 shows an example of how the CF matrix is represented with the group obtained for each book.

Table 2. Example collaborative filtering matrix

	Book1	Book2	Book3	Book4	Book5
User1	4	0	0	0	2
User2	0	3	0	0	0
User3	0	1	3	0	5
	Clus 1	Clus 2	Clus 1	Clus3	Clus4

Books Recommendation and Visualization. We generate a recommendation list made up of books that a user has not read and rated, and which belong to the same cluster, the books with a high rating prediction are used to compile the recommendation list, and then those are recommended to the target user. The idea is to optimize the recommendation algorithm such that it generates faster recommendations without affecting the recommendation quality.

For a given user, the recommender generates a list of books made up of the identifiers of the books that may interest him/her the most. With this base information, we query the system's database in order to retrieve relevant attributes of each book.

The system database contains the book's data, obtained from the Kaggle dataset, and other metadata that was obtained from DBPedia. Thanks to this additional data, we were able to create a result preparation and visualization service. The service returns the user with basic information on each book, but also it allows the user to refine the results, due to the links associated with key metadata such as country, type of work, genre, author, and country. In the next section, we illustrate the type of output that the user receives from our system.

3   Results

In this section, we describe the experimental settings to evaluate the effectiveness of the approach. We have tested our recommendation algorithm on the book dataset. We used cross-validation to obtain improved results.

3.1   Experimental Results

To analyze the behaviour of the system and the quality of the predictions, we use Mean Absolute Error (MAE) [28], and to measure the quality of recommendations, we use Precision, Recall, and F-measure.

The results were compared with two different algorithms: traditional CF based on items (IBCF), and the Bayesian non-negative matrix factorization (BNMF) algorithm, using the same sample of users. IBCF estimates the user's rating for the target item based on ratings given by the user to other similar items [29]. BNMF is based on factorizing the rating matrix into two non-negative matrices whose components provide an understandable probabilistic meaning [26].

During the experiments, we set the following hyperparameters for each CF algorithm.

- IBCF was used with the cosine similarity to determine the nearest neighbours to the target book and predict the target user's rating. The number of neighbours of a book was $nn = 30$.
- With BNMF a vector of K components to each user and each item is necessary, therefore we have the following hyperparameters: $k = 8$, $\alpha = 0.8$ and $\beta = 3$, $number\_of\_iterations = 120$.

– Cluster-based CF (the proposed approach) was started with: number of latent factors (optimal number of clusters) $k = 4$, $\alpha = 0.02$ and $\beta = 0.02$, $number\_of\_iterations = 80$.

These hyperparameters were selected to maximize the accuracy of the CF algorithms for the quality measures used.

Table 3 contains the prediction quality values for the dataset used in the experiments with each CF approach.

Table 3. MAE Results

Algorithm	MAE
IBCF	0.6804
BNMF	0.5932
Cluster-based CF	0.5684

According to results shown in Table 3, our approach based on clustering provides more accurate predictions, since the MAE value is lower compared with IBCF and BNMF. We believe that this improvement is because the proposed approach, unlike baselines used, predicts based on those items most similar to the target item that belong to the same cluster.

In addition to obtaining acceptable predictions, our approach has the advantage of providing understandable item vectors since they are clustered according to their similar features. This allows us to easily explain the recommendations.

Figure 1 contains the quality values for Precision and Recall. We can observe that Cluster-based CF and IBCF provide better precision than the BNMF algorithm. On the other hand, when the number of recommendations increases, the precision is better with Cluster-based CF compared to other algorithms. This figure shows also that when the number of recommendations increases, BNMF exhibits better performance in recall compared to IBCF and Cluster-based CF algorithm.

Figure 2 shows the F-Measure value obtained for each algorithm. F-Measure combines precision and recall to measure the performance of the recommender system. The F-measure value of Cluster-based CF is the highest among the three algorithms when the number of recommendations is greater than 5. Moreover, Fig. 2 shows that when the number of recommendations increases, the F-measure value of both approaches (IBCF and Cluster-based CF) increases.

From the results shown in Figs. 1 and 2, it seems that Cluster-based CF is better than the IBCF and BNMF in terms of MAE, precision and F-measure. Moreover, cluster-based CF shows a behaviour similar to BNMF in recall when the number of recommendations increases.

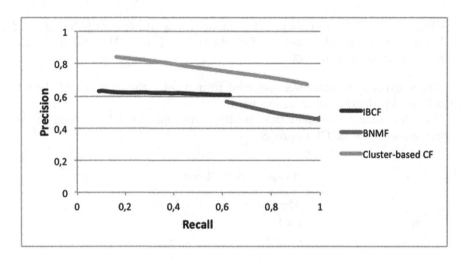

Fig. 1. Precision and recall results of each CF algorithm

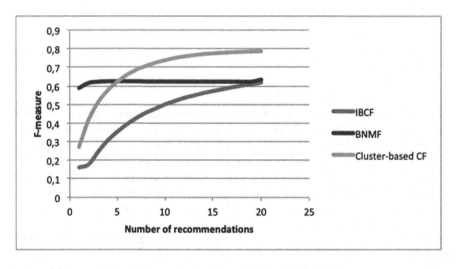

Fig. 2. F-measure results of each CF algorithm

3.2   Output Presentation

Figure 3 illustrates how recommendations are displayed to a target user. Here our recommendation proposal generates the top-3 list of books that could interest him/her the most. If the predicted rating for a given recommended book meets the relevance threshold of 4, then it will be displayed to the target user.

By providing extra and relevant information about each top book, users could be able to understand and refine results using facets like author, country, type of work, and genre. Likewise, if the user wishes, he/she could go to Wikipedia or DBpedia to review additional information on a specific book. Finally, a rating

Fig. 3. Top-3 of the recommended books for a target user. The screenshot is what the target user receives when interacting with the system.

heatmap of each work is generated automatically, so the user can know which is the book with the highest proportion of ratings by each scale value $[1:5]$.

We believe that this type of output will allow users to understand the recommendations and support the suggestions provided by the algorithm.

3.3   Discussion

The cluster-based CF approach mainly allows dealing with the coldstart (new-item) problem. Every time the system receives a new book, it will be classified using the clusters; thus the system could recommend to the user a set of books based on the prediction of ratings for similar books belonging to the same cluster. However, as occurs in most recommendation systems based on CF, one of the limitations of our approach occurs when there are unregistered users, who have not yet rated any book (new user coldstart problem). To alleviate this problem, in the future we will try to complete the proposed approach by clustering user information too, in such a way that we obtain a hybrid approach.

The experimental results also show that our approach can achieve good results when the user-item matrix is sparse. On the other hand, the scalability issue has been addressed by grouping books sharing common features so that only a smaller subset of books needs to be considered during the recommendation.

4 Conclusions

This paper presented a CF-based recommendation approach designed to alleviate the cold-start problem of new items. The proposal employs a clustering algorithm to compute several features of books and build an item list that provides recommendations close to the users' preferences. In addition, the approach allows the user to understand the recommendation output which is enhanced with the data collected from a knowledge graph. In this way, our approach allows users to get easily interpretable results and provides them with a better understanding of the recommendations.

We tested the cluster-based CF approach using the book dataset and two CF baselines: the IBCF memory-based algorithm and BNMF model-based algorithm. The results showed an improvement in the proposed approach with respect to other CF algorithms in MAE. Likewise, it gets better precision results, especially when the number of recommendations is low. Hence, the results obtained with cluster-based CF are considered acceptable, since the approach allows predicting the rating a book could have considering the explicit feedback given by users and books metadata.

As future work, we plan: a) to extend the proposal to face the cold-star problem of new-user by using domain knowledge and connecting open or queryable data on the web, b) to make more experiments applying other model-based algorithms by using large-scale datasets, and c) to extend the proposed approach to large-scale cases like distributed ones to determine if the quality of the recommendations improves and the user experience.

References

1. Hernando, A., Bobadilla, J., Ortega, F., Gutiérrez, A.: A probabilistic model for recommending to new cold-start non-registered users. Inf. Sci. **376**, 216–232 (2017). https://doi.org/10.1016/j.ins.2016.10.009
2. Chen, R., Hua, Q., Chang, Y.S., Wang, B., Zhang, L., Kong, X.: A survey of collaborative filtering-based recommender systems: from traditional methods to hybrid methods based on social networks. IEEE Access **6**(October), 64301–64320 (2018). https://doi.org/10.1109/ACCESS.2018.2877208
3. Shi, Y., Lin, H., Li, Y.: IU-PMF: probabilistic matrix factorization model fused with item similarity and user similarity. In: International Conference on Cloud Computing and Security, pp. 747–758 (2017)
4. Valdiviezo-Diaz, P., Ortega, F., Cobos, E., Lara-Cabrera, R.: A collaborative filtering approach based on naïve bayes classifier. IEEE Access **7**, 108581–108592 (2019). https://doi.org/10.1109/access.2019.2933048
5. Mohammadpour, T., Bidgoli, A.M., Enayatifar, R., Javadi, H.H.S.: Efficient clustering in collaborative filtering recommender system: hybrid method based on genetic algorithm and gravitational emulation local search algorithm. Genomics **111**(6), 1902–1912 (2019). https://doi.org/10.1016/j.ygeno.2019.01.001
6. Chicaiza, J., Valdiviezo-Diaz, P.: A comprehensive survey of knowledge graph-based recommender systems: technologies, development, and contributions. Information **12**(6), 232 (2021). https://doi.org/10.3390/info12060232

7. Rastegarpanah, B., Crovella, M., Gummadi, K.P.: Exploring explanations for matrix factorization recommender systems. In: FATREC 2017. No. 1 (2017). https://doi.org/10.18122/B2R717

8. Adak, F., Ucar, M.: A book recommendation system using decision tree-based fuzzy logic for e-commerce sites. In: HORA 2021–3rd International Congress on Human-Computer Interaction, Optimization and Robotic Applications, Proceedings (2021)

9. Gulzar, Z., Leema, A.A., Deepak, G.: PCRS: personalized course recommender system based on hybrid approach. Procedia Comput. Sci. **125**, 518–524 (2018). https://doi.org/10.1016/j.procs.2017.12.067

10. Orama, J.A., Borràs, J., Moreno, A.: Combining cluster-based profiling based on social media features and association rule mining for personalised recommendations of touristic activities. Appl. Sci.(Switzerland) **11**(14) (2021). https://doi.org/10.3390/app11146512

11. Tey, F.J., Wu, T.-Y., Lin, C.-L., Chen, J.-L.: Accuracy improvements for cold-start recommendation problem using indirect relations in social networks. J. Big Data **8**(1), 1–18 (2021). https://doi.org/10.1186/s40537-021-00484-0

12. Yang, H., Gao, H.: User recommendation in online health communities using adapted matrix factorization. Internet Res. **31**(6), 2190–2218 (2021). https://doi.org/10.1108/INTR-09-2020-0501

13. Zriaa, R., Amali, S.: A comparative study between k-nearest neighbors and k-means clustering techniques of collaborative filtering in e-learning environment. Innovations in Smart Cities Applications Volume 4 , pp. 268–282 (2021). https://doi.org/10.1007/978-3-030-66840-2_21

14. Mondal, B., Patra, O., Mishra, S., Patra, P.: A course recommendation system based on grades. In: 2020 International Conference on Computer Science, Engineering and Applications, ICCSEA (2020). https://doi.org/10.1109/ICCSEA49143.2020.9132845

15. Huang, Y.: Research on design and application of online english education platform based on web. Int. J. Antennas Propag. **2021** (2021). https://doi.org/10.1155/2021/7648856

16. Kaur, S., Challa, R., Kumar, N., Solanki, S., Sharma, S., Kaur, K.: Recommendation generation using typicality based collaborative filtering. In: Proceedings of the 7th International Conference Confluence 2017 on Cloud Computing, Data Science and Engineering, pp. 210–215 (2017).https://doi.org/10.1109/CONFLUENCE.2017.7943151

17. Alok, S., Jagadev, K., Mohanty, S.: A collaborative filtering approach for movies recommendation based on user clustering and item clustering, Communications in Computer and Information Science, 906 (2018)

18. Jeyasekar, A., Akshay, K., Karan: Collaborative filtering using Euclidean distance in recommendation engine. Indian J. Sci. Technol. **9**(37), 1–5 (2016)

19. Yusefi Hafshejani, Z., Kaedi, M., Fatemi, A.: Improving sparsity and new user problems in collaborative filtering by clustering the personality factors. Electron. Commer. Res. **18**(4), 813–836 (2018). https://doi.org/10.1007/s10660-018-9287-x

20. Liu, Z., Han, X.: Deep learning in knowledge graph. In: Deng, L., Liu, Y. (eds.) Deep Learning in Natural Language Processing, pp. 117–145. Springer, Singapore (2018). https://doi.org/10.1007/978-981-10-5209-5_5

21. Zhao, M., et al.: Construction of an industrial knowledge graph for unstructured chinese text learning. Appl. Sci. **9**(13), 2720 (2019). https://doi.org/10.3390/app9132720

22. Bader, S.R., Grangel-Gonzalez, I., Nanjappa, P., Vidal, M.-E., Maleshkova, M.: A knowledge graph for industry 4.0. In: Harth, A., Kirrane, S., Ngonga Ngomo, A.-C., Paulheim, H., Rula, A., Gentile, A.L., Haase, P., Cochez, M. (eds.) ESWC 2020. LNCS, vol. 12123, pp. 465–480. Springer, Cham (2020). https://doi.org/10.1007/978-3-030-49461-2_27

23. Muhammad-Ali, S., Bain-Khusnul, K., Eka-Mala, S., Satoto, B.D.: Integration k-means clustering method and elbow method for identification of the best customer profile cluster. IoP Conf. Ser.: Mater. Sci. Eng. **336**, 012017 (2018). https://doi.org/10.1088/1757-899x/336/1/012017

24. Shahapure, K.R., Nicholas, C.: Cluster quality analysis using silhouette score. In: 2020 IEEE 7th International Conference on Data Science and Advanced Analytics (DSAA), pp. 747–748 (2020). https://doi.org/10.1109/DSAA49011.2020.00096

25. Huang, L., Tan, W., Sun, Y.: Collaborative recommendation algorithm based on probabilistic matrix factorization in probabilistic latent semantic analysis. Multimedia Tools Appl. **78**(7), 8711–8722 (2018). https://doi.org/10.1007/s11042-018-6232-x

26. Bobadilla, J., Bojorque, R., Hernando, A., Hurtado, R.: Recommender systems clustering using bayesian non negative matrix factorization. IEEE Access **3536**, 1–1 (2018). https://doi.org/10.1109/ACCESS.2017.2788138

27. Pujahari, A., Sisodia, D.S.: Pair-wise preference relation based probabilistic matrix factorization for collaborative filtering in recommender system. Knowl.-Based Syst. **196**(3), 105798 (2020), cited By :22

28. Wang, W., Lu, Y.: Analysis of the mean absolute error (MAE) and the root mean square error (RMSE) in assessing rounding model. IoP Conf. Ser.: Mater. Sci. Eng. **324**(1), 012049 (2018). https://doi.org/10.1088/1757-899x/324/1/012049

29. Thakkar, P., Varma, K., Ukani, V.: Outcome fusion-based approaches for user-based and item-based collaborative filtering. In: Satapathy, S.C., Joshi, A. (eds.) ICTIS 2017. SIST, vol. 84, pp. 127–135. Springer, Cham (2018). https://doi.org/10.1007/978-3-319-63645-0_14

Handwritten Signature Verification System Using Convolutional Neural Network for Real-Time Applications

Cristian Maza-Merchán[(⊠)] [iD] and Jorge Cordero[iD]

Universidad Técnica Particular de Loja, Loja, Ecuador
{cjmaza2,jmcordero}@utpl.edu.ec

Abstract. The handwritten signature is the most common method used to verify the legality of documents and plays a critical role in indicating a person's identity. Traditionally, a person determines the validity of a signature by manually comparing it to a stored record of genuine signatures. Manual verification is time-consuming and depends on the skill of the verifier to detect forgeries. This work aims to develop a system for handwritten signature recognition using pattern recognition techniques. This work pretends to contribute to banks and companies to validate a document's signature automatically. Handwritten signature verification systems have been approached using different methods; however, solutions with artificial intelligence stand out for their superior performance. The proposed model is based on a shallow convolutional neural network and trained with the CEDAR handwritten signature dataset. The model can recognize the handwritten signatures of 55 users, verifying their legality against forgeries with an Equal Error Rate of 1.716%, improving the performance described by other methods working on the same dataset. The developed system is lightweight and allows verification to be performed in real time. Additionally, this paper provides insightful analysis for hyperparameter optimization of the model.

Keywords: Handwritten signature verification · Writer-independent signature verification · Convolutional neural networks

1 Introduction

The handwritten signature is the most common method of verifying the legality of documents and plays a fundamental role in identifying a person and evidencing consent. One basic premise of handwriting is that no two persons write exactly the same [1]. Therefore, a person's signature is unique and widely accepted as a biometric trait. With the advancement of technology, the use of biometric characteristics for the authentication and identification of individuals is becoming more and more common. Identification refers to establishing a person's identity, while authentication or verification refers to confirming or denying a person's claimed identity. The handwritten signature is an essential biometric trait, mainly due to its ubiquitous use to verify a person's identity in legal, financial, and administrative areas [2].

M. Botto-Tobar et al. (Eds.): ICAT 2022, CCIS 1755, pp. 103–117, 2023.
https://doi.org/10.1007/978-3-031-24985-3_8

Handwritten signatures are used daily to prove the authenticity of documents such as checks. Although digital payments are growing, checks that require a handwritten signature are still predominant. According to the American Bankers Association (ABA), losses for check fraud kept increasing and accounted for 47% or $1.3 billion of industry deposit account fraud losses in 2018 [3]. Traditionally, a person determines the genuineness of a signature by manually comparing it to a database of genuine signatures. Manual verification takes significant time, and it is an entirely subjective process that is highly dependent upon the expertise of the human verifier [4]. An automated verification process would enable banks and other financial institutions to significantly reduce check and money order forgeries, which account for a significant monetary loss yearly [5].

Handwritten signature systems are easy to use, non-invasive, can be changed easily whenever a signature is compromised, and are well accepted by society [6]. The Handwritten Signature Verification (HSV) has been studied for many decades. However, it is a challenging task that is still being researched for better-performing and viable solutions. Besides being accurate and secure, the signature verification process should be very fast, i.e., real-time verification can be done [4]. Currently, HSV systems have several limitations and challenges that must be overcome before they can be implemented in real-world applications.

A handwritten signature can be forged, unlike physiological biometric traits that cannot be replicated or imitated. Forgeries are commonly classified into random, simple, and skilled (or simulated) [2]. Random forgeries are those in which there is no information about the user and his signature, so a completely different signature is used. Simple forgeries are those in which the forger knows the user's name but does not know the user's signature, so if the genuine signature contains the user's name, the forgery may have some similarity. Skillful forgeries are those in which the forger knows the user's signature, and the forgery closely resembles the genuine signature. Skilled forgery is considered the most dangerous because forgers will be given time to mimic as closely as possible the genuine signature in terms of static and dynamic information [7].

Depending on the acquisition method, signature verification systems are divided into two categories: online (dynamic) and offline (static) [2]. In the online acquisition method, data such as writing pressure and writing speed are collected; however, special equipment such as a graphics tablet and a stylus is required. In the offline acquisition method, the signature is acquired by scanning or photographing after being written on paper. Nowadays, most researchers focus on online signature verification because it gives better accurate results [8]. On the other hand, offline signatures are the most widely used today because they do not require additional equipment and are easier to use.

Depending on the framework used, HSV systems can be divided into Writer-Dependent (WD) and Writer-Independent (WI). The writer-dependence distinction refers to whether the model has a different classifier for each identity or a single classifier for all identities [9]. WD systems require one binary classifier for each user, and this approach is the most common in HSV systems. Although WD systems achieve good results for the HSV task, requiring a classifier for each user increases the complexity and the cost of the system operations as more users are added [10]. In a WI system, a single classifier is used for all users. Compared to the WD approach, WI systems are less complex but generally obtain worse results [11].

The HSV problem has been approached from different perspectives. In the past, these systems used handcrafted feature extractors to find a good feature representation. The features extracted were fed into a classifier in order to recognize signatures. Artificial intelligence (AI) solutions have been the most notable in the last few years due to their excellent performance. Methods using artificial intelligence techniques, such as Deep learning, have been shown to have superior results in their application for handwritten signature verification [2]. Deep learning solutions do not necessarily require handcrafted features since features can be learned directly from raw data (image pixels). Convolutional neural networks (CNNs) are being used in computer vision tasks due to their powerful feature learning capabilities [12] and are well suited for modelling the global aspects of handwritten signatures [13].

In the literature, the majority of state-of-the-art systems are based on CNNs. Alajrami et al. [14] feed signature images directly into the network, performing minimal preprocessing. Although the system obtains 99.7% accuracy, comparing it with other algorithms is problematic because it was trained and tested using a private dataset, and no other metrics were provided. Hafemann et al. [15] proposed a model that learns the visual cues of a signature in order to differentiate it from forgeries and then evaluate it with signatures where no forgeries are available. This work obtained state-of-the-art results in many public datasets. The authors released two trained models as a contribution to the research community. Souza et al. [11] used features extracted using a CNN with a Support Vector Machine classifier. This model was evaluated using a global and user threshold scenario, outperforming other methods in some public datasets. Jain et al. [4] proposed using a shallow CNN with a simple but efficient architecture. The proposed architecture was tested on public and private datasets, improving accuracy and Equal Error Rate over state-of-the-art methods.

There are still many limitations in HSV systems regarding scalability and accuracy. Since people's signatures vary due to various factors, a dataset with several signatures of the same individual is required to achieve an accurate verification. For security reasons, it is not easy to make a signature dataset of real documents such as banking [5]. HSV systems that rely on several samples have a big problem regarding scalability, as adding a new user requires several genuine signatures. Because genuine signatures vary slightly among themselves, it is necessary to take a margin of error in which a signature is still considered genuine, thus leaving room to accept forgeries as genuine signatures.

High number of writers, small number of training samples per writer with high intraclass variability, and heavily imbalanced class distributions are among the challenges and difficulties of the offline HSV problem [16]. Usually, skilled forgeries are used to increase the accuracy of HSV systems. In a realistic scenario, during training we only have access to genuine signatures for the users enrolled in the system [5]. Similarly, to obtain good results, HSV systems usually use dozens of samples of a user's genuine signature. Obtaining good results without relying on a large amount of data is necessary, as this is another limitation holding the use of HSV systems in real applications.

This paper has been divided into four sections, following the IMRaD structure. Section 2 describes the research methods. Section 3 shows and discusses the results. Section 4 presents the conclusions.

2 Method

This project method is based on the Cross Industry Standard Process for Data Mining (CRISP-DM) methodology, described in [17]. Figure 1 shows the tasks proposed for each phase. First, project objectives are determined to establish the scope of the project. Handwritten signature datasets are reviewed, and preprocessed signature images are used to train the model selected. The model's performance is evaluated before proceeding with the deployment.

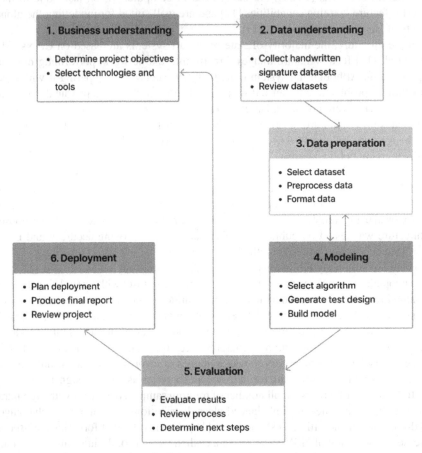

Fig. 1. Methodology phases and proposed tasks.

2.1 Business Understanding

This project aims to develop a handwritten signature verification system to be used in real time by a mobile device. The system needs to perform two tasks: recognition and verification; convolutional neural networks are the technology selected for the tasks.

This work can help banks, companies, and courts to validate a document's signature automatically. The system only needs the photo of a signature as input, and it will identify the user who signed and verify if the signature is genuine or a forgery. The contribution of this work is developing an automatic verification system that intends to be more accurate than manual verification.

2.2 Data Understanding

This phase focuses on identifying, collecting and analyzing datasets that will help achieve the project objective. After a literature review, the datasets most commonly used in the handwritten signature verification task were identified. Table 1 shows a review of the datasets analyzed.

Table 1. Commonly used signature datasets review.

Dataset	Samples	Description
SVC2004 [18]	40 users, 20 genuine signatures, 20 skilled forgeries	- Online acquisition: signature information is contained in text files as x,y coordinates - Open access
GPDS [19]	4000 users, 24 genuine signatures, 20 skilled forgeries	- Offline acquisition - Upgrades and replaces GPDS-960 which is no longer available - Requires access request
CEDAR [20]	55 users, 24 genuine signatures, 24 skilled forgeries	- Offline acquisition: png images scanned at 300 dpi in 8-bit grayscale - Open access
MCYT [21]	330 users, 25 genuine signatures, 25 skilled forgeries	- Online acquisition using a graphics tablet - Each user was asked to make 5 forgeries of 5 other users - Requires access request
PUC-PR [22]	60 users, 40 genuine signatures, 10 skilled and 10 simple forgeries	- Offline acquisition: built with checks from a Brazilian bank - Requires access request

2.3 Data Preparation

In this phase, the dataset is selected, preprocessed and formatted. Online and offline acquisition datasets were analyzed in the previous section. Online acquisition datasets already contain digitized signature information. Since this work objective is to enter a signature using a mobile photo, the input data (from a camera) will be different from the training data (from a graphics tablet); thus, online acquisition datasets are discarded.

Also, it is noticeable that only two datasets are open access while the rest require an access request. With all these considerations, the selected dataset is CEDAR, as it contains images in png format, is open access and contains a high number of genuine signatures and skillful forgeries with a moderate number of users.

Figure 2 shows the preprocessing steps used. The input image is converted to grayscale, and noise is removed to avoid erroneous pixels. Then, the signature is centered by cropping and resizing the image to 64 × 128 pixels. The centered image is binarized, converting all its information to binary values 0 and 1. The resulting information of all the signatures is stored in a text file. The text file will be used to train and evaluate the model. This preprocessing can be used on a photo from a mobile device. This way, input data will be the same as training data.

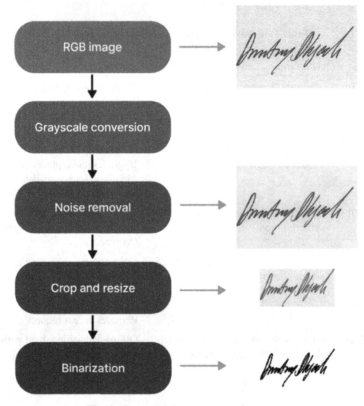

Fig. 2. Proposed data preprocessing steps.

2.4 Modeling

In this phase, the algorithm is selected, the data set is divided into training and validation sets, and the model is built and trained. The algorithm selected is the shallow CNN defined in [4]. The network architecture is shown in Table 2. The input layer has three dimensions:

height, width, and the number of channels. In this case, to pass the binary data of a 64 × 128 pixels image, the shape required is 64 × 128 × 1. Then, the convolutional base is defined using a three-set pattern of a Conv2D layer and a MaxPooling2D layer. Dense layers take a vector as input (1-Dimension), so a Flatten layer is required to convert the previous matrix (a 3D tensor) to a vector. Dense layers perform the classification, so the number of classes is considered. Since genuine signatures and forgeries are considered two different classes, the single model (writer-independent) designed for 55 users will have 110 classes. The first dense layer has a dimension twice the number of classes plus the number of the input dimensions (2D for a binary image), and the last dense layer has a dimension equal to the number of classes, 222 and 110, respectively.

Table 2. Network architecture of the CNN model.

Layer (type)	Kernel shape/Pool size	Param #	Output shape
Input	–	0	64 × 128 × 1
Convolutional (ReLU)	7 × 7	2000	58 × 122 × 40
Pooling (Max)	2 × 2	0	29 × 61 × 40
Convolutional (ReLU)	5 × 5	30030	25 × 57 × 30
Pooling (Max)	3 × 3	0	8 × 19 × 30
Convolutional (ReLU)	3 × 3	5420	6 × 17 × 20
Pooling (Max)	3 × 3	0	2 × 5 × 20
Flatten	–	0	200
Dense (ReLU)	–	44622	222
Dense (Softmax)	–	24530	110
Total trainable params: 106,602			

The dataset is split into 70–30%, 17 samples for training and 7 for validation. Contrary to most CNN applications, where it is beneficial to have more samples, an HSV system will have few samples for each user in a realistic scenario. The model is built and trained in a Google Colab notebook using the Tensorflow library in Python. Training parameters were selected based on the results of hyperparameter optimization. The model's performance is directly influenced by the hyperparameter configuration [23], which can improve algorithms' performance, producing new state-of-the-art results [24]. A 4 parameters sweep was performed using Weights & Biases [25]. Since the training time is low, the method selected for the sweep is the grid method, which means it will try every possible combination of parameters. Table 3 shows the training parameters considered for the hyperparameter optimization.

2.5 Evaluation

The metrics used for evaluating a handwritten signature verification system are: False Accepted Rate (FAR), False Rejected Rate (FRR), and Equal Error Rate (EER). FAR

Table 3. CNN training parameters for hyperparameter optimization.

Parameter	Value(s)
Epochs	[10, 15, 20, 25, 30]
Batch size	[32, 64, 128]
Optimizer	[Adam, SGD]
Learning rate	[0.01, 0.005, 0.001, 0.0005, 0.0001]
Number of classes	55
Samples per class	17
Sweep method	Grid

indicates the percentage of forgeries accepted as genuine by the system. FRR indicates the percentage of genuine signatures that are rejected as forgeries. Considering a high threshold to reject forgeries (low FAR) will result in many genuine signatures being rejected (high FRR). Similarly, considering a low threshold will result in many forgeries being accepted as genuine, and the system will have a high FAR with a low FRR. A threshold where both errors are equal is considered to achieve a balance and get a low value on both errors. EER is the point where both errors are equal, which is desirable in biometric verification systems. The system is required to achieve a low EER. The results of the evaluation can be found in the Results and Discussion section.

2.6 Deployment

In this phase, a plan for deploying the model is developed. The trained model is not useful if a user cannot access it. The model is implemented as a cloud processing service where the user can access it through a mobile application. Amazon's cloud computing service (AWS) is selected to run the CNN model in real-time on an EC2 instance. Finally, a mobile application is developed as an interface for the user to access the verification system. Figure 3 shows the deployment plan. The system's deployment and review are left as future work.

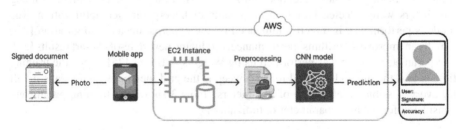

Fig. 3. Proposed system's deployment.

3 Results and Discussion

3.1 Hyperparameter Optimization

Figure 4 shows the results from every parameter combination previously mentioned in Table 3. Since there are 150 possible parameter combinations, 150 models were trained. The average training time is 78.65 s. The sweep was conducted in a virtual machine from the free tier of Google Colab using Weights & Bias and it had duration of about 3 h and 17 min. All the experiments are evaluated based on the EER obtained. An EER value of null indicates that the model isn't predicting properly and its accuracy is zero. There are 22 experiments with a null EER, which means 22 models are unusable since its accuracy is close to zero.

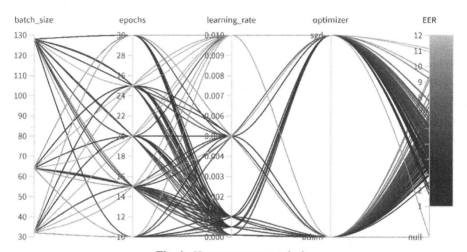

Fig. 4. Hyperparameter analysis.

On most combinations, Adam and SGD optimizers produced similar results. Adam showed more consistent results than SGD, as SGD worked much better and worse than Adam on some configurations. All models trained for 30 epochs reported high accuracy (above 70%), and only 67% of the models trained for 10 epochs reported an accuracy above 70%. However, all the models reported similar EER values. On average, models trained for 10, 15, 20, 25, and 30 epochs presented an EER between 2.5 and 7. The more epochs, the more accurate, but this is not necessarily good as overfitting can occur; this is why EER is the preferred metric over accuracy for this verification system. Batch size does not seem to correlate with the system's accuracy or EER.

The highest learning rate tested (0.01) reported 20 models with an accuracy of zero. The remaining models reported high EER (between 4 and 7). Learning rates of 0.005 and 0.001 reported the best results in terms of EER (between 2 and 6.5) for both optimizers. Adam works better than SGD with 0.005 and SGD better than Adam with 0.001. The EER starts rising again with lower learning rates. Learning rates of 0.0005 and 0.0001 report an EER between 4 and 9. These results show that, of all the learning rates tested, high and low learning rates produce models with high EER. An intermediate value like 0.001 works best for the proposed CNN architecture.

Optimized Model. Based on the hyperparameter optimization, the final model is built with the parameters in Table 4. The parameters of the model with the lowest EER were selected. The table also shows some of the model's metrics, such as accuracy, loss, EER and runtime.

Table 4. Parameters of the implemented model.

Parameter	Value
Architecture	sCNN
Batch size	64
Dataset	CEDAR (70–30%)
Classes	110
Samples per class	17
Epochs	30
Optimizer	SGD
Learning rate	0.001
Log step	20
Val log step	50
Runtime	71 s
EER	1.716
Accuracy	0.99465
Loss	0.02581

3.2 Experiment

Experiments are performed on the model to demonstrate its functionality. The system is tested with a genuine signature and a forgery of the same user. Figure 5 shows a) a genuine signature and b) a forgery of user #51 taken from the validation dataset.

Figure 6 shows the result obtained with a) a genuine signature as input to the system. The input data showed is the resulting image of the preprocessing performed. The system accurately recognizes the user who signed and also verifies, with 100% accuracy, that it is a genuine signature. Figure 6 b) shows the result obtained with a forgery as input. The system accurately recognizes the user and, with 99.99% accuracy, that it is a forgery.

3.3 False Accepted Rate

To calculate the FAR, only forgeries are considered and it indicates how many are accepted by the system while changing the threshold from 0 to 99% accuracy. Figure 7

a)   Genuine signature   b)   Forgery

Fig. 5. Signatures of user #51.

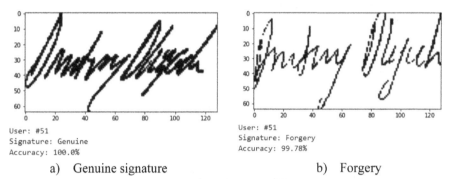

User: #51
Signature: Genuine
Accuracy: 100.0%

User: #51
Signature: Forgery
Accuracy: 99.78%

a)   Genuine signature   b)   Forgery

Fig. 6. Verification system output.

shows the FAR of the model. All 385 forgeries are accepted when the threshold is set to 0% accuracy. When the threshold is increased to 1%, the accepted forgeries drop to 14.28%. As the threshold increases, fewer forgeries are accepted. When the threshold is set to 99%, only 0.78% of forgeries are accepted.

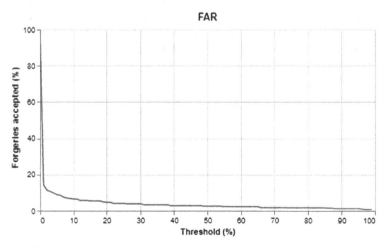

Fig. 7. False Acceptance Rate as a function of the accuracy threshold.

3.4 False Rejected Rate

To calculate the FRR, only genuine signatures are considered and it indicates how many are rejected by the system while changing the threshold from 0 to 99% accuracy. Figure 8 shows the FRR of the model. When the threshold is set to 99% accuracy, 13.51% of genuine signatures are rejected. As the threshold is lowered, fewer genuine signatures are rejected. At a threshold below 54%, all genuine signatures are accepted.

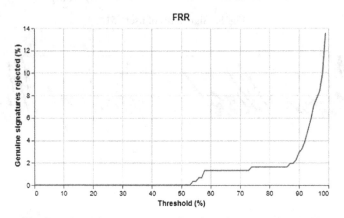

Fig. 8. False Rejection Rate as a function of accuracy threshold.

3.5 Equal Error Rate

The EER is the point where the two graphs intersect (FAR = FRR). A low EER is desired so that both errors are low, achieving a balance between rejected genuine signatures and accepted forgeries. Figure 9 shows the FAR and FRR plots overlapped, where the EER point is located at their intersection. The EER achieved is 1.716% with a threshold of 86% accuracy. Therefore, the developed verification system accepts 1.716% of forgeries as genuine and rejects 1.716% of genuine signatures as forgeries.

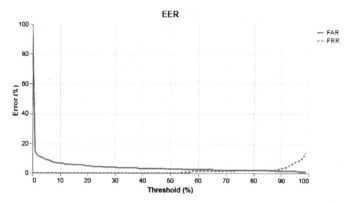

Fig. 9. Model's Equal Error Rate.

The performance of the system is compared with related work that uses the same data set. Table 5 shows a EER comparison.

Table 5. State-of-the-art performance on CEDAR database.

Reference	EER (%)
Chen and Srihari [26]	7.9
Kumar et al. [27]	8.33
Bharathi and Shekar [28]	7.84
Guerbai et al. [29]	5.6
Hafemann et al. [15]	4.63
Present work	1.716

4   Conclusions

Convolutional neural networks are used in applications requiring pattern recognition and contribute to the task of handwritten signature verification, considerably improving the results obtained with other methods. A shallow convolutional neural network is a lightweight model because the training and inference process takes little time, consuming fewer hardware resources than other CNN. This model contributes to the real-time verification of handwritten signatures in real-world implementations.

The handwritten signature verification system developed has an equal error rate of 1.716%. With this system, 98.284% of genuine signatures are recognized and accepted, while 98.284% of forgeries are rejected. This work also provided analysis for hyperparameter optimization for this model's architecture. Important parameters and their correlation with the EER were identified. A limitation of the developed system is the number of samples required since 17 genuine signatures and 17 forgeries were used to obtain good results. In a real scenario, getting so many signatures or skillful forgeries to train the model is impossible.

In future work, further hyperparameter optimization is proposed to improve the model and train it with a smaller number of samples. Training parameters such as dataset split ratio, input size, and the number of samples are of interest for future hyperparameter optimization. Also, the system's deployment is left as future work. The deployment plan includes the development of a mobile application for the user to use the model in real-time using the mobile camera. Finally, a usability analysis is planned to validate the functioning of the developed system in the real world.

References

1. Stewart, L.F.: The process of forensic handwriting examinations. Forensic Res. Criminol. Int. J. **4**, 00126 (2017)
2. Hafemann, L.G., Sabourin, R., Oliveira, L.S.: Offline handwritten signature verification—literature review. In: 2017 Seventh International Conference on Image Processing Theory, Tools and Applications (IPTA), pp. 1–8. IEEE (2017)
3. American Bankers Association: ABA Deposit Account Fraud Survey Report. American Bankers Association (2020)
4. Jain, A., Singh, S.K., Singh, K.P.: Handwritten signature verification using shallow convolutional neural network. Multimedia Tools Appl. **79**(27–28), 19993–20018 (2020). https://doi.org/10.1007/s11042-020-08728-6
5. Prakash, G.S., Sharma, S.: Offline signature verification and forgery detection based on computer vision and fuzzy logic. IAES Int. J. Artif. Intell. (IJ-AI) **3**, 156–165 (2014)
6. Barbantan, I., Vidrighin, C., Borca, R.: An offline system for handwritten signature recognition. In: 2009 IEEE 5th International Conference on Intelligent Computer Communication and Processing, pp. 3–10. IEEE (2009)
7. Mohammed, R.A., Nabi, R.M., Sardasht, M., Mahmood, R., Nabi, R.M.: State-of-the-art in handwritten signature verification system. In: 2015 International Conference on Computational Science and Computational Intelligence (CSCI), pp. 519–525. IEEE (2015)
8. Jindal, U., Dalal, S., Dahiya, N.: A combine approach of preprocessing in integrated signature verification (ISV). Int. J. Eng. Technol. **7**, 155–159 (2018)
9. Alvarez, G., Sheffer, B., Bryant, M.: Offline signature verification with convolutional neural networks. Technical report (2016)
10. Kumar, A., Bhatia, K.: A survey on offline handwritten signature verification system using writer dependent and independent approaches. In: 2016 2nd International Conference on Advances in Computing, Communication, and Automation (ICACCA) (Fall), pp. 1–6. IEEE (2016)
11. Souza, V.L.F., Oliveira, A.L.I., Sabourin, R.: A writer-independent approach for offline signature verification using deep convolutional neural networks features. In: 2018 7th Brazilian Conference on Intelligent Systems (BRACIS), pp. 212–217. IEEE (2018)
12. Jagtap, A.B., Hegadi, R.S., Santosh, K.C.: Feature learning for offline handwritten signature verification using convolutional neural network. Int. J. Technol. Hum. Interact. (IJTHI) **15**, 54–62 (2019)
13. Hatkar, P.V, Salokhe, B.T., Malgave, A.A.: Offline handwritten signature verification using neural network. Methodology **2**, 1–5 (2015)
14. Alajrami, E., et al.: Handwritten signature verification using deep learning. Int. J. Acad. Multidiscipl. Res. (IJAMR) **3** (2020)

15. Hafemann, L.G., Sabourin, R., Oliveira, L.S.: Learning features for offline handwritten signature verification using deep convolutional neural networks. Pattern Recogn. **70**, 163–176 (2017)
16. Souza, V.L.F., Oliveira, A.L.I., Cruz, R.M.O., Sabourin, R.: A white-box analysis on the writer-independent dichotomy transformation applied to offline handwritten signature verification. Expert Syst Appl. **154**, 113397 (2020)
17. Wirth, R., Hipp, J.: CRISP-DM: towards a standard process model for data mining. In: Proceedings of the 4th International Conference on the Practical Applications of Knowledge Discovery and Data Mining, pp. 29–39. Manchester (2000)
18. Yeung, D.-Y., Chang, H., Xiong, Y., George, S., Kashi, R., Matsumoto, T., Rigoll, G.: SVC2004: first international signature verification competition. In: Zhang, D., Jain, A.K. (eds.) ICBA 2004. LNCS, vol. 3072, pp. 16–22. Springer, Heidelberg (2004). https://doi.org/10.1007/978-3-540-25948-0_3
19. Vargas, F., Ferrer, M., Travieso, C., Alonso, J.: Off-line handwritten signature GPDS-960 corpus. In: Ninth International Conference on Document Analysis and Recognition (ICDAR 2007), pp. 764–768. IEEE (2007)
20. Kalera, M.K., Srihari, S., Xu, A.: Offline signature verification and identification using distance statistics. Int. J. Pattern Recogn. Artif. Intell. **18**, 1339–1360 (2004)
21. Ortega-Garcia, J., et al.: MCYT baseline corpus: a bimodal biometric database. IEE Proc. Vision Image Sig. Process. **150**, 395–401 (2003)
22. Cinthia, O.d.A., et al.: Bases de Dados de Cheques BancáriosBrasileiros (2000)
23. Yang, L., Shami, A.: On hyperparameter optimization of machine learning algorithms: theory and practice. Neurocomputing **415**, 295–316 (2020). https://doi.org/10.1016/J.NEUCOM.2020.07.061
24. Feurer, M., Hutter, F.: Hyperparameter optimization. In: Hutter, F., Kotthoff, L., Vanschoren, J. (eds.) Automated Machine Learning. TSSCML, pp. 3–33. Springer, Cham (2019). https://doi.org/10.1007/978-3-030-05318-5_1
25. Biewald, L.: Experiment Tracking with Weights and Biases (2022). https://www.wandb.com/
26. Chen, S., Srihari, S.: A new off-line signature verification method based on graph. In: 18th International Conference on Pattern Recognition (ICPR 2006), pp. 869–872 (2006). https://doi.org/10.1109/ICPR.2006.125
27. Kumar, R., Sharma, J.D., Chanda, B.: Writer-independent off-line signature verification using surroundedness feature. Pattern Recogn. Lett. **33**, 301–308 (2012). https://doi.org/10.1016/j.patrec.2011.10.009
28. Bharathi, R.K., Shekar, B.H.: Off-line signature verification based on chain code histogram and support vector machine. In: 2013 International Conference on Advances in Computing, Communications and Informatics (ICACCI), pp. 2063–2068 (2013). https://doi.org/10.1109/ICACCI.2013.6637499
29. Guerbai, Y., Chibani, Y., Hadjadji, B.: The effective use of the one-class SVM classifier for handwritten signature verification based on writer-independent parameters. Pattern Recogn. **48**, 103–113 (2015)

A Comparison of Machine Learning Algorithms to Predict Cervical Cancer on Imbalanced Data

Christian Ortiz-Torres, Ruth Reátegui(✉)(iD), Priscila Valdiviezo-Diaz(iD), and Luis Barba-Guaman(iD)

Universidad Técnica Particular de Loja, 101608 Loja, Ecuador
{caortiz,rmreategui,pmvaldiviezo,lrbarba}@utpl.edu.ec

Abstract. Cervical cancer is a leading cause of death in women. The present research analyzes, explores, compares and identifies the best method for predicting cervical cancer by applying machine learning techniques. The data is from the University Hospital of Caracas, Venezuela where a selection of variables was made according to the literature in order to predict cervical cancer. Seven algorithms were applied: decision tree (DT), random forest (RF), logistic regression (LR), XGBoost (XG), Naive Bayes (NB), multilayer perceptron (MLP) and K-nearest neighbors (KNN). Furthermore, three imbalanced data techniques were applied: SMOTETomek, SMOTE, and ROS for Hinselmann, Schiller, Cytology and Biopsy as target variables. In addition, accuracy, precision, recall, f-score and AUC were used to evaluate the results. Random forest was the algorithm with the highest results in accuracy, precision and f-score, with 94.57%, 72.46% and 60.70% respectively. Logistic regression and Naive Bayes had the highest values for recall and AUC with 68.37% and 79.11% respectively.

Keywords: Machine learning · Cervical cancer · Prediction · Imbalanced data techniques

1 Introduction

Cervical cancer is one of the most frequently cancers diagnosed in women worldwide [1]. In Latin America and the Caribbean the mortality rates are three times higher than in North America because the inequities in wealth, gender and access to health services in the Region [2].

With the development of modern technology, an increasing number of studies apply machine learning in the health field. Cervical cancer prediction using machine learning has a promising future and nowadays exist some works related to this disease. For example, [3–7] used the data collected at Hospital Universitario de Caracas in Caracas, Venezuela to predict cervical cancer. This data is available in the UCI Machine Learning Repository [8]. Those works used different algorithms, such as KNN algorithm [3], extreme gradient boosting algorithm

© The Author(s), under exclusive license to Springer Nature Switzerland AG 2023
M. Botto-Tobar et al. (Eds.): ICAT 2022, CCIS 1755, pp. 118–129, 2023.
https://doi.org/10.1007/978-3-031-24985-3_9

[4], decision tree algorithm [5], logistic regression, decision tree, random forest, adaboosting [6], and random forest [7].

Furthermore, in [9] used data from a center in Jakarta, Indonesia. This work applied logistic regression, classification trees, multilayer perceptron and an ensemble model with a soft-voting method. In [10] the authors worked with data from the Shohada Hospital Tehran. They applied support vector machine, QUEST, C&R tree, multi-layer perceptron and radial basis function algorithms.

Some risk factors for cervical cancer are shown in Table 1. Due to the number of factors, some authors worked with feature selection techniques to improve cervical cancer prediction. For example, in [11] the authors propose the Chicken Swarm Optimization method to eliminate redundant features and with Random Forest algorithm they obtained the best performance. Moreover, in [12,13] they share some types of feature selection techniques such as filter and wrapper methods to determine important attributes for cervical cancer prediction. Also, [5] worked with recursive feature elimination (RFE) and least absolute shrinkage and selection operator (LASSO) for feature selection.

Some works used imbalanced data, therefore, some authors such as [5,7,14–16] apply SMOTE or SMOTETomek to balance the data. Also, in [17] performs k-fold cross validation to balance the data and uses the Hill climbing algorithm for feature selection. In this work they split the data 50–50 for KNN algorithm and 25–75 for Decision Tree and Random Forest algorithms.

Because the importance of analyze cervical cancer with machine learning techniques, this work compares some supervised algorithms and imbalanced data techniques to predict cervical cancer.

2   Methodology

The present work followed some steps describes below.

2.1   Dataset

The data set used in this research is from the Hospital of Caracas, Venezuela [8] and contains information of 858 patients and 36 variables. These variables have integer and Boolean values.

2.2   Pre-processing

The data has 36 variables, 4 of them are target variables: Hinselmann, Schiller, Cytology and Biopsy. Also, 26 variables have missing values, therefore, variables such as STDs:Time since first diagnosis and STDs:Time since last diagnosis were eliminated because more than 50% of values were missing. Moreover, imputation with the mean value was performed with the following 7 variables: First sexual intercourse, Number of pregnancies, Smokes (years), Smokes (packs/year), Hormonal Contraceptives (years), IUD (years) and Number of sexual partners.

Table 1. Cervical cancer risk factors.

#	Risk factors
1	Family pathological history
2	Early age of sexual debut
3	Sexual promiscuity or high-risk partners
4	Immunosuppression
5	History of co-infection by sexually transmitted disease
6	Use of contraceptive pill
7	Lack of adherence to the population screening program
8	Tobacco use
9	Multiparity and first pregnancy at an early age
10	Type of childbirth
11	Type of human papillomavirus (HPV) infection
12	Weak or compromised immune system
13	Chlamydia infection
14	Economic status
15	A diet low in fruits and vegetables
16	Previous abnormal Pap test or cervical biopsy
17	No Pap smear in the last 5 years
18	Lack of previous Pap smear
19	Uncircumcised male partner
20	Vitamin deficiency

Finally, the remaining variables with missing information were replaced by the mean without imputation.

Python programming language was used for data processing, where the data set was divided into 70% for training samples and 30% for test samples.

Based on the literature review, 25 relevant variables were selected for the prediction task, see Table 2.

2.3 Imbalanced Data Techniques

The data used in this work is imbalanced; therefore three imbalanced data techniques were selected: SMOTE and ROS algorithms corresponding to the oversampling technique, and a hybrid SMOTETomek method using oversampling and under sampling techniques. Data balancing was applied on the training data as shown in Table 3, in column "Target feature" the number zero refers to the number of negative samples and the number one refers to the number of positive samples for each target variable.

2.4 Algorithms

Seven algorithms were applied for cervical cancer prediction: decision tree (DT), random forest (RF), logistic regression (LR), XGBoost (XG), Naive Bayes (NB), multi-layer perceptron (MLP), K-nearest neighbors (KNN).

Table 2. Variables used in the prediction task.

#	Variables
1	Age
2	Number of sexual partners
3	First sexual intercourse
4	STDs
5	STDs (number)
6	STDs:condylomatosis
7	STDs:cervical condylomatosis
8	STDs:vaginal condylomatosis
9	STDs:vulvo-perineal condylomatosis
10	STDs:syphilis
11	STDs:pelvic inflammatory disease
12	STDs:genital herpes
13	STDs:molluscum contagiosum
14	STDs:AIDS
15	STDs:HIV
16	STDs:Hepatitis B
17	STDs:HPV
18	STDs: Number of diagnosis
19	Hormonal Contraceptives
20	Hormonal Contraceptives (years)
21	Smokes
22	Smokes (years)
23	Num of pregnancies
24	Dx:HPV
25	Smokes (packs/year)

2.5 Evaluation

For the evaluation of results, accuracy, precision, recall, f-score and AUC metrics were applied.

3 Results

This section details the results obtained of applied 3 different techniques to balance data for the prediction task.

3.1 SMOTETomek

Table 4 and Fig. 1 show the results of the predictions applying the SMOTETomek technique.

Table 3. Imbalanced data techniques.

SMOTETomek		SMOTE		ROS	
Dimension	Target variable	Dimension	Target variable	Dimension	Target variable
(1146, 25)	Hinselmann	(1158, 25)	Hinselmann	(1158, 25)	Hinselmann
	0 = 573		0 = 579		0 = 579
	1 = 573		1 = 579		1 = 579
(1080, 25)	Schiller	(1104, 25)	Schiller	(1104, 25)	Schiller
	0 = 540		0 = 552		0 = 552
	1 = 540		1 = 552		1 = 552
(1122, 25)	Citology	(1142, 25)	Citology	(1142, 25)	Citology
	0 = 561		0 = 571		0 = 571
	1 = 561		1 = 571		1 = 571
(1112, 25)	Biopsy	(1128, 25)	Biopsy	(1128, 25)	Biopsy
	0 = 556		0 = 564		0 = 564
	1 = 556		1 = 564		1 = 564

For Hinselmann variable, RF had the highest values for accuracy, precision and f-score with 94.57%, 72.46% and 54.85% respectively. LR and NB algorithms had the best values for recall with the 57.58% and AUC with the 79.11% respectively.

For Schiller variable, RF had the highest values for accuracy, precision and f-score with 89.15%, 65.56% and 58.19% respectively. LR and XG algorithms had the best values for recall with 61.87% and AUC with 75.56% respectively. For Cytology variable, XG had better results in accuracy, precision and f-score with 93.41%, 59.74% and 53.55% respectively. NB algorithm had the highest values for recall and f-score metrics with 58.55% and 53.68% respectively.

For Biopsy variable, RF had the highest values for accuracy, precision and AUC with 91.86%, 63.29% and 72.99% respectively. LR algorithm had the highest values of recall and f-score with 64.69% and 56.72% respectively.

NB algorithm had the lowest accuracy and f-score values, for all the target variables, with values in the ranges between 18%-22% and 17%-22% respectively.

As we can see, RF had the best results for the accuracy and precision, but the highest values of both metrics were obtained for the Hinselmann target variable.

3.2   SMOTE

Table 5 and Fig. 2 show the results of the predictions applying the SMOTE technique.

For Hinselmann, RF had the highest values for accuracy, precision, f-score with 94.57%, 72.46% and 54.85% respectively. LR and NB algorithms had the highest values for recall and AUC with 59.31% and 78.60%.

For Schiller, RF had the highest value accuracy, precision and f-score with 89.53%, 69.48% and 60.70% respectively. LR and XG algorithms had the highest values for recall and AUC with 62.72% and 72.81% respectively.

For Cytology, XG had the highest values of accuracy, precision and f-score with 93.02%, 57.23% and 53.19% respectively. LR had the highest values of recall and AUC with 56.79% and 52.73% respectively.

Table 4. Results with SMOTETomek.

Target variable	Algorithms	Accuracy	Precision	Recall	F-score	AUC
Hinselmann	Decision Tree	88,37%	50,07%	50,09%	50,03%	49,71%
	Random Forest	**94,57%**	**72,46%**	53,37%	**54,85%**	60,39%
	Logistic Regression	64,34%	51,70%	**57,58%**	45,38%	64,20%
	XGBoost	94,19%	64,12%	53,16%	54,38%	54,71%
	Naive Bayes	18,22%	53,11%	56,76%	17,77%	**79,11%**
	MLP	78,29%	50,51%	51,49%	48,67%	52,11%
	KNN	70,93%	49,36%	47,60%	45,08%	52,50%
Schiller	Decision Tree	80,23%	52,43%	53,15%	52,59%	52,80%
	Random Forest	**89,15%**	**65,56%**	56,40%	**58,19%**	68,99%
	Logistic Regression	74,42%	55,77%	**61,87%**	55,59%	58,19%
	XGBoost	88,76%	63,73%	56,18%	57,78%	**75,56%**
	Naive Bayes	22,09%	54,04%	54,97%	22,04%	64,39%
	MLP	75,97%	52,43%	54,19%	52,17%	56,38%
	KNN	58,53%	51,14%	53,03%	45,26%	54,00%
Citology	Decision Tree	89,15%	50,45%	50,45%	50,45%	50,45%
	Random Forest	92,64%	55,56%	52,30%	52,84%	41,33%
	Logistic Regression	79,84%	51,86%	54,90%	50,96%	52,51%
	XGBoost	**93,41%**	**59,74%**	52,72%	**53,55%**	33,58%
	Naive Bayes	22,48%	53,49%	**58,85%**	21,56%	**53,68%**
	MLP	79,84%	49,44%	48,64%	47,92%	43,81%
	KNN	69,38%	48,95%	46,21%	44,36%	42,66%
Biopsy	Decision Tree	87,21%	54,14%	54,34%	54,23%	54,16%
	Random Forest	**91,86%**	**63,29%**	54,43%	55,86%	**72,99%**
	Logistic Regression	79,46%	56,23%	**64,69%**	**56,72%**	58,20%
	XGBoost	91,47%	60,90%	54,22%	55,45%	70,23%
	Naive Bayes	21,71%	52,83%	55,32%	21,23%	70,49%
	MLP	77,13%	53,54%	58,59%	52,93%	55,98%
	KNN	68,60%	52,82%	58,83%	49,38%	62,54%

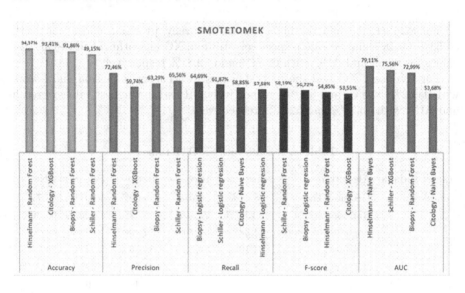

Fig. 1. Best result with SMOTETomek.

For Biopsy, RF had the highest values of accuracy, precision and AUC with 92.25%, 66.64% and 74.34% respectively. LR had the highest values for recall and f-score with 68.37% and 59.69% respectively.

Like the previous results, NB algorithm had the lowest values of accuracy and f-score with ranges between 18% - 24% and 17%-23% respectively. Also, RF had the best results for accuracy and precision, and the highest values were for the Hinselmann target variable.

3.3   ROS

Table 6 and Fig. 3 show the results of the predictions applying the ROS technique.

For Hinselmann, RF had the highest values of 93.80% for accuracy. DT had the highest values for precision and f-score with 53.65% and 52.42% respectively. LR had the highest value for recall with 60.45%, and NB had the highest value for AUC with 78.35%.

For Schiller, RF had the highest values for accuracy, precision and AUC with 89.15%, 65.56% and 71.34% respectively. LR and XG had the highest value of recall and f-score with 64.44% and 59.83% respectively.

For Cytology, RF had the highest values for accuracy and precision with 93.02% and 57.23% respectively. NB had the highest values of recall and AUC with 57.82% and 52.87% respectively. XG algorithm present the highest f-score with a value of 54.33%.

For the Biopsy, RF had the highest values for accuracy, precision and AUC with values of 91.86%, 63.29% and 78.67 respectively. LR and XG had the highest value for recall and f-score with 65.86% and 59.07% respectively.

Table 5. Results with SMOTE

Target variable	Algorithms	Accuracy	Precision	Recall	F-score	AUC
Hinselmann	Decision Tree	88,37%	50,07%	50,09%	50,03%	49,90%
	Random Forest	**94,57%**	**72,46%**	53,37%	**54,85%**	64,12%
	Logistic Regression	61,24%	52,00%	**59,31%**	44,40%	63,11%
	XGBoost	93,41%	47,25%	49,39%	48,30%	51,38%
	Naive Bayes	18,22%	53,11%	56,76%	17,77%	**78,60%**
	MLP	76,36%	50,15%	50,47%	47,68%	51,96%
	KNN	70,16%	50,99%	53,92%	46,77%	51,01%
Schiller	Decision Tree	80,62%	53,83%	55,07%	54,17%	54,74%
	Random Forest	**89,53%**	**68,48%**	58,32%	**60,70%**	70,53%
	Logistic Regression	72,87%	55,83%	**62,72%**	55,21%	60,01%
	XGBoost	88,76%	59,50%	52,77%	53,06%	**72,81%**
	Naive Bayes	22,09%	54,04%	54,97%	22,04%	64,40%
	MLP	75,19%	52,12%	53,76%	51,67%	64,72%
	KNN	62,02%	53,20%	58,39%	48,55%	56,39%
Citology	Decision Tree	89,53%	50,70%	50,66%	50,68%	50,66%
	Random Forest	92,25%	54,35%	52,10%	52,52%	38,35%
	Logistic Regression	77,52%	52,28%	**56,79%**	50,88%	**52,73%**
	XGBoost	**93,02%**	**57,23%**	52,51%	**53,19%**	31,74%
	Naive Bayes	24,42%	52,37%	56,75%	23,00%	48,45%
	MLP	78,68%	50,43%	51,15%	48,87%	41,29%
	KNN	64,73%	48,42%	43,74%	42,23%	41,03%
Biopsy	Decision Tree	87,98%	58,40%	59,60%	58,93%	59,29%
	Random Forest	**92,25%**	**66,64%**	54,64%	56,30%	**74,34%**
	Logistic Regression	81,78%	58,27%	**68,37%**	**59,69%**	59,61%
	XGBoost	91,47%	56,44%	51,79%	51,93%	68,38%
	Naive Bayes	21,71%	52,83%	55,32%	21,23%	71,61%
	MLP	78,68%	55,02%	61,85%	55,09%	63,51%
	KNN	70,16%	53,17%	59,67%	50,33%	60,50%

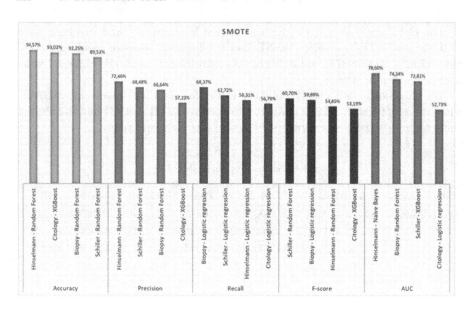

Fig. 2. Best result with SMOTE.

The NB algorithm continues with the lowest accuracy and f-score results with ranges between 18%-22% and 17%-22% respectively.

With ROS, RF had the best accuracy and precision, but unlike SMOTE-Tomek and SMOTE, the highest precision value was obtained with RF for the Schiller target variable.

Table 6. Results with ROS.

Target variable	Algorithms	Accuracy	Precision	Recall	F-score	AUC
Hinselmann	Decision Tree	92,25%	**53,65%**	52,14%	**52,52%**	52,15%
	Random Forest	**93,80%**	47,27%	49,59%	48,40%	66,01%
	Logistic Regression	69,77%	52,54%	**60,45%**	48,41%	62,88%
	XGBoost	93,41%	47,25%	49,39%	48,30%	55,33%
	Naive Bayes	18,22%	53,11%	56,76%	17,77%	**78,35%**
	MLP	75,19%	50,95%	53,22%	48,35%	67,10%
	KNN	82,95%	51,69%	53,95%	51,28%	52,47%
Schiller	Decision Tree	84,11%	50,24%	50,18%	50,09%	50,22%
	Random Forest	**89,15%**	**65,56%**	56,40%	58,19%	**71,34%**
	Logistic Regression	75,97%	57,17%	**64,44%**	57,53%	57,89%
	XGBoost	87,21%	61,61%	58,74%	**59,83%**	70,57%
	Naive Bayes	22,09%	54,04%	54,97%	22,04%	62,25%
	MLP	77,52%	52,15%	53,35%	52,07%	56,23%
	KNN	67,44%	51,97%	54,58%	49,42%	54,48%

(continued)

Table 6. (*continued*)

Target variable	Algorithms	Accuracy	Precision	Recall	F-score	AUC
Citology	Decision Tree	87,98%	49,86%	49,84%	49,82%	49,84%
	Random Forest	**93,02%**	**57,23%**	52,51%	53,19%	40,23%
	Logistic Regression	78,29%	49,17%	47,82%	47,19%	48,04%
	XGBoost	90,31%	54,48%	54,20%	**54,33%**	37,42%
	Naive Bayes	20,54%	53,41%	**57,82%**	19,91%	**52,87%**
	MLP	78,68%	47,95%	44,90%	45,76%	48,26%
	KNN	78,68%	50,43%	51,15%	48,87%	47,41%
Biopsy	Decision Tree	87,60%	54,55%	54,55%	54,55%	54,58%
	Random Forest	**91,86%**	**63,29%**	54,43%	55,86%	**78,67%**
	Logistic Regression	77,13%	56,06%	**65,86%**	55,91%	58,42%
	XGBoost	89,92%	60,25%	58,23%	**59,07%**	74,06%
	Naive Bayes	21,71%	52,83%	55,32%	21,23%	65,10%
	MLP	74,81%	52,80%	57,33%	51,42%	67,08%
	KNN	79,07%	53,30%	57,21%	53,09%	55,74%

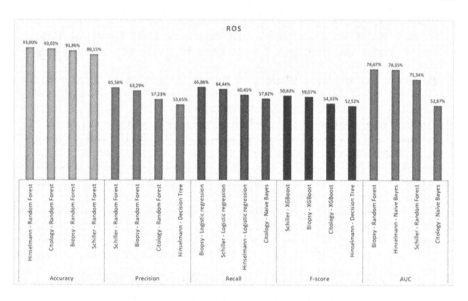

Fig. 3. Best result with ROS

4 Conclusion

In this work, in most of the experiments, random forest presented the highest values for accuracy, precision and f-score. The highest accuracy of 94.57% and precision of 72.46% was obtained applying SMOTETomek and SMOTE techniques for the Hinselmann variable. The highest f-score of 60.70% was obtained applying SMOTE for the Schiller variable. Naive Bayes presented the highest AUC value of 79.11% applying SMOTETomek for the Hinselmann variable.

The above mentioned, let us to assume that Hinsselman and Schiller could be considered as target variables to obtain the highest values for cervical cancer prediction. Also, SMOTETomek and SMOTE are the imbalanced data techniques that allow us improve the prediction. The improvement with those balance techniques were also demonstrated in the works of [5,7].

This work used a literature review to select the variables from the original data set. For future works, a feature selection or transformation techniques could be applied in order to improve the result based on the predictor variables.

References

1. WHO Cervical Cancer. https://www.who.int/news-room/fact-sheets/detail/cervical-cancer. Accessed 16 Sep 2022
2. PAHO. https://www.paho.org/en/topics/cervical-cancer. Accessed 16 Sep 2022
3. Suresh, K.: Classification study and prediction of cervical cancer. In: Chiplunkar, N.N., Fukao, T. (eds.) Advances in Artificial Intelligence and Data Engineering. AISC, vol. 1133, pp. 329–347. Springer, Singapore (2021). https://doi.org/10.1007/978-981-15-3514-7_27
4. Kaushik, K., et al.: A machine learning-based framework for the prediction of cervical cancer risk in women. Sustainability **14**(19) (2022) https://doi.org/10.3390/su141911947
5. Tanimu, J. J., Hamada, M., Hassan, M., Kakudi, H. A., Abiodun, J. O.: A machine learning method for classification of cervical cancer. Electronics **11**(3) (2022). https://doi.org/10.3390/electronics11030463
6. Yin, Q.: The application of machine learning in cervical cancer prediction. In: ACM International Conference Proceeding Series, pp. 12–19 (2021). https://doi.org/10.1145/3468891.3468894
7. Ijaz, M. F., Attique, M., Son, Y.: Data-driven cervical cancer prediction model with outlier detection and over-sampling methods. Sensors **20**(10), 15 (2020). https://doi.org/10.3390/s20102809
8. UCI Machine Learning Repository. https://archive.ics.uci.edu/ml/index.php. Accessed 17 Sep 2022
9. Curia, F.: Cervical cancer risk prediction with robust ensemble and explainable black boxes method. Health Technol. **11**(4), 875–885 (2021). https://doi.org/10.1007/s12553-021-00554-6
10. Asadi, F., Salehnasab, C., Ajori, L.: Supervised algorithms of machine learning for the prediction of cervical cancer. J. Biomed. Phys. Eng. **10**(4), 513–522 (2020)
11. Tripathi, A.K., Garg, P., Tripathy, A., Vats, N., Gupta, D., Khanna, A.: Prediction of cervical cancer using chicken swarm optimization. In: Khanna, A., Gupta, D., Bhattacharyya, S., Snasel, V., Platos, J., Hassanien, A.E. (eds.) International Conference on Innovative Computing and Communications. AISC, vol. 1087, pp. 591–604. Springer, Singapore (2020). https://doi.org/10.1007/978-981-15-1286-5_51
12. Nithya, B., Ilango, V.: Evaluation of machine learning based optimized feature selection approaches and classification methods for cervical cancer prediction. SN Appl. Sci. **1**(6), 1–16 (2019). https://doi.org/10.1007/s42452-019-0645-7

13. Nithya, B., Ilango, V.: Machine learning aided fused feature selection based classification framework for diagnosing cervical cancer. In: 2020 Fourth International Conference on Computing Methodologies and Communication (ICCMC), pp. 61–66 (2020)
14. Deng, X., Luo, Y., Wang, C.: Analysis of risk factors for cervical cancer based on machine learning methods. In: 2018 5th IEEE International Conference on Cloud Computing and Intelligence Systems (CCIS), pp. 631–635 (2019). https://doi.org/10.1109/CCIS.2018.8691126
15. Sharma, M.: Cervical cancer prognosis using genetic algorithm and adaptive boosting approach. Health Technol. **9**(5), 877–886 (2019). https://doi.org/10.1007/s12553-019-00375-8
16. Geeitha, S., Thangamani, M.: A cognizant study of machine learning in predicting cervical cancer at various levels-a data mining concept. Int. J. Emerg. Technol. **11**(1), 23–28 (2020)
17. Parikh, D., Menon, V.: Machine learning applied to cervical cancer data. Int. J. Math. Sci. Comput. **5**(1), 53–64 (2019). https://doi.org/10.5815/ijmsc.2019.01.05

An Electronic Equipment for Automatic Identification of Forest Seed Species

Miguel Tupac[ID], Reiner Armas[ID], and Guillermo Kemper[(✉)][ID]

Universidad Peruana de Ciencias Aplicadas, Av. Prolongación Primavera 2390,
Santiago de Surco, Lima, Perú
{u201415209,u201322040}@upc.edu.pe, guillermo.kemper@upc.pe

Abstract. This work proposes an electronic equipment which identifies forest seeds for academic and research purposes. Existing integral solutions are prohibitively costly for silviculture laboratories used in forestry teaching. Thus, they must identify the seed by visual inspection, causing visual fatigue and results with low reliability. The state of the art proposes solutions using support vector machines, achieving a 98.82% accuracy for sunflower seeds. Other solutions extract morphological attributes of mussel seeds to identify up to 5 species with an accuracy of 95%. Most solutions only identify a single seed type with similar sizes. In this context, an electronic equipment is developed. It consists of an image acquisition enclosure, an electromechanical device to move a camera so different sizes of seeds can be imaged at different distances, and a single-board computer to control the image processing and artificial intelligence (convolutional neural network) algorithms. The equipment achieves an accuracy of 95%, which is satisfactory for potential users and silviculture specialists.

Keywords: Image processing · CNN · Identification · Forest seeds · Electronic equipment

1 Introduction

Educational silvicultural centers and laboratories allow students and teachers to learn and research about the geometric, morphological and color attributes of forest seeds. This information is important, because it helps to identify and distinguish between seed species through visual inspection and the knowledge acquired at the educational centers.

On many occasions, distinguishing the seed's features may be challenging, due to requiring the experience and continuous accompaniment of teachers and forestry specialists along the teaching and learning process. Teachers may not be able to aid every single student, so there is a need for having automatic machines to identify the seeds under study. Moreover, even if teachers can aid students, there is a high subjectivity in fgresult in an elevated rate of seeds wrongly identified by students, which hinders their learning process.

Table 1 shows the different attributes of some seeds, which students must learn to visually identify using the parameters established by their teachers.

M. Botto-Tobar et al. (Eds.): ICAT 2022, CCIS 1755, pp. 130–142, 2023.
https://doi.org/10.1007/978-3-031-24985-3_10

Table 1. Main attributes of certain seeds [1]

Especie	Tamaño	Forma	Color	Cubierta
Abies pinsapo	6-12 mm/5-7 mm	Aovado-triangular	Parda	Lisa-lustrosa
Acer opalus	2,5-3,5 mm	Circular	Glauca	Estriada
Alnus glutinosa	3 mm	Angulosa	Marrón	Lisa sin brillo
Arbutus unedo	2-3 mm	Alargada-angulosa	Pardo	Agrietada
Celtis australis	5-8 mm	Redonda	Pardo-claro	Reticular
Cistus ladanifer	1 mm	Globoso-poliedro	Marrón oscuro	Lisa
Crataegus monogyna	5-8 mm	Ovoide	Pardo-amarillento	Rugosa
Genista umbellata	2-3 mm/1,6-2,2 mm	Lenticuliforme	Amarilla-verde claro	Lisa sin estrófilo
Juniperus oxycedrus	5-7 mm	Alargada-angulosa	Pardo-amarillento	Rugosa
Myrtus communis	2-3 mm	Ariñonada	Crema	Lisa brillante
Pinus pinaster	7-8 mm	Oblonga	Negro	Ligeramente rugosa
Prunus mahaleb	4-6 mm	Alargada-apuntada	Blanco-grisáceo	Sutura lateral
Quercus canariensis	7-18 mm/8-20 mm	Alargado	Castaño-amarillento	Lisa y lustrosa

Currently, there are no portable forest seed identification equipment; existing ones usually cost more than 5000 dollars and require special transportation. These limitations force the educational laboratories and centers to visually identify the seeds, generating eye fatigue in students, teachers, and specialists. With this in mind, the present work proposes a useful equipment for forestry academics and researchers. The electronic device is portable, can distinguish between 15 different forest seed types, has a friendly graphical user interface for user interaction and seed visualization.

Scientific literature has proposals which attempt to solve this problem. In [2], authors present an identification algorithm which performs well with medium and large seeds but underperforms with small ones. There is no proposal of a portable device. Authors in [3] use a support vector machine (SVM) to identify only sunflower seeds. [4] proposes a mussel seed classifier using morphological features. Authors compare different algorithms: SVM, artificial neural networks (ANN), logistic regression (LR) and K-Nearest Neighbor (kNN). The algorithm achieved an accuracy of 95% for the 5 mussel species under evaluation. The work at [5] proposes a classification method for 4 rice types based on shape, color and texture features. It uses neural networks, achieving an accuracy of 97.6%. In [6], authors propose an algorithm to evaluate the quality of corn seeds using SVM. First, they extract geometric attributes such as the length of the long axis, length of the short axis, perimeter, area and length-width ratio of each seed. These features feed a radial basis function SVM, achieving a good performance.

On the other hand, in [7] an algorithm to classify 4 wheat varieties grown in Turkey by making use of image processing and K-NN classifier is proposed. In this case only an algorithm and not a portable classification equipment is proposed.

Finally, the work at [8] proposes an Android mobile application called "Museed". The algorithm distinguishes between 7 types of seeds with a precision of 97% and handles seeds which are very close to each other.

Most solutions identify seeds from a single crop, proposing only an algorithm or method without a portable physical device which may handle different seed species and sizes. Thus, the main contribution of this work is the electronic equipment capable of identifying different forest seed species and sizes, achieving a precision of at least

95%. The following sections describe the equipment, the classification algorithm and the results.

2 Description of the Proposed Equipment

Figure 1 shows the block diagram of the proposed equipment. First, the device images the seeds which are located in acquisition platforms. Next, it runs the image processing algorithms in the single-board computer, which controls the complete process, from the moment the user initiates the acquisition until the identification result visualization. The following sections describe each part of the device.

2.1 Structure of the Electronic Equipment

Figures 2 and 3 show exterior views of the device. It has a power button, LED indicators, a sliding box with the seed platforms and the graphical interface for user interaction and result visualization.

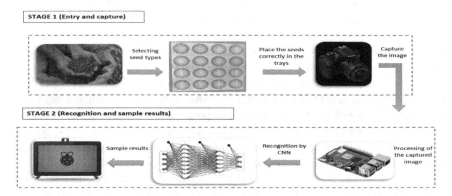

Fig. 1. Electronic equipment block diagram.

2.2 Image Acquisition

The image acquisition enclosure has a three-level platform to place the forest seeds: one for small seeds, one for medium seeds and one for large seeds. It also has an electromechanical system to move the camera so it can image each level. Figure 3 shows the platform. Smaller seeds are closer to the camera so that there is an adequate pixel density for the different seed sizes.

The electromechanical system has a stepper motor coupled to an endless screw, a pair of guiding axes and a camera bracket, as seen in Fig. 4. This system horizontally displaces the camera to take one image at each platform level, generating 3 images. The enclosure also has a white LED light to illuminate the interior.

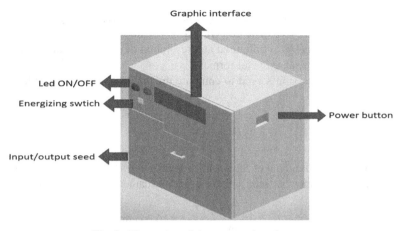

Fig. 2. Illustration of the proposed equipment.

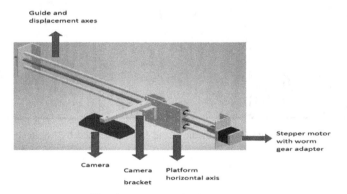

Fig. 3. External view of the prototype.

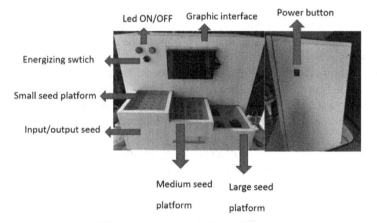

Fig. 4. Electromechanical system.

The camera's aspect ratio and resolution were used in order to design the enclosure and define the platform sizes. The camera was a Logitech C922 Pro Stream, with a diagonal field of view of 78°, configured at a resolution of 640 × 480 pixels and a 4/3 aspect ratio to ensure a squared pixel format.

The following expression served to compute the distance (D) between the camera and each platform [9]:

$$D = \frac{H}{\tan(\alpha/2)} \tag{1}$$

where H is half of the diagonal of the acquisition area covered by the field of view, α.

The minimum distance between a platform and the camera was computed as follows:

$$D_{min} = \frac{26.46/2}{\tan(78°/2)} = 16.34 \, \text{cm} \tag{2}$$

This was done considering the worst-case scenario: the platform closest to the camera had a diagonal of 26.46 cm. This platform holded the smallest seeds.

Using this result as a starting point, the distances between the camera and each platform were: 15 cm for the small seeds, 18 cm for the medium seeds and 21 cm for the large seeds.

Figure 5 shows the different platforms with seeds. The platform for the small seeds had a size of 19.4 cm × 18 cm, the one for the medium seeds was 20 cm × 19 cm and the one for the large seeds, 20 cm × 18.6 cm. The device was able to hold 16 small seeds, 25 medium seeds and 4 large seeds. The size with the most variety of species was the medium one.

The platform color was chosen after comparing different colors and hues. Red showed the best contrast between the seeds and the background. This was done in order to minimize errors during the seed segmentation process.

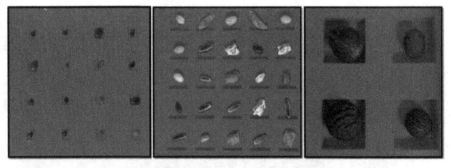

Fig. 5. Example of test image (small, medium and large) obtained by Logitech C920 digital camera.

2.3   Image Processing and Forest Seed Identification

The algorithm was developed in Python, running in the single-board computer: a Raspberry Pi 4B. Figure 6 shows the algorithm stages, described in the following sections.

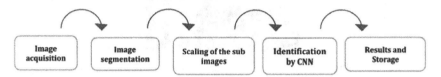

Fig. 6. Block diagram of the proposed algorithm

Image Acquisition

Images were 640×480 pixels in RGB format (24 bits per pixel) and consisted in the three primary color components: $I_R(x, y)$, $I_G(x, y)$ and $I_B(x, y)$. (x, y) correspond to the spatial coordinates. These components serve to segment the seeds and train the convolutional neural network.

Image Segmentation

First, the RGB image was converted to HSV [10], resulting in $I_H(x, y)$, $I_S(x, y)$ and $I_V(x, y)$. Then, the background pixels were eliminated applying two binary masks to the HSV components, as follows:

$$I_1(x, y) = \begin{cases} 1 \,, \ I_H(x, y) \leq 8 \wedge 140 \leq I_S(x, y) \leq 255 \wedge 90 \leq I_V(x, y) \leq 255 \\ \\ 0 \,, \qquad\qquad\qquad\quad in\ other\ case \end{cases} \tag{3}$$

$$I_2(x, y) = \begin{cases} 1 \,, \ 160 \leq I1_H(x, y) \leq 180 \wedge 140 \leq I1_S(x, y) \leq 255 \wedge 90 \leq I1_V(x, y) \leq 255 \\ \\ 0 \,, \qquad\qquad\qquad\qquad in\ other\ case \end{cases}$$

$$\tag{4}$$

Both masks were used to build a resulting mask:

$$I_3(x, y) = NOT(I_1(x, y)\ OR\ I_2(x, y)) \tag{5}$$

where *OR* and *NOT* are pixel-wise logical addition and negation.

A 7×7 median filter [10] was applied to mask $I_3(x, y)$ to avoid eliminating pixels inside of the seeds, resulting in a final mask $I_4(x, y)$ (see Fig. 7). This last mask is applied to each color component in the original RGB image, resulting in the image shown in Fig. 8.

Fig. 7. Resulting $I_4(x, y)$ mask for seed segmentation.

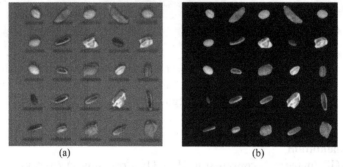

(a)   (b)

Fig. 8. (a) Original RGB image, (b) Original RGB image with segmented seeds

The stable illumination inside the acquisition enclosure allowed finding fixed thresholds to eliminate the background and effectively segment the seeds.

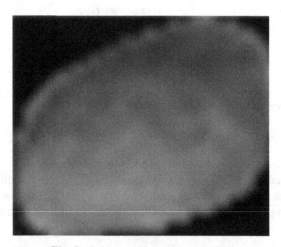

Fig. 9. Subimage of a segmented seed

Next, a labeling algorithm with 8-connectivity [10] was employed to extract each individual seed. Labeling was done with the $I_4(x, y)$ mask. Each resulting subimage contained a single seed, represented by $IR_n(x, y)$, $IG_n(x, y)$ and $IB_n(x, y)$ where $n = 1, 2, \ldots, N$ and N is the total number of seeds in a platform. Figure 9 shows a segmented seed sub-image.

Image Rescaling

The seed sub-images have different sizes which are dependent on the seed location and orientation, but the convolutional neural network requires them to be all of the same size in order to be used as inputs. Thus, bicubic interpolation was employed to resize all the sub-images. Table 2 shows the final image sizes for each seed size. The rescaled sub-images are $IER_n(x, y)$, $IEG_n(x, y)$ and $IEB_n(x, y)$.

Table 2. Final resolution of the segmented and rescaled subimages

Size type	Image resolution
Small	60×60 pixels
Medium	80×80 pixels
Big	120×120 pixels

Convolutional Neural Network (CNN) Architecture and Configuration

The following steps were followed to achieve the forest seed identification algorithm:

- Generate an image database with images of the 3 seed sizes.
- Design a network architecture to achieve optimal results.
- Define an adequate training parameter configuration.
- Analyze the confusión matrices to evaluate the CNN performance.

Database

Data augmentation was employed with Python. Data augmentation consists of generating synthetic images starting from an original image and applying transformations to it, such as rotations, inversions, scaling, cropping, etc. 500 original images per seed type were acquired and 6 more images were generated for each of these, resulting in 3000 images. The following parameters were employed in the data augmentation process [11]:

- Rotation_range: sets the random rotation range to apply to the image, from 0° to 360°. This was fixed to 30°.
- Horizontal_flip: activates the application of a horizontal flip. This was set to "TRUE" in order to activate it.
- Zoom_range: sets the random zoom range to apply to the image, from 0 to 1. This was fixed to 0.3.

- Width_shift_range: sets the random width shift range to apply to the image, from 0 to 1. This was fixed to 0.2.
- Height_shift_range: sets the random height shift range to apply to the image, from 0 to 1. This was fixed to 0.2.

CNN Architecture

After creating the database, the CNN architecture was developed to achieve an acceptable identification performance. The structure is shown in Fig. 10.

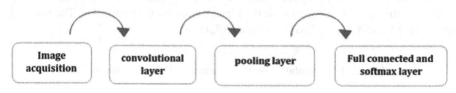

Fig. 10. CNN structure

Each step is now described in detail [11]:

- Input image: the network was configured according to the input image size (small, medium and large – see Table 2); this was set by the INPUT_SIZE parameter in the Conv2D function. The image was a scaled sub-image containing a single seed, defined by the primary components, $IER_n(x, y)$, $IEG_n(x, y)$ and $IEB_n(x, y)$.
- Convolutional layer: three convolutional layers were employed. The first one consisted of 32 9 × 9 filters to cover larger image sizes. The second layer consisted of 64 5 × 5 filters and the last layer, 64 3 × 3 filters. All layers used ReLU activations.
- Pooling layer: each convolutional layer used max-pooling at the output, with a pool size of 2. The last pooling layer had a flatten layer at the output, to convert it to a 1-D vector.
- Dense layer (fully-connected layer): two fully-connected layers were employed. The first one used ReLU activation and a 50% dropout; the second (and last) layer used Softmax activation to output the seed classification.

CNN Training Configuration

Table 3 shows the parameters used during the CNN training.

Table 3. Configuración del entrenamiento de la CNN

MaxEpochs	MiniBatchSize	InitialLearnRate	L2	LearnRateDropPeriod
30	50	0.001	0.0004	8

The parameters are described as follows [12]:

- MaxEpochs: maximum number of epochs during training; this was set to 30.
- MiniBatchSize: subset of training samples employed to verify the loss gradient and update weights; this was set to 50 as in the corn classification work.
- InitialLearnRate: initial learning rate used in training. If the rate is too small, training will be slow, so it was set to 0.001.
- L2: regularization factor (weight decay) which aids in avoiding overfitting. It was set to 0.0004 according to the rice classification work.
- LearRateDropPeriod: number of epochs until learning rate reduction. Among many tested values, the best results were obtained using a period of 8 epochs.

3 Results

The algorithm validation process was done using 750 images per seed type. From the total of 3000 images, 75% were used for training and 25% for validation. Each seed was manually labelled and classified in the 3 size groups:

- The large seeds were: aguaje, chambira and walnut (*nogal*).
- The medium seeds were: boliche, huanacoste, melia, black ear (*oreja de negro*), moringa, phoenix palm (*palmera fenix*), green palm (*palmera verde*), ponciana and tipa.
- The small seeds were: huarango, molle serrano, papelillo, white pine (*pino blanco*), pink pine (*pino rosado*) and tara.

Table 4 shows an example for each of the seed sizes.

Table 4. Examples of seeds (small, medium and large)

Species	Color	Size (cm)	Texture	Shape	Image
Aguaje (Large)	Brown and black	3.4 x 3.6	Smooth	Globe-shaped and ovoid	
Tipa (Medium)	Brown	1.5 x 1.8	Smooth	Ovoid	
White pine (small)	Brown	0.9 x 0.8	Smooth	Ovoid	

Since there was a CNN for each seed size, the size classification allowed to evaluate the performance of each one using confusion matrices. The ground truth consisted of manual labels done by forest engineers with coincident appreciations [2]. Figures 11, 12 and 13 show the confusion matrices for each seed size.

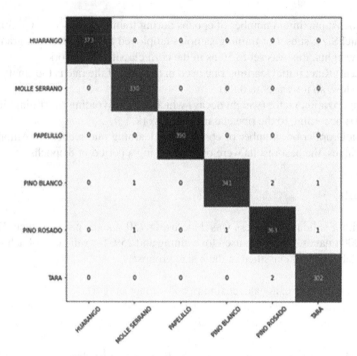

Fig. 11. CNN validation results (small seeds)

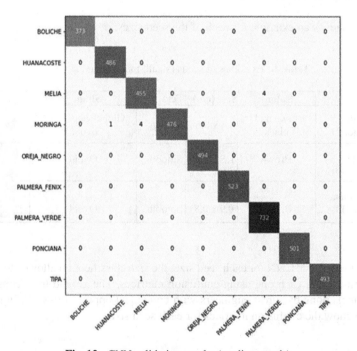

Fig. 12. CNN validation results (medium seeds)

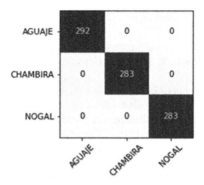

Fig. 13. CNN validation results (large seeds)

Classification of small seeds resulted in an average error of less than 0.5%. This is mostly due to the confusion between white pine seeds and pink pine seeds, and between tara and pink pine seeds. Medium seed classification achieved an average error of 0.3%, mostly because of confusions between moringa and melia seeds, and melia and green palm seeds. Finally, large seed classification achieves a 0% error. This might be explained due to these images having the largest pixel count in each object, which helps the CNN. Moreover, there are fewer varieties of large seeds.

The equipment's performance was also compared to the experts' opinions using the Cohen's Kappa index (K) [13], which measures the agreement level between different observers. A $K = 0.94$ was achieved for small seeds, $K = 0.96$ for medium seeds and $K = 1$ for large seeds. The three results represent a "very good" agreement level [13].

Conclusions

The low error percentages and high Cohen's Kappa values obtained in the validation indicate that the proposed device is very successful for silviculture experimentation and is suitable to be used in educational forestry institutions.

The image acquisition enclosure design, using different distances between the camera and the acquisition platforms according to the seed size was a very important factor for the successful seed identification. Additionally, the red background of the platform where the seeds are positioned helped significantly to correctly segment the objects.

The use of the Python programming language in single-board computers such as the Raspberry facilitated the implementation of computational algorithms, since it provides a large number of libraries for image processing, machine learning and deep learning, among others.

Finally, future works will aim to improve the identification capacity of the proposed device, training algorithms with a larger variety of forest seeds which are important to forestry specialists and researchers.

Acknowledgements. The authors would like to thank the Dirección de Investigación of Universidad Peruana de Ciencias Aplicadas for funding and logistical support with Code UPC-D-10-2022.

References

1. Navarro, R.M., Gálvez, C.: Manual para la identificación y reproducción de semillas de especies vegetales autóctonas de Andalucía, Consejería de Medio Ambiente, Sevilla, 390 p. (2001)
2. Armas, R., Túpac, M., Kemper, G., Del Carpio, C.: Un algoritmo de clasificación de semillas forestales basado en procesamiento digital de imágenes y redes neuronales convolucionales, Memorias de la Décima Novena Conferencia Iberoamericana en Sistemas, Cibernética e Informática (CISCI 2020), Orlando, USA (2020)
3. JayaBrindh, G., Gopi Subbu, E.S.: Ant Colony technique for optimizing the order of cascaded SVM classifier for sunflower seed classification. IEEE Trans. Emerg. Top. Comput. Intell. 2(1) (2017). https://doi.org/10.1109/TETCI.2017.2772918
4. Coelho-Caro, P.A., Saavedra-Rubilar, C.E., Staforelli, J.P., Gallardo-Nelson, M.J., Guaquin, V., Tarifeño, E.: Mussel classifier system based on morphological characteristics. IEEE Acces (2018). https://doi.org/10.1109/ACCESS.2018.2884394
5. Chaugule, A.A., Mali, S.N.: Identification of paddy varieties based on novel seed angle features. Comput. Electron. Agric. 123, 415–422 (2016). https://doi.org/10.1016/j.compag.2016.03.012
6. Yuanyuan, Z., Jilong, Z., Lingshen, F.: Research on quality evaluation of maize seed shape based on support vector machine. In: 2nd IEEE International Conference on Computer and Communications (ICCC), Chengdu, China (2017). https://doi.org/10.1109/CompComm.2016.7924791
7. Günes, E.O., Aygün, S., Kırcı, M., Kalateh, A., Çakır, Y.: Determination of the varieties and characteristics of wheat seeds grown in Turkey using image processing techniques. In: The Third International Conference on Agro-Geoinformatics, Beijing, China (2014). https://doi.org/10.1109/Agro-Geoinformatics.2014.6910610
8. Gao, K., White, T., Palaniappan, K., Warmund, M., Bunya, F.: Museed: a mobile image analysis application for plant seed morphometry. In: IEEE International Conference on Image Processing (ICIP). Beijing, China (2017). https://doi.org/10.1109/ICIP.2017.8296798
9. Casabona, P., Legonía, G.: Desarrollo de un equipo portátil orientado a la automatización del diagnóstico rápido de dengue por flujo lateral, basado en algoritmos computacionales de procesamiento digital de imágenes. Tesis para optar el título profesional de ingeniero electrónico, Universidad Peruana de Ciencias Aplicadas, Lima, Peru (2021)
10. Gonzales, R., Woods, R.: Digital Image Processing, 4th edn. Pearson, London (2017)
11. López, M.: Detección de personas enimágenes de profundidad mediante redes neuronales convolucionales. Tesis para optar el título profesional de ingeniero electrónico de comunicaciones, Universidad de Alcalá (2019)
12. Torres, J.: Python Deep Learning: Introducciónpráctica con Keras y TensorFlow 2, Alfaomega Marcombo (2020)
13. Landis, J.R., Koch, G.G.: The measurement of observer agreement for categorical data. Biometrics (1977)

Automatic Evaluation of Physiotherapy Activities Using Deep Learning Techniques

Enrique V. Carrera$^{(\boxtimes)}$ ⬤, Xavier Arequipa ⬤, and Bryan Hernández ⬤

Departamento de Eléctrica, Electrónica y Telecomunicaciones
Universidad de las Fuerzas Armadas – ESPE, Sangolquí 171103, Ecuador
{evcarrera,xaarequipa,bshernandez}@espe.edu.ec

Abstract. Physiotherapy activities are necessary in patients with physical disabilities or to restore their functional abilities after injury or surgery. However, home-based therapy requires some mechanisms for automatic evaluation of the correct execution of physiotherapy exercises. Although novel tools and equipment exist to support physical therapy sessions at home, low-cost implementations could fail if patients perform the exercises incorrectly or at an unusual pace. Thus, this work proposes to determine the precision of physical therapy exercises using low-cost motion sensors and deep learning techniques, evaluating the most successful classification architectures based on supervised learning. In particular, the proposed system will classify the type of execution of some common exercises in physiotherapy sessions, labeling them as correct execution, fast execution, or low-amplitude execution. The accuracy and sensitivity results are very promising, as we have obtained an accuracy greater than 95% and an average sensitivity greater than 94% using recurrent neural networks. We hope that works like this will help to improve the effectiveness of physiotherapy sessions at home, leaving aside the need for trained clinicians or restricted schedules.

Keywords: Physiotherapy activities · Exercise evaluation · Motion sensors · Deep learning techniques

1 Introduction

Physiotherapy activities are commonly prescribed for patients who are physically disabled or to restore their functional capabilities after injury or surgery. In physical therapy sessions, a clinician instructs patients on the exercises to perform and then monitors their performance in a clinical setting. However, this type of physiotherapy treatment is restricted by the availability of trained clinicians and free schedules [10]. In order to increase the flexibility of physical therapy activities, home-based therapy is often used as a complement to clinic-based treatments. But as you can imagine, poor supervision promotes increased risk because patients may perform exercises incorrectly [12], reducing the effectiveness of physiotherapy exercises, delaying the physical recovery of the patient, or even increasing the risk of re-injury.

M. Botto-Tobar et al. (Eds.): ICAT 2022, CCIS 1755, pp. 143–154, 2023.
https://doi.org/10.1007/978-3-031-24985-3_11

Therefore, it is important to evaluate each of the exercises performed by the patients at home and to assess the effectiveness of every physiotherapy session. For all these reasons, there is currently a demand for novel tools and equipment to support home-based physical therapy, such as robotic assistive devices, exoskeletons, haptic devices and virtual gaming environments [3,9,10,19]. In fact, several previous studies have already addressed this need by taking into account various metrics such as energy expenditure, exercise duration, among others [4,6,18].

However, the above approaches can be quite costly or even misleading if the patient performs the exercises incorrectly or at an unusual pace [16]. In the latter case, the two most common types of errors that patients make during their exercise sessions are: (i) they perform the movements too quickly, or (ii) they perform the exercise with a small amplitude without fully executing the movement [17]. The first mistake is due to the fact that patients do not maintain the position for the necessary time because they want to quickly complete the required number of repetitions, while the second mistake is due to physical incapacity or due to negligence, sloppiness, carelessness, etc.

Based on the previous discussion, this work proposes to determine the precision of physiotherapy exercises using low-cost motion sensors [12] and deep learning techniques [8], evaluating the most successful classification architectures based on supervised learning [1]. The proposed system will be able to classify the type of execution of some common exercises in physiotherapy sessions, labeling them as correct execution, fast execution, or low-amplitude execution. Since the recordings are sequences of motion-sensor measurements [13], different deep learning architectures are adapted to correctly label each physical therapy exercise.

The accuracy and sensitivity results are very promising, as we have obtained an accuracy greater than 95% and an average sensitivity greater than 94% when recurrent neural networks where used. This is a significant improvement over previous similar works that achieved 93% accuracy using much more complex dynamic time warping algorithms [17] or statistical modeling [14]. In this proposal, recurrent neural networks allow us to achieve high accuracy despite using low-cost motion sensors and employing a simpler design based on this well-known deep learning technology [7].

The rest of this paper is organized as follows. Section 2 introduces low-cost motion sensors as tools for monitoring physical therapy exercises, as well as describing the main deep learning techniques. Section 3 presents the proposal for the automatic evaluation of physiotherapy activities using several deep learning architectures. The main results and their implications are discussed in Sect. 4. Finally, Sect. 5 concludes the paper and analyzes some future works.

2   Background

Before describing the proposed system for the automatic evaluation of physical therapy activities using deep learning techniques, this section presents the most significant concepts associated with motion sensors, physiotherapy exercises, and machine/deep learning.

2.1 Motion Sensors

Current systems for human motion analysis range from consolidated gait laboratories, based on video motion capture, to game platforms such as Kinect, or even innovative and low-cost alternatives suitable for autonomous use at home. In fact, the use of cameras and computer vision algorithms for human motion analysis is a fairly well-established field that has had notable contributions [11]. Today, these specialized laboratories use various cameras with infrared illuminators and triangulation algorithms to track the three-dimensional positions of reflective markers moving within a calibrated field of view. The main problem with these professional systems is their high cost and the complexity of installation and use.

A cheaper and simpler alternative is the Kinect sensor introduced by Microsoft in 2010, although there is now a second version that slightly outperforms its predecessor in precision. Kinect is an input device for motion capture on the Xbox game console [3]. This device features a standard digital video camera, a depth sensor based on structured infrared illumination and a directional microphone [5]. This motion sensor has been used in bio-mechanical and clinical research showing several interesting results.

Finally, the availability of micro-electromechanical systems packed as miniaturized sensors, combined with integrated processing and communication technologies, have allowed the development of portable sensing devices to monitor the human body movements [12]. These sensors present some technological requirements (*e.g.*, sensing capabilities, signal bandwidth, throughput) and other general challenges (*e.g.*, device portability, system usability, data reliability). Although a portable sensor provides a simple method of collecting motion data relative to the body segment where it is worn, by combining a network of sensors to form a full-body model, joints' motion could be inferred. Thus, the integration of multiple sensors within the same device (*e.g.*, accelerometer, gyroscope, and magnetometer) allows the implementation of robust sensor fusion algorithms to provide reliable and detailed information in a wide range of dynamic conditions and application contexts. In fact, data produced by these embedded sensors can be exploited to analyze various characteristics of the human motion [11], and dedicated algorithms have been developed for tasks such as activity recognition, exercise recognition and evaluation, gait analysis, jump analysis, etc.

2.2 Physiotherapy Exercises

Physiotherapy is a treatment method that uses body movements to help people restore, maintain and/or maximize their physical motion, strength, and general well-being. Although each physical therapy program is unique and adapted to every patient, there are three general types of physical therapy exercises [3]:

– Balance exercises seek to control the stationary body as well as the body in motion. These exercises improve the awareness of joint position as the center of gravity changes.
– Range of motion exercises are movements of a joint from its fully flexed position to its fully extended position. These movements can be passive, active-assisted or active, depending on the level of assistance of the physiotherapist to the patient.
– Strengthening exercises ensure that the muscles have normal strength to prevent future injuries. Normally, strengthening exercises overload the muscle to the point of muscle fatigue, encouraging the growth of that particular muscle.

In this work, we will evaluate actively performed range of motion exercises, since they are the most common physiotherapy exercises executed by patients at home and in which low-cost portable devices can be used.

2.3   Machine and Deep Learning

In last years, various machine learning methods have been applied in several fields and have been very well received within the research community. Undoubtedly, the possibility of learning from examples facilitates the development of new applications, instead of revealing the implicit rules of a problem or proposing complex specific processing methods [20]. Within machine learning techniques, supervised learning algorithms stand out over unsupervised, reinforced and/or self-supervised learning approaches [1]. In general, the models created through machine learning algorithms are applied to classification or regression tasks with many useful and successful applications.

Moreover, the use of deep learning models has generated a great attention in the last decade. These models are mainly based on neural networks that can be of three types [7]: deep neural networks, convolutional neural networks and recurrent neural networks. Deep neural networks are structures that contain tens or even hundreds of hidden layers of neurons. Convolutional neural networks apply filtering structures that optimize image classification and recognition. Finally, recurrent neural networks have connections that feedback the output of a set of neurons to the inputs of previous layers. This feedback of information allows to maintain a state (*i.e.*, memory) that makes them suitable for classification or regression tasks on sequential data or time-series. Within the different recurrent neural networks, two models have demonstrated their applicability under various conditions [8]: the first one is LSTM (Long Short-Term Memory) that uses memory cells with input, output and forget gates, while the second model, a little bit newer, is GRU (Gated Recurrent Unit) that includes reset and update gates.

In particular, this work will use classification models based on *(i)* deep neural networks that employ autoencoders as feature extractors, *(ii)* convolutional neural networks that require the spectrograms of the time signals as inputs, and *(iii)* recurrent neural networks that classify data sequences of variable length.

All these models will learn to determine the type of execution for various physiotherapy exercises.

3   Proposal

The general scheme of the system proposed in this work is shown in Fig. 1. The processing of the system begins with the labeled data set of the motion-sensor measurements, which are then preprocessed and adapted for the three types of algorithms of deep learning to analyze, specifically deep neural networks (DNN), convolutional neural networks (CNN) and recurrent neural networks (RNN). At the end of the training process, the results of accuracy, sensitivity and precision are compared. The entire system was implemented on an i7 laptop with 16 GB of RAM, running Matlab 2022a.

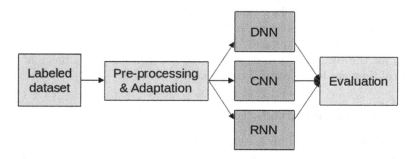

Fig. 1. General structure of the system utilized for the evaluation of physiotherapy exercises.

3.1   Data Set

The data set used in this work is the Physical Therapy Exercises Dataset, publicly available in the UCI Machine Learning Repository [17]. This data set was created to study the automatic detection of physiotherapy exercises using portable motion sensors. The sensors used in this case are the MTx sensor units manufactured by XSens Technologies, where each unit contains three tri-axial sensors: an accelerometer, a gyroscope, and a magnetometer [18]. All these sensors are sampled 25 Hz and the time series data is filtered by the sensor manufacturer's software using the default settings during data acquisition.

In this particular data set, the recorded data contains information from five MTx sensor units corresponding to the execution of multiple physical therapy exercises. Therefore, the data set includes 45 (*i.e.*, 5 sensors × 9 axes) normalized time series for training sessions and simulated exercise sessions with predetermined patterns. In other words, the original data set is already divided into training and testing sets, where the training set contains template recordings and the testing set contains the simulated physical therapy exercises.

The exercises and the experimental procedure were determined in collaboration with a physiotherapy specialist. In total there are eight types of physiotherapy exercises involving only arm or only leg movements, each of which has three types of execution (*i.e.*, correct, fast and low-amplitude). Each execution of each type was performed multiple times by five subjects.

3.2   Pre-processing and Adaptation

Since the data set provided by the UCI Machine Learning Repository is already filtered and normalized, the system begins packing the data into the structures required by each of the deep learning architectures discussed below. Moreover, instead of using the training and testing split suggested by the original repository, we create a single structure with all the samples and then apply a 70–30 random split for the training and testing sets, respectively.

For the input to the deep neural network, we create an array of 45×13615 values, where each column has a label indicating normal, fast, or low-amplitude. For the convolutional neural network, each column of the previous matrix is converted to a spectrogram and saved as a JPG image of 227×227 pixels. Finally, for the recurrent neural network, the 45 measurements made at some instant of time are fed in parallel to the neural network.

3.3   Deep Learning Architectures

Figure 2 shows the four deep learning architectures used for the evaluation of physiotherapy exercises. Although the overall analysis of these architectures implies a complete study of the parameter space, we will describe them only in terms of the configurations that achieve the best performance.

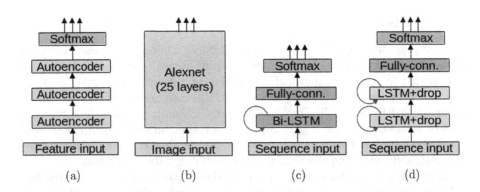

Fig. 2. Structure of the four deep-learning architectures used for the evaluation of physiotherapy exercises: (a) DNN based on autoencoders, (b) CNN with transfer learning over Alexnet, (c) Bidirectional LSTM, and (d) Multi-layer LSTM.

First, we have used a deep neural network based on autoencoders (Fig. 2a), which allow us to extract features in an unsupervised way. The original 45 input features are reduced to 25, 15, and finally 5 latent variables, and then classified through a softmax layer that identifies any of three classes (*i.e.*, correct, fast, and low-amplitude executions).

The second deep learning architecture is an Alexnet-based convolutional neural network (Fig. 2b). This network is already trained for the Imagenet challenge [15], and we use transfer learning to classify the 227×227 pixel spectrogram images into just three classes. Note also that although Alexnet is the simplest convolutional neural network with good performance in the Imagenet competition, it has 25 layers (according to the nomenclature adopted by Matlab) among convolutional, normalization, pooling, relu, dropout, fully-connected and softmax layers.

Finally, to evaluate the recurrent neural networks, we have tested two architectures: the first one is a bidirectional LSTM network (Fig. 2c), and the second structure is a two-layer LSTM network that includes dropout layers on the outputs of the recurrent layers (Fig. 2d). The bidirectional LSTM network contains 500 neurons in its recurrent layer, while the two-layer LSTM network contains 250 and 100 neurons in its two recurrent layers, respectively. In both cases, the recurrent neural networks discriminate only three classes with a many-to-one mapping [8].

3.4   Evaluation

As mentioned before, the evaluation of these deep learning models is based on a holdout methodology, where 70% of the samples are used for training and 30% of them for testing. The metrics to be compared are based on the confusion matrix created by the classifier [1], emphasizing the values of accuracy, sensitivity, and precision.

In order to facilitate the presentation of results in the confusion matrix, we have associated 'class 1' with a correct execution of the exercises, 'class 2' with a fast execution, and 'class 3' with a low-amplitude execution. It is also important to note that these three classes are unbalanced in the original data set and we are using them in that way.

4   Main Results

In this section, the main classification results for the three general deep learning architectures are presented. Results of the time dedicated to training in these architectures are also compared.

4.1   Deep Neural Network

The first classifiers to be evaluated is a neural network made up of 3 autoencoders that reduce the input feature vector to only 5 latent variables and then classified them using a simple softmax layer. The autoencoders employ unsupervised learning and were trained separately with 1000, 275 and 200 epochs. After training the autoencoders, a softmax layer is added, ant it is also trained during 10000 epochs. Finally, a fine-tuning process adjusts the weights of all the stack of layers presented in (Fig. 2a). The entire training process takes almost 16 min and the results of its confusion matrix are presented in Table 1.

Table 1. Confusion matrix for the deep neural network: unsupervised autoencoders + softmax layer.

Autoencoders	Target 1	Target 2	Target 3	Precision
Output 1	1484	262	30	83.6%
Output 2	181	440	91	61.8%
Output 3	82	143	1371	85.9%
Sensitivity	84.9%	52.1%	91.9%	**80.7%**

As we can see, the results presented in Table 1 have a classification error of 19.3%. There are also classes like the second one (*i.e.*, fast exercise) that, due to the reduced number of samples, have low sensitivity and precision, approximately 52% and 62%, respectively. Therefore, unsupervised extraction of features using autoencoders does not guarantee a good mapping separation in the latent space of these three classes.

4.2   Convolutional Neural Network

In the case of convolutional neural networks, instead of creating a new network from scratch, we use Alexnet, a convolutional network trained to recognize 1000 different objects in a set of one million images [2]. Through transfer learning, the last layers of the network are changed to classify only three classes and the weights of those last layers are adjusted using a fine-tuning process. Due to the complexity of the network (*i.e.*, 25 layers), the training of this model takes much longer that the other architectures analyzed here. In fact, 40 epochs took about 10 h and 18 min.

Table 2. Confusion matrix for the convolutional neural network: Alexnet + transfer learning.

Alexnet	Target 1	Target 2	Target 3	Precision
Output 1	1518	175	29	88.2%
Output 2	128	607	52	77.1%
Output 3	66	84	1426	90.5%
Sensitivity	88.7%	70.1%	94.6%	**86.9%**

Table 2 shows the results of the convolutional neural network classification. As we can see, this deep learning model performs better than the autoencoder-based network. The classification error is reduced to 13.1% but the sensitivity and precision of the second class are still low, approximately 70% and 77%, respectively. Although using spectrogram images is better that feature extraction through autoencoders, the model still cannot reach high accuracy.

4.3 Recurrent Neural Networks

For the case of recurrent neural networks, we have evaluated two versions: a bidirectional LSTM network and a two-layer LSTM network. The bidirectional LSTM neural network was trained for 350 epochs, obtaining the confusion matrix shown in Table 3. This training process took a little bit more than 39 min.

Table 3. Confusion matrix for the bidirectional recurrent neural network that uses 500 LSTM cells.

BiLSTM	Target 1	Target 2	Target 3	Precision
Output 1	1654	64	15	95.4%
Output 2	47	784	30	91.1%
Output 3	13	39	1438	96.5%
Sensitivity	95.5%	88.4%	97.0%	**94.9%**

We can see in Table 3 that the classification error drops to 5.1%, reaching an average sensitivity and precision of approximately 94% for both metrics. Definitively, recurrent neural networks are a better option for classifying time series, as is the case with the samples obtained from the motion sensors.

On the other hand, the two-layer LSTM network was trained for 500 epochs, taking a little more than 22 min to train. The confusion matrix for this second recurrent neural network is shown in Table 4. We can see that this last alternative learns faster that the bidirectional LSTM network and presents the lowest classification error, specifically 4.5%. Likewise, the average sensitivity of the model is 96.6% and its average precision 95%.

Table 4. Confusion matrix for the two-layer recurrent neural network with 200 and 100 LSTM units at the corresponding layers.

2×LSTM	Target 1	Target 2	Target 3	Precision
Output 1	1662	57	10	96.1%
Output 2	34	790	26	92.9%
Output 3	18	40	1447	96.1%
Sensitivity	97.0%	89.1%	97.6%	**95.5%**

Finally, it is important to summarize the most significant results and provide an overall comparison of all deep learning architectures previously analyzed for the evaluation of physiotherapy exercises. Thus, Table 5 presents the average accuracy and the total training time of the four deep learning architectures.

We can see that the two-layer LSTM network is the best option for the evaluation of physiotherapy exercises, not only due to its high accuracy but also due to the relative low training times, even considering that the motion sensors used in this work are very low cost. Although there is room of improvement, we are convinced that the current results are clear proof of the advantage of using recurrent neural networks in this type of applications.

Table 5. Accuracy and training time of the four deep learning architectures evaluated in this work.

Architecture	Accuracy	Training time
Autoencoders	80.7%	15 m 50 s
Alexnet	86.9%	10 h 18 m 11 s
BiLSTM	94.9%	39 m 28 s
2×LSTM	95.5%	22 m 15 s

5   Conclusions

Home-based physiotherapy requires some mechanism for automatic evaluation of the correct execution of the exercises performed by the patients. Therefore, this work shows that low-cost implementations, based on simple motion-sensor units, could accomplish this goal in an effective way. In addition to low-cost motion sensors, four deep learning architectures were tested as possible classifiers of determine the correct or incorrect execution of the physiotherapy exercises. The results show that recurrent neural networks are powerful tools to classify sequential data or time series. In particular, a two-layer LSTM network is capable of reaching an accuracy greater than 95%, with average sensitivity and precision of around 96% and 95%, respectively.

These are very promising results, even considering that inexpensive motion sensors are used to assess the quality of the physiotherapy exercises performed by patients at home. Obviously, the deep learning techniques deserve much of the credit for this successful behavior. Based on this, we hope that works like this will help to improve the effectiveness of physical therapy sessions at home, leaving aside the need for trained clinicians or restricted schedules.

Some future works that we have planned in our research group include the testing of other models of recurrent neural networks, as well as the evaluation of the influence of the quality of motion sensors on the performance of this type of applications. In addition, we would like to see how these algorithms behave in a more controlled environment where the number of samples for each exercise is completely balanced.

References

1. Alpaydin, E.: Machine Learning. MIT Press, Cambridge (2021)
2. Andrade, F., Carrera, E.V.: Supervised evaluation of seed-based interactive image segmentation algorithms. In: 20th Symposium on Signal Processing, Images and Computer Vision (STSIVA), pp. 1–7. IEEE (2015)
3. Chang, Y.J., Chen, S.F., Huang, J.D.: A kinect-based system for physical rehabilitation: a pilot study for young adults with motor disabilities. Res. Dev. Disabil. **32**(6), 2566–2570 (2011)
4. Cuellar, M.P., Ros, M., Martin-Bautista, M.J., Le Borgne, Y., Bontempi, G.: An approach for the evaluation of human activities in physical therapy scenarios. In: Agüero, R., Zinner, T., Goleva, R., Timm-Giel, A., Tran-Gia, P. (eds.) MONAMI 2014. LNICST, vol. 141, pp. 401–414. Springer, Cham (2015). https://doi.org/10.1007/978-3-319-16292-8_29
5. Debnath, B., O'brien, M., Yamaguchi, M., Behera, A.: A review of computer vision-based approaches for physical rehabilitation and assessment. Multimedia Syst. 1–31 (2021)
6. Decroos, T., Schütte, K., De Beéck, T.O., Vanwanseele, B., Davis, J.: AMIE: automatic monitoring of indoor exercises. In: Brefeld, U., et al. (eds.) ECML PKDD 2018. LNCS (LNAI), vol. 11053, pp. 424–439. Springer, Cham (2019). https://doi.org/10.1007/978-3-030-10997-4_26
7. Goodfellow, I., Bengio, Y., Courville, A.: Deep Learning. MIT Press, Cambridge (2016)
8. Grossberg, S.: Recurrent neural networks. Scholarpedia **8**(2), 1888 (2013)
9. Hassan, H., et al.: Automatic feedback for physiotherapy exercises based on PoseNet. Inform. Bull. **2**(2), 10–14 (2020)
10. Liao, Y., Vakanski, A., Xian, M., Paul, D., Baker, R.: A review of computational approaches for evaluation of rehabilitation exercises. Comput. Biol. Med. **119**, 103687 (2020)
11. Milosevic, B., Leardini, A., Farella, E.: Kinect and wearable inertial sensors for motor rehabilitation programs at home: state of the art and an experimental comparison. Biomed. Eng. Online **19**(1), 1–26 (2020)
12. Raso, I., Hervás, R., Bravo, J.: m-Physio: personalized accelerometer-based physical rehabilitation platform. In: Proceedings of the Fourth International Conference on Mobile Ubiquitous Computing, Systems, Services and Technologies, pp. 416–421. Citeseer (2010)
13. Taylor, P.E., Almeida, G.J., Kanade, T., Hodgins, J.K.: Classifying human motion quality for knee osteoarthritis using accelerometers. In: 2010 Annual International Conference of the IEEE Engineering in Medicine and Biology, pp. 339–343. IEEE (2010)
14. Williams, C., Vakanski, A., Lee, S., Paul, D.: Assessment of physical rehabilitation movements through dimensionality reduction and statistical modeling. Med. Eng. Phys. **74**, 13–22 (2019)
15. You, Y., Zhang, Z., Hsieh, C.J., Demmel, J., Keutzer, K.: Imagenet training in minutes. In: Proceedings of the 47th International Conference on Parallel Processing, pp. 1–10 (2018)
16. Yurtman, A., Barshan, B.: Detection and evaluation of physical therapy exercises by dynamic time warping using wearable motion sensor units. In: Gelenbe, E., Lent, R. (eds.) Information Sciences and Systems 2013, vol. 264, pp. 305–314. Springer International Publishing, Cham (2013). https://doi.org/10.1007/978-3-319-01604-7_30

17. Yurtman, A., Barshan, B.: Automated evaluation of physical therapy exercises using multi-template dynamic time warping on wearable sensor signals. Comput. Methods Programs Biomed. **117**(2), 189–207 (2014)
18. Yurtman, A., Barshan, B.: Detection and evaluation of physical therapy exercises from wearable motion sensor signals by dynamic time warping. In: 22nd Signal Processing and Communications Applications Conference (SIU), pp. 1491–1494. IEEE (2014)
19. Zhang, W., Su, C., He, C.: Rehabilitation exercise recognition and evaluation based on smart sensors with deep learning framework. IEEE Access **8**, 77561–77571 (2020)
20. Zhou, Z.H.: Mach. Learn. (2021). Springer Nature

Multivariable Control Approach Applied to the Embryo Incubation Process of Gallus Gallus Domesticus

Alvaro Balseca[1], Marco Herrera[2], and Oscar Camacho[3(✉)]

[1] Universidad Técnica de Ambato, Av. Los Chasquis, Ambato, Ecuador
abalseca9373@uta.edu.ec
[2] Escuela Politécnica Nacional, Ladrón de Guevara, Quito E11, 253, Ecuador
marco.herrera@epn.edu.ec
[3] Colegio de Ciencias e Ingenierías, Universidad San Francisco de Quito, Quito, Ecuador
ocamacho@usfq.edu.ec

Abstract. In this paper, a multivariable control using fuzzy logic and genetic algorithms (GA) is developed to control the incubation process of "gallus gallus domesticus" embryos. The incubation process is a system with high interactions among its input and output variables. A dynamic decoupling is used through Relative Gain Array (RGA) analysis to reduce these interactions. The proportional-integral (PI) controllers and the linear decoupler are designed from single-variable control structures obtained from a parametric identification for systems that can approximate first order and first order with a delay (FOPDT). Comparative performance analysis of PI, PI-Fuzzy, and PI-Fuzzy tuned with Genetic Algorithms controllers are evaluated using the integral squared error (ISE) and integral absolute error (IAE) through experimental tests using the NODEMCU ESP-WROOM-32 embedded system.

Keywords: Multivariable control · Fuzzy logic · Genetic algorithms

1 Introduction

The poultry industry is one of the largest producers of raw materials and derivatives worldwide; this is due to the high consumption of chicken meat and eggs, which is why it has been seen the need to potentiate technology in its different stages, especially in the incubation process. Therefore, according to their nature, these processes present a multivariable behavior due to the number of variables involved, which leads to the development of control algorithms to improve the performance of the controller and, thus, of the multivariable process, which through classical control techniques is difficult to achieve, [1–3].

The incubation process of gallus gallus domesticus embryos is formed according to its nature by the artificial generation of the body heat poultry and the process of producing ambient relative humidity. Therefore, for this work, the heat energy generated by convection and the evaporation of water produced by electrical

© The Author(s), under exclusive license to Springer Nature Switzerland AG 2023
M. Botto-Tobar et al. (Eds.): ICAT 2022, CCIS 1755, pp. 155–170, 2023.
https://doi.org/10.1007/978-3-031-24985-3_12

resistances are the inputs to the process. At the same time, temperature and humidity are the outputs. Thus, the artificial embryo incubation is a multivariable process with high interactions between its inputs and outputs, which complicates the design and implementation of single-variable control algorithms, [4,5].

A mathematical model equivalent to the incubation process can be approximated through a first order system with dead time, [6]. Therefore, these systems can be classified according to their temperature control and humidity control, differentiated mainly by different controller designs, such as Proportional Integral (PI), Proportional Integral Derivative (PID), and fuzzy control. To improve the performance of the incubation process, fuzzy controllers with different design perspectives have been developed. For instance, in [7] uses a control system for an egg incubator based on IoT technology through the design of a fuzzy controller, where the inputs are the error (Err) and the derivative of the error (ΔErr). In contrast, in the study of [8], a prototype of the hen egg incubation system is built, whose temperature is controlled by Mamdani Fuzzy Logic Control, where its inputs are temperature and humidity. Its outputs are two regulators for resistive and inductive loads through a PWM signal to control a lamp and a fan, respectively. The controller is a multivariable control design with two inputs and two outputs (TITO). All these studies research to improve the performance of the controller through classical control tools such as PID and provide intelligence to the process such as fuzzy control, [9].

This work develops a fuzzy PI controller tuned through Genetic Algorithms (GA). The proposed scheme blends the advantages of these techniques: the accuracy and easy implementation of the PI, the artificial intelligence of the Fuzzy, and the parameter optimization of the GA. The controller uses an approximate first-order plus dead time (FOPDT) model obtained from the parametric identification method by the least squares criterion. In addition, a decoupling network is used to reduce the interaction between variables. This work is organized as follows: In Sect. 2, the nonlinear and approximate model of the process is presented. Then, in Sect. 3, the study of model interactions and variable paring is performed, and the decoupling of the process model is developed. Next, in Sect. 4, the proposed control system is developed; in Sect. 5, the experimentally obtained results are presented; and finally, the conclusions are presented.

2   Dynamic Model

The schematic of the incubation system is shown in Fig. 1, which consists of temperature and humidity processes. This system has two phase modulators for resistive loads, which generate heat energy and humidity by evaporation. Therefore, the inputs to the process are the voltages of the electrical resistors U_1 and U_2, and the outputs of the temperature and humidity sensors are Y_1 and Y_2. Now, applying the equations of the thermal and water energy balance, the Eqs. (1)–(2) are obtained, [10,11].

$$m_a C_e \frac{dT_i}{dt} = Q_a + Q_e - Q_w - Q_E - Q_o - Q_h \tag{1}$$

$$\rho V_H \frac{dD_b}{dt} = D_e - D_v + D_o \qquad (2)$$

The control signal is the voltages of the electrical resistors U_i, m_a is the mass of air inside the incubator, C_e is the specific heat of the air, V_H is the effective volume of humidity which approximates the total volume inside the incubator, Q_a is the heat energy required to heat the air inside the incubator, Q_w, Q_e, Q_E, Q_o and Q_h are the heat energy lost through the walls, heat energy required by the embryos, heat energy needed for the enthalpy change of the air (opening and closing the door), heat energy lost through the air renewal holes inside the incubator and heat lost by humidification, T_i is the temperature

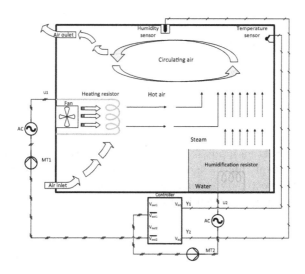

Fig. 1. Incubation system scheme

Table 1. Incubation system parameters

Symbol	Description	Value	Unit
m_a	Air mass inside the incubator	0.155	Kg
C_e	Specific heat of air	1000	$\frac{J}{Kg \cdot {}^\circ C}$
V_H	Effective humidity volume	0.155	m^3
Q_a	Heat energy to heat the incubator air	3053.5	J
Q_w	Heat energy lost through the walls	17.85	J
Q_e	Heat energy required by the embryos	864.63	KJ
Q_E	Heat energy required for open/close door	2730	J
Q_o	Heat energy lost for renovation of air	1.85	J
Q_h	Heat energy lost by humidification	11.29	KJ
T_i	Temperature inside the incubator	37.7	$^\circ C$
D_e	Evaporation system humidity rate	65	$\%$
Q_v	Ventilation system humidity rate	2	$\%$
Q_o	Outdoor air humidity rate	20	$\%$

inside the incubator, ρ is the air density, D_e is the humidity flow supplied by the evaporation system, D_v is the humidity flow to the outside due to the air exchange by the ventilation system and D_o is the humidity flow gained from the outside, [10]. The design is established through the parameters in Table 1.

According to the nature of the incubation process, the dynamic behavior is performed at the operating point which is 37.7 °C for temperature and 65% for humidity.

2.1   Approximate Model of the Incubation System

The least squares criterion identification method is used to find an approximate linear model. At the operating point, a variation in the input signal ΔV is made, and the behavior of the output signal ΔY is analyzed. The result can be approximated to a first-order model or a first-order plus dead time (FOPDT), as shown in the Eqs. (3)–(4), [12,13].

$$\frac{Y(s)}{U(s)} = \frac{K}{\tau s + 1} \tag{3}$$

$$\frac{Y(s)}{U(s)} = \frac{K e^{-t_0 s}}{\tau s + 1} \tag{4}$$

where $U(s)$ is the System input, $Y(s)$ is the system output, K is the Static gain, τ is the time constant, and t_0 is the Dead time. The parameters K, τ, and t_0 turn out to be the vector of parameters to be estimated and are obtained from a linear regressor structure given by Eq. (5).

$$\hat{y}(n) = \varphi^T(n)\theta \tag{5}$$

where: $\hat{y}(n)$ is the predicted system output with respect to real output $y(n)$, $\varphi^T(n)$ is the linear regression vector and $\theta = \begin{bmatrix} K & \tau & t_0 \end{bmatrix}$ is the vector of parameters to be estimated. The difference between the real experimentally obtained data $y(n)$ and the predicted output $\hat{y}(n)$ is the error $e(n)$. To minimize the error $e(n)$, the fitness function is minimized, [14].

To find the parameter vector θ with the lowest prediction error, a first order plus dead time approximation is included in the regressor to predict its dynamics. It is represented in Eq. (6).

$$\hat{G}(s) = \frac{\hat{\theta}(1)e^{-\hat{\theta}(3)s}}{1 + (\hat{\theta})(2)} \tag{6}$$

Equation (6) will converge until its prediction error is minimum. In order to prediction algorithm to be recursive, it is necessary to establish an initial parameter vector θ_o and a learning a, resulting in Eq. (7).

$$J(\theta) = \theta_o \cdot \hat{\theta} \cdot a \tag{7}$$

System identification is established through initial parameters and search criteria presented in Table 2.

Table 2. Initial parameters and search criteria for parametric least-squares identification

Parameter	Value
K_0	10
τ_0	1
t_0	0.01
a (Learning)	$0.2 \cdot \begin{bmatrix} 0.1 \\ 0.5 \\ 0.1 \end{bmatrix}$
Minimum global error	$8 \cdot 10^{-8}$
Iterations	5000

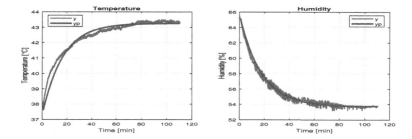

Fig. 2. Time responses of temperature and humidity for a variation on $+U_1$

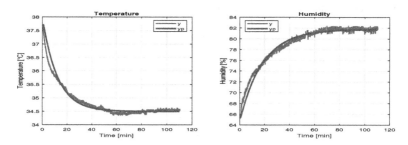

Fig. 3. Time responses of temperature and humidity for a variation on $-U_1$

In order to find a linear model representation, a $\pm 20\%$ variation on input U_1 (Heating resistor), the time responses of outputs Y_1 (Temperature) and Y_2 (Humidity) are shown in the Figs. 2 and 3, and a $\pm 20\%$ variation on the U_2 (Humidification resistor), the time responses of outputs Y_1 and Y_2 are shown in the Figs. 4 and 5. [15].

The results of each identification experiment have uncertainty; therefore, an average of the parameters found that are linked to each of the inputs is performed to obtain an approximate model of the system dynamics. In summary, these

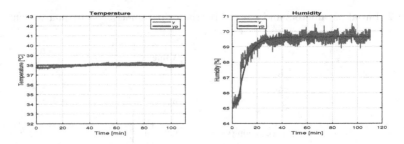

Fig. 4. Time responses of temperature and humidity for a variation on $+U_2$

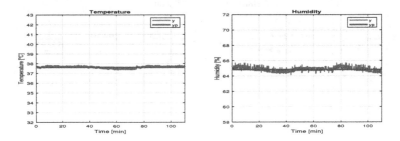

Fig. 5. Time responses of temperature and humidity for a variation on $-U_2$

incubation system approximation models are given by:

$$G_{11}(s) = \frac{0.5513}{14.47s + 1} \tag{8}$$

$$G_{12}(s) = 0.042643 \tag{9}$$

$$G_{21}(s) = -\frac{1.723}{17.96s + 1} \tag{10}$$

$$G_{22} = \frac{1.087e^{-3.53s}}{7.229s + 1} \tag{11}$$

Equations (8)–(11) represent the multiple inputs and outputs (MIMO) of the incubation process with different dynamic behaviors.

3 Interaction and Decoupling of Variables

In order to choose a decoupling method, it is essential to determine the degree of interaction among the input and output variables of the system. For this, the open-loop structure is schematized through the unions between the transfer

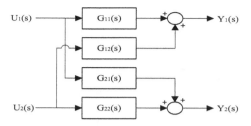

Fig. 6. Scheme of interaction among inputs/outputs

functions to form a block diagram as shown in Fig. 6, [16]. According Fig. 6, the Eqs. (8)–(11) can be rewritten as a transfer function matrix:

$$\begin{bmatrix} Y_1(s) \\ Y_2(s) \end{bmatrix} = G(s) \begin{bmatrix} U_1(s) \\ U_2(s) \end{bmatrix} \tag{12}$$

where:

$$G(s) = \begin{bmatrix} \dfrac{0.5513}{14.47s+1} & 0.042643 \\ -\dfrac{1.723}{17.96s+1} & \dfrac{1.087e^{-3.53s}}{7.229s+1} \end{bmatrix} \tag{13}$$

In order to establish the degree of interaction among variables, the Relative Gain Array (RGA) is used [17]. Therefore, it is required to obtain the static gain matrix of the system as $G(0) = \lim_{s \to 0} G(s)$. The RGA is expressed as:

$$\Lambda = G(0) \circ \left(G(0)^{-1} \right)^T = \begin{bmatrix} 0.8908 & 0.1092 \\ 0.1092 & 0.8908 \end{bmatrix} \tag{14}$$

From Eq. (14) it is concluded to pair Y_1 with U_1 and Y_2 with U_2. In this way, an approach to the control of multivariable systems using a decoupling of their variables can be addressed, [18]. Thus, it is necessary to use a decoupling block to reduce the degree of interaction of the variables as a result of making the control loops independent, resulting in several single-variable subsystems. The schematic of the decoupling block and the system is shown in Fig. 7.

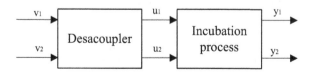

Fig. 7. Variable decoupling scheme

where, V_1 and V_2 are the decoupled variables. In an ideal case, it is expected to obtain a null interaction among the input and output variables of the system, therefore the following relationships are obtained:

$$\frac{Y_1(s)}{V_2(s)} = 0 \quad \frac{Y_2(s)}{V_1(s)} = 0 \tag{15}$$

Therefore, to design the variable decoupling network is based on Eq. (16). Where, $G(s)$ is the transfer function matrix, $D(s)$ is the decoupler and $Q(s)$ is the apparent process.

$$G(s)D(s) = Q(s) \tag{16}$$

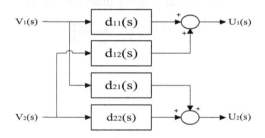

Fig. 8. Decoupler scheme for 2×2 system

The structure of the decoupler for a 2×2 system is shown in Fig. 8 and can be written in matrix from Eq. (16).

$$\begin{bmatrix} g_{11}(s) & g_{12}(s) \\ g_{21}(s) & g_{22}(s) \end{bmatrix} \begin{bmatrix} d_{11}(s) & d_{12}(s) \\ d_{21}(s) & d_{22}(s) \end{bmatrix} = \begin{bmatrix} q_1(s) & 0 \\ 0 & q_2(s) \end{bmatrix} \tag{17}$$

From the Eq. (17), it is observed that $Q(s)$ has elements in the main diagonal and solving it obtains the following:

$$\frac{d_{22}(s)}{d_{12}(s)} = -\frac{g_{11}(s)}{g_{12}(s)}; \quad \frac{d_{11}(s)}{d_{21}(s)} = -\frac{g_{22}(s)}{g_{21}(s)} \tag{18}$$

Then, the decoupling matrix has the following form:

$$D(s) = \begin{bmatrix} -\frac{g_{22}(s)}{g_{21}(s)} & 1 \\ 1 & -\frac{g_{11}(s)}{g_{12}(s)} \end{bmatrix} \tag{19}$$

Replacing the transfer functions of the incubation system, the decoupling matrix is found, then a plant model for first order systems plus dead time must be approximated to a second order system through the first Taylor approximation, [12], then:

$$e^{-t_0 s} = \frac{1}{t_0 s + 1} \tag{20}$$

Thus, the transfer functions of the decoupler are given by:

$$d_{11}(s) = -\frac{g_{22}(s)}{g_{21}(s)} = \frac{19.52s+1.087}{43.97s^2+18.54s+1.723}$$
$$d_{22}(s) = -\frac{g_{11}(s)}{g_{12}(s)} = \frac{0.5513}{0.617s+0.04264} \tag{21}$$

Using the decoupler with a 10% variation on V_1. The new dynamics of the temperature system is approximated by the identification by the least squares criterion and the following transfer function shown in Eq. (17) is obtained.

$$\frac{Y_1(s)}{U_1(s)} = \frac{0.3942}{18.07s^2 + 8.501s + 1} \tag{22}$$

For a variation of 10% on V_2, the system for the humidity variable can be approximated as:

$$\frac{Y_2(s)}{U_2(s)} = \frac{-15.99e^{-7.4s}}{19.5s2 + 1} \tag{23}$$

With these new approximate models, the system is considered independent and the execution of the design of a decentralized diagonal control by single-input single-output (SISO) system control strategies is possible, [17,19].

4   Control Strategies

This section presents a Proportional Integrative (PI) controller, a PI-Fuzzy controller and a PI-Fuzzy controller tuned with Genetic Algorithms (GA) for both temperature and humidity variables.

4.1   PI Controller

From Eq. (17) and Eq. (18), the PI controllers for temperature and humidity are designed through Eq. (19):

$$G_c(s) = K_p \left(1 + \frac{1}{T_i s}\right) \tag{24}$$

where K_p is the proportional gain and T_i is the time integral which multiplied by K_p, it is gives the integrative gain K_i, as shown in Fig. 9.

The temperature PI controller is designed using the pole assignment method, where the parameters are calculated through Eq. (20) and Eq. (21):

$$K_p = \frac{2\zeta^2 \omega_n^2 + \omega_n^2 - 1}{K} \tag{25}$$

$$K_i = \frac{\zeta_n^3}{K} \tag{26}$$

The damping ratio ζ and the undamped natural frequency ω_n are unknowns, which can be found from the maximum overshoot M_p and the settling time t_s.

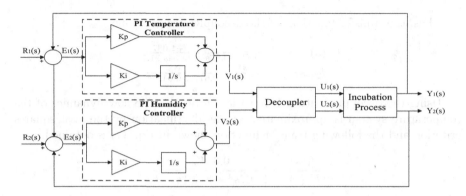

Fig. 9. PI controller scheme of incubation process

Therefore, the parameters are: $M_p = 5\%$ and $t_s = 25\,\text{min}$ and obtain $K_p = 4.829$ and $K_i = 0.019$. To design the PI humidity controller, the Smith & Corripio method is used [20]. This method is designed for first order models plus dead time, where the $K_p = \frac{\tau}{2KL} = -0.0826$ and $K_i = \tau = -0.0042$ parameters take the following values from Eq. (22) and Eq. (23) respectively.

4.2   Fuzzy PI Controller

In order to control the temperature and humidity variables, the fuzzy logic improves the performance of the PI controller, and an independent fuzzy controller is designed for both variables. This controller has two inputs and one output: the proportional error $e_p(t)$, the integral error $e_i(t)$ and the control action $V_i(t)$ respectively. The scheme of the Fuzzy PI controller is illustrated in Fig. 10. In order to design the Fuzzy PI controller, it is based on qualitative knowledge about the process to be controlled. The same is designed through Matlab/Simulink software and the use of Fuzzy Logic Toolbox as in [21].

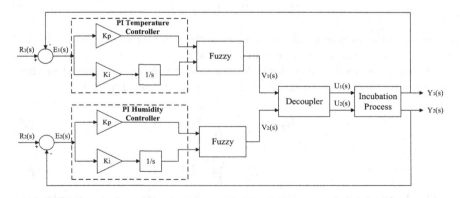

Fig. 10. Schematic of the Fuzzy-PI controller of the incubation process

Table 3. Fuzzy control rules

$\int e(t)/e(t)$	N	Z	P
N	N	Z	P
Z	N	Z	P
P	N	Z	P

For the input and output variables described previously, three membership functions (MFs) were chosen to smooth the control action through the following description: negative (N), zero (Z), and positive (P). The range of the universe of discourse for the input and output variables are the following: $e_p(t)$ of $[-160 \quad 160]$, $e_i(t)$ of $[-750 \quad 750]$ and V_1 of $[-100 \quad 200]$. The input ranges are determined according to the maximum error established in the controller's development. The output range is chosen according to the range of action of the input to the decoupler. Each membership function is symmetrical triangular, with 50% overlap only for the zero (Z) membership function. The fuzzy inference rules were established from the studies of [21,22] and are presented in Table 3.

For the Humidity Fuzzy PI controller, three membership functions (MFs) were chosen: negative (N), zero (Z), and positive (P). The range of the universe of discourse for the input variables $e_p(t)$ and $e_i(t)$ is $[-2 \quad 2]$, which is determined through the maximum error that has been established in the development of the controller. For the output variable V_2 is $[-1 \quad 0]$, whose range is chosen according to the range of action control of the input to the decoupler. Each membership function is a symmetrical triangular type with 50% overlap only for the zero (Z) membership function.

4.3 Tuning Through Genetic Algorithms

Genetic Algorithms (GA) are a powerful tool of Artificial Intelligence (AI) that aims to find and optimize solutions based on theories of natural evolution [21]. Therefore, AG is characterized by having operations such as selection, crossover, and mutation of chromosomes or individuals. For this work, heuristic analysis and the optimization technique are used to find optimal values for tuning the Fuzzy-PI controller, searching to minimize the fitness function, where the initial parameters are the K_p and K_i found by Smith & Corripio method for FODTP systems for humidity control, and the method by pole assignment for temperature control. The fitness function is determined from the performance index ISE, IAE, and TVu, as in the studies of [12,23].

The GA search criteria for each controller are: 50 individuals with a chromosome length of 6, 10 generations, selection of 50% of the best fit population and a mutation probability of 2%. These parameters were chosen through simulations looking for the best performance of the controllers, at the end the results were: $K_p = 3.8710$ y $K_i = 0.0323$ for temperature and $K_p = 0.8710$ y $K_i = -0.100$ for humidity.

4.4   Implementation of Controllers

The controllers are implemented in an artificial incubation test module. The experiments are performed using the NODEMCU ESP-WROOM-32 Xtensa Dual-Core 32-bit 240 MHz NODEMCU embedded system. The temperature and humidity setpoints (SP) were sent through an electronic display board via SPI and I2C communication to the embedded system. The readings were recorded with the Ds18b20 sensor for temperature and the DHT21 sensor for humidity. In this way, the NODEMCU ESP-WROOM-32 board is in charge of calculating the control actions required to control the incubation module. Figure 11 shows the operating scheme used for the respective tests performed.

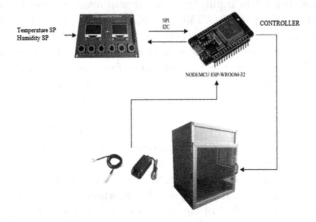

Fig. 11. Operating diagram of the incubation module

5   Tests and Results

This section presents the experimental results of the tests performed to compare the performance of the controllers. First a reference change test is performed for an operating range of [36 45] °C on temperature and [60 80]% on humidity. On the other hand, in the second test, an analysis of the system response to an unmodeled disturbance is carried out.

5.1   Reference Tracking Test

In this test, three reference changes in temperature and two changes in humidity are tracked. When the system is stable at the operating point of 37.7 °C temperature, the first positive change of +5% (1.87 °C) is made at 90[min], and the second positive change of +5% (1.87 °C) at 133[min] and finally a change of −15% (5.63 °C) at 165[min]. For humidity, the first reference change of +10% (6.5%)

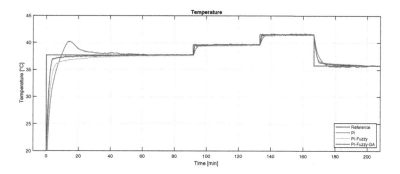

Fig. 12. Temperature control performance in reference tracking test

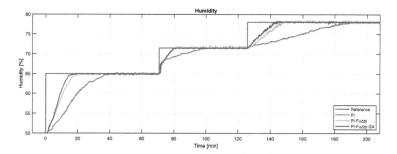

Fig. 13. Humidity control performance in reference tracking test

Table 4. Performance of temperature and humidity controllers for reference tracking test

Index	PI	Fuzzy-PI	Fuzzy-PI-GA
$ISE_T\ (x10^3)$	44.46	29.71	20.59
$IAE_T\ (x10^3)$	7.48	7.69	5.45
$ISE_H\ (x10^3)$	222.48	108.80	96.75
$IAE_H\ (x10^3)$	35.54	19.40	18.58

is performed at $72[min]$ and the second change of $+10\%$ (6.5%) at $125[min]$. Figures 12 present each controller's performance. It is observed that the temperature controllers follow the reference normally, but the Fuzzy-PI controller tuned with AG presents better performance. In addition, Fig. 13 indicates the response for the humidity reference tests, where the controllers follow the reference; however, the PI controller has a very slow response. On the other hand, the Fuzzy-PI controller has an acceptable response; however, the settling time is slightly longer than the Fuzzy-PI-AG. The values of ISE and IAE support this characteristic in Table 4.

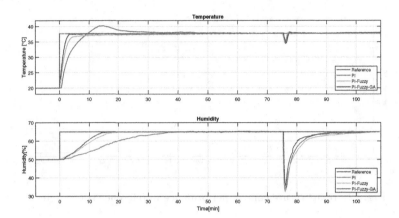

Fig. 14. Temperature and Humidity control performance in Regulatory Test

Table 5. Performance of temperature and humidity controllers with a disturbance

Index	PI	Fuzzy-PI	Fuzzy-PI-GA
$ISE_T\ (x10^3)$	12.18	18.01	12.01
$IAE_T\ (x10^3)$	1.95	3.18	1.91
$ISE_H\ (x10^4)$	14.153	37.495	1.872
$IAE_H\ (x10^3)$	13.28	42.97	s3.18

5.2 Regulatory Test

The incubation process can cause disturbances, mainly caused by operators inspecting embryo growth. This test recreates this phenomenon by opening the incubator door for one minute to produce a disturbance of -18% ($3.23\,°C$) for temperature and -21.8% (-32.67%) for humidity. Figure 14 shows the test response time before a disturbance in temperature and humidity, where the three controllers respond immediately before that uncertainty. To corroborate the result, Tables 5 describe the values of the performance indexes ISE and IAE, giving the experimental results of the process.

5.3 Conclusions

In this work, three controllers were implemented to recreate the artificial incubation process with the best performance of the controllers and the control action. First, the single-variable models were found through the identification by the least squares criterion, designing a decoupling network through the RGA analysis, which eliminates the existing interaction between the process variables, originating independent control loops. The controllers presented are the PI controller, and from this the PI based on fuzzy logic was implemented and tuned by GA. Finally, these controllers were compared through the ISE and IAE indices, where the Fuzzy-PI-AG controller presented lower values in the indices for monitoring the reference change and regulation.

Acknowledgment. This work was supported by the Universidad San Francisco de Quito through the Poli-Grants Program under Grant 17461.

References

1. Ramos, J.M.P., Cedeño, E.A.L.: Estudio de las tecnologías de control utilizadas en las incubadoras avícolas. E-IDEA J. Eng. Sci. **2**(4), 13–23 (2020)
2. Ali, M., Abdelwahab, M., Awadekreim, S., Abdalla, S.: Development of a monitoring and control system of infant incubator. In: 2018 International Conference on Computer, Control, Electrical, and Electronics Engineering (ICCCEEE), pp. 1–4. IEEE (2018)
3. Mueller, C.A., Burggren, W.W., Tazawa, H.: The physiology of the avian embryo. In: Sturkie's Avian Physiology, 7th edn, pp. 1015–1046. Academic Press (2022)
4. Widhiada, W., Antara, I., Budiarsa, I., Karohika, I.: The robust PID control system of temperature stability and humidity on infant incubator based on arduino at mega 2560. In: IOP Conference Series: Earth and Environmental Science, vol. 248, no. 1, p. 012046. IOP Publishing (2019)
5. Pérez, C.S., Guzmán, J., Molina, J.S., Berenguel, M.: "Modelado y control multivariable de temperatura y humedad en un invernadero. In: de VIII Congreso Ibérico de agroingeniería, pp. 856–865. España, Algorfa (2015)
6. El Hadj Ali, J., Feki, E., Zermani, M.A., de Prada, C., Mami, A.: Incubator system identification of humidity and temperature: comparison between two identification environments. In: 2018 9th International Renewable Energy Congress (IREC), pp. 1–6 (2018)
7. Aldair, A.A., Rashid, A.T., Mokayef, M.: Design and implementation of intelligent control system for egg incubator based on IoT technology. In: 2018 4th International Conference on Electrical, Electronics and System Engineering (ICEESE), pp. 49–54. IEEE (2018)
8. Lestari, I.N., Mulyana, E., Mardi, R.: The implementation of Mamdani's fuzzy model for controlling the temperature of chicken egg incubator. In: 2020 6th International Conference on Wireless and Telematics (ICWT), pp. 1–5. IEEE (2020)
9. Kutsira, G., Nwulu, N., Dogo, E.: Development of a small scaled microcontroller-based poultry egg incubation system. In: 2019 International Artificial Intelligence and Data Processing Symposium (IDAP), pp. 1–7. IEEE (2019)
10. Sansomboonsuk, S., Phonhan, C., Phonhan, G.: Automatic incubator. Energy Res. J. **2**(2), 51–56 (2011)
11. Harb, S.K., Habbib, Y.A., Kassem, A.M., El Raies, A.-R.: Energy consumption for poultry egg incubator to suit small farmer. Egypt. J. Agric. Res. **88**(1), 193–210 (2010)
12. Herrera, M., Gonzales, O., Leica, P., Camacho, O.: Robust controller based on an optimal-integral surface for quadruple-tank process. In: IEEE Third Ecuador Technical Chapters Meeting (ETCM), pp. 1–6. IEEE (2018)
13. Chacón, W., Vallejo, J., Herrera, M., Camacho, O.: Regulation of nonlinear chemical processes with variable dead time: a generalized proportional integral controller proposal. Int. J. Adv. Sci. Eng. Inf. Technol. **11**(4), 1501–1506 (2021)

14. van den Bosch, P.P., van der Klauw, A.C.: Modeling, Identification and Simulation of Dynamical Systems. CRC Press, Boca Raton (2020)
15. Herrera, M., Camacho, O., Leiva, H., Smith, C.: An approach of dynamic sliding mode control for chemical processes. J. Process Control **85**, 112–120 (2020)
16. Morilla, F., Garrido, J., Vázquez, F.: Control multivariable por desacoplo. Revista Iberoamericana de Automática e Informática industrial **10**(1), 3–17 (2013)
17. Bhat, V.S., Thirunavukkarasu, I., Priya, S.S.: Design and implementation of decentralized PI controller for pilot plant binary distillation column. Int. J. Chem. Tech. Res. **10**(1), 284–294 (2017)
18. Garrido, J., Vázquez, F., Morilla, F.: Multivariable PID control by decoupling. Int. J. Syst. Sci. **47**(5), 1054–1072 (2016)
19. Garrido, J., Vázquez, F., Morilla, F.: Diseño de sistemas de control multivariable por desacoplo con controladores PID. In: X Simposio CEA de Ingeniería de Control, pp. 64–71 (2012)
20. Smith, C.A., Corripio, A.B.: Principles and Practices of Automatic Process Control. Wiley, New York (2005)
21. Cruz, P.P.: Inteligencia artificial con aplicaciones a la ingeniería. Alfaomega (2011)
22. Song, B., Xiao, Y., Xu, L.: Design of fuzzy PI controller for brushless dc motor based on PSO-GSA algorithm. Syst. Sci. Control Eng. **8**(1), 67–77 (2020)
23. Aguas, X., Revelo, J., Herrera, M., Cuaycal, A., Camacho, O.: A fuzzy-PD controller for wall-following of a mobile robot: experimental validation. Revista Digital Novasinergia **2**(2), 49–57 (2019)

Discovering Visual Deficiencies in Pilots Candidates Using Data Mining

Sonia Cárdenas-Delgado$^{(\boxtimes)}$ ⓘ, Mauricio Loachamín-Valencia,
Stalin Crisanto-Caiza, and Danny Lasso-Ayala

Universidad de las Fuerzas Armadas ESPE,
Av. General Rumiñahui s/n, 171-5-231B Sangolquí, Ecuador
{secardenas,mrloachamin,socrisanto,dflasso1}@espe.edu.ec

Abstract. Organizations are applying data mining and knowledge discovery techniques, so they must integrate and transform their data for analytical processing. The decision making is a process that can be carried out with the support of data mining techniques. Discover patterns and characteristics related to visual deficiencies in pilot candidates can contribute to aviation safety processes. This work presents the design of a technological tool to the selection process of pilots candidates in aviation schools. This includes modules to facilitate the registration of the participants' data; the integration of the results obtained from traditional and technological visual tests; and the data analysis module. To discover visual deficiencies in pilot candidates, the collected data was integrated and analysed using data mining. To validate the prototype, we applied the protocol established in the project. The results of the analysis were satisfactory for the team of specialists due to the confidence margin obtained. These preliminary results allow us to demonstrate the usefulness of the proposed technological tool and to continue with its development.

Keywords: Aviation · Visual test · Data mining · Visual deficiencies

1 Introduction

Clinical decision support systems have undergone a great evolution and are becoming a key tool for doctors to improve their diagnoses. This type of decision in the medical field is a process that can be carried out with the support of technological tools based on different techniques such as deductive reasoning, data analysis, data mining, machine learning, diffuse logic, classifiers, among others [13].

Participants information can be recorded and stored using different techniques. Database types and engines are available for data storage. A relational database prioritizes the relationships that exist between different entities or tables. Non-relational databases add an important feature that is the inclusion of any type of data, including text [2].

M. Botto-Tobar et al. (Eds.): ICAT 2022, CCIS 1755, pp. 171–183, 2023.
https://doi.org/10.1007/978-3-031-24985-3_13

Storage technologies and automated solutions that allow access, integration, and analysis of different types of data are growing exponentially. This collection of large amounts of data and the search for trends within it has created new paradigms such as BigData and SmartData. Facing the challenge of managing structured and unstructured data in the current scenario of the digital world is mandatory for organizations [2].

Data mining applications used for healthcare have proven to be very effective in addressing the analysis of medical knowledge and expertise [19]. Applications that employ data mining techniques require the construction of scalable and reliable models. The challenge is to apply techniques that help users in the analysis of knowledge. Data mining is used to discover knowledge, that is, from the analysis of large amounts of data, significant relationships, patterns and rules can be discovered automatically [9,12].

In the medical field, the sources of information are innumerable and the use of Big-Data and Data-Mining have become important tools for data management and decision-making. The data that is collected in the field of health is related to the clinical information of the patient, medications, diseases, medical images, diagnoses and research. The collection of data is generated thanks to the use of sensors, by social networks, blogs, websites and other platforms [7].

Vision is one of the most important senses that a professional pilot must possess. To pilot aircraft each of the qualities of vision is required, so it is necessary to evaluate visual acuity, visual field width, depth vision, normal color vision and retinal adaptation capacity [6,17].

From this perspective, the aviation schools of the country's Armed Forces do not have a technological tool that integrates the data from the different visual assessment tests that are applied prior to the entry of pilot applicants. The objective is to contribute to the mitigation of subjectivity when determining the applicants who do or do not have the visual qualities suitable for piloting aircraft and to improve the selection process.

In the present work, we focus on the lack of support systems for the analysis of the results in the different visual tests that are applied to the personnel of the aspiring pilots, as part of the selection process for admission to the aviation schools of the Armed Forces of our country. We conducted a preliminary literature review and the study of related works. The results obtained from the research allowed the design of a technological tool that integrates all the results of the traditional and technological visual tests, which will be analyzed through specific associative rules from the field of knowledge of Ophthalmology and Aviation. The objective is to support decisions through information and knowledge management in order to reduce subjectivity within the pilot applicant selection process. The proposal will include modules for the integration of data from different sources, inference rules, knowledge base and user interface.

The article is organized in the following manner. Section 2 presents the background obtained from the study of works related to Artificial Intelligence, data Mining techniques in Medicine and Ophthalmology for the detection of different diseases and visual deficiencies. Next, Sect. 3 The methods and materials used for the development of the presented tool and the analysis of different visual tests during the selection process of aspiring pilots. The Sect. 4 includes the experimental study. The Sect. 5 presents the results. The Sect. 6 summarize the conclusions, and finally, the Sect. 7 is briefly described the future works.

2   Background

During the process of studying and reviewing the literature, several works have been found that use different techniques in the medical field to support decision-making. These works show positive results with a precision range from 84% to 93% in some cases. Systems in the medical area focus on collecting data through patient medical register, but these data must to be analyzed comprehensively to improve patient care and support medical decision-making. Currently there are several data analysis techniques that are used in the medical field to support decision making, some of them are Data Mining, Neural Networks, Correlations, Regression, Fuzzy Logic.

Sundar proposes a simple data mining model for heart disease prediction. His model used the next techniques in data mining: Naive Bayes classification and k-means clustering algorithm. Basically, the system generates a recommendation based on the values of the test attributes [22].

Firwan et al. [8] conducted a review of feature selection and classification approaches for heart disease prediction. The authors determined the classification is a data mining task that can be utilized to predict heart disease. The researchers used many methods for data mining such as: (1) filters (it selects variables based on ranks and criteria), (2) wrapper (through search techniques makes a sub dataset and evaluates with a supervised learning algorithm), (3) embedded (It interact with the classifier, it focus in relationship between features), and (4) hybrid (combines several feature selection).

The study [5] describes two databases that are related to the ophthalmological field. The first is an ophthalmological data warehouse that allows the management of electronic medical records and diagnostic images belonging to an ophthalmological hospital. Its operation is carried out in real time and allows to identify in an easier and faster way the different conditions that a patient may suffer called Smart Eye Database (SMEYEDAT). The second, called IRIS, is a system that allows the registration of ophthalmic data to drive improvements in the provision of eye care services. IRIS automatically aggregates clinical data to provide real-time analysis.

Examples of two medical decision support systems are presented in [10]. The first, a system created for the diagnosis of peripheral neuropathy using fuzzy logic. For which he does, they used 24 entries in the different fields of the system, these fields symptoms and diagnostic test results; it is important to know the percentage of accuracy that this system achieved, 93% accuracy compared to the experts. The second, called DXplain, a system that is based on records prepared electronically that provides a diagnosis with probability based on clinical symptoms, with 84% accuracy that was based on a diagnostic test validated with 30 clinical cases.

Using the machine learning approach, Gupta et al. [11] propose a recommender system that analyzes symptoms and tries to recommend the best medicine. First, They analyzed data with the philosophy "Exploratory Data Analysis (EDA)" and then they implemented three data mining algorithms: decision tree classifier, Random forest classifier, and Naive Bayes classifier.

Bhuvaneswari et al. [3] propose an effective prediction model for diseases by reducing the dimensions and applying clustering with different Machine Learning algorithms. Their model used different dimensionality reduction algorithms such as: Principal Component Analysis (PCA), Linear Discriminant Analysis (LDA), Locally Linear Embedding (LLE) and Singular Value Decomposition (SVD).

Furthermore, in [18] machine learning techniques was used for personalized medicine approaches in immune-mediated chronic inflammatory diseases. Also, these authors determined that through unsupervised models (algorithm Principle component analysis) can provide a more personalized treatment for patients.

This research studied identification and prediction of chronic diseases using machine learning approach. The author used algorithms such as convolutional neural network (CNN) and K-nearest neighbor (KNN) to find symptom matches in a data set with aims of predicting disease [1].

Jayasri and Aruna presents and evaluation corresponding to a medical database of people suffering from diabetes, where it combines hierarchical decision algorithms such as decision trees, association rules and classification of multiclass outliers using the MapReduce framework. For which the Hadoop and MapReduce platforms were developed that were used in combination with the innovative data mining algorithms, that is, the decision tree (DT) care network, the association rules (AR) and the multiclass classification technique based on outliers. Through this proposed hierarchical technique, the database of diabetic patients will be effectively analyzed since a classification technique called the multiclass outlier technique is executed from the MapReduce platform [15].

Sundari and Subaji aims to resolve the problem of data scarcity in the recommendation system. For which it uses two-level preprocessing techniques to reduce the size of the data at the element level. Additional resources are added to the data to extend deep learning and analysis. The advantage of the proposed method is the recommendation that is generated, according to the user's interest pattern and avoiding recommending obsolete articles. User information is grouped based on similar item gender and tag function. In general, it reduces dimensions, which is an initial way of preparing data, to analyze hidden patterns. To improve performance, the proposed method used Apache's association rule mining approach and Mllib FP-Growth in a distributed environment. To reduce the computational cost of tree construction in FP-Growth, the candidate data set is stored in the form of an array. Experiments were performed using the MovieLens dataset. The observed results show that the proposed method achieves a 4% increase in accuracy compared to previous methods [23].

Ristoski et al. [20] presented Data mining and knowledge discovery in databases (KDD) is a field of research that deals with obtaining high-level insights from data. Tasks performed in that field are knowledge intensive and can often benefit from the use of additional knowledge from various sources. Therefore, many approaches have been proposed in this area that combine Semantic Web data with data mining and knowledge discovery processes. This survey article provides a comprehensive overview of those approaches at different stages of the knowledge discovery process. As an example, we show how linked open data can be used in various stages to build content-based recommendation systems. The survey shows that while there has been plenty of exciting research work, the full potential of the Semantic Web and Linked Open Data for data mining and KDD has yet to be unlocked.

Itani et al. they argue that data mining continues to play an important role in medicine; specifically, for the development of diagnostic support models used in expert and intelligent systems. It is mentioned that physicians are still reluctant to use decision support tools. One of the causes of this situation is social pressure, but there are also concerns about reliability and credibility. Therefore, this study emphasizes the importance of collaboration between data miners and clinicians. The study lays the groundwork for such interaction, focusing on the details of diagnostic aid and related data modeling goals. In this sense, an overview of the requirements expected by clinicians, both experts and end users, is proposed. In fact, it is suggested that the interaction with the doctors occurs from the first steps of the process and throughout the development of the predictive models [14].

In the work of Santos et al. [21] present an evaluation of the different open source data mining tools: KNIME, R, RapidMiner, Scikit-learn and Spark. He also mentions that, in the health industry, traditional statistical approaches are considered the main technique of data analysis and data mining as the secondary technique due to the limited exposure to the data mining area by medical researchers. And health professionals. These techniques are mainly based on mathematics, the great advantage of data mining is that it has a greater breadth with techniques such as machine learning, database systems and visualization, which provides important advances over statistical techniques. Traditional. The study concludes that KNIME and RapidMiner are the best solutions due to their higher coverage of identified healthcare requirements compared to the other tools. However, in evaluating these two solutions, it has been concluded that RapidMiner is a better solution than KNIME if RapidMiner meets the data requirements of the specific healthcare application under investigation.

Lebedev et al. [16] proposed a system called "SechenovDatamed", designed to support medical decision-making based on providing timely access to complete and reliable information on the patient's health. For the realization of the system, intelligent search tools were used that implement semantic search mechanisms, natural language processing, interfaces to operate the system from mobile devices and portable devices, multilingual support and automatic translation into the main languages and knowledge extraction technologies. from unstructured textual content (text mining). As a result, the system has a database and knowledge storage subsystem, a subsystem for processing search queries and issuing clinical recommendations for the rational use of pharmacotherapeutic drugs, an automatic learning subsystem to create medicine knowledge bases based on evidence, subsystem to provide access from mobile devices.

3   Material and Method

Based on the study carried out and the meetings with the project specialists allowed the identification of needs and the design and development of the proposal. The design of a technological tool that includes the integration of structured and unstructured data. This data is recorded from different traditional and technological visual tests. All the data is integrated into a repository and data mining techniques are applied.

The different components that make up the prototype of the decision support system have been designed, applying the prototyping methodology, the use cases, the user interfaces, the database design and the system architecture were designed.

Moreover, based on the Business Intelligence Philosophy [4], we followed the following steps:

- Collection and reception of data, the API REST architecture used to allows the communication and exchange of data, which have the JSON format in a way that allows an adequate reading and subsequent storage of the information.
- Loading the data, a NoSQL database designed and created to allow the persistence of the data of all the visual test modules (traditional and nontraditional) that are integrated with the application, MongoDB was used for this.
- Data exploration, the data resulting from each type of visual test performed were recorded and analyzed. The algorithm for checking the association rules was created by applying the criteria defined by specialist doctors and using Python.

- Discovery of patterns and trends, based on the data sent by the applicant and the stored history, patterns and trends will be searched for by means of inference rules to find common facts and features.
- Reporting and visualization of information, the user web interface was created for queries and generation of reports that allow displaying the result of data analysis. The React interfaces library was used to build the interfaces.
- Evaluation of the Solution, the validity of the solution demonstrated by applying the classic and technological visual tests on a sample selected by the specialists, that is, a control group that includes military personnel aspiring to pilots from different branches of the Armed Forces. These tests are carried out jointly with project researchers, medical specialists, candidates and developers. Finally, the results obtained from the study based on the criteria and recommendations of the specialists and the established protocol are analyzed.

3.1 Architecture

The system architecture scheme describes the operation and the relationship between its components, as shown in Fig. 1.

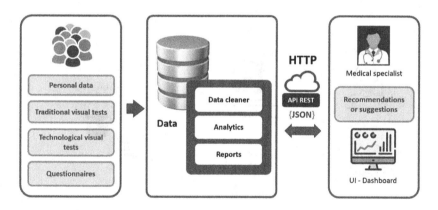

Fig. 1. Architecture scheme

3.2 Data Analysis Module

The Fig. 2 shows the scheme of the data analytics process that compose the proposed technological solution.

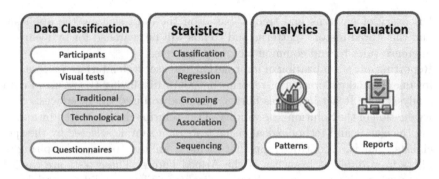

Fig. 2. Data analysis scheme

3.3   Database Scheme

The database integrated relational and non-relational data from the different results of the visual tests (traditional and virtual-technological), as shown in Fig. 3.

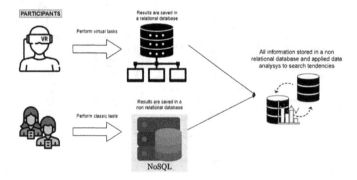

Fig. 3. Database schema

3.4   Software

The tools that are being used in the development of the software are listed below.

– Apache Spark: It is used in an open source programming framework, the different APIs and modules that facilitate data processing, and the integration with various programming languages are used.

- MongoDB, facilitates the administration of NoSQL data, allows to take advantage of the structure called BSON for its integration.
- To implement the decision support system, web development technologies were applied so that different users can record the data.

3.5   Interfaces

This section shows the main user interfaces: login (See Fig. 4.), test data, registration of visual test results for each type (See Fig. 5.), and the interface that allows generating the data analysis and obtain a recommendation to evaluators in the pilot candidate selection process (See Fig. 6.).

Fig. 4. Screen - sign in

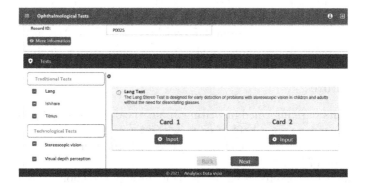

Fig. 5. Screen - input and export data

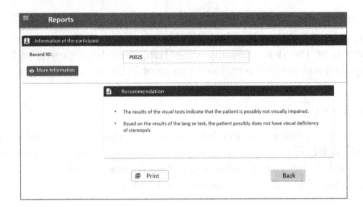

Fig. 6. Screen - results

4 Experimental Study Design

To validate the developed prototype, a protocol was applied. The study was conducted in a session that was divided into three stages. The steps were performed sequentially. In stage one, the participants were informed about the objectives of the project, filled out and signed the informed consents, approximately 5 min. In the second stage, they performed two traditional visual tests (Lang and Ishihara), an average of 3 min each test. In the third stage, the candidates performed two technological tests, these consisted of two virtual tasks (assessment of visual perception of depth and color), an average of 3 min each test. The study was performed in an average of 12 min.

4.1 Participants

The experimental tests were applied to a control group of participants. The sample was selected by specialists. The group was conformed of military personnel. They were five aspiring pilots from different branches of the Armed Forces. The age of the participants ranged between 18 and 20 years, all of them were men.

4.2 Procedure

All participants were informed in writing about the objectives and procedures of the study. They were completely free to withdraw from the study at any time, and the study was carried out in accordance with the principles established in the Declaration of Helsinki.

The evaluator registered each participant through the application interfaces. Then, each traditional visual test was performed and the participants' answers were registered. These answers were also recorded in digital audio files for later recognition and verification.

The analysis process was based on the rules defined together with the project specialists. The evaluation parameters are extracted from the generated knowledge base.

5   Results

The recommendations obtained by the application as a result of the data analysis were validated by the team of evaluators and specialists who usually participate in the assessment process for the selection of aspiring pilots. They agreed with the results obtained in the tests performed on the control group of the selected sample.

The analysis of the data was based on the results obtained in each type of visual test, traditional and technological. In another study of this same project, the correlations between these types of visual tests were demonstrated. The application has a module that executes the analysis of the recorded answers.

The data analysis module was generated to integrate the results of each test and obtain the patterns of visual deficiencies. The results obtained had an average margin of certainty 91.5%.

The results of the tests carried out were satisfactory for the team of specialists. These results allow to demonstrate the usefulness of the proposed technological tool. In addition, the developed prototype could be a complementary tool in the selection process for aspiring pilots. The validity of the proposal is demonstrated with the preliminary tests carried out, the results obtained in the visual evaluation.

Training for handling the prototype of the application was given to specialists and evaluators. After using, they stated that the interface was friendly and easy to use.

6   Conclusions

A review and study of the related literature has been carried out. In addition, several tools and techniques have been analyzed to propose the design and model of the alternative technological solution.

The prototype of the developed application is a decision-making support tool during the selection process of aspiring pilots. Meetings were held with the team of researchers, specialists, and developers to identify the system requirements, design the interfaces, the database, and define the inference rules.

A preliminary version of the proposed technological is presented, the architecture, the database, the data analytics module. Data mining techniques were implemented to generate recommendations that support decisions in the visual assess process, based on the patterns found and on the technical foundations of international aeronautics about the visual capabilities that an individual must possess to pilot a plane aircraft.

The results obtained from the tests carried out were satisfactory for the team of specialists. These results demonstrated the validity and usefulness of the proposed technological tool. The developed prototype could be a complementary tool in the pilot candidate selection process.

The users were the specialists, doctors and evaluators. They stated that the application interface was friendly and easy to use.

7   Future Work

In the next phase, the proposed will be implemented, and the respective validations will be carried out with two groups of participants, a control group and a non-control group of participants.

Other visual tests will be included in the knowledge base to improve the identification of characteristics and patterns that allow discovering visual deficiencies in pilot candidates.

In addition, future work is related to the application of machine learning techniques so that the system is capable of learning and adapting, through the implementation of algorithms and statistical models that facilitate the analysis and extraction of inferences from patterns about deficiencies. vision in pilot candidates. Furthermore, it is planned to apply machine learning techniques to obtain a functional prototype to support decision-making in the selection of aspiring pilots of the Armed Forces.

Acknowledgment. The authors would like to thanks to "Universidad de las Fuerzas Armadas ESPE" of Ecuador for the funded given to project "VisioStereo-Diagnostic-PIS-10".

References

1. Alanazi, R.: Identification and prediction of chronic diseases using machine learning approach. J. Healthc. Eng. **2022** (2022)
2. Bathla, G., Rani, R., Aggarwal, H.: Comparative study of noSQL databases for big data storage. Int. J. Eng. Technol. **7**(2.6), 83–87 (2018)
3. Bhuvaneswari, A., Sam, R.P., Bindu, C.S.: EPMD: effective prediction model for diseases by reducing the dimensions and applying clustering with different machine learning algorithms. J. Jilin Univ. **40**(06-2021) (2021)
4. Cano, J.L.: Business Intelligence: competir con información. Banesto, Fundación Cultur [ie Cultural] (2007)
5. Cheng, C.Y., et al.: Big data in ophthalmology. Asia-Pac. J. Ophthalmol. **9**(4), 291–298 (2020)
6. DGAC: Normas para el otorgamiento del certificado médico aeronáutico. Technical report, Dirección General de Aviación Civil (2012). Accessed 10 June 2022
7. European Institute of Health and Social Welfare. www.esn-eu.org. Accessed 10 June 2021
8. Firdaus, F.F., Nugroho, H.A., Soesanti, I.: A review of feature selection and classification approaches for heart disease prediction. IJITEE (Int. J. Inf. Technol. Electr. Eng.) **4**(3), 75–82 (2021)
9. Gordan, M., et al.: State-of-the-art review on advancements of data mining in structural health monitoring. Measurement, 110939 (2022)

10. Guo, X., Swenor, B.K., Smith, K., Boland, M.V., Goldstein, J.E.: Developing an ophthalmology clinical decision support system to identify patients for low vision rehabilitation. Transl. Vis. Sci. Technol. **10**(3), 24–24 (2021)
11. Gupta, J.P., Singh, A., Kumar, R.K.: A computer-based disease prediction and medicine recommendation system using machine learning approach. Int. J. Adv. Res. Eng. Technol. (IJARET) **12**(3), 673–683 (2021)
12. Han, J., Pei, J., Tong, H.: Data Mining: Concepts and Techniques. Morgan Kaufmann, Burlington (2022)
13. Instituto Europeo de Salud y Bienestar Social: The challenge of big data in health systems, http://institutoeuropeo.es. Accessed 19 June 2022
14. Itani, S., Lecron, F., Fortemps, P.: Specifics of medical data mining for diagnosis aid: a survey. Expert Syst. Appl. **118**, 300–314 (2019)
15. Jayasri, N., Aruna, R.: Big data analytics in health care by data mining and classification techniques. ICT Express **8**(2), 250–257 (2022)
16. Lebedev, G., et al.: Technology of supporting medical decision-making using evidence-based medicine and artificial intelligence. Procedia Comput. Sci. **176**, 1703–1712 (2020)
17. Nakagawara, V.B., Wood, K.J., Montgomery, R.W.: A review of recent laser illumination events in the aviation environment. Technical report, FFA Civil Aerospace Medical Institute (2006). Accessed 10 June 2022
18. Peng, J., Jury, E.C., Dönnes, P., Ciurtin, C.: Machine learning techniques for personalised medicine approaches in immune-mediated chronic inflammatory diseases: applications and challenges. Front. Pharmacol. 2667 (2021)
19. Pramanik, S., Galety, M.G., Samanta, D., Joseph, N.P.: Data mining approaches for healthcare decision support systems. In: Dutta, P., Chakrabarti, S., Bhattacharya, A., Dutta, S., Shahnaz, C. (eds.) Emerging Technologies in Data Mining and Information Security, vol. 490, pp. 721–733. Springer, Singapore (2022). https://doi.org/10.1007/978-981-19-4052-1_71
20. Ristoski, P., Paulheim, H.: Semantic web in data mining and knowledge discovery: a comprehensive survey. J. Web Semant. **36**, 1–22 (2016)
21. Santos-Pereira, J., Gruenwald, L., Bernardino, J.: Top data mining tools for the healthcare industry. J. King Saud Univ.-Comput. Inf. Sci. (2021)
22. Sundar, S.K.: A simple data mining model for heart disease prediction. J. Glob. Pharma Technol. (2009)
23. Sundari, P.S., Subaji, M.: An improved hidden behavioral pattern mining approach to enhance the performance of recommendation system in a big data environment. J. King Saud Univ.-Comput. Inf. Sci. (2020)

An Electronic Equipment for Measuring Color Difference Between Tissues Based on Digital Image Processing and Neural Networks

José Calderón⑩, Benghy Lipa⑩, and Guillermo Kemper$^{(\boxtimes)}$ ⑩

Universidad Peruana de Ciencias Aplicadas, Av. Prolongación Primavera 2390,
Santiago de Surco, Lima, Perú
{u201615390,u201623659}@upc.edu.pe, guillermo.kemper@upc.pe

Abstract. This work proposes an electronic equipment aimed at measuring the color difference between fabrics for a homogeneous selection of these. The proposed method analyzes tissues with different illuminants so that, by taking measurements with a camera, the impact of effects such as metamerism can be reduced, resulting in a more accurate method that represents reality. For this, an enclosure was designed and built to allow constant lighting conditions and spotlights with standard lighting were installed. On the software side, the camera was manually configured to ensure persistent measurements over time and the colors obtained from the RGB color space were converted to CIELAB. For the calculation of the color difference, the Delta E (CMC) color difference equation was used because this is the standard used in the textile industry. Finally, a neural network was trained to estimate the color difference between the fabrics. To validate the results, the measurements obtained with the proposed equipment were compared with those obtained using a colorimeter to measure the colors of the fabrics and calculate whether their color difference is significant. The developed equipment achieved an accuracy of 95% in the correct identification of fabrics that are homogenous in color.

Keywords: Color difference · Fabric color · Textile image processing · Illuminants · Metamerism

1 Introduction

Objects, like fabric, are perceived as being of different colors under different lighting conditions. However, there is another effect pertaining to color perception called metamerism. This is a phenomenon whereby two color samples appear the same in some circumstances and different in others. For this case, there are two types of metamerism. The first, illuminant metamerism, which is when two samples appear identical under one lighting but different under another. And the second, observer metamerism, which is when two samples appear under one lighting, but different for different observers. These are caused in part due to the differences in the recipe of the dye used [1]. These effects, together, are called observer subjectivity. There's also physical limitations such

© The Author(s), under exclusive license to Springer Nature Switzerland AG 2023
M. Botto-Tobar et al. (Eds.): ICAT 2022, CCIS 1755, pp. 184–196, 2023.
https://doi.org/10.1007/978-3-031-24985-3_14

as color blindness or loss of perception due to age or visual fatigue which can result in an erroneous measurement of the true color of an object; which is one of the most important parameters in textile quality control [2].

The current domestic color difference detection method is mainly based on the human eye or the use of some portable instrument to measure and analyze the fabrics when they are out of production, such as the use of color matching cabinets, commonly called "light boxes". These are used to verify the difference of the color from a standard light source to check the difference. A light box like the TU300C consists of a fixture with different standard light sources such as D65, TL84, CWF, UV and F7A [3]. The process of detection consists of a visual evaluation of the fabrics under different light sources by the evaluator with the cabinet. The advantage of this instrument is that it has different light sources, which facilitates the perception of color. However, this method presents shortcomings such as a possible effect called metamerism of the observer. Also, if the evaluator performs several evaluations over a long period of time, it could cause visual fatigue that would lead to a less reliable analysis.

In the product presented by Yuntao, Chen, Haoran, Yang and Zhaokui [4] a fabric color difference detection device based on machine vision recognition technology is proposed. The system is formed by a conveyor belt and a detection box. To start the system, a detection box is placed above the front of the belt and a second box below the rear. Standard light sources of constant and uniform brightness are installed inside the boxes. A high-resolution CCD sensor camera inside each box interfaces with an external image processing computer. This computer controls an alarm on the system and the conveyor belt. While this system achieves accurate results and is applicable to large-scale production. However, its size and installation time make it only suitable for fabric producers and not customers. In addition, the system proposed by the authors only allows detecting the color difference on the same fabric to find inconsistencies but does not allow comparing several different fabrics; therefore, it cannot be used as a suitable selection factor for purchasing.

In the proposal submitted by Li, Ning and Jing [5] the idea of using a T-S fuzzy neural network for the conversion of an RGB color space to CIELAB for the detection of color difference in textile factories is proposed. The advantage of this process is the processing performed for the conversion since it does not utilize much computational load. It replaces the traditional formulas for the color space conversion process and avoids the complicated calculations required, which makes it more efficient [5]. However, using a scanner [5] for taking samples, its only light source is white lighting. This could result in not taking the spectral range of the color as mentioned in [6] and [8]. This is because the illuminant temperature is an important factor to obtain an accurate color value.

On the other hand, in the work presented by Goñi and Salvadori [7] the authors develop a computer vision system (CVS) for food color measurement. For this, they created a cabinet for image acquisition with 4 fluorescent tubes installed on the walls and a diffuser. They also created a program for image processing in MATLAB. The system has the capability of being calibrated without the use of a colorimeter. The results when comparing the measurements of the system with those made with a colorimeter gave an average color difference of 2.45. This work only uses one illumination to make the measurements and is therefore vulnerable to metamerism and, considering that the usual threshold for quality control is a color difference of 1, the accuracy could be low for certain applications.

From the work carried out in the same field, it is observed that most of the studies carried out use a single type of illuminant as a light source, which makes them vulnerable to metamerism, or use illuminants that are not within the standards. Furthermore, color measurement geometry standards are usually not taken into consideration when making the measurements. Added to that, these systems depend on the use of an expert or on having a computer or laptop connected, which raises their costs and does not allow them to function on their own. In conclusion, the system proposed in this work solves the aforementioned problems by making use of various standard illuminants and meeting measurement geometry standards. Finally, this system is able to work on its own since it does all the calculations and processing on the Raspberry Pi 4B single board computer.

2   Description of Electronic Equipment

In Fig. 1 the block diagram of the proposed method for calculating the color difference is shown. This method consists of image acquisition and a image processing algorithm. The image acquisition block consists of 3 sub-blocks. The first sub-block represents the types of illuminants used for the acquisition of each image according to the standard ISO 11664-2:2007(E)/CIE S 014-2/E:2006 [8]. The second subblock represents the positioning of the illuminants, chosen according to the first subblock, as well as the positioning of the tissue, camera and illuminants for their acquisition according to the standard color measurement instrument geometry CIE 176:2006 [9]. The third sub-block registers the image of the fabric in RGB (Red, Green, Blue) format, which has a .JPG extension. The image acquisition block is followed by the image processing algorithm block which consists of 3 sub-blocks. The first subblock represents the average of pixels to find the fabric color of the captured image, under the different lighting conditions in RGB. The second sub-block determines the conversion of this color averaging to the color space La^*b^*. Finally, the third sub-block uses a neural network to predict the homogeneity of the colors of the samples according to the color difference ΔE_{CMC} described in the standard ISO105-J03:2009 [10].

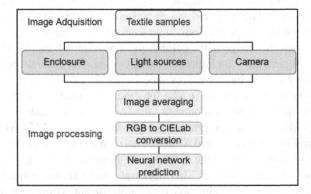

Fig. 1. Block diagram of the proposed method.

2.1 Image Acquisition

Data acquisition is a crucial step in the field of image processing in terms of performance, according to the applied techniques. To do this, a set of fabrics, illuminants and their positioning have been chosen based on standards. For the acquisition of images, the following points were taken into consideration.

Illuminants

Three types of light sources were selected. The first is the incandescent type illuminant, which was chosen because it has a color rendering index of 100 and has a complete light spectrum. In addition, it meets the illuminant A standard and ensures that tissue colors are measured as faithfully as possible [8]. The second light source chosen was a fluorescent illuminant, because it presents a completely different spectrum than the incandescent light and allows the sample to be evaluated as if the fabrics were in different scenarios. In addition, it complies with the F2 illuminant standard. Finally, the 6500K LED type illuminant, also known as the cold light LED. This light was picked because it represents most environments today, as this low-power technology grows popular and replaces others. These illuminant types were selected to simulate the different lighting conditions in which the fabric will be observed.

Enclosure

After selecting the types of illuminants to be used in the capture of the images, it is important to also determine the positioning of these, as well as the proper placement of the tissue and the camera. For this, the standard color measurement instrument geometry 45°/0° was chosen. This stipulates that the sample must be illuminated at a 45° angle and that the measuring device (camera) has to be directly on top, at an angle of 0° [9].

Camera

For a correct color measurement, the camera (Raspberry Pi v2.1 camera) must be 0° from the perpendicular line to the textile, with its position fixed. It is important to determine how the image is captured. This image capture is done with a resolution of 640 × 480 pixels ($N = 640, M = 480$). This is so that it is small enough to be processed quickly and large enough not to lose too much detail. In addition, the capture is done with an ISO value of 100, as low as possible to reduce noise in the image, and a shutter speed of 20 ms. In addition, the camera is set to have static white correction values, which means disabling the automatic white balancing correction and setting the red and blue gains manually. The values of 4.2 and 1.5 were chosen respectively. Lastly, the waiting time before the camera captures the image after each illuminant is turned on is controlled.

The acquired image can then be expressed in its primary RGB components $I_R(x, y), I_G(x, y) e I_B(x, y)$, where (x, y) the spatial coordinates for $x = 0, 1, \ldots, M - 1$, $y = 0, 1, \ldots, N - 1$.

Taking the previous points about angle of illumination and angle of measurement into consideration, the enclosure shown in Fig. 2 is designed. The position of the camera and the angle from which the samples are illuminated are shown in Fig. 3. Thus, the images of the fabric under each illuminant are captured. In such manner, all the measurements are taken under the same physical and lighting conditions.

Finally, Fig. 4 shows an external view of the prototype.

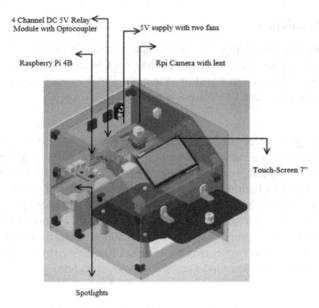

4 Channel DC 5V Relay
Module with Optocoupler

5V supply with two fans

Raspberry Pi 4B

Rpi Camera with lent

Touch-Screen 7"

Spotlights

Fig. 2. Illustration of the proposed equipment.

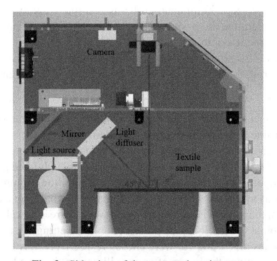

Camera

Mirror   Light
         diffuser
Light source

Textile
sample

45°

Fig. 3. Side view of the proposed equipment.

2.2   Image Processing Algorithm

This section, which represents the image processing algorithm, is responsible for calculating the value of the colors of the fabrics in the CIELab color space. This is done for the same fabric under different illuminations, based on the images captured by the camera in RGB format. To do this, the following steps are performed.

Fig. 4. External view of the prototype.

Image Averaging

Pixel averaging is performed to find the fabric color in the captured image. After that, a color averaging of the different images of the fabric taken under the same lighting is performed:

$$A_R = \frac{1}{M \times N} \sum_{x=0}^{M-1} \sum_{y=0}^{N-1} I_R(x, y) \qquad (1)$$

$$A_G = \frac{1}{M \times N} \sum_{x=0}^{M-1} \sum_{y=0}^{N-1} I_G(x, y) \qquad (2)$$

$$A_B = \frac{1}{M \times N} \sum_{x=0}^{M-1} \sum_{y=0}^{N-1} I_B(x, y) \qquad (3)$$

RGB to CIELAB Conversion

The averaged colors A_R, A_G and A_B are converted to CIELAB L* a* b* model. First, the conversion from RGB to XYZ color space is performed for each illuminant. The procedure is described below:

Step 1: Value normalization between [0,1].

$$AN_R = \frac{A_R}{255} \qquad (4)$$

$$AN_G = \frac{A_G}{255} \qquad (5)$$

$$AN_B = \frac{A_B}{255} \qquad (6)$$

Step 2: Conversion to the XYZ color space:

$$ANP_R = \begin{cases} \left(\frac{AN_R+0.55}{1.055}\right)^{2.4} \times 100 \, , \, AN_R > 0.04045 \\ \\ \frac{AN_R}{12.92} \times 100 \quad , \quad othercase \end{cases} \tag{7}$$

The same procedure is applied to AN_G and AN_B, generating ANP_G and ANP_B respectively.

Then, the conversion to the XYZ color space is applied:

$$\begin{bmatrix} X \\ Y \\ Z \end{bmatrix} = \begin{bmatrix} 0.4124 \ 0.3573 \ 0.1805 \\ 0.2126 \ 0.7152 \ 0.0722 \\ 0.0193 \ 0.1192 \ 0.9505 \end{bmatrix} \begin{bmatrix} ANP_R \\ ANP_G \\ ANP_B \end{bmatrix} \tag{8}$$

Step 3: XYZ normalization considering the illuminants:

$$X_{norm} = \frac{X}{X_r} \tag{9}$$

$$Y_{norm} = \frac{Y}{Y_r} \tag{10}$$

$$Z_{norm} = \frac{Z}{Z_r} \tag{11}$$

where X_{nrm}, Y_{nrm}, Z_{nrm}, are the normalized values XYZ according with each illuminant used in this proposed equipment (see Table 1)

Table 1. Tristimulus reference values according to illuminant

Iluminate	X_r	Y_r	Z_r
D65 (Cold light LED)	95.047	100.00	108.883
A (Incandescent)	109.850	100.00	35.585
F2 (Fluorescent)	99.187	100.00	67.395

Step 4: Conversion to the CIELab color space.

The values X_{norm}, Y_{norm}, Z_{norm} are converted using the following expressions:

$$X1_{norm} = \begin{cases} \sqrt[3]{X_{norm}} \quad , \, X_{norm} > 0.008856 \\ \\ 7.787 \times X_{norm} + \frac{16}{116} \, , \quad othercase \end{cases} \tag{12}$$

For Y_{norm} and Z_{norm} the same expresión is applied, obtaining $Y1_{norm}$ and $Z1_{norm}$.

Lastly, the values L^*, a and b are calculated as shown:

$$L^* = (116 \times Y1_{norm}) - 16 \tag{13}$$

$$a^* = 500 \times (X1_{norm} - Y1_{norm}) \tag{14}$$

$$b^* = 200 \times (Y1_{norm} - Z1_{norm}) \tag{15}$$

2.3 Neural Network Training

This section describes the process by which the neural network was designed and trained. This neural network is responsible for predicting whether the measured fabrics meet the color difference requirements. The following steps were performed for the training:

Measurements for the Training Dataset

Training a neural network requires a large amount of data from which the network can learn. For this, 100 pieces of cloth of different colors were chosen. To take the measurements to be used in the training as a baseline, the FRU brand WR-10QC colorimeter was used. This equipment allows color measurements to be made in the CIELAB color space with a precision of $\Delta E < 0.03$. With the colorimeter, several measurements were made on the fabrics, which were averaged, obtaining a set of 100 CIELAB color values. The same fabrics were measured with the enclosure designed and the 300 colors measurements (3 for each fabric) saved.

Calculation of Color Difference

From the L* a* b* values obtained with the colorimeter, the CMC color difference formula proposed by the Color Measurement Committee (referred to as CMC) is used, which is explained in ISO 105-J03:2009 [10]. This parameter presents the following equation:

$$\Delta E_{CMC} = \sqrt{\left(\frac{\Delta L^*}{k_l S_l}\right)^2 + \left(\frac{\Delta C^*}{k_c S_c}\right)^2 + \left(\frac{\Delta H^*}{S_H}\right)^2} \tag{16}$$

Equation (16) presents the color difference from considering the HSV color space, since many instruments do not use this color space. For the calculation of this equation, the C^* and H^*, considered, which represent the chroma and the saturation, respectively, of the HSV space. Besides, k_l y k_c son coeficientes para ajustar la capacidad relativamente amplia de luminosidad and chroma, respectively. For the dyeing industry $k_l = 2$ and $k_c = 1$ while ΔL^*, ΔC^* and ΔH^* correspond to the differences in lightness, chroma and hue between the sample and the standard. For the calculation of these last parameters, the following equations are used (comparing two color samples 1 and 2):

$$\Delta L^* = L_1^* - L_2^* \tag{17}$$

$$\Delta a^* = a_1^* - a_2^* \tag{18}$$

$$\Delta b^* = b_1^* - b_2^* \tag{19}$$

$$C_1^* = \sqrt{a_1^{*2} + b_1^{*2}} \tag{20}$$

$$C_2^* = \sqrt{a_2^{*2} + b_2^{*2}} \tag{21}$$

$$\Delta C_{ab}^* = C_1^* - C_2^* \tag{22}$$

$$\Delta H^* = \sqrt{\Delta a^{*2} + \Delta b^{*2} - \Delta C_{ab}^{*\,2}} \tag{23}$$

$$S_l = 1 \tag{24}$$

$$S_c = 1 + K_1 C_1^* \tag{25}$$

$$S_H = 1 + K_2 C_2^* \tag{26}$$

For the calculation of these last parameters were considered $K_1 = 0.048$ and $K_2 = 0.014$, which are the ones used in the textiles industry.

Creation of Dataset

For the creation of the training dataset, the color differences ΔE_{CMC} were calculated (using the formulas mentioned above) with the colorimeter measurements of each possible permutation of fabric pairs. From this, it is obtained a list of 9900 pairs of fabrics with their color difference and measurements obtained with the built enclosure. From this dataset, 500 samples were chosen in the area of interest, around a color difference of 1, which will be used for training the neural network. The members of the training dataset were chosen such as to ensure that the ratio of samples that were measured to have a color difference lower than 1 and those that didn't were equal to reduce any bias in the data.

The dataset created has 19 elements per sample, composed of two fabrics' color measurements and the color difference between the textiles, as measured by the colorimeter ($\Delta E_{colorimeter}$). Each textile is measured 3 times, each time illuminated under a different light source (Incandescent, Fluorescent, and Cold Light LED), obtaining 3 CIELab values. Each CIELab has 3 values: L, a^* and b^*. The structure of the dataset created is shown in Fig. 5.

Neural Network Design

To train the neural network, it must be able to accept the measurements made, so it will have 18 units in the input layer; 3 for each color L* a* b*. On the other hand, the output layer should only be able to indicate if the fabrics meet the quality requirement, which will be indicated by 0 and 1, so only one sigmoid activation unit is needed.

Unlike the input and output layers, the number of hidden layers, the number of units in them, and their activation functions vary from case to case depending on where the neural network will be implemented. Through an empirical process, a structure of 3 hidden layers, one of 72 and the rest of 150 units, was reached (see Fig. 6). This design

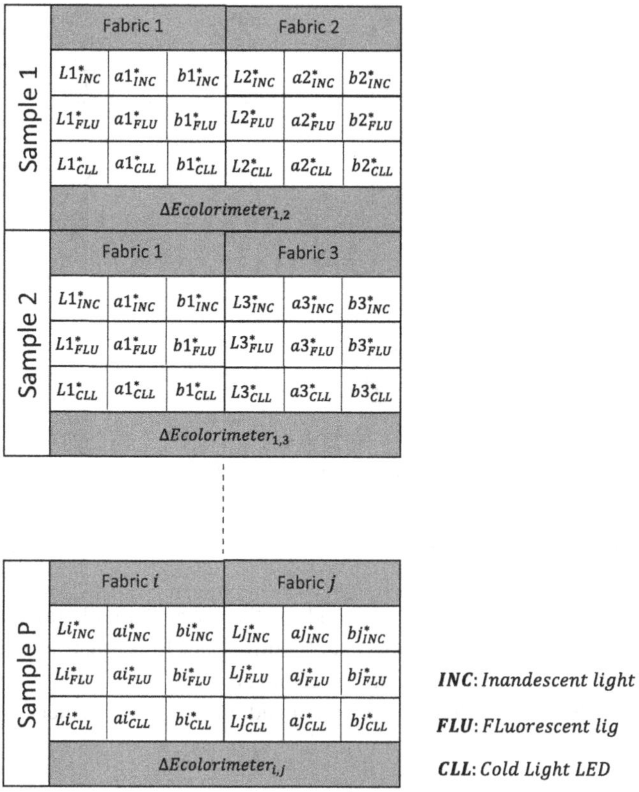

Sample 1

Fabric 1			Fabric 2		
$L1^*_{INC}$	$a1^*_{INC}$	$b1^*_{INC}$	$L2^*_{INC}$	$a2^*_{INC}$	$b2^*_{INC}$
$L1^*_{FLU}$	$a1^*_{FLU}$	$b1^*_{FLU}$	$L2^*_{FLU}$	$a2^*_{FLU}$	$b2^*_{FLU}$
$L1^*_{CLL}$	$a1^*_{CLL}$	$b1^*_{CLL}$	$L2^*_{CLL}$	$a2^*_{CLL}$	$b2^*_{CLL}$
$\Delta Ecolorimeter_{1,2}$					

Sample 2

Fabric 1			Fabric 3		
$L1^*_{INC}$	$a1^*_{INC}$	$b1^*_{INC}$	$L3^*_{INC}$	$a3^*_{INC}$	$b3^*_{INC}$
$L1^*_{FLU}$	$a1^*_{FLU}$	$b1^*_{FLU}$	$L3^*_{FLU}$	$a3^*_{FLU}$	$b3^*_{FLU}$
$L1^*_{CLL}$	$a1^*_{CLL}$	$b1^*_{CLL}$	$L3^*_{CLL}$	$a3^*_{CLL}$	$b3^*_{CLL}$
$\Delta Ecolorimeter_{1,3}$					

Sample P

Fabric i			Fabric j		
Li^*_{INC}	ai^*_{INC}	bi^*_{INC}	Lj^*_{INC}	aj^*_{INC}	bj^*_{INC}
Li^*_{FLU}	ai^*_{FLU}	bi^*_{FLU}	Lj^*_{FLU}	aj^*_{FLU}	bj^*_{FLU}
Li^*_{CLL}	ai^*_{CLL}	bi^*_{CLL}	Lj^*_{CLL}	aj^*_{CLL}	bj^*_{CLL}
$\Delta Ecolorimeter_{i,j}$					

INC: *Inandescent light*

FLU: *FLuorescent lig*

CLL: *Cold Light LED*

Fig. 5. Dataset structure

was found to be large enough to learn from the database, but not large enough to cause overfitting; that is, maintaining its ability to generalize.

The activation function of the hidden layers chosen was the hyperbolic tangent or tanh. This type was used as opposed to the more widely used Rectified Linear Unit (ReLU) since the CIELAB color space is spherical and the way the human eye perceives it, and the color difference formulas are not linear. Furthermore, it was found in tests that the inclusion of ReLU units frequently caused overfitting.

Training

The dataset that was created was randomly divided into 2 parts with a ratio of 7:3. The largest dataset was used for training the neural network and the other to test its accuracy. Adam was used for training, a stochastic optimizer that works well in the vast majority of cases; as well as being efficient and faster than other popular methods like RMSprop. The mini-batches method, which is to train the network with small batches of data instead of all the training data at once, was also applied to accelerate learning. A mini-batch size of 16 was used. The neural network was trained for 5000 epochs since it was not seen to be significant after this value and overfitting is to be avoided. Finally, the learning rate used, which brought the best results was 0.0001.

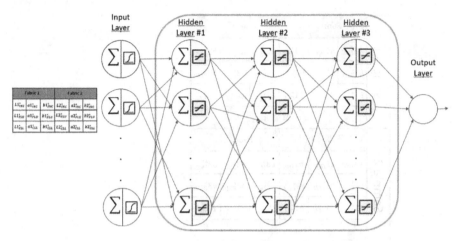

Fig. 6. Neural network structure

3 Results and Discussion

To ascertain the accuracy of the device created and the neural network trained, 30 samples of fabric pairs which tested positive (had a color difference lower than 1) and 30 negative samples were measured with the designed enclosure. The results are shown in Fig. 7. The Fig. 8 shows how the system is controlled and the output presented.

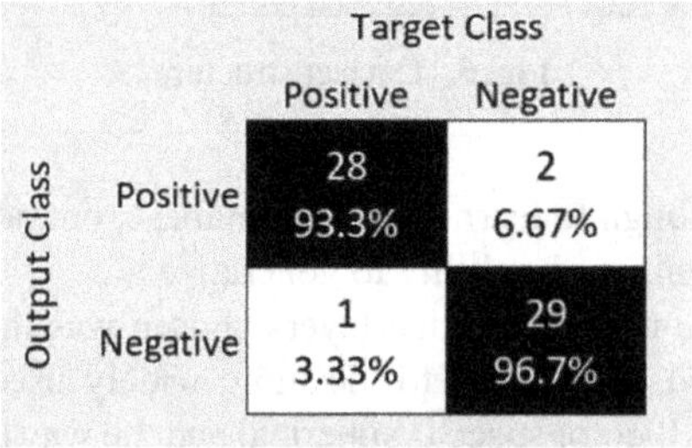

		Target Class	
		Positive	Negative
Output Class	Positive	28 / 93.3%	2 / 6.67%
	Negative	1 / 3.33%	29 / 96.7%

Fig. 7. Confusion matrix.

Discussion

From the results, it can be seen that the system is capable of measuring color differences that agree with visual analysis and is even capable of showing which fabrics are similar, even when this is difficult for the human eye. On the other hand, it can be seen how the different lights can obtain different details from the fabrics. However, there's also room for improvement. The CIELab color space's wideness makes it so the system struggles with colors and tones that differ too much from what it's been trained with.

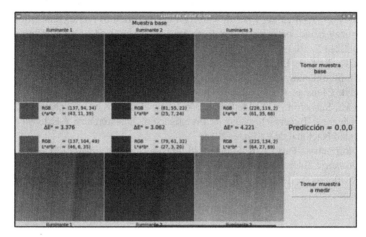

Fig. 8. The system's GUI showing a prediction of a negative sample.

Conclusions

- The developed equipment currently achieves an accuracy of 95% in the correct identification of fabrics that are homogenous in color, regardless of the issue of metamerism
- The system is capable of measuring color differences that agree with visual analysis and is even capable of detecting which fabrics are similar, even when this is difficult for the human eye
- The electronic equipment is portable and works independently. It doesn't need a PC or specialized personnel to operate, only an electric outlet.
- The CIELab color space's wideness makes it so the system struggles with colors and tones that differ too much from what it's been trained with.
- An improvement could be increasing the size of the training dataset, measuring more textiles to increase the information the neural network learns from.

References

1. Lockuán Lavado, F.E.: La industria textil y su control de calidad. Tejeduría (2012a)
2. Li, X., et al.: Machine vision of textile testing and quality research. J. Intell. Fuzzy Syst. **38**(1), 319–325 (2020). https://doi.org/10.3233/jifs-179407
3. TESTEX INSTRUMENTS LTD.: Color Matching Cabinet TU300C/D (n.d.). Recuperado de: https://www.testextextile.com/product/color-light-box-tu300cd/
4. Yuntao, Z., Chen, L., Haoran, D., Yang, P., Zhaokui, Z.: Fabric color difference detection device based on machine vision recognition technology (International Patent No. CN210401196 (U)). European Patent Office (2020). https://worldwide.espacenet.com/public ationDetails/biblio?FT=D&date=20200424&DB=&locale=en_EP&CC=CN&NR=210401 196U&KC=U&ND=8

5. Li, P.-F., Ning, Y.-W., Jing, J.-F.: Research on the detection of fabric color difference based on T-S fuzzy neural network. Color. Res. Appl. **42**(5), 609–618 (2017). https://doi.org/10.1002/col.22113
6. Huertas, R., Roa, R., López, M., Robledo, L., Melgosa, M.: Comparación entre fuentessimuladora e iluminantes. In: VII Congreso Nacional de Color. Dpto. De Óptica. Ed. Mecenas, Facultad de Ciencias. Universidad de Granada. 18071 Granada (2007)
7. Goñi, S.M., Salvadori, V.O.: Medición de color de alimentos en el espacio CIELAB a partir de imágenes. Terceras Jornadas de Investigación, Transferencia y Extensión. La Plata: Universidad Nacional de La Plata (2015)
8. CIE: Colorimetry—Part 2: CIE Standard Illuminants for Colorimetry (2006a)
9. CIE: Geometric Tolerances for Colour Measurements (2006b)
10. ISO 105-J03:2009: Textiles – Tests for colour fastness-Part J03: Calculation of colour differences

Artificial Intelligence-Based Banana Ripeness Detection

Jorge Enríquez$^{(\boxtimes)}$ and Mayra Macas

Department of Computer Science, Universidad de las Fuerzas Armadas ESPE,
Quito, Ecuador
{jsenriquez3,mamacas1}@espe.edu.ec

Abstract. This paper aims to construct an artificial intelligence model that detects the level of ripeness of bananas according to three categories of the Von Loesecke scale: totally green, yellow with green tips and yellow with brown spots. The manual methods typically used to classify the degree of ripening of bananas are unreliable since they are very subjective; therefore, it is necessary to automate this procedure. The features leveraged by our model are extracted using the HSV (Hue, Saturation, Value) color model obtained from the images. The Multiclass Support Vector Machine (SVM) model based on OVO (one-vs-one) with an Radial Basis Function (RBF) kernel function is implemented as the proposed classifier. The used dataset comprises 1242 images divided into 80% for training and 20% for test data. The accuracy obtained using the proposed model was 98.89%, outperfoming the state-of-the-art methods (We have published the source code at https://github.com/Jorge260399/AI-bases-framework.).

Keywords: Banana ripeness · HSV · SVM multiclass · RBF · Artificial intelligence

1 Introduction

Nowadays, with the imminent growth of the world population, it is estimated that the agricultural sector will need to produce 50% more food [1]. Due to the decrease in available labor for agricultural work, it is necessary to implement solutions through the use of technologies that enable automation and increase productivity by using artificial vision systems for monitoring agricultural sectors, among others [26]. Bananas are known for being one of the most consumed fruits, as they have a high potassium content and also contain magnesium and phosphorus. Overall, when a banana reaches its highest maturation phase according to the Von Loesecke scale, it also reaches its highest nutritional value [6]. In Ecuador, a third of the world's banana exports originate. Therefore, the cultivation of bananas is considered the most important agricultural activity for the country's economy.

M. Botto-Tobar et al. (Eds.): ICAT 2022, CCIS 1755, pp. 197–211, 2023.
https://doi.org/10.1007/978-3-031-24985-3_15

The manual methods that determine the degree of ripeness of bananas are usually of low precision and unreliable since they are based on the evaluator's experience. Therefore, automation of such a process is necessary. A subset of artificial intelligence called machine learning (ML) has recently emerged as a promising solution for enabling and facilitating agriculture [21]. More precisely, ML minimizes farming losses by providing rich recommendations and insights about the various crops. Some of the most used methods for predicting the degree of ripeness in fruits are Support Vector Machines (SVMs), Artificial Neural Networks (ANNs), Random Forest (RF), and the K-Nearest Neighbor (KNN) algorithm [10,14].

Although KNN is one of the simplest classification algorithms to understand and interpret, it has a high computational cost as it stores the entire training data set. In addition, KNN is commonly used to solve economic prediction problems and construct recommender systems, among others. Similarly, using ANNs (in particular deep NN - DNN) in image classification problems is also expensive in terms of storage and processing capabilities due to the exponentially increased number of trainable parameters induced by the forward-facing direction in which inputs are processed [18]. Contrary to that, SVMs are considered suitable for image classification since they are relatively indifferent to the number of data items, while the classification complexity does not depend on the dimensionality of the feature space enabling them to learn a potentially larger set of patterns [15].

This work aims to create an artificial intelligence model based on SVM that allows the detection of the ripening state of bananas by extracting the HSV color model from images. The Von Loesecke maturation scale is used to determine the degree of ripeness. In particular, we performed a comparative analysis between the four types of kernels of the SVM, e.i, linear SVM, polynomial SVM, RBF, and hyperbolic tangent (sigmoid). The dataset contains 1242 instances generated from two sides (front and back view) of 258 bananas. The proposed artificial intelligence model can classify three different levels of ripeness (i.e., totally green, yellow with green tips and yellow with brown spots). Our key contributions can be summarized as follows: (i) We design and implement an intelligent system for banana ripeness detection, which can be trained on image datasets generated by a banana plantation. The proposed intelligent model is built upon a Multi-Class Support Vector Machine and extracts the HSV (Hue, Saturation, Value) color model from the images to determine the degree of ripeness according to the Von Loesecke maturation scale. To the best of our knowledge, this is the first attempt to solve the problem of classifying bananas according to the level of ripeness to enable agriculture automation in Ecuador. (ii) We conduct an extensive experimental analysis on data collected from a banana plantation. The results demonstrate the superior performance of the proposed model over state-of-the-art baseline techniques. (iii) Last but not the least, we publish the source code of our model at https://github.com/Jorge260399/AI-bases-framework. The layout of the manuscript is as follows: Sect. 2 Related work, Sect. 3 Background, Sect. 4 Framework and Methodology, Sect. 5 Experiments and Analysis and Sect. 6 Conclusion and Future Work.

2   Related Work

A considerable amount of research has focused on automating the inspection of fruits for defect detection, maturity phase identification, and category recognition. The authors in [14] introduced a Multi-Class SVM (MSVM) model for the ripening level classification of strawberries. The proposed system obtained an accuracy of 85.64% over a dataset of 300 image samples of strawberries at different ripening stages. Aiming to construct a sweet bell pepper maturity stage classification system, Elhariri et al. [8] employed MC-SVM with linear kernel function on a dataset composed of 175 images. They considered the bell pepper surface color as the fundamental factor in the feature extraction stage and achieved 93.89% of accuracy during experimentation. A banana maturity stage classification system was developed using ANNs in [19]. The authors stated that their model achieved an accuracy of around 100% using 300 samples (i.e., 104 green, 57 yellowish, 97 mid-ripen, and 42 overripen banana). Nonetheless, there is notable evidence of overfitting to the data, suggesting that regularization techniques could enhance results. Using the same model, Ahmad et al. [2] proposed a system for the classification of the ripening level of Chinese fruit. They have used the RGB model for feature extraction and a segmentation technique called Euclidean distance metric. The result obtained was the ability to recognize ripe, unripe and overripe fruit with an accuracy of 97.33%. Riskiawan et al. [25] introduced an automatic detector for the ripening stage of cocoa using KNN and three levels of maturity (i.e., ripe, medium and raw). They implemented some digital image processing techniques such as: image segmentation, RGB color extraction and the application of an HSL filter to improve the data set quality. However, the size of the used dataset is limited (it includes only 46 images), resulting in an overfitting problem.

More recently, Gayathri et al. [10] used CNNs to develop a classification system for the ripening state of papaya. Although this model achieved a high accuracy (96.5%), the employed dataset is not big enough (only 300 images divided into three categories: ripe, unripe, and partially ripe), leading to overfitting. Thakur2020 et al. [29] and Gunawan et al. [12] applied the same model to predict the strawberry and apple ripening stages, respectively. Even though performance evaluation reached a higher accuracy, the authors did not consider any regularization technique to avoid overfitting. The aforementioned classification techniques, however, have the following shortcomings within the context of the problem that we examine: (i) The classifiers are not robust because dissimilar fruit images may have similar or identical shapes and color features; (ii) The proposed recognition systems can classify different types of fruits [8,23,25,27] but they are not appropriate for banana ripeness detection; and (iii) Intelligent systems such as [10,12,19,29] do not consider any regularization technique to avoid overfitting. Therefore, they are unrealistic and possibly do not work correctly in a real environment. (iv) Furthermore, studies such as [10,12,29] omit that DL techniques are mostly black boxes, meaning that determining why an ANN makes a particular decision is a difficult task. Since DL is heavily dependent on the employed data, obtaining representative, valid, and accurate samples should be the primary concern when building a classifier, particularly in recognition systems. Finally, DL typically is computational demanding. Advanced parallel computing, such as GPUs and high-performance chips, promoted the popularity and rising of DL, yet DL also heavily depends on them. To overcome these shortcomings, this paper presents an efficient artificial intelligence-based framework for banana ripeness detection. More specifically, our framework uses an MSVM model based on OVO with an RBF kernel function trained on image datasets generated by a banana plantation.

3 Background

3.1 Machine Learning in Agriculture

The digital transformation of agriculture has converted diverse management aspects into artificially intelligent systems to generate value from the ever-increasing data originating from numerous sources. ML has considerable potential to address numerous challenges in establishing knowledge-based farming systems. The application of ML in agriculture allows more efficient and precise farming with less human resources, while ensuring high-quality production. In addition, ML-enabled systems allow anticipating possible errors and monitoring the crops individually based on the data obtained from previous crops [4]. For more details about ML in agriculture, we refer the interested readers to [4] (Fig. 1).

Fig. 1. Each banana bunch represents a stage during the ripening process [11].

3.2 Von Loesecke Scale

Generally, the so-called Von Loesecke ripening scale is employed to classify banana ripening. Von Loesecke and Willard [30] established seven ripening subclasses corresponding respectively to the following peel color stages: totally green (1), green with yellow lines (2), more green than yellow (3), more yellow than green (4), yellow with green tips (5), totally yellow (6), and yellow with brown spots (7). The evaluation of the subclass is accomplished through visual inspection based on a set of photographs representative of the different stages of ripening (see Fig. 3). This comparative method is highly subjective given that color analysis relies on several factors, such as angle of observation, the lighting of the environment, and observer accuracy. As such, it is harming the standardization in the grading process [11].

3.3 Support Vector Machine

Vapnik and his co-workers introduced the SVM algorithm in the late 1970s. SVM is one of the most widely used kernel-based learning algorithms in various ML applications, primarily image classification [15]. In SVMs, the main objective is solving a convex quadratic optimization problem to obtain a globally optimal solution in theory and thus overcome the local extremum dilemma of other ML techniques. SVM belongs to nonparametric supervised methods that are insensitive to the underlying data distribution. This is one of the advantages of SVMs compared to other statistical methods wherein data distribution should be known in advance [28]. SVM is a linear binary classifier identifying a single boundary between two classes. The basic assumption regarding linear SVM is that the multidimensional data are linearly separable in the input space.

The performance of SVM broadly relies on the appropriate selection of a kernel function that generates the dot products in the higher-dimensional feature space. This space can theoretically be of an infinite dimension where linear discrimination is possible. There is a wide variety of kernel types, among which Linear, RBF, Polynomial, and Sigmoid stand out, as they can be used regardless of the type of problem [3]. The *linear kernel* is the simplest of the SVM kernels since it is based on a linear function for its operation. Its use is recommended when the linear separation of the data is simple and the only hyperparameter that must be adjusted is C (regularization). The *RBF kernel* is very similar to the Gaussian distribution. Its use offers two advantages: (i) only two hyperparameters (gamma γ and the C regularization) need to be configured and; (ii) its flexibility allows generating from a linear classifier to a more complicated one. The *polynomial kernel* is a more generalized form of the linear kernel. This function not only identifies the similarity that exists between the characteristics of the input data but also the possible combinations between them. This kernel has two hyperparameters: the degree of the polynomial and C. The *sigmoid kernel* comes from neural networks, which have an activation function called the bipolar sigmoid function. It is necessary to emphasize that this kernel is equivalent to a two-layer neural network and perceptron and has the same hyperparameters as RBF. The binary nature of SVMs usually brings complications on their use for multiclass scenarios, as in the problem we examine. To address this, a multiclass task needs to be broken down into a series of simple SVM binary classifiers using methods such as one-vs-one (OVO) [17] and one-vs-all (OVA) [9].

4   Framework and Methodology

In this section, we offer details on each component module (i.e., Data collection, Preprocessing, Feature extraction, Modelling, Training, and Evaluation.) of the proposed framework (see Fig. 2).

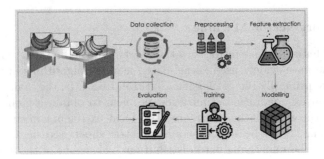

Fig. 2. Overview of the proposed framework.

4.1   Data Collation

Images of the following three ripeness stages of bananas were obtained and manually labeled: totally green, yellow with green tips, and yellow with brown spots. Specifically, data samples of export banana variants in Taiwan from [20] were utilized. A DSLR camera captured the RGB images of bananas with 320×213 size. The dataset contains 516 instances generated from two sides (front and back view) of 258 bananas. Following, we identified only 305 images as suitable for our study. Overall, there are three classes (i.e., totally green, yellow with green tips, and yellow with brown spots) with 209, 41, and 55 samples, respectively. In order to balance the dataset, we used the data augmentation techniques, resulting in approximately 400 images per class with a total of 1242 samples[1].

4.2   Preprocessing

The non-local means (NLM) algorithm was employed for image denoising. In greater detail, the NLM denoising method is based on the concept that any noisy pixel located in the center of an image patch may be denoised by building relevant statistics from patches having similar structures located anywhere in the image $\mu = (\mu_1, \mu_2, \mu_3)$ and a certain pixel ρ [5]:

$$\hat{\mu}_j(\rho) = \frac{1}{C(\rho)} \sum_{q \in B(\rho,q)} \mu_j(q) w(\rho, q), \quad C(p) = \sum_{q \in B(\rho,r)} w(\rho, q), \tag{1}$$

---

[1] The labeled dataset can be found at https://github.com/Jorge260399/Banana_Ripeness_Dataset_Augmented.

where $j = 1, 2, 3$ and $B(\rho, q)$ indicates a neighborhood centered at ρ with size $(2r + 1) \times (2r + 1)$ pixels. This neighborhood is limited to a square of fixed size due to computation restrictions. The weight $w(\rho, q)$ depends on the squared Euclidean distance $d^2 = d^2(B(\rho, f), B(q, f))$ of the $(2f + 1) \times (2f + 1)$ color patches centered respectively at ρ and q:

$$d^2(B(\rho, f), B(q, f)) = \frac{1}{3(2f + 1)^2} \sum_{j=1}^{3} \sum_{k \in B(0,f)} (\mu_i(\rho + k) - \mu_i(q + k))^2 \quad (2)$$

That is, the restored value of each pixel is computed as the average of the most resembling pixels, where the resemblance is calculated in the color image. Therefore, each channel value for every pixel is the average of the same pixels. Moreover, an exponential kernel is used to compute the weights:

$$w(\rho, q) = e^{-\frac{max(d^2 - 2\sigma^2, 0.0)}{h^2}}, \quad (3)$$

where σ denotes the standard deviation of the noise and h is the filtering parameter set depending on the value of σ. The weight function is employed for averaging similar patches up to noise. More precisely, when the square distances are smaller than σ^2 the patches are set to 1, while larger distances decrease rapidly due to the exponential kernel. The weight of the reference pixel p in the average is set to the maximum of the weights in the neighborhood $B(\rho, r)$. This setting avoids the excessive weighting of the reference point in the average. Otherwise, $w(\rho, p)$ should be equal to 1 and a larger value of h would be necessary to ensure the noise reduction. By applying the above averaging procedure we recover a denoised value at each pixel p. Finally, for removing the background, we use the open source tool Rembg [22].

4.3   Feature Extraction

Color Feature Extraction: The color of an image is defined through any of the popular color spaces such as RGB, L*a*b*, and HSV (Hue, Saturation, Value). It has been reported that the HSV model describes colors similarly to how the human eye tends to perceive color [24]. Besides, it is employed to separate image luminance from color information. Thus, the HSV color space gives the best color histogram feature among the different color spaces. Accordingly, the RGB banana image was converted to HSV color space. A color histogram represents the distribution of colors in an image through a set of bins, where each histogram bin corresponds to a color in the color space. A color histogram for a given image is represented by a vector: $H = H[0], H[1], H[2], ..., H[j], ...H[n]$, where j is the color bin in the color histogram and $H[j]$ represents the number of pixels of color j in the image, and n is the total number of bins used in the color histogram. Each pixel in the image is assigned to a suitable. Consequently, the value of each bin gives the number of pixels that have that specific color.

Textural Feature Extraction: Image texture refers to a set of metrics designed to quantify the perceived texture of an image. It provides information regarding the spatial distribution of color or pixel intensities in the entire image or a selected region. Texture analysis is a method of quantifying intuitive qualities described by terms like rough, smooth, silky, or bumpy in the form of a function representing the spatial variation in pixel intensities. In this sense, the roughness or bumpiness of an image regards variations in its pixel intensity values or gray levels. We employ gray level co-occurrence matrices (GLCMs) based on texture in this work. The GLCM functions characterize an image's texture by creating a GLCM and using it to extract statistical measures. More precisely, the GLCM is created by calculating the occurrence frequency of pixels with specific values that have a particular spatial relationship. Special features of banana images were extracted to describe co-occurrence matrices (CMs) data, including angular second moment, contrast, correlation, the sum of squares (variance), inverse difference moment, sum average, sum variance, squared sum entropy, entropy, difference variance, difference entropy, information measures of correlation, maximal correlation coefficient [13]. Principal Component Analysis (PCA) was performed for dimensionality reduction to reduce the complexity of a model and avoid overfitting.

4.4   Modeling: Multiple Classes Classification

In our study, there exist three ripeness stages of banana; thus, multi-class SVM (MSVM) is used. Particularly, the classification of three ripeness stages of banana can be considered as constructing three binary classifiers and combining them into one multi-class classifier. As we mention in Sect. 3.3, many methods can be used to construct a multi-class classifier such as OVO [17] and OVA [9]. For one classification of N classes, N binary tests are needed for OVA, while $N(N-1)/2$ binary tests are required for OVO [7]. However, in most cases, OVO needs less time than OVA because the binary SVMs of OVO are trained for two information classes and involve much fewer SVs. Besides, a number of binary SVMs of OVO share the same SVs, which also reduces the computational complexity [7]. Therefore, for efficiency, OVO multiclass strategy is used in this work to construct the banana ripeness classifier. Two types of OVO-based MSVMs are considered to classify the ripeness stages of bananas, namely, directed acyclic graph MSVM (DAGMSVM) and voting-based MSVM (VBMSVM).

The DAGMSVM needs to train $N(N-1)/2$ to binary SVMs. In the test phase, it uses the rooted binary directed acyclic graph (DAG), which consisting of $N(N-1)/2$ internal nodes and N leaves, to combine these binary SVMs. The VBMSVM is also a $N-class$ OVO MSVM consists of $N(N-1)/2$ binary SVMs. One SVM C_{ij}, where $i \neq j, i = 1,...,N; j = 1,...,N$, is designed for distinguishing the ith class from the jth class. Each SVM C_{ij} is trained with all examples in the ith class with positive label, and the examples in the jth class with negative label [16].

Typically, a dataset is divided into two subsets. The first subset is used to *fit the model* and is referred to as the *training dataset*. The second subset is used to *evaluate the model* and is referred to as the *test dataset*. Samples from this subset are provided as input to the model and predictions are made and compared to the expected values. The objective is to estimate the ML's performance on new data (i.e., data not used while training the model). Further details about the training and evaluation stages will be provided in the following sections.

5   Experiments and Analysis

5.1   Experimental Setup and Data Preprocessing

Experiments were performed on a Linux server (Ubuntu distribution v20.04) with 40 GB of storage and 7 GB of RAM. All the procedures/models were implemented in Python 3.8.10. As mentioned in Sect. 4.1, the dataset selected for our study is unbalanced. Therefore, *Data Augmentation* techniques were implemented using the ImageDataGenerator class for image preprocessing from the Keras library to obtain approximately 400 images per image class, resulting in 1242 images in total. *The Data Augmentation* techniques applied were flipping, shifting, rotation, shearing, zooming, and closest fill mode. Subsequently, the preprocessing of the images was carried out using the NLM technique (see Sect. 4.2) employing the OpenCV library, to eliminate noise from the images, using the following minimum parameters recommended by the library: $h = 10$, templateWindowSize $= 7$, and searchWindowSize $= 21$. The next step was to remove the background of the images using a tool called Remg [22], which is based on a U^2-Net deep network for the detection of objects.

5.2   Feature Extraction

Feature extraction was carried out considering the color and texture of the images. For the extraction of the *color features*, the image was transformed into the HSV color space. Then a color histogram was made using the following parameters: image, channels $= [0, 1, 2]$, mask $=$ None, histSize $= [8, 8, 8]$, ranges $= [0, 256, 0, 256, 0, 256]$. These parameters indicate the image for which the histogram is going to be calculated, the image channels considered, the image mask, the size of the histogram for each channel determined by the number of bins and the range of possible pixel values, respectively. Then, the image (i.e., the pixel intensity level) was normalized to enhance contrast. The result of performing this procedure is obtaining a color vector with a size of 512 values. For the extraction of the *textural features*, the Mahotas library was used. Since the employed approach is based on the technique of spatial dependence of gray tones, it was necessary to transform the image to gray scale. Subsequently, the textural features were obtained for four types of adjacency (horizontal, vertical, left, and right diagonals), the mean was calculated, and a feature vector with a size of 13 values was obtained. Finally, the Principal Component Analysis (PCA) technique was applied to reduce the dimensionality of the features. In greater detail, creating a PCA object specifying the desired number of components, in our case 19 components, uses an adjustment method that allows identifying the key characteristics that mainly explain the variance of the dataset.

5.3 Parameter Setting and Model Training

In Sect. 4.4, we specify that two types of OVO-based MSVMs (i.e., DAGMSVM, VBMSVM) are built to classify the banana ripening stages. The hyperparameters considered for VBMSVM and DAGMSVM are: *C (regularization)* which indicates the supported classification error, *decision function shape* for which we always used *'ovo'* as a multiclass strategy, *degree* which indicates the power of the function when using the polynomial kernel, and *gamma* which defines the influence of the calculation of the approved division line (considered only by the RBF and sigmoidal kernels). The aforementioned hyperparameters were optimized through the grid search strategy, and k-fold cross-validation was also used to estimate the model's performance, performing tests with the value of k in the range of 5–10. In VBMSVM (see Algorithm 1), each prediction made is passed to each classifier, and the predicted class is stored to assign the class that gets the maximum number of votes. On the other hand, for DAGMSVM, in each prediction, the rejected class is removed until there is only one class left to be assigned.

Algorithm 1. VBMSVM Model training

Input: X, Y
1: Train, Test ← X, Y   ▷ Split in training and testing data
2: Applying PCA for dimensionality reduction of feature space
3: Define grid parameters
4: Best estimator ← Using grid search
5: Build the model ← Best estimator
6: Train model using VBMSVM classification method ← Train Data
7: Define scoring
8: **for** i in range (5,11) **do**   ▷ Testing between 5-10 fold cross-validation
9:      Cv ← i
10:     Using the k-fold cross-validation ← Cv, scoring values and train data
11: **end for**
12: Select the cv value that allows to obtain better accuracy
13: Evaluating the model ← Test data
14: **return** accuracy, f1-score, precision, recall

5.4 Baseline Methods

We compared MSVM with an ensemble method and a neural network model: (i) The Random Forest (RF) ensemble method includes multiple decision trees and is based on majority vote for classification. The hyperparameters considered for this technique were: *n_estimators* which indicates the number of trees in the forest, *criterion* which is the function to measure the quality of a division, *max_depth* which is the maximum depth of the tree and *max_features* which are the number of features to be considered for finding the best division. The best values for the aforementioned hyperparameters were found using the grid search strategy. For this technique, it was also necessary to adjust the performance through k-fold cross-validation, performing several tests by varying the value of k in the range 5–10. (ii) The neural network model was implemented using the Tensorflow library, is CNN-based and leverages Transfer Learning (TL). In particular, VGG16 was used as a pre-entry model, composed of thirteen convolutional layers and five max-pooling layers. In addition, a flat layer, two dense layers with a relu activation function, and one dense layer with a softmax activation function were considered. The selected hyperparameters of the proposed model were a sparse categorical cross-entropy *loss function*, the 'adam' *optimization* algorithm and, finally, the accuracy *metric*. The best model performance was achieved using a value of 50 epochs and batch size of 32.

Table 1. Models summary

Experiment N°	Technique	Accuracy	F1	Precision	Recall
	VBMSVM Linear Kernel	98.19	98.19	98.22	98.19
	VBMSVM Polynomial Kernel	98.09	98.09	98.13	98.09
1st Experiment:	VBMSVM RBF Kernel	98.39	98.39	98.42	98.39
Concatenated	VBMSVM Sigmoid Kernel	97.88	97.88	97.95	97.88
Color Features	DAGMSVM Linear Kernel	98.09	98.09	98.10	98.09
and Textural	DAGMSVM Polynomial Kernel	98.19	98.19	98.24	98.19
Features	DAGMSVM RBF Kernel	98.09	98.09	98.15	98.09
	DAGMSVM Sigmoid Kernel	97.88	97.88	97.95	97.88
	Random Forest	98.09	98.09	98.14	98.09
	VBMSVM Linear Kernel	97.48	97.47	97.51	97.48
2nd Experiment:	VBMSVM Polynomial Kernel	98.69	98.69	98.72	98.69
Concatenated	VBMSVM RBF Kernel	98.39	98.39	98.44	98.39
Color Features	VBMSVM Sigmoid Kernel	96.37	96.37	96.49	96.37
and Textural	DAGMSVM Linear Kernel	97.07	97.07	97.14	97.07
Features with	DAGMSVM Polynomial Kernel	98.69	98.69	98.72	98.69
PCA	DAGMSVM RBF Kernel	98.89	98.89	98.93	98.89
	DAGMSVM Sigmoid Kernel	96.47	96.47	96.57	96.47
	Random Forest	96.98	96.98	97.13	96.98
3rd Experiment: Deep Learning	CNN-based TL	48.19	37.07	30.38	48.19

5.5 Experimental Evaluation and Discussion

Here, we evaluate and discuss the performance of the models (i.e., DAGMSVM, VBMSVM, RF, and CNN-based TL) on a sizeable set of appropriately preprocessed banana images (see Sect. 5.1) in terms of accuracy, precision, recall and F1 score. The results are reported for comparison in Table 1. We used the settings and configurations described in Sect. 5.3 for MSVM and in Sect. 5.4 for the Random Forest technique and the CNN-based TL model. Furthermore, for DAGMSVM, VBMSVM and RF, we considered the following scenarios (i.e., feature spaces): (i) Color Features and Textural Features (see Sect. 5.2) concatenated, where a feature space of 525 was used, (ii) Color Features and Textural Features concatenated with PCA, where the feature space consisted of 19 features obtained by applying PCA. In particular, when implementing Random Forest, the following hyperparameters were set: $criterion =$ 'entropy', $max\_depth = 8$, $max\_features =$ 'sqrt', $n\_estimators = 100$ without PCA and $criterion =$ 'entropy', $max\_depth = 8$, $max\_features =$ 'auto', $n\_estimators = 115$ with

PCA. The results were 98.09% accuracy, 98.09% of F1 score, 98.12% precision, 98.09% recall without applying PCA, and 96.98% accuracy, 96.98% F1 score, 97.13% accuracy and 96.98% recall when applying PCA.

When implementing MSVM (i.e., DAGMSVM, VBMSVM), the hyperparameters were tuned based on the kernel type: linear, polynomial, RBF, and sigmoidal. For the *linear kernel*, without applying PCA and using the *VBMSVM* strategy, the best model was identified by fitting the hyperparameters to C = 10 and decision function shape = 'ovo'. The achieved performance metrics were 98.19% accuracy, 98.19% F1 score, 98.22% precision, and 98.19% recall. When applying PCA with the same strategy and hyperparameters, the highest performance metrics achieved were 97.48% accuracy, 97.47% F1 score, 97.51% precision, and 97.48% recall. For the *polynomial kernel*, without applying PCA and using the *DAGMSVM* strategy, the best model was identified by adjusting the hyperparameters to C = 1000, decision function shape = 'ovo' and degree = 3. The achieved performance metrics in this case were 98.19% accuracy, 98.19% F1 score, 98.24% precision, and 98.19% recall. For both strategies, when applying PCA with the same configurations besides changing C to 100, the following metrics were measured: 98.69% accuracy, 98.69% F1 score, 98.72% precision and 98.69% recall.

For the *RBF kernel*, without applying PCA and using the *VBMSVM* strategy, the best model was identified by adjusting the hyperparameters to C = 10, decision function shape = 'ovo', and gamma = 'scale'. The corresponding performance metrics were 98.39% accuracy, 98.39% F1 score, 98.42% precision, and 98.39% recall. When applying PCA with the *DAGMSVM* strategy and the same hyperparameters, the metrics of highest performance were 98.89% accuracy, 98.89% F1 score, 98.93% precision and 98.89% recall. For the *sigmoidal kernel*, without applying PCA with both strategies, the same results were obtained. However, by adjusting the hyperparameters to C = 1000, decision function shape = 'ovo', and gamma = 'auto', the performance metrics were 97.88% accuracy, 97.88% F1 score, 97.95% precision and 97.88% recall. Finally, when applying PCA with the *DAGMSVM* strategy and modifying only the hyperparameter C = 100, the results were as follows: 96.47% accuracy, 96.47% F1 score, 96.57% precision, and 96.47% recall. Unlike the aforementioned models, the CNN-based TL model consists of the following stages. First, the data set (see Sect. 4.1) was properly curated. The data was then shuffled (i.e., randomly ordered) to ensure that the network fully generalizes to the dataset. Then, the values obtained from the images were normalized, re-scaling the pixel values from the 0–255 range to the 0–1 range, which were used to feed the model. The results obtained using this model were 48.19% accuracy, 37.07% F1 score, 30.38% precision, 48.19% recall.

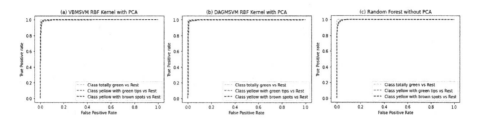

Fig. 3. (a) VBMSVM Kernel RBF with PCA, (b) DAGMSVM Kernel RBF with PCA, (c) Random Forest without PCA.

As shown in Table 1, the VBMSVM RBF Kernel, DAGMSVM RBF Kernel with PCA, and RF without PCA models achieved the best performance for each experimental scenario. Figure 3 shows the multiclass ROC curve of the mentioned models, where they showed a certain superiority when distinguishing the totally green class from the rest. Whereas, for the yellow with green tips classes and yellow with brown spots, it is observed that the curves closest to the upper left corner belong to the DAGMSVM RBF Kernel model, followed by the VBMSVM RBF Kernel model, and lastly, the Random Forest model. Therefore, both variants of the MSVM technique outperformed RF (see Fig. 3(c)). In addition, among the MSVM techniques, it can be seen that DAGMSVM (see Fig. 3(a)) allows the classes yellow with green tips and yellow with brown spots to be recognized more precisely than VBMSVM (see Fig. 3(b)). Besides, Fig. 4 shows the effectiveness of the VBMSVM and DAGMSVM techniques compared to the CNN-based TL model. We can see also that the DAGSVM RBF Kernel technique outperformed both VBMSVM RBF Kernel and CNN-based TL.

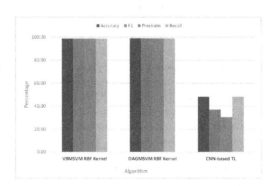

Fig. 4. Comparison of the third experiment with the best models of the previous experiments.

6   Conclusion and Future Work

In this study, an artificial intelligence model was developed to detect the level of ripeness of bananas according to three categories of the Von Loesecke scale:

totally green, yellow with green tips and yellow with brown spots. The constructed model used the DAGMSVM classification technique and the RBF kernel, making use of an 8-fold cross-validation, which allowed obtaining an accuracy of 98.89%. For future work, we plan to collect banana samples of different ripeness stages in Ecuador by preparing a fully controlled environment to avoid the interference of unfavorable environmental conditions. In addition, we plan to examine more deep learning techniques such as CNNs, given their reputation as the ideal models for solving computer vision problems thanks to their ability to extract detailed representations of the content of images.

References

1. El estado de los recursos de tierras y aguas del mundo para la alimentación y la agricultura - Sistemas al límite. FAO, December 2021
2. Ahmad, K.A., Abdullah, N., Osman, M.K., Sulaiman, S.N., Abdullah, M.F., Hussain, Z.: Classification of starfruit ripeness using neural network technique. In: 2020 10th IEEE International Conference on Control System, Computing and Engineering (ICCSCE). IEEE, August 2020
3. Al-Mejibli, I.S., Abd, D.H., Alwan, J.K., Rabash, A.J.: Performance evaluation of kernels in support vector machine. In: 2018 1st Annual International Conference on Information and Sciences (AiCIS). IEEE, November 2018
4. Benos, L., Tagarakis, A.C., Dolias, G., Berruto, R., Kateris, D., Bochtis, D.: Machine learning in agriculture: a comprehensive updated review. Sensors $21(11)$, 3758 (2021)
5. Buades, A., Coll, B., Morel, J.-M.: Non-local means denoising. Image Process. On Line 1, 208–212 (2011)
6. Chandler, S.: The nutritional value of bananas. In: Gowen, S. (ed.) Bananas and Plantains, pp. 468–480. Springer, Dordrecht (1995). https://doi.org/10.1007/978-94-011-0737-2_16
7. Chen, J., Wang, C., Wang, R.: Adaptive binary tree for fast SVM multiclass classification. Neurocomputing $72(13–15)$, 3370–3375 (2009)
8. Elhariri, E., El-Bendary, N., Hussein, A.M.M., Hassanien, A.E., Badr, A.: Bell pepper ripeness classification based on support vector machine. In: 2014 International Conference on Engineering and Technology (ICET). IEEE, April 2014
9. Galar, M., Fernández, A., Barrenechea, E., Bustince, H., Herrera, F.: An overview of ensemble methods for binary classifiers in multi-class problems: experimental study on one-vs-one and one-vs-all schemes. Pattern Recogn. $44(8)$, 1761–1776 (2011)
10. Gayathri, S., Ujwala, T.U., Vinusha, C.V., Pauline, N.R., Tharunika, D.B.: Detection of papaya ripeness using deep learning approach. In: 2021 Third International Conference on Inventive Research in Computing Applications (ICIRCA). IEEE, September 2021
11. Gomes, J.F.S., Vieira, R.R., Leta, F.R.: Colorimetric indicator for classification of bananas during ripening. Scientia Horticulturae 150, 201–205 (2013)
12. Gunawan, K.C., Lie, Z.S.: Apple ripeness level detection based on skin color features with convolutional neural network classification method. In: 2021 7th International Conference on Electrical, Electronics and Information Engineering (ICEEIE). IEEE, October 2021

13. Haralick, R.M., Shanmugam, K., Dinstein, I.: Textural features for image classification. IEEE Trans. Syst. Man Cybern. **SMC-3**(6), 610–621 (1973)
14. Indrabayu, I., Arifin, N., Areni, I.S.: Strawberry ripeness classification system based on skin tone color using multi-class support vector machine. In: 2019 International Conference on Information and Communications Technology (ICOIACT). IEEE, July 2019
15. Joachims, T.: 11 making large-scale support vector machine learning practical. In: Advances in Kernel Methods: Support Vector Learning, p. 169 (1999)
16. Li, D., Yang, W., Wang, S.: Classification of foreign fibers in cotton lint using machine vision and multi-class support vector machine. Comput. Electron. Agric. **74**(2), 274–279 (2010)
17. Liu, Y., Bi, J.-W., Fan, Z.-P.: A method for multi-class sentiment classification based on an improved one-vs-one (OVO) strategy and the support vector machine (SVM) algorithm. Inf. Sci. **394–395**, 38–52 (2017)
18. Macas, M., Chunming, W., Fuertes, W.: A survey on deep learning for cybersecurity: progress, challenges, and opportunities. Comput. Netw. **212**, 109032 (2022)
19. Mazen, F.M.A., Nashat, A.A.: Ripeness classification of bananas using an artificial neural network. Arab. J. Sci. Eng. **44**(8), 6901–6910 (2019)
20. Mesa, A.: Banana project dataset (2021)
21. Meshram, V., Patil, K., Meshram, V., Hanchate, D., Ramkteke, S.D.: Machine learning in agriculture domain: a state-of-art survey. Artif. Intell. Life Sci. **1**, 100010 (2021)
22. University of Alberta. Rembg (2020). https://github.com/danielgatis/rembg. Accessed 02 Mar 2022
23. Pardede, J., Husada, M.G., Hermana, A.N., Rumapea, S.A.: Fruit ripeness based on RGB, HSV, HSL, l∗a∗b∗ color feature using SVM. In: 2019 International Conference of Computer Science and Information Technology (ICoSNIKOM). IEEE, November 2019
24. Piedad Jr., E., Larada, J.I., Pojas, G.J., Ferrer, L.V.V.: Postharvest classification of banana (musa acuminata) using tier-based machine learning. Postharvest Biol. Technol. **145**, 93–100 (2018)
25. Riskiawan, H.Y., Puspitasari, T.D., Hasanah, F.I., Wahyono, N.D., Kurnianto, M.F.: Identifying cocoa ripeness using k-nearest neighbor (KNN) method. In: 2018 International Conference on Applied Science and Technology (iCAST). IEEE, October 2018
26. Saleem, M.H., Potgieter, J., Arif, K.M.: Correction to: automation in agriculture by machine and deep learning techniques: a review of recent developments. Precision Agric. **22**(6), 2092–2094 (2021)
27. Septiarini, A., Hamdani, H., Hatta, H.R., Kasim, A.A.: Image-based processing for ripeness classification of oil palm fruit. In: 2019 5th International Conference on Science in Information Technology (ICSITech). IEEE, October 2019
28. Sheykhmousa, M., Mahdianpari, M., Ghanbari, H., Mohammadimanesh, F., Ghamisi, P., Homayouni, S.: Support vector machine versus random forest for remote sensing image classification: a meta-analysis and systematic review. IEEE J. Sel. Top. Appl. Earth Observ. Remote Sens. **13**, 6308–6325 (2020)
29. Thakur, R., Suryawanshi, G., Patel, H., Sangoi, J.: An innovative approach for fruit ripeness classification. In: 2020 4th International Conference on Intelligent Computing and Control Systems (ICICCS). IEEE, May 2020
30. Von Loesecke, H.W.: Bananas: chemistry, physiology, technology. Technical report, Interscience Publishers (1950)

U–Net vs. TransUNet: Performance Comparison in Medical Image Segmentation

Roberto Castro$^{(\boxtimes)}$ ⓘ, Leo Ramos ⓘ, Stadyn Román ⓘ, Mike Bermeo ⓘ, Anthony Crespo ⓘ, and Erick Cuenca ⓘ

Yachay Tech University, Urcuquí, Ecuador
{roberto.castro,leo.ramos,stadyn.roman,mike.bermeo,
brian.crespo,ecuenca}@yachaytech.edu.ec

Abstract. Image segmentation is a fundamental task in computer-aided diagnosis systems. Correct image segmentation can help healthcare professionals to have better arguments to define a diagnosis and a possible treatment. Among the existing methods and techniques for this task is the TransUNet architecture. This architecture comes from the U-Net architecture, its predecessor, and has the characteristic of incorporating transformers in its encoder. This paper analyzes TransUNet and contrasts its performance with its predecessor. For this purpose, the architectures were implemented, trained, and tested using the Medical Segmentation Decathlon dataset, which provides new challenges and tasks different from those usually addressed. The experimental results reveal the superiority of TransUNet over U-Net in both spleen and left atrium segmentation by reducing the loss in 83% and 72% in the training and testing set, respectively, in the spleen task; and 94% and 92% in the left atrium task. Likewise, in the dice score, TransUNet achieved a superiority of 3.42% and 0.34% for the spleen and left atrium task, respectively, over U-Net.

Keywords: Image segmentation · Supervised learning · Deep learning · Artificial intelligence

1 Introduction

Artificial Intelligence (AI) has a crucial role in medicine, as machines can process many data more optimally and rapidly than humans and identify patterns that they cannot [1]. One of the AI fields used in medicine is computer vision, precisely, medical imaging. Medical imaging allows doctors to analyze various structures to find signs or indications of some disease [2], such as breast cancer detection in women [3] or brain tumor detection [4]. Several imaging techniques have been developed for these applications, such as Magnetic Resonance Imaging (MRI), Computed Tomography (CT) [5], Digital Mammography, and more [6].

Thanks to these approaches, more precise and accurate diagnoses and treatment plans can be obtained in less time [7,8].

Image segmentation is a process that uses an automatic or semi-automatic method to extract the Region of Interest (ROI) [9] for image processing purposes. It consists of taking an image and partitioning it into regions that have similar features and properties [10,11], for example, specific human organs [12].

Classical computer vision techniques have been widely used in medical image processing [13,14]. However, these techniques have limitations when dealing with some typical image segmentation problems, such as trying to segment an object partially covered by another object (i.e., occlusion) [15] and lack of training data, which often leads to an over-fitting problem [16]. Also, these algorithms often do not take advantage of all the information in the image; in fact, many of them only work with 2D and grayscale images [17]. This can significantly affect the quality of the result, as they may omit critical information.

Deep Learning (DL) is a part of the family of AI-based Machine Learning (ML) methods. DL has displaced many of the classical image segmentation techniques. The fast evolution of these approaches allowed the scientific society to achieve better results in terms of result quality, computing requirements, memory capacity, among others [18]. In addition, ML and DL techniques propose solutions and alternatives, such as data augmentation and transfer learning [16,19], to deal with many of the segmentation challenges that classical techniques do not. Furthermore, using ML techniques, specifically DL, provides state-of-the-art solutions to these problems and constant performance improvements [16].

This paper aims to test the TransUNet architecture in conjunction with the U-Net architecture with the tasks of spleen and left atrium segmentation in medical images to analyze its validity, feasibility, and performance, facing a not previously addressed dataset.

2   Related Work

2.1   Medical Image Segmentation Using Neural Networks

Convolutional neural networks (CNNs) have been used to detect many conditions and diseases in medical image segmentation. For example, Niu et al. [20] tested various classifiers, such as SVM, and deep CNNs with images obtained through endoscopy, obtaining better results detecting cancerous cells than human examiners. Also, they developed a system that could automatically detect upper gastrointestinal cancer in real-time. In CT imaging, SVM obtained an accuracy of 96% in segmenting the ROI from the images, allowing the examiners to extract vital information to help the diagnosis.

Sharma and Kaur [21] carried out research work on optimizing the detection of liver tumors and segmentation using neural networks. They used a region-based segmentation on CT scan images to classify tumors by comparing two optimization algorithms, particle swarm optimization (PSO), and seeker optimization algorithm (SOA). They found that PSO was a better algorithm, with an accuracy of 93.3% in classification and detection with an elapsed time of 42.4 s. At the same time, SOA obtained 60% accuracy in classification and detection using elapsed time of 48.7 s.

Xia et al. [22] proposed a fusion scheme that combined the features of multi-scale transformations and deep CNNs. This method used Gauss-Laplace filtering for multi-scaling and a CNN capable of obtaining and fusing high frequency and low-frequency images. They concluded that their method improves various quantitative parameters compared to other existing methods, obtaining, for example, a spatial frequency of 13.640 in medical abdomen images, which was the second-best value, just 0.224 units behind the best value. Recently, Pereira et al. [23] used a smaller convolution kernel in a CNN model to improve the speed of the neural network. They also implemented recalibration and recombination to adapt to the image information and thus improve the results. This did not only improve the extraction speed but also facilitated the acquisition of image features, but resulted in lower accuracy of segmentation, getting scores of at most 0.90 in brain tumor images.

2.2   Medical Image Segmentation Using U-Net

Ronneberger et al. [24] proposed the U-Net model that takes advantage of data augmentation to efficiently use small datasets, which is a necessity in medical imaging. This architecture consisted of a contracting path to capture context and a symmetric expanding path for precise localization. The authors tested the network's performance with different medical image datasets, like images of fly and brain cells, obtaining accuracies of 92% with cultured cells and 77% with brain cells, outperforming the state of the art in that time by 9% and 31% respectively. The authors also found that U-Net was very fast, with the segmentation of a 512×512 image taking less than a second on a single GPU.

Çiçek et al. [25] proposed a variation of U-Net, called 3D U-Net, which enabled 3D volumetric segmentation. The core structure is the same as classic U-Net, but all 2D operations are replaced with corresponding 3D operations, resulting in a 3-dimensional segmented image. The advantage of doing this is that the network can segment images using very few annotated examples because 3D images have many repeating structures and shapes, enabling a faster training process even with few data. The authors obtained an accuracy above 80% in the segmentation of 3D kidney images and demonstrated that their network was well suited for 3D images. Since then, 3D U-net has seen extensive use in medical imaging, going from diagnosis of the cardiac and bone structures, vertebral column, and brain and liver tumors [26].

Khanna et al. [27] proposed a new variation of U-Net combining it with ResNet. They implemented a new network called Residual U-Net that was capable of removing false positives for lung CT segmentation. Their idea was to implement a U-Net architecture composed of residual blocks to overcome the problem of performance degradation and use various data augmentation techniques to improve the generalization capability of the method. They achieved competitive results over the existing methods with accuracies of 98.63%, 99.6%, and 98.68%

for three different medical imaging datasets. In the same way, Chen et al. [28] proposed QSMGAN, which consisted of a 3D U-Net architecture with increased receptive field and refined using a Wasserstein generative adversarial network (WGAN) with gradient penalty. This method allowed to detect brain tumors in patients using radiation-induced cerebral microbleeds and could outperform normal 3D U-Net and non-learning methods, getting a structural similarity index measure (SSIM) of 0.952, higher than the rest of the methods.

2.3 Medical Image Segmentation Using TransUNet

Chen et al. [29] proposed the TransUNet model, which combines the strengths of both Transformers and the U-Net architecture, using tokenized image patches for the encoding process. The decoded images are combined with the high-resolution CNN feature maps to enable precise localization. The authors found that the addition of transformers served as strong encoders for medical image segmentation tasks, with the combination of U-Net to enhance finer details. Furthermore, TransUNet achieved superior performances to other competing methods, obtaining an accuracy of 89.71% on ACDC, a dataset for cardiac image segmentation.

Lin et al. [30] proposed a deep medical image segmentation framework called Dual Swin Transformer U-Net (DS-TransUNet). This framework incorporated the advantages of hierarchical Swin Transformer into both encoder and decoder of the architecture to enhance semantic segmentation in medical images, using a new convolutional block, the Swin Transformer block, to retrieve more information in the decoding process. The authors found that DS-TransUNet was very effective for medical image segmentation, obtaining a precision of 91.6% in the Kvasir dataset, a dataset of gastrointestinal medical images obtained by endoscopy. DS-TransUNet outperformed state-of-the-art methods, including U-Net and some of its variations, like Res-UNet and Double U-Net.

3 Materials and Method

3.1 Dataset Description

The Medical Segmentation Decathlon dataset (MSD) [31] is used for this study. This dataset was designed and tested using different image segmentation algorithms, with the added difficulty that the tasks to which these algorithms were subjected were not previously addressed. The MSD is available under an open-source license, and the macro dataset is divided into multiple subgroups. Specifically, the MSD contains data of ten human body areas: brain, heart, liver, hippocampus, prostate, lung, pancreas, hepatic vessel, spleen, and colon, for a total number of 2633 three-dimensional images. The data comes from multiple anatomies of interest, multiple modalities, and multiple sources and institutions; in addition, all imaging data were acquired through routine clinical scanning.

Regarding the data format, each of the ten datasets is available in TAR format, which includes the directories with the images and labels of the training set and the images of the testing set. Additionally, each image is in the Neuroimaging Informatics Technology Initiative or NIfTI format. Also, a JSON file contains the information required to use the dataset. This file includes the imaging modality that can be MRI, or CT, the number of training and testing images, and the name of each image with its respective label, as seen in Fig. 1.

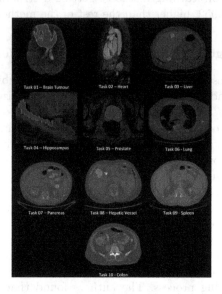

Fig. 1. Exemplar images and labels for each dataset. Blue, white, and red correspond to labels 1, 2, and 3, respectively, of each dataset. Not all tasks have 3 labels. Source: [32] (Color figure online)

3.2   Architectures Under Study

U-Net Model. This model, from its conception, was intended to offer the scientific community a point-to-point convolutional solution to solve segmentation tasks related to medical imaging [24]. This structure is made up of an encoding part or "contracting path" connected to a decoding section or "expansive path".

Since this architecture was originally intended for single-channel images (See Fig. 2), it progressively generates a compact and detailed version of the input as feature maps. This process is carried out through the application of well-defined blocks of layers. On the one hand, two blocks are applied sequentially, each composed of a 3×3 convolutional layer in conjunction with a RELU activation function. After this, a downsampling process is carried out by a 2×2 max pooling operation with a stride of two, which at the same time doubles the number of filters previously used. This process is applied until a representation of 1024 channels is reached. lot .bar

At this point, after a convolutional bottleneck, the inverse process for dimensionality recovery begins. Within the expansive path, these feature maps are still subjected to the same convolution layers with RELU function, with the variation that the max pooling operations are replaced by deconvolutional layers, also known as upsampling layers. In this way, the dimensionality of the image is progressively increased, while the number of channels is halved in each upsampling process. Once the 64 channels are reached, a last 1×1 convolutional layer is applied to give rise to the segmentation mask predicted by the model, returning as many channels as classes involved in the problem.

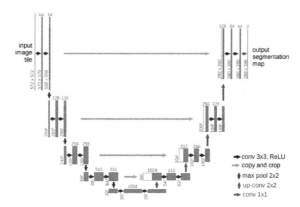

Fig. 2. Composition of the U-Net convolutional model. Source: [24]

It should be noted that in order to solve the loss of context inherent to convolutional approaches aimed at solving segmentation problems, the authors of this model propose the reincorporation of information from the contracting path into the expansive path. This action is performed employing three skip connections that, taking advantage of the symmetry of the architecture, perform a trimming and concatenation process of zones where the number of channels coincides between the encoder and the decoder.

TransUNet Model. For this U-Net-inspired model, the authors seek to incorporate notions beyond the classical convolutional approach that has dominated the field of image segmentation [29]. In this way, and seeking to use much more recent techniques, they propose a hybrid model by employing a Transformer-based portion within the encoding section of the network.

Detailing the general architecture included in Fig. 3, the TransUNet encoder is composed of both a convolutional portion and an attentional structure. In the first instance, given an input image, the convolutional architecture generates its corresponding compressed version as a feature map. At this point, a patch embedding process of size 1×1 is applied so that the Transformer architecture

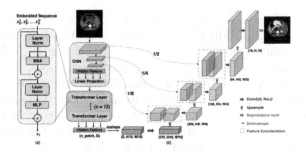

Fig. 3. General overview of the TransUNet model. (a) CNN-Transformer hybrid encoder. (b) Cascade Upsampler. Source: [29].

processes this new version of the raw image. This component corresponds more specifically to the encoder used for the ViT model [33].

Once the encoder output is obtained, the architecture known as Cascade Upsampler is presented. Similar to the original U-Net model, from the application of blocks composed of a convolutional layer, an upsampling process, and a relu activation function, it is sought to recover the original dimensions of the input image, finally obtaining the desired segmentation mask.

As an additional detail, following the methodology of the U-Net derived architectures, different skip connections are included at different resolution levels. This concatenation of information comes from different stages along the convolutional encoder towards the feature maps obtained during the upsampling process.

3.3   Dataset Challenge Selection and Preprocessing

Among the ten different challenges proposed by the dataset selected for the present work, we chose to address the areas dedicated to spleen and left atrium segmentation. Although these specific datasets consists of multiple CT 3D images, the organization in charge of the challenge does not make the ground-truths of the test sets available to the public, so for the present work, a part of the training set was used as test samples.

Spleen Challenge. The 3D volumes of the selected challenge consisted of images of dimension $N \times 512 \times 512$, where N was a non-fixed number defining the depth of the volume. Due to this fact, it was decided to work with models operating with 2D images, so N slices of 416×416 pixels were obtained from each three-dimensional composition.

Then, since not all instances of the dataset contained the body of interest to be segmented, we removed those images that did not provide relevant segmentation knowledge for the models. Thus, the challenging images were separated into training and testing sets, consisting of 840 and 211 slices, respectively. As an additional step, due to the high resolution of the images and taking into consideration the limited amount of VRAM memory available for training, we proceeded to symmetrically crop each of the instances together with their respective segmentation masks. After this step, 416×416 pixel images were obtained, taking care not to affect the sections involving the body of interest.

Heart Challenge. Unlike the previous challenge, the images to be processed present slices of 320×320 pixels each. Considering this fact, these images were not cropped due to their smaller size. As for the preprocessing for this data set, the three-dimensional volumes were again decomposed into their corresponding two-dimensional anatomical slices, eliminating those that did not include the body of interest. Thus, 1080 images were used in the training phase, while 271 were reserved for the testing phase.

3.4   Model Specifications, Hyperparameters and Training

Regarding specific aspects of the models studied, on the one hand, the official implementation of the original authors was used for the TransUNet model[1]. Among the different variants available, we chose to use a model composed of a ViT-Base architecture of 12 transformer blocks and 12 attention heads, together with a ResNet-50 convolutional network.

For the U-Net model, we chose to use the same construction as shown in Fig. ??, by changing only the number of initial filters, from 64 to 32 filters. This decision was taken so that, before both architectures generate the respective segmentation mask, they have a similar number of filters, seeking to balance scenarios as much as possible to achieve a more relevant contrast.

Once the models were built, and the dataset was prepared, the training parameters were defined. The same hyperparameter settings were used for both U-Net and TransUNet. A batch size of 10 slices was defined since it was the maximum possible size before a VRAM memory overflow of the graphics card used for training (NVIDIA A100 GPU). Since the task is to solve a binary classification task, a binary cross-entropy was set as a loss function, defined as follows for each of the n batches:

$$l_n = -[y_n * log x_n + (1 - y_n) * log(1 - x_n)] \tag{1}$$

where y_i corresponds to the respective targets and X_i to the scores generated by the network.

In addition, the Adam optimizer was used to adjust the learnable parameters. However, for the spleen segmentation challenge, a learning rate of 0.00095 was used, while for the heart segmentation task, it was decided to reduce this hyperparameter to 0.00006. These values were selected after a previous phase, where different alternatives were evaluated for this section.

---

[1] https://github.com/Beckschen/TransUNet (accessed on March 2022).

4   Results and Discussion

Regarding the metrics defined for the evaluation and comparison between models, it was decided to consider the evolution of the loss, both in the training and testing phases, over 30 epochs. Mainly, this decision was made to verify the effective training of the models and their viability to generalize knowledge to previously unseen instances. Additionally, the Sorensen-Dice Coefficient (dice score) was chosen to quantify the quality/precision of the predictions concerning the ground-truths of the test set.

4.1   Spleen Segmentation

Starting by analyzing the results during the training phase, as shown in Fig. 4a, both models show training curves that denote a satisfactory progressive adjustment of the learnable parameters. However, it should be noted that in terms of convergence, the TransUNet model shows a much earlier stabilization, being close to epoch number 20. On the other hand, U-Net reaches a similar situation only when the training process reaches the last five epochs.

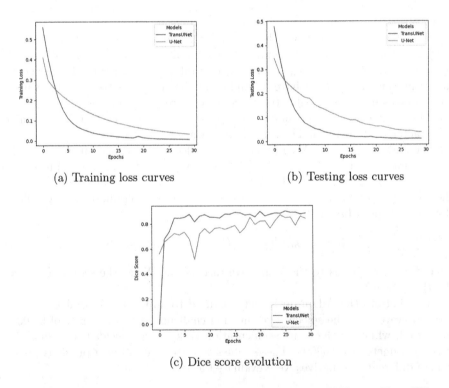

(a) Training loss curves

(b) Testing loss curves

(c) Dice score evolution

Fig. 4. Curves of loss and dice score for spleen segmentation: U-Net vs. TransUNet.

The same scenario is shown for the test set (See Fig. 4b). Again, a much more accelerated convergence by the TransUNet model is highlighted. In addition, the U-Net curve stands out for the presence of specific peaks that are not very pronounced, unlike its contender. Thus, the classical model's higher incidence of overfitting can be inferred. Focusing now on the evolution of the dice score shown in Fig. 4c, the results previously analyzed are reflected. As expected, this metric remains unstable throughout the initial epochs, becoming increasingly stable as the model converges. Therefore, in the case of TransUNet, this desired scenario is obtained early in contrast to the U-Net architecture.

Table 1 shows the three evaluation indicators defined for this work, TransUNet emerges as the best option for this task. A margin of improvement of approximately 3.42% in terms of the maximum score achieved by this model stands out. In addition, the minimum training loss achieved in contrast to U-Net is reduced by approximately 83% and by 72% in the case of the test group.

Table 1. Table of results contrasting the performance of the U-Net and TransUNet architectures facing the spleen segmentation challenge.

	Dice score	Train loss	Test loss
U-Net	0.8696	0.0314	0.0391
TransUNet	**0.8993**	**0.0053**	**0.0108**

In further support of the results shown, Fig. 5 displays a contrast of the performance between U-Net and TransUNet in generating their corresponding predictions for a randomly extracted image from the test set along with its ground-truth. The accuracy of both models is more than evident, however, pointing out the error made by U-Net in segmenting an additional area away from the object of interest.

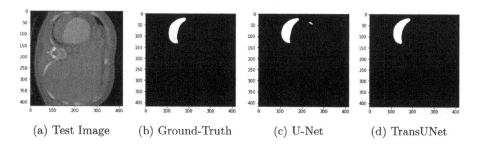

(a) Test Image   (b) Ground-Truth   (c) U-Net   (d) TransUNet

Fig. 5. Comparison of the predictions generated by the trained models with respect to the original image and its corresponding ground-truth for the spleen segmentation task.

4.2 Left Atrium Segmentation

Turning to the results concerning the left atrial segmentation challenge, Fig. 6a shows the adequate training of both models. Again, the same scenario is repeated regarding the convergence of the models, with the results obtained by TransUNet being even more favorable. For epoch 30, the U-Net graph does not reach a flat trend that denotes the optimal stabilization of the model.

As expected, the pattern previously seen extends to the evolution of loss for the test set, as shown in Fig. 6b. TransUNet again stands out for requiring fewer epochs to reach a loss stability phase. Despite the previously mentioned behavior regarding the loss both using the training and test set, the situation regarding the dice score is considerably competitive, as shown in Fig. 6c. Both graphs are very similar, so a simple graphical analysis does not allow highlighting one model over the other.

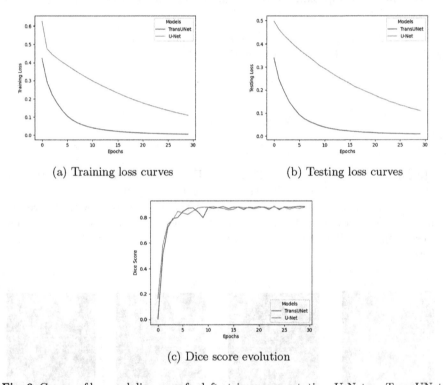

(a) Training loss curves   (b) Testing loss curves

(c) Dice score evolution

Fig. 6. Curves of loss and dice score for left atrium segmentation: U-Net vs. TransUNet.

Table 2 shows the metrics results. For this scenario, TransUNet reduces the minimum loss achieved during the training process by 94% and by 92% for the test set. However, the margin of improvement in the dice score metric is much more modest, showing a margin of improvement of approximately 0.34% concerning U-Net.

Table 2. Table of results contrasting the performance of the U-Net and TransUNet architectures facing the left atrium segmentation challenge.

	Dice score	Train loss	Test loss
U-Net	0.8866	0.1099	0.1098
TransUNet	**0.8901**	**0.0056**	**0.0088**

Finally, as for the spleen segmentation challenge, the reader is provided with a visual contrast of the predictions elaborated by the trained models from an image belonging to the test group (see Fig. 7). In this case, unlike its hybrid counterpart, the U-Net model does not recognize the three portions of the body of interest contained in the input image, generating an incomplete segmentation mask concerning the ground-truth and the prediction of the TransUNet model.

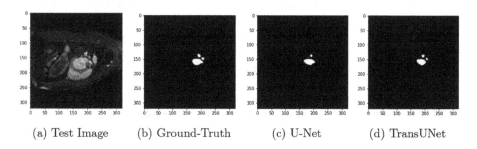

(a) Test Image   (b) Ground-Truth   (c) U-Net   (d) TransUNet

Fig. 7. Comparison of the predictions generated by the trained models with respect to the original image and its corresponding ground-truth for the left atrium segmentation task.

5   Conclusions and Future Work

This work evaluated two image segmentation architectures: U-Net, a purely convolutional architecture, and TransUNet, a hybrid model. The objective was to evaluate these architectures by testing them with two medical image segmentation tasks: spleen segmentation and left atrium segmentation, both belonging to "The Medical Segmentation Decathlon" dataset.

Visual results show that TransUNet can better segment both the spleen and left atrium in most cases. On the other hand, U-Net may present erroneous segmentation masks, either segmenting additional structures that do not correspond to the region of interest or not segmenting all the components of interest, delivering incomplete segmentation masks on some occasions.

Regarding the quantitative results related to spleen segmentation, TransUNet improved in approximately 3.42% of the dice score results compared to U-Net. Also, the loss was significantly lower in TransUNet, being 83% and 72% lower than that of the convolutional model, in the training and testing phase, respectively. Regarding the left atrium segmentation, similar results were observed since the loss in TransUNet was 94% lower in the training phase and 92% lower in the testing phase in contrast to U-Net. However, the improvement of the dice score was discrete since TransUNet only outperformed U-Net by approximately 0.34%. It is also important to mention that TransUNet showed a much earlier stabilization in terms of convergence while U-Net reached a similar situation in the later epochs.

While the present study compared U-Net and TransUNet with two segmentation tasks, the number of segmentation tasks can be increased to better contrast the architectures. TransUNet demonstrated a more significant improvement in the spleen segmentation task regarding Dice Score. The images for this task are of 416×416 resolution. On the other hand, TransUNet's superiority was reduced in the left atrium segmentation task, for which the images are 320×320 resolution. A hypothesis arises from this: TransUNet seems to show better performance as the image dimensions are larger, in contrast to U-Net. This hypothesis could be corroborated or refuted by extending the number of tasks with images of different dimensions to have a better conclusion about the performance of the architectures. Also, additional techniques, such as data augmentation, can be incorporated to improve the final results.

Acknowledgement. The authors are grateful for the valuable support given by the SDAS Research Group (www.sdas-group.com - Last accessed: 07 - Jun - 2022).

References

1. Patel, D., Shah, Y., Thakkar, N., Shah, K., Shah, M.: Implementation of artificial intelligence techniques for cancer detection. Augment. Hum. Res. **5** (2020)
2. Rengier, F., et al.: 3D printing based on imaging data: review of medical applications. Int. J. Comput. Assist. Radiol. Surg. **5**(4), 335–341 (2010)
3. Yuan, X., Wang, Y., Yuan, J., Cheng, Q., Wang, X., Carson, P.L.: Medical breast ultrasound image segmentation by machine learning. Ultrasonics **91**, 1–9 (2019)
4. Kharrat, A., Benamrane, N., Messaoud, M.B., Abid, M.: Detection of brain tumor in medical images. In: International Conference on Signals, Circuits and Systems, pp. 1–6. IEEE (2009)
5. Chuquín, S., Cuenca, E.: Computerized tomography images processing using artificial intelligence techniques. In: Botto-Tobar, M., Cruz, H., Díaz Cadena, A., Durakovic, B. (eds.) CIT 2021. LNNS, vol. 405, pp. 205–218. Springer, Cham (2022). https://doi.org/10.1007/978-3-030-96043-8_16
6. Norouzi, A., et al.: Medical image segmentation methods, algorithms, and applications. IETE Tech. Rev. **31**(3), 199–213 (2014)
7. Krupinski, E.A., Jiang, Y.: Anniversary paper: evaluation of medical imaging systems. Med. Phys. **35**(2), 645–659 (2008)
8. Rietzel, E., Chen, G.T.Y., Choi, N.C., Willet, C.G.: Four-dimensional image-based treatment planning: target volume segmentation and dose calculation in the presence of respiratory motion. Int. J. Radiat. Oncol.* Biol.* Phys. **61**(5), 1535–1550 (2005)

9. Pal, N.R., Pal, S.K.: A review on image segmentation techniques. Pattern Recogn. **26**(9), 1277–1294 (1993)

10. Jyothi, S., Bhargavi, K.: A survey on threshold based segmentation technique in image processing. Int. J. Innov. Res. Dev. **3**(12), 234–239 (2014)

11. Kaur, D., Kaur, Y.: International journal of computer science and mobile computing various image segmentation techniques: a review. Int. J. Comput. Sci. Mob. Comput. **3**(5), 809–814 (2014)

12. Wu, J., Ye, F., Ma, J.-L., Sun, X.-P., Xu, J., Cui, Z.-M.: The segmentation and visualization of human organs based on adaptive region growing method. In: International Conference on Computer and Information Technology Workshops, pp. 439–443. IEEE (2008)

13. Huang, T.S., et al.: Computer vision: evolution and promise. In: CERN European Organization for Nuclear Research-Reports-CERN, pp. 21–26 (1996)

14. Ávila-Tomás, J.F., Mayer-Pujadas, M.A., Quesada-Varela, V.J.: Artificial intelligence and its applications in medicine II: current importance and practical applications. Atencion Primaria **53**(1), 81–88 (2020)

15. Hoiem, D., Efros, A.A., Hebert, M.: Recovering occlusion boundaries from an image. Int. J. Comput. Vision **91**(3), 328–346 (2011)

16. Goceri, E.: Challenges and recent solutions for image segmentation in the era of deep learning. In International Conference on Image Processing Theory, Tools and Applications, pp. 1–6 (2019)

17. Kang, W.-X., Yang, Q.-Q., Liang, R.-P.: The comparative research on image segmentation algorithms. In: International Workshop on Education Technology and Computer Science, vol. 2, pp. 703–707. IEEE (2009)

18. O'Mahony, N., et al.: Deep learning vs. traditional computer vision. In: Arai, K., Kapoor, S. (eds.) CVC 2019. AISC, vol. 943, pp. 128–144. Springer, Cham (2020). https://doi.org/10.1007/978-3-030-17795-9_10

19. Hesamian, M.H., Jia, W., He, X., Kennedy, P.: Deep learning techniques for medical image segmentation: achievements and challenges. J. Digit. Imaging **32**, 582–596 (2019)

20. Peng-Hui Niu, L.-L., Zhao, H.-L.W., Zhao, D.-B., Chen, T.: Artificial intelligence in gastric cancer: application and future perspectives. World J. Gastroenterol. **26**, 5408–5419 (2020)

21. Sharma, A., Kaur, P.: Optimized liver tumor detection and segmentation using neural network. Int. J. Recent Technol. Eng. **2**(5), 7–10 (2013)

22. Xia, K., Yin, H., Wang, J.: A novel improved deep convolutional neural network model for medical image fusion. Cluster Comput. **22** (2019)

23. Pereira, S., Pinto, A., Amorim, J., Ribeiro, A., Alves, V., Silva, C.A.: Adaptive feature recombination and recalibration for semantic segmentation with fully convolutional networks. IEEE Trans. Med. Imaging **38**(12), 2914–2925 (2019)

24. Ronneberger, O., Fischer, P., Brox, T.: U-net: convolutional networks for biomedical image segmentation. In: Navab, N., Hornegger, J., Wells, W.M., Frangi, A.F. (eds.) MICCAI 2015. LNCS, vol. 9351, pp. 234–241. Springer, Cham (2015). https://doi.org/10.1007/978-3-319-24574-4_28

25. Çiçek, Ö., Abdulkadir, A., Lienkamp, S.S., Brox, T., Ronneberger, O.: 3D U-net: learning dense volumetric segmentation from sparse annotation. In: Ourselin, S., Joskowicz, L., Sabuncu, M.R., Unal, G., Wells, W. (eds.) MICCAI 2016. LNCS, vol. 9901, pp. 424–432. Springer, Cham (2016). https://doi.org/10.1007/978-3-319-46723-8_49

26. Siddique, N., Paheding, S., Elkin, C.P., Devabhaktuni, V.: U-net and its variants for medical image segmentation: a review of theory and applications. IEEE Access **9**, 82031–82057 (2021)

27. Khanna, A., Londhe, N., Gupta, S., Semwal, A.: A deep residual U-net convolutional neural network for automated lung segmentation in computed tomography images. Biocybern. Biomed. Eng. **40**(3), 1314–1327 (2020)

28. Chen, Y., Jakary, A., Avadiappan, S., Hess, C., Lupo, J.: QSMGAN: improved quantitative susceptibility mapping using 3D generative adversarial networks with increased receptive field. Neuroimage **207**, 116389 (2019)

29. Chen, J., et al. TransUNet: transformers make strong encoders for medical image segmentation. Computing Research Repository, abs/2102.04306 (2021)

30. Lin, A.-J., Chen, B., Xu, J., Zhang, Z., Lu, G.: DS-TransUNet: dual swin transformer U-net for medical image segmentation. abs/2106.06716 (2021)

31. Antonelli, M., et al.: The medical segmentation decathlon. arXiv preprint arXiv:2106.05735 (2021)

32. Simpson, A.L., et al.: A large annotated medical image dataset for the development and evaluation of segmentation algorithms. arXiv preprint arXiv:1902.09063 (2019)

33. Dosovitskiy, A., et al.: An image is worth 16x16 words: transformers for image recognition at scale. Computing Research Repository, abs/2010.11929 (2020)

Access Control Through Mask Detection and Estimation of People Capacity in Covered Premises

Rodrigo Silva$^{(\boxtimes)}$, Andrés Zapata, and Darwin Alulema

Departamento de Eléctrica, Electrónica y Telecomunicaciones, Universidad de las Fuerzas Armadas – ESPE, Sangolquí 171103, Ecuador
{rsilva,amzapata3,doalulema}@espe.edu.ec

Abstract. The health emergency due to the COVID-19 pandemic requires the search for technological and intelligent solutions that facilitate the control of biosecurity measures such as social distancing, to use of a mask, and capacity in covered spaces. This work aims to develop a prototype based on artificial vision algorithms, capable of performing the automatic mask detection and people counting who go to covered premises such as bars, restaurants, gyms, cinemas, and micro-market among others. The prototype implements SSD-MobileNet object detection and SORT tracking algorithms that work on the electronic device NVIDIA Jetson Nano, equipped with two video cameras to perform mask detection and people counting respectively, as well as speakers, for emission of audible alert messages about the use of mask and the capacity estimation within the premise and an external web server too in which people counter information is displayed.

Keywords: COVID-19 · Artificial vision · Mask detection · People counter · MobileNet

1 Introduction

The health emergency caused by Coronavirus meant a dramatic global change in the socioeconomic field and especially in health; so, it was necessary to take some preventive measures to try to reduce the spread of COVID-19 virus among people. In a few months, the Coronavirus managed to expand rapidly among many countries in the world, so on March 11th 2020, the World Health Organization declared of COVID-19 pandemic presence, urging countries to take measures and join efforts to control the largest public health of the world in modern times [1].

Among the most important measures adopted to avoid the massive virus contagion, there is the use of masks and social distancing, which in many countries have been adopted in a mandatory way, and even its non-compliance is a reason for economic sanctions for noncompliance [2]. The attempt of the local authorities in Ecuador to create social awareness among citizens has had a slight impact, since the non-compliance with prevention measures is a situation that is experienced daily, and which has resulted in hospitals working at the limit of their capacity, and even exist people waiting for

M. Botto-Tobar et al. (Eds.): ICAT 2022, CCIS 1755, pp. 227–239, 2023.
https://doi.org/10.1007/978-3-031-24985-3_17

outpatient care or in intensive care units, facts that generated concern even though the vaccination plan of the government of Ecuador has advanced at an accelerated pace [3].

In context, technology could play an important role in providing solutions for the control measures prevention, whose task involves somewhat difficult but necessary actions, since the use of masks and compliance with the capacity allowed by the effect of social distancing within closed spaces, can contribute greatly to stopping the infection wave. For this reason, the development of autonomous smart devices, capable of performing the automatic mask detection placed on people's faces and people controlling capacity in places of mass access, could become a great technological challenge in the eagerness to try to counteract the advance of the pandemic. The present work proposes to implement a prototype which the access people control can be carried out at the main entrance of premises or closed spaces, by detecting the use of masks and also to account people capacity within them.

This article is structured with the following sections: (ii) Our proposal, this section describes the conceptual idea of the prototype through the models for mask detection and people counting; (iii) models implementation, training and inference actions of the models on the Nvidia Jetson Nano card are described to implement our mask detector and people counter; (iv) tests and results, to validate the prototype, performance tests of the prototype are carried out in controlled real environments, and (v) conclusions and future work that emerges for the development of new applications.

2   Our Proposal

In this paper, we propose to develop a prototype portable and autonomous device whose scheme architecture general is shown in Fig. 1. The algorithms processing is done through an NVIDIA Jetson Nano development card, equipped with external devices such as video cameras, speakers, and Wi-Fi server connectivity, which it allow to reproduce audible and visual information as warning signs of the system, both for access through mask detection, and too the capacity estimation through the people account.

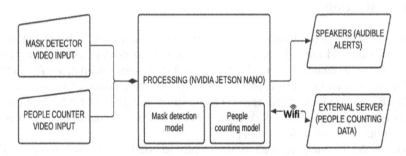

Fig. 1. Prototype general scheme

2.1   Mask Detection Model

The implementation mask detection model shown in Fig. 2 requires the retraining of the MobilenetV1 object detector model [4] for mask detection and Nvidia card inference made through a Docker container with Tensor RT framework considering three conditions detection: a) face with mask b) face without a mask and c) face with a misplaced mask.

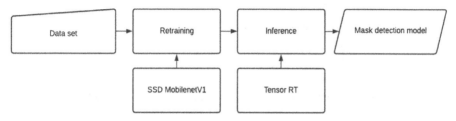

Fig. 2. Mask detection model

2.2 People Counting Model

The people counting model is shown in Fig. 3. It consists of two parts: MobilnetV1 people detection algorithm and SORT algorithm [5] for tracking objects operating on each frame that is being processed with a combination of these algorithms, it is possible to count in real time the people who enter or leave an enclosed space and then present the estimate of the capacity expressed in percentage through audible messages, which alert people by capacity is incomplete or full, and too at administrator place through a monitor screen.

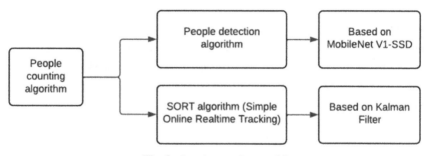

Fig. 3. People counting model

3 Model Implementation

3.1 Mask Detector

Mask detection is implemented by transferring learning from a pre-trained model of Mobilenet network [6] through a Docker or container provided by Nvidia Jetson-inference. The container implements Pytorch for the transfer learning task and Tensor RT for the inference the object detection models that based train on a dataset obtained from Kaggle [7] with 853 marked images of three classes that are: a) face with a maskb) face without mask and c) face with the mask used incorrectly, to shown in Fig. 4.

Fig. 4. Faces with masks and labeling for training taken from (Kaggle, 2020)

3.2 Training

The dataset previously obtained from Kaggle is converted to VOC PASCAL (Pattern Analysis, Statistical Modeling, and Computational Learning) format. In this case, the imaging data is divided, 10% for testing and 90% for training, which is a conventional assignment used for detection model training. The MobileNet SSD network retraining Docker in mask detection is located in a Python script which is configured with the parameters shown in Table 1. This new training was done on the Jetson Nano card whose performance in terms of image processing per second and the training duration by epoch are shown in Table 2.

Table 1. Retraining parameters

Argument	Value	Description
--data	data/	Dataset directory location
--model-dir	models/	Control points of the trained model directory
|--batch-size	4	Images number taken in each iteration
--epochs	50	Times number for training

Table 2. Training duration

	Images/s	Time/epoch [s]
Jetson Nano	≈5	≈2 min 50 s
Training duration	≈2 h 22 min	

3.3 Inference

For inference to be made with TensorRT, it is necessary to change the model to ONNX (Open Neural Network Exchange) format, which uses a script provided by the NVIDIA container. Once we have the model in ONNX format it's possible to run it through *detectnet.py* file, this script makes inference to the model and allows mask detection in real-time as shown in Fig. 5.

Fig. 5. Detection model inference on Nvidia card

3.4 People Counter

People counter shown in Fig. 6 implements two algorithms: people detector based on the MobilenetV1-COCO network and SORT object tracking detector based on Faster RCNN networks and Kalman filter. A Tensorflow trained model is used for people detection and then performing the inference via Tensor RT so that it can run on the Nvidia card.

As a strategy to perform people counting as shown Fig. 7(a) an algorithm is implemented that serves to discriminate the tracker path from one zone to another, considering the image division of the frame into two regions, one as input and in the reverse case as output as shown Fig. 7(b).

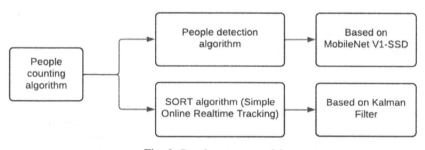

Fig. 6. People counter model

3.5 Audible Messages Implementation

Audible messages are shown in Fig. 8 act as alarms that are triggered only by validation parameters in certain video frames.

```
for t, trk in enumerate(trackers):
        if t not in unmatched_trks:
        d = matched [np.where(matched[:, 1] == t)[0], 0]
        trk. update(boxes[d, :][0])
        xmin, ymin, xmax, ymax = boxes [d, :][0]
        cy = int ((ymin + ymax) / 2)
        #IN count
        if idstp[trk.id][0][1] < H // 2 and cy > H // 2 and trk.id not in idcnt:
        incnt += 1
        idcnt. append(trk.id)
        #OUT count
        elif idstp[trk.id][0][1] > H // 2 and cy < H // 2 and trk.id not in
idcnt:
        outcnt += 1
```

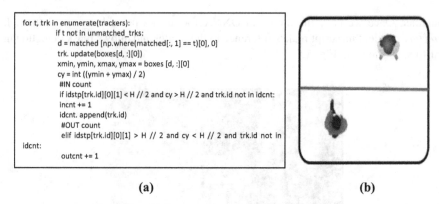

(a)   **(b)**

Fig. 7. People counter deployment. (a) Tracking algorithm (b) tracker reference

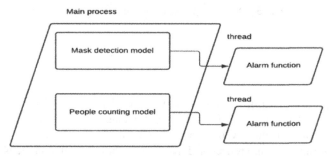

Fig. 8. Alarm message model

The alarm function of the mask detector is implemented with the code shown in Fig. 9(a) where the validation parameter is the confidence percentage in the detection of each object class, to ensure reliable class detection, with a masked face and without it. Validation is performed when detection exceeds 90% confidence percentage, while for the incorrectly used mask class, a 60% confidence percentage is established due to the performance of the detection model.

```
if (len(detections)==1):
        if(detection. Confidence>0.90):
                if(detection. ClassID==2):
                alarma.sin_mascarilla()
                if(detection. ClassID==1):
                alarma.con_mascarilla()
        if(detection. Confidence>0.40):
                if(detection. ClassID==3):
                alarma.mal_mascarilla()
```

```
CNT = incnt-outcnt
if(CNT == round(0.5*CAPACITY)):
        alarm.capacity50()
if(CNT == round(0.75*AFORO)):
        alarm.capacity75()
if(CNT > CAPACITY):
        alarm.aforolleno()
```

(a)   **(b)**

Fig. 9. Alarm message deployment (a) mask detector alarm code (b) people counter alarm code

People counter code shown in Fig. 9(b) is used, which establishes the criterion for activating audible messages when the capacity of the premises is at 50, 75, and 100% occupied. For this, validations based on the number of people who are inside the premises or enclosed space are required.

3.6 Capacity Server Deployment

A particular server is used, on which a simple interface is built where the two values associated with the people account are: people number who are inside the establishment and capacity alert is at 50%, 75% or if the capacity is full Fig. 10(a). For sending of the data to the server, the code shown in Fig. 10(b) was implemented, in which CNT counter data is sent, this contains the people number who are inside the establishment and the text string that has two states, incomplete capacity, and full capacity. These validations are carried out in SORT algorithm using the CNT values, which is the number who are inside the establishment, and the capacity configurable value, which depends on the capacity allowed in the environment test it is going to be put into operation.

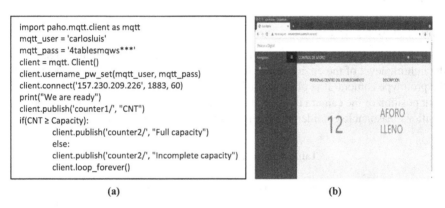

(a)   (b)

Fig. 10. Capacity server (a) server displaying (b) connection to server code

3.7 Prototype Assembly

The prototype uses two video cameras, an IMX 219 camera connected at Jetson Nano video port for mask detector and a Logitech C70 camera to the USB port for the people counter. Wireless adapter type USB Wi-Fi for connection of the prototype at a web server on internet, audio adapter type USB 2.0 to jack 3.5 mm for connection of speakers, as are shown in Fig. 11.

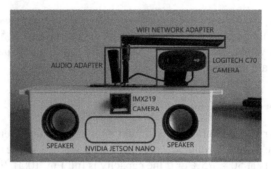

Fig. 11. Prototype assembly

4 Tests and Results

With the idea this prototype can be installed and tested in real environments such as bars, restaurants, gyms, and micro-markets, among others, multiple recurrent lab tests were first performed, both with mask detector and people counter.

4.1 Mask Detector Test

Mask detector tests criteria consider the position of the camera concerning a light source, the lighting level of the environment during the daytime, and the distance person from the prototype camera. It is observed in Table 3 that there are detection problems in the front position of the camera in front of the light source, while in the lateral and opposite positions reasonable confidence percentages are obtained with mask detection.

Table 3. Tests concerning light position

Relative position to the light source	With mask (% confidence)	Incorrectly used mask (% confidence)	No mask (% confidence)
Front (BACKLIGHT)	60%	Erroneous detection	Erroneous detection
Left side	98%	66%	98%
Right side	98%	68%	98%
Opposite	99%	75%	99%

As can be seen, in Table 4, the illumination percentage varies at different daytime concerning solar lighting, which results in variation in the confidence percentages of detections. However, it is important to mention that this variation range is not so wide, so for the prototype operation, it can be configured between ranges within the validations of percentages confidence.

In test detection in Table 5, reasonable values were obtained in the detection percentages at a distance of 0.8 to 1 m. This parameter is important because it can draw a maximum distance where the person is located for detection and obtain a reliable detection.

Table 4. Screening tests at different times and lighting level

Hour	With mask (% confidence)	Incorrectly used mask (% confidence)	No mask (% confidence)
8:00 (with lighting)	91%%	45%	92%
10:00	92%	56%	95%
12:00	99%	72%	98%
14:00	99%	70%	99%
16:00	96%	63%	96%
18:00 (with lighting)	95%	55%	93%
20:00 (with lighting)	92%	52%	92%

Table 5. Distance screening tests

Distance [m]	With mask (% confidence)	Incorrectly used mask (% confidence)	No mask (% confidence)
0.2	80%	27%	80%
0.4	89%	45%	88%
0.6	97%	68%	97%
0.8	99%	75%	99%
1	98%	65%	98%
1.2	95%	55%	94%
1.4	92%	42%	93%
1.6	88%	36%	88%
1.8	85%	No detection	84%
2	85%	No detection	83%

4.2 People Counter Test

In Table 6 we can see that the people detection camera should be located in a height range of 2.75 to 3.5 m. While at heights less or greater than, range errors occur in the count of the people number, so such a range is recommended for the people counter operation correct.

4.3 Real Scenery Test

To carry out these tests it was necessary to account for the integrated operation of the mask detection model, such as the people counter, audible alerts, and the presentation of the values associated with the counter on the external server. The device operation has the first objective to control the people's entry based on the allowed capacity, and

Table 6. People counter tests

Distance [m]	Income		Exit	
	Correct detection and counting	No detection	Correct detection and counting	No detection
2	6	4	8	2
2.25	7	3	8	2
2.5	9	1	10	0
2.75	10	0	10	0
3	10	0	10	0
3.25	10	0	10	0
3.50	10	0	10	0
3.75	10	0	10	0
4	8	2	9	1

once met this parameter, verify the use of mask, because it may not make sense that if the capacity is full, people should no longer enter the detection of mask and the work synchronism of both functionalities is also ensured.

The provision of elements indicated in Fig. 12(a) takes into consideration a real environment of the closed premises. The camera for mask detection is located inside the test establishment, Fig. 12(b) which will be at a prudent distance from the camera of the person counter, this allows the mask detection function after counting entry of the person.

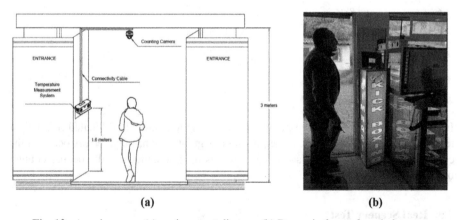

(a)   (b)

Fig. 12. A real scenery (a) environment diagram (b) Person in front of mask detector

The Fig. 13 shows the results with the images of the mask detector associated with the people counter and the capacity information viewer.

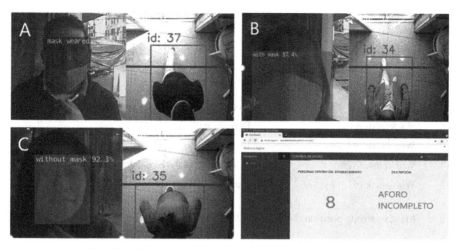

Fig. 13. Mask detection and people counting in real scenery

Finally, some results of people arriving at the closed premises we observe in Table 7 with the different possible results of mask use and the audible messages created in the respective capacity situation.

Table 7. System results operating in a real scenario

User	Mask detection	People account	Audible messages alarms
1	With mask (96.2%)	Income (1)	Mask detected, Welcome
2	No mask (93.3%)	Income (2)	Put on your mask
3	With mask (82.1%)	Income (3)	Mask detected, Welcome
4	With mask (91.1%)	Income (4)	Mask detected, Welcome
5	With mask (85.8%)	Income (5)	Mask detected, Welcome
6	With mask (93.3%)	Income (6)	Mask detected, Welcome Capacity at 50%
7	No detection	Departure (5)	
8	No detection	Departure (4)	
9	With a mask (88.1%)	Income (5)	Mask detected, Welcome
10	Mask in wrong position (43.8%)	Income (6)	Put on your mask correctly
11	No mask (94.7%)	Income (7)	Put on your mask
12	With mask (94.8%)	Income (8)	Mask detected, Welcome

(*continued*)

Table 7. (*continued*)

User	Mask detection	People account	Audible messages alarms
13	With mask (92.1%)	Income (9)	Mask detected, Welcome Capacity at 75%
14	With mask (88.0%)	Income (10)	Mask detected, Welcome
15	No detection	Departure (9)	
16	With mask (93.3%)	Income (10)	Mask detected, Welcome
17	With mask (87%)	Admission (11)	Mask detected, Welcome
18	With mask (91.9%)	Income (12)	Mask detected, Welcome 100% capacity
19	Mask in wrong position (56.5%)	Admission (13)	Capacity at 100%, Do not enter

5 Conclusions

The prototype tests were satisfactory with good performance can be obtained in the speed of image processing, taking into account the computational limitations of the Nvidia card, although there are more complex algorithms in which the problem of occlusion can be mitigated, however, these algorithms also require more processing power than the hardware used.

Mask detection and people count performance, are determined by the lighting level of the environment, and play a preponderant role, so it is necessary to accommodate both the camera position to avoid the effect of backlight, as well as the distance of the person concerning it. For detection training, it is important to configure their parameters based on the computational capacity of the device, so care must be taken with the training iterations number as well as with the processed images batch because prolonged working time raises the temperature. It could be verified that an increase could cause errors that sometimes prevent concluding with the training process.

Future Work
The application models based on Artificial Intelligence are increasing, however, the focus on its development is rarely oriented to solve social problems. That is important because AI has a great field in security applications, an aspect in our country that has great deficiencies. Due to this, as future work, it is proposed to use the same conception of the present project, oriented on weapons detection within closed establishments, with alerts that can be generated, when it endangers the situation of the users of an establishment. These alerts can be sent to external servers at the time of weapons detection or dangerous objects, so that security agents, whether public or private, can take immediate action in the face of these facts. It can also be reoriented towards its application on public transport since today the use of a mask and the control of capacity within transport units is one of the main supervisory factors in the current pandemic.

References

1. Díaz, F., Toro, A.: SARS-CoV-2/COVID-19 the virus, the disease and the pandemic. Medicina Labotatorio **24**(3) (2020)
2. Sedano, F., Rojas, C., Vela, J.: COVID-19 from the perspective of primary prevention. Scielo (2020)
3. Chauca, R.: Covid-19 in Ecuador: political fragility. Scielo **28**(2), 587 (2020)
4. Andrew, G.H., Zhu, M.: MobileNets: efficient convolutional neural networks for mobile vision applications. arXiv:1704.04861v1 [cs.CV] (2017)
5. Bewley, Z. Ge, L. Ott, F.R., Upcroft, B.: Simple online and realtime tracking. In: 2016 IEEE International Conference on Image Processing (ICIP), pp. 3464–3468 (2016)
6. Andrade, H., Sinche, S., Hidalgo, P.: Model to detect the correct use of masks in real-time. J. Inf. Technol. Res. **9**(17) (2021)
7. Bewley, A., Ge, Z.: Simple online and real-time tracking. Queensland, Sydney (2017). arXiv: 1602.00763v2 [cs.CV] (2016)

Customer Segmentation in Food Retail Sector: An Approach from Customer Behavior and Product Association Rules

Juan Llivisaca[1,2]([✉]) [ID] and Jonnatan Avilés-González[3] [ID]

[1] Dirección de Posgrado, Universidad Politécnica Estatal del Carchi, Av. Universitaria y Antisana, Tulcán, Ecuador
`juan.llivisaca@ucuenca.edu.ec`
[2] Department of Applied Chemistry and Systems of Production, Faculty of Chemical Sciences, University of Cuenca, 010107 Cuenca, Ecuador
[3] Facultad de CCTT, Centro de Investigación en Ingeniería de Producción y Operaciones, Universidad del Azuay, Av. 24 de Mayo 7-77 y Hernán Malo. Apartado 01.01.981, Cuenca, Ecuador

Abstract. In competitive markets, customer segmentation improves customer loyalty and business performance, but in practice, these analyses are carried out using simple relationships in dashboard, or Microsoft Excel' sheets, which do not show customer behavior. Data segmentation in the era of big data has changed this paradigm with some techniques that try to decrease bias. In this research, four segmentation techniques are tested with a large set of data from a retail store. CLARA (Clustering Large Applications Algorithm) and Random Forest algorithms both were the best. Through the RFM (Recency, Frequency, Monetary) approach, eight customer segments were found, where *Champions* customers spend more money and return frequently to the retail store. In addition, each segment of customer buys following a model, this was demonstrated with the a priori algorithm. Finally, some strategies are given into which products should go together and how to distribute them so that customers can find them, as well as the best-selling products.

Keywords: Data mining · Clustering algorithm · Random forest · Retail · A priori

1 Introduction

The retail sector is dedicated to the retail sale of many products such as food, household appliances, jewelry, etc. The main advantage it has is the flexibility to adapt to customer changes; so, any company that is dedicated to this business should know that managing a good diversification of products, customer portfolio, and a good store along with an adequate level of inventories can lead to increase market and competitive. Retail customers seek these companies for their variety of products and for the ease of purchasing a product. Therefore, having a physical store is one of the critical factors involved in the customer's purchase decision, since it provides the customer with a comfortable place

M. Botto-Tobar et al. (Eds.): ICAT 2022, CCIS 1755, pp. 240–254, 2023.
https://doi.org/10.1007/978-3-031-24985-3_18

to make their purchase, which ultimately ensures that the customer will return, and thus increase sales [1].

The store design considers which customers will be served and in what quantity. The number of customers entering a store is used to segment customers. For this purpose, retail stores have adopted the use of barcode scanners to obtain information about the product purchased, which has allowed the retailer to use the information to make decisions on procurement, shelf space and decision in advertising campaigns. The data obtained from each payment is used to define the consumer's buying pattern and thus organize the products according to the consumer's preference [1]. However, this technique is limited, because it only categorizes customers using information such as age, gender, or education level. But information about how often the customer buys, what kind of products the customer buys, or how much money the customer spends is not considered if no customer segmentation is performed. Customer segmentation tries to find clusters that have similarities and differences between groups. Generally, this segmentation is based on historical data, and on observing customers' buying behaviors, to evaluate them and discover high-value customers [2]. In competitive markets, customer segmentation improves customer loyalty and business level, but in practice, these long-lasting relationship analyses are carried out by applying profitable customer databases and without a holistic analysis [3]. Therefore, segmenting customers to find potential customers plays a significant role in a retailer's expansion and competitiveness.

In customer segmentation research, some clustering algorithms have been determined such as decision trees, fuzzy c-means, genetic algorithms, particle swarm K-means, affinity propagation algorithms, spectral clustering algorithms, and Gaussian mixtures, K-means, Mahalanobis distances, among others [2, 4–6]. Each of these proposals can be applied considering the number of clusters, bandwidth, scalability, and geometric distance. It is known that fuzzy c-means algorithms, and genetic algorithms, are more used in environments where the size of groups is equal, while affinity propagation algorithms, spectral clustering algorithms, Gaussian mixtures, are used more in non-planar distance geometry and with groups that have connectivity constraints. Despite this variety of algorithms, the two most used algorithms are K-means algorithm and decision trees. These two algorithms are applied in many situations and with a few clusters these work quite well. Khalili-Damghani [3] proposed a decision tree that follows a flowchart approach, where each internal node in the tree contains a question about a particular feature and each branch shows the result of the experiment. In this study, this algorithm gave good classification results due to the classification rules that were placed, and it was possible to classify a group of data based on economic indicators. While in the study of Espinosa and Zúñiga [7], it can be noted that the decision trees facilitated the classification of a group of data giving a performance of 91.38% which shows the robustness of this algorithm. On the other hand, the K-means algorithm is very popular because of its ease of use. This technique selects the initial cluster centroids using sampling based on an empirical probability distribution. The distance to the centroids is based on euclidean distance and associates the members of each cluster considering this variable. Anitha and Patil [4], suggest a customer segmentation considering K-means, with this they found a method to identify profitable and high-value customers. While Saraf et al. [6], using K-means managed to obtain four clusters of different customers that help to know the buying patterns of customers as well as how they bill each cluster so that strategies can be applied to serve these customers and positively lengthen the customer life cycle.

On the other hand, in customer segmentation, it is common to take an approach with variables such as *Recency, Frequency, and Monetary*, which are: the customer's most recent purchase (R), frequency of purchases (F), and money spent (M). RFM can be defined as the segmentation of customer analysis that not only provides information about the customer's frequent purchase pattern but also about the recent purchase and the profit earned [8]. A high measure of RFM indicates the presence of a high-value customer and conversely with a low measure. Parikh and Abdelfattah [2], in their research, performed data segmentation and found five defined clusters. Cluster 5 was identified as the highest spender but had a low frequency. While cluster 3 spent the least money, they are the ones who made the most recent purchases. From this work, it can be noted that the customers who spend the most are not the ones who buy the most or the most recent purchases, in addition to which customers the business should concentrate on in order to formulate different strategies. In [5], their study did an RFM analysis of customers, and determined that only eight transactions are enough to classify a customer this is interesting because in a retail business there are many customers but few transactions. However, in [9] not only transactions were considered for their RFM, but they proposed one more metric to the RFM, and that was to measure the trend of customers dynamically.

Many retailers distribute their products intuitively, without any study to validate their decisions. So, in data mining, one of the main tasks is to find association rules and discover useful patterns in large volumes of data [10]. These associations are not evident with a simple descriptive analysis of the data, and usually, different association algorithms must be used to find these patterns. The *A priori* algorithm proposed in 1993 has been the most widely used to find these associations, the power of an association rule being measured by support and confidence. Moreover, for an association rule to be considered interesting, these two parameters must be together [11]. Support measures the number of transactions in which the items are present according to the association rule, i.e., whether the items are together in the data relative to the total number of transactions. Confidence represents the actual probability that a set of items coexists with another set of items in a data set, it measures the accuracy of the association rule used. This measure indicates the percentage of transactions containing the ascending term and the consequent term in relation to the number of transactions containing the antecedent part [10].

From the previous paragraphs, retail store optimization and customer categorization in retail stores becomes an important research topic, because there is a big problem in identifying high-value customers while having an adequate distribution of products in the stores. Something that small retail stores do not have. Therefore, the following research question is posed: *Could customer categorization be based on customers' consumption behavior, considering which products they purchase?*

This paper is organized as follows: Sect. 2 presents the methodology of work, and describes the data set used in this research, Sect. 3 describes the results to apply four clustering algorithms and rules associations, and Sect. 4 is a discussion of results and comparison of others research, finally, Sect. 5 presents the conclusion and future work.

2 Methodology

2.1 Exploratory Analysis and Data Preprocessing

The first step was to review scientific articles, which resulted in the recognition of different studies with models and methods oriented to segment customers, and associate products in cases of retail stores selling food products. Meanwhile, the data obtained are from a small retail store in Cuenca - Ecuador. The database used was part of a research on retail trade in the city of Cuenca. Data set includes all transactions carried out in the retail trade corresponding to September, October, November, and December 2020, it was 60,596. The database has nine features, these are, Issue Date, Consumer ID, Transaction Number, Product Code, Quantity Purchased, Unit Price, Product Name, Category, and Unit of Measurement. The first six features are numeric and the last three are string features. As for the customers, there were 1,001 customers at the beginning of the database. Exploratory Analysis and Data Preprocessing (EAD) consisted of cleaning the data in the database, and statistical graphs were used to find anomalies and thus use the appropriate statistical techniques. In addition, a coding and text mining of the variables was performed in order to have a uniform description of the products, the string features must be converted to numeric features. Likewise, all the product codes were revised so that they have values of product price or quantity purchased. Meanwhile, the products purchased by customers were placed in four categories. Category 1 included products such as beef, chicken, pork, seafood, and sausages. Category 2 includes products such as fruits, vegetables, legumes, and eggs. Category 3 includes dairy products, bakery products, confectionery, canned goods, rice, sugar, salt, oils, alcoholic and non-alcoholic beverages, condiments, and sauces. In Category 4, there is any type of product that is not in the previous categories. It is important to note that the brands of the products were not relevant at the time of the study.

2.2 Segmentation of Customers

The RFM approach was used to segment customers, and different classification algorithms were used to evaluate the performance of each in the case study. The RFM values (refers to Recency, Frequency, Monetary value), complaints registered, their purchases, products, and date since the last store visit, contribute to highly accurate segmentation [6]. The calculation of the RFM value corresponds to the following equation [12]:

$$RFM \ score = (rs \times rw) + (fs \times fw) + (ms \times mw) \tag{1}$$

where rs = recency score and rw = recency weight, fs = frequency score and fw = frequency weight, ms = monetary score and mw = monetary weight.

In this section, eight categories have been placed for customers which are: "Champions", "Loyal Customers", "Potential Loyalist", "New Customers", "Promising", "Need Attention", "About to Sleep", "At Risk", "Can't Lose Them", and "Lost". These data categories were placed according to descending RFM scores.

Because of the literature review, it was decided to use four classification algorithms. The first uses the centroid method (K-means) to know the effect of variability in the data, the second uses the K-medoids clustering method (CLARA) which is more robust, and the third is a hierarchical algorithm that allows knowing the effect of not assigning a cluster number previously and finally Random Forest which is a machine learning algorithm for large volumes of data. K-means algorithm Clusters the data by attempting to separate the samples into n groups of equivalent variances. Unlike some of the other clustering algorithms, K-means requires that the number of k clusters is provided. In order to define the number of clusters [6] describe in their publication that the Elbow method, which is the most popular heuristic. In this case, the Elbow Method was taken, which for any unsupervised learning algorithm, determining the number of clusters is elementary. The Elbow method is the most popular method to determine the optimal value of k, and the silhouette method was used. The objective of the K-means is to segment the existing data into K- clusters, such that the total Euclidean distance between the cluster centroid and the respective data points is minimized. Here is a mathematical equation to represent the same:

$$\min_{B_j c_j} \sum_{i=L}^{k} \sum_{xi \in B} \left\| x_i - B_j \right\|_{L_2}^{2} \tag{2}$$

where: Bj is K clusters, y Cj centroids. L2 is euclidean distance.

When there is a large amount of data or the presence of outliers there are sophisticated algorithms that handle this problem, for example, K-medoids with the use of Partitioning Around Medoids (PAM), but the drawback of this algorithm is its high run time cost [13]. To overcome this, the Clustering Large Applications Algorithm (CLARA) is presented, which combines the idea of K-medoids with resampling in order to work with large volumes of data more efficiently [14]. The algorithm CLARA repeatedly applies PAM on a subsample with n' ≪ n objects. Afterwards the remaining objects are assigned to their closest medoid. The CLARA method considered a sample of 60 data in order to perform the clustering and the distance to the medoids was performed considering the Manhattan method. As with the previous algorithm, Silhouette width and Dunn were used to internally validate the Clusters generated.

Hierarchical clustering is a general family of clustering algorithms that create nested clusters by successively merging or splitting them [6]. This algorithm does affinity clustering, and the clusters can be of different sizes. The algorithm looks for hierarchies in the data and generates the Clusters based on this, this is represented using dendrograms. In the hierarchical algorithm, the agglomerative method was used.

While the selected distance, the available methods were analyzed, such as complete distance, average distance, single distance, Ward.D2, euclidean distance, Mcquitty, etc. To choose the appropriate method, the correlation index was used and the highest one was selected. Since this will better represent the distance of the data to the centroids. In addition, an internal validation of clusters generated with the use of the algorithm was performed, for this, the Silhouette width, and Dunn were used [15].

The Random Forest algorithm is a supervised learning technique whose purpose is to generate a decision on a set of data, using for this purpose a segment of these data (training) usually chosen by bootstrapping [7]. The main advantages of the Random Forest algorithm according to Cánovas-García [16] are: that it can be used for classification, for this each tree chooses a class and the result of the model is the class with the highest number of "votes" in all trees. Besides, this is an easier training model, in order to compare against complex techniques, but with similar performance. Finally, it maintains its accuracy with large missing data. For the Random Forest algorithm, 70% of the data was taken for training the model, and 30% for testing. As for classification, we tested whether the eight categories of the selected RFM clients were able to be reached using this algorithm. The algorithm requires the number of trees and the number of random variables to be found as candidates in each branch and the maximum number of nodes selected from the hyperparameters analyzed.

2.3 Association Rules

Association rules are widely used in machine learning. In this step of the methodology, the products that are most purchased by each of the identified customer segments were identified. Once this was done, with the *A priori* algorithm, the respective association rules were obtained. This algorithm is included in the rules association rules package of the R statistical software. For data analysis, it was necessary to create a matrix with the transactions of each customer segment where each row represents a transaction and each column an item. Then, diagrams were created with the five best-selling products for each segment. The confidence level and support value for each rule were adjusted to 0.01 and 0.6 respectively so that the results obtained were the products that are frequently sold together, and the rules are as reliable as possible. It was considered necessary to obtain, in addition to the indicators that the algorithm yields by default, the indicators of leverage and conviction, which help to determine the direction of the rule and to choose the optimal product mix. Also in rules, a process of verification was developed to know whether there were duplicate and redundant rules and remove them from the study. The rule that has more products always has lower support and is considered redundant since it does not provide additional information. Likewise, two rules are identical when they have the same antecedent and consequent [1].

3 Results

3.1 Exploratory Analysis and Data Preprocessing

The results described below were developed with the R program (version 4.2.1). In EAD, from the database, we had 60,596 transactions corresponding to 1,001 different customers. Each customer has an identification code and those customers who purchase products were considered. Customers who did not have complete information were eliminated; in the end, only 853 customers were analyzed. From the verification of the quantities of the variables price and quantity paid, three data that have a value of zero were eliminated. The analysis of outliers, in this case, was not performed, because we want to know how these data affect customer segmentation, on the other hand, in the case study there may be customers who buy very high quantities of products and do so frequently. However, all outliers were identified.

3.2 RFM Analysis

In the RFM analysis, the starting point is the refined dataset of EAD. To start the RFM analysis, the final analysis date was set as December 31, 2020, since at that date the company performs a quarterly evaluation of its annual business strategy. A pre- processing of the RFM was performed using the R program, with the "rfm" library and "ggplot2" for the graphs (Fig. 1). To understand the behavior of customers, 101 reference days were counted (09/21/2020 to 12/31/2020). Customers as active are those who in the mentioned period have visited the retailer at least four times in the quarter, sleeping is those who have visited the retailer between 4 to 2 times in the quarter and inactive customers are those who have visited the retailer less than 2 times in the quarter. In Fig. 1, it can be seen that the majority are inactive customers, followed by sleeping customers, and finally active customers. This is common in small retailers. If we analyze the frequency of transactions, only 4,094 of the visits are made by registered customers. While the total number of transactions analyzed is 60,596, this implies that it is only capturing about 6.76% of the transactions made by returning customers. It can be noted that many customers are inactive, but to look at this segment in more detail, in the RFM analysis, eight categories were proposed which represent more detail of the retail situation. The data was distributed as follows: *Champions* (9.50%), *Loyal customer* (17.94%), *Potential Loyal* (18.41%), while *Lost* (8.32%), *At Risk* (1.29%), *About to sleep* (5.04%), *Need Attention* (0.82%) and *Others* (38.69%) have a low percentage, which is good for the retail business. In terms of average monetary spending, the *Champions* segment is the one that spends the most (USD 43 average per transaction). On the other hand, the customer with ID 102000000000, is the one who has visited the retail business the most, while the customer with ID 301231767 is the one who spends the most in the retail business (Table 1).

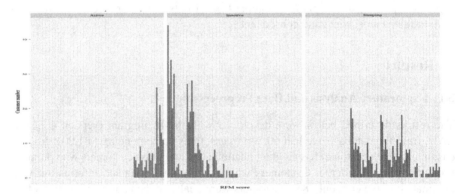

Fig. 1. Pre-processing of transactions.

3.3 Algorithms of Segmentations

In this section, four segmentation algorithms were tested. The first algorithm was K-means, which took as input data the results of the RFM. From the data, a statistical

Table 1. Top 5 customer in RFM.

Customer ID	Recency	Frequency	Monetary
102000000000	21.0	114	18.60
301231767	24.0	21.0	41.3
102914041	22.0	20.0	34.1
103547758	26.0	14.0	37.2
103584082	27.0	12.0	46.1

normality test was run for the Recency, Monetary, and Frequency variables. It is desired to know if these variables have any correlation, so it was necessary to calculate a correlation coefficient, therefore, a normality test was run on the variables. The results are shown in Table 2, and it is found that the variables do not follow a normal distribution. With these data, a Spearman's test can be performed to see if there is a correlation between the variables. The relationship between Recency and Frequency is the highest and most significant (-0.57), between Recency and Monetary it does not exist (-0.017) as well as between Frequency and Monetary (0.039). This indicates that K-means clustering can be performed since the groups formed are representatives.

Table 2. Normality test.

Variable	Kolmogorov-Smirnov	P-value (*)
Recency	0.13612	2.2 e−16
Frequency	0.47005	2.2 e−16
Monetary	0.22957	2.2 e−16

(*) $\alpha = 0.01$

K-means is an iterative clustering algorithm that initially randomly assigns data points to clusters, unlike hierarchical clustering. The number of clusters is always a problem to determine in this algorithm. But as suggested by many authors, Elbow Method can be used for any unsupervised learning algorithm, therefore determining the number of clusters is elementary, likewise, the silhouette method which analyzes how well the resulting clusters are separated can be used [6]. From Fig. 2, it can be seen that the optimal number of Clusters was 2, while in Table 3, the results are summarized, and based on these it is decided to take 3 clusters.

As can be seen with only two clusters, the segmentation is not good since the second cluster collects the information with more clients. Therefore, these values are improved by considering the three clusters, since the clustering is improved, and more information is obtained. In the clustering based on K-means, it was performed with the "stats" package of R. The result is shown in Fig. 3, where the three clusters formed can be seen. However, it is noticeable that due to the presence of data with very high frequencies (outliers), there are few clients in cluster 3. Moreover, cluster 1 has good recency, but a low frequency

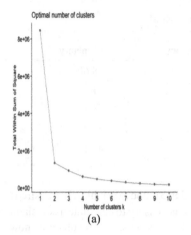

(a)

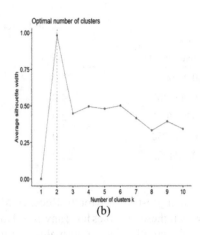

(b)

Fig. 2. a) Elbow method, b) Silhouette method.

Table 3. Resultados con K = 2 y K = 3

Cluster	Recency	Frequency	Monetary
1	51.73	4.804	20.81
2	21	2675	12.34
1	21	2675	12.34
2	79.86	1.503	20.21
3	33.41	6.953	21.2

Note: average values.

and high monetary. In this group are the category of customers *Champions, Potential Loyal, and Loyalty*. In cluster 2, it can be seen that the Recency is low, frequency is high, as well as the monetary is low. In this group, there are customers *Need Attention and At risk*, in the last cluster 3, it is noticed that there are low values of recency and frequency, but high monetary, these are customers who have been few times to the business but have spent a high monetary value, the category of *Lost, About to sleep and Others* are in this group.

The second algorithm used to improve clustering was the CLARA algorithm. This algorithm is a non-hierarchical algorithm that handles a lot of data, and its resolution is based on the K-medoids proposal. In addition, to improve the clustering, the Manhattan distance method is used, as this helps to avoid overlapping the groups. The number of clusters K = 3 is placed, a sample (60 data) is selected for clustering and the following results are obtained (Fig. 3). This Clustering shows that the centroids are not affected by very large or small values. The clusters are formed dynamically. However, the overlapping of the Clusters is noticed.

In this algorithm, cluster 1 is formed by *Loyal* customers, its average dissimilarity is 3.415, its maximum dissimilarity is 29.449 and it is composed of 294 customers.

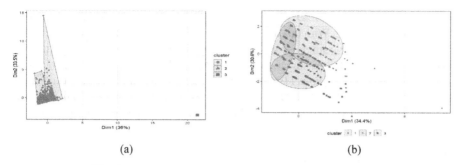

(a)   (b)

Fig. 3. a) Results of K-means k = 3, b) Results of CLARA.

Cluster 2 is formed by *Potential Loyal* customers, its average dissimilarity is 2.941, its maximum dissimilarity is 5.915 and it is composed of 301 customers. Cluster 3 is formed by *Other* customers, its average dissimilarity is 2.876, its maximum dissimilarity is 12.894 and it is composed of 258 customers. The uniform size of the clusters can be noticed by partitioning the data, while the dissimilarity, it is seen that cluster 1 has the highest dissimilarity. This implies that the *Loyal* customer segment differs from the other clusters.

On the other hand, the third algorithm that was used is the hierarchical Clustering algorithm. In this algorithm to perform the clusters, the best possible distance is chosen, and the complete method was the one that best fits the data. This distance is calculated, as the distance between all pairs formed by one observation of cluster A and one of cluster B. The average value of all of them is selected as the distance between the two clusters (mean inter-cluster dissimilarity). The hierarchical algorithm does not require calculating the number of clusters and when the respective dendrogram is available, a cut of the dendrogram is performed. The cut was made at h=5 so that three groups defined in the clustering can be counted. For better visualization of the dendrogram, it can be seen in **Appendix 1**. The Clustering by the hierarchical algorithm, there are two groups marked (blue and green) and cluster 1 (red) is not noticeable. In cluster 1 are the data with higher recency and higher frequency, in this group are the *Lost* group, while in cluster 2 are the customers of type *Champions Potential Loyal and Loyalty*, and cluster 3 are the rest of the groups such as *Need Attention, At risk, and About to sleep.*

To validate if the number of clusters placed is adequate, the silhouette method was calculated to know if the classification is correct. The average silhouette method is like the Elbow method, but instead of minimizing the total inter-cluster sum of squares, the average silhouette coefficient or silhouette index (SI) is maximized. Silhouette quantifies how well an observation has been assigned. The SI coefficient varies between -1 to 1, if the values are close to 1, it can be mentioned that the observation was performed correctly, and if it is less than zero the observation was poorly performed [17]. The silhouette coefficients for this algorithm were: cluster 1 (0.34), cluster 2 (0.35), and cluster 3 (0.32), likewise the data that are misclassified in cluster 1 (2 customers), cluster 2 (21 customers), and cluster 3 (16 customers).

The fourth algorithm tested for classification was the random forest. For this algorithm, a training sample (597 data) and a test sample (256) were taken. The number of trees was 100, which is sufficient for classification [7]. A Depth of 10 and mtry max of 10 were also determined. With this algorithm, the highest classification in each category was achieved. With the training group it was possible to classify all the categories and there were no errors in the classification. The results are *About-To-Sleep* (9 customers), *At Risk* (2 customers), *Champions* (19 customers), *Lost* (23 customers), *Loyal Customers* (43 customers), *Need Attention* (0 customers), *Others* (111 customers), and *Potential Loyalist* (49 customers). This shows that this algorithm had the best-ranking design.

3.4 Associations Rules

In the association rules, the data was prepared in such a way that it can be read by the algorithm a priori. Products are listed by the invoice numbers for association rule mining and coded transactions made by customers. *A priori* algorithm is used to find high and low-value customers. These customers are employed to retrieve the products that customers may purchase, after purchasing a relevant product. For that, the *A priori* algorithm finds the associations that exist among the products purchased by customers in the clusters. After that, *A priori* algorithm was applied to identify the associate rules under the minimum support of 0.01 and the minimum confidence of 0.6. The top 3 rules are depicted in **Appendix 2.** All these rules were ordered by the confidence indicator, which indicates the probability that a product A is purchased, given that a product B was purchased.

From the analysis of the best-selling products, it can be noted that most customers buy up to five products, being these products the best sellers: avocado, ripe plantain, tomatoes, philippine banana, eggs, and ginger syrup. For the best-selling product we have the following rule {pickle} => {avocado}, this means that if a customer buys a pickle, he/she is very likely to buy avocado.

In the analysis by segments, the customer segment (*Champions*) is composed of 81 customers, who spend an average of USD 43 on each purchase. In this group, it can be noted that most of them buy category 2, which is vegetables and fruits, and most of them buy one product or a maximum of three products from this category. For example, tomato has been purchased 2,636 times. So, it can be understood that in this segment there are people who buy food for the home, and they do it frequently. For example, if they buy an avocado and peeled pearl onion, they have a very high probability of buying tomatoes. As for the segment known as *Loyal customers*, the association rule, with more confidence, indicates that onion and tamarillo are purchased in conjunction with tomato. This group also buys fruits and vegetables, as well as chicken and meat (categories 1 and 2). Products such as beef, tamarillo and tomatoes were purchased 1,580 times. As for the *Potential Loyal* segment, only 6 rules were created, and the behavior of the two groups described above is very marked. This group of customers is the highest in the segmentation (157 customers) and together with the *Loyal* (153 customers) is the most representative group. In the *At risk* and *Need Attention* groups, customers who buy category 3 products, e.g., eggs, and milk has been purchased about 741 times. This group is the one to watch out for as they are the people who can get lost. As for the Lost group, it can be noted that they are customers who buy products that are not edible (category 4), but they buy them only once or after some time. It is made up of 71 customers, none of whom make frequent purchases. Most of them buy beer and products such as snacks. Likewise, the segment of customers *About to sleep* has the most preferred for the purchase of products of category 3 and chocolates. This group is composed of 43 customers. The *Other* group was not analyzed since it does not show a marked trend.

4 Discussion

In the proposed research in the retail store, the large data is a problem when analyzing the information. However, many proposals have been developed to deal with this problem. Some of these techniques were used in this work. The RFM analysis contributed to knowing the consumer preferences, and as mentioned by [1], this behavior was searched. In Fig. 1, many customers are inactive or are sleeping in the retail business, so it is possible to capture these customers by giving them the possibility of discounts or promotions such as membership cards with benefits. The business should consider a rewards system to increase the percentage of returning customers. As in [2], the RFM study found eight categories of customers, in contrast to the aforementioned research, the *Champions* group is the one that spends the most on average (USD 43) and returns the soonest (10 days). While the *At risk* is the second group that most spends on average (USD 26) and they are a considerable number of customers, therefore, the retail business must consider a marketing campaign for this group so that they are not lost.

On the other hand, as for the ranking algorithms that were used, Table 4 summarizes the comparison of these. It is known that the average Silhouette width uses the average distance of observation and by comparing with all others in the nearest group. In addition, once misclassification is suspected, it is necessary to know how many observations have fallen into these false positives. As for the Dunn indicator, which measures the ratio of the minimum distance of the observations to the maximum distance between the observations. Therefore, high Dunn index numbers are preferred since this implies having compact and well-separated clusters because the minimum separation between clusters will be high and the maximum separation between clusters will be low. Considering this, for the K-means algorithm, a value of 0.134 was obtained, for the CLARA algorithm a value of 8.338393e-05 was obtained, while for the Hierarchical agglomerative it is 0.0511.

Table 4. Comparison between clustering methods

Clustering method	Measurement	Cluster 1	Cluster 2	Cluster 3
K-means	Silhouette	0.47	0	0.57
	False positive	1	1	1
CLARA	Silhouette	0.39	0.44	0.36
	False positive	3	0	1
Hierarchical Agglomerative	Silhouette	0.34	0.35	0.32
	False positive	2	21	16

Note: False positive is misclassified data.

As can be seen, the numeric data show the best algorithm for classification is K-means, followed by CLARA, and finally the Hierarchical method. These results are similar to those obtained in [2, 4–6], while it was the opposite since in the latter study the Hierarchical method was the best, but in our research, it was the one with the lowest score. For the choice of any of these three algorithms, it is considered that in the presence of data that has a lot of bias, it is necessary to opt for a robust method. Therefore, for the case study, the CLARA method can be chosen, due to the high number of average Silhouette width and low false positives, although the Dunn index is lower. In these classification algorithms, Random Forest was considered, which is a supervised method and requires the use of samples and a defined number of trees. As mentioned by [3], a good choice for classification is classification trees and a robust method is Random Forest as in the works of [7, 16], the method gave good results. In the case of this research, the classification of this algorithm coincides remarkably where it can be evidenced that there is a perfect classification.

Finally, as for the analysis of the rules of association based on the market basket, the top of these rules can be noted (Appendix 2). It can be noted that customers purchase products from category 1 (beef, chicken and pork, seafood, and sausages) and category 2 (fruits, vegetables, legumes, and eggs) regardless of the segment to which they belong since they are considered elementary in the basic market basket. As for the *Lost* group, according to the rules analyzed, they are one-time customers and non-commodities products. As for the *Others* group, no rules were found that define this group, i.e., the data do not follow any purchase pattern, this could be because many of these customers are people who do not register data or have bought in the store only once, and their purchase was perhaps influenced by the loss of the pandemic caused by Covid-19. With the use of the rules of association, the retail business is given an idea of how to distribute its products and what items should not be missing for its customers, as well as the possibility of creating promotions that include these products. In addition, with these association rules, the retail business can control the flow of customers by placing each product as close as possible or as far away as possible, depending on the objective of the business, whether it is to sell more products (the customer will spend more time in the store, thus increasing the probability of purchasing more products) or to attract customers (the customer will be able to find everything he/she is looking for immediately).

5 Conclusion

The research question posed at the beginning of this research was: Could customer categorization be based on customers' consumption behavior, considering which products they purchase? And it has been shown that customer categorization does follow a pattern based on their recency, frequency, and monetary behavior. In addition, customer clustering is affected by data with high variability, so robust algorithms should be used to avoid misclassifications. On the other hand, the store design is a critical factor in retail store management, which is associated with high investment and maintenance costs. Therefore, having an analysis of the consumer's purchase history and knowing which products are purchased the most and whether they are purchased individually or in groups is important so that shelf space and other equipment are occupied by items that will benefit both the customer and the company. If a business has the necessary products distributed optimally, the customer will likely return and go from being a champion or loyal customer.

For future research, it is recommended that the horizon of analysis might be extended, and the purchase consumer´s behavior, outside the pandemic period, can be compared in order to contrast whether consumption remains the same. In addition, the analysis of brands is important; in this study they were not considered since there was no catalog of business brands. Besides, the seasonality of the data is not considered since the case study, strategy to acquire products is done in a controlled manner and has a product acquisition model that contemplates seasonality.

Appendix

Appendix 1: https://n9.cl/appendix-1

Appendix 2: https://n9.cl/appendix-2

References

1. Joe, T., Sreejith, R., Sekar, K.: Optimization of store layout using market basket analysis. Int. J. Recent Technol. Eng. **8**, 6459–6463 (2019). https://doi.org/10.35940/ijrte.B2207.078219
2. Parikh, Y., Abdelfattah, E.: Clustering algorithms and RFM analysis performed on retail transactions. In: 2020 11th IEEE Annual Ubiquitous Computing, Electronics and Mobile Communication Conference, UEMCON 2020, pp. 506–511. Institute of Electrical and Electronics Engineers Inc. (2020)
3. Khalili-Damghani, K., Abdi, F., Abolmakarem, S.: Hybrid soft computing approach based on clustering, rule mining, and decision tree analysis for customer segmentation problem: real case of customer-centric industries. Appl. Soft Comput. J. **73**, 816–828 (2018). doi:https://doi.org/10.1016/j.asoc.2018.09.001
4. Anitha, P., Patil, M.M.: RFM model for customer purchase behavior using K-Means algorithm. J. King Saud Univ. Comput. Inf. Sci. **34**, 1785–1792 (2022). doi:https://doi.org/10.1016/j.jksuci.2019.12.011
5. Rahim, M.A., Mushafiq, M., Khan, S., Arain, Z.A.: RFM-based repurchase behavior for customer classification and segmentation. J. Retail. Consum. Serv. **61**, 102566 (2021). https://doi.org/10.1016/j.jretconser.2021.102566
6. Saraf, E., Pradhan, S., Joshi, S., Sountharrajan, S.: Behavioral segmentation with product estimation using K-means clustering and seasonal ARIMA. In: 2022 6th International Conference on Trends in Electronics and Informatics, ICOEI 2022 – Proceedings, pp. 1641–1648. Institute of Electrical and Electronics Engineers Inc. (2022)
7. Espinosa Zúñiga, J.J.: Aplicación de algoritmos Random Forest y XGBoost en una base de solicitudes de tarjetas de crédito. Ing. Investig. y Tecnol. **21**, 1–16 (2020). doi:https://doi.org/10.22201/fi.25940732e.2020.21.3.022
8. Hu, Y.H., Yeh, T.W.: Discovering valuable frequent patterns based on RFM analysis without customer identification information. Knowl.-Based Syst. **61**, 76–88 (2014). https://doi.org/10.1016/j.knosys.2014.02.009

9. Yoseph, F., Heikkila, M.: Segmenting retail customers with an enhanced RFM and a hybrid regression/clustering method. In: Proceedings - International Conference on Machine Learning and Data Engineering, iCMLDE 2018, pp. 77–82. Institute of Electrical and Electronics Engineers Inc. (2019)
10. Dahbi, A., Jabri, S., Balouki, Y., Gadi, T.: A new method to select the interesting association rules with multiple criteria. Int. J. Intell. Eng. Syst. **10**, 191–200 (2017). https://doi.org/10.22266/ijies2017.1031.21
11. Cheng, W.Z., Li Xia, X.: Fast algorithm for mining association rules. In: Proceedings of IEEE International Conference Software Engineering Service Science ICSESS, pp. 513–516 (1994). doi:https://doi.org/10.1109/ICSESS.2014.6933618
12. Yoseph, F., Heikkila, M.: Segmenting retail customers with an enhanced RFM and a hybrid regression/clustering method. In: Proc. - Int. Conf. Mach. Learn. Data Eng. iCMLDE 2018, pp. 77–82 (2019). doi:https://doi.org/10.1109/iCMLDE.2018.00029
13. Schubert, E., Rousseeuw, P.J.: Faster k-medoids clustering: improving the PAM, CLARA, and CLARANS Algorithms. In: Amato, G., Gennaro, C., Oria, V., Miloš, R. (eds.) Similarity Search and Applications, pp. 171–187. Springer International Publishing, Cham (2019)
14. Everitt, B., Landau, S., Leese, M., Stahl, D.: Cluster Analysis. Wiley, Hoboken, NJ, Estados Unidos (2011)
15. Paranavithana, I.R., Rupasinghe, T.D., Prior, D.D.: Unsupervised learning and market basket analysis in market segmentation. In: Lecture Notes in Engineering and Computer Science, pp. 122–127. Newswood Limited (2021)
16. Cánovas-García, F., Alonso-Sarría, F., Gomariz-Castillo, F., Oñate-Valdivieso, F.: Modification of the random forest algorithm to avoid statistical dependence problems when classifying remote sensing imagery. Comput. Geosci. **103**, 1–11 (2017). doi:https://doi.org/10.1016/j.cageo.2017.02.012
17. Amat Rodrigo, J.: Clustering y heatmaps: aprendizaje no supervisado. https://www.cienciadedatos.net/documentos/37_clustering_y_heatmaps

Bibliometric Analysis of Web of Science Database STEM Fields in Engineering and Mathematics. Ecuador's Case Study

Jhair Aldás-Onofre[1][(⊠)] 🆔 and Bernardo Cordero[2] 🆔

[1] Industrial and Process Engineering, Quito, Ecuador
jhair.aldas@ute.edu.ec
[2] Industrial Engineering Msc, Quito, Ecuador
bernardo.cordero@unmsm.edu.pe

Abstract. The scientific production in Ecuador has been increasing considerably over the last two decades; the actual research proceeds to conduct the specific bibliometric analysis of the publications in STEM subjects in Engineering and Mathematics from the Web of Science Core Collection in 1990–2021. Through 4 steps of a data preprocessing structured methodology, were outcome two datasets of which 4 650 publications became inputs to quantitative analysis of Engineering and Mathematics Web of Science Categories, each verifying Price's Law ($R^2 = 0.9485$) establishing the exponentially increasing of documents published and a Pareto's Law approximation percent of articles published within 63 research areas. 86.69% of all publications are in the English language from both clusters (data set) analyzed. Khorami, Majid is the author with more relevance. As a result, university institutes contribute more to research publications. Escuela Politécnica Nacional del Ecuador is prominent.

Keywords: Bibliometric analysis · STEM field · Engineering · Mathematics · Country research output

1 Introduction

Bibliometric analysis is an alternative technique to studying the different research fields properly with criteria of scientific output such as the definition of terms and search criteria [1, 2]. The concept of bibliometric analysis was first described in 1977 by Dr. Eugene Garfield, founder of the Institute for Scientific Information (ISI) [3]. Institute was founded in the 1960s in Philadelphia based on categorizing, retrieving, and tracking scientific-academic information through indicators and data intake belonging to the different scientific articles [4]. Then, in Table 1, the contributions that refer to bibliometric study framed in STEM for the world and Ecuador are presented. STEM is part of an analysis of the current situation regarding the most recent contributions.

M. Botto-Tobar et al. (Eds.): ICAT 2022, CCIS 1755, pp. 255–270, 2023.
https://doi.org/10.1007/978-3-031-24985-3_19

Table 1. State of the art review

Author/s	Year	Title and Reference	Contribution
Chérrez, K.	2020	Bibliometric analysis of the Hispano-American scientific production on occupational health indexed in Web of Science (2015–2019) [5]	- The analysis of scientific productivity (%) of the region (9.1%) is low compared to the world (90.9%) - Poor research interest due to socioeconomic shortcomings - Research gap between the country and the Spanish-American Country
Limaymanta Alvarez, C. et al.	2020	Bibliometric and scient metric analysis of the scientific production of Peru and Ecuador from Web of Science (2009–2018) [6]	- Although Peru has a more extensive research production than Ecuador, considerable growth is expected - The leading institutions that contribute the most are the Universities - The thematic categories in Ecuador are pedagogy and environment
Marín Velásquez, T., et al.	2020	Analysis of Latin American journals indexed by Redalyc in the Engineering area: relationship with socioeconomic indicators [7]	- In Ecuador, only one engineering journal is indexed in Redalyc - The most significant download of engineering journals: Brazil, Cuba, and Mexico - Investment in research about GDP. Ecuador ranks fourth with 36% of investment in Latin America between 2015 and 2018

(continued)

Table 1. (*continued*)

Author/s	Year	Title and Reference	Contribution
Herrera-Franco, G., et al.	2021	Scientific Research in Ecuador: A Bibliometric Analysis [2]	- From 2011 to 2021, there is an 85% growth in production - In Ecuador, three universities are among the top 1 000 in the QS World University Rankings (world score) - Six universities within the Top 100 South American ranking
Schirone, M.	2022	STEM Information Literacy: A Bibliometric Mapping (1974–2020) [8]	- There are 6 221 key documents (worldwide) after data clean - Key documentation 'Journal of academic librarianship' (12,9%) - Keywords as high relevance degree (centrality)

Note: Area of study of the publications part of Library and Information Sciences, unlike the author Chérrez [5] with the area of Occupational Health and Safety.

Bibliometric information is a product of qualitative and quantitative research that allows data to be transformed into graphic charts. [9], of this the themes according to what is needed, managing their analysis with historical data. Various applications of this branch of science show evidence in the methodologies used for systematized bibliographic research on tax issues. [10], in the academic treatment of teaching based on the Pedagogical Content Knowledge (PCK) [11] and through the features offered by the VOSViewer software to study different forms of biomass drying in the case of sugar [12].

Within the bibliometric analysis it is based on three following theories:

– Theory 1 - Bradford's Law. Primary sources are divided into three regions. Zone 1 is the most active region, also known as the central region; compared to Zones 1 and 2, Zone 2 is moderately active, while Zone 3 is barely productive [13]. This theory allows the grouping of a few journals concerning many sources, done in clusters [14].
– Theory 2 - Lotka's Law. A formula establishes that the total author's frequency is proportional to the inverse square of the number of publications [15]. A causal relationship describes the large research production with a small group of actors.
– Theory 3 - Price's Law. Analyze the efficiency of a specific discipline or a particular country based on scientific production whose growth is exponential [16]; the latter is described by a regression representation curve [17], whether there is growth or obsolescence of the topics to be discussed.

The bibliometric analysis studies trends mainly in co-authorship: authors, organizations, countries; bibliographic coupling and citation: prolific author; fields search, and research areas. Between the terms bibliometrics and scientometrics, the difference in concise is the object of study, whereas, for bibliometrics, they are: books, journals, articles, documents, authors, and users for scientometrics. The study of the scientific community's subjects, fields, disciplines, and spheres [17] mentions that bibliometric analysis examines scientific dynamism within a given period by observing scientific production. For this investigation of Bibliometric Analysis, subjects included in Science, Technology, Mathematics, and Engineering (STEM) will be analyzed.

The components of this investigation go beyond just academic disciplines. Governments worldwide, through educational programs, seek to promote STEM disciplines at all levels of training of the subject to meet future technological, energetical, and environmental elements needs, among others. [18] Since 2001, knowledge of STEM subjects concerning innovation and development has been acquired. The knowledge-based economy, according to the National Science Foundation (NSF) of the United States [19]. This research seeks Ecuadorian scientific production about STEM.

Some definitions of STEM have included other branches of the social sciences such as economics, anthropology, and psychology. Other acronyms are disciplines such as arts (STEAM) and robotics (STREAM), according to the indicator [18]. Additionally, it can be seen that in all forms of STEM, the transversality presented by computer science in the meaning of STEM/CS [20] within the disciplines as mentioned earlier.

Following the International Association of Educators (NAFSA) of the STEM fields that the Department of Education's Classification of Instructional Programs of the United States establishes that integrating 'Mathematics' and 'Engineering'; in the field 'Mathematics' is considered multidisciplinary and interdisciplinary study by the metrics of scientific databases [21]. Mathematics is treated as interdisciplinary knowledge [22] but as transdisciplinary teaching [23].

In the vast group of disciplines, it is permanently updated to resolve problems in each domain in a transversal and collaborative way [24]. Therefore, this research seeks to cover the most representative categories of the platform and thereby analyze the most critical bibliometric aspects.

The so-called primary collection of the Web of Science (WoS) or Web of Science Core Collection™, which houses scientific literature from the year 1900 [25] (see Table 2) and whose first indexing became known as the Science Citation Index (SCI) was in 1960 [26]. In contrast, it has evolved by the standards of information sciences, and the volume of knowledge generation per publication ranked as high impact whose contribution has been allusive to Ecuador since 1990; these converge in 5 indices subject to the degree of subscription obtained by the institution for the use of the WoS database [27].

Table 2. WoS core collection index

Collection	Description*	Reference
Science Citation Index Expanded™	Since 1990, originally SCI and was updated in 2018 as SCI-EXPANDED	[25]

(continued)

Table 2. (*continued*)

Collection	Description*	Reference
Social Sciences Citation Index™ (SSCI)	Since 1990, journals that prove necessary levels of editorial rigor and best practices	[28]
Emerging Sources Citation Index™ (ESCI)	Since 2017, it has been excluded for it has no impact factor	[28]
Conference Proceedings Citation Index™ (CPCI-S)	Since 2008, it has indexed conferences and citations	[28]
Book Citation Index™ (BKCI-S)	Since 2011, it has indexed conferences and citations	[28]

Note: (*) Analysis time to consider according to institutional underwriting.

WoS has 12 categories related to the knowledge of the branch of Mathematics, aimed at fields that involve a great application of mathematical principles in problem-solving. The Engineering branch includes a range of 41 categories that meet quality and impact criteria in the indexes, also known as the WoS Index. For which the Journal Citation Reports (JCR) platform of the ISI.

The JCR establishes the methodology for calculating the impact factors for scientific journals in each WoS category [25]. Of the 254 varieties in which more than one group can consist, 41 correspond to Engineering and 12 to Mathematics (see Table 3); and each of them corresponds to 7 metrics respectively, for this research.

Table 3. WoS core collection categorization

Collection*	Description
Category	By 2020 the JCR attributes one or more categories to each journal among the 254 existing
Group	By 2020 51 groups allow directing each category according to the JCR
Edition	The WoS Index is according to subscription
# of journals	The number of journals contains in a research category
Citable items	Types of documents considered academic contributions by the JCR are the denominator of the journal's impact factor calculation
Total citations	The total amount of times a journal has been cited by all journals registered in the database every year
Median impact factor	The statistic index yields the median of the impact factors of every journal within its category

Note: (*) Analysis time to be considered according to the institutional subscription. Adapted from [29].

To determine the relevance of Ecuadorian scientific production in the branches of Engineering and Mathematics. Scientific documents with the SCI-EXPANDED, SSCI, CPCI-S, and BKCI-S indexes will be counted. The proportionate value of the median impact factor will be calculated with the JCR methodology for each category up to 2020, taken as a reference.

Therefore, to determine the relevant Ecuadorian scientific production of Engineering and Mathematics STEM fields, it is necessary to consider the median impact for SCI-EXPANDED, SSCI, CPCI-S, and BKCI-S indexes. It excludes the Emerging Sources Citation Index™ (ESCI) [30]. In contrast to other publications, the aggregate impact factor with the average and this statistic are excluded in this research.

2   Methodology

This four-step implementation was used for the present study (see Fig. 1):

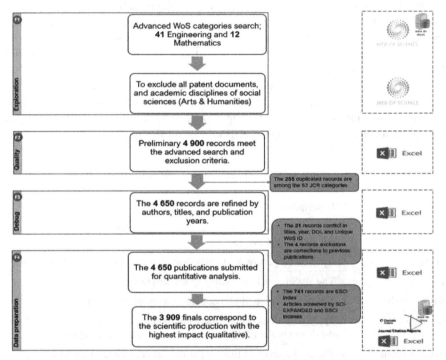

Fig. 1. Proposed model for bibliometric analysis. Based on the PRISMA technique to schematize the bibliometric flowchart. [5] Process-Driven Approach (PDA) process-based model. [31] Platform architecture for data ingestion and analytics [32].

Phase 1 (F1) – Exploration: WoS Advanced Search Strategy
Ecuador is the country of affiliation of all scientific production susceptible to analysis,

the better-known categorizations of the JCR for all relevant academic contributions for each discipline, and fixed the time interval that dates until the year 2021; for Engineering, categories are formulated as the following:

*(**cu**=ecuador) **AND** ((**TASCA**==("agricultural engineering" **OR** "automation control systems" **OR** "construction building technology" **OR** "engineering aerospace" **OR** "engineering biomedical" **OR** "engineering chemical" **OR** "engineering civil" **OR** "engineering electrical electronic" **OR** "engineering environmental" **OR** "engineering geological" **OR** "engineering industrial" **OR** "engineering manufacturing" **OR** "engineering marine" **OR** "engineering mechanical" **OR** "engineering multidisciplinary" **OR** "engineering ocean" **OR** "engineering petroleum" **OR** "fisheries" **OR** "food science technology" **OR** "forestry" **OR** "imaging science photographic technology" **OR** "information science library science" **OR** "instruments instrumentation" **OR** "materials science characterization testing" **OR** "mechanics" **OR** "medical laboratory technology" **OR** "metallurgy metallurgical engineering" **OR** "microscopy" **OR** "mining mineral processing" **OR** "nuclear science technology" **OR** "optics" **OR** "quantum science technology" **OR** "regional urban planning" **OR** "remote sensing" **OR** "robotics" **OR** "spectroscopy" **OR** "telecommunications" **OR** "thermodynamics" **OR** "transportation science technology" **OR** "water resources")) **NOT** (**PY**==("2022")))*   (1)

Let be **cu** = country, **TASCA** = categories, **PY** = year; **AND, OR, NOT** Boolean operators. Date of all consultations 2022/03/28.

Under the same variables, the categories for Mathematics:

*(**cu**=ecuador) **AND** ((**TASCA**==("computer science artificial intelligence" **OR** "computer science theory methods" **OR** "logic" **OR** "mathematical computational biology" **OR** "mathematics" **OR** "mathematics applied" **OR** "mathematics interdisciplinary applications" **OR** "physics mathematical" **OR** "psychology mathematical" **OR** "social sciences mathematical methods" **OR** "statistics probability")) **NOT** (**PY**==("2022")))*   (2)

From the information extracted from the Core Collection Subject Categories of the WoS, a common category between Engineering and Mathematics is attributed, which will be incorporated mostly into Mathematics given its treatment of transdisciplinary knowledge which will be analyzed a posteriori. The types of Operations Research Management Sciences are formulated as the following:

*(**cu**=ecuador) **AND** ((**TASCA**==("operations research management science"))*   (3)

In the formal declaration of exclusions from scientific production that are part of this study, it will not contemplate patents of any kind assimilated with the limitations of the institutional subscription used that does not display in its search services to the bases of the Derwent World Patents Index™ (DWPI). This group includes productions that may be related to social sciences, arts, and humanities, which are beyond the scope of STEM disciplines. The exclusions are:

$$NOT \, (DT==("tv \; review \; radio \; review" \; OR \; "item \; about \; an \; individual" \; OR$$
$$"bibliography" \; OR \; "retraction" \; OR \; "reprint" \; OR \; "fiction \; creative \; prose" \; OR \tag{4}$$
$$"biographical \; item" \; OR \; "poetry")$$

Sean **DT**=documents.

Phase 2 (F2) – Quality: Verification of the Results
Obtaining the data as a process is susceptible to improvement, recognizing the particularities and constant modifications suffered by the scientific databases, for which case in question of the WoS collection. The four search iterations were processed in one month: the next point, two updates through full use of the graphical interface of the platform. Finally, the two parameterizations directly with the field label through Boolean operators.

Phase 3 (F3) – Debug: Cleaning the Data Set
In this phase, it has been noted that the resulting download is consistent with the parameters entered in the search strategy, proving the amount of the requested information is by the requirement. The purification of the data will revolve around six bibliometric fields that will be the basis to give the unique character to each record within the data set (see Table 4).

Table 4. List of fields for search

Basic fields	Description
Author Full Names	All records contemplate this field, and all matching data is automatically extracted in addition to the title, year of publication, DOI, and Unique WoS ID
Title	Any record whose data is duplicated will be removed
Publication Year	Catalog with the period set up in the advanced search and be a constant of belonging in all records
WoS Categories	At least the records hold two of the five categories assigned for segmentation into 2 clusters
Web of Science Index	All data must have at least one of the three indexes of this field representing the JCR impact metric as qualitative, relevant information
Research Areas	That all records have this quantitative information

With this, segmentation criteria are implemented to form two clusters: 'Engineering' and 'Mathematics'. For data processing, the data set of the second will be taken as a reference given transdisciplinarity.

Phase 4 (F4) – Data Preparation: Sorting of Data for Analysis of Results
The information is then divided between quantitative (Excel Spreadsheet) and qualitative (VOSViewer and R Studio). Both are impact factors.

3 Results

Product of the debugged base product of the model of Fig. 1 (4 650 quantitative base and 3 909 qualitative base), the required visualizations are analyzed one by one according to each result illustrated below:

Scientific Production in Engineering and Mathematics
For this section, the 'Publication Year' column was taken from the database produced from the proposed model (cleaned base), grouping the annual count of all publications. They result in the characteristic curve under Price's Law (see Fig. 2). For this case, the best resulting projection is exponential.

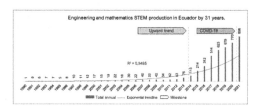

Fig. 2. Evolution of scientific production – Mathematics and Engineering in Ecuador.

Among the localized milestones, the first is the most accelerated growth from the end of 2013 onwards ($R^2 = 0.9485$ – Price's Law [33]). Consequently, the milestone of COVID-19 where the increase in scientific production was also observed.

Languages of Publications
Like the previous section, under the debugged 'Language' and 'Category' fields (see Fig. 3). The researcher developed a feature to distinguish between Mathematics and Engineering.

The most used languages within Ecuadorian research reference for fields of English Engineering (72.86% of total publications). Mathematics: English (13.83%). The second most used language is Spanish with 11.83% and 0.62% of production for Engineering and Mathematics, respectively. Briefly, 86.69% of all publications are in the English language from both clusters analyzed.

Fig. 3. Distribution of languages by cluster – Mathematics and Engineering in Ecuador.

Articles with Status Open Access
The 'Open Access Designations' field of the cleaned base is contemplated, for which the different distinctions (e.g., Bronze, gold, hybrid) are quantified according to the scientific production (see Fig. 4).

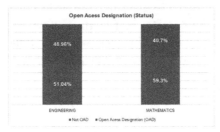

Fig. 4. Scientific production of free access for the community – Mathematics, and Engineering in Ecuador.

The identified total records are 2 080 for Engineering and 399 for Mathematics. They are considered publications that cannot be accessed unless a subscription payment or the purchase of the scientific publication.

Relevant Production – Mathematics and Engineering
To check the importance of the SCI-EXPANDED indicator for Engineering and Mathematics. They are compared for the indexes (see Fig. 5).

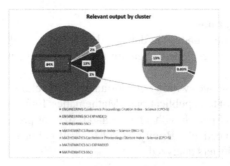

Fig. 5. Comparison between discipline and discipline - Mathematics and Engineering in Ecuador.

This figure illustrates the impact of Engineering (84%) on Mathematics (13%) for the indicator studied. Therefore, scientific production in Ecuador is relevant for the two disciplines.

Contribution by Research Areas

For the present analysis of the purified base, the count of the main areas of the 'Research Area' field is considered. Consequently, a specific topic studied was recounted (e.g., Engineering, Computer Science) (See Fig. 6).

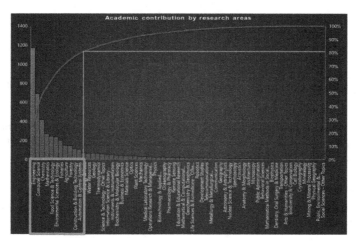

Fig. 6. Pareto diagram result of scientific production (63 categories) - Mathematics and Engineering in Ecuador.

The illustration follows that under principle 80–20 Pareto analysis to locate a few vital [34]. The most representative areas are: (1) Engineering; (2) Computer Science; (3) Chemistry; (4) Mathematics; (5) Food Science & Technology; (6) Environmental Sciences & Ecology; (7) Fisheries; (8) Agriculture; (9) Forestry; (10) Construction & Building Technology; (11) Automation & Control Systems. These areas are considered of vital importance for both disciplines in Ecuador. Additionally, by types of publications, it is illustrated in Fig. 7 its distribution.

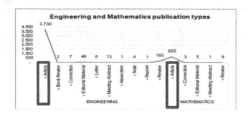

Fig. 7. Comparative scientific production - Mathematics and Engineering in Ecuador.

The prevalence of the scientific articles fields represent with 'Article' of Engineering (3 730–80.22%) and Mathematics (655–14.09%) respectively, where it stands for 94.30% of total publications is representative. Therefore, this is the most offered product.

Author Keyword Cloud
The result of processing the data referring to the group 'Author Keywords' of the debugged database, you have the Fig. 8, using R Studio™.

Fig. 8. Keyword Cloud - Engineering and Mathematics Disciplines Ecuador.

Therefore, it can be deduced that the words most often are Ecuador, Machine Learning, and Optimization, which refers to the studies taught under Ecuadorian talent and Machine Learning (ML) topics.

Co-authorship by Authors, Universities, Collaborations
Similarly, as described previously, in the field 'Authors', the co-authors with the highest prevalence are illustrated in Fig. 9.

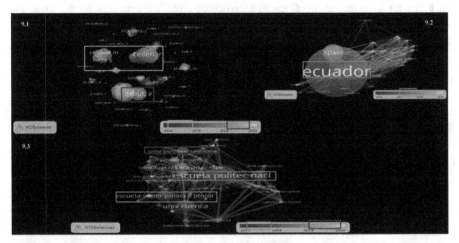

Fig. 9. Co-authors/IES/Countries with greater collaboration - Engineering and Mathematics Disciplines Ecuador.

From the Fig. 9.1, the most representative co-authors are identified: (1) 'zurita, g'; (2) 'celleri, r'; (3) 'cerrada, m' y (4) 'debut, a', of the latter with the greatest impact within the years 2019–2020. From Fig. 9.2, the data illustrate that in the same country, 'ecuador', there was a great collaboration for elaborating scientific production between 2017–2018. From Fig. 9.3, the organizations that contribute the most to research are the Instituciones de Educación Superior (IES), data analyzed from 'Addresses' of the refined base. The universities with the highest research link are: 'escuela politec nacl' (Escuela Politécnica Nacional del Ecuador) and 'escuela super politecn litoral' (Escuela Superior Politécnica de Litoral), two universities that have a higher prevalence but between the years 2017–2018. Otherwise for 'univ fuerzas armadas espe' (Universidad de las Fuerzas Armadas - ESPE) with the highest participation between 2019–2020.

Collaboration Network of the Most Prolific Author
From the refined base, the 'Authors' field is analyzed as the most representative author in more scientific articles and citations of other publications (see Fig. 10).

Fig. 10. Most outstanding authors - Disciplines of engineering and mathematics Ecuador.

Therefore, all the authors described are within the engineering area; the author with more relevance, Khorami, Majid h-Index in Publons score 26 [35].

4   Discussion

For scientific research in Ecuador, the authors Rodríguez et al. [36] conclude a notable slowdown in South America for the number of documents produced 'Number of Documents'. However, about publications in journals indexed for SCOPUS, there is a growth from 2013 compared to the decade 2000–2010 as such a higher percentage of publication 'Publication Rate'. In a similar situation, publications related to the number of inhabitants correlate to the 89% growth of the indicator 'Number of Documents/Millions of habitants' between 2011 and 2020.

In another research, the authors Cortés et al. [37] mention that within the comparative analysis between 103 countries selected for the study, the continents with the highest 'Average researchers (per million people)' (1996–2015) index are (1) Asia, (2) LATAM, (3) Africa; predominant country India with 10.5, China (9.4); in LATAM Brazil, Colombia, and Mexico with 2.1, 1.4 and 1.0 respectively. Therefore, Latin America has a more prominent presence in the countries mentioned earlier worldwide, surpassing even countries such as Malaysia and Iran [37].

Regarding the use of Scopus, WoS, and Scielo scientific journal collection platforms for analysis exclusively in Ecuador, researchers Zhimnay et al. [38] mention that for the indicator of production per year concerning the three databases studied.

WoS started with a considerable gap with Scopus in 2013; however, in 2018, it decreased this gap, reaching more excellent proximity to Scopus, deducing then that WoS production is relatively significant like Scopus. Therefore, the use of WoS is relevant to the present research since it groups more databases, such as Wiley, Chinese Science Citation FSTA, Medline. [39], primary collection WoS, Russian Science Citation Index, KCI – Korean Journal Database [40].

In the same way, it is also essential for the study of STEM binding exclusively for Engineering and Mathematics within a method suitable for the use of bibliometric analysis. This study gives the depth of STEM and its areas of knowledge before the respective analysis in WoS of the 53 categories, surpassing Scopus again by detailing a better standardization.

5 Conclusions

According to the scientific production in Ecuador, there is no state of the art in Engineering and Mathematics subjects from STEM. Unlike the total scientific output that gives more breadth to other areas not linked to STEM.

There are categories belonging to the WoS catalog of Engineering and Mathematics subjects related to STEM, 41 and 12.

The 'Research Area' criteria are more relevant than the WoS categories. It allows its best bibliometric analysis for STEM subjects of scientific production and eases the dissemination of information in specific crucial areas of research.

It is possible to use technological tools to group enough bibliometric information needed for dissemination. The use of the graphic modeler VOSViewer, Excel spreadsheet, and the annual publication of JCR evaluator indicators is illustrated within the proposed model and its service within a data architecture.

This research is essential since it allows us to visualize aspects of STEM and its relationship with academic production in Ecuador. Therefore, the qualitative and quantitative analysis of the scientific output in Engineering and Mathematics, languages of the publications, articles with Open Access status, production Engineering – Relevant Mathematics, contribution by research areas, author's keywords, and collaborations. This study is necessary for further research as it is a starting point for future analyses with more STEM categories and databases not considered in the current paper.

References

1. Fahimnia, B., Sarkis, J., Davarzani, H.: Green supply chain management: a review and bibliometric analysis. Int. J. Prod. Econ. **162**, 101–114 (2015)
2. Herrera-Franco, G., Montalván-Burbano, N., Mora-Frank, C., Bravo-Montero, L.: Scientific research in ecuador: a bibliometric analysis. Publications **9**(4), 55 (2021)
3. Arshad, A.I., et al.: Antibiotics: a bibliometric analysis of top 100 classics. Antibiotics **9**(5), 1–16 (2020)
4. Baykoucheva, S., From the science citation index to the journal impact factor and web of science. In: Managing Scientific Information and Research Data, Elsevier, pp. 115–121 (2015)
5. Chérrez, K.: Análisis bibliométrico de la producción científica Hispanoamericana sobre Salud Ocupacional indexada En Web Of Science (2015–2019). Universidad Internacional del Ecuador (2020)

6. Limaymanta Alvarez, C.H., Zulueta-Rafael, H., Restrepo-Arango, C., Alvarez-Muñoz, P.: Análisis bibliométrico y cienciométrico de la producción científica de Perú y Ecuador desde Web of Science (2009–2018). Inf. Cult. Soc. (43), 31–52 (2020)
7. Marín Velásquez, T.D., Arriojas Tocuyo, D.D.J.: Análisis de revistas de América Latina indexadas en Redalyc del área de Ingeniería: relación con indicadores socioeconómicos. Métodos Inf. **11**(21), 001–021 (2020)
8. Schirone, M.: STEM information literacy: a bibliometric mapping (1974-2020). In: Kurbanoğlu, S., Špiranec, S., Ünal, Y., Boustany, J., Kos, D. (eds.) ECIL 2021. CCIS, vol. 1533, pp. 385–395. Springer, Cham (2022). https://doi.org/10.1007/978-3-030-99885-1_33
9. Analuisa, I., Caicedo, S., Evaluación bibliométrica de los antimicrobianos y las contribuciones en WOS (2000–2021). In: Congreso de investigación aplicada a ciencia de datos II congreso nacional de R Users Group – Ecuador, p. 13 (2022)
10. Proaño Ponce, W.P., Alay Barcia, T.V.: Gestión del conocimiento para el análisis de obligaciones fiscales establecidas en las asociaciones del ámbito socio-económico en Jipijapa. Ecuadorian Sci. J. **4**(2), 56–62 (2020)
11. Ruiz Pino, D.D.P., Barrios, N.: Chemistry teacher's PCK: state of the art. In: Botto-Tobar, M., Cruz, H., Díaz Cadena, A. (eds.) CIT 2020. AISC, vol. 1327, pp. 461–475. Springer, Cham (2021). https://doi.org/10.1007/978-3-030-68083-1_34
12. RincónQuintero, A.D., Del PortilloValdés, L.A., MenesesJácome, A., Sandoval-Rodríguez, C.L., Rondón-Romero, W.L., Ascanio-Villabona, J.G.: Trends in technological advances in food dehydration, identifying the potential extrapolated to cocoa drying: a bibliometric study. In: Botto-Tobar, M., Cruz, H., Díaz Cadena, A. (eds.) CIT 2020. LNEE, vol. 763, pp. 167–180. Springer, Cham (2021). https://doi.org/10.1007/978-3-030-72212-8_13
13. Arslan, H.M., Chengang, Y., Siddique, M., Yahya, Y.: Influence of senior executives characteristics on corporate environmental disclosures: a bibliometric analysis. J. Risk Financ. Manag **15**(136), 1–21 (2022)
14. Brodin Danell, J.A., Danell, R., Vuolanto, P.: Fifty years of complementary and alternative medicine (CAM) – a bibliometric analysis of publication activity and general content of the publications. J. Scientometr. Res. **9**(3), 268–276 (2020)
15. Dharmani, P., Das, S., Prashar, S.: A bibliometric analysis of creative industries: current trends and future directions. J. Bus. Res. **135**(June), 252–267 (2021)
16. Demir, E., Akmeşe, F., Erbay, H., Taylan-Özkan, A., Mumcuoğlu, K.Y.: Bibliometric analysis of publications on house dust mites during 1980–2018. Allergol. Immunopathol. (Madr). **48**(4), 374–383 (2020)
17. Rodríguez-Rojas, Y.L., Luque Clavijo, A.M., Castro Rojas, M.L.: Metodologías para el fortalecimiento de líneas en grupos de investigación académicos o empresariales. Rev. Lasallista Investig. **16**(2), 142–159 (2019)
18. QS World University Rankings: What is STEM? 29-ene-2021. [Online]. Available: https://www.topuniversities.com/courses/engineering/what-stem. Accessed 22 Mar 2022
19. Hallinen, J.: STEM education curriculum, 21 October 2021. [Online]. Available: https://www.britannica.com/topic/STEM-education. Accessed 21 Mar 2022
20. U.S. Department of Education: Science, Technology, Engineering, and Math, including Computer Science (2022). [Online]. Available: https://www.ed.gov/stem. Accessed 30 Mar 2022
21. NAFSA: DHS Adds 22 Fields to STEM Designated Degree Program List. 21-ene-2022. [Enlínea]. Disponible en: https://www.nafsa.org/regulatory-information/dhs-adds-22-fields-stem-designated-degree-program-list. Accessed 21 Mar 2022
22. Rogora, E., Tortoriello, F.S.: Interdisciplinarity for learning and teaching mathematics. Bolema Bol. Educ. Matemática **35**(70), 1086–1106 (2021)
23. Testov, V.A., Perminov, E.A.: The role of mathematics in transdisciplinarity content of modern education. Obraz. i Nauk. **23**(3), 11–34 (2021)

24. Zuo, Z., Zhao, K.: The more multidisciplinary the better? – the prevalence and interdisciplinarity of research collaborations in multidisciplinary institutions. J. Informetr. **12**(3), 736–756 (2018)
25. Calahorrano, L., Monge-Nájera, J., Wang, M.-H., Ho, Y.-S.: Ecuador publications in the science citation index expanded: institutions, subjects, citation and collaboration patterns. Rev. Biol. Trop. **68**(1), 98–107 (2020)
26. Blakeman, K., Bibliometrics in a digital age: help or hindrance. Sci. Prog. **101**(3), 293–310 (2018)
27. Franco, F.: Bibliometría como instrumento para fortalecer los servicios bibliotecarios. México D.F. (2019)
28. Web of Science Group: Web of Science Core Collection (2022). [Online]. Available: https://mjl.clarivate.com/collection-list-downloads
29. Clarivate Analytics: InCites Journal Citation Reports Help. [Online]. Available: http://help.incites.clarivate.com/incitesLiveJCR/glossaryAZgroup/g5/8199-TRS.html. Accessed 29 Mar 2022
30. Kiesslich, T., Beyreis, M., Zimmermann, G., Traweger, A.: Citation inequality and the journal impact factor: median, mean, (does it) matter? Scientometrics **126**(2), 1249–1269 (2021)
31. Schäffer, E., Stiehl, V., Schwab, P.K., Mayr, A., Lierhammer, J., Franke, J.: Process-driven approach within the engineering domain by combining business process model and notation (BPMN) with process engines. In: Procedia CIRP, vol. 96, pp. 207–212 (2021)
32. López-Martínez, F., Núñez-Valdez, E.R., García-Díaz, V., Bursac, Z.: A case study for a big data and machine learning platform to improve medical decision support in population health management. Algorithms **13**(4), 1–19 (2020)
33. Sisa, I., Abad, A., Espinosa, I., Martinez-Cornejo, I., Burbano-Santos, P.: A decade of Ecuador´s efforts to raise its health research output: a bibliometric analysis. Glob. Health Action **14**(1) (2021)
34. Dutta, S., Jaipuria, S.: Reducing packaging material defects in beverage production line using Six Sigma methodology. Int. J. Six Sigma Compet. Advant. **12**(1), 59 (2020)
35. Publons: Majid Khorami (2022). [Online]. Available: https://publons.com/researcher/4421268/majid-khorami/. Accessed 08 Apr 2022
36. Rodríguez, V., Flores-Sanchez, M., Zambrano, C.H., Rincón, L., Paz, J.L., Torres, F.J.: Analysis of Ecuador's SCOPUS scientific production during the 2001–2020 period by means of standardized citation indicators. Heliyon **8**(4), e09329 (2022)
37. Cortés, J.D., Guix, M., Carbonell, K.B.: Innovation for sustainability in the Global South: bibliometric findings from management & business and STEM (science, technology, engineering and mathematics) fields in developing countries. Heliyon **7**(8), e07809 (2021)
38. Zhimnay Valverde, C., Fernandez, J., Albarracín, J., Sádaba-Rodriguez, I., Sucozhanay, D.: Mapping of scientific production in social sciences in Ecuador. In: INTED 2019 Proceedings, vol. 1, no. May 2020, pp. 9501–9509 (2019)
39. Clarivate. Web of Science Core Collection. [Online]. Available: https://clarivate.com/webofsciencegroup/solutions/web-of-science-core-collection/. Accessed 26 May 2022
40. Araujo-Bilmonte, E., Huertas-Tulcanaza, L., Párraga-Stead, K.: Análisis de la producción científica del Ecuador a través de la plataforma Web of Science. Cátedra **3**(2), 150–165 (2020)

Image Processing Method to Estimate Water Quality Parameter

José Alonso Ruiz Navarro[1]([✉]), Félix Melchor Santos López[2],
Jhon Manuel Portella Delgado[2], and Eulogio Guillermo Santos de la Cruz[3]

[1] School of Science and Engineering, Pontifical Catholic University of Peru Lima,
Lima, Peru
ruizn.ja@pucp.edu.pe
[2] Department of Engineering, Pontifical Catholic University of Peru Lima,
Lima, Peru
{fsantos,jportella}@pucp.edu.pe
[3] Faculty of Industrial Engineering, National University of San Marcos, Lima, Peru
esantosd@unmsm.edu.pe

Abstract. Human settlements in rural areas face multiple sanitary challenges including water quality, the control of which is usually deemed as secondary due to the lack of materials or appropriate equipment. Hence, the measurement of water quality parameters, including the concentration of free chlorine, is extremely important. This paper proposes a sensing system for the measurement of free chlorine concentration based on the traditional colorimetric method, with N,N-diethyl-p-phenylenediamine as the reagent. The major hardware components are a dark room and a stationary digital camera. Using the proposed image processing method, the algorithm quantifies the pigmentation change and subsequently estimates the free chlorine concentration of the sample. Following this, a regression model is derived from the compiled data, which enables the evaluation of new samples in terms of free chlorine concentration. This model has an estimation error of less than 7% and a working range of 0.26 ppm to 1.50 ppm.

Keywords: Image processing · Water · Quality · Model · Chlorine

1 Introduction

Chlorine usage is considered to be a standard method for water disinfection due to its simplicity and easy availability of chlorine. Over the years, various methods have been developed to measure free chlorine, which is considered to be a relevant indicator for water sanitary conditions. From visual inspection to digital sensing, the variety of available methods is not vast, but big enough for some use cases such as industry, laboratory analysis and field tests. A majority of these methods rely on a procedure called colorimetry, which involves a chemical reaction that induces a change of color in a given sample. This method can be implemented with multiple chemicals depending on the parameter under evaluation. In the

M. Botto-Tobar et al. (Eds.): ICAT 2022, CCIS 1755, pp. 271–282, 2023.
https://doi.org/10.1007/978-3-031-24985-3_20

case of free chlorine, there is a small variety of reagents, such as potassium starch or o-toluidine. This paper describes the design process of a system that evaluates water quality of a given sample based on its free chlorine concentration, via a chemical reaction with N,N-diethyl-p-phenylenediamine (DPD). The obtained image is then preprocessed. Finally, the change in color is quantified using image processing (computer vision) and the result is used as input to estimate the concentration in the sample.

This publication's structure has a literature review as starting point. Other publications were analyzed in order to evaluate their relevance for this work. The ones where the analysis or conclusions have any relation to this paper area, were deconstructed to allow the extraction of relevant qualitative and quantitative data from each one of them, making a strong emphasis in some results which were summarized. Secondly, we describe the system proposal, defining all the requirements it should fulfill. The experiment that took place to design a model using the presented image processing method is presented, mentioning all the materials used in it like any physical and electric components included. The analysis process, which the recompiled data from the experiment went through, is detailed and presented in three stages - a preprocessing stage, a processing stage and a model determination stage. Subsequently, all the numeric results of these experiments and their interpretations are reported. Finally, we present the authors' conclusions.

2   Literature

There are various approaches to the measurement and detection of chlorine in water. Estimation of free chlorine concentration can be achieved by traditional colorimetric methods, which involve adding chemicals such as DPD, o-toluidine or potassium starch to a water sample, which then react with the chlorine present in it. The concentration of the products obtained from these chemical reactions is related to the concentration of chlorine. However, the most significant change is that the presence of the new chemical is revealed by the tonality of the water sample, which loses its transparency and acquires a specific color. The intensity of this color is indicative of the concentration of the resultant chemical, and therefore, the concentration of free chlorine. The evaluation of this color intensity is traditionally performed via the naked eye. This method is low-cost, but is inevitably susceptible to variables such as light conditions and the operator's vision.

Newer methods for measurement have been developed over time, which include the use of amperometric sensors. This approach is based on the reaction of chlorine with certain metals. Amperometric sensors usually consist of a probe; immersion of this probe in water triggers a reaction with an inner anode and cathode, generating the flow of an electric current between these electrodes. This method relies on the relation between the intensity of the current and the free chlorine concentration. These sensors are commercially sold by manufactures such as Bürkert [2], Endress+Hauser [5] and Sensorex [18]. Other innovations include digital colorimeters which are tristimulus devices and emit a light beam of a certain wavelength through the sample. The absorbance of this medium, i.e., the sample, is measured and is then used to estimate the concentration of free chlorine in the sample.

Digital image colorimetry is yet another method, and is related to the traditional colorimetric method. The chemical reaction takes place in a cuvette, following which a digital image is taken and processed in order to quantify the color intensity. This process determines whether a relationship exists between the concentration label and the values of the image. This method is applied not only to estimate free chlorine concentration, but also to evaluate the presence of other parameters in many chemical analyses. A structured review of the literature is summarized in Table 1 and allows us to differentiate between digital image colorimetry techniques. The colorimetry methods adopted by researchers till date can be grouped according to the ways in which features are extracted from an image - direct measurement or formulation. The former involves directly measuring mean values in a traditional RGB colorspace [12,15,21] or transforming the image to another colorspace such as HSV or CieLab [1,3,8,11]. The latter involves using the mean values of many colorspaces as inputs and plugging them into a predefined equation, which computes an estimated value for the given parameter [4,9,10,17]. A significant criteria for differentiation is the inclusion of a preprocessing stage where the mean values of colors in an image are compared or compensated with a reference. This process is included in order to increase the robustness of the image processing algorithm against variables such as illumination variation, distance between the camera and the sample and the incidence angle of light to the sample, regardless of whether these are being handled manually or by hardware. Examples of the inclusion of a preprocessing stage are [6,7,9,17,21]. Lastly, it is important to note that artificial intelligence [14,16,19] has been also applied to digital image colorimetry, and the mean values of RGB or HSV are commonly used as inputs. Nevertheless, machine learning is used in this context primarily to solve classification rather than regression problems.

From the papers listed in Table 1, it can be concluded that several researchers typically extract features from the Red-Blue-Green (RGB) colorspace, either solving a regression or classification problem using image processing or implementing machine learning methods. Despite this, alternative colorspaces such as HSV or CieLab are also used. It is also important to note that compensation or normalization using a reference is a relevant step in image processing to avoid the influence of illumination variations.

3   System Proposal and Requirements

In this paper, we propose a design for a sensing system (shown in Fig. 1) for free chlorine concentration estimation using image processing, specifically digital image colorimetry. The system's working range must include the value 0.5 ppm (i.e., 0.5 mg/L), because this is typically the lowest value considered to be healthy by sanitary institutions such as Dirección General de Salud Ambiental (DIGESA) in Peru.

Table 1. Literature review

Ref. N°	Algorithm description	Processing formulation	Parameter
[20]	Logarithmic scale of proportion between a reference and target	$T = \log(I_{blank}/I_{new})$ $I = (R+G+B)/3$	Various
[10]	Grayscaling	$gsv = (R_{av} + G_{av} + B_{av})/3$	Blood hematocrit
[19]	Machine learning for classification	RGB, HSV and Lab mean values as inputs	Peroxide
[21]	Self-referencing to avoid luminosity variations	$R_{norm} = R_{samp}/R_{ref}$ $R'_{norm} = R_{norm}/\|RGB\|$	Various
[11]	Direct measurement of image values	Hue and Saturation	pH and nitrite respectively
[15]	Direct measurement of image values	Red	Arsenic and mercury
[9]	Distance in Lab colorspace (classification)	$\Delta E = \sqrt{\Delta L^2 + \Delta A^2 + \Delta B^2}$	Various
[16]	Machine learning for classification	RGB mean values as inputs	Various
[6]	Logarithmic scale of proportion between a reference and target	$I_x = \log(X_o/X_s)$ where $X = R, G$ or B	Mercury
[17]	Distance in XYZ colorspace (classification)	$\Delta L = \sqrt{\Delta X^2 + \Delta Y^2 + \Delta Z^2}$	Various

4 Experiment

4.1 Materials

The samples were prepared with commercial bleach, which was highly diluted to a concentration of approximately 2 ppm. This was mixed with tap water, which was measured to have low chlorine concentration, in order to acquire our baseline values. The chemical reactions between 10 ml water samples and commercial doses of DPD were triggered, during which the reagent was added to the sample in a glass cuvette. The free chlorine concentration of each sample was then determined using a Free Chlorine Checker. All the necessary equipment (Checker, cuvette and reagent) were manufactured by Hanna Instruments.

4.2 Physical Set up

The physical set up consisted of a dark room (shown in Fig. 2), which was designed and modeled using the CAD software Autodesk Inventor 2021. The model, which was designed as multiple separate parts that fit together, was then 3D printed using the raw material polylactic acid (PLA). The model had two different slots (shown in Fig. 2)- the first was designed for inserting a piece of white cardboard paper as the photographic background, while the second was circular and designed to keep the glass cuvette in place, therefore maintaining

Fig. 1. Dark room's 3D CAD model.

a constant distance between all the components such as the background, the cuvette and the camera.

All lighting came from an artificial source, i.e., two LED strips inside the dark room, allowing us to maintain full control over the illumination. These strips were controlled using the digital output pin of a microcontroller. In order to avoid blinding the digital camera when the lights were turned on, a circuit (as depicted in Fig. 3), was used to decrease the glow of the LED strips. Instead of turning the lights on abruptly by activating an optocoupler, the digital pin started charging a resistor-capacitor circuit, the transient voltage of which was used as a control signal for the base of a Bipolar Junction Transistor. This allowed the gradual flow of electric current between the collector and emitter. This current then flowed through the LED strips. A five-pin relay connected the capacitor to a resistor with no source to start the discharge phase, therefore slowly reducing the brightness of the LED strips. We consider this step particularly important, because it allowed us to obtain images with a consistent, high intensity and to avoid blinding the digital camera, which could lead to image distortions, particularly in the case of colors.

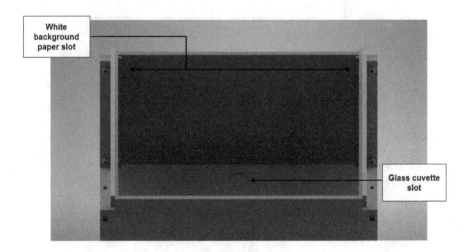

Fig. 2. Slots for placing the white background and a glass cuvette.

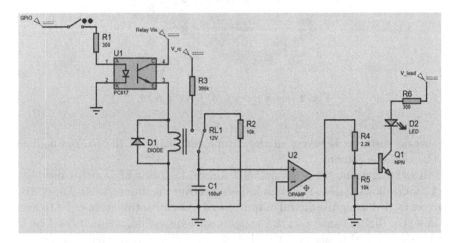

Fig. 3. Diagram of the described circuit.

4.3 Procedure

The water samples were prepared using a combination of tap water and highly diluted commercial bleach. The former had a low free chlorine concentration, while the latter was diluted in three stages to reduce the original 50000 ppm concentration to 2.5 ppm. Each of these stages consisted of mixing a small sample of an input chemical (commercial bleach in the first step) with clean tap water. This resulted in a chemical with a lower concentration of chlorine, which was used as the starting point for the next stage. This allowed us to obtain a more greatly diluted bleach solution at each stage, finally resulting in a more suitable chlorine concentration. As discussed before, commercial doses of DPD reagent were added to 10 ml water samples in glass cuvettes with a free chlorine concentration of 2 ppm or less. The cuvette was placed in the respective slot inside the dark room and an image was taken after the inner LED lights were gradually turned on.

4.4 Analysis

Preprocessing. All images went through preprocessing, primarily to manage minor variations in illumination. These variations were detected using the white background as reference, which should theoretically remain constant in all images.

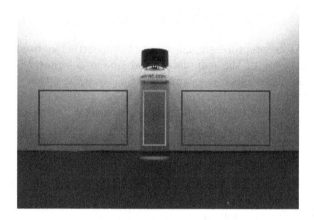

Fig. 4. Preprocessing ROI (blue) and processing ROI (green). (Color figure online)

It was under this assumption that we proceeded to apply some "compensation", making the background uniform in all pictures. First, target values were estimated, i.e., the mean values in the white background area for the RGB colorspace (Fr, Fg, Fb) of all pictures. Then, a compensation factor was calculated for each channel for each picture. This factor was then applied to all the pictures. Taking the red channel as an example, this procedure could be formulated as follows:

The target value was calculated taking in account all the pictures.

$$T_r = \frac{\sum_{i=1}^{n} Fr_i}{n} \tag{1}$$

where in (1), "Fr_i" is the mean red value in the white background for an specific "i" picture among "n" pictures.

A compensation factor was calculated for each picture in order to normalize the white background used as a reference.

$$Kr_i = \frac{T_r}{Fr_i} \tag{2}$$

where in (2) "Kr_i" stands for the compensation factor for a "i" image in the red channel. Finally the correction is applied to the corresponding channel image as follows:

$$R'_i = R_i * Kr_i \tag{3}$$

Processing. After preprocessing, features were extracted from each picture to quantify the color of the sample (digital image colorimetry). The feature extracted in our algorithm was saturation (S). To achieve this, the image was first converted from its original colorspace (RGB) to HSV. The mean S value was then extracted from each sample in the area denoted by the green rectangle in Fig. 4.

Model Determination. The relation between the selected feature (S) and free chlorine concentration is shown in Fig. 5. A fifth degree polynomial that was determined using least-squares regression was used as the best fitting curve to model the data. The polynomial is shown in Eq. (4):

$$P(x) = 5.5259 * 10^5 x^7 - 1.0894 * 10^6 x^6 + 8.9499 * 10^5 x^6$$
$$-3.9593 * 10^5 x^4 + 1.0155 * 10^5 x^3 - 1.5059 * 10^4 x^2 \tag{4}$$
$$+1.1967 * 10^3 x - 39.2$$

where x is the mean saturation value in the processing ROI. The performance of this model is evaluated in later sections. A comparison between this model's predictions and the target values is shown in Fig. 6.

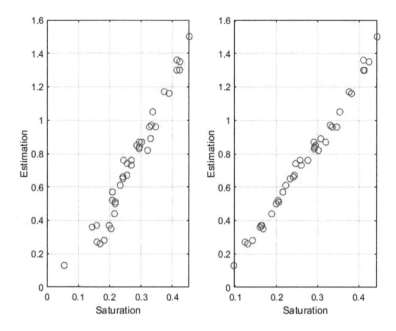

Fig. 5. Data points with (right) and without (left) preprocessing.

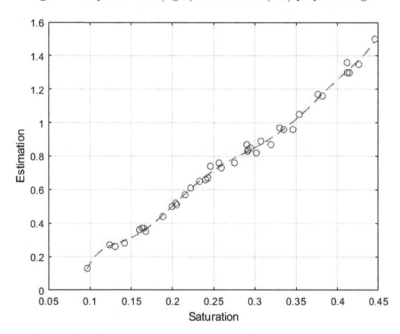

Fig. 6. Plot of the points and the fitted model.

5   Results

The model shown in prior sections for chlorine concentration estimation was determined using the least-squares method; in other words, the coefficients of polynomial P(x) minimize a loss function which is defined as shown in equation (5), where "n" is the number of data points.

$$\sum_{k=1}^{n}(P(x_k) - y_k)^2 = L \tag{5}$$

Model Performance. The estimated model shows a relative error less than 7% within a working range of 0.26 ppm to 1.50 ppm. In order to demonstrate the precision of the model, the correlation between target values and predicted values is shown in Fig. 7, which includes the values obtained if no preprocessing methods were applied. The correlation coefficient with no preprocessing was found to be 0.9913, whereas preprocessed data led to a model with correlation coefficient of 0.9975, which is closer to 1, the value in the ideal scenario. A comparison between both cases is shown in Fig. 7.

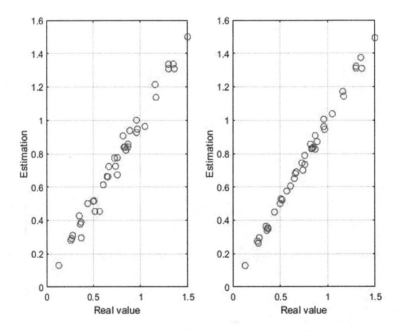

Fig. 7. Plots showing the impact of the preprocessing method in the correlation.

These results show the effectiveness of this methodology. Preprocessing results in a better relationship between free chlorine concentration and saturation mean value.

6   Conclusions

A literature review was undertaken to identify similar studies with promising results. Among these, several studies undertook image preprocessing to ensure lighting correction, color compensation and normalization. Not only were these methods taken into consideration, but also the specific colorspaces applied.

Our proposed image preprocessing and processing techniques, in combination with the recommended physical set up, derived a polynomial model for our specific use case. This tested model describes a relationship between the quantification value for an image and the measured concentration of free chlorine, and shows a maximum relative error of 6.54%. However, these methods can be applied by other authors in varying physical configurations in future studies to develop their own specific models for free chlorine estimation. These results showcase an improvement in comparison to contributions reporting error of 10% [20] and a correlation closer to 1 than works reviewed in [13].

References

1. Bayram, A., Horzum, N., Metin, A.U., Kılıç, V., Solmaz, M.E.: Colorimetric bisphenol-a detection with a portable smartphone-based spectrometer. IEEE Sens. J. **18**(14), 5948–5955 (2018)
2. Bürkert: Type 8232 - Chlorine sensor. https://www.burkert.com/en/type/8232
3. Coleman, B., Coarsey, C., Asghar, W.: Cell phone based colorimetric analysis for point-of-care settings. Analyst **144**(6), 1935–1947 (2019)
4. Coleman, B., Coarsey, C., Kabir, M.A., Asghar, W.: Point-of-care colorimetric analysis through smartphone video. Sens. Actuators, B Chem. **282**, 225–231 (2019)
5. Endress+Hauser: Memosens CCS51D: Digital free chlorine sensor. https://www. endress.com/en/field-instruments-overview/liquid-analysis-product-overview/ free-chlorine-digital-sensor-ccs51d
6. Firdaus, M.L., Aprian, A., Meileza, N., Hitsmi, M., Elvia, R., Rahmidar, L., Khaydarov, R.: Smartphone coupled with a paper-based colorimetric device for sensitive and portable mercury ion sensing. Chemosensors **7**(2), 25 (2019)
7. Guan, B., Zhao, J., Jin, H., Lin, H.: Determination of rice storage time with colorimetric sensor array. Food Anal. Methods **10**(4), 1054–1062 (2017)
8. Jalal, U.M., Jin, G.J., Shim, J.S.: Paper-plastic hybrid microfluidic device for smartphone-based colorimetric analysis of urine. Anal. Chem. **89**(24), 13160–13166 (2017)
9. Kılıç, V., Alankus, G., Horzum, N., Mutlu, A.Y., Bayram, A., Solmaz, M.E.: Single-image-referenced colorimetric water quality detection using a smartphone. ACS Omega **3**(5), 5531–5536 (2018)
10. Kim, S.C., Jalal, U.M., Im, S.B., Ko, S., Shim, J.S.: A smartphone-based optical platform for colorimetric analysis of microfluidic device. Sens. Actuators, B Chem. **239**, 52–59 (2017)
11. Luka, G., Nowak, E., Kawchuk, J., Hoorfar, M., Najjaran, H.: Portable device for the detection of colorimetric assays. Royal Soc. Open Sci. **4**(11), 171025 (2017)
12. McCracken, K.E., Angus, S.V., Reynolds, K.A., Yoon, J.Y.: Multimodal imaging and lighting bias correction for improved μpad-based water quality monitoring via smartphones. Sci. Rep. **6**(1), 1–13 (2016)

13. McCracken, K.E., Yoon, J.Y.: Recent approaches for optical smartphone sensing in resource-limited settings: a brief review. Anal. Methods 8(36), 6591–6601 (2016)
14. Mercan, Ö.B., Kılıç, V., Şen, M.: Machine learning-based colorimetric determination of glucose in artificial saliva with different reagents using a smartphone coupled μpad. Sens. Actuators, B Chem. 329, 129037 (2021)
15. Motalebizadeh, A., Bagheri, H., Asiaei, S., Fekrat, N., Afkhami, A.: New portable smartphone-based pdms microfluidic kit for the simultaneous colorimetric detection of arsenic and mercury. RSC Adv. 8(48), 27091–27100 (2018)
16. Mutlu, A.Y., Kılıç, V., Özdemir, G.K., Bayram, A., Horzum, N., Solmaz, M.E.: Smartphone-based colorimetric detection via machine learning. Analyst 142(13), 2434–2441 (2017)
17. Priye, A., Ball, C.S., Meagher, R.J.: Colorimetric-luminance readout for quantitative analysis of fluorescence signals with a smartphone cmos sensor. Anal. Chem. 90(21), 12385–12389 (2018)
18. Sensorex: FCL Amperometric Free Chlorine Sensor. https://sensorex.com/product/fcl-free-chlorine-sensor/
19. Solmaz, M.E., Mutlu, A.Y., Alankus, G., Kılıç, V., Bayram, A., Horzum, N.: Quantifying colorimetric tests using a smartphone app based on machine learning classifiers. Sens. Actuators, B Chem. 255, 1967–1973 (2018)
20. Šafranko, S., Živković, P., Stanković, A., Medvidović-Kosanović, M., Széchenyi, A., Jokić, S.: Designing colorx, image processing software for colorimetric determination of concentration, to facilitate students' investigation of analytical chemistry concepts using digital imaging technology. J. Chem. Educ. 96(9), 1928–1937 (2019)
21. Wang, X., Chang, T.W., Lin, G., Gartia, M.R., Liu, G.L.: Self-referenced smartphone-based nanoplasmonic imaging platform for colorimetric biochemical sensing. Anal. Chem. 89(1), 611–615 (2017)

Use of the Student Engagement as a Strategy to Optimize Online Education, Applying a Supervised Machine Learning Model Using Facial Recognition

Noboa Andrés⬤, Gonzalez Omar⬤, and Tapia Freddy(✉)⬤

Ecuador Departamento de Ciencias de la Computación,
Universidad de las Fuerzas Armadas ESPE, Sangolqui, Ecuador
{aenoboa1,ofgonzalez1,fmtapia}@espe.edu.ec

Abstract. The engagement of a student is a vital part of an online learning environment, however, because of the spatial separation between instructors and students in an online environment, it is often very difficult to measure the level of engagement in online learning. Higher levels of engagement are often related to a better sense of well-being, and are more related to emotions like happiness. In this paper, two state-of-the-art models that can help measure engagement and emotions are tested, in this case, we investigated suitability of two popular models: XCeption Architecture proposed for the DAiSEE dataset, and the DeepFace Emotion Recognition model. Both models are then applied in a real-life test, using real students in an online class, we measured their emotions using the models and then compared the results to obtain the effectiveness of correctly measuring the engagement and emotions of the students. We interpret the findings from our experimental results based on psychology concepts in the field of engagement.

Keywords: Engagement · Machine learning · Online environment · XCeption · DAiSEE · DeepFace · Emotion recognition

1 Introduction

People's life has changed quickly, and they need to keep learning new knowledge, and new skills. In this case, traditional school education and traditional classroom teaching cannot meet their needs fully. With the development of computer technology, network technology, and multimedia technology, online learning has emerged. Different from traditional classroom learning, online learning break through the limit of time and space, with its flexibility, mobility, and convenience, thus becoming an important way to learn. However, from the data obtained from MOOC (Massive Open Online Course) platforms, the completion rate of the courses is less than 10% and the participation of the students is relatively low [6].

In the words of Hu et al. [6], one of the most important characteristics of an online learning environment is the Engagement of a student. It's composed of 3 dimensions:

M. Botto-Tobar et al. (Eds.): ICAT 2022, CCIS 1755, pp. 283–295, 2023.
https://doi.org/10.1007/978-3-031-24985-3_21

behavioral engagement, cognitive engagement, and emotional engagement. In the online learning environment, the relationship and communication between teachers and students are not enough to get emotional engagement from the student. Therefore, it is crucial to carry out an analysis of the 'engagement' of a student in the online environment; for this, the use of a supervised model of machine learning is proposed, which allows measuring with certainty how engaged a student really is.

Nowadays, Facial emotion recognition fundamentally identifies emotions and reactions based on situations as well as the environment to which they belong [12]. In addition, a technology that goes hand in hand with the previous term and is presented in the proposed articles [4] is machine learning, which is one of the emerging technologies that are considered to have an impact of 90% in the next 4 years [11].

Taking this background into account, the present work focuses on developing a supervised machine learning model for facial emotion recognition to measure 'Student Engagement' in students who are in an online learning environment. The processes for the execution of the project will be to perform the training of a Convolutional Neural Network (CNN) model using images of faces that are in a freely accessible data set to perform the classification of engagement, Dataset for the Affective States in E-Environments (DAiSEE), we will also test a commonly used open-source tool "Deep Face" to measure other relevant emotions, then we validate the classification results obtained by both models using common validation techniques such as the matrix of confusion, we then apply the models to generate results based on the emotions of the students. Finally, we generate conclusions from the data obtained with the intervention of two expert psychologists.

The following are key highlights of this paper:

- Measure the level of engagement of a student from the facial emotions presented in a real environment using an Xception neural network.
- Use of techniques applied in psychology such as the EVEA test to fact-check the moods of students in a real environment.
- Develop an application that allows the inference of the emotional states of a student using their web cam applying both Xception and DeepFace.
- Compare the predicted results with the emotions obtained by the EVEA test using common evaluation techniques such as the Confusion Matrix.

This article is composed of five sections: the first section, related work, the second section architecture and implementation, four-section evaluation and results, and finally, conclusions and future work.

2 Related Work

Three relevant databases were consulted for the collection of related works on the subject. Association for Computing Machinery (ACM), Institute of Electrical and Electronics Engineers (IEEE), and ScienceDirect. For data collection, the following search string was proposed (Machine Learning or ML) and (Emotion Recognition) and (Facial Recognition) and (Online Environment or Online Education) and (DaisEE or Student

Engagement dataset) with the following inclusion criteria: journals, early access articles, and research articles between the years 2018-2021. Courses, standards, and Conferences were not taken into account. For the present work, the 12 most relevant and important works have been considered on the subject in the last 4 years.

The fields of Face Recognition (FR) and Facial Expression Recognition (FER) in Computer Vision are still evolving because of different challenges that are posed when recognizing an Image: pose variation, poor lighting, or even movement can play an important factor. In the case of FR, the most prevalent algorithms being studied are as follows: Multi Support Vector Machine (Multi-SVM), and Convolutional Neural Networks (CNN).

Tamil et al. [16] intends to tackle these challenges with a proposed Hybrid Robust Point Set Matching Convolutional Neural Network (HRPSM_CNN) to effectively recognize faces from data, this method works by detecting faces using the Viola-Jones algorithm, then features are extracted and detected by the HRPSM_CNN, this proposed method proves to be more efficient than traditional ones with an accuracy rate of 97% for easy to identify conditions, and an accuracy of 95 % in the case of harder situations like poor lighting and weather.

As a way to easily apply FER in supervised learning domains, DeepFace, proposed by Serengil et al. [15] offers an open-source framework that can help with the easier testing and implementation of FR models, the study discusses the implementation of many state-of-the-art algorithms like: VGG-Face, FaceNet, OpenFace, DeepFace, DeepID and Dlib, this helpful tool can aid with an easy way to switch up FR models on the fly.

Dewan et al. [3] demonstrate the feasibility of using Deep Learning methods to predict the different levels of engagement using facial features, by applying Local Directional Patterns (LDP) and KPCA to capture different features, they achieve a really high accuracy of 90.89% on two-level engagement detection and 87.25% on three-level engagement detection using the DAiSEE data set, it is mentioned how Engagement and affects can be linked, moreover, the work mentions increased importance of recognizing the levels of user engagement, with many actual useful applications, like being able to adjust the teaching strategy and obtaining real-time feedback, further optimizing the use of online education for instructors.

In the article by Kuruvayil et al. [9], they chose to use the meta-learning concept since they mention that there are a lack of sufficient samples with real conditions, such as partial occlusions, different head positions, and inadequate lighting conditions to be able to perform facial emotion recognition. Meta-learning using prototypical networks (metric-based meta-learning) has been proven to be well-fit for few-shot problems without severe overfitting. They used the CMU Multi-PIE dataset which contains images with partial occlusions, varying head poses, and illumination levels for training and evaluating the model. The proposed method is called ERMOPI (Emotion Recognition using Meta-learning across Occlusion, Pose, and Illumination). The proposed method achieved 90% accuracy for CMU Multi-PIE database images and 68% accuracy for AffectNet database images.

Abedi et al. [1] present and mention the existence of psychological evidence for the incorporation of affect states in engagement level detection, a proposed Temporal Convolutional Network (TCN) serves to analyze affect and behavioral features which are concatenated to one feature vector for all the frames of a video, with this Architecture, they accomplish a Mean Squared Error (MSE) of 0.0708 on the DAiSEE with their proposed method, there is also a mention of how difficult it is to measure disengagement as an anomaly. Also worthy of note, the actors highlight the use of the circumplex model (Fig. 1) of both positive and negative values of valence and arousal, which can help represent if a person is being engaged in a certain task.

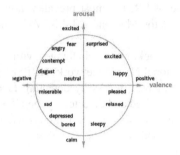

Fig. 1. Circumplex Model of Affect with both positive and negative emotional states [1]

In the article by Pronav et al. [11] they focused on developing a Deep Convolutional Neural Network (DCNN), model that classifies 5 human emotions (happy, angry, neutral, sad, and surprised) the proposed CNN consists of 4 layers composed of convolutional, pooling dropout and fully connected to extract the features from input data. The model uses an Adam optimizer to reduce the loss function and is tested to have an accuracy of 78.04%.

As a point of comparison, the potential for shallower neural networks in FER tasks is tested by [17], achieving an accuracy of 93.4 % on the DAiSEE dataset, using a shallow depth of 50 layers, the method helps avoid the vanishing gradient problem and the inclusion of residual layers helps to reduce the high loss found in deeper networks.

It is worth noting, that the related works found didn't measure engagement in a real-life scenario, instead of using preexisting data sets for engagement measurement.

3   Architecture and Implementation

This section presents the architectural proposal and describes the aspects of the development of the application using the Deep Face system, which allows deep learning facial recognition. In addition, we also applied the **XCeption** Architecture [2] a model trained on the DAiSEE Dataset through deep learning with an XCeption network (Fig. 2), this model applies the techniques of transfer learning, taking advantage of what XCeption has to offer, this will allow measuring the engagement of real students in 4 distinct labels identically as presented in the DAiSEE dataset: with 0 being a "Very Low" level of engagement, "1" being Low, 2 as High and finally "3" to represent the highest possible level of Engagement.

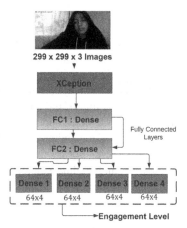

Fig. 2. XCeption architecture

The proposed architecture is based on Yogesh et al. [8] Xception implementation, removing the top classification layers of XCeption, with a new classification head, with two Fully Connected (FC) layers between the average pooling layer and classification.

The Exit flow of the architecture is as follows (Fig. 3), the final (Dense) layer of the model serves as the output of the engagement classification prediction.

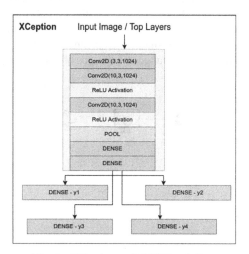

Fig. 3. XCeption on DAiSEE exit flow

Therefore, it is indicated which tools will be used, identifying the details related to the architecture of the system and its implementation.

3.1 Tools

The main language used was Python, which has several libraries suitable for the development of machine learning tools. In addition, Raschka's article [13] mentions that Python is the most preferred language for scientific computing, data science, and machine learning, boosting both performance and productivity by enabling the use of low-level libraries and clean high-level APIs. For proper training of the data from the Daisee dataset, the Tensor Flow library was used since it has benefits such as creating and training models through intuitive high-level APIs such as Keras, with immediate execution. In addition, OpenCv was used, which is an open-source library that can be used to perform tasks such as face detection, object tracking, and landmark detection.

3.2 Architecture

The DeepFace framework allows the possibility of analyzing facial features with the facial expression module, of the available emotions: **happy, neutral, surprise, sad, angry and fear** and **disgust**, we tested the feasibility of this module within a real-life environment.

As presented in Fig. 4, the architecture is composed of two sections user layer and the application layer: i) the user layer, where it is necessary to interact with the interface of the web application developed with the React framework (Figs. 5 and 6) in order to access the webcam, ii) the application layer, composed of the Flask web server as its main back-end, which is located in a container that will receive the frames of the user's face through the webcam. The responses sent by the server to the user will originate from the feeding of the Daisee data to the development platform, where through the TensorFlow, OpenCV libraries, and the DeepFace and XCeption models, they will be sent a JSON format with the percentages of the possible emotions of the user, to the backend in Flask.

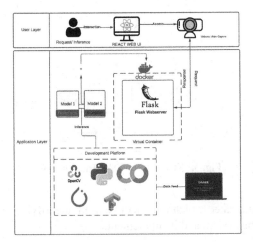

Fig. 4. End to end architecture of the proposed application

Fig. 5. Front-end of the proposed application

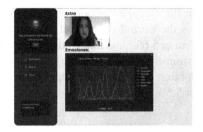

Fig. 6. Front-end of the proposed application

4   Evaluation

This section describes the parameters that were considered to carry out the evaluation (demographics, time, tools), the proposed scenarios, and each proposed session, in order to implement and subsequently analyze the results, with the aim of obtaining data to measure the engagement of students through their emotions.

We will work with a number of 18 students between 16 and 19 years of age belonging to the Unidad Educativa Dr. Arturo Freire.

4.1   Scenario Definition

Scenario 1. The study of the first scenario will be done to verify the functionality of the models applied within the application, therefore the following sessions will be defined:

– **High School Students between the Age range of 16–19 years old**: Students will engage in an online lecture, then they will complete a survey based on a rating scale of their frame of mind "Escala de Valoracion del Estado de Animo (EVEA)" [14] to verify which emotion they had during the class.

The objective will be to measure their engagement with the lecture. Various emotions that could affect how they perceive the lecture will be reviewed, such as sad, happy, disgust, anger, fear, neutral, and finally engagement itself. Said emotions will be verified and compared with the result of a Deep Face Emotion Model and an XCeption model, following that, we will draw conclusions based on the EVEA test that the students will complete.

To predict the various emotions from the videos, we made use of 10-second clips for each student, as mentioned by White Hil et al. [18] that labeling videos of this length proves to be a reliable predictor. For the experiment we extracted 10 consecutive frames per clip using the open-source tool "FFm-peg", we then applied the Viola-Jones algorithm for face extraction, and finally, we predicted the emotion for each clip using both models.

5 Results

5.1 DeepFace Results

The results generated from the DeepFace model (Fig. 7) indicate that the dominant emotion in the classroom is the neutral emotion at 38.9%, the happiness emotion at 27.8%, sadness at 22.2%, fear at 5.6%, and finally anger at 5.6%

The results generated from the survey indicate that the dominant emotion in the classroom is the neutral emotion at 83.3%, the happiness emotion at 5.6%, disgust at 5.6%, and finally sadness at 5.6%.

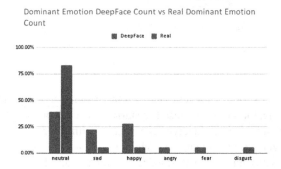

Fig. 7. Dominant emotion DeepFace vs Real dominant emotion

Comparing the predicted vs. actual results, using a confusion matrix (Table 1) it's noted that the most favorable result was obtained for the neutral emotion, with an accuracy of 33.33%. The way in which the DeepFace model failed to predict different results could be due to the different changes in illumination and camera quality.

Table 1. Confusion matrix deep face test for various emotions (in percentages).

		Predicted					
		0	1	2	3	4	5
Actual	0	0.0	0.0	0.0	5.56	0.0	0.0
	1	0.0	0.0	0.0	0.0	0.0	0.0
	2	0.0	0.0	0.0	0.0	5.56	0.0
	3	0.0	5.56	0.0	0.0	22.22	0.0
	4	0.0	0.0	0.0	0.0	33.33	5.56
	5	0.0	0.0	0.0	0.0	22.22	0.0

5.2 XCeption vs Real Engagement Results

The results generated from the XCeption model, which measures engagement on a scale of 0 to 3, indicate that engagement levels 2 and 3 present 44.4%, while scales 0 and 1 present a minimum percentage of 5.56%, we can see the parallel between both real(surveyed) values and the predicted Engagement values (Figs. 8 and 9).

In the case of the Real Levels, the results indicate a very similar occurrence of high levels of engagement, it is difficult, however, to make a discernible difference in the occurrences between levels 2 and 3.

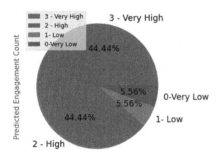 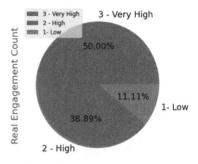

Fig. 8. Predicted levels of engagement   **Fig. 9.** Real levels of engagement

Both the predictions and real levels surveyed levels of engagement show a most common level of high and very high presence (Fig. 10), this is in line with the work of Geng et al. [5], and the DaiSEE data set itself since an overwhelming majority of the videos are labeled level 2 and 3 for high and very high respectably, creating class imbalance. This suggests a higher level of engagement in online learning is present in the real world, at least when the students are asked to turn on their cameras.

The confusion matrix for the predictions goes as follows (Table 2), the most favorable results were from the engagement labels 2 (16.67%) and 3 (27.78%) respectively. Being very difficult to differentiate the two in a real-life classroom environment. It is worth noting that doing this task as a binary classification could be much more doable, as noted by Liao et al. [10].

Table 2. Confusion matrix for student's engagement levels (in percentages).

| | | Predicted | | | |
		Very Low	Low	High	Very High
Actual	Very Low	0.0	0.00	5.56	0.00
	Low	0.00	0.00	5.56	0.00
	High	0.00	5.56	16.67	22.22
	Very High	0.00	5.56	11.11	27.78

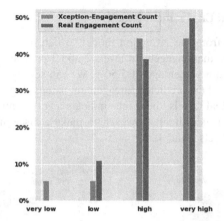

Fig. 10. Dominant engagement level count (in percentages)

5.3 EVEA Test

In the EVEA test section, the results indicate that the level of anxiety among the students is 3.083/10, anger-hostility 1.069/10, sadness and depression 1.94/10 and finally, happiness 4.22/10, these results were obtained by taking into account the averages of the EVEA test, it can be seen that the levels of happiness (Fig. 11) are the highest compared to the other emotions, according to the psychologists who worked on the project, the level of happiness may have a relationship with the level of engagement as mentioned in the article [7]. Therefore, the students had an almost regular level of engagement in an online environment.

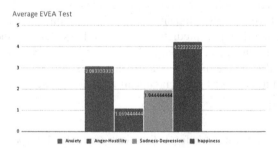

Fig. 11. Average results for the Evea test

We also measured the Spearman correlation coefficient as a way to obtain a measure of the affiliation that can exist between variables, in this case, the different affect emotions present in the EVEA test and the relations that can exist with engagement values, this coefficient has been used to identify strong relationships in emotion intensity predictions, such as in the work of Xie et al. [19]. The Spearman correlation is defined as:

$$\rho = 1 - \frac{6 \sum d_i^2}{n(n^2 - 1)} \tag{1}$$

where ρ is the Spearman coefficient in (1), it can be $+1$ or -1 depending on how strong a relationship between variables can be in our data, measuring ρ between the results in the test and the engagement predictions and the results of the EVEA test is as follows, Where the asterisks represent the value p for statistical significance, this is indicated in (Table 3)

Table 3. Correlation table with asterisks (*) indicating statistically significant scores for the student group ($n = 18$). *** p < .1; ** p < .05; *** p < 0.01.**

	Engagement	Anxiety	Anger-hostility	Sadness-depression	Happiness
Engagement	1***	0.44**	0.15	0.26	0.15
Anxiety	0.44**	1***	0.63	0.58*	0.43
Anger-hostility	0.15	0.63***	1***	0.87***	0.37
Sadness-depression	0.26	0.58***	0.87***	1***	0.41***
Happiness	0.15	0.43*	0.37	0.41*	1***

5.4 Future Work

In future work, it would be feasible to determine what factors can influence the recognition of students' emotions. In addition, the recognition of other emotions could be added depending on the area where the model is applied. Finally, the inclusion of state-of-the-art FER and FR models with different architectures like shallow networks can be applied to increase the precision when recognizing emotions.

6 Conclusions

At the end of the analysis of the emotions of the students, through the Xception generated model, the DeepFace model, it was determined that the majority of the students present a neutral emotion, and this has a relationship with the surveys carried out directly to the students. It should be noted that the other emotions in the models vary, this is due to the accuracy of the models with 33.3% and 27.7%, respectively.

Regarding the EVEA Test, the results indicate that the students presented a moderate percentage of happiness and low anxiety during class, and this is directly related to the engagement level where 88.9% of the student sample presents a level 2–3 of engagement and 11.1% presents a level 1, according to the psychologists who participated in the project. The online environment will be adequate only if there is a healthy environment taking into account factors such as interpersonal interactions between peers and teaching strategies.

References

1. Abedi, A., Khan, S.: Affect-driven engagement measurement from videos. arXiv preprint arXiv:2106.10882 (2021)
2. Chollet, F.: Xception: deep learning with depthwise separable convolutions. In: Proceedings of the IEEE Conference on Computer Vision and Pattern Recognition (CVPR), July 2017
3. Dewan, M.A.A., Lin, F., Wen, D., Murshed, M., Uddin, Z.: A deep learning approach to detecting engagement of online learners. In: 2018 IEEE SmartWorld, Ubiquitous Intelligence and Computing, Advanced and Trusted Computing, Scalable Computing and Communications, Cloud and Big Data Computing, Internet of People and Smart City Innovation (Smart-World/SCALCOM/UIC/ATC/CBDCom/IOP/SCI), pp. 1895–1902. IEEE (2018)
4. Dhall, A., Sharma, G., Goecke, R., Gedeon, T.: EmotiW 2020: driver gaze, group emotion, student engagement and physiological signal based challenges, pp. 784–789. Association for Computing Machinery, New York (2020). https://doi.org/10.1145/3382507.3417973
5. Geng, L., Xu, M., Wei, Z., Zhou, X.: Learning deep spatiotemporal feature for engagement recognition of online courses. In: 2019 IEEE Symposium Series on Computational Intelligence (SSCI). pp. 442–447. IEEE (2019)
6. Hu, M., Li, H., Deng, W., Guan, H.: Student engagement: one of the necessary conditions for online learning. In: 2016 International Conference on Educational Innovation through Technology (EITT), pp. 122–126 (2016). https://doi.org/10.1109/EITT.2016.31
7. Joo, B.K., Lee, I.: Workplace happiness: work engagement, career satisfaction, and subjective well-being. Evidence-Based HRM: Glob. Forum Empir. Scholarsh. **5**(2), 206–221 (2017). Emerald Publishing Limited. https://doi.org/10.1108/EBHRM-04-2015-0011, https://doi.org/10.1108/EBHRM-04-2015-0011
8. Kamat, Y.: Edumeet (2020). https://github.com/yogesh-kamat/EduMeet
9. Kuruvayil, S., Palaniswamy, S.: Emotion recognition from facial images with simultaneous occlusion, pose and illumination variations using metalearning. J. King Saud Univ. Comput. Inf. Sci. (2021). https://doi.org/10.1016/j.jksuci.2021.06.012, https://www.sciencedirect.com/science/article/pii/S1319157821001452
10. Liao, J., Liang, Y., Pan, J.: Deep facial spatiotemporal network for engagement prediction in online learning. Appl. Intell. **51**(10), 6609–6621 (2021). https://doi.org/10.1007/s10489-020-02139-8
11. Pranav, E., Kamal, S., Satheesh Chandran, C., Supriya, M.: Facial emotion recognition using deep convolutional neural network. In: 2020 6th International Conference on Advanced Computing and Communication Systems (ICACCS), pp. 317–320 (2020). https://doi.org/10.1109/ICACCS48705.2020.9074302
12. Prospero, M.R., Lagamayo, E.B., Tumulak, A.C.L., Santos, A.B.G., Dadiz, B.G.: Skybiometry and affectnet on facial emotion recognition using supervised machine learning algorithms. In: Proceedings of the 2018 International Conference on Control and Computer Vision. ICCCV 2018, pp. 18–22. Association for Computing Machinery, New York (2018). https://doi.org/10.1145/3232651.3232665
13. Raschka, S., Patterson, J., Nolet, C.: Machine learning in python: main developments and technology trends in data science, machine learning, and artificial intelligence. Information **11**(4), 193 (2020). Multidisciplinary Digital Publishing Institute. https://doi.org/10.3390/info11040193, https://www.mdpi.com/2078-2489/11/4/193
14. Sanz Fernandez, J., Gutierrez, S., Garcia Vera, M.P., Sanz Fernandez, J., Gutierrez, S., Garcia Vera, M.P.: Propiedadespsicométricas de la Escala de Valoración del Estado de Ánimo (EVEA): una revisión (2014). Sociedad Española para el Estudio de la Ansiedad y el Estrés (SEAS). https://eprints.ucm.es/id/eprint/58409/

15. Serengil, S.I., Ozpinar, A.: Hyperextended lightface: a facial attribute analysis framework. In: 2021 International Conference on Engineering and Emerging Technologies (ICEET), pp. 1–4. IEEE (2021). https://doi.org/10.1109/ICEET53442.2021.9659697
16. Tamilselvi, M., Karthikeyan, S.: An ingenious face recognition system based on hrpsm_cnn under unrestrained environmental condition. Alex. Eng. J. **61**(6), 4307–4321 (2022)
17. Thiruthuvanathan, M.M., Krishnan, B., Rangaswamy, M.: Engagement detection through facial emotional recognition using a shallow residual convolutional neural networks. Int. J. Intell. Eng. Syst. **14**(2) (2021)
18. Whitehill, J., Serpell, Z., Lin, Y.C., Foster, A., Movellan, J.R.: The faces of engagement: automatic recognition of student engagementfrom facial expressions. IEEE Trans. Affect. Comput. **5**(1), 86–98 (2014)
19. Xie, H., Feng, S., Wang, D., Zhang, Y.: A novel attention based CNN model for emotion intensity prediction. In: Zhang, M., Ng, V., Zhao, D., Li, S., Zan, H. (eds.) NLPCC 2018. LNCS (LNAI), vol. 11108, pp. 365–377. Springer, Cham (2018). https://doi.org/10.1007/978-3-319-99495-6_31

Crime Data Analysis Using Machine Learning Models

Vivas Kumar[✉] [iD]

Universidad de Las Fuerzas Armadas-UFA, Sangolquí 171103, Ecuador
akvivas@espe.edu.ec

Abstract. Crime statistics in Ecuador show us that in recent years the number of cases for different types of crimes has increased. Although the different state entities have criminal data, analyzes are not always carried out to predict new cases. This work proposes an analysis of the information based on automatic learning algorithms that allows extracting knowledge about the relationships between the different variables that affect criminal acts. These results can be used as tools for the country's authorities and organizations to better control and prevent crime. Using machine learning algorithms, crime counts by province can be predicted using techniques that are based on multiple regression or other techniques. Using monthly counts of different types of crimes over several years, three machine learning algorithms are implemented: Multiple Linear Regression (MLR), Decision Tree Regression (DTR), and Random Forest Regression (RFR). These models are trained and tested for use in predicting new crimes, especially rapes, burglaries, and personal thefts. The R-squared, adjusted R-squared, and root mean square error (RMSE) metrics are used to evaluate and compare the proposed regression models. The results show that the RFR model achieves a better fit to the data with an adjusted R-squared value of 0.965746 for the case of home burglaries and a value of 0.974088 for thefts. In addition, this model presents the lowest RMSE value for the three types of crimes. The best adjusted R-squared value for the rape case was obtained using the MLR model with a value of 0.929960. The most affected provinces in absolute counts are Guayas and Pichincha, whose crime levels remain at alarming levels.

Keywords: Machine learning · Data crime · Regression models

1 Introduction

Crime rates in Ecuador for the last few years have been alarming. According to INEC data [1], in January 2022, there were 2219 cases of theft, 348 rapes, and 665 home robberies throughout the country. These examples are some of the crimes defined in the country by the Ministry of Defense [2].

The role of data analyst is to extract knowledge from information. This can be done using different statistical and machine learning tools. For example, for analysis of crime data, time series can be used to predict future crime counts for specific regions or an entire country [3]. These models are very useful for understanding the information and through their analysis, decision-making by the authorities and crime control entities is facilitated.

The main objective of this work is to apply models based on machine learning to predict the future crime count in specific regions or any geographical unit that has data. This can be used to predict likely future crime hotspots. This makes it possible to increase the efficiency and effectiveness of the organizations in charge of enforcing order and the law, improving their abilities to combat crime. The data is analyzed descriptively, and predictions are made using multiple linear regression (MLR), decision tree regression (DTR), and random forest regression (RFR) techniques. Experimental results show that the RFR prediction model is better than the other two techniques for predicting crime, based on historical data per month from 2014 to 2021.

1.1 Types of Crimes

According to the Organic Penal Code [2], multiple crimes are typified, in this work the following are analyzed.

Rape. It is carnal access, with total or partial introduction of the virile member, orally, anal or vaginally, or the introduction, vaginally or anally, of objects, fingers or other organs, to a person of either sex.

Home Robbery. The person who, with lies or clandestinely, enters or stays in the home, business, dependency or place inhabited by another, against the express or presumed will of whoever has the right to exclude it and seizes something or foreign object on said property.

Theft. The person who, through threats or violence, subtracts or seizes another's thing or object, whether the violence takes place before the act to facilitate it, at the time of committing it or after it is committed to seek impunity.

1.2 Related Work

Sing et al. [4] proposes an efficient method called Stacking and Assembly Based Crime Prediction Method (SBCPM) based on SVM algorithms to identify suitable crime predictions by implementation of methods based on machine learning, using Matlab. The proposed method achieved a classification accuracy of 99.5% on the test data.

KB Sundhara Kumar and N. Bhalaji [5] apply classification methods to predict the nature of a crime, that is, determine whether the crime is a violent crime or a non-violent crime. They use Gradient Boosting and Random Forest algorithms enhanced through Boruta's algorithm that optimizes the accuracy of the predicted results. They also analyze the accuracy, precision and recovery values of these algorithms for crime records. The study finds that in feature selection, the Boruta algorithm performs better than the Chi-Square algorithm.

McClendon and Meghanathan [6] use an open-source data mining software, WEKA, and conduct a comparative study between patterns of violent crime for non-normalized community and crime data provided by the repository of the University of California-Irvine and true crime statistics for the state of Mississippi. Using linear regression algorithms, additive regression, among others, they conclude that, in general, the linear regression algorithm was the one that best performed among the selected algorithms.

Anchal and Rajasree [7], use an approach that uses the dynamic time warping technique and the Mahanolobis distance model to use records and statistics to analyze crime trends and predict future crimes.

Svedha and Thiyagarajan [8], develop an interview system that helps gather knowledge through language. They focus on the knowledge extraction element of crime using natural language. Two formats were used to assess the approach: police and victim narrative reports. MAE (82%) and RMSE (80%) values are obtained.

Muzammil et al. [9], propose a crime prediction model by comparing three algorithms: Naive Bayes, Random Forest and Gradient Boosting Decision Tree. Pattern identification is performed through exploratory data analysis (EDA). The accuracies of the Naive Bayes, Random Forest and Gradient Boosting Decision Tree techniques are 65.82%, 63.43% and 98.5%, respectively. It is concluded that the Gradient Boosting Decision Tree model is better than the other two techniques to predict crime.

Hossein et al. [10], show that only 10 percent of criminals commit 50 percent of all crimes in the city of San Francisco. Their proposed system predicts crimes by analyzing data sets containing records of previously committed crimes and their patterns. The system is based on two main algorithms: i) decision tree and ii) k-nearest neighbor. Random Forest algorithm and Adaboost are used to increase prediction accuracy.

2 Methods

The information obtained on the INEC digital platform is compiled in.csv format to be later preprocessed and adjusted to the requirements of the regression models in Python.

The proposed models are applied: MLR, DTR and RFR. Then, with the test data, the fit and accuracy of the data is measured. For this, the values of R squared, adjusted R squared, and the mean squared error are used. These models are used to predict crime counts for the different provinces of Ecuador in each month. OpenStreetMap is used to graph the predictions using the R language, showing the crime counts in each of the provinces.

2.1 Models and Metrics

The machine learning methods used in this work along with their metrics are explained below.

MLR. MLR is a regression algorithm that relates a single continuous dependent variable to multiple continuous or categorical independent variables. The representation of the MLR model is given as:

$$Y = \beta_0 + \beta_1 X_1 + \beta_2 X_2 + \cdots + \beta_p X_p + \epsilon \tag{1}$$

where Y represents response, the dependent variable, X_j represents the jth predictor and β_j quantifies the association between variable and the response.

Once a valid regression model is obtained, it is possible to predict the value of the response variable y for new values of the predictor variables x. It is important to note that predictions should generally be limited to the range of the data, that is, to the levels of the data on which the model has been trained [11]. This must be considered since, although linear models can be extrapolated, only in this region is it certain that the conditions for the model to be valid are met [12]. The following equation is used to calculate predictions

$$\hat{y}_i = \hat{\beta}_0 + \hat{\beta}_1 x_{i1} + \hat{\beta}_2 x_{i2} + \cdots + \hat{\beta}_p x_{ip} \tag{2}$$

In machine learning, once the best model obtained with the data has been selected, its ability to predict new observations with data that has not been used to train it must be verified, in this way it is verified if the model can be generalized [13]. A commonly employed strategy is to randomly split the data into two groups: training data and test data. The model fitting is done with the training data and to estimate the accuracy of the predictions the test data is used. The appropriate size of the partitions depends largely on the amount of data available and the confidence that is needed in the estimation of the error. One of the most used settings is 80% for training data and 20% for test data. The diagram of the process to be followed for the MLR models is presented in Fig. 1.

Fig. 1. Flowchart of the MLR model applied to crime data.

DTR. Decision tree regression is a machine learning method that is widely used for data classification and for building multiple regression models. The regression tree uses a tree-like graph or model and is built through an iterative process that divides each node into child nodes according to certain rules. Initially, the process starts with the entire data set, which makes up the root node, from this the algorithm creates different limits that are obtained from the data at various successive levels of the tree. To train a model, recursive partitioning and multiple regressions are performed on the training dataset. From the root node of the tree, the data division process is repeated at each internal node of a tree rule until the stopping criterion is met, which can be determined by some factors such as: reaching a maximum depth for the tree in question, that each region contains a minimum quantity of observations, that the tree has a maximum number of terminal nodes or that the incorporation of more nodes does not reduce the error by a certain minimum percentage [14]. This tool is attractive as it can satisfy both good prediction accuracy and easy interpretation, and therefore it has received a lot of attention in the machine learning literature [15]. The information gain, is calculated for each division performed and thus the best division is chosen, based on the gain with the highest value. The variety of DTR methods depend on the formula used to calculate the information gain.

When it is required to make decision trees for classification, the leaf nodes are the proper labels of the data, on the other hand, the leaf nodes for the regression are the average values of the data belonging to each region that result from the divisions on the way from the root to the corresponding leaf node. Also, the difference between the entropy in the data slice before the split and the total entropy of the partitions after the data slice is split is what we have called the information gain. Consider, S1 is the data segment before partition and S2 is the set of partitions after partition, we can define,

$$IG(X) = Entropy(S1) - Entropy(S2) \tag{2}$$

where $IG(X)$ is the gain information for X.

The entropy of segment $S1$ is calculated by,

$$Entropy(S1) = \sum_{i=1}^{n} -p_i log_2(p_i) \tag{3}$$

where n is the number of class levels and p_i is the percentage of data in the class level. To calculate the entropy for $S2$ the weighted sum of the entropy in all partitions must be performed,

$$Entropy(S2) = \sum_{i=1}^{n} -wi * Entropy(P_i) \tag{4}$$

where wi is the allocation which depends on the proportion of records that fall in the partition, P_i is partition i.

Some of the most important parameters that need to be configured in the Python sklearn package to apply DTR model are:

Criterion. This parameter configures the way in which the data is divided to create the branches of the tree, by default it uses the criterion "mse", mean square error.

Splitter. Strategy used for the division in each node, the default configuration is "best" which would be the best option (other option is "random").

max_depth. Refers to the maximum tree depth. By default, the algorithm expands nodes until all leaves are pure or contain less data. However, this can lead to an overfitting of the model, so it is preferred to "prune" the tree by setting this parameter to some tested value.

A flowchart of this process is presented in Fig. 2.

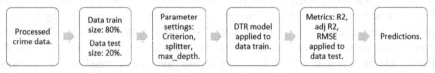

Fig. 2. Flowchart of the DTR model applied to crime data.

RFR. If repetitions of the DTR algorithm are performed, so that a forest of decision trees is obtained, then we would be building the basis of the RFR algorithm [16]. RFR is a method based on joint learning, that is, it elaborates several algorithms or the same algorithm several times to produce a much more robust algorithm [17]. Basically, to train an RFR, we randomly choose k data points from the previously created training set and apply DTR to these points. These two steps are repeated n times, thus obtaining a forest of n decision trees built on n sets of randomly chosen data points [18]. To make a prediction, new data is provided, and the decision trees work to calculate the prediction of the dependent variable. All these results are averaged to obtain the final prediction [19].

DTR algorithms bring with them high correlation values, in that sense, we can think of RFR algorithms as a decorrelation of the trees, which makes the average of the resulting trees less variable and therefore more reliable.

Node purity increase is a measure that quantifies the total increase in node purity due to splits in which the predictor participates. For this, the decrease achieved in the measure used as a division criterion (Gini index, entropy or other) is recorded in each division of the trees. For each of the predictors, the average descent achieved in the set of trees that make up the ensemble is calculated. This determines the contribution of the predictor to the model.

Some of the most important parameters that need to be configured in the Python sklearn package to apply RFR model are:

n_estimators. It refers to the number of trees that the algorithm builds before taking the maximum vote or taking average predictions. In general, a larger number of trees increases performance and makes predictions more stable but also slows down the computation.

Criterion. Defines the selection measure that will be used to divide the data in the best possible way. By default, this parameter is configured with the Gini index. Another option is to configure this parameter with the information gain, for which the "entropy" option must be chosen.

max_depth. Refers to the depth of the tree that by default is configured for nodes to expand until all leaves are pure or until leaves contain less than the minimum number of samples.

max_features. Refers to the maximum number of features that the random forest considers splitting a node. Sklearn implements some options like using all the features or only a fraction of them.

A flowchart of this process is presented in Fig. 3.

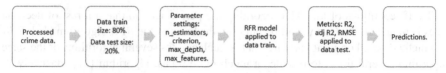

Fig. 3. Flowchart of the RFR model applied to crime data.

Metrics. The metrics used to evaluate the regression models:

R square. The R-squared value for any regression model is a measure of the fit for a regression model. The fit refers to how close the regression curve is to the data and its value is between 0 and 1. The formula for calculating the value of R squared is given by

$$R^2 = 1 - \frac{SS_{res}}{SS_{total}} \tag{5}$$

where SS_{res} is the sum of the squared residuals, that is, the sum of the squares of the differences between the actual value and the predicted value for the dependent variable, in addition, SS_{total} is the sum of the squares of the differences between the value real value and the average value of the real values for the same variable.

Adjusted R Square. This value is used to measure the goodness of fit for a regression model. Especially when there are many predictors in a model, the R-squared value also increases, however this is misleading. Therefore, it is necessary to adjust the value of R squared. Its formula is

$$AdjR^2 = 1 - (1 - R^2)\frac{n-1}{n-p-1} \tag{6}$$

where n is, the data sample size and p is the number of independent variables.

Root Mean Squared Error (RMSE). Root Mean Square Error measures the amount of error between two sets of data. In other words, it compares a predicted value and an observed or known value [20]. Its formula is

$$RMSE = \sqrt{\frac{\sum_{i=1}^{n}(P_i - O_i)^2}{n}} \tag{7}$$

where P_i are the predicted values and O_i are the observed values.

Data. The database was taken from the INEC digital platform that contains the counts of the different types of crimes by province. These counts are registered per month from January 2014 to January 2022, so there are 97 observations for each crime. Some types of crimes that are recorded on the platform are: theft, theft of vehicle accessories, motorcycle theft, car theft, home theft, theft from economic units and rapes. For this work, the counts of crimes typified as rapes, home robberies and thefts were taken. The sequences of rapes in the period 2014 - 2021 in each province are shown in Fig. 4. It is expected that the most populous provinces are those with the highest number of crimes counts, such as Guayas and Pichincha. Replacing the few missing data that the database presented with the mean of the corresponding records was part of the preprocessing [21]. On the other hand, to apply the MLR, DTR and RFR models, it was necessary to introduce dummy variables that represent whether the data groups belong to a given province. This causes the number of entries to increase considerably, thus the data contains 2328 entries and 24 columns corresponding to the independent variables. Independent variables are related to one dependent variable at a time. Rape, personal theft, and home theft are the crimes considered in this study and are used as dependent variables for the models. Excel and Python were used for data preprocessing. To apply the MLR, DTR and RFR models, python sklearn library was used.

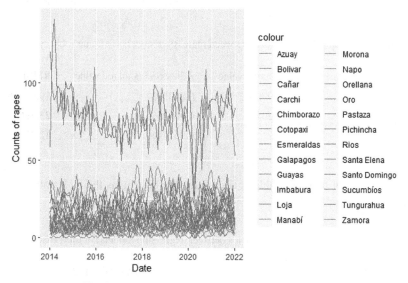

Fig. 4. Sequences of rapes in the period 2014–2021.

3   Results and Discussion

The regression models obtained with the data for the dependent variables of rapes, home robberies and thefts are analyzed through the regression algorithms used, MTR, DTR and RFR. These models can predict counts of these types of crimes by month and province. To mathematically evaluate and compare these models, the R-squared, adjusted R-squared, and mean squared error values in the test set values are used. Table 1 shows the results for rape crimes. The model that best fits these data is the MLR and in the same way it obtains the lowest RMSE value.

Table 1. Comparison of metrics between regression models for rape cases.

Regression model used	R-squared value	Adjusted-R squared value	RMSE
MLR	0.932853	0.929960	5.892508
DTR	0.878955	0.873739	8.842932
RFR	0.911513	0.907701	6.207299

For the case of home robberies in Table 2, the model that best fits is the RFR, which obtains an adjusted R-squared value very similar to the DTR model. However, the RMSE value for the DTR model is much higher than the RMSE value for the RFR model.

Table 2. Comparison of metrics between regression models for home robbery cases.

Regression model used	R-squared value	Adjusted-R squared value	RMSE
MLR	0.849996	0.843533	29.649762
DTR	0.962043	0.960408	25.396365
RFR	0.967161	0.965746	12.254011

For the case of thefts in Table 3, the model that best fits is the RFR and shows the lowest RMSE value of all.

Table 3. Comparison of metrics between regression models for theft cases.

Regression model used	R-squared value	Adjusted-R squared value	RMSE
MLR	0.952541	0.948612	50.562411
DTR	0.967067	0.966078	54.318198
RFR	0.975158	0.974088	34.308689

The following figures are the map diagrams drawn using the leaflet library in R with the OpenStreetMap package for the types of crimes studied. The predictions are made for June 2022 and show the counts for rapes, home robberies and thefts using the RFR model. The counts for all provinces of the country except Galapagos are used, since this province does not present significant values. It should be noted that the diameter of the circumferences is proportional to the number of counts for the crimes.

Figure 5 shows the rape counts for the 23 provinces. We can see that the most affected province is Pichincha with its capital Quito.

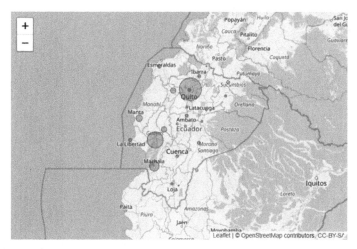

Fig. 5. Leaflet map plot for the number of rape cases by province in June 2022.

Figure 6 shows the counts of home robberies for the 23 provinces, in general we can see that Pichincha and Guayas are the most affected provinces together with their capitals, Quito and Guayaquil, respectively.

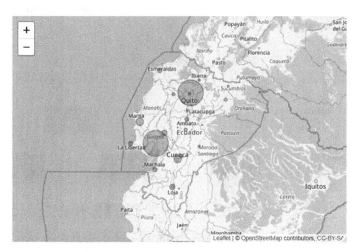

Fig. 6. Leaflet map plot for the number of home robberies cases by province in June 2022.

Figure 7 shows the theft counts for the 23 provinces. In general, we can see that Guayas is the most affected province together with its capital, Guayaquil.

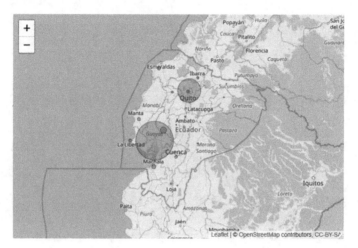

Fig. 7. Leaflet map plot for the number of theft cases by province in June 2022.

For decision tree regression, DTR, Fig. 8 shows the tree created by the model. We can see that the tree has a depth of 3 and the number of terminal nodes is 8. The variables provincia_Guayas, provincia_Pichincha, provincia_Oro and month have been used as predictors. It is always possible to improve the conditions for a decision tree through techniques such as pruning in order to reduce the variance of the model and thus improve its predictive capacity.

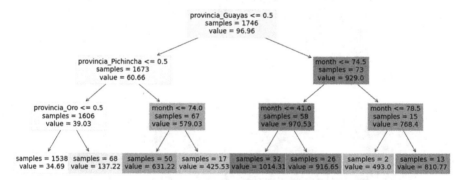

Fig. 8. Resulting decision tree for the DTR model applied to theft cases.

Since the random forest regression is based on decision trees, the predictor variables are expected to be the same as for the decision tree regression. Figure 9, through the importance of characteristics diagram, we can see that the most influential variables are the same as the predictor variables of the decision tree.

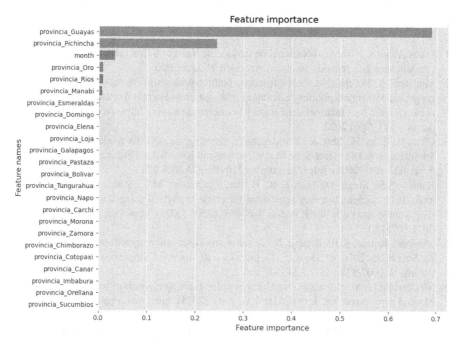

Fig. 9. Importance by purity of the nodes associated with the RFR model for theft cases.

4 Conclusion

This work has performed the regression analysis applying different machine learning algorithms in order to predict counts for crime data. To show the results, programming languages such as Python and R have been used through their tools such as sklearn, leaflet and OpenStreetMap.

Since three different techniques have been used: MLR, DTR and RFR, metrics were used to compare their efficiency. The best adjusted R-squared values were: 0.929960 for rape data using the MLR algorithm, 0.965746 for burglary data using the RFR algorithm, and 0.974088 for theft data using the RFR algorithm.

With the given results, predictions were made for June 2022 on the counts for each of the types of crimes studied. In the case of rapes, the most affected province is Pichincha with a total of 91 cases. In the case of home robberies, the most affected province is Pichincha with a total of 162 cases. In the case of thefts, the most affected province is Guayas with a total of 937 cases. This data-driven analysis can help police and other organizations make the right decisions about which regions require more attention and crime control. The models used are known for their power and efficiency, therefore they produce good predictions and are widely used at all levels of research. For a better performance of this type of studies, it is expected that the data collection in the country of origin be broader and consider showing more disaggregated data so that the quality of the models can be improved.

References

1. Datos Abiertos – Servicio Nacional de Gestión de Riesgos y Emergencias. https://www.ges tionderiesgos.gob.ec/datos-abiertos/. Accessed 21 June 2020
2. Ministerio de Defensa Nacional – Instancia político-administrativa del Gobierno de Ecuador encargada de dirigir la política de defensa y administrar las Fuerzas Armadas; armonizando las acciones entre las funciones del Estado y la institución militar. https://www.defensa.gob.ec/. Accessed 11 April 2022
3. Chen, P., Yuan, H., Shu, X.: Forecasting crime using the ARIMA model. In: Proceedings - 5th International Conference on Fuzzy Systems and Knowledge Discovery, FSKD 2008, vol. 5, pp. 627–630 (2008). https://doi.org/10.1109/FSKD.2008.222
4. Kshatri, S.S., Singh, D., Narain, B., Bhatia, S., Quasim, M.T., Sinha, G.R.: An empirical analysis of machine learning algorithms for crime prediction using stacked generalization: an ensemble approach. IEEE Access **9**, 67488–67500 (2021). https://doi.org/10.1109/access. 2021.3075140
5. Sundhara Kumar, K.B., Bhalaji, N.: A study on classification algorithms for crime records. In: SmartCom 2016. CCIS, vol. 628, pp. 873–880. Springer, Singapore (2016), doi: https:// doi.org/10.1007/978-981-10-3433-6_104
6. Mcclendon, L., Meghanathan, N.: Using machine learning algorithms to analyze crime data. Mach. Learn. Appl. Int. J. (MLAIJ) **2**(1), 1–12 (2015). https://doi.org/10.5121/mlaij.2015. 2101
7. Rani, A.: Crime trend analysis and prediction using mahanolobis distance and dynamic time warping technique. Int. J. Comput. Sci. Inf. Technol. **5**(3), 4134–4135 (2014). www.ijcsit. com
8. Awodele, O., Ernest, O.E., Olufunmike, O.A., Oluwawunmi Ugo-Ezeaba Anita A, S.O.: A real-time crime records management system for national security agencies. Europ. J. Comput. Sci. Inf. Technol. **3**(2), 1–12 (2015). www.eajournals.org
9. Khan, M., Ali, A., Alharbi, Y.: Predicting and preventing crime: a crime prediction model using san francisco crime data by classification techniques. Complexity **2022**, 1–13 (2022). https://doi.org/10.1155/2022/4830411
10. Hossain, S., Abtahee, A., Kashem, I., Hoque, M.M., Sarker, I.H.: Crime prediction using spatio-temporal data. In: Chaubey, N., Parikh, S., Amin, K. (eds.) COMS2 2020. CCIS, vol. 1235, pp. 277–289. Springer, Singapore (2020). https://doi.org/10.1007/978-981-15-6648- 6_22
11. Singh, R., Umrao, R.K., Ahmad, M., Ansari, M.K., Sharma, L.K., Singh, T.N.: Predic-tion of geomechanical parameters using soft computing and multiple regression approach. Measurement **99**, 108–119 (2017). https://doi.org/10.1016/j.measurement.2016.12.023
12. Farhadian, H., Katibeh, H.: New empirical model to evaluate groundwater flow into circular tunnel using multiple regression analysis. Int. J. Min. Sci. Technol. **27**(3), 415–421 (2017). https://doi.org/10.1016/J.IJMST.2017.03.005
13. Bandekar, S.R., Vijayalakshmi, C.: Design and analysis of machine learning algorithms for the reduction of crime rates in India. Procedia Computer Science **172**, 122–127 (2020). https:// doi.org/10.1016/J.PROCS.2020.05.018
14. Ahmad, M.W., Reynolds, J., Rezgui, Y.: Predictive modelling for solar thermal energy sys-tems: a comparison of support vector regression, random forest, extra trees and regression trees. J. Clean. Prod. **203**, 810–821 (2018). https://doi.org/10.1016/J.JCLEPRO.2018.08.207
15. Yang, L., Liu, S., Tsoka, S., Papageorgiou, L.G.: A regression tree approach using mathemat-ical programming. Expert Syst. Appl. **78**, 347–357 (2017). https://doi.org/10.1016/J.ESWA. 2017.02.013

16. Speiser, J.L., Miller, M.E., Tooze, J., Ip, E.: A comparison of random forest variable selection methods for classification prediction modeling. Expert Syst. Appl. **134**, 93–101 (2019). https://doi.org/10.1016/J.ESWA.2019.05.028

17. Chen, Y., Zheng, W., Li, W., Huang, Y.: Large group activity security risk assessment and risk early warning based on random forest algorithm. Pattern Recogn. Lett. **144**, 1–5 (2021). https://doi.org/10.1016/J.PATREC.2021.01.008

18. Alves, L.G.A., Ribeiro, V.H., Rodrigues, F.A.: Crime prediction through urban metrics and statistical learning. Phys. A Stat. Mech. Appl. **505**, 435–443 (2018). https://doi.org/10.1016/J.PHYSA.2018.03.084

19. Li, Y., Yan, C., Liu, W., Li, M.: A principle component analysis-based random forest with the potential nearest neighbor method for automobile insurance fraud identification. Appl. Soft Comput. **70**, 1000–1009 (2018). https://doi.org/10.1016/J.ASOC.2017.07.027

20. Yeşilkanat, C.M.: Spatio-temporal estimation of the daily cases of COVID-19 in worldwide using random forest machine learning algorithm. Chaos Solitons Fractals **140**, 110210 (2020). https://doi.org/10.1016/J.CHAOS.2020.110210

21. Gunturi, S.K., Sarkar, D.: Ensemble machine learning models for the detection of energy theft. Electric Power Syst. Res. **192**, 106904 (2021). https://doi.org/10.1016/J.EPSR.2020.106904

Machine Vision

Gene Therapy as a Solution to Genetic Diseases Through DNA Manipulation

Milton Temistocles Andrade-Salazar$^{(\boxtimes)}$ ⓘ, Verónica Martínez-Cepedaⓘ,
Luis Ortiz-Delgadoⓘ, Sandra Margoth Armijos-Hurtadoⓘ,
Holger Alfredo Zapata-Mayorgaⓘ, Patricia Denisse Villacis-Aguirreⓘ,
and Vanessa Johana Unda-Ilaquizeⓘ

Universidad de las Fuerzas Armadas ESPE, Sangolqu, Santo Domingo de los
Tsáchilas, Ecuador
{mtandrade,vimartinez1,laortiz9,smarmijos1,hazapata,
pdvillacis,vjunda}@espe.edu.ec

Abstract. The objective of the study was to investigate the advances in gene therapy to determine if its future methods will be the best solution when treating any genetic disease. This expectation is based on the fact that the treatment corrects the genomic sequence, eradicating it completely without the risk of its reappearance. The continuous development of this technique means ending "incurable" diseases and also treating "rare" diseases. The clinical trials carried out show that it has been possible to cure cancers and neuronal diseases that, through standard treatments, only relieve the symptoms and prolong the life of the patient without improving their quality of life. The cost of treatment, in the face of long-term critical illnesses, does not guarantee a cure or a better quality of life. Biosafety committees have been created with protocols that guarantee the safety of the treatment. A documentary research was carried out, content analysis was used as a technique. In conclusion, gene therapy is an innovation in both the medical and technological fields, as it offers a single application service to cure patients.

Keywords: Gene therapy · Genetic diseases · Genome sequencing · Bioethics

1 Introduction

Gene therapy consists of taking a DNA sample from a patient, to apply a process of correcting the defective genome that causes the disease, to reinsert it into the individual with the purpose of reversing the alteration of the genomic sequence and thus providing It forms a treatment for the patient and even a cure for the disease, the impact of this technique in the medical field lies in its applicability to critical illnesses or sometimes misnamed incurable diseases such as cancer,

Supported by Universidad de las Fuerzas Armadas ESPE.

diabetes, HIV, or other autoimmune diseases such as multiple sclerosis, rheumatoid arthritis, lupus, among others. In short, gene therapy is the means by which scientists can replace a defective gene with a healthy one, add genes that help the body deal with a disease, or deactivate genes that are causing some type of imbalance in the body of the person. Based on these expectations, the following approach is made: gene therapy in the future will be the method with the highest rate to cure diseases; because it is the best solution of all the possible ones, but at the same time it is the most complex, considering that sending genetic material to the cells that are needed to take effect, is of great difficulty.

[1] state that worldwide the population suffering from genetic diseases represents 7%, this causes a high morbimortality rate due to the fact that there are more than 10000 variants or different diseases, meaning a challenge in the medical field; as a solution to this problem the advance of science and technology generated gene therapy, whose purpose is to correct the genetic cause of a condition with a single application of this technique.

When gene therapy was approved in 1990, it is in the United States from 2007 and in Europe from 2012 where this type of treatment began to have greater prominence and practice; Since then, numerous clinical studies have been carried out, in monogenic, multigenic, infectious diseases, viral hepatitis, cirrhosis and malignant tumors that use different types of gene therapy, such as somatic therapy, which treats the patient by applying different strategies such as: ex vivo, in in situ, in vivo.

Germline gene therapy that modifies the DNA of gamete genes; it is a way of treating the disease, carrying out the genetic alterations in the pre-embryonic stage. The result of this therapy is not only that the individual is cured of the genetic disease, but that some of the individual's gametes may also have the altered trait. One protocol that might be feasible in human germline gene therapy involves removal of an embryo during the blastocyst stage of development and injection with transgenic cells. Somatic gene therapy uses three different strategies in the application process:

1.1   The Ex Vivo Strategy

Consists of extracting cells with altered genes from the patient, taking them to the laboratory, repairing them and reimplanting them in the patient's body. This strategy has a drawback, which is that the corrected cells have a short life, and therefore tend to disappear, generating the need for periodic treatments.

1.2   In Situ Strategy

Consists of the introduction of repairing or corrective genes directly into the cells of the organ itself where the problem has been identified. This strategy is excellent when the defect to be corrected is located; it does not work, that is, it cannot correct widespread problems. Currently this treatment is applied in different diseases, for example, to treat fibrocystic pancreas. In situ, it lacks safe and efficient pathways that allow repairing or corrective genes to be implanted in certain organs.

1.3 The in Vivo Strategy

Consists of administering the vectors containing the corrective genes directly into the blood. Once in the body, the vectors seek to meet their target cells to transfer the genetic information.

In gene therapy, the medium that will be used to transmit the therapeutic gene to the cells is very important, a medium that is known as a "vector"; This must meet some essential characteristics for the gene therapy process to have a correct execution. Among them: be reproducible and stable, allow the entry of genetic material into cells, recognize and act on specific cells, be able to regulate the expression of the therapeutic gene, lack elements that induce an immune response, be harmless or instead be that secondary effects are produced, these are of minimal effects. These vectors are associated in two groups:

Viral: These are modified to make them harmless inside the cells, in this group we find: retroviruses, adenoviruses, adeno-associated viruses and herpesviruses.

Non-viral: They are certain types of polymers which are less toxic, but at the same time less effective when entering cells; These include particle bombardment, direct DNA injection, cationic liposomes, and gene transfer via receptors.

The part of the body where a chemical causes adverse effects is called the target tissue. But a target "tissue" can actually be an entire organ, tissue, cell, or just a subcellular component.

Common health problems like heart disease, type 2 diabetes, and obesity don't have a single genetic cause; they are influenced by multiple (or polygenic) genes in combination with lifestyle and environmental factors, such as exercise, diet, or exposure to pollutants. Conditions caused by many contributing factors are known as complex or multifactorial diseases.

According to [2] in Latin America, 865 diseases have been reported, of which 93.1% are multifactorial, of which arterial hypertension represents 33.2%; 4.9% are chromosomal, with Down Syndrome being the most representative with 97.7%, becoming the first cause of mental retardation and the third cause of morbidity in Ecuador. Within the disabilities it represents 11% of the problems; Thus, one of every 527 children is born with Down Syndrome only in the city of Quito, with an upward trend as the mother's age increases, which is generally from 35 years [3].

Table 1 shows the different types of diseases, categorized as being multifactorial or chromosomal.

Table 1. Chromosomal and multi factorial diseases.

Chromosomal	Multi factorial
Down's Syndrome	Schizophrenia
Turner's syndrome	Arterial hypertension
Kinefelter's syndrome	Arteriosclerosis
Patau syndrome	Alzheimer disease
Edward's syndrome	Asthma
Cri-du-Chat or cat meow syndrome	Mellitus diabetes
Angelman syndrome	Various types of cancer, obesity

2   Gene Therapy and Its Technical Limitations

There are many technical aspects to refine in gene therapy, this is due to the lack of complete knowledge of the genome in terms of its regulation mechanisms; So far, there is no complete sequencing of the genes and how they interact with each other. This knowledge is very important to be able to act efficiently in this microenvironment. Genes introduced into patients often do not reach the target cells.

It is worth mentioning that viral vectors are derived from viruses found in the environment, so several of them can infect cells of the body in a non-specific way; which becomes a serious impediment if you want the gene to be expressed in a certain proportion of a specific organ or tissue.

At the same time, viruses present the difficulty of depositing their DNA load randomly within the DNA, which can be harmful if it interferes with a gene that is functioning regularly, since it could incite the activation of oncogenes, with the consequence of having the appearance of cancer cells. It would also be necessary to determine how much the cell can withstand an increase in the amount of DNA, which will increase when the new genes are introduced, so that, despite this increase, it can continue to function normally.

Additionally, it has been detected that another problem usually arises, and that is that many times the genes introduced do not work optimally and eventually stop working. This fact is related to the immune response triggered by viral vectors, which induces the immune system to eliminate the cells that the vectors have influenced with the normal gene.

The entities responsible for authorizing the different clinical studies are very demanding in terms of the innocuousness of the viruses used, i.e. that they are harmless; this is understandable considering that most of the time pathogenic viruses are used. At present, new methods are still being investigated to guarantee this innocuousness.

3 Gene Therapy and Its Ethical Limitations

These are related in a high percentage with the possibility of developing germ cell gene therapy, the same one that has generated great controversies, since when the changes made in them are transmitted to the following generations, the genetic spectrum of the human species is affected, and an error in perception or technology can have unintended and unpredictable consequences. For this reason, this type of therapy has been totally prohibited by different international organizations such as the WHO, UNESCO and the Council of Europe, among others.

Gene therapy, being a new paradigm in world medicine, will have very enthusiastic followers who will make it the tool to treat and eradicate any type of disease; but, it also has its detractors who will make gene therapy seem like something extraterrestrial. In any case, if all the prejudices, knowledge problems and technical difficulties are overcome, gene therapy can redefine the practice of medicine in the medium term, taking into account that only 8 years ago the first protocols in this new paradigm were obtained Of medicine.

It is important to know the real benefits of gene therapy to justify its practice and application. One of its benefits or advantages compared to other treatments is reflected in its potential to prevent subsequent morbidity, in the long term, and with a single treatment. This entails a one-time cost which, although it may seem high, must be weighed against the sum of the events generated by the disease and the continuous care over many years. The value or cost of applying gene therapy should be seen as a multidimensional concept, since aspects such as the improvement in the quality of life and the reduction of the years lost due to the anomalies generated by the disease must be considered, as well as the economic impact generated by the disease and the therapy or treatment as such, and the family, social, school or work impact of the patient.

The Fig. 1, shows the general process to be followed in the application of ex vivo gene therapy.

GENE THERAPY

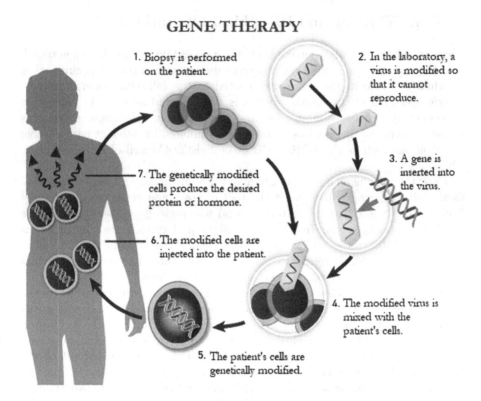

1. Biopsy is performed on the patient.

2. In the laboratory, a virus is modified so that it cannot reproduce.

3. A gene is inserted into the virus.

4. The modified virus is mixed with the patient's cells.

5. The patient's cells are genetically modified.

6. The modified cells are injected into the patient.

7. The genetically modified cells produce the desired protein or hormone.

Fig. 1. Ex vivo gene therapy procedure

In Latin America, research in this regard is quite scarce since economic resources are very limited, not so in the world of developed countries. Historically, research funding in Latin America has been known to be insufficient. In addition, both the products and the procedures related to gene therapy, especially those aimed at rare diseases, are expensive. To date, the results of clinical studies designed, conducted, and funded by local agencies have rarely been published [4].

The WHO considers that a disease acquires the character of "rare" if it affects less than 5 out of every 10,000 inhabitants, therefore, they are disorders with a low incidence, that is, 0.0005%. This means that around the world there are around 490 million people who suffer from some type of rare disease.

The 80% of the human application of gene therapy comes from the United States, the United Kingdom, Switzerland, Germany and France; fundamentally because phase III and IV studies require special industrial support to cover the costs of supplies and logistics, money that probably cannot be invested for this purpose in Latin America [4].

Gene therapy and the methodologies involved are in constant development, have yielded favorable results and have provided solutions to medical needs, however, it gives rise to bioethical considerations as there are issues to be addressed such as enhancement therapy, whose character ceases to be therapeutic and no longer seeks to correct but to improve the characteristics of the human being.

A beneficial factor for patients who require the application of gene therapy is the cost, in comparison with conventional medical procedures that are extensive and costly, besides not guaranteeing that the patient will be cured, this treatment implies a fair investment, since only a single dose is needed, its effects are prolonged during the patient's life and it completely avoids dependence on chronic treatments.

Gene therapy is supposed to be the best solution in treating genetic diseases to cure patients, decrease morbidity worldwide, alleviate the burden on the medical system and thus improve society's quality of life. The present scientific study based on a project of exploratory scope has the general objective of investigating the advances of gene therapy in the field of medicine, making use of sources of information related to the subject.

4   Methodology

Gene therapy is a proposal with great acceptance in the field of medicine thanks to its successful clinical trials, since it has meant a revolt in the way of dealing with the treatment of genetic diseases, since it has opened a new paradigm to cure diseases, which until now only existed treatments oriented to reduce their symptoms.

Gene therapy is the set of techniques that use the transfer of genetic material, or any other method that makes it possible to edit or modify the patient's genetic information, to prevent or cure genetic diseases. It is undoubtedly the best of all possible alternatives, but probably also the most complex. It goes directly to the root of the problem by transferring the correct version of a defective gene, which is causing the disease. Among the main obstacles to this approach is the difficulty of targeting the genetic material specifically to those cells or tissues where the gene needs to perform its function, or that the regulation of the introduced gene approximates the way the gene is regulated in healthy people [5]

In addition to the functions already mentioned, it is possible to inhibit genes that are causing a disease, thus preventing their multiplication and completely blocking future diseases such as cancer or viruses such as HIV.

Among the main obstacles to gene therapy is the difficulty of directing the genetic material specifically to those cells or tissues where the gene needs to perform its function, or that the regulation of the gene introduced is close to the way in which it is regulated in healthy people.

In order to put gene therapy into practice, a number of factors must be considered, among which are the following:

- To know which is the target tissue, the one that is going to receive the therapy.
- To know if it is possible to treat the affected tissue in situ.
- Which is the appropriate vector that will be used to introduce the gene into the target tissue.

– What is the efficacy of the new gene, and to know what response the receptor organ or tissue will have with the entry of the modified gene.

The Figure 2 summarizes the process of applying gene therapy to patients with CTNNB1 problems. This gene provides instructions for producing a protein called beta-catenin. This protein is present in many types of cells and tissues, where it is found primarily at the junctions that connect neighboring cells (adherent junctions).

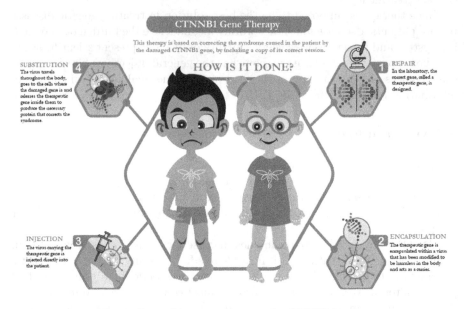

Fig. 2. Gene therapy process to the CTNNB1 gene

Gene therapy has a wide field of action, but we can visualize it in three main areas: monogenic, multigenic and infectious diseases.

Monogenic Diseases, also known as hereditary Mendelian diseases, are caused by the mutation or alteration in the DNA sequence of a single gene. Worldwide there are more than 6000 monogenic hereditary diseases, with a prevalence rate of one case per 200 births. Below is the following table with the most common monogenic diseases, see Table 2.

Table 2. Most common monogenic hereditary diseases.

Diseases	Information
Cystic fibrosis	Genetic disorder, in which the lungs and digestive system become clogged with mucus
α and β-Thalassemias	An inherited blood disorder characterized by the formation of an abnormal form of hemoglobin. It causes tiredness, yellowish skin, dark urine, abdominal swelling, and facial bone deformities
Fragile X syndrome	Caused by mutations in the FMR1 gene that provides instructions for transcription of the protein-FMRP, which plays a role in synapse development, thus affecting brain development
Hemophilia A	Deep internal bleeding, joint damage
Spinal Muscular Atrophy	It is a group of genetic diseases that damages and kills motor neurons
Sickle cell anemia	An inherited blood disorder in which red blood cells take on a crescent/sickle shape
Huntington's disease	A condition that leads to progressive degeneration of nerve cells in the brain
Autosomal recessive polycystic kidney disease	It is produced by alterations in the PKHD1 gene, which encodes the protein fibrocystin or polyductin, involved in the functioning of this primary cilium
Myotonic Dystrophy Type 1 (Steinert's)	It is the most common muscular dystrophy in adults
Duchenne/Becker muscular dystrophy	They are X-linked recessive disorders characterized by proximal muscle weakness caused by degeneration of muscle fibers
Marfan syndrome	Genetic disorder that affects the connective tissues (tissue that supports the skeleton and internal organs). It commonly affects the eyes, heart, blood vessels, and skeleton
Neurofibromatosis Type 1 (NF1)	It is a disease caused by the mutation of a gene on chromosome 17 that is responsible for the production of the protein neurofibromin 1, which is necessary for normal functioning in many types of human cells
Progeria or Hutchinson-Gilford syndrome	It consists of the appearance of signs of aging in children between their first and second year of life

Multigenic Diseases, also known as multifactorial hereditary diseases, they are derived from several small genetic mutations that can cause some of the most frequent diseases that can be known; in these there is the influence of genes and the environment. Among the most common diseases can be found: heart disease, diabetes, hypertension, coronary disease, Alzheimer's, arthritis, among others. Cancer is a disease resulting from a process of acquired and inherited mutations in cellular genes.

Infectious Diseases, also called contagious, it can be the clinical expression of an infection caused by a microorganism such as bacteria, viruses, fungi, among others. There is a wide variety of these types of diseases that can be treated effectively by gene therapy. HIV is one of the diseases that has been most treated by this procedure, whose results are quite significant. Other infectious diseases: Human Papilloma Virus (HPV), listeriosis, among others.

The present research had at the beginning an exploratory scope because in its first stage an in-depth examination of the different strategies and conceptualizations of gene therapy and the impact it generates in the different diseases of people is carried out. It then moves on to the descriptive stage, in that it is necessary to describe and contextualize the characteristics of the intervening elements. Then it enters the correlational scope, as it is necessary to know the degree of relationship or association between the different diseases and the tentative gene therapy procedures to be applied.

The technique used in this research is the documentary analysis where significant information has been collected, the same that has been obtained from different scientific sources, in which a deep analysis of the documents addressed and intimately related to Gene Therapy was performed; the information was collected from academic documents, obtaining truthful results on clinical and technological advances with modern processes and methods thus acquiring real data and information available to arrive at possible reflections.

It is relevant to carry out a documentary treatment based on the interpretation and analysis of the information in the documents in order to outline. To refute this report [6], indicate that to carry out the documentary analysis: "data are collected from secondary sources. Books, bulletins, journals, magazines, brochures, and newspapers are used as sources to collect data on the variables of interest".

The instrument used is the reading card, to make a correct selection of the bibliographic material required for the documentary analysis.

The present research through the documentary analysis carried out determines several characteristics about the progress and future of gene therapy worldwide, the impact generated both in the present and in the future is due to the positive results that most of the clinical trials have yielded through the application of gene therapy in its different methodologies.

5   Results

The treatment of several rare diseases is ceasing to be a problem due to the presence of gene therapy, but there is a latent problem that is difficult for developing countries to solve, and that is the high cost of this type of treatment.

The managing partner of life sciences consultancy Trinity Partners Herman Sánchez explains that there is a correlation between the patient population and the price of therapy: the fewer potential patients there are, the more expensive the treatments. As can be seen in Figure 3MIT, prices range between 373,000 dollars (almost 321,000 euros) and one million dollars (more than 860,000 euros), while the maximum number of patients per year only reaches about 7,500. [7]

The Figure 3 shows the general process to be followed in the application of ex vivo gene therapy.

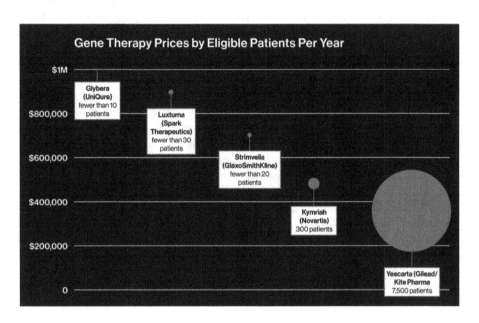

Fig. 3. Gene therapy price related to patients per year

As long as there is less demand from patients requiring gene therapy, proprietary pharmaceutical companies have a greater opportunity to increase the cost. This analysis shows that the number of treatments carried out influences the prices that the beneficiaries will have to pay, the greater the accessibility, the lower the cost.

The different studies carried out worldwide show that the objective of gene therapy is to reduce morbimortality and to improve the patient's quality of life. The benefit of gene therapy is that it only requires a single application to definitively solve the condition, so that the symptoms would not only be alleviated but completely eradicated. From an overall perspective, the health system would decrease the dependence on treatments in chronic patients and increase its rate of discharged patients.

Gene therapy promises great advances in the future, conventional therapy has several limitations, and there are several "incurable" diseases, this situation would change completely if gene therapy is within the reach of any medical institution that is capable of carrying it out. As for example diseases of the central nervous system, due to a deficient dispensing system to cross the blood-brain barrier, it causes an instability in the molecules and a systemic administration of extreme sensitivity and care. The clinical trials carried out show positive results, demonstrating that gene therapy through an in vitro and in vivo methodology cure CNS anomalies, from the human genome itself, without requiring other interventions. However, despite being an immediate solution to this and other ailments, more clinical trials should be carried out for a more complete study, to obtain more knowledge about vector transfer and for its application to be more effective, since this aspect is one of the most significant technical problems in the development of gene therapy; In addition, the development of new generation vectors is needed to solve the implicit biosafety problems when using Gene Therapy.

[8] add that other technical problems have also been found; germline gene therapy has been the reason for the creation of specialized bioethics commissions on the subject, which have generated strict protocols, since the experimental phase, despite its potential, does not compensate for the associated risks. And like any other scientific advance, the patient should only be exposed to procedures that have a balance between the benefits to be received and the possible risks. For this same reason, bioethics committees also govern the standards of clinical trials; Due to the magnitude of the dangers, all experimental projects are continuously supervised by expert review teams. On the other hand, somatic gene therapy, its experimental therapeutic treatment does not entail protocols that signify a danger or alert to ethics, rather, it supposes the solution and eradication of most genetic diseases.

It is clear that the development of gene therapy needs financing that influences the speed of showing results, the results that have already been obtained in experimental clinical practices strengthen this cooperation network, in recent years the capacities of experts have been taken advantage of in gene therapy. Juan Bueren, researcher at the U710 CIBERER at the CIEMAT and the IIS-FJD, proposes promoting the deepening of knowledge that will determine once and for all the success of this therapeutic practice that is highly demanded by the needs of the world population. The high cost and complexity of the method of these therapies would work more effectively if the creation of Mixed Experimental and Clinical Research Units to carry out quality preclinical research is supported. It is necessary to advance in basic science to deepen the foundations of advanced therapies and thus be able to improve them in terms of efficacy and safety before using them in public and private health systems.

6 Conclusions

This project concludes that gene therapy and the methodologies involved are in constant development, which has yielded favorable results and has provided solutions to medical needs; however, it gives rise to bioethical considerations as there are issues to be addressed, such as enhancement therapy, which is no longer therapeutic in nature and no longer seeks to correct but to improve human characteristics.

There are still many limitations to these therapies, but it is a discipline in continuous development. It can be said that gene therapy has broadened horizons to new therapeutic cells, to a new notion of medicine and to the alteration of the human genome.

To cure genetic diseases, scientists must first determine which gene or which set of genes causes each disease. This new research provides innovative strategies to diagnose, treat and cure genetic diseases.

The use of somatic gene therapy was introduced in the 1990 s, although in its beginnings it did not have significant trials, with the passing of time it continues to be a very competent way for its scientific advances.

Germline therapy causes ethical problems because its virtues do not outweigh the risks associated with it.

Gene therapy will revolutionize the practice of medicine. The role of physicians and patients will change in the coming years and it is all due to this therapy. This technique has the capacity to cure many of the diseases that have plagued our society for years.

References

1. Abarca Barriga, H.H., Chávez Pastor, M., Trubnykova, M., Serna-Infantes, L., Jorge, E., Poterico, J.A.: Factores de riesgo en las enfermedades genéticas. Acta Médica Peruana **35**(1), 43–50 (2018)
2. Conejo, V.V., Carmona, Y.G., Blanco Díaz, A.T., Varela, L.M.-D., Castro, H.F., Avellaneda, D.M.: Las enfermedades genéticas en el contexto latinoamericano desde la óptica de los estudiantes de la escuela latinoamericana de medicina. Panorama Cuba y Salud 12(3), 10–17 (2017)
3. Terapia genética para el síndrome de down., (2013)
4. Linden, R., Matte, U.: A snapshot of gene therapy in Latin America. Genet. Mol. Biol. **37**, 294–298 (2014)
5. Mazorra-Carillo, J.L.: La terapia génica: una posible solución a las enfermedades crónico-degenerativas. Transregiones **3**, 107–114 (2022)
6. Ly, C.T., Siesquen, I.S.: Técnicas e instrumentos de recolección de datos (2012)
7. Mullin, E.: Terapias génicas: cuánto más rara es la enfermedad más alto es el precio (2017)
8. García Miniet, R.S., González Fraguela, M.E.: Terapia génica: perspectivas y consideraciones éticas en relación con su aplicación. Revista Habanera de Ciencias Médicas, 7(1), (2008)

Security

Vulnerability of CAPTCHA Systems Using Bots with Computer Vision Abilities

Julio Villares-Jimenez[(✉)], Jordy Quinatoa-Medina, Germán Rodríguez-Galán, Daniel Nuñez-Agurto, and Benjamin Santillán-Tituaña

Universidad de las Fuerzas Armadas ESPE, Sede Santo Domingo de los Tsáchilas, Santo Domingo, Ecuador

{jjvillares,jjquinatoa2,gerodriguez10,adnunez1,
absantillan1}@espe.edu.ec

Abstract. CAPTCHA stands for Completely Automated Public Turing test to tell Computers and Humans Apart. They are machine-controlled challenge-response tests used to determine when the user is a human or an automatic program (bot). Attacks perpetrated by malicious bots are one of the most common problems in web systems. To counter these attacks, CAPTCHA systems can be implemented. However, the growth of technologies such as Artificial Vision has caused many of the CAPTCHAS systems to be broken very easily. On the other hand, the implementation of automated processes in computer security has marked an additional complement in the process of searching for vulnerabilities in web systems. In this context, this article aims to automate searching tasks and analyze web systems vulnerabilities through Robotic Process Automation (RPA) tools and artificial vision techniques. As part of the bot development, the UiPath tool in its Community Edition version and the Google Cloud Platform API for artificial vision techniques were used. In the results, the functioning of the developed bot was systematically evaluated by broken the CAPTCHA system based on images of a test page. This proposal is intended to demonstrate that CAPTCHA systems, specifically of the hCAPTCHA type, can be broken using artificial vision techniques in conjunction with the automated processes of a bot.

Keywords: CAPTCHA · RPA · BOTs

1 Introduction

The evolution of information and technology has been a fundamental part of the development of updated systems that meet new technological needs. Many companies use client-server architectures for their businesses due to their ease of access and efficiency. However, like most computer tools, web systems have been exposed to various attacks produced by cybercriminals with excellent knowledge and high preparation in their environment.

Automated systems (bots) have intensified the integration of company processes and people's daily activities; some bots can execute simple tasks to handle

M. Botto-Tobar et al. (Eds.): ICAT 2022, CCIS 1755, pp. 329–343, 2023.
https://doi.org/10.1007/978-3-031-24985-3_24

all the business logic of a company. For this reason, research carried out, such as that of Missouri Enterprise, mentions that an organization, when integrating bots into the main processes, can reduce production costs by up to 50%, comply with the process cycle time from 30% to 50% and improve productivity levels from 10% to 16%. This case study serves as a reference to contextualize the improvements produced by implementing RPA-based technologies [1].

A typical attack on web systems is a Denial of Service (DDoS) attack, which is why many companies use CAPTCHA systems to counter them. According to the research carried out and supported by Institutions from China and the United Kingdom, they presented an Artificial Intelligence model capable of exploiting text-based CAPTCHA systems through a desktop GPU in an estimated 0.05 s. Within the study, the operation of 33 text-based CAPTCHA systems was verified; 11 are used in 32 of the 50 most popular websites in the world [2].

It is also important to mention that many computer attacks are perpetrated while carrying out daily activities within an organization, generating high traffic of helpful information for cybercriminals. All this, added to the minimum actions carried out in managing vulnerabilities within companies, means that threats become a reality and are undetectable in their initial phase. Acting immediately to solve problems after detecting a possible vulnerability within computer systems can prevent economic and information losses to the company.

The existing problems within the analysis of vulnerabilities and execution of searches in web systems lie in need for human intervention to implement their processes in such a way that it affects the estimated time to solve a computer attack and patch it in the shortest time. On the other hand, the creation of malicious bots has caused companies to apply CAPTCHA systems to many of their applications to counteract these attacks, but with the application of techniques based on artificial vision, these systems can be violated [3].

In this context, this work's main objective is to automate searching and analyzing vulnerabilities in web systems through RPA tools. For this, a bot is developed that demonstrates the existing vulnerabilities in CAPTCHA systems, specifically in hCaptcha-type systems, through UiPath software and artificial vision techniques.

Our proposal has been structured as follows; The first section presents the introduction of the research. The second section corresponds to the materials and procedures for developing the bot with artificial vision abilities. The third section details the results obtained in the execution of the bots and the comparison of the RPA tools used in this work [4]. Finally, the conclusions and future work of the project are detailed.

2   Structure and Methodology

For our proposal, it is crucial to determine the RPA tool to be used, to implement the bot in the shortest possible time. It is essential to highlight the comparative analysis to obtain the most suitable tool.

2.1   Selection of the RPA Tool

For the analysis and development of this project, the results obtained by the two most essential consultants of current technologies, Forrester Wave and Gartner, have been considered. These two consultants present statistical data on the different technological solutions and products on the market that implement software. Figure 1 shows the results obtained in the Gartner Magic Quadrant based on surveys conducted up to June 2021 and the results obtained in the Forrester Wave in the first quarter of 2021. The final result gets the market-leading tool, UiPath software.

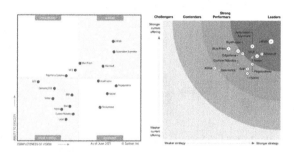

Fig. 1. Gartner Magic Quadrant for Robotic Process Automation (RPA) conducted in July 2021. Identification of RPA Leaders in The Forrester Wave in Q1 2021

The main reason the results obtained in the Gartner Magic Quadrant and the Forrester Wave of Leaders are taken as a reference is because of the guarantee offered by their studies and the high standards required by RPA technologies. As the study's primary objective focuses on searching for vulnerabilities in CAPTCHA systems based on images, it is essential to mention that the chosen RPA tool must have an image analysis module.

For the development of the bot, the UiPath tool was used in its Community Edition version, it has limited tools, but it contains many other features that allow the development of a functional program. This edition was used since implementing bots to automate website vulnerability search tasks does not require very complex processes, so purchasing an UiPath Enterprise Edition would be unnecessary. Additionally, the UiPath Community Edition is tailored to the development needs of those new to robotic process automation.

2.2   BOT for the Analysis of Vulnerabilities in CAPTCHA Systems

Many web pages use CAPTCHAS systems to counteract attacks carried out by malicious bots and thus protect the security of web services. However, today many systems can be easily compromised due to the significant increase in technologies such as Artificial Intelligence. Our proposal aims to demonstrate that these CAPTCHA systems can be violated precisely with the implementation of automated bots.

Based on the previous analysis to select the RPA tools, the bot was developed to violate CAPTCHA systems based on images. The design and development process was divided into two parts: the first part explains the configurations necessary to obtain the key provided by the Google API (Cloud Vision API), allowing the use of artificial vision technologies from the Google platform. Cloud. The second part details the bot development process in the UiPath Community Edition software. Figure 2 shows a graphic scheme of how our bot works.

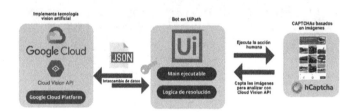

Fig. 2. Development phases of the proposed bot to break the security of a CAPTCHA system.

This proposal analyzed the images of the CAPTCHA system (hCAPTCHA type) by comparing each image that appears in the hCAPTCHA matrix with the images of the dataset that implements the Google Cloud Vision API. The Google API is the tool that provides the necessary artificial vision technologies, analyzes the images, and determines the characteristics of the figure. A script in JSON format was used to establish the connection of the API with the bot, providing the exchange of information between said projects. The bot's development was executed in two parts; the first consisted of a main. xaml file, which includes the executable section of the bot, and the second part is made up of the captcha solver-xaml file, where the logic of the operation and the web page analysis were established.

2.3   Integration with Google Cloud Platform

In the bot's development, artificial vision technologies have been implemented to solve the CAPTCHA system, and the advantages of the Google Cloud Platform were used. This platform offers many cloud computing services to develop complete, optimizable, and functional applications that require an acceptable cost for their use. Despite this, Google also offers the advantage of using many of its services for a limited time. For the proposal, the platform's trial version was used, where Google offers $300 US dollars as a credit for the use of its services within a maximum period of 3 months, after which the company will begin to invoice.

After obtaining the account, the project was created by clicking on the APIs and Services section, where the service search option appears, and the "Google Vision" option is typed. It can click on the Google Cloud Vision API to enable said service when the option is displayed. This API uses machine learning techniques to interpret the images with precision very close to reality, offering, as a result, the summary of the characteristics of the image, the detection of faces and objects, and obtaining metadata of the figure.

Only after this instance has the API been enabled, but the project has yet to be created. To create a new artificial vision project, click on the "My first project" section and enter the data requested in the form. An APP was created within the API to obtain the credentials that will be used for the link with the bot. After modeling the consent screen, it is essential to provide permission to access the previously created application. These permissions allow users to create requests to the APP to obtain access to the private data of their own Google accounts. As a next step, enabling the Cloud Vision API option is vital since it contains machine vision features. Finally, the option "Create a Credential" was clicked in the credentials section, resulting in the content shown in Fig. 3.

Fig. 3. Obtaining the access key to the app created in the API, whose technology provides the artificial vision skills to the bot.

This key is placed in the bot's input arguments and provides the link to the Google Cloud API. In the same way, to establish said data exchange between the Google Cloud API and the bot developed in UiPath, a script was developed in request format, which consists of a JSON object, and includes a single list of requests and one or more request objects. Type AnnotateImageRequest.

2.4   Development of the Bot in the RPA UiPath Tools

Once the current configuration has been integrated with the machine vision capabilities, the next step is the development of the bot. For this, the UiPath robotic process automation tool was used. One of the advantages provided by this tool is how easy it is to create activities since it handles each process in the form of "blocks", and these contain secondary blocks made up of more activities.

The creation of the bot has been based on the analysis of the hCAPC-THA system that has the website "https://www.map24.com/contact/". This page corresponds to a website specialized in publishing news, health advice, sports articles, and everything related to the art of publishing. The website has a "Contacts" section where the image-based hCAPTCHA system is located.

There are different ways to start development by creating new projects within UiPath. First, the option to create a "Processes" project to develop a new one and establish the automation of tasks from scratch. There is the "Library" option for creating a new project from reusable and published components as script libraries. Another option is "Test Automation" to create test projects from scratch. Finally, there is the "Template" option for developing projects from others previously created and stored as reusable templates.

For the Main development 4, the option of a new "Processes" project was used. It is essential to know that in UiPath, each development block corresponds to an activity that contains the instructions that the bot will carry out and those that will be executed in sequence. In the case of the bot, the main block executes a set of secondary activities according to a defined and unique order. Since the bot establishes a communication with the Google Cloud Vision API, a call to the JsonPayload.txt file will be made through the activity that allows reading a text file. As the bot analyzes the CAPTCHA system of a specific website, an activity has been implemented to open the browser at a specific URL. Once the browser is opened, a container is attached to it and executes multiple tasks within it Figs. 4, 9 and 10.

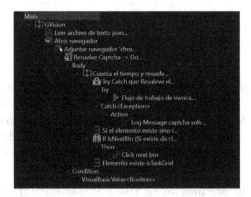

Fig. 4. Overview of the structure of the Main.xaml file

This section defines the analysis logic of the CAPTCHA system, for which a block has been established that allows the activities contained to be executed first and repeat them when certain conditions are met. For this instance, it is essential to establish a sequence of child activities executed in a particular order and then execute the activities in a TryCatch workflow, which contains the activities executed in an exception-handling block.

Within the Try-Catch, a workflow block was established, which synchronously invokes the activity stream that sends a list of input arguments. This workflow allowed dividing the activities developed in the analysis logic for the CAPTCHA resolution with the logic implemented in the Main file. At this point, the activities established in the captcha solver are called and executed in the Try. The Catch is given where the error message is established in the execution.

After the bot can select each of the CAPTCHA images, it must click on the "Next" button to solve the following panel of figures; here, it is essential to verify if the button element exists, then the existence of the button is verified, the specified element can be clicked, to continue with the resolution of the second panel of images provided by the CAPTCHA.

With the development of the Main, it is essential to establish the logic of how the bot will behave within the web page. All the logic required to carry out the activities that a human develops without problems within a web page has been implemented in the captcha solver file. Activities as simple as clicking on a button, scrolling to the site, selecting images, or simply accepting a checklist, which for a machine can involve thousands of lines of programming, but for humans, it is simple. According to this, the captcha solver file is considered the core of our proposal since here is the essential part of establishing the CAPTCHA analysis based on images and obtaining the results.

In this context, Fig. 5 shows the main scheme of the tasks the bot will carry out; these have been organized in a general sequence block and comprise a set of secondary activities structured in a tree. To analyze a specific section of the web page, the "UI Explorer" provided by UiPath was used to determine the position of an element on the screen and extract the selectors that make up the CAPTCHA structure.

The main bot schema comprises a primary activity block of sequences, where the secondary activities are executed in a defined order. For better understanding, Fig. 5 shows the main block called "CAPTCHA Logic", which contains an activity block that attaches the browser page and keeps it open. All the analysis activities were carried out within the web page to maintain the order of execution. For this, a block of activities in the sequence was used again.

An activity block was implemented that contains the tasks executed in a Try-Catch type exception handling; if they do not meet the established conditions, they are repeated until they are true. As certain activities can be repetitive until their conditions are met, orderly and systematic execution is essential; for this reason, a sequence block was used again, and activities such as clicking on the button that opens the CAPTCHA were added to verify the existence of the images to be analyzed.

Once the sequence activity was established, a block was implemented that models a condition. In order to fulfill the task, we must obtain the images based on the text indicated by the CAPTCHA. A sequence block was used, which

Fig. 5. Structured schema of the captchasolver.xaml file

analyzes the image to be searched according to the specified filter criteria and obtains the value of an attribute determined by the UI Explorer and detailed in its destination selector. The analysis process of the CAPTCHA images is carried out based on the matrix of figures presented to the user. Since there are nine figures, the condition must be repeated nine times to determine if it matches the model image.

A message has been considered to indicate to the user which word is being analyzed within the image matrix. For this, a LogMessage type block writes the specified diagnostic message at the determined level. At this point, the components that make up the CAPTCHA have been analyzed, but it is necessary to analyze how to determine the correct images based on the word being searched. A For-Each type block allowed the execution of a series of secondary activities on each element of an enumeration.

With For-Each, activities have been programmed in sequence to search an input string for occurrences of a regular expression. The activity that allowed sending a request and obtaining the image to be analyzed with the API has been configured through the serialization of information established in the previously configured JSON file. Finally, multiple arguments have been assigned within the same activity to obtain a response from the request and deserialize the JSON string to a JObject.

Up to this point, the image has been obtained and analyzed using the artificial vision API, but it is still necessary to establish what would happen if the image found matches the CAPTCHA word. In this case, an If type condition was established, which determines the correspondence of the image with the word to click on each of the correct elements, then the algorithm deletes the analyzed image from the project's root folder. In this case, if it meets the established conditions, the bot analyzes the existence of the "Verify" button. The satisfactory verification condition is automatically established with this verification, and the button to pass the test is clicked.

3   Results and Discussion

3.1   Results

Performance tests were run to verify that hCAPTCHA-type challenges are safe and stop bot attack attempts. The effectiveness and correct functioning of the bot was evaluated [5]. This test measured the bot's execution times, demonstrating its effectiveness when entering the web page "https://www.map24.com/contact/" the resolution time was also verified with the time of resolution by a human. Figure 6 shows the execution times of the bot in a maximum period of 20 repetitions. It can be seen that these times are variable. These variations are results obtained from different aspects that were analyzed during the execution of the process.

Fig. 6. Graph of timelines used by the bot to solve the CAPTCHA challenge

In the first three runs, a downward trend is displayed concerning time. It is because the images presented at the beginning within the CAPTCHA had the same characteristics (the three runs had images of animals), which implies that the API's machine vision model was trained correctly, understanding images faster.

The time went up considerably on the fourth run because new images were presented in the CAPTCHA, implying a new computer vision analysis. In addition, the word the bot takes for the analysis was divided into two parts, which meant that the bot only got the final part and needed to analyze it correctly. In the fifth, sixth, and seventh runs, there is an upward trend concerning time because the CAPTCHA challenge presented new images that had to be analyzed by the computer vision model.

From the 8th to the 11th execution, there is an upward trend concerning time because images appeared that had the word that the bot takes for the analysis divided into two parts, which is why the bot only obtained the final part and did not parse correctly. In run No. 12, the CAPTCHA resolution time decreased significantly because the bot could identify the presented images faster. In runs No. 13 and No.14, there is an upward trend concerning time since similar images (figures of dogs) with identical colors were presented, making it challenging to analyze the figures in the vision API correctly.

In executions No. 15 to 17, the time is considerably low since the artificial vision model that the API has was trained correctly with the images presented and solved the challenge faster. In execution No. 18, the resolution time increased considerably due to the appearance of images with similar characteristics and identical colors, hindering the correct analysis of the artificial vision model that the API has.

Finally, in runs No. 19 and No. 20, there was a downward trend concerning time because the CAPTCHA showed images that had already appeared previously, so the computer vision model solved the challenge faster.

Based on all the times obtained and their variations, it is essential to note that no execution was more significant than the first since the bot could analyze the previously received image with the help of the artificial vision model.

Once the bot's performance was evaluated, its operation was analyzed on different web pages. UiPath offers the development of new projects from previously developed codes. This way, reusing the code for new systems is more feasible [6]. In this context, a new bot was developed to analyze the official hCAPTCHA website.

When establishing the performance tests on the web pages "https://www.map24.com/contact/" and "https://www.hcaptcha.com/", it was shown that the hCAPTCHA images that do not have textures on the figure are more likely to be violated, unlike the images that present textures and distortions, making it challenging to analyze the figures. Figure 7 shows the distortions and textures of the images analyzed in the two web pages.

Fig. 7. Image presented in the CAPTCHA system of the online magazine page vs Image with distortions and textures presented in the CAPTCHA system of the official hCAPCTHA page.

To analyze the behavior related to the resolution of the hCAPTCHA system in the two web pages, the following evaluation criteria have been evaluated and compared in Table 1.

Table 1. Comparative analysis of the resolution of the hCAPTCHA system in web pages

Evaluation criteria	map24.com	hcaptcha.com
Detection of images provided by hcaptcha	YES	YES
Resolution of hCAPTCHA	YES	NO
Types of images	It has sharper images that facilitate object recognition	Has images with textures that make it difficult to recognize objects
Average execution time	24 s	Undetermined

Initially, when establishing the functional tests on the website "https://www.hCAPTCHA.com/", the CAPTCHA system that it had was broken. However, as of July 23, 2022, Intuition Machines, Inc. Owner of the registered trademark of hCAPTCHA, observed possible attempts to attack its system and implemented images with wavy background textures, representing an additional difficulty in the analysis of the images by the bot. Therefore, as of this date, it was impossible to violate the official hCAPTCHA page using the same bot with artificial vision.

3.2 Discussion

There are different tools to solve CAPTCHA systems based on images. These solutions have been based on extensions for web browsers and the use of APIs [7]. The alternatives that have been analyzed were: "Buster, CAPTCHA Solver for Humans" and "Anti-CAPTCHA Solving."

Buster CAPTCHA Solver for Humans: It is an extension for web browsers (Chrome, Firefox, Mozilla, Opera) that helps solve CAPTCHA systems that appear on a web page. This extension allows us to solve text-based challenges and reCAPTCHA V2. The process for reCAPTCHA V2 resolution is shown in Fig. 8, through the download of audios found as a second resolution option and processed through Natural Language Processing (NLP) APIs. They allow the automatic transcription of the audio to text within the corresponding box, achieving the resolution of the CAPTCHA challenge [8].

Anti-CAPTCHA Solving: It is a paid online service to solve any CAPTCHA based on images through the use of real humans. To solve any challenge, the application uploads the CAPTCHA system to a server, where it is assigned to a human worker to solve the challenge and send it back to the client application. This process takes approximately 18 s.

The two solutions (Buster and Anti-CAPTCHA) offer other resolution alternatives for CAPTCHA systems. On the one hand, the free alternative implements a browser extension based on an open-source project. On the other hand, a CAPTCHA system resolution service with a monthly payment.

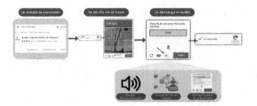

Fig. 8. How the Buster CAPTCHA Solver for Humans extension works

Fig. 9. How the Anti-CAPTCHA Solving service works

In analyzing the possible alternatives for the resolution of CAPTCHAs systems, it is essential to establish a comparative analysis between the solutions presented and our proposal to provide new knowledge that will serve future research. A qualitative analysis of criteria has been established, and the authors' points of view are exposed based on the usability experience of the three solutions. Table 2 shows the parameters evaluated for each tool.

Table 2. Comparative analysis of the solutions found to solve CAPTCHA

Parameters evaluated	Buster CAPTCHA Solver				Anti-Captcha Solving				Bot with computer vision			
	User 1	User 2	Prom.	Qualification	User 1	User 2	Prom.	Qualification	User 1	User 2	Prom.	Qualification
Execution time	6	7	6.5	Medio	8	7	7.5	Alto	3	4	3.5	Bajo
Usability	8	7	7.5	Alto	9	8	8.5	Alto	7	6	6.5	Medio
Effectiveness	5	4	4.5	Medio	8	9	8.5	Alto	7	5	6	Medio
Automation Solution	6	5	5.5	Medio	1	2	1.5	Medio	9	10	9.5	Alto
Browser Compatibility	8	7	7.5	Alto	6	7	6.5	Medio	7	9	8	Alto
	TOTAL		6.3		**TOTAL**		6.5		**TOTAL**		6.7	

A qualitative analysis was applied based on the experience of use of the first two authors of this proposal (students who developed a thesis related), and the final qualification was established through the HIGH, MEDIUM, and LOW criteria. HIGH corresponds to the solution offering solid and outstanding characteristics in said parameter compared to the other solutions. MEDIUM corresponds to the solution offering features that can be improved and could be more outstanding compared to the other solutions. LOW corresponds to the solution offering inefficient characteristics compared to the other solutions.

To better understand each selected parameter, the values and description of the evaluated parameters have been determined:

Execution Time: Time is one of the most critical parameters evaluated during this proposal's execution since the automation of a task requires a fast process compared to the tasks that a human can perform. In this context, a HIGH rating was given to the solution that executed a task in less time, MEDIUM to the solution that performed the task reasonably but did not offer an immediate response, and LOW to the solution that performed the automation of task in a long time compared to the other solutions.

Usability: Usability plays a vital role in the correct performance of a computer tool; therefore, as a tool is functional, it must also provide a good user experience, so the user should feel comfortable and adapt to the operation. A HIGH rating was given to the solution with a user-friendly and easy-to-use interface, MEDIUM to the solution with an unfriendly interface that required more than one attempt to understand its operation, and LOW to the solution of common understanding for the user and that required many attempts to understand its operation.

Effectiveness: This parameter is associated with the time criterion since, as a process is executed, it is essential to execute it with the fewest possible number of errors and much better if the task is executed on the first attempt. For this reason, a HIGH rating was given when the presented solution executed the task on the first attempt and without errors, MEDIUM when the presented solution required two attempts to execute a task and produced errors on its first attempt, and LOW for the solution that required more than three execution attempts and had multiple errors when executing the task.

Solution for Automation: The solutions presented had the objective of automating repetitive processes. Therefore the selected tool had to offer an automated software solution to reduce the margin of error that humans can have. For this reason, a HIGH rating was given to the tool that effectively solved the CAPTCHA system in an automated manner, MEDIUM to the tool that required two or more attempts to pass the CAPTCHA challenge, and LOW to the tool that did not solve the CAPTCHA system or that implemented other non-automated means to resolve.

Browser Compatibility: Since CAPTCHA systems are implemented on websites, the presented solution must be compatible with most existing web browsers. Therefore, a HIGH rating was given to a solution that was compatible with more than three web browsers, MEDIUM to a solution that was compatible with at least two web browsers, and LOW to a solution that applied to only one web browser.

All tools have excellent functionality features, "Anti-CAPTCHA Solving" is not considered an optimal solution to work as RPA because humans solve the resolution of CAPTCHA systems. On the other hand, "Buster CAPTCHA

Solver" has strengths in usability and compatibility parameters. While the bot developed in this proposal, "Bot with Artificial Vision", presents an effective solution to CAPTCHA's challenges based on images due to the implementation of easily accessible technologies such as artificial vision.

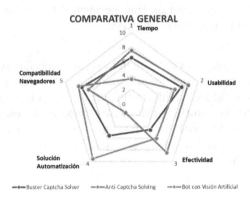

Fig. 10. General analysis of the tools to solve CAPTCHA systems

The figure above shows the general analysis of the presented solutions, evidencing that each has its strengths and weaknesses, taking the evaluated parameters as a reference.

4   Conclusions and Future Work

Security in CAPTCHAs systems is vital for web pages where the user must enter or send data. Therefore, according to the analyzed literature, the most used CAPTCHA systems in web pages are those based on text, video, images, or audio, which fulfill their role of counteracting malicious bot attacks. Like many computer systems, CAPTCHAs are exposed to cyber attacks, even more so if implemented to prevent malicious bots from accessing web pages. The computer attacks most used to violate this type of security are language recognition systems, character recognition systems (OCR), and syntactic analyzers.

A bot capable of breaking the challenges of CAPTCHA systems of the hCAPTCHA type was developed using the website "www.map24.com" (French online magazine) as a reference with the implementation of artificial vision techniques provided by the Google Cloud Vision API and the UiPath companion tool in its Community Edition version.

Based on the tests, it is concluded that the bot developed in UiPath solves the CAPTCHA challenge as long as the image presented by the hCapctha meets certain conditions (clear image, without textures, transparent backgrounds).

In the execution of the performance tests, the time the bot required to solve the CAPTCHA challenge was variable (from highest to lowest) since the images presented sequentially were similar (dogs, animals, boats, cats, others.). It has shown that CAPTCHA systems of the hCAPTCHA type can be easily violated using artificial vision techniques.

As the proposal demonstrates, the bot can occasionally fail because the hCAPTCHA images can present textures, patterns, and distortions that make analysis difficult. For the detection to achieve 100% effectiveness, it is recommended to incorporate new images with these characteristics into an updated dataset, presenting this proposal as future work.

References

1. Universidades, y P.F.: Retos operaciones logística y supply chain (2022). https:// retos-operaciones-logistica.eae.es/author/retos-en-supply-chain-2
2. Ye, G.: Yet another text captcha solver: a generative adversarial network based approach. In: Proceedings of the 2018 ACM SIGSAC Conference on Computer and Communications Security, Ser. CCS '18, Toronto, Canada: Association for Computing Machinery, 2018, pp. 332–348, ISBN: 9781450356930. https://doi.org/10.1145/3243734.3243754
3. Escabias, P.R.: Captchas: debilidades y fortalezas (2013). https://e-archivo.uc3m.es/handle/10016/18365
4. Callisaya Uchani, Z.A.: Captcha para la seguridad de la información en las aplicaciones web. INF-FCPN-PGI Revista PGI, 7, pp. 112–115, Nov. (2021). https://ojs.umsa.bo/ojs/index.php/inf_fcpn_pgi/article/view/123
5. Fernández, A.L.: Reconocimiento de captchas con redes neuronales, Nov. (2019). https://riull.ull.es/xmlui/bitstream/handle/915/14736/Reconocimiento%5C%20de%5C%20CAPTCHAs%5C%20con%5C%20redes%5C%20neuronales.pdf?sequence=1
6. Bursztein, E., Bethard, S., Fabry, C., Mitchell, J.C., Jurafsky, D.: How good are humans at solving captchas? a large scale evaluation. In: 2010 IEEE Symposium on Security and Privacy, pp. 399–413 (2010). https://doi.org/10.1109/SP.2010.31
7. TM, U.: Ponga los robots a trabajar y ponga sus tareas en piloto automático (2022). https://www.uipath.com/es/desarrollo/edicion-community
8. Intuition Machines, I.: Detener más bots. empieza a proteger la privacidad de los usuarios (2022). https://www.hcaptcha.com/

Military Leadership in the Ecuadorian Army

Sandra Patricia Galarza Torres [ID], Alvaro Patricio Carrillo Punina[(✉)] [ID],
Joffre Eduardo Aragón Taco, and Diego Mauricio Noroña Gallo [ID]

University of the Armed Forces ESPE, Sangolquí, Ecuador
{spgalarza,apcarrillo}@espe.edu.ec

Abstract. The success of nations' defense and security operations depends on the prevailing military leadership style. Over the past decade, insecurity has increased in Ecuador due to the proliferation of drug trafficking and international criminal groups. In addition, the Ecuadorian state is going through an economic crisis that comes from the pandemic, corruption, unemployment, poverty, bankruptcy of companies, low oil prices, strong political opposition, high public debt, natural disasters, among other aspects. These facts limit the delivery of financial resources to the Armed Forces for the effective fulfillment of operations. Likewise, the current laws hinder the performance of the new roles played by the Armed Forces combating the country's internal insecurity and supporting risk management. The objective of this research is to identify the dimensions, characteristics, and styles of dominant leadership in the Ecuadorian Army. The study has a qualitative and quantitative approach, the research is descriptive, inferential, correlational, transversal, exploratory and non-experimental. The research is based on the military leadership model established by Castro-Solano. The techniques used are the survey applied to a sample in two groups of officers and the in-depth interview conducted with experts. The results determine that the transformational leadership predominant in the group of operational officers, the leadership of complete range in the officers of the tactical group and, the Laissez-faire has a low presence in both groups.

Keywords: Characteristics of the leader · Leadership dimensions · Leadership styles · Full-ranking leadership · Transformational leadership

1 Introduction

Leadership is an important social dimension in the management of organizations [1]. It is the set of qualities, habits, and values that allows an individual to influence and motivate a group of people to achieve higher ends [2–6]. In the field of Armed Forces, leadership is an aspect that affects the development of military operations [7–9]. Military leadership is the process performed by the commander to influence, motivate, and develop capabilities in the soldiers of the military units to successfully fulfill the missions imposed by the superior command [10, 11].

In the history of Ecuador, the Armed Forces play a historic role in the construction of the state through the exercise of distinct roles, however, they do not have a current military doctrine to aimed at addressing the new unconventional, natural, and anthropic threats [12]. Thus, the end of the Cold War unleashes the proliferation of unconventional threats such as organized crime and drug trafficking and, since 2008, these events have grown strongly in Ecuador, since the country is located among drug producers [13–15].

Currently, the Armed Forces operate to mitigate the risks generated by the presence of threats: a) natural risks: landslides, floods, floods, sinkholes and earthquakes and b) citizen insecurity: crime, drug trafficking and organized crime. The Armed Forces must strengthen their strategic capabilities to play new roles, considering that the formation of the military leader requires training, organizational power, and self-acceleration, therefore, the military needs to develop the traits of ambition, management and tenacity, confidence, psychological openness, realism, and appetite for learning [16].

Military leadership should strengthen group commitment, considering the honor, responsibility, reciprocity, honesty, knowledge, experiences, and quality of command perceived by subordinates [17, 18]. Military academies are leader-forming and require ongoing studies on the leadership styles of officers at different ranks to prepare successful military personnel.

The documentary review identifies some studies on military leadership and its relationship with other variables, such as "Military leadership and its relationship with the combative morale of the Second Division of the Colombian National Army" [19], "Prototypes of leadership in civilian and military population" [20], "Analysis of leadership from military maneuver exercises" [21], "Influence of leadership styles on the innovative behavior of Peruvian cadets" [22], "Body development and leadership in the military training process" [23], "Implicit theories of leadership, quality of the relationship between leader and follower (LMX-leader/follower exchange) and satisfaction" [24], Relationship between leadership styles, values and organizational culture: a study with civilian and military leaders" [25].

These studies use the transformational, transactional, and Laissez-faire leadership theories [26], implicit leadership theories [27], situational leadership theory [28] and Castro-Solano military leadership model [29]. The research design defined is mixed exploratory, non-experimental, descriptive, correlational, and inferential. The techniques applied are surveys, interviews and statistics of reliability coefficients, correlations, and factor analysis. Finally, studies identify the predominant leadership style in various military units and determine the relationships between leadership and other social variables.

Therefore, this research identifies the dimensions, characteristics, and style of leadership dominant in the Ecuadorian Army and answer the guiding questions: Do Ecuadorian army officers have a leadership style that allows them to face the new challenges of the Armed Forces? differences between the military leadership of officers of different hierarchical grades? Therefore, this article contains the theoretical and empirical support of the research, the description of methods, the presentation and discussion of the results and the statement of conclusions.

2 Materials and Methods

The research design has qualitative and quantitative approach. It is a study applied, non-experimental, cross-sectional, documentary exploratory, descriptive, inferential, and correlational. The study applies Castro-Solano's leadership model in military populations that has seven dimensions to define the qualities of the leader: charisma, inspiration, intellectual stimulation, individualized consideration, contingent reward, direction by exception and Laissez Faire. Castro-Solano's model applies Bass's leadership styles: transformational leadership (charisma, intellectual stimulation, inspiration, and individualized consideration), transactional leadership (contingent reward and direction by exception) and leadership of complete range (when the leader uses both styles) [29, 30].

The dominant leadership style depends on the percentile identified in the Castro-Solano Military Population Scale that establishes the level of strengths and weaknesses that each group studied has. This study applies the surveys designed by Castro-Solano: style questionnaire, characteristics questionnaire and leadership dimensions questionnaire. The study segments two groups of military officers: *operational* group (army colonels and majors) and *tactical* group (lieutenant and captains).

The sample size formula for finite populations determines a sample of 210 officers (40 from the task force and 170 from the tactical group) in a universe of 305 officers composed of fifty-four operative group officers (19%) and 251 tactical group officers (81%), with 99% confidence, 5% sampling error, 50% probability of occurrence and 50% probability of non-occurrence. Questionnaires entered Google Forms sent by mail to randomly selected officers.

In addition, three experts in military leadership and unconventional, natural, and anthropic threats participate in the in-depth interview. Survey information must cover in the SPSS version 22 statistical package. In the processing of interviews and the identification of military leadership style are using Microsoft Excel. Finally, the study uses Cronbach's Alpha correlation coefficient to support the reliability of the surveys and the Principal Components Analysis (PCA) to propose the model that describes the predominant characteristics of leadership in Ecuadorian Army officers.

3 Results and Discussions

3.1 Survey Reliability

Table 1 presents Cronbach's Alpha coefficient that measures the degree of reliability of the instrument used to collect information through the survey. The questionnaires of leadership-tactical dimensions, characteristics of the leader-operational, characteristics of the leader-tactical, stiles of leadership-operational and stiles of leadership-tacticians have a high degree of reliability (greater than 0.8) and the questionnaire of leadership-operational dimensions presents a moderately important level of reliability (between 0.6 and 0.8). In summary, the instruments used in this research are solidly dependable.

Table 1. Cronbach's alpha coefficient

Survey	Cronbach's alpha
Leadership-operational dimensions	0.622
Leadership-tactical dimensions	0.816
Characteristics of the leader-operational	0.839
Characteristics of the leader-tacticians	0.932
Leadership-operational styles	0.817
Leadership-tactical styles	0.934

3.2 Dimensions of Military Leadership

Dimensions of Leadership: Operational Group

Table 2 reveals the predominance of leadership dimensions in the operational group of Ecuadorian Army officers (average value mayor than 8): inspiration, charisma, intellectual esteem, and individualized consideration.

Table 2. Leadership dimensions: operational group

Dimensions	Average
Inspiration	9,25
Charisma	8,95
Intellectual Estimation	8,85
Individualized Consideration	8,53
Direction by Exception	7,15
Laissez Faire	5,98
Contingent Reward	5,70

From these dimensions the characterization of military leadership is:

The military leader can influence and develop in the subordinates the fulfillment of a higher vision. The leader stimulates and guides the effort according to the common objectives and the importance of the mission. The leader innovates in the subordinates' new ways of thinking and even changes the expectations and beliefs that the soldier has. The military leader attends, cares for and advises his followers.

Dimensions of Leadership: Tactical Group

The analysis of the information from the survey applied to 170 officers belonging to the tactical group determines the dominant dimensions of military leadership (average

Table 3. Leadership dimensions: tactical group

Dimensiones	Promedio
Intellectual estimation	9,19
Inspiration	9,01
Charisma	8,56
Individualized consideration	8,41
Direction by exception	7,71
Laissez faire	7,52
Contingent reward	7,51

valor greater than 8): intellectual estimation, inspiration, charisma and, individualized consideration. See Table 3.

The characterization of the military leadership of the tactical group is:

The military leader induces in the subordinate's new ways of thinking and even changing their own expectations and beliefs. The military leader can influence and develop in the subordinates the fulfillment of a higher vision. The leader stimulates and guides the effort according to the common objectives and the importance of the mission. The military leader attends, advises and cares for his subordinates.

3.3 Characteristics of the Military Leader

Characteristics of the Leader: Operational Group

The survey of the characteristics of the military leader addresses the criteria that must predominate in the officer to conduct military operations in the face of new threats and direct the personnel of new generations. Table 4 (through Pareto 80/20) identifies the predominant characteristics of the military leader in the operational group: intellectual competences; leadership capacity and command gift; rectitude, authenticity, and honesty; and initiative, enthusiasm, and motivation.

Table 4. Characteristics of the leader: operational group

Characteristics	Weight	Peso acumulado
Intellectual competences	6,03%	6,03%
Steering ability/control gift	6,03%	12,06%
Righteousness, authenticity, and honesty	5,86%	17,92%
Initiative, enthusiasm, and motivation	5,36%	23,28%
Be responsible	5,36%	28,64%

(continued)

Table 4. (*continued*)

Characteristics	Weight	Peso acumulado
Loyalty	5,19%	33,84%
Emotional intelligence	5,19%	39,03%
Be fair	5,03%	44,05%
Be an example to others	5,03%	49,08%
Interest in subordinates/understanding	4,86%	53,94%
Character, poise, and security	4,86%	58,79%
Charisma and influence	4,69%	63,48%
Respect	4,52%	68,01%
Fitness	3,85%	71,86%
Creative ideas and innovative approaches to solving problems	3,85%	75,71%
Critical thinking	3,85%	79,56%
Fellowship and solidarity	3,35%	82,91%
Maturity	3,02%	85,93%
Accept errors	2,85%	88,78%
Expression in speaking and good manners	1,84%	90,62%
Achievement orientation	1,68%	92,29%
Orientation to the organization	1,68%	93,97%
Questioning the conventional way of doing things	1,51%	95,48%
Being selfless	1,34%	96,82%
Orient and cede power	1,17%	97,99%
Happiness and joy	1,01%	98,99%
Use of informal communication channels	1,01%	100,00%
Total	100,00%	

Characteristics of the Leader: Tactical Group

Table 5 presents the predominant characteristics of the military leader in the tactical group: intellectual characteristics; capacity of direction and gift of command; concern for subordinates and understanding; initiative, enthusiasm, and motivation; be the example for others.

Table 5. Characteristics of the leader: tactical group

Characteristics	Weight	Peso Acumulado
Intellectual competences	5,08%	5,08%
Steering ability/control gift	4,92%	10,01%
Interest in subordinates/understanding	4,83%	14,83%
Initiative, enthusiasm, and motivation	4,67%	19,50%
Be an example to others	4,60%	24,10%
Righteousness, authenticity and honesty	4,50%	28,60%
Be fair	4,41%	33,01%
Respect	4,41%	37,42%
Be responsible	4,38%	41,80%
Character, poise, and security	4,34%	46,14%
Loyalty	4,28%	50,42%
Fitness	4,05%	54,47%
Charisma and influence	3,83%	58,30%
Emotional intelligence	3,76%	62,07%
Accept errors	3,64%	65,70%
Critical thinking	3,47%	69,18%
Maturity	3,28%	72,46%
Fellowship and solidarity	3,22%	75,68%
Creative ideas and innovative approaches to solving problems	3,22%	78,89%
Expression in speaking and good manners	3,15%	82,05%
Orientation to the organization	2,93%	84,97%
Achievement orientation	2,77%	87,74%
Happiness and joy	2,67%	90,41%
Empowerment	2,67%	93,08%
Being selfless	2,51%	95,59%
Questioning the conventional way of doing things	2,35%	97,94%
Use of informal communication channels	2,06%	100,00%
Total	100,00%	

3.4 Military Leadership Style

Military Leadership Style: Operational Group

Table 6 and Fig. 1 presents the analysis of the transformational leadership of the operational group that registers a 75th percentile, that is, the group has a high proficiency in transformative leadership skills in the way of conducting work. The leadership style in the operational group promotes change, the cohesion of the group, strongly motivates and takes care of the leader-subaltern treatment to achieve the objectives set. In the group, strong skills prevail in the dimensions of charisma and stimulation and moderate skills in the dimensions of inspiration and consideration.

The transactional style of leadership in the operational group of officers has a 25th percentile, therefore, the group has low skills to lead through the transactional style. In the operational group of officers prevails a low exchange of promises and favors between leader-follower and low negotiation of transactions to achieve the proposed objectives. Finally, the results reveal that the operational group has a low presence of Laissez Faire, which registers a 25th percentile.

Table 6. Military leadership styles: operational group

Leadership	Average	Percentile	Dimensions	Average	Percentile	Questions
Transformational	4,60	75	Charisma	4,71	75	3, 33, 21, 34
			Stimulation	4,55	75	25, 23, 30, 28, 29, 4, 15
			Inspiration	4,58	50	24, 19, 22
			Consideration	4,55	50	13, 17, 14
Transactional	2,72	25	Reward	2,70	25	11, 10, 8, 16, 12
			Direction	2,74	25	26, 2, 7, 5, 9, 18
Laissez faire	1,88	25	Absence of command	1,88	25	31, 20, 1, 32, 27, 6

Military Leadership Style: Tactical Group

Table 7 and Fig. 2 identifies that the officers of the tactical group have a leadership style of complete range, since the transformational leadership and transactional leadership have percentiles of fifty. The military leader of the tactical group possesses moderate skills of transformational leadership in the way of conducting the work, the military leader promotes the change, the cohesion of the group, strongly motivates his followers, takes care of the leader-subaltern treatment to achieve the group objectives set and, the leaders have moderate skills to make exchanges of promises between the leader and follower to achieve institutional objectives.

The tactical group has moderate skills in the dimensions of charisma, stimulation, recompense, and direction, since these have percentiles of fifty. Meanwhile, the skills of inspiration and consideration are low. However, Laissez Faire denotes a 25th percentile, the absence of command is extremely low.

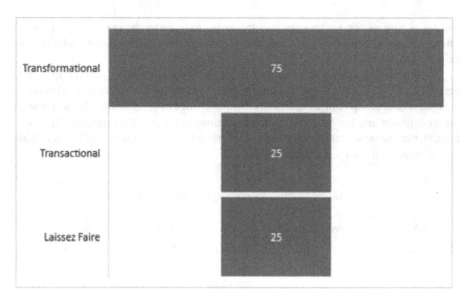

Fig. 1. Military leadership styles: operational group

Table 7. Military leadership styles: tactical group

Leadership	Average	Percentile	Dimensions	Average	Percentile	Questions
Transformational	4,21	50	Charisma	4,32	50	3, 33, 21, 34
			Stimulation	4,16	50	25, 23, 30, 28, 29, 4, 15
			Inspiration	4,23	25	24, 19, 22
			Consideration	4,12	25	13, 17, 14
Transactional	3,04	50	Reward	3,03	50	11, 10, 8, 16, 12
			direction	3,06	50	26, 2, 7, 5, 9, 18
Laissez faire	1,95	25	Absence of Command	1,95	25	31, 20, 1, 32, 27, 6

3.5 Interview Analysis

The analysis of the interviews determines that the military leader must develop skills and abilities so that the subordinate loses fear within the values, principles, patriotic spirit, and image projected by the leader. The military must fulfill the tasks imposed according to the training acquired. The military leader must build trust, spirit of body, integration, and loyalty. The military leader must be intelligent, creative, visionary, and resilient to

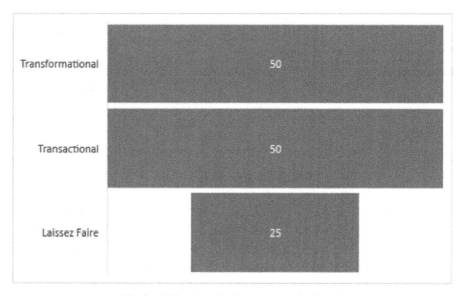

Fig. 2. Military leadership styles: tactical group

make decisions in critical situations and face VICA scenarios and the wars of the XXI century.

Military leadership must be participatory and act according to the different generational characteristics of subordinates. The leader must promote honesty, decency, patriotism, integrity, and credibility. In the Ecuadorian army, each military grade requires developing leadership skills and experiences to successfully fulfill the missions of the superior command.

Experts propose that the Armed Forces should implement innovative training, analysis, and planning techniques in the technical and physical fields. The military leader in the Ecuadorian Army must develop skills and knowledge of cyber defense, geopolitics, and technological innovation. The military leader must strategically prepare to face non-traditional, asymmetric, hybrid and changing threats. In addition, the military leader must strengthen communication skills, exemplariness, critical management, high performance, moral integrity, and body spirit to maintain trust, delegate work and generate respect from his subordinates.

3.6 Dimension Reduction Analysis

The processing of the 210 surveys of leader characteristics applied in the operational and tactical groups the SPSS statistical package. The Dimension Reduction Analysis (ACP) exposes the model of dominant characteristics of military leadership in the Ecuadorian Army. Likewise, Table 8 of the KMO and Barlett Test determines the feasibility of performing the ACP. Table 9 describes that 52.84% of the total variance explains the model of military leadership of Ecuadorian Army officers and can represented in three components.

Table 8. KMO and Barlett test

Kaiser-Meyer-Olkin sampling adequacy measure		,914
Bartlett sphericity test	Aprox. Chi-square	2669,146
	Gl	351
	Sig	0,000

a. It is based on correlations

Table 9. Total variance explained

Initial eigenvalues[a]				Sums of extraction of loads squared		
Component	Total	% Variance	% accumulated	Total	% Variance	% accumulated
1	2,159	40,485	40,485	9,424	34,905	34,905
2	,420	7,882	48,366	2,234	8,275	43,181
3	,238	4,471	**52,838**	1,282	4,747	47,928
4	,218	4,094	56,931	1,221	4,522	52,450
5	,201	3,778	60,709	1,116	4,134	56,584
6	,179	3,364	64,073			
7	,161	3,028	67,100			
8	,154	2,893	69,994			
9	,140	2,624	72,618			
10	,136	2,547	75,165			
11	,123	2,314	77,480			
12	,116	2,168	79,647			
13	,105	1,976	81,624			
14	,103	1,940	83,563			
15	,098	1,833	85,396			
16	,094	1,757	87,154			
17	,086	1,617	88,771			
18	,084	1,571	90,342			
19	,080	1,506	91,849			
20	,074	1,389	93,237			
21	,066	1,232	94,469			
22	,059	1,113	95,582			
23	,057	1,074	96,656			

(*continued*)

Table 9. (*continued*)

Initial eigenvalues[a]				Sums of extraction of loads squared		
Component	Total	% Variance	% accumulated	Total	% Variance	% accumulated
24	,051	,965	97,621			
25	,047	,873	98,494			
26	,046	,856	99,350			
27	,035	,650	100,000			

Table 10 describes the characteristics that are part of each component and that have relationship with each other. COMPONENT 1: felicity and joy, solidarity, adequate language and good manners, disinterest, maturity, use of informal communication channels, creative ideas, and original approaches to solve problems, questioned of the conventional way of doing things, prepared to cede power, critical thinking, emotional intelligence, orientation to the achievement and, orientation to the organization. COMPONENT 2: charisma and influence; rectitude, authenticity, and honesty; Initiative enthusiasm and motivation; justice and acceptance of errors. Finally, COMPONENT 3 contains: responsibility.

Consequently, COMPONENT 2 contains dimensions of Transformational Leadership, so it is the most suitable to develop and strengthen the skills and abilities of the leader's training to overcome crises, face new threats and manage subordinates with new generational traits.

Leadership in the most experienced officers (operational group) is characterized by the fact that the military leader can influence and develop in the followers a superior vision that they must fulfill, while, for officers with less seniority (tactical group) military leadership focuses on the ability to induce in the follower's new ways of thinking and even change their own beliefs. In both cases, the dimensions of transformational leadership prevail, linking leader-follower to a moral commitment to a cause that goes beyond one's own interests [8]. Thus, the characterization of the dominant military leadership in the officers of the Ecuadorian Army is:

The military leader can influence and develop in the followers a superior vision that they must fulfill. The leader innovates in the follower's new ways of thinking and even changing their own expectations and beliefs. The military leader streamlines and guides the effort according to common objectives and the importance of the mission. The military leader attends, cares for and advises his followers.

Table 10. Rotated component matrix

Components	1	2	3
Intellectual competences	,054	,306	−,014
Interest in subordinates/understanding	,166	,237	,238
Character, poise, and security	,086	,195	,699
Carisma e influencia	,286	**,565**	,291
Steering ability/control gift	−,030	,270	,157
Righteousness, authenticity, and honesty	,067	**,507**	−,004
Initiative, enthusiasm, and motivation	,102	**,544**	,108
Be fair	,081	**,621**	,164
Accept errors	,320	**,712**	,063
Be an example to others	,167	,410	−,067
Be responsible	,172	,073	**,693**
Respect	,256	,213	,230
Happiness and joy	**,687**	,446	,139
Fellowship and solidarity	**,603**	,246	,294
Expression in speaking and good manners	**,676**	,223	,061
Loyalty	,358	−,123	,283
Fitness	,401	,034	,108
Being selfless	**,772**	,267	,258
Maturity	**,622**	,068	,416
Use of informal communication channels	**,781**	,307	,128
Creative ideas and original approaches to solving problems	**,732**	−,005	−,143
Questioning the conventional way of doing things	**,794**	,253	,051
Empowerment	**,756**	,240	,222
Critical thinking	**,731**	−,112	−,096
Emotional intelligence	**,662**	−,223	−,020
Achievement orientation	**,779**	,158	,196
Orientation to the organization	**,776**	,155	,095

4   Conclusions

The actions of the leaders influence the actions of their followers to achieve the objectives and the common mission, so the achievement of results is a responsibility of the leader. Sundry authors consider the transformational leverage as the most effective in times of crisis because it helps to adapt to change, and this style shapes the culture through motivation, commitment, and fidelity to achieve both personal and group innovation. The joint presence of the characteristics, dimensions, and styles of transformational and transactional leadership does not affect the domain of the characteristic leadership of the group and allows to successfully face different situations.

The military leadership of the operational group is transformational, promoting change and innovation in its troops by motivating followers to transcend their personal goals to reach important levels of performance. The leader acts through charisma, synthesizing the information of the medium and promoting the cohesion of the group. In this case, leadership is charisma, influencing others by creating a vision that replaces the individual goals of followers with those of the leader. The military leader is an expert in the intellectual stimulation of his followers because it leads to generate innovative solutions to the usual problems, this being fundamental aspect to face critical situations. This leader inspires followers to adhere to the vision to involve them in change projects. The military leader of the operating group protects cares for and watches over the welfare of the troops.

The military leader of the tactical group is moderately transformational and transactional, has charisma, influences others by creating a vision that replaces the individual goals of the followers with those of the leader. The military leader is an expert in the intellectual stimulation of his followers because it leads to generate innovative solutions to the usual problems, this being fundamental aspect to face critical situations. This leader rewards his followers for a job well done and constantly controls that the activities conducted comply with the laws and regulations and, the military leader reinforces and sanctions the performance of the subordinate.

This study determines the main characteristics that define the military leadership of the Ecuadorian army, these being, charisma and influence; rectitude, authenticity, and honesty; initiative, enthusiasm, and motivation; justice and acceptance of errors. These aspects make it possible to establish strategies to strengthen the dominant leadership and confront unconventional threats such as organized crime and drug trafficking. Finally, it proposed to conduct studies on the characteristics, dimensions and leadership styles in Ground Force officers who have other grades.

References

1. Carrillo-Punina, A.P., Galarza Torres, S.P.: Reportes de Sostenibilidad de Organizaciones Sudamericanas. Ciencias Administrativas **103** (2022). https://doi.org/10.24215/231 43738e103
2. House, R., Aditya, R.: The social scientific study of leadership: Quo Vadis? J. Manag. **23**(3), 409–473 (1997)
3. Galarza-Torres, S.P.: Leadership and performance in Ecuadorian Savings and Credit Cooperatives. Tesis. Universidad Nacional de La Plata, La Plata (2019). https://sedici.unlp.edu.ar/handle/10915/79854
4. Carrillo, Á., Sierra, C.: Modelosorganizacionales en el marco de cultura, poder y liderazgo. Yura: Relaciones Internacionales (8), 89–113 (2016). http://world_business.espe.edu.ec/wp-content/uploads/2016/10/Art%C3%ADculo-8.5-Alvaro-Carrilo-Carlos-Sierra.pdf
5. Carrillo Punina, Á.P., Galarza Torres, S.P., Franco Pombo, M., ArocaJácome, R.: Predominant cultural dimensions in the university of the armed forces ESPE. In: Botto-Tobar, M., Cruz, H., Díaz Cadena, A., Durakovic, B. (eds.) CIT 2021. LNNS, vol. 406, pp. 422–435. Springer, Cham (2022). https://doi.org/10.1007/978-3-030-96046-9_32

6. Carrillo Punina, Á.P., Galarza Torres, S.P., Franco Pombo, M., Aroca Jácome, R.: Organizational culture from the focus of values in competition: current and desired situation in the university of the armed forces ESPE. In: Botto-Tobar, M., Cruz, H., Díaz Cadena, A. (eds.) CIT 2020. AISC, vol. 1327, pp. 42–56. Springer, Cham (2021). https://doi.org/10.1007/978-3-030-68083-1_4

7. Hamad, H.: Transformational leadership theory: why military leaders are more charismatic and transformational? Int. J. Leadersh. 3(1), 1–8 (2015)

8. Avolio, B.J., Bass, B.M.: Individual consideration viewed at multiple levels of analysis: a multi-level framework for examining the diffusion of transformational leadership. Leadersh. Q. 6(2), 199–218 (1995)

9. Wong, L., Bliese, P., McGurk, D.: Military leadership: a context specific review. Leadersh. Q. 14(6), 657–692 (2003)

10. Bradley, O.: Liderazgo. Mil. Rev. 49–54 (2012)

11. Jason, M. P.: Reevaluandoel liderazgo del Ejército en el siglo XXI. Mil. Rev. 33–41 (2009)

12. Andrade-Vásquez, M.: Doctrina y estructura militar ecuatoriana: de cara o de espaldas a las amenazas del siglo XXI. URVIO Revista Latinoamericana de Estudios de Seguridad 29, 09–121 (2021). https://doi.org/10.17141/urvio.29.2021.4322URVIO

13. Rivera Vélez, F.: Ecuador: tradicionespolíticas, cambio de época y Revolución Ciudadana. En La actualidad política de los países andinos centrales en el gobierno de izquierda, pp. 55–88. Instituto de Estudios Peruanos, Lima (2014)

14. Espinosa, C.: Una amenazasilenciosa: el narcotráfico en el Ecuador. Polemika 1(1), 136–42 (2013). https://bit.ly/3dAKcO8

15. Bargent, J.: Ecuador: autopista de la cocaína hacia Estados Unidos y Europa. Insight Crime (2019). http://bit.ly/30DsV1G

16. Kolditz, T.: Why the military produces great leaders. Harv. Bus. Rev. 6. Recuperado de https://hbr.org/2009/02/why-the-military-produces-grea

17. Charan, R.: Six personality traits of a leader. Military.com (2018). Recuperado de https://www.military.com/veteran-jobs/careeradvice/on-the-job/6-traits-for-improved-leadership-skills.html

18. Monsalve-Castro, C., Chamorro Rojas, L., LuzardoBriceño, M.: Liderazgo militar y su relación con la moral combativa de la Segunda División del Ejército Nacional de Colombia. Revista Facultad de Ciencias Económicas: Investigación y Reflexión 26(2), 115–127 (2018). https://revistas.unimilitar.edu.co/index.php/rfce/article/view/3049/3065

19. Olid Martínez, P.: Liderazgo militar [Military leadership]. Mil. Rev. 20–29 (2002)

20. Castro Solano, A., Becerra, L., LupanoPerugini, M.: Prototipos de liderazgo en población civil y militar. Interdisciplinaria 24(1), 65–94 (2007). https://www.redalyc.org/pdf/180/18024103.pdf

21. Beramendi, M., Muratori, M., Zubieta, E.: Análisis del liderazgo a partir de ejercicios de maniobra militar. Pensamiento Psicológico 13(1), 105–118 (2015). https://www.redalyc.org/pdf/801/80140030008.pdf

22. Norena-Chávez, D., Céliz Kuong, J., Guevara, R.: Influencia de los estilos de liderazgo en el comportamiento innovador de cadetes peruanos. Revista Científica General José María Córdova 19(33), 29–50 (2021). https://www.redalyc.org/journal/4762/476268269002/html/

23. Sandoval, L.E., Otálora, M.C.: Desarrollo corporal y liderazgoen el proceso de formación militar. Revista Científica General José María Córdova 13(16), 33–53 (2015). https://www.redalyc.org/articulo.oa?id=476247224003

24. Castro-Solano, A.: Teorías implícitas del liderazgo, calidad de la relación entre líder y seguidor (LMX-intercambio líder/seguidor) y satisfacción. Anuario de Psicología 39(3), 333–350 (2008)

25. Nader, M., Castro S., A.: Relación entre los estilos de liderazgo, valores y cultura organizacional: un estudio con líderes civiles y militares. Anuario de Psicología **40**(2) 237–254 (2009). https://www.redalyc.org/pdf/970/97017660007.pdf

26. Bass, B., Avolio, B., Atwater, L.: The transformational and transactional leadership of men and women. Appl. Psychol. Int. Rev. **45**(1), 5–34 (1996)

27. Eden, D., Leviatan, U.: Implicit leadership theory as a determinant of the factor structure underlying supervisory behavior scales. J. Appl. Psychol. **60**, 736–741 (1975)

28. Hersey, P., Blanchard, K.H.: Management of Organizational Behavior: Utilizing Human Resources. Prentice Hall, Englewoods Cliffs (1982)

29. Castro, A.: Técnicas de evaluación psicológica en ámbitos militares, motivación, valores y liderazgo. Editorial Paidos SAICF, Buenos Aires (2005)

30. Galarza Torres, S.P., Carrillo Punina, Á.P., Cueva Ochoa, B.E., LandázuriRecalde, F.P.: Influence of the discrepancy between the real and ideal leader and the quality of the LMX relationship: case of the ecuadorian savings and credit banks. In: Botto-Tobar, M., Cruz, H., Díaz Cadena, A., Durakovic, B. (eds.) CIT 2021. LNNS, vol. 406, pp. 362–372. Springer, Cham (2022). https://doi.org/10.1007/978-3-030-96046-9_27

Analysis of Key Variables for Ecuadorian Defense Industry Development

Angie Fernández Lorenzo[1][(✉)] [iD], Oscar Lenin Chicaiza Sánchez[1] [iD],
Marco Antonio Hernández Arauz[1] [iD], Darwin Manolo Paredes Calderón[2] [iD],
and Zlata Dolores Borsic Laborde[1] [iD]

[1] Department of Economic, Administrative and Commercial Sciences, Universidad de Las
Fuerzas Armadas-ESPE, Quito, Ecuador
aafernandez2@espe.edu.ec
[2] Ecuadorian Army, Quito, Ecuador

Abstract. The present work is a practical application of the theoretical advances developed by the authors about the model or system of the defense industry in Ecuador. After defining the usefulness of the quintuple helix approach for the determination of actors related to the model (government, academia, civil society, business sector, and natural environment), among other elements of contextualization to the Ecuadorian case, in the present work identified the key variables that should be taken into account for the development of the natural defense industry. 9 national and international experts with recognized experience in the subject participated in the exercise, with whom 13 variables were determined to study. The MICMAC prospective method was applied for the processing of the direct relationship matrices completed by the experts, showing that the most important variables are: economy; technology; defense market; consumer needs; quality, productivity, and competitiveness; innovation, and links with the private sector. It was also determined that the most important relationships are established between the economy variable and that of quality, productivity, and competitiveness. The results obtained will allow us to continue deepening the analysis of the particular conditions of Ecuador to develop its defense industry sector and lay the foundations for modeling the relationships between the actors related to these key issues.

Keywords: Defense · Industry · Variables · Key variables · MICMAC method · Ecuador

1 Introduction

Article 158 of the Constitution of the Republic [1] states that "...*The Armed Forces and the National Police are institutions for the protection of the rights, freedoms, and guarantees of citizens. The Armed Forces have as a fundamental mission the defense of sovereignty and territorial integrity*".

Nations face threats such as organized crime, drug trafficking, migration, etc., which brings great challenges to security and defense, which is why today the world is aware of the importance of scientific and technological activities to guarantee safety.

M. Botto-Tobar et al. (Eds.): ICAT 2022, CCIS 1755, pp. 360–372, 2023.
https://doi.org/10.1007/978-3-031-24985-3_26

Governments have adapted to nations' different ways of managing the nation, so much so that today democracy has high participation in the development of a country, however, this security depends on the investment offered to the industrial sector.

In Ecuador, investment programs have been incorporated that are oriented to the strengthening and development of the Armed Forces, an example of this is shown in the National Defense Policy "White Book" [2], which has among its strategic objectives to 2030 *"Contribute to the national development through activities of intersectoral cooperation, research, and innovation in the defense industries"*.

In the Strategic Institutional Defense Plan 2017 to 2021 [3], the main challenge is to develop useful defense equipment that allows reducing the outflow of foreign exchange due to imports of military material and equipment, in Ecuador, there is a plan aimed at the sector, however, several years have passed since its approval and its application in the industry since it is being too delayed compared to other countries in the world.

Perhaps it is not only necessary to analyze the industrial sector but also the National Defense sector in general. The answer is probably related to several factors that positively or negatively affect this fraction, since the whole world is going through a situation that took it by surprise, as a result of the pandemic, the impact on the economy destabilized first-class countries. In a world such as China and the United States, however, the impact is being much greater for poor countries that are or were developing, if before their objectives included development, becoming commercially independent, lowering their country risk, etc., now With Covid-19, a new priority arises, which is health, and a large part of the resources of each country is being directed to this sector, leaving aside sectors such as education, defense, research, work, the environment, among others that are essential for the development of each country.

In the case of Ecuador, the state must provide resources for education, health, work, and defense with the aim of safety safeguard citizens, to understory spending, reference must be made to all those state funds that are earmarked for the maintenance or strengthening of the Armed Forces to safeguard the order of the state against any externality. This item includes military and civilian salaries, investment, infrastructure, operating expenses, social security, supplies including weapons, ammunition, war material, etc.

In previous works by the authors, progress has been made in theorizing the defense industry model or system, combining actors such as the government, academia, civil society, the business sector, and the natural environment, based on the quintuple helix approach. [4]. The determination of the strategies of actors, based on the prospective approach of Godet [5], must start from the survey and identification of the associated key variables.

Considering the above, in this paper, it is proposed to determine the key variables or aspects to be taken into consideration for the development of the national defense industry, based on a holistic and comprehensive approach.

2   Materials and Methods

The research developed is of an applied type with a mixed approach, based on the analysis of bibliographic information that allowed conceptualizing the variables to be studied; and on the other hand, apply the MICMAC structural analysis method [5] with the participation of experts, the completion of matrices and their mathematical processing.

Nine national and international experts (Mexico, Brazil, Chile, Cuba, and Spain) were chosen to participate in the study, five of them with a doctorate a nest with a master's degree. After the process of evaluating the level of expertise applying the method of Barroso and Cabero [6], an expert coefficient K of 0.825 was obtained, which is adequate to consider the criteria of the specialists in the study.

The 13 variables shown in Table 1 were defined, which were validated by the experts and will be analyzed later.

Table 1. Studied variables

No	Variable	Description
V1	Politics	One of the primary duties of the State is to "guarantee and defend national sovereignty" in militthe ary, territorial, administrative, and civil aspects. The government as head of state directs, controls, and administers its institutions through the determination of policies and laws
V2	Economy	The economy is fluctuating and directly affects the different sectors of the country. How the defense sector distributes and uses scarce resources to fulfill its objectives, including those aimed at the defense industry
V3	Technology	Tools, instruments, machines, organizations, methods, techniques, systems must be adapted in the defense industry to face the requirements and threats of a globalized world
V4	Defense market	The market is open and consequently competitive. The critical resource that will define the country's competitiveness and that will attract the necessary capital and technology is the local availability of qualified labor available in the defense industry
V5	Consumer needs	Consumers in the defense industry are scarce, so the market must meet their requirements and thus increase their purchasing decisions
V6	Relationship with suppliers	Necessary actions and mechanisms in favor of generating competitive advantages for the National Defense Industry, not only in cost or in meeting requirements, but also continuous improvement of the product or service

(continued)

Table 1. (*continued*)

No	Variable	Description
V7	Quality, productivity, and competitiveness	The capacity of the national defense industry to improve its production processes, reduce costs and satisfy the needs of its consumers. The competition of defense products and services in an international market
V8	International cooperation and foreign support	Strategic association between two or more countries to promote actions that contribute to the development of the defense industry through the transfer of knowledge and technology. Cooperation and integration help to avoid conflicts and reduce technological dependency on developed countries that supply military goods
V9	Innovation	Technological development of defense industry products, the existence of new products, services, technology, or processes. Innovation provides a competitive advantage to the defense industry, which in turn facilitates cooperative knowledge transfer between different public, private, national, and international actors
V10	Environmental impact	The evolution of the defense industry adapted to the circular economy, which considers a regenerative production process, concerning the inputs used and therefore has a low environmental impact in terms of greenhouse gas emissions. This will allow the defense industry to be more competitive and to maintain itself in the medium and long term
V11	Culture	The values, customs, beliefs, and practices of a country influence the judgments or opinions of consumers when purchasing military goods or services from the defense industry
V12	Link with academy	Indispensable relationship with academic institutions and research centers to promote and drive processes of scientific research, generation, innovation, dissemination, and transfer of technology aimed at meeting the real needs of the defense industry

(*continued*)

Table 1. (*continued*)

No	Variable	Description
V13	Link with the private sector	Relationship of the defense industry with private industries to generate investment in new methods and processes that promote the productive development of the national industry, the actions and activities must be aimed at establishing associations to increase the country's productivity and competitiveness

Source: Own elaboration

Table 2 shows the structure of the matrix of direct relationships between variables that were completed by each expert, considering the following scale:

0: There is no relationship between the variables
1: There is a weak relationship between the variables
2: There is a median relationship between the variables
3: There is a strong relationship between the variables
4: There is a potential relationship between the variables

Table 2. Direct relationship matrix

Var	V1	V2	V3	V4	V5	V6	V7	V8	V9	V10	V11	V12	V13
V1													
V2													
V3													
V4													
V5													
V6													
V7													
V8													
V9													
V10													
V11													
V12													
V13													

Source: Own elaboration

After the completion of the matrices by the experts, the mathematical analysis was carried out with the MICMAC software [5], with which indirect and hidden relationships between variables are calculated, to determine their classification and determination of the keys.

3 Results

3.1 Conceptualization of Variables Related to the Defense Industry in Ecuador

Politics

The Dictionary of the Royal Academy defines politics as "*the science or art of governing and enacting laws and regulations to maintain public peace and security and preserve order and good customs*" [7]. According to Solozabal, politics in the public sphere is delimited by the activity of the State, where means and ends are specially combined [8].

Politics is understood as a government action on a community to conceive social coexistence. By relating politics to defense, it is determined that the decisions, policies, or laws that are defined have a direct impact on the defense industry, the Joint Command is the highest body for planning, preparation, and strategic management of military and security operations. Advice on military policies at all levels.

Economy

Two important terms underlie this definition: scarcity and efficiency, which is why Samuelson and Nordhaus added that "*The essence of economic theory is to recognize the reality of scarcity and then find a way to organize society in such way, that produces the most efficient use of resources*" [9].

The economy plays an important role in each sector of the country, such as the relationship with the defense industry whose impact turns out to be. In this way, if there is an international financial crisis there will be an imbalance that would seriously affect poor and developing economies of development since this results in a limitation of resources for the fulfillment of the objectives.

While its positive impact is in the distribution and investment capacity of those few resources in projects that generate competitiveness in the international market and, as a consequence, the progress of the country's economy.

Technology

Technology, according to García [10], has its particularity in the use of generated and tested knowledge, applying it to a specific reality to transform or generate resources.

Technology and innovation have become the new tools applied in defense industries around the world, this has helped to make production faster, more efficient, and more complex due to the threats of a globalized world.

It is clear that technology is essential in the production of defense materials, however, as companies have a limited capacity to produce them, it is necessary to form a long supply chain to accumulate a sufficient degree of knowledge, experience, and means, these relationships require the participation of foreign companies to meet production needs and thus increase spending.

Therefore, a greater budget allocation must be made for research and development since, in an increasingly globalized market, the innovation that a country can contribute to a product provides that added value in such a competitive market. This investment will help the defense industry generate technology-based goods and services, both for internal use and for possible exports.

Defense Market

The market for civil products and services, unlike the defense market, has countless consumers, which is why it is based on the law of supply and demand. For its part, the defense market offers products and services for the only client is the national one. For this reason, the legislative bodies of the governments are the ones that determine and demand from the defense industry products that only conform to the specifications of the exclusive consumer.

To all this, if the Defense Industry does not generate products and services that are competitive in the national and international market, it becomes irrelevant to its demands.

With the evolution of technology, defense requirements have also evolved, now countries are looking for technologically advanced materials or systems, which represents a disadvantage for the country if we compare Ecuador with countries such as Russia, China, among others, whose industry develops highly advanced products that are potentially in demand in the international defense market.

Consumer Needs

On the consumer side, institutions and governments are the ones who seek to guarantee the security of their nation, which is why they become the main consumers of the defense industry.

In the case of the defense market and industry, consumers are important because they are scarce.

Relationship with Suppliers

Ecuador's main supplier in China, among other South American countries such as Argentina and Chile.

In 2019, Ecuador invested $101.9 million in the purchase of military equipment, including twin-engine helicopters, basic training aircraft, larger and smaller caliber weapons, radars for the surveillance, alarm and airspace control system, boats for operations of the jungle, among other things, among the suppliers in China.

Foreignareeing its main suppliers, therefore, to be able to produce defense material at an international level, it is necessary to make a high investment.

Quality, Productivity, and Competitiveness

Productivity is the ability of the industry to produce in the same way it measures production efficiency, it is directly related to competitiveness. According to Carro & González *"Productivity improves the production process. Improvement means a favorable comparison between the number of resources used and the number of goods and services produced"* [11].

Productivity then improves processes and this implies a reduction in costs, and therefore establishes economic growth for the industry that allows it to be competitive in an international market.

International Cooperation and Foreign Support

Cooperation can be defined as those agreements through which companies share resources, capabilities, or activities, to carry out an exchange of knowledge that allows them to improve their positions in the market and strengthen their competitive advantages according to Briones, Bernal & de Nieves [12].

In Ecuador, specifically the Ministry of Defense in its Institutional Strategic Planning 2017–2021 [3]:

"It defines institutional objectives, from which strategies are derived aimed at strengthening the strategic capabilities of the Armed Forces, to guarantee the sovereignty and territorial integrity; develop new joint strategic capacities to achieve an efficient participation in the different missions entrusted; promote the development of defense research, innovation, and technology transfer in support of achieving relative technological autonomy; and increase regional integration and international cooperation in the field of defense".

To establish international relations, the actions of the Ministry of Foreign Affairs are necessary, in this way it will be possible to develop joint strategies that facilitate an exchange not only of products or services but also of communications and information technology. Ecuador cooperates with the United States in the framework of the fight against drug trafficking materialized in organized crime organizations, but without neglecting cooperation with China or other emerging powers worldwide.

Innovation

Innovation represents a competitive advantage and in turn facilitates the transfer of cooperative knowledge between people, institutions, universities, and research centers in such a way that it promotes the growth of the industry.

When talking about innovation, reference is also made to the technological part, so that technological development allows innovation to be a differentiating strategy in industries, technological innovation is developed in various fields, among them are advanced materials, aero-structures, tactical and operational simulation, optoelectronics, microelectronics.

Environmental Impact

Currently, the environmental impact is becoming increasingly evident, for this reason, the concern of countries to reduce pollution becomes an essential point for sustainable development, identification of actions that enable the reduction of greenhouse gas emissions. They have increased.

The UN has incorporated strategies so that all countries have the concept of sustainable development as a reference [13].

The green economy and the circular economy are mechanisms that are helping to fight against those systems that do not give priority to environmental problems. Currently, the new mechanism that is being used the most is the circular economy, which considers a regenerative production process concerning the inputs used and therefore has a low environmental impact in terms of greenhouse gas emissions.

Culture

Culture can be understood as the set of values, customs, beliefs, and practices that constitute the way of life of a specific group.

The Ecuadorian culture greatly influences the industry, it allows societies to adapt to a certain time and space to survive, the fact that this culture is shared from generation to generation has determined the way of thinking of being and living people, including the specifications to buy an artifact, although a large part of society has created a very close link with the importation of goods or services because they find the quality, benefit, and cost that they seek and believe not found in national products.

This consequently results in a negative point for the Ecuadorian industry since it is a culture that is transmitted to other generations, thus creating an environment of distrust in national products.

However, this situation has a much greater impact on the defense industry, because the culture of national clients is based on the non-existence and inability to produce quality defense products and services, which forces a country to acquire such elements abroad, leaving aside the possibility of creating them domestically.

Link with Academy

Over the years, education has determined the development and growth of the country. Nowadays, educational institutions together with industry experts collaborate in the generation of ideas for products and services that represent the growth of the industry. However, it is convenient that from the educational beginnings a more dynamic and adaptive education is established to collaborate and solve the needs of the industry effectively and immediately.

For this, there must be mutual interest between academia and industry so that students align their research efforts with the real needs of industry, with tto accelerate and market records.

Link with the Private Sector

The role of the private sector in the country's market economy turns out to be fundamental for the development of sectors such as industry.

The private sector includes all those organizations or individuals that are not part of the State as such, therefore, their economic activities, decisions, and budgets are autonomous and are governed by the laws of the country. It promotes access to international markets and consequently increases employment and the opportunity to reduce the country's unemployment rate.

Its participation in the defense industry can become active since, the investment in research, development, innovation, and use of new methods or processes, speeds up and facilitates collaboration in the production of defense supplies.

3.2 Results of the Application of the MICMAC

After applying the MICMAC method, the classification of variables was obtained, as follows:

I Motor variables: V3
II Bind variables: V2; V4; V5; V7; V9; V13
III Autonomous variables: V1, V11
IV Resulting variables: V6; V10
V Platoon variables: V8; V12

Figure 1 shows the plane of the variable:

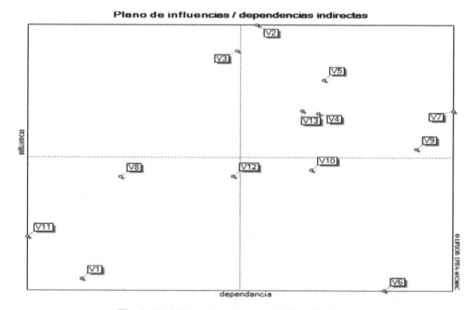

Fig. 1. Variables plane. Source: MICMAC software

According to the classification of Godet's methodology [5], the key variables resulting in the study are:

– Economy (V2)
– Technology (V3)
– Defense market (V4)
– Consumer needs (V5)
– Quality, productivity, and competitiveness (V7)
– Innovation (V9)
– Link with the private sector (V13)

Gráfico de influencias indirectas

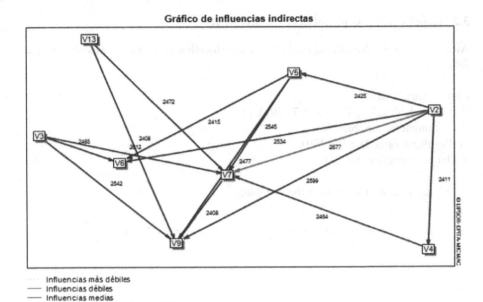

Influencias más débiles
Influencias débiles
Influencias medias
Influencias relativamente importantes
Influencias más importantes

Fig. 2. Graph of relationships between variables. Source: MICMAC software

Figure 2 shows another of the important results of the application of the MICMAC, the graph of the strongest relationships between variables.

As can be seen, the strongest relationships in the system are between the variables economy (V2) and quality, productivity, and competitiveness (V7).

4 Discussion

The results obtained with the application of the MICMAC method and based on the criteria of the experts participating in the study were very interesting.

Despite what could be considered a priori, the Political variable was discriminated against in the study, which has its explanation in that in the country in recent years the issue of the defense industry has been present in the different regulatory documents at the level of the national government, Ministry of Defense or Joint Command of the Armed Forces [2, 3].

In this sense, the results were fundamentally directed towards the economic field, determining that V2 "Economy" was set as the most influential in the system (it can be viewed as the one located at the top of the plane between variables); explained by the need to stimulate resources towards the development of the defense industry in the country, which have remained contracted in recent years, with indices with countries in the region [14] and as a sign of a sustained crisis in the economy Ecuadorian [15].

The relationship graph shows the strong relationship of this variable with one of an internal character to the system (quality, productivity, and competitiveness), which becomes the most dependent of those studied (it is displayed on the right of the plane), and therefore both in an issue to be addressed carefully by the future decision-makers of the system, and its specific business sector.

Similarly, the importance of analysis and relations with the defense market, and consumers, in particular, was identified, denoting that the future defense industry system should be born precisely with the study of the needs of consumers and other associated issues, giving it an economic and marketing approach. To this is added that the variable link with the private sector was also prioritized by the experts and the MICMAC process, considering that this will be an important strategic ally that will benefit considering that they would become the pioneers in venturing into this important field.

The determination of the technology and innovation variables as keys to the future development of the defense industry is logical, considering that they are the basis for the development of a sector as innovative as this one. According to Martí [16], *"the defense industry is characterized by its innovative tendency (…) companies have to dedicate an important part of their resources to research, development, and innovation"*; hence, it is recognized that the development of technology and innovation strategies constitutes an opportunity for the development of companies associated with defense [17].

5   Conclusions

Based on previous studies and the theoretical and contextual analysis carried out, 13 variables were defined to study related to the defense industry model or system in Ecuador, all of them important for a better understanding of the subject and the developmental mechanisms in the defense industry practice, which until now have not been studied in the country.

With the application of the MICMAC prospective method that included the participation of nine specialists in the subject, the key variables of the studied system were identified, and the most important relationships between them; being an interesting contribution for the deepening in the studies on the subject in the national context.

The analysis of the results allows us to identify that Ecuador, to develop its defense industry system, must prioritize issues related to the allocation of resources from the General State Budget, the creation or strengthening of companies that implement strategies that tend to achieve quality, productivity and competitiveness based on innovation processes and access to advanced technologies; without losing sight of relationships with consumers in the defense market and the private sector.

References

1. Ecuador. Constitution of the Republic. Montecristi: Constituent Assembly (2008)
2. Ecuador. National Defense Policy - White Book. Quito: Ministry of Defense (2018)
3. Ecuador. Institutional strategic plan 2017–2021. Quito: Ministry of Defense (2017)
4. Carayannis, E.G., Barth, T.D., Campbell, D.F.J.: The Quintuple Helix innovation model: global warming as a challenge and driver for innovation. J. Innov. Entrepreneurship 1(2), 1–12 (2012). https://doi.org/10.1186/2192-5372-1-2
5. Godet, M.: The Toolbox of Strategic Foresight. LIPSOR, Paris (2000)

372	A. Fernández Lorenzo et al.

6. Barroso, J., Cabero, J.: The use of expert judgment for the evaluation of ICT: the coefficient of expert competence. Pedagogy Mag. **65**(2), 25–38 (2013). https://recyt.fecyt.es/index.php/BORDON/article/view/22403
7. Royal Spanish Academy: Politics concept (2022). https://dle.rae.es/pol%C3%ADtica
8. Solozabal, J.J.: A note on the concept of politics. J. Polit. Stud. (New Era) **42**, 137–162 (1974). https://dialnet.unirioja.es/descarga/articulo/26809.pdf
9. Samuelson, P., Nordhaus, W.: Economy. McGraw Hill, New York (2005)
10. García, F.: The technology its conceptualization and some reflections regarding its effects. Methodol. Sci. **2**(1), 13–28 (2010). http://www.ammci.org.mx/revista/pdf/Numero2/2art.pdf
11. Carro, R., González, D.: Productividad y Competitividad. Administración de las Operaciones. Universidad Nacional de Mar del Plata, Mar del Plata (2012)
12. Briones, A.J., Bernal, J.A., de Nieves, C.: Interorganizational relations in the defense industry: its influence on innovation and cooperation and its effect on competitiveness. J. Global. Competitiveness Gov. **11**(3), 20–37 (2017). https://doi.org/10.3232/GCG.2017.V11.N3.01
13. UN: Sustainable Development Goals (2015). https://www.un.org/sustainabledevelopment/es/objetivos-de-desarrollo-sostenible/
14. Borsic, Z.D., Fernández, A., Paredes, DM., Montoya, S.N.: Comparative analysis of defense industry models in South American countries. Smart Innov. Syst. Technol. **2** (2022, in press)
15. ECLAC: An economic study of Latin America and the Caribbean. Main determinants of fiscal and monetary policies in the post-COVID-19 pandemic era. United Nations, Santiago de Chile (2020). https://repositorio.cepal.org/bitstream/handle/11362/46070/89/S2000371_es.pdf
16. Martí, C.: The defense industry. Main characteristics and efficiency of a strategic sector. Industr. Econ. (388), 169–182 (2013). https://dialnet.unirioja.es/servlet/articulo?codigo=4368296
17. Riola, J.M.: The defense technology and Innovation strategy, an opportunity for the naval sector. Naval Eng. (945), 45 (2016). https://dialnet.unirioja.es/servlet/articulo?codigo=5489750

The Prioritization of External Security as a Means of Guaranteeing Multidimensional Security and Economic Growth

Henry Cruz[✉]🆔 and Lili Salcedo Vallejo🆔

Universidad de Las Fuerzas Armadas - ESPE, Sangolquí, Ecuador
{hocruz,lcsalcedo}@espe.edu.ec

Abstract. Security represents a complex concept that pragmatically seeks to define actions to reach stability in territorial established spaces. In this context, the present work shows an up-to-date analysis of security both from the external point of view as well as from the multidimensional one, establishing, in this way, security levels of priority. For this, the reach of a security application is verified by taking into account as reference historic occurrences from World War I (WWI) to our days. The obtained results show that external security has a greater relevance relative to other types of security, which have allowed, among other aspects, to guarantee the survival of states and their populations. Moreover, the carried-out study allows us to infer that external security incentives economic growth, the same that propitiated the increase of economic welfare of certain world powers based, in effect, on a war economy.

Keywords: External security · Multidimensional security · War economy · Economic growth

1 Introduction

Security is a topic that is conceptualized as the lack of risk or threat, provides a sense of safety, it is feeling safe and taken care for. All these premises have one direct relation and applicability in the survival and development of states and their populations. The sensation of security combines these two aspects and allows nation-states to position themselves in the global context.

Besides, security disposes of a personal needs satisfaction hierarchy that goes from biological survival to self-fulfillment [1]. The requirement of satisfaction of individual needs generates collective aspirations that later materialize themselves when political objectives and the survival of the State are reached. To fulfill national or state goals, if necessary, force should be employed, and one of the channels frequently used is the war, which is considered a means to guarantee external security [2, 3].

Within this context, the satisfaction of individual well-being needs has been divided into several security requirements and from various contexts and dimensions, generating a securitization effect [4]. This tendency of relating security to the satisfaction of

© The Author(s), under exclusive license to Springer Nature Switzerland AG 2023
M. Botto-Tobar et al. (Eds.): ICAT 2022, CCIS 1755, pp. 373–385, 2023.
https://doi.org/10.1007/978-3-031-24985-3_27

human needs and their environment is not totally delimited, it generates controversies and imprecisions on how to define the reach of security in contemporaneity [5]. From this, it emerges the necessity of establishing what type of security guarantees the well-being of both the human being and its environment, which is the priority of its application [6]. Because of this, this work is divided into the following contents. Section 2 presents a chronological analysis of external and multidimensional security from WWI to our days. Section 3 verifies the relation of the economy relative to external security, using as a source of information the two world wars. Section 4 generates a discussion of the obtained results, and lastly, Sect. 5, shows the main conclusions done.

2 Security as a Means to Guarantee the Existence of the State and the Human Being

2.1 External Security as a Priority in World Wars

The concepts of security have varied significantly as much as the history of humanity. In contemporaneity, the beginning and the ending of world wars have produced different conceptions of security. At the end of WWI, the fall-out of the German empire generated as a consequence a nationalist environment where the conception of external security is presented as a priority, considering the vital space as a geopolitical foundation of German expansionism. The results of wear out of this first great war produce an effect of reassurance of the frontiers and a national development focus on defense, both in Japan and in the United States (US) where there was an already existing national security doctrine [7].

In World War II (WWII), external security again is presented as a necessary alternative where there is a requirement to sustain war efforts and to strengthen the structure of military power looking to reach the survival of belligerent states. At the end of WWII the winning military powers impose a new security approach, in Japan, for example, it overturned internal security where public security imposes itself through the police force and external security is presented as an element of external competition based on cooperation and alliances [8]. The same effect is produced in the German state where it begins a new security approach that prohibits militarism and nationalism to overall avoid the state suffering all over again the already lived traumas of this nation and with the end to reach Europe's stability [9].

2.2 The Focus of Internal Security Post External Security

With the end of WWII, it begins a new process of militarization due to the mistrust within the wining powers, these incentives the development of new doctrines with the tendency to strengthen external security. As a result, the Cold War takes place, the same that is presented as a dispute to establish the new world order, in one case to impose a unipolar scheme, and in another a bipolar one; it is necessary to precise that the latter has begotten a multipolar scheme [10]. In this sense, also national security doctrines strongly emerged. This type of doctrine was initially developed and implemented by the US, and, its model was replicated throughout all of Latin America, a region where internal security prevails in search of countering the socialist and communist ideologies promoted by the former Union of Soviet Socialist Republics (USSR) [11].

The national security doctrine prompts new concepts of security related to establishing alliances that allow amplifying security zones at a continental and regional level, in this way emerge hemispheric and intercontinental security. In fact, the US promoted the creation of the Interamerican Treaty of Reciprocal Assistance in 1947 and the North Atlantic Treaty Organization (NATO) in 1949 [12]. Moreover, the former USSR promoted the Treaty of Friendship, Cooperation, and Mutual Assistance in 1955, and Russia sponsors the Collective Security Treaty Organization (CTSO) which was created in 1992.

In Central America and South America, from the sixties until the nineties the scenario became violent. In fact, in Guatemala (1960–1996) and El Salvador (1980–1992), civil wars take place, as well as in Nicaragua where the Sandinista Revolution (1979–1990) resulted in internal bloodshed; Also in the '90s guerrillas in Mexico emerge. In South America, on the other hand, guerrillas movements are introduced in Colombia, Ecuador, Peru, Bolivia, Paraguay, Chile, Argentina, and Brazil, all these armed groups present left ideological tendencies that intend to forcefully impose a new social and political order in the region. In addition, guerrilla movements also appear in the Caribbean in Cuba and Puerto Rico. In all these cases internal security prevails as the way to avoid the consolidation of communist regimes.

2.3 Multidimensional Security as a Response to Internal Post-conflict

Since the fall of the Berlin Wall and the consolidation of the perestroika the security approach is divided into two tracks: one that maintains external security as the end, and, the other, that is focused on multidimensional security where the man (the human) is the center of the application of security. In fact, multidimensional security or securitization puts the human being and the search for its well-being at the center of attention [13]. In Latin America, this concept is applied as a response to the fight against organized crime, drug trafficking, and corruption, to generate other types of security such as food security, and energy security, among others.

This approach to multidimensional security establishes that many aspects construct security and each one has a particular reach and scope of application. In this sense, it is important to define and establish which are the characteristics that each dimension present, and, overall, how to guarantee their compliance, which altogether assures global security.

Global security is made up of different types of security that underpin or undermine it, those components are related and have an interdependence between them, providing in this way a cause-effect; for example, the weakening of economic security will affect food security and influence the decrease of personal security because crime indicators will rise. For this reason, it is imperative to distinguish, classify and dispose of a particular strategy to solve each one of them and that contributes at the same time to strengthening the whole group. Multidimensional security aims precisely this, that is to say, that the whole represents the well-being of the human, in this way human security is built, the same that is oriented towards protecting, maintaining the freedoms and the survival of the human being, whose main challenges could be:

- Provide economic security because the gap between rich and poor is growing and this produces hunger and death, and contributes to the destruction of the environment.
- Prioritize environmental security because the uncontrolled production of goods and the extraction of resources destroy and degrade the habitat.
- Guarantee food security because the damage to the environment and the unequal distribution of well-being have increased scarcity for the majority of the world population.

Another component that underpins the well-being of humans is public security, this is a responsibility of the state, which has to guarantee the integrity of its citizens and properties. This type of security is inherently part of modernity and seeks the maintenance of peace, the rule of law, and public order. The main challenges in the present are [14]:

- Combating organized crime that is generating preoccupation in society and reduces state institutionalism.
- Eliminating the production and traffic of drugs that damage the citizens and finance organized crime.
- Neutralizing cybercrime is an activity that is not controlled and that gets to destabilize economies at all levels.

In this sense, it could be inferred that to guarantee public security it is required of:

- Institutions that assure the rule of law such as the judicial branch, maintain the order and ensure compliance with the law such as the armed forces, police, and security bodies of the state.
- Tools that allow to effectively impose the rule of law, that is to say, norms that rule over a civilized society and;
- The will of the society to attack and comply with established norms, avoid anarchy, corruption, power abuse, etc. This is also related to providing and adopting cultural norms and forms of education to society in general, all of these in benefit of the abidance and compliance with the law.

2.4 External Security and Multidimensional Security

After the analysis done on prior items, it was verified that world wars have focused on guaranteeing the survival of states through external security being this a priority; in these periods the focus was state-centric security. Under this point of view, state security represents global security, and with this, human security is also guaranteed, in the same way, the rest of the securities within the multidimensional context become of secondary importance and depend on the maintenance of external security.

During the Cold War, the efforts of world powers are directed to impose unipolarity, bipolarity, and multipolarity. In this sense, external security is imposed, and efforts are concentrated on developing military technology to support and ensure the future survival of states that seek to impose the world order. In this context, internal security in other regions of the world, such as Latin America, better represents a component that underpins external security.

After the fall of the Berlin Wall the scope of the unipolar world order feeds the multidimensionality of security that pretends to reduce the requirement to bolster external security, however, the Gulf War (1990–1991), the Iraq War (2003–2011), the Afghanistan War (2001–2021), as well as the Russian-Ukrainian conflict (2022), demonstrate that external security is still a priority. In fact, even though the United Nations (UN) promotes multiple dimensions of security, the five permanent members of the Security Council that possess veto power are between the states with a higher military budget [15], expense or investment that underpins to maintain of the survival of these states and humanity in general, entrenching external security as a top priority. Therefore, Fig. 1 graphs the relationship and levels of priority, considering external security on top of other securities with a multidimensional scope.

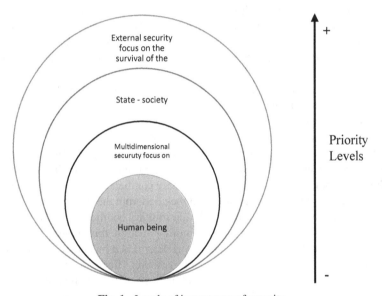

Fig. 1. Levels of importance of security

3   Economic View of Wars Within External Security

In humanity's history, the relationship between economy, states development, and the addressing of war efforts have motivated several positions/ schools of thought. All this is because the economy, as the nature and motive of war shift with such frequency as civilization progresses. In general, external security is linked and has a direct relationship to the maintenance and equipment of military forces, as well as the management of war efforts.

In the initial conception of economic science, Adam Smith determined that the military is unproductive employment. Therefore, the budget for this sector should be minimum [16]. With the same approach, with a neoclassical character, Walras rejected war considering the supremacy of individualism on the top of national interests [17], highlighting the nature of Capitalism and economic Liberalism, this thought was strengthened by the critics of Pareto to militarism. Under the same tendency of rejection of military conflict, founded on dialectic materialism, the Marxist school of thought and its authors establish that capitalism is a fundamental factor in the development of war; and for the neo-Marxists, militarism constitutes the support needed for the existence of capitalism [18].

As it is observable, conceptions that oppose the development of war exist, the same ideas that confronted other stances of theoretical character as the mercantilist school of thought, that based on the principles of wealth accumulation, analyzes wars as necessary situations in the procurance of the balance of power and the increase nation-states' wealth as a result of territorial expansion [19]. This school of thought is deeply linked to the historic German school for which war is the only needed path for growth and development of the nation-state [20].

It is important to mention that one of the most relevant authors at the time of the two world wars, John Maynard Keynes, who despite not criticizing in favor or against war, presents strategies to finance it to avoid unmeasured inflation rates through the increase of tax rates [21]. In light of these concepts, it is evident that historically the liberal economy has rejected military conflicts due to their economic consequences, however, other conceptions such as the neo-Marxist of the German Historic School do exist, they conceptualize wars and/or other military conflicts as the elements that trigger economic dynamization in great nations and they underpin the lived realities of each of these nation-states within the two most relevant military conflicts until the present.

In WWI, states lived the need to finance military action, this prevented budget limitations on defense and national security, as was determined by classic economists. The main participants of the conflict destined public resources financing machinery, military personnel, weapons, troops mobilization, and more [22]. The public military spending relative to the GDP increased during the war period as presented in Fig. 2; considering basic Keynesian premises, this increase in public spending can propel an indirect increase of demand by provoking an increase in consumption, the same that incites an increase of investment. In light of the public spending on defense, this sort of expense is somewhat different than a mere increase in public spending due to demand. It depends on the response capacity that countries involved in the conflict can have, a response based on the military production they generate, the innovation on military equipment, the military development, and their self-production capacity; in other words, the development of the military and weapon industry, better known as the war industry.

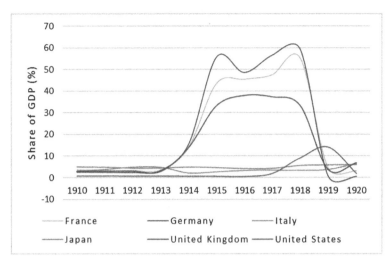

Fig. 2. Military expenditure as a share of GDP – Period 1910–1920

This capacity to reorganize the economic policy of countries in conflict and their industry, orienting it to military production to assign resources, both to the war efforts and to the needs of the civil population, is what is determined as war economy [18]. The results of the variation of the GDP relative to the increase of public military spending during the war period in some participant countries in WWI are shown in Fig. 3. From the analysis of data is established that not all countries have the capacity of reconfiguring their productive sector and becoming war economies.

Moreover, it is evident that Germany (after 1915) and the United Kingdom during WWI are presented as war economies because their national production has a similar tendency to its military spending, showing the capacity of their military production in each country, in these cases spending becomes an investment. On the other hand, France does not dynamize its economy under military spending, on the contrary, the GDP grows when the spending decreases, this reflects that the industry was not able to reorganize itself to respond to the military necessities of the time.

A third relation is visible between the GDP and the military spending of the US, which in the moment of intervention shows a slight tendency relation between 1917 and 1920. However, the US's GDP does not only respond to spending on the military sector, at least in the analyzed years. Nonetheless, its intervention and supremacy relative to other European countries were evident later because it became the main source of financing for these countries, imposing as a result a new economic and political world order [21].

On the other hand, even though the causes that ignited WWII are different than the ones of WWI, the actors involved are the same belligerent powers. As in WWI, in WWII it was also required financing for the active participation in the conflict, but by the already lived experience, some countries generated economic policies that pushed for a war economy even before the beginning of the armed conflict. Precisely, Germany prepared itself to implant a war economy in 1934 approximately. In Fig. 4, it can be verified an increase in military spending relative to the GDP, specifically during the

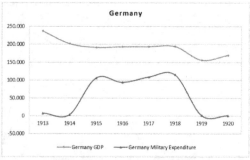

a. GDP vs. Military expenditure of Germany

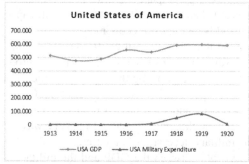

b. GDP vs. Military expenditure of United Kingdom

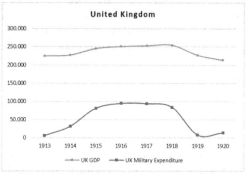

c. GDP vs. Military expenditure of United States of America

d. GDP vs. Military expenditure of France

Fig. 3. GDP vs. Military expenditure in WWI (million 1990 International Geary-Khamis dollars) a. Germany, b. United Kingdom, c. United States of America, d. France.

years in which the conflict took place from 1939 to 1945. The countries that assigned more resources relative to their gross product were Germany and Japan.

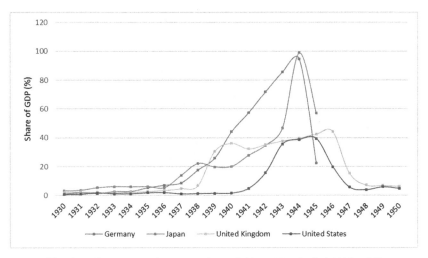

Fig. 4. Military expenditure as a share of GDP (%) – Period 1930–1950

During WWII, the relation GDP-military spending between the main powers maintained a similar tendency as presented in Fig. 5. This demonstrates a direct relation between these variables.

In this way, it is visible that the four economies represented in Fig. 5 are the ones with a product development-oriented toward satisfying military needs and maintaining war efforts. Germany joined the conflict with a war economy, but since 1941 its production did not dynamize even after an increase in military spending. The US, since WWI maintained its military production allowing it to bolster its alliances at the beginning of WWII, becoming a producer and exporter of military machinery and weapons, a situation that is reflected in the relational dynamic between its GDP and military spending. Japan incremented military spending but its production was not influenced immediately by this, it rather became a war economy by the end of the conflict and later it was consolidated by developing a solid post-war economy. Finally, Great Britain, despite already developing a war economy in WWI, in the second military conflict presents a weaker relation between the GDP and military spending, considering that other factors influence the production in this country.

a. GDP vs. Military expenditure of Germany

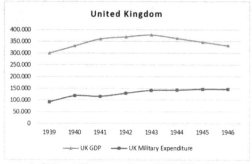

b. GDP vs. Military expenditure of United Kingdom

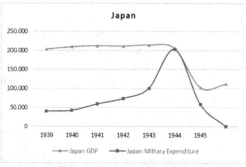

c. GDP vs. Military expenditure of Japan

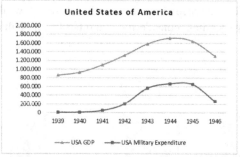

d. GDP vs. Military expenditure of United States of America

Fig. 5. GDP vs. Military expenditure in WWII - (million 1990 International Geary-Khamis dollars). a. Germany; b. United Kingdom; c. Japan; d. United States of America.

4 Discussion of the Results

Security is a complex concept that departs from the individual requirement of stability, it is observed that human security has a relation with the environment and as a whole, it points to the survival and development of states. Because of this, is that external security prevails, this is evident in the importance that the humankind has given to world wars, the assurance of military power, industrial and technological production for defense, as well as the creation of doctrines that support and/or push external security. The investment that states make in external security is compensated with the survival, stability, and guarantees to continue with the welfare state.

In this way, the relation GDP- military spending (or defense investment) is not a bidirectional relation independent of other variables, within this relation multiple factors can be influential such as the level of technological development of nations, wealth of the economies, productive adaptability capacity and, in a special form, macroeconomic policies implemented both for conflict financing and the productive development of states. However, further away from post-war effects such as the loss of human capital, physical, cultural, wealth, and the theories of economic interdependency as a factor in the prevention of military international conflicts [23], this relation GDP- military spending allows us to infer to what level do world conflict dynamizes great economies. For this reason, it is always latent the possibility of an external conflict, underpins external security.

The relation presented between military spending and GDP, the existence of war economies, the necessity for the development of world powers, the growing oxygenation required by the capitalist model, the concentration of capital and wealth, and the exhaustion of productive markets show the requirement to strengthen and prioritize external security. It also exposes the possibility of the emergence of conflicts to achieve the dynamization of the economy with a vision of dominating the global economy. The constant possibility of military confrontation demands states' capacity to assign a permanent public budget for the national defense sector, prioritizing the investment in external security research.

5 Conclusions

Security is a concept that departs from the satisfaction of individual needs, that later become collective needs, which are satisfied by policies implemented by nation-states. For this reason, the requirement for human well-being has a direct relation with the welfare and survival of the environment, this is to say the nation-state that takes in the individual or the individuals (citizens).

External security presents a primacy over multidimensional security, if the state with welfare survives through the application of external security, the citizens (the human beings) survive as well with welfare, despite the multiple dimensions or the various reaches of security.

External security has a direct relation to economic support. In WWI, the supremacy of the UK and the US as war economies is evident. In both cases, there is a GDP growth with rates of 12,08% and 24,38% between 1914 and 1918, respectively. In WWII, the

US again was able to consolidate itself as a war economy, with an emphasis on the years when the military conflict took place. The American GDP presents a growth of 90% from 1939 to 1945, showing the importance of increasing external security spending.

External security, war, and the economy have a direct relation. For example, the US as a war economy is strengthened especially during the world wars due to the increase of weapons and military machinery exportation as a product of an investment policy in the defense sector. Japan, on the other hand, consolidates itself as a war economy after strengthening its economy at the end of the conflicts. Its growth rate from 1913 to 1919 was 41%, and from 1949 it presents an economic recovery after WWII.

We can infer that the spending in underpinning external security and defense could be considered an investment and a priority of the state; after the analysis made since WWI military powers have established policies oriented to maintaining the welfare of the state by sustaining military power and war efforts, this to achieve an economic positioning and the compliance to national development goals.

Acknowledgment. This work was supported partially for the project PIJ-012 "Sistema semi-automatico, virtual e interactivo de enfocado a la mejora de procesos de enseñanza aprendizaje en la Universidad de las Fuerzas Armadas - Espe y unidades académicas especiales AGE-ESMIL-ESFORSE y unidades militares", belong to Universidad de las Fuerzas Armadas - ESPE.

References

1. Wahba, M.A., Bridwell, L.G.: Maslow reconsidered: a review of research on the need hierarchy theory. Organ. Behav. Hum. Perform. **15**(2), 212–240 (1976)
2. Baker, J.P.: Maslow, Needs, and War. Army War Coll Carlisle Barracks Pa (2012)
3. Von Clausewitz, C.: On war. In: On War. Princeton University Press, Princeton (2008)
4. McSweeney, B.: Identity and security: Buzan and the Copenhagen school. Rev. Int. Stud. **22**(1), 81–93 (1996)
5. Collins, A. (ed.): Contemporary Security Studies. Oxford University Press, Oxford (2022)
6. Buzan, B., Hansen, L.: The Evolution of International Security Studies. Cambridge University Press, Cambridge (2009)
7. Kennedy, R.A.: Woodrow Wilson, World War I, and an American conception of national security. Dipl. Hist. **25**(1), 1–31 (2001)
8. Shuichi, W.: Article nine of the Japanese constitution and security policy: realism versus idealism in Japan since the Second World War. In: Japan Forum, vol. 22, no. 3–4, pp. 405–431. Taylor & Francis Group, Oxfordshire (2010)
9. Duffield, J.: World Power Forsaken: Political Culture, International Institutions, and German Security Policy After Unification. Stanford University Press, Stanford (1998)
10. Krauthammer, C.: The unipolar moment. Foreign Aff. **70**, 23 (1990)
11. Schoultz, L.: National Security and the United States Policy toward Latin America. Princeton University Press, Princeton (2014)
12. Long, T.: Historical antecedents and post-World War II regionalism in the Americas. World Polit. **72**(2), 214–253 (2020)
13. Cruz, H.: La securitización ¿percepción o realidad tangible? Un análisis multidimensional. Revista De La Academia Del Guerra Del Ejército Ecuatoriano **13**(1), 11 (2020)
14. United Nations Office on Drugs and Crime UNDOC Annual Report. https://www.unodc.org/unodc/en/about-unodc/annual-report.html?ref=menutop. Accessed 03 Feb 2022

15. statista.com. https://www.statista.com/statistics/266892/military-expenditure-as-percentage-of-gdp-in-highest-spending-countries/#main-content. Accessed 02 Feb 2022
16. Smith, A.: Una investigaciónsobre la naturaleza y las causas de la riqueza de las Naciones, 2nd edn (1776)
17. Fontanel, J., Chatterji, M.: Introduction: the controversial economic question of peace and war. In: Fontanel, J., Chatterji, M. (eds.) War, Peace and Security (Contributions to Conflict Management, Peace Economics and Development, vol. 6. Emerald Group Publishing Limited, Bingley, pp. 1–12 (2008)
18. Coulomb, F.: Economic Theories of Peace and War. Ed. Routlegde, Nueva York (2004)
19. Langa, A.: La Economía Política de la Guerra, pp. 119–224. In Paz y Conflictos, Icaria, España (2013)
20. Langa, A.: Los conflictos armados en el pensamiento económico. IECAH. http://ibdigital.uib.es/greenstone/sites/localsite/collect/cd2/index/assoc/iecah004/4.dir/iecah0044.pdf. Acceded 08 Feb 2022
21. Guerrero, F.: Economías de guerra: algunas ideas sobre la importancia de la Primera Guerra Mundial desde el punto de vista económico. In Economía Informa Nro. 392 (2015)
22. Feinstein, C.H., Temin, P., Toniolo, G.: The World Economy between the World Wars. OUP Catalogue, Oxford University Press, no. 9780195307559 (2008)
23. Eloranta, J.: From the great illusion to the Great War: military spending behaviour of the Great Powers, 1870–1913. Eur. Rev. Econ. Hist. **11**(2), 255–283 (2007)

Comparative Study of Deep Learning Algorithms in the Detection of Phishing Attacks Based on HTML and Text Obtained from Web Pages

Eduardo Benavides-Astudillo[1,2(✉)] , Walter Fuertes[1,2] ,
Sandra Sanchez-Gordon[1] , German Rodriguez-Galan[1,2] ,
Verónica Martínez-Cepeda[2] , and Daniel Nuñez-Agurto[2]

[1] Escuela Politécnica Nacional, Quito, Ecuador
debenavides@espe.edu.ec
[2] Universidad de las Fuerzas Armadas ESPE, Sangolquí, Ecuador

Abstract. Phishing webpages are a type of cyber-attack whose objective is to try to deceive people through fraudulent web pages to harm its victims, commonly in an economical way. Every day new fraudulent web pages are created, so one of the standard methods to detect these recent attacks is the use of Artificial Intelligence algorithms based on the HTML content of a web page. Therefore, this work aims to perform a comparative analysis between Deep Learning algorithms to know if it is more effective to detect an attack, either using HTML code or the text obtained from this code. The content of a large text Dataset was obtained using Web Scraping techniques. Then the Deep Neural Network (DNN), Recurrent Neural Network (RNN), Convolutional Neural Network (CNN), and Recurrent Convolutional Neural Network (RCNN) algorithms were executed, feeding them first with HTML code and then with text. The average of the metrics obtained with HTML was 85%, and the overall metrics obtained for text averaged 84%. In conclusion, it is determined with this study that it makes no difference whether the algorithm is fed with HTML or text because when analyzing with text, the unnecessary features of HTML are eliminated, but simultaneously, the essential elements of HTML are also lost.

Keywords: Phishing · Deep learning · HTML code content · Text content · Web scraping

1 Introduction

1.1 Social Engineering

With the arrival of the Covid-19 pandemic, the number of people using digital services for shopping, education, and health, among others, has increased exponentially. However, with the massification of these services, the number of social engineering attacks has also increased [1]. Social Engineering is the type of cyber-attack for which the attacker

M. Botto-Tobar et al. (Eds.): ICAT 2022, CCIS 1755, pp. 386–398, 2023.
https://doi.org/10.1007/978-3-031-24985-3_28

tries to deceive the end-user, using digital media and the internet, to obtain from this user: money, usernames, or passwords, among other damages.

Different hardware and software tools may exist to detect a cyber-attack; however, the Social Engineering attackers always target the weakest link, the human being, either because of their reckless behavior [2] or their naive personality traits [3].

1.2 Phishing

There are different types of social engineering attacks, but the phishing attack is the one that prevails over the others [4]. Two phishing attacks stand out: first, there are phishing web pages, followed by phishing e-mails [5]. Both Phishing pages and Phishing e-mail attacks try to trick the end-user, asking them for anything from sensitive information to money transfers to affect them or their organizations [5]. However, Phishing e-mail attacks are less elaborate than Phishing web page attacks and, for that reason, less effective. Even today, many fraudulent e-mails serve only to include a link to a phishing web page in their body and to reach more people; this research is focused on detecting phishing web page attacks.

1.3 Phishing Detection Methods

The primary method in detecting Phishing pages is called Blacklists, a list in which the URLs of pages previously seen as Phishing are stored. However, the problem with Blacklists is that the Phishing page must have already been previously identified as malicious, i.e., it will not be able to locate a new Phishing URL. Machine Learning solutions address this problem by detecting with acceptable accuracy if a page has a high probability of being phished based on the similarity of features of pages previously identified as Phishing. An advantage of traditional Machine Learning algorithms over more profound Machine Learning algorithms is that they do not need a large amount of data to reach an acceptable accuracy; also, the processing time of these algorithms is shorter [6]. On the other hand, Deep Learning, a branch of Machine Learning, needs an enormous amount of data and, at the same time, more computational processing [2]. However, a characteristic of these Deep Learning algorithms is that the greater the amount of data entered, the greater the accuracy obtained, surpassing even traditional Machine Learning Algorithms. Also, an expert must select the main features in Traditional Machine Learning Algorithms. Deep Learning Algorithms have been used previously, but they have primarily been used in recent years due to higher processing capacity and data availability.

According to [7], several applications use Deep Learning algorithms to deal with this type of attack, but among them, two stand out, RNN and CNN. For this reason, in this study, the implementation of RNN, CNN, and a combination of these two, called RCNN, was performed; in addition, to have another reference, the DNN algorithm was implemented, and finally, four algorithms were implemented.

1.4 Related Works

In [8], a combined hybrid approach between CNN and LSTM is used, similar to the one we use in this work, which produces better accuracy when detecting the probability that a page is Phishing or Ham. However, it does not analyze the text of the web pages but only the URLs. In [9], text, images, and frames features are extracted; however, almost the entire article is oriented to working with URLs and needs to indicate how the characteristics were extracted from text. In [10], a model for Phishing page detection is proposed, using RNN-GRU (Graph Convolutional Network) and reaching a high accuracy percentage; however, the framework is oriented to URLs only. The authors of [11] use Deep Learning algorithms to detect a Phishing attack but analyze the text obtained from the e-mails. However, they do not analyze the content of web pages.

When reviewing the works published in Journals in the previous paragraph, it can be seen that, although all of them use Deep Learning algorithms, most are analyzing the URLs of web pages or oriented to the text obtained from the body of e-mails. Thus, our proposal is justified because it aims to conduct a comparative study of the execution of Deep Learning algorithms on the text obtained from Phishing web pages.

1.5 Hypothesis

It is hypothesized in this work that it does not matter whether the Deep Learning algorithms are fed with HTML code or with text obtained from that HTML code. In other words, the accuracy will not vary significantly between text and HTML code. This hypothesis stems from our observation of the detection of phishing e-mail attacks [6]. The body of the e-mail message containing words such as won, money, and credit card, among others, is considered for detection.

1.6 Objectives

Thus, the main objective of this study is to determine the extent to which the detection of phishing attacks changes based on HTML code and text extracted from HTML. For this, the following specific objectives must be achieved:

1. To obtain a sufficiently large Dataset with URLs and HTML codes of Phishing and Ham pages, extract the HTML code from each collected web page and extract the relevant text from the previously obtained HTML code.
2. To run four Deep Learning algorithms with the HTML code and text obtained and evaluate the resulting metrics in detecting the algorithms in the clean Dataset.
3. To determine if there is an improvement in accuracy when evaluating algorithms with Clean text rather than HTML code.

1.7 Datasets

Three data sources were used to obtain Phishing and Ham pages: 7,983 records were obtained from Phishtank, 10,488 from Phishload, and 180,000 from.

Malicious_URL_Dataset from Kaggle. Of these databases, the only one with the URL address and the HTML content of each record was Phishload, while only the URL address was available for the others. See Table 1.

The rest of this document is structured as follows: Sect. 2 shows the methodology used; in Sect. 3 the results are presented; in Sect. 4, the results found are discussed;

Table 1. Phishing and Ham Datasets.

Dataset	Phishing	Ham	URL	HTML
Phishtank [12]	7,983	0	Yes	No
Phishload [13]	9,312	1,176	Yes	Yes
Malicious_URL_Dataset [14]	90,000	90,000	Yes	No

and finally, in Sect. 5, the conclusions of this study and the proposed future work are presented.

2 Methodology

The methodology is divided into three groups: data collection, data cleaning, and execution of the selected Deep Learning algorithms. See Fig. 1.

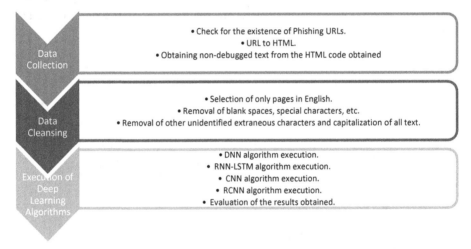

Fig. 1. Research methodology.

2.1 Data Collection

Our study is oriented to web pages' detection; using the text contained in them, it was necessary to implement the URL to HTML and HTML to text algorithms.

The data were obtained from three different sources, so converting the URL formats to a single ISO format was necessary. Thus, the data in ISO format can now be parsed by Python., i.e., from simply having the type domain.com, switch to the format http://domain.com. Next, were followed the steps specified in Fig. 2.

Fig. 2. Steps in data collection.

Check for the Existence of URLs. One of the characteristics of the web pages created to carry out Phishing attacks is that they disappear after a short time. For this reason, it was necessary to carry out an algorithm to check if these pages were still active, keep only those active websites, and delete the others. All the algorithms were carried out in Python. It should be noted that this process was the one that took the longest execution time on the server, even though this server is up to 60 times faster than a personal computer. Thus, one of the processes that could take up to 100 days on our personal computer was carried out on the server in only two days.

URL to HTML. Since the Phishtank and Malicious_URL records did not have their HTML content, it was necessary to create an algorithm to obtain this code. The result is shown in Fig. 3.

```
1  print(df1.at[1,'htmlContent'])
<!DOCTYPE html PUBLIC "-//W3C//DTD HTML 4.01 Transitional//EN" "http://www.w3.org/TR/html4/loose.dtd">
<html xmlns="http://www.w3.org/1999/xhtml"><head>
<script type="text/javascript">var ue_t0=ue_t0||+new Date();</script>


<!--btech-iplc-->
    <script type="text/javascript">
      new Image().src="http://g-ecx.images-amazon.com/images/G/01/gno/images/orangeBlue/navPackedSprite
g";
      new Image().src="http://g-ecx.images-amazon.com/images/G/01/x-locale/common/transparent-pixel._V1
    </script>
    <meta content="on" http-equiv="x-dns-prefetch-control" />
    <link href="http://g-ecx.images-amazon.com" rel="dns-prefetch" />
    <link href="http://z-ecx.images-amazon.com" rel="dns-prefetch" />
    <link href="http://ecx.images-amazon.com" rel="dns-prefetch" />
```

Fig. 3. HTML code obtained from a web page.

HTML to Text. Once each web page's HTML code was obtained, the text was extracted. More than 12,000 records were obtained, of which about 6,000 are Phishing, and 6,000 are Ham. This text obtained is not yet valid for input to the Deep Learning algorithms, which is why preprocessing is carried out in Preprocessing.

2.2 Preprocessing

Up to this point, the text obtained from each web page has already been achieved; however, analyzing it with our Deep Learning algorithms still needs to be more helpful

Fig. 4. Steps in preprocessing.

because they still contain pages in English with unwanted or non-alphabetic characters. Putting all the text in English is necessary, which is why we continue with the preprocessing steps described in Fig. 4.

Text only in English. Our algorithm is based on detecting attacks utilizing the text on the webpage, so it was necessary to carry out an algorithm to keep only those records whose text is only in English. Only about 10,000 records remained between Phishing and Ham, thus maintaining the data balance between the two classes, Phishing and Ham. See Fig. 5.

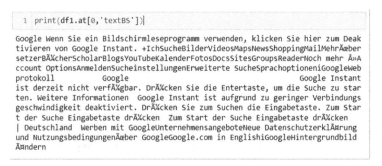

Fig. 5. Text record from a non-English page.

Delete Blank Spaces and Others. In order to have clean text that does not affect later when feeding the Deep Learning algorithms, white spaces, special characters, punctuation marks, and usernames had to be deleted.

Delete Junk Characters. With the previous step, many characters not used in our algorithm were deleted; however, some junk characters could still affect performance. Also, in this step, the numbers in the text were deleted.

So far, the text is clean, but in upper and lower case; however, it is necessary to transform all text to upper case to prevent the algorithms from treating the exact words differently, for example, play, Play, and PLAY. The upper function was used to transform all the text to the upper case.

It would be essential to delete the Stop Words or empty words, which are words without meaning, such as articles, pronouns, prepositions, and others. However, we decided to filter out these words later in implementing the Deep Learning algorithms.

Up to this point, we already have got text clean and ready to be entered into the Deep Learning algorithms. See the Fig. 6.

```
1  print(df1.at[1,'text_html_cleaned'])
```

AMAZONCOM ONLINE SHOPPING FOR ELECTRONICS APPAREL COMPUTERS BOOKS DVDS MORE A DIFFERENT VERSION OF TH IS WEB SITE CONTAINING SIMILAR CONTENT OPTIMIZED FOR SCREEN READERS AND MOBILE DEVICES MAY BE FOUND A T THE WEB ADDRESS WWWAMAZONCOMACCESS AMAZONCOM HELLO SIGN IN TO GET PERSONALIZED RECOMMENDATIONS NEW CUSTOMER START HERE A FREE TWODAY SHIPPING SEE DETAILS YOUR AMAZONCOM A A A A A A TODAYS DEALS A A GI FTS WISH LISTS A A GIFT CARDS A YOUR DIGITAL ITEMS A A YOUR ACCOUNT A A HELP SHOP ALL DEPARTMENTS SEA RCH ALL DEPARTMENTSAMAZON INSTANT VIDEOAPPLIANCESAPPS FOR ANDROID ARTS CRAFTS SEWINGAUTOMOTIVEBABYBEA UTYBOOKSCELL PHONES ACCESSORIESCLOTHING ACCESSORIESCOMPUTERSELECTRONICSGIFT CARDSGROCERY GOURMET FOOD HEALTH PERSONAL CAREHOME KITCHENINDUSTRIAL SCIENTIFICJEWELRYKINDLE STOREMAGAZINE SUBSCRIPTIONSMOVIES TVMP DOWNLOADSMUSICMUSICAL INSTRUMENTSOFFICE PRODUCTSPATIO LAWN GARDENPET SUPPLIESSHOESSOFTWARESPORTS OUTDOORSTOOLS HOME IMPROVEMENTTOYS GAMESVIDEO GAMESWATCHES A A CART CART WISH LIST ALL LISTS REGISTRI ES AEURO WISH LIST AEURO GIFT ORGANIZER AEURO WEDDING REGISTRY AEURO BABY REGISTRY AEURO AMAZON REMEM BERS UNLIMITED INSTANT VIDEOS PRIME INSTANT VIDEOS UNLIMITED STREAMING OF THOUSANDS OFMOVIES AND TV S HOWS WITH AMAZON PRIME LEARN MORE ABOUT AMAZON PRIME AMAZON INSTANT VIDEO STORE RENT OR BUY HIT MOVIE S AND TV SHOWSTO STREAM OR DOWNLOAD YOUR VIDEO LIBRARY YOUR MOVIES AND TV SHOWSSTORED IN THE CLOUD WA

Fig. 6. Text record ready for input to Deep Learning algorithms.

3   Results

3.1   Execution of Deep Learning Algorithms

Once the text was cleaned, the Deep Learning algorithms were run on this data. The columns that were entered for the execution of each of the algorithms were:

- html_Content: It has stored HTML code obtained from each URL.
- text_html_cleaned: It has stored all the clean and preprocessed text.
- isPhish: Indicates whether that record corresponds to a Phishing page or not.

The Deep Learning algorithms chosen to enter and execute the data were the following:

1. Deep Neural Network (DNN)
2. Recurrent Neural Network (RNN)
3. Convolutional Neural Network (CNN)
4. Recurrent Convolutional Neural Networks (RCNN)

These algorithms are similar to those used in the paper [15], in which a selection problem is solved, with 20 classes. Our solution is focused on two classes (Phishing or Ham). First, each of the algorithms was run with the HTML code and then with the clean text to determine which of them (HTML or text) the best results were obtained.

Deep Neural Network. To vectorize the input data, we use the TFIDF technique with the TfidfVectorizer function, in which we worked based on a maximum number of words of 275,000. In addition, we further refined the text in this algorithm, leaving aside the common Stop Words of the English vocabulary. The values resulting from the execution of the algorithm are shown as follows:

DNN on text

DNN on text

	precision	recall	f1-score	support
0	0.86	0.82	0.84	1213
1	0.83	0.86	0.85	1236
accuracy			0.84	2449
macro avg	0.84	0.84	0.84	2449
weighted avg	0.84	0.84	0.84	2449

Recurrent Neural Network. In the execution of RNN, we used a maximum word input of 275,000 words, with a sequence of 500 words in each. In addition, for word representation, we used the Glove 6B 50D file [16].

RNN on text

RNN on text

	precision	recall	f1-score	support
0	0.85	0.72	0.78	1213
1	0.76	0.88	0.81	1236
accuracy			0.80	2449
macro avg	0.81	0.80	0.80	2449
weighted avg	0.80	0.80	0.80	2449

Convolutional Neural Network. In the execution of CNN, we use the same parameters as in RNN to compare the accuracy with those same parameters, i.e., we also use a maximum word input of 275,000, with a sequence of 500 words in each. We use the Glove 6B 50D file to represent the words.

CNN on text

CNN on text

	precision	recall	f1-score	support
0	0.88	0.77	0.82	1213
1	0.80	0.89	0.84	1236
accuracy			0.83	2449
macro avg	0.84	0.83	0.83	2449
weighted avg	0.84	0.83	0.83	2449

Recurrent Convolutional Neural Networks. The combination of Deep Learning algorithms can give a better result. In this case, the RCNN implementation is used, which uses the best features of RNN and CNN.

RCNN on text

	precision	recall	f1-score	support
0	0.90	0.76	0.82	1213
1	0.80	0.92	0.85	1236
accuracy			0.84	2449
macro avg	0.85	0.84	0.84	2449
weighted avg	0.85	0.84	0.84	2449

4 Discussion

4.1 Deep Neural Network

In all the metrics analyzed (precision, recall, f1-score, and accuracy), better results were obtained using HTML rather than Clean text, even in the two classes analyzed, phishing and ham. See Fig. 7.

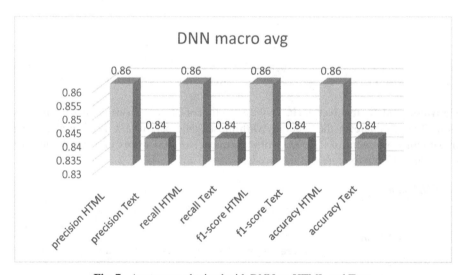

Fig. 7. Avg macro obtained with DNN on HTML and Text.

4.2 Recurrent Neural Network

Only in this algorithm can it be seen that in all the metrics analyzed (precision, recall, f1-score, and accuracy), better results were obtained by entering Clean text instead of HTML text, even in each of the two classes analyzed. See Fig. 8.

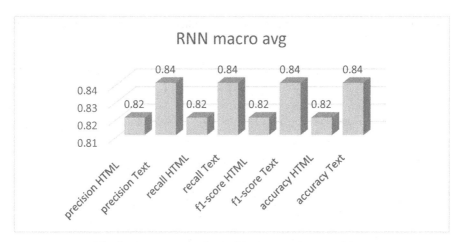

Fig. 8. Avg macro obtained with RNN on HTML and Text

4.3   Convolutional Neural Network

As with DNN, it can be observed that in all the metrics analyzed (precision, recall, f1-score, and accuracy), better results were obtained, even in each of the two classes analyzed. See Fig. 9.

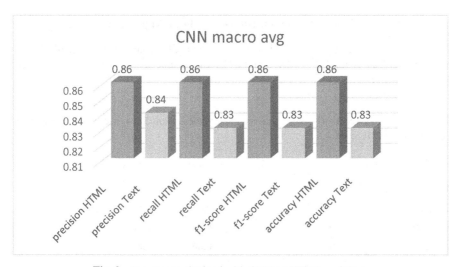

Fig. 9. Avg macro obtained with CNN on HTML and Text.

4.4   Recurrent Convolutional Neural Networks

The pattern of improvement is repeated in all the metrics analyzed (precision, recall, f1-score, and accuracy), in which better results were obtained, even in each of the two classes analyzed. As a comparative measure with other Deep Learning algorithms. See Fig. 10.

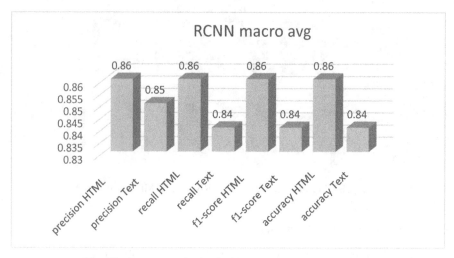

Fig. 10. Avg macro obtained with RCNN on HTML and Text.

4.5 Comparison Among the Application of the Four Algorithms

Table 2 shows the values obtained when running each of the four algorithms with HTML code. It can be seen that DNN, CNN, and RCNN give similar results of 86% in all their metrics, while RNN was the worst performer with 82%.

Table 2. Precision, recall, f1-score, and accuracy values obtained with each Deep Learning algorithm on HTML code.

	DNN	RNN	CNN	RCNN	Average
Precision HTML	**0.86**	0.82	**0.86**	**0.86**	0.85
Recall HTML	**0.86**	0.82	**0.86**	**0.86**	0.85
f1-score HTML	**0.86**	0.82	**0.86**	**0.86**	0.85
Accuracy HTML	**0.86**	0.82	**0.86**	**0.86**	0.85

Table 3 shows the values obtained when running each of the four algorithms with text code. It can be seen that DNN, RNN, CNN, and RCNN give very similar results at 84%; however, it can be observed that with CNN, in general, a point is lowered in the percentage, while with RCNN, a point is raised in the text precision metric.

Based on the averages obtained from both Table 2 and Table 3, it can be seen that the best average is obtained with HTML with 85% over text with 84%. In the words of these

Table 3. Precision, recall, f1-score, and accuracy values obtained with each Deep Learning algorithm on Text.

	DNN	RNN	CNN	RCNN	Average
Precision text	0.84	0.84	0.84	**0.85**	0.84
Recall text	0.84	0.84	0.83	**0.84**	0.84
f1-score text	0.84	0.84	0.83	**0.84**	0.84
Accuracy text	0.84	0.84	0.83	**0.84**	0.84

authors, it cannot be determined that when running the algorithms with either HTML or text, one is better than the other because the percentage difference of 1 point is slight. When running the same algorithms with the same data, the percentages obtained vary by a low percentage.

5 Conclusions and Future Work

This study was conducted to determine that there is no difference in inputting HTML code or clean text to any of the four Deep Learning algorithms. For this, we first obtained a clean text from HTML code, then ran four Deep Learning algorithms with either HTML code or text. Finally, we evaluate and show the results obtained.

Although the text obtained from the HTML code removes many irrelevant features, many relevant features are also lost. One example is a deleted link that always points to an external phishing page. This deleted phishing link would be essential to determine if a page is Phishing. For this reason, it can be determined that it is irrelevant whether to any Deep Learning algorithm we input HTML code or text obtained from that code.

Since our algorithm has to input a clean dataset with text instead of HTML code, training and testing Deep Learning algorithms is faster because the database size is reduced from 600 Mbytes in HTML to 30 Mbytes in Clean text.

For this study, the Deep Learning algorithms were fed directly with text obtained from the HTML code. An algorithm will be developed to have the text semantically and syntactically analyzed before it is fed into the algorithms, to improve the accuracy and precision of phishing page detection. In this way, we will take advantage of the richness of grammatical structures and the meaning of words.

Our model was implemented on a few more than 10,000 records; However, we plan to analyze about 100,000 records in total, on which the accuracy of implemented algorithms will be analyzed again. Also, the number of layers and nodes of each Deep Learning algorithm implemented will be varied until the most optimal one is found. Other parameters will also be varied in each of the algorithms. Create a multi-layer model in which the model presented in this work contributes to the different layers of URL and behavioral detection.

References

1. Andrade, R.O., Cazares, M., Fuertes, W.: Cybersecurity Attacks During COVID-19: an analysis of the behavior of the human factors and a proposal of hardening strategies. In: Daimi, K., Peoples, C. (eds.) Advances in Cybersecurity Management, pp. 37–53. Springer, Cham (2021). https://doi.org/10.1007/978-3-030-71381-2_3

2. Benavides-Astudillo, E., et al.: Analysis of Vulnerabilities Associated with Social Engineering Attacks Based on User Behavior, pp. 351–364 (2022). https://doi.org/10.1007/978-3-031-03884-6_26

3. Benavides-Astudillo, E., et al.: A framework based on personality traits to identify vulnerabilities to social engineering attacks, pp. 381–394 (2022). https://doi.org/10.1007/978-3-031-03884-6_28

4. Benavides, E., Fuertes, W., Sanchez, S., Nuñez-Agurto, D.: Caracterización de los ataques de phishing y técnicas para mitigarlos. Ataques: una revisión sistemática de la literatura. Cienc. y Tecnol. 13(1), 97–104 (2020). https://doi.org/10.18779/CYT.V13I1.357

5. Benavides, E., Fuertes, W., Sanchez, S., Sanchez, M.: Classification of phishing attack solutions by employing deep learning techniques: a systematic literature review. In: Rocha, Á., Pereira, R.P. (eds.) Developments and Advances in Defense and Security. SIST, vol. 152, pp. 51–64. Springer, Singapore (2020). https://doi.org/10.1007/978-981-13-9155-2_5

6. Ona, D., Zapata, L., Fuertes, W., Rodriguez, G., Benavides, E., Toulkeridis, T.: Phishing attacks: detecting and preventing infected E-mails using machine learning methods. In: 2019 3rd Cyber Secur. Netw. Conf. CSNet 2019, pp. 161–163, October 2019. https://doi.org/10.1109/CSNET47905.2019.9108961

7. Macas, W., Mayra; Wu, Chunming; Fuertes, "A survey on deep learning for cybersecurity: Progress, challenges, and opportunities," Elsevier (2022). https://www.sciencedirect.com/science/article/abs/pii/S1389128622001864?dgcid=author. Accessed 04 Jun 2022

8. Adebowale, M.A., Lwin, K.T., Hossain, M.A.: Intelligent phishing detection scheme using deep learning algorithms J. . Enterp. Inf. Manag. (2020). https://doi.org/10.1108/JEIM-01-2020-0036

9. Yang, P., Zhao, G., Zeng, P.: Phishing website detection based on multidimensional features driven by deep learning. IEEE Access 7, 15196–15209 (2019). https://doi.org/10.1109/ACCESS.2019.2892066

10. Tang, L., Mahmoud, Q.H.: A deep learning-based framework for phishing website detection. IEEE Access 10, 1509–1521 (2022). https://doi.org/10.1109/ACCESS.2021.3137636

11. Alhogail, A., Alsabih, A.: Applying machine learning and natural language processing to detect phishing e-mail. Comput. Secur. 110, November 2021. https://doi.org/10.1016/J.COSE.2021.102414

12. PhishTank > Developer Information. https://phishtank.org/developer_info.php. Accessed 09 Apr 2022

13. Phishload - Download. https://www.medien.ifi.lmu.de/team/max.maurer/files/phishload/download.html. Accessed 09 Apr 2022

14. Malicious URLs dataset | Kaggle. https://www.kaggle.com/datasets/sid321axn/malicious-urls-dataset. Accessed 09 Apr 2022

15. K. Kowsari, K. J. Meimandi, M. Heidarysafa, S. Mendu, L. Barnes, and D. Brown, "text Classification Algorithms: A Survey," Inf. 2019, Vol. 10, Page 150, vol. 10, no. 4, p. 150, Apr. 2019, doi: https://doi.org/10.3390/INFO10040150

16. GLOVE 6B 50D Word Embeddings | Kaggle. https://www.kaggle.com/datasets/adityajn105/glove6b50d. Accessed 09 Apr 2022

Ground Robot for Search and Rescue Management

Mélany Yarad Jácome[1] , Fernando Alvear Villaroel[1(✉)] ,
and Junior Figueroa Olmedo[2(✉)]

[1] Universidad de Las Fuerzas Armadas ESPE, Av. El Progreso S/N, Sangolquí, Ecuador
{mjyarad,faalvear}@espe.edu.ec
[2] Instituto Superior Universitario Sucre, Teodoro Gómez de la Torre S14-72 y Joaquín
Gutiérrez, Quito, Ecuador
jfigueroa@tecnologicosucre.edu.ec

Abstract. The incursion in the field of robotics represents the change of the productive matrix of Ecuador, this prototype is directed towards the field of search and rescue known as SAR (Search and Rescue), presents a versatile structure based on land mobile robots, its structure has four engines for mobilization, as well as 4 independent joints that allow it to maneuver on uneven terrain or obstacles, which also allow it to continue operating even after a rollover. The handling of this prototype is based on the use of wireless technologies such as 2.4 GHz radiofrequency modules and Wifi, so it is considered an ROV (Remotely Operated Vehicle) type robot; by means of the video camera and image processing techniques, the reality of the environment where the robot is moving is interpreted and from this information and control algorithms the mobile robot determines the best route to start its navigation process; which is essential for the search and rescue team.

Keywords: Control algorithm · Processing · ROV · SAR · Wifi

1 Introduction

The main objective of the construction of this robot is to solve problems that seriously affect human society such as natural disasters, since they are unpredictable; around the world robots occupy a very important space because they represent a vital point for SAR teams.

Robots are presented as tools to help perform activities that put at risk the rescue personnel, but one of its major drawbacks is the construction of the same by the large investment it represents. At the Instituto Superior Universitario, the student Jean Zhamungui, together with his teachers, put into practice the knowledge acquired during his professional training, for the construction of a rescue robot.

The field that achieved a great development with the help of robotics is Risk Management, since it presents a continuous change based on the experiences, data obtained both currently and historically; its objective is to foresee future risks and try to mitigate each one of them. Robotics is found as an aid tool both in software and hardware, this work represented many risks in its beginnings, exposing the personnel to dangerous places to obtain information, which only counted on their experience to make adequate decisions.

M. Botto-Tobar et al. (Eds.): ICAT 2022, CCIS 1755, pp. 399–411, 2023.
https://doi.org/10.1007/978-3-031-24985-3_29

2 Background

The operations in which rescue robots intervene are based on the plan known as "Search and Rescue (SAR)", which is developed by a group of specialized people or institutions to promote a series of guidelines, guides, methodologies and designated protocols [1]. Based on the events occurred as the earthquake in Manabi - Ecuador occurred in April 2016, and several sequels that have been occurring after the disaster, it has been considered to investigate the SAR field based on technologies that are easily accessible to not generate large costs in production and are useful for specialized teams in the field. We are considering improving the model of an articulated robot to enter under rubble. Ecuador is in a high-risk zone due to its location within the Pacific Ring of Fire, which causes problems such as volcanic eruptions, landslides, floods, earthquakes, etc.

Given these precedents, this project is based on the investigation of characteristics and specific qualities where it is intended to generate a robot model for the study of its functions and applications in the S.A. field. R, using technologies that are in the country and are easily accessible, as several drawbacks are presented by lack of materials or high costs in construction; it is intended to maintain a wireless communication using technologies such as radio frequency and WI-FI, this robot will be the combination of 2 types of land mobile robots such as the robot with wheels and articulated, these features will allow this model to mobilize with greater speed and in turn will present capabilities to cross obstacles.

3 Statement of the Problem

Natural disasters are a constant threat that affect a general level since they can arise at any time or place, since they are unpredictable, ways are sought in which to act in such circumstances; Dr. Robin Muphy is the one who promotes robotic technologies to intervene in various natural disasters [2].

Based on the problem mentioned, such as natural disasters, and welcoming the new robotic technologies present today, the aim is to provide a solution to the S.A.R field, by asking ourselves the following question: How do robots influence the management of search and rescue activities in the event of a natural disaster?

4 Justification

It is intended to improve a hexapod robot, which presents a versatile structure and an articulated design that allows access to irregular terrain, where a robot with only tires could not enter, its flexibility allows that in case of falling and being upside down it can continue working under the same parameters; since its design and actuators maintain the same posture since several existing prototypes do not have a similar feature, which is a disadvantage for a robot dedicated to rescuing people.

Being a remote operation vehicle, it will be able to detail the information perceived through the sensors and the vision camera, significantly increasing the chances of a timely and successful rescue.

5 Objectives

5.1 Main

The objective of this project is the design and construction of a remote operation vehicle for exploration in areas that are difficult to access in the event of a natural disaster.

5.2 Specifics

- Design and apply a remote operation robot for the search and rescue field.
- Identify the operations to which the robot may be exposed
- Evaluate the results.

6 Hypothesis

The persons in charge of rescue operations will be those who use the remote operation robot in such a way that they do not influence high-risk investigations.

7 Arguments

In recent years several models of robots have been implemented to mitigate various adversities that may occur to personnel performing these activities, their models vary according to the needs that have presented the different SAR groups, in the field you can find information on various models presented for different activities from manipulators robots to robots reptadores; articulated models such as the RBD-10 can manipulate within uncomfortable or inaccessible places for staff. Also, you can find different models with other features such as wheels combining different articulations for its operation as is the case of Rising STAR [3].

7.1 Literature Review

i. Terrestrial Mobile Robots

Mobile robots have different structures and shapes that allow them to develop their proposed activities, this type of robots have different forms of locomotion which can be by wheels, sliding belt (caterpillar), legs or even crawling; mobility for this class of robots presents several complications due to the irregularity of the terrain in which it performs its activity [4].

The aspects considered for the design of this type of robots are maneuverability, traction, stability, efficiency, type of maintenance, type of control, among the main ones. In general, wheeled robots have simple structures, consume less energy and move faster than other locomotion mechanisms (e.g., legged robots or tracked vehicles). From the control point of view, less control effort is required, due to their simple mechanisms and reduced stability problems. Although it is difficult to overcome rough terrain or uneven ground conditions, wheeled mobile robots are suitable for a variety of environments in practical applications. They are used in almost all indoor service robot applications and also outdoors when the terrain is not too rough [5, 6]. The main problems in the design of wheeled mobile robots are traction, maneuverability, stability, and control that depend on wheel types and configurations (drive systems) [6].

Robots with legs can move on uneven terrain, because they have a greater degree of freedom as shown in Fig. 1, this provides good stability depending on the number of legs it has, but also generates that the control is more complex, there are different types of joints that allow you to get the degrees of freedom.

Mobile robots have different structures and shapes that allow them to develop their proposed activities. These types of robots have different types of locomotion which can be by means of wheels, sliding belt (caterpillar), legs or even crawling; mobility for this class of robots presents several complications due to the irregularity of the terrain in which it carries out its activity [3].

The aspects that are considered for the design of this type of robots are maneuverability, traction, stability, efficiency, type of maintenance, type of control, among the main ones.

Fig. 1. Robot with legs

ii. **Fields of application of robots in risk management**

Robin Murphy, director of the Center for Robot-Assisted Search and Rescue (CRASAR) at Texas A&M University, is one of the people who has promoted the study of robots to collaborate in the event of disasters, his services are carried out with his 3 types of robots, the aerial ones that allow visibility and analysis of areas where GPS cannot be used, the terrestrial ones in the shape of a snake which allow burrows to be dug. The aquatic ones that allow to examine submerged structures or recover victims, all the models have their specific functions, but they work as a team, Robin's ideal is not only to wait for a catastrophe to happen but also to prevent it [2].

Its objectives are focused on collecting information through its built-in sensors or cameras, also allowing the transport of various implements such as an emergency kit, there are models that even have the ability to transport a person inside while preserving their integrity, others that they allow to manipulate with their final effector, models known to be used by the police as bomb deactivators, others that present weapons to neutralize enemies.

Fig. 2. Amitiel Prototype

The field of risk management is broad since it fulfills various functions that vary according to the required need, robots such as Amitiel, which is displayed in Fig. 2, seek to help personnel deal with unsafe conditions that could arise, its design with wheels allows it to be practical for certain types of activities that your model allows [7].

7.2 Experiment Setup

This project presents characteristics for the conformation of the prototype, which are implemented based on the study of different designs, qualities and preferences of the people to whom the project is directed; The prototype is made up of mobile parts, i.e. the joints or commonly called legs which allow maneuvering on uneven terrain, also consists of four modified servomotors, with their respective tires which allow the overall mobility of the prototype, consists of two IP cameras that allow maintaining the visualization of the environment in which it is located, also consists of two infrared sensors for obstacle detection, in Fig. 3 you can see the design of the prototype.

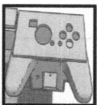

Fig. 3. Prototype design

For the construction of this prototype, based on the specifications obtained, the design is created in the SolidWorks platform, where the robot chassis is designed and will have specific places to place the respective sensors, cameras, servomotors, batteries, electronic board, micro controller, among others.

For the construction of the prototype, once the 3D model is developed, the printing is done with the help of a 3D printer, the assembly of the prototype once printed is done by joining the electromechanical components, for the union of the joints it is done with the MG996R servomotors, as final effector has a MG995 servomotor modified as a DC motor, as shown in Fig. 4.

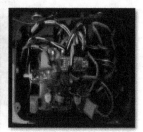

Fig. 4. Robot structure

7.3 Electronic Connections

The following shows the corresponding connection for each pin of the control card to the respective sensors and actuators, the colors shown in Fig. 5 show the order of the wires for their respective connection.

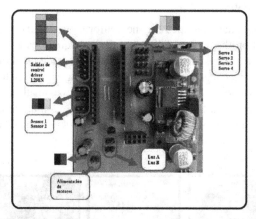

Fig. 5. Overall connection

a) Transmitter
   The diagram in Fig. 6 shows the configuration used for programming the transmitter, in which the buttons and the joystick used to control the robot are detailed.
b) Receiver
   Figure 7 shows the configuration that was used for programming the receiver, in which there is control of the electromechanical elements such as motors, servomotors, we also have control of the lights; reception of infrared sensors, cameras ESP 32 CA

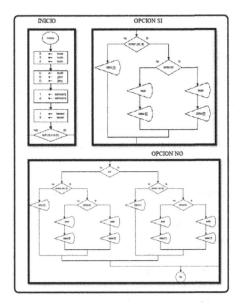

Fig. 6. Transmitter scheme

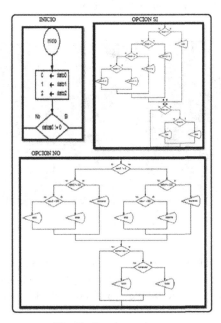

Fig. 7. Receiver scheme

8 Results

8.1 Design and Construction

This prototype is based on the investigation of characteristics or specific qualities according to the needs to be solved in the field of risk management, which is taken into account the characteristics of a hybrid mobile robot with wheels and legs that allow avoiding small obstacles, such that accompanied by a high torque motor can overcome obstacles of greater height and joints that allow maneuvering them to maintain a balance, these characteristics are determined with information from various models that exist in the field.

For the control of the prototype we chose to use the Arduino and Rasberry microcontrollers; with their respective programming environments. The programming for manual control consists of 3 data designated as data 1, 2 and 3 which will be sent to identify the function to be performed.

The control part is made by several modules, which are organized in a Bakelite that allows to connect in an orderly manner the power supply and control part of the prototype; to facilitate the control of the robot reception, the electronic board as shown in Fig. 8, allows to control the PWM of the servomotors and DC motors, on the other hand, the Sharp sensors allow to detect objects at a distance of 10 to 80 cm depending on its configuration and the lipo battery of 3000 mAh.

Fig. 8. Control elements

The component that allows communication between the robot and the controller is the NRF24L01 module, while the IP cameras of the ESP 32cam development module allow the robot's environment to be viewed through Wi-Fi communication on a local network.

Figure 9 shows the coupling of the servomotors to the chassis with the respective fastening, to assemble the arm a star type coupling is used which is held together with the servomotor forming a joint, the servomotor modified to DC enters in the same way in the arm slot and is adjusted with four screws, to generate less vibration due to the length and weight of each leg a roller is added between the union of the servomotor and the arm, likewise in the middle of the union of the rim and the DC servomotor.

Once the servomotors have been coupled to the chassis, the cable covers are fitted with two bolts.

Fig. 9. Joint union

For the construction of this type of robot, the following points are taken into consideration:

- In the event of an accident, the teams considered to be the main ones are those for removal, penetration or extrication.
- Robots are necessary tools that provide valuable information that can be used by the teams in charge, their acceptance indicates that robots promote trust, since their integrity will not be at risk
- Risk activities in which personnel must expose their integrity can lead to errors due to the pressure generated by the environment in which they find themselves, robots can help detail information that a person may overlook during an inspection.
- Tires are considered the most suitable form of mobility for this type of work, since they have good mobility and speed; however, it must be considered that the type of tire must vary according to the terrain that is presented.

8.2 Machine Vision Exploration and Navigation

There are a multitude of techniques for the autonomous navigation process, but in this case, we exclude those that employ artificial intelligence and opt for a traditional approach. The basic operation of the algorithm consists of drawing lateral lines that are isolated and that delimit the shortest route to follow to reach the target. The process of isolating the lines is generally carried out using color, which is the feature that best distinguishes them from the rest of the image.

But such lateral lines do not provide all the information necessary to guide the vehicle, or at least from that perspective, since it is not possible to see the real distances in the image, so a perspective-to-image transformation is performed, after which taking the frontal image of the robot a virtual image parallel to the ground is generated, which is commonly known as a bird's eye view.

This transformation is implemented in the OpenCV library and uses source and target coordinates which are the reference points. The library does not calculate the coordinates automatically, so it is necessary to make multiple adjustments until the desired result is obtained. This has mainly a problem, although a priori it may seem that the transformation is performed satisfactorily, a distortion can be observed when an object with a known geometric shape is placed in front of the camera, so it is necessary to make further adjustments until the distortion is mitigated.

For the enhancement process of the image captured by the camera, we chose to use a filter very similar to the so-called "median filter", with which we obtained a 5x5 kernel and a fairly clear image as can be seen in Fig. 10 for further interpretations. After several tests we managed to implement a bilateral filter, which was effective in removing noise while keeping the edges defined, all at the cost of a slight loss of performance.

Fig. 10. Joint union Mean and median filters with 5×5 kernel applied on a frame.

The following examples are a small representation of the tests performed and the wide variety of results they provide. As can be seen in the images in Fig. 11, a small difference in the thresholds, in this case the second threshold, has a large impact on the result, hence it is critical to find suitable values. This, once again, depends greatly on the previous filtering, therefore, all settings must be adjusted accordingly.

Fig. 11. Joint union. Edge extraction by Canny with the second threshold low or high.

In order to interpret the dividing lines between the edges of walls and objects relative to the floor, the probabilistic Hough transform was used as shown in Fig. 12, which is implemented in the OpenCV library. In the image on the right, a reduced maximum segment size has been used, together with a reduced maximum inter-segment distance and a high threshold. This leads to the interpretation of the edges obtained above as a huge number of segments that perfectly define the edges of the path that the robot will face. On the other hand, if a good adjustment of these parameters is made, it is possible to obtain an image like the one on the right, in which each edge is interpreted using at most one or two segments.

Fig. 12. Obtaining the lines by means of the probabilistic Hough transform, applied on the same frame, but modifying the threshold, the maximum length of the segments and the maximum length between segments.

Subsequently, the most prominent corners of a specific region of the image are detected using the Shi-Tomasi algorithm, which is an evolution of the Harris corner detection algorithm. The implementation of this method has as input a grayscale image and allows to indicate the number of corners to be found, a threshold value between 0 and 1 for the selection of the quality of these corners and a minimum Euclidean distance between the detected corners. As can be seen in Fig. 13, the identification of the edges by this function is very effective and allows the edge to be perfectly defined by the points. Thanks to the configuration parameters, it is possible to have a high control of the type of representation desired, going from a large number of points per section, very close, to a very simplified representation formed by a very reduced number of them, counting practically one per corner.

Fig. 13. Edge and corner detection using the Shi-Tomasi algorithm.

8.3 Conclusions and Recommendations

The present prototype obtained several modifications by the tests in which it was subjected, from which it was obtained a change of tires by ones of greater diameter and different carving, allowing to cross different terrains, the change of motors by modified servomotors to DC increase the force to cross obstacles, while the control made by means of two IP cameras, allowed to maintain a panoramic vision of the environment, but it is important to indicate that it depends on the characteristics of the WI-FI equipment for its coverage and transmission of data; In addition, a pair of infrared sensors are used to detect obstacles that may not be recognized by the processing of the images captured by the camera.

The nature of this work has been an involvement of mathematical concepts that allow the creation and control of mobile robotic systems for processes involving exploration, supervision, rescue and security in a hostile environment; where the navigation process of the mobile robot focuses on image processing techniques with artificial vision, presiding most of the use of sensors. This has been a key aspect in the approach of the work, the intention was to move away from complex or computationally expensive techniques based on artificial intelligence, showing that the use of simple mathematical functions used with ingenuity is feasible; therefore, this has been the most extensive part and the one that has been the most deepened.

This approach is becoming increasingly viable thanks to the enormous variety of options provided by artificial vision libraries, as is the case of OpenCV, which has served as a base; therefore, it is intended to convey a change of mentality and loss of fear generated by this type of technology and an approach to developers, so that the results obtained are simple applications and gradually the difficulty that characterizes them will be placed on a par with the difficulties inherent in the use of sensors.

Regarding the work carried out, the greatest challenge has been to understand the range of possibilities existing in the field of artificial vision and the thoughtful choice of a set of strategies for route planning to be followed. For this purpose, a large number of tests have been carried out using a large number of combinations and a large amount

Fig. 14. Robots in operation

of information has been sought, since it is necessary to have a set of basic notions to understand the dimension of the problem.

The current cameras are development modules, which have certain configurations that could improve visibility, but are limited by the WI-FI connection, for which it is recommended to have a more robust equipment as shown in Fig. 14 to avoid data loss and improve communication between the operator and the prototype.

The maintenance and repairs of the robot structure allow the replacement of spare parts such as the microcontroller, shield or electromechanical elements in a simpler way.

References

1. Garay, B.A.: multimedia.uned, Abril (2016). https://multimedia.uned.ac.cr/pem/montanismo/5busqueda/index.html
2. Hernández, I.: El mundo, 9 Oct (2015). https://www.elmundo.es/ciencia/2015/10/09/5616a6 2e268e3e15768b463b.html
3. Agencia EFE, "EFE," 10 Feb (2019). https://www.efe.com/efe/america/tecnologia/crean-un-robot-aracnido-para-la-busqueda-y-rescate-de-personas-en-mexico/20000036-3893585
4. Kessel, N., Cicely, E.: ASTM INTERNATIONAL, Mayo (2015). https://www.astm.org/SNEWS/SPANISH/SPMJ13/nelsonenright_spmj13.html
5. N. R. S. D. Siegwart R.: Introduction to Autonomous Mobile Robots. MIT Press, London (2011)
6. Figueroa, A.P.J.: Diseño y Elaboración de Guías de Laboratorio para la Plataforma Móvil Labview Robotics SBRIO Starter Kit de National Instrument., Sangolquí: Escuela Politécnica del Ejército, (2012)
7. Earl, B.: METRO ECUADOR, 4 Enero (2016). https://www.metroecuador.com.ec/ec/noticias/2016/01/04/exhiben-robot-que-ayudar-rescate-personas-terremotos-tsunamis.html
8. Hernández, I.: El mundo, 10 Septiembre (2015). https://www.elmundo.es/ciencia/2015/10/09/5616a62e268e3e15768b463b.html

A Virtual Shooting Range, Experimental Study for Military Training

Mauricio Loachamín-Valencia(✉) [ID], José Mejía-Guerrero,
Víctor Emilio Villavicencio Álvarez, Sonia Cárdenas-Delgado,
and Darwin Manolo Paredes Calderón

Universidad de las Fuerzas Armadas ESPE, Av. General Rumiñahui s/n,
171-5-231B Sangolquí, Ecuador
{mrloachamin,jlmejia4,vevillavicencio,secardenas,dmparedes}@espe.edu.ec

Abstract. In the field of security and defence, training is considered one of the key factors to improve the skills of soldiers in tactical operations. Technological and communications advances have allowed the development of new technological tools to be effective and have a significantly lower operating cost. This work presents the design of a virtual shooting range, simulating an open polygon that includes the recreation of real scenarios from each region of the country, 3D objects, silhouettes, targets and weapons. The first-person shooter avatar soldier modelled as a 3D object, placed in a location and orientation relative to the virtual environment. It includes four virtual environments: Amazon jungle, rural, coastal and snowy. The preliminary results obtained in usability showed that the participants perceived realism in the scenarios and the 3D objects that compose them. The assessment in relation to the devices used shows that the virtual reality glasses and the VR gun controllers facilitated the visualization and interaction with the virtual scenarios during the training. The overall usability average was 4.90/5. Participants show no symptoms of cyber-sickness after training. This work could be a useful and complementary tool to train military personnel, improve the skills of soldiers to carry out tactical operations. It could even be a low-cost technological alternative, it would reduce the risk, increase the time and number of training sessions.

Keywords: Simulator · Military training · Virtual reality · Virtual shooting range

1 Introduction

In the field of security and defence, training is considered one of the key factors to improve the skills of soldiers to carry out tactical operations. Increasing concern over rising training costs, time, risk to life, and scarcity of training ranges has forced organizations to adopt converging technologies such as simulation models, and several simulators in military training. Technological and communications advances have allowed these tools to be effective and have a significantly lower operating cost [23].

M. Botto-Tobar et al. (Eds.): ICAT 2022, CCIS 1755, pp. 412–425, 2023.
https://doi.org/10.1007/978-3-031-24985-3_30

Military training can be broadly classified into two categories individual and collective training. Individual training provides specific skills and knowledge to each soldier. Collective training is directed towards accomplishment of assigned tasks by a group in an integrated and synchronised. The traditional training methods provide individual and collective training, however they involve huge costs, time, risk of life and impact on the environment [2].

Simulation technology is being applied extensively in the technologically advanced countries as an effective training tool for both individual and collective training using computer simulation models, interaction and immersion devices, virtual, augmented and mixed [20]. Technology advancements have allowed more trainees to be included and significantly lower the cost if compared to the field exercises. A simulation represents the dynamic behaviour of events occurring in the different scenarios. It is a tool to examine existing systems and to predict system performance under varying conditions without incurring much cost or risk of actual application.

A shooting training range is a physical field destined to the practice of various tactical strategies for the correct use of short and long range weapons. At a firing range, training and instruction is provided in ballistics, area security, handling, assembly, disassembly, safety, draw, grip, posture alignment and weapon maintenance. The shooting training range can be located in closed environments using virtual simulators or in outdoor environments that have strict internal security regulations [18].

Virtual reality is a type of human-computer interaction providing a virtual environment that can be explored through direct interaction with our senses. A virtual environment allows to interact with a simulated environment in 3D in which the user is immersed environment through the use of a head mounted display (HMD), CAVE, or other visualization devices; and by means of data input devices, such as treadmills, hand-operated sensors, gloves, game-pads and joystick. A virtual range is an area intended for target practice with the use of weapons without real ammunition.In most virtual environments be VR guns are used [6,12].

This work describes the design of a virtual shooting range simulator applied to military training in Ecuador, using Virtual Reality Technology. Also, for this purpose, a review of the related literature has been carried out to know about the possibilities offered by the new technologies such as Virtual Reality, modern interaction devices, techniques and methodologies used in the field of security and defense.

The paper is structured as follows. Section 2 a Background that includes related work. Section 3 describes the scope of the research applied methodology for the design and development of the VR system, architecture. Section 4 displays VR environments and modeled 3D objects measurements and a brief description of the experimental protocol performed. Section 5 the results obtained in the applied questionnaires are shown. Finally, Sect. 6 presents the conclusions and future work of research.

2   Background

In many countries of the world, virtual firing range systems are used to train their soldiers, and studies show that it can be an effective technique because it improves combat skills in shooting, strengthens practice and improvement in precision. However, the budget allocated for tactical and operational activities of the Armed Forces is increasingly reduced. This limits the number of training sessions in the real shooting ranges, ammunition and hours of training that are required.

The Armed Forces and the National Police are the institutions responsible for training citizens who serve their country. One of the most important areas within the instruction is the preparation for the use of weapons. Over the years, various methods of training for the use of weapons have been created. The most commonly used drill is the firing range, which involves isolated terrain with multiple targets of different sizes located at different distances [19].

The goal of shooting instruction is to train military personnel to properly use individual weapons and increase their level of effectiveness in combat shooting techniques and tactics. The physical space should not be so easy to find and requires specialized security to ensure that third parties are not harmed during training.

The shooter gets an evaluation according to the sector of the target where his shot hits. There are two types of shooting ranges: indoor and outdoor. Indoor shooting ranges can be isolated buildings or part of larger buildings. The basic components they contain consist of shooting lanes, silhouettes and bullet traps, which are responsible for stopping bullets, as well as elements such as safety protections for the user, acoustic insulation and appropriate lighting [8,11].

Outdoor firing ranges are large fields that reach distances of up to 1,000 m or more, for the use of long-range weapons. The silhouettes and bullet retaining walls are basic elements in these establishments, in addition, climatic factors such as lighting and wind must be considered because they can influence the direction of the ammunition. Flags are equally important elements as they show the direction of the wind, which must be considered by the person taking the shot [5]. Rifles, shotguns, rifles and pistols are normally used in these scenarios.

Simulators are currently the most widely used training method in military and defense institutions [7]. These allow physical and mental training for soldiers to face serious combat situations, without the need to put them in real danger. They are used when there is no real system, or when it is very expensive to build or manipulate; facilitates the control of experimental conditions without taking greater risks; the experiment can be repeated as many times as necessary without incurring additional costs.

Military training simulators reproduce the environment where tactical combat actions will be carried out, whether on land (armored tanks, firing ranges, etc.), sea (warships, submarines) or air (combat aircraft). Worldwide, the Armed Forces are including simulators that allow validating and testing new technologies or attack and/or defense configurations, including techniques such as virtualization, emulation, simulation, analytical models, among others [4].

The goal of shooting instruction is to train military personnel to properly use individual weapons and increase their level of effectiveness in combat shooting techniques and tactics. The instructions are carried out in day and night conditions and in different scenarios [14].

Virtual combat shooting ranges are an increasingly common tool used for shooting training. They have a series of advantages, including the ability to implement virtually any training scenario in a relatively safe manner, at a relatively low cost [14].

The work [16] highlights the importance of realism in the virtual shooting range as it increases the quality of the shooting training conducted. They used the Unity environment, to simulate a projectile impact damage to basic building materials have been performed. A series of simulations were conducted in the prepared virtual scenes, with the parameters selected so as to make the results correspond to experiment results from a real-life shooting range as registered on video. Their results suggest that realism is an important aspect of a virtual shooting range, raising the quality of the training taking place with its use and teaching the shooter proper sensibility regarding shots fired using various types of firearms against certain objects.

In recent years, interest in research in shooting training systems has increased. The cost of traditional military shooting training system is rather high, and it can only train one person at one time. Basing on it, in [22] have designed and realized a Shooting Training System for Police Force. They used Virtual Reality technology. The authors analyzed the teaching function of Shooting Training System and included multi-people simultaneously training. They suggest that the proposal proved to be flexible and low-cost.

In [24] showed that virtual environments offer added value in human learning, through a learning method that includes a prototype with Virtual Reality for training in the calibration procedure of the Felin IR sight, including an infrared observation device. First they have practiced using 2D software, then virtually until they made no mistakes and finally they have applied their knowledge in a real situation on the shooting range and the results have shown better knowledge using the VR prototype.

On the other hand, the study conducted by [21], compares the symptoms of cybersickness while the participants were standing on a moving platform and shooting at hostile ships and using virtual reality (VR) and augmented reality (AR) devices. They obtained better accuracy and response time to the instruction to start shooting in the VR condition. The use of VR or AR devices in smooth motion conditions was feasible because symptoms increased over time but were not different with respect to devices or motion. They suggest conducting more research to determine if this holds up under more extreme movement.

After carrying out a systematic review of the literature, certain successes, gaps and challenges have been detected. In works like [9] a multimedia shooting training system using optoelectronic solutions is shown. The design allows small arms targeting to be taught, monitored and evaluated and soldiers to be prepared to fire live ammunition in open fields for combat targets and silhouettes. In others studies have used laser capture for a shooting simulator using VR and computer vision. In addition, for live military student shooting military training, an interactive 3D virtual reality system is shown in [1] that uses a serious learning environment based on games that integrate invisible laser infrared technology, full-scale rifle guns 1:1 with back effects. Their results showed learning motivation and positive impacts on live shooting performance scores.

These works demonstrate the efforts that have been invested in research and development initiatives for this type of simulators, however, there are still challenges to overcome. Some of the gaps found have been the lack of information on pedagogical methods, study to detect positions, analysis of psychological aspects and the lack of automatic evaluations before, during and after simulation training [17,25].

3   Scope of the Research

The paper presents the design of a virtual shooting range, simulating an open polygon that includes the recreation of real scenarios from each region of the country, 3D objects, silhouettes, targets and weapons. The first-person shooter avatar soldier modeled as a 3D object, placed in a certain location and orientation relative to the virtual environment.

3.1   Methodology

The phases of the methodology proposed by Kaur [13], have been used for the design and development of this project, see Fig. 1.

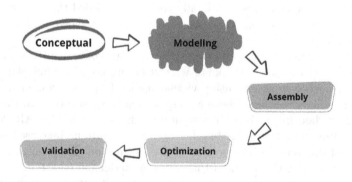

Fig. 1. Kaur methodology [13]

- **Conceptual:** In this phase, meetings have been held with the project's researchers and military personnel specializing in shooting. The meetings allowed knowing the requirements, to define the system architecture, the processes that are executed during the instruction, instruments and materials used, specification of 3D objects, silhouettes, targets and weapons.
- **Modeling:** In this phase, the elements of the scenarios of each region of the country, 3D objects such as silhouettes, targets and weapons and the shooter avatar soldier are defined, designed and modeled.
- **Assembly:** In this phase, all the components have been integrated: 3D objects, VR devices, user interface, database and the training configuration module.
- **Optimization:** Virtual environments, colors and textures of 3D objects, sound and positions were optimized.
- **Validation:** Preliminary tests were carried out to validate the requirements and functionality of each of the components, the results were analyzed and improvements were made.

3.2   Architecture

This section shows the building blocks of the virtual shooting range simulator in an open environment. The organization of computer system components and the operations that guide their operation. The organization determines the functional units that make up the system, the structure of its inter-connectivity, the control of interfaces and instructions, operations, and integration of devices and application programs that specify the virtual training task. In Fig. 2 the blocks that integrate the architecture can be seen.

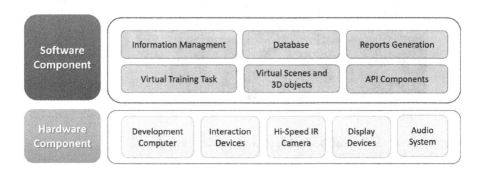

Fig. 2. System architecture

Hardware Components

For development, we used a workstation with liquid-cooled 8-core Intel Core i7 processor. NVIDIA GeForce RTX 3060Ti graphics card (8 GB GDDR6 dedicated), 32 GB memory, 1 TB PCIe SSD + 2 TB HDD.

For interaction, two types of devices are used: a VR gun and touch controllers. For visualization, an Oculus HMD and a room with a projection system are used.

For shot detection, a high speed IR camera and loudspeakers are used for the reproduction of sound and instructions.

Software Components

A virtual task was designed for training. The environments are configured and programmed with Unity, JavaScript and C#.

The virtual scenes and 3D objects were modeled in Blender. The 3D objects that are integrated into the virtual environments are silhouettes, the shooter's arms, the targets and the weapon.

API components, packages and installers of the devices were used for their configuration and integration between them.

Information management includes registration of participant data and configuration of training.

The training configuration interface allows you to register participants, select scenarios, weapons and objectives.

– Scenarios and weapons: This option allows us to choose the type of scenario, its description and the type of weapon with its respective description, see Fig. 3(a).
– Targets: this option contains the type of targets, the targets animation and the amount of ammunition, the add session button configures us and extracts them from the database, see Fig. 3(b).

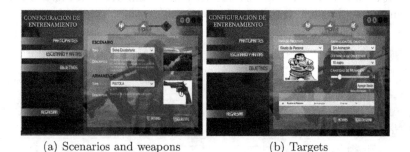

(a) Scenarios and weapons   (b) Targets

Fig. 3. Training Configuration Interfaces

The database was designed considering the system requirements, the use cases and the users. The tool to model the database, attributes and entities was Power Designer version 16.5.4.1.

For the dynamic generation of reports and managing users, Angular 13 was used. It connects to the database through the navigation menu, enters the different system options: instructor management, participant management according to the training carried out with their respective weapons, scenarios and targets used, and the results of the score obtained during shooting practice.

4 Virtual Environments

The virtual environments were generated in a three-dimensional space with the UNITY video game engine, the version used was that of 2018.4.36, the scale is the default of 1:100, vertical and horizontal alignments were considered, on the x axis, and, z. The modeled scenery were Amazon rainforest, rural, coastal and snowy.

To model the virtual jungle scenario, a jungle area of Zamora Chinchipe was taken as a base, see Fig. 4(a). The VR modeled environment shows the details based on the Unity "Klen" asset, see Fig. 4(b).

(a)   (b)

Fig. 4. (a) Image obtained from Google Maps of a jungle area of Zamora Chinchipe (b) virtual modeling of the jungle area.

To model the virtual scenario of the rural area, the Pasochoa park was taken as a base, the image was obtained from Google Maps, see Fig. 5(a). The VR modeled environment shows details based on the Unity "Mini Nature" asset, see Fig. 5(b).

(a)   (b)

Fig. 5. (a) Image obtained from Google Maps of a rural area (Pasochoa) (b) virtual modeling of the rural area.

To model the virtual scenario of the coastal zone, an area of the province of Santa Elena was taken as a base, the image was obtained from Google Maps, see Fig. 6(a). The VR modeled environment shows details based on the Unity "Desert Rocks" asset, see Fig. 6(b).

(a)   (b)

Fig. 6. (a) Image obtained from google maps of a sector of the province of Santa Elena. (b) Virtual modeling of the coastal area.

To model the virtual scenario of the snowy area, an area of the Chimborazo volcano was taken as a base, the image was obtained from Google Maps, see Fig. 7(a). The VR modeled environment shows details based on the Unity "Winty Asset", see Fig. 7(b).

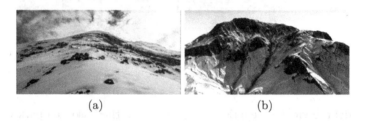

(a)   (b)

Fig. 7. (a) Image obtained from google maps of an area of the Chimborazo Volcano. (b) Virtual modeling of the snowy area.

4.1   3D Object Modeling

The 3D objects modeled to be integrated in each virtual environment were:

- Arm with gun, the modeling of the arm has been done with a camouflage texture. The participant can observe the arms as if they were his own. The hand was modeled and holds the weapon at the moment of interaction.
- Avatar, a soldier outfitted in his outfit was modeled for inclusion in the environment.
- War tank, the modeling of the tank was done in Blender, its texture is camouflage.
- Targets, the three shooting targets that were modeled are: silhouette of a person (Fig. 8(a)), silhouette of a bottle within a person (Fig. 8(b)), and a precision target (Fig. 8(c)).

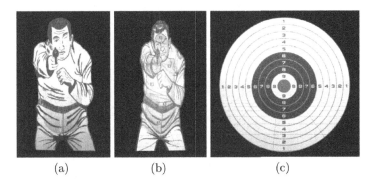

(a)   (b)   (c)

Fig. 8. Modeling of 3D objects

4.2 Component Integration

Virtual environments, components and shooting targets were integrated (Fig. 9). In addition, visualization and interaction devices have been integrated into the virtual scenarios. The information administration, database and report management interfaces are integrated with the entire system for its functionality.

Fig. 9. Integrated components in virtual environments

4.3 Experimental Protocol

The preliminary experimental tests were carried out at the CICTE-ESPE facilities. Bio-safety regulations were respected to protect the participants during the practice and the research staff. Disposable caps and alcohol were used to disinfect the devices and the hands of the participants. The questionnaires used

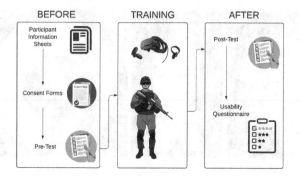

Fig. 10. Experimental protocol

are widely used in this field Cybersickness-SSQ [15] and Usability [10]. The sample of participants was five, three officers and two volunteers. The protocol was divided into three stages (Fig. 10).

- **Before**, the participants learned about the objectives of the project through the informative sheet, and signed the informed consent if they agreed to participate. Then, they answered the cybersickness questionnaire before the training. The Fig. 11(a) shows a participant filling out the questionnaire.
- **Training**, The instructor records the participant's data and sets up the training session. The participants performed the training task using the VR system. The Fig. 11(b) shows a participant performing the training.
- **After**, the participants answered the cyber-sickness questionnaire and a usability questionnaire that includes aspects of interaction, experience, and satisfaction.

(a)   (b)

Fig. 11. Participant in training

5   Results

The preliminary results obtained in each of the assessed aspects through the usability questionnaire show that the participants found it easy to use the application (4.90/5). Regarding the environment, the participants perceived realism in the scenarios and the 3D objects that compose it, as shown by the obtained average of 4.95/5. The evaluation in relation to the devices used shows that the virtual reality glasses and the VR gun controllers facilitated the visualization and interaction with the virtual scenarios during the training (score obtained 4.85/5).

A questionnaire was applied to identify possible symptoms of cyber-sickness that may occur after training using virtual reality devices. The participants answered the questionnaire before carrying out the training and another one afterwards. Figure 12(a) and Fig. 12(b) show the results. The participants did not present discomfort or symptoms after training; rather a curious fact that was found was that some participants improved their condition after using the VR system. These results are consistent with the work carried out by [3], which shows that the use of Oculus HMDs is a suitable device for virtual reality military training applications.

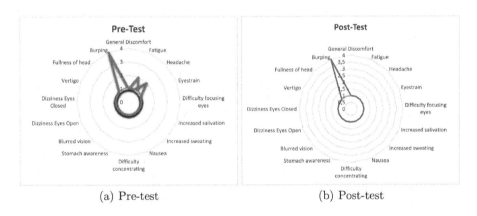

(a) Pre-test   (b) Post-test

Fig. 12. SSQ Questionnaire results

6   Conclusions and Future Works

Several meetings were held with specialists and researchers to learn about shooting techniques and define the system requirements. The prototype of the virtual firing range system was developed to train military personnel. The training includes four virtual environments: amazon jungle, rural, coastal and snowy. Each environment integrates components and 3D objects agreed with the specialists. The virtual environments were configured and programmed using Unity, JavaScript, and C#. The 3D objects were modeled in Blender. The results obtained about the usability, interaction, and satisfaction of the application show that the participants perceived realism in the scenarios and were able to identify the 3D objects in the environment.

The project is still in the development phase. In future works, the developed software will be integrated with specialized hardware that is under construction (gun with infrared sensor and pneumatic kit). In addition, tests will be carried out with the same software but in a room with a projection system that will be implemented.

The results obtained show that this work could be a useful and complementary tool to train military personnel, improve the skills of soldiers to carry out tactical operations. It could even be a low-cost technological alternative, it would reduce the risk, increase the time and number of training sessions.

Acknowledgments. The authors would like to thanks to *Universidad de las Fuerzas Armadas ESPE* of Ecuador for the funded given to project "Development and implementation of a Virtual shooting range for military training with smaller caliber weapons. PIM-02".

References

1. Bhagat, K.K., Liou, W.K., Chang, C.Y.: A cost-effective interactive 3d virtual reality system applied to military live firing training. Virtual Reality **20**(2), 127–140 (2016)
2. Brunyé, T.T., et al.: A review of us army research contributing to cognitive enhancement in military contexts. J. Cogn. Enhancement **4**(4), 453–468 (2020)
3. Cárdenas-Delgado, S., Loachamín-Valencia, M., Calderón, M.P.: VR-System ViPoS: VR system with visual and postural stimulation using HMDs for assessment cybersickness in military personnel. In: Rocha, Á., Guarda, T. (eds.) MICRADS 2018. SIST, vol. 94, pp. 71–84. Springer, Cham (2018). https://doi.org/10.1007/978-3-319-78605-6_6
4. Cárdenas-Delgado, S., Loachamín-Valencia, M., Guanoluisa-Atiaga, P., Monar-Mejía, X.: A VR-system to assess stereopsis with visual stimulation: a pilot study of system configuration. In: Botto-Tobar, M., Cruz, H., Díaz Cadena, A. (eds.) CIT 2020. AISC, vol. 1326, pp. 328–342. Springer, Cham (2021). https://doi.org/10.1007/978-3-030-68080-0_25
5. Centers for Disease Control and Prevention: Protecting Workers at Indoor Firing Ranges. Tech. rep, Occupational Safety and Health Act (2013)
6. Friedman, D., Leeb, R., Pfurtscheller, G., Slater, M.: Human-computer interface issues in controlling virtual reality with brain-computer interface. Hum. Comput. Interact. **25**(1), 67–94 (2010)
7. Gacek, J., Marciniak, B., Woźniak, R.: Major conditions of shooting range operation in poland. Problemy Mechatroniki: uzbrojenie, lotnictwo, inżynieria bezpieczeństwa **9** (2018)
8. General Services Administration: Indoor firing range: Design, Operations and Maintenance Criteria. Tech. rep., U.S. General Services Administration (2013)
9. Hlosta, P., Rolek, W., Swiderski, W., Olpinski, W.: Preliminary analysis of shooting training systems: Spartan. In: Electro-Optical and Infrared Systems: Technology and Applications XVII. vol. 11537, p. 115370Q (2020)

10. Hodrien, A., Fernando, T., et al.: A review of post-study and post-task subjective questionnaires to guide assessment of system usability. J. Usability Stud. **16**(3), 203–232 (2021)
11. Kardous, C.A., Murphy, W.J.: Noise control solutions for indoor firing ranges. Noise Control Eng. J. **58**(4), 345–356 (2010)
12. Karray, F., Alemzadeh, M., Abou Saleh, J., Arab, M.N.: Human-computer interaction: overview on state of the art. Int. J. Smart Sens. Intell. Syst. **1**(1), 137–159 (2017)
13. Kaur, K., Maiden, N., Sutcliffe, A.: Design practice and usability problems with virtual environments. In: Proceedings of Virtual Reality World 96 (1996)
14. Kazior, D., Bereska, D., Ilewicz, W.: Implementation of a realistic damage model in a simulated environment. Problemy Mechatroniki: uzbrojenie, lotnictwo, inżynieria bezpieczeństwa 10 (2019)
15. Kennedy, R.S., Lane, N.E., Berbaum, K.S., Lilienthal, M.G.: Simulator sickness questionnaire: an enhanced method for quantifying simulator sickness. Int. J. Aviat. Psychol. **3**(3), 203–220 (1993)
16. Ladha, S., Chandran, S., Miles, K.: Vision assited safety enhanced shooting range simulator. In: Proceedings of Computer Vision, Pattern Recognition, Image Processing and Graphics, National Conference (NCVPRIPG) (2010)
17. Liu, X., Zhang, J., Hou, G., Wang, Z.: Virtual reality and its application in military. In: IOP Conference Series: Earth and Environmental Science. vol. 170, p. 032155. IOP Publishing (2018)
18. North Atlantic Treaty Organisation: Virtual Reality: State of Military Research and Applications in Member Countries. Tech. rep., NATO Research Study Group 28 (2003)
19. Osodlo, V., Rakhmanov, V., Krykun, V., Tarasenko, N., Aristarkhova, M.: Officers' foreign language training in educational and information environment of the higher military educational institution. Rev. Educ. **10**(1), e3317 (2022)
20. Parvinen, P., Hamari, J., Pöyry, E.: Introduction to the minitrack on mixed, augmented and virtual reality. In: Proceedings of the 51st Hawaii International Conference on System Sciences, pp. 1395–1396 (2018)
21. Pettijohn, K.A., Peltier, C., Lukos, J.R., Norris, J.N., Biggs, A.T.: Virtual and augmented reality in a simulated naval engagement: preliminary comparisons of simulator sickness and human performance. Appl. Ergonomics **89**, 103200 (2020)
22. Shi, B.: Design and realization of shooting training system for police force. In: Nunes, I.L. (ed.) AHFE 2018. AISC, vol. 781, pp. 175–183. Springer, Cham (2019). https://doi.org/10.1007/978-3-319-94334-3_19
23. Silva Achancaray, J.A.: La gestión de las tecnologías de la información y comunicaciones y el desarrollo de simuladores de armas en el comando de educación y doctrina del ejército (2017)
24. Taupiac, J.D., Rodriguez, N., Strauss, O., Rabier, M.: Training soldiers to calibration procedures in virtual reality, the felin ir sight use case. In: 13emes Journées de la Réalité Virtuelle (j. RV) (2018)
25. Zhang, M., Li, X., Yu, Z., Chen, Z., Sun, Y., Li, Y.: Virtual range training based on virtual reality. In: Proceedings of the 4th International Conference on Contemporary Education, Social Sciences and Humanities, Atlantis Press. vol. 10 (2019)

Recovery of Level III Ballistic Plates by Reinforcing and Renewing Their Structural Components

Cesar Tapia[1], Darwin Urbina[2], Carlos Mena[3,4], Xavier Sánchez Sánchez[4](✉), and Edison Haro[4]

[1] Centro de Mantenimiento de la Aviación del Ejército CEMAE, PO BOX 170809, Quito, Ecuador
[2] Centro de Mantenimiento Fluvial CEMAFLU, PO BOX 220202, Puerto Francisco de Orellana, Ecuador
[3] Centro de Investigación y Desarrollo de la Fuerza Aérea CIDFAE, PO BOX 180110, Ambato, Ecuador
[4] Departamento de Ciencias de la Energía y Mecánica, Universidad de las Fuerzas Armadas ESPE, PO BOX 171-5-231B, Sangolquí, Ecuador
xrsanchez@espe.edu.ec

Abstract. The research focuses on recovering level III ballistic plates, consisting of a soft part (Aramid) and a rigid part (ballistic ceramic), that have completed their useful life by reinforcing and renewing their structural components, using composite material lamination methods. For this, a procedure based on reverse engineering was carried out to study the internal configuration of the plates and the characterization of each of the components. As a result, it was determined that Kevlar 49 has lost its mechanical properties by degradation, while the ceramic material maintains its physical and mechanical properties. Finally, level III ballistic plates were manufactured with different configurations and using colloidal silica nanofillers to perform impact tests. It was determined that the most resistant configuration has Dyneema as the soft part, improving 9.48% by weight and 7.61% resistance to ballistic impact.

Keywords: Ballistic Plates · Aramid · Dyneema · Colloidal Silica · Composite Materials

1 Introduction

Combat individual protection equipment has been developed and studied over the years. Zahari et al. (2018) carried out a parametric study with nine configurations of ballistic plates, determining that the "titanium-aluminum" specimen had the highest specific energy absorbed [1]. Kosla et al. (2020) generates a method for preparing ballistic armor with hybrid silicone-ceramic compounds (HSC) of great flexibility with success in impact tests [2]. Kevlar/HH rubber composites in two and four-layer configurations increase impact resistance by 53% and 73% compared to pure Kevlar fabric [3]. Santos de la Luz et al. (2020) made a comparison between the ballistic performance of the Dyneema compound, and the epoxy compound reinforced with 30% natural fibers extracted from pineapple leaves (PALF).This proved additional protection to level IIIA armored vests made with Kevlar using the introduction of PALF composite board [4]. The ballistic effect is determined in the sequence of layers that provide the resistance to perforation with hybrid panels. [5].

The members of the armed forces have bulletproof vests made internally with level III ballistic plates, which have a useful life of 5 years. [6], The purpose of this research is to determine the physical, mechanical, and impact characteristics of each component (rigid part and soft part), and to provide an alternative use. From the results of ballistic tests on ceramics using different projectiles, Medvedovski (2010) determined that the ballistic performance of armor ceramics is defined by their microstructure and phase composition [7]. It is necessary to improve the microstructure and phase composition by replacing the soft part through lamination processes with vacuum curing at 60 °C and reusing the rigid part with the application of colloidal silica nanofillers, to prolong the useful life of the ballistic plates.

Various investigations on ballistic plates have been carried out using Kevlar – ceramics, and modifications, obtaining results of a different nature as shown in Tables 1, 2, and 3.

Table 1. Studies of new technologies in ballistic plates.

Company	Research	Field	Result
DUPONT TM[8] (EEUU)	Invention and innovation of kevlar.	Different fields of industry are best known for their use in ballistics and body armor.	Extraordinarily strong plastic material.
SANDA BALLISTIC.[9] (CHINA)	Research and develop high-tech armor products.	Patented technologies in sectors such as bulletproof vests and armored vehicles.	Customized ballistic solutions based on customers needs.

Table 2. Research work on the use of Kevlar for Ballistic Protection

Research	Conclusion
Manufacture of Kevlar Panels from thermo-curing processes [10].	It depends on the different temperatures and configurations of the materials.
Calculation and simulation of a ceramic-based multilayer armor [11].	A comparative steel-ceramic study was made, which showed a value of almost 30% with alumina and 50% with SiC.
Numerical simulation of ballistic tests on carbon fiber laminates and post-impact resistance study [12].	Simulation with the structural software LS-Dyna of the resistance of a carbon fiber laminate against ballistic impacts.

Table 3. Colloidal silica nanofillers in ballistic plates

Research	Conclusion
Nano-silica on the mechanical properties of acrylic polyurethane coatings [13].	Regardless of the type of putty, the microhardness of transparent varnishes increases linearly. When a 6% of weight filler was used to reinforce the clear coat, a 100% increase was observed. It is also understood that the nano-silica particles allow effective improvement of the corrosion resistance of the clear coat. The results show that the thickness loss of the nano-silica type is lower, resulting in higher corrosion resistance.
Absorption energy behavior of hybrid composite laminates with nano-fillers [14].	Laminates containing nanofillers that can effectively cover the surface of the fiber cloth and effectively seal the spaces between the fiber bundles have higher energy absorption capabilities. Although the aluminum powder completely seals the cavity, resulting in the lens having the highest impact energy absorption capacity.

2 Materials, Equipment and Tests

2.1 Materials and Equipment

The materials used in the research with their characteristics can be found in Table 4.

Table 4. Materials

Materials	Description	Application
Colloidal silica 406 (SiO2)	Nanofillers are made up of sand and quartz. Its function is to act as a hard filler for holes [14].	Fills possible holes in the ceramic matrix composite material.
Epoxy Resin 2000 – hardener 2060	They are cured using a catalyst or hardener, also called a two-component system. The resin used in this investigation belongs to this group [15].	Protect and give shape to the fibers that reinforce it. It is constituted as a composite material of polymeric matrix reinforced with aramid or Dyneema fibers.

(*continued*)

Table 4. (*continued*)

Materials	Description	Application
Nylon Bagging Film P/N: 01–14805	Bagging film is a flexible, high-strength nylon material.	Used to compact and seal all other bagging and laminating materials.
Breather Bleeder P/N: 01–14810	100% non-woven polyester breathing fabric that is designed to allow airflow throughout the vacuum process.	Absorbent of the excess resin that emanates from the laminate due to the action of pressure.
Peel-Ply P/N: 09–00100	100% polyamide fabric that is applied as the last layer of the laminate, does not adhere to resins.	They acted as superficial protectors.
Yellow Sealant Tape	Closure tape.	Provides a joint between the mold and the Nylon Bagging Film, compacting the vacuum bagging process.
Aramid sheets 49	Fiber with excellent properties, low density and high resistance.	It resists impact loads and works by reinforcing composite materials with a polymeric matrix.
Dyneema sheets	It has a higher impact resistance than all thermoplastics.	Highly functional and sustainable.
Plasticine Roma N°1 Grey-Green	This material has been designated as a support material for ballistic tests to recognized standards such as NIJ, HOSDB, SK and ISO.	Material used to determine impact trauma and simulate the consistency of human muscles, by the provisions of the American standard NIJ 0101.06 [16].

To perform the tests, obtain mechanical properties, and measure linear dispalcement a Faithful Model SH4 Magnetic Stirrer and digital balance, SHIMADZU 5K universal testing machine, and a MITUTOYO micrometer, which is a composite material curing equipment for composite material manufacturing, were used. For image analysis, a MEIJI microscope was combined with the Pax It program. The SMART OXIDES application of the BRUKER S2 PUMA team in RX fluorescence and the Shooting Tunnel of the Santa Bárbara EP - Factory.

2.2 Tests

To determine the effects produced the comparative method was applied creating the necessary environmental conditions with different configurations of specimens as shown in the diagram of Fig. 1. In other words, the materials of the ballistic plate (Ceramic, Kevlar). Then, the physical and mechanical characteristics of each component (Ceramic, Kevlar) are maintained through tensile and bending tests, and the mechanical characteristics between the old Kevlar and the new one are analyzed. Subsequently, the Kevlar assembled with the ceramic is laminated under vacuum at 60 °C and the fillers are added, to finally carry out the impact tests.

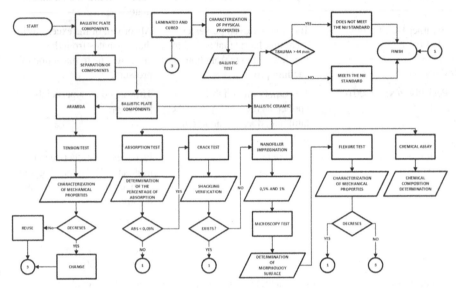

Fig. 1. Test methodology

ASTM D3039/M-14 is used for tension tests with a load cell of 5 tons and a test speed of 10 mm/min. On the other hand, with ASTM C373, the absorption test is applied as shown in Fig. 2, where the weight data is taken before and after remaining submerged in water first for five hours and then for 24 h.

Fig. 2. a) Drying of samples in an oven for the absorption test b) Immersion of the samples in boiling water for the absorption test and c) Data collection of the weight of the samples for the determination of absorption.

The apparent density is the relationship between the volume and the dry weight, for which the Archimedes principle is used for displacement of volume (voids, pores and cracks are considered). To determine cracks, a cracking test was carried out, where after subjecting the ballistic ceramics to a sudden change in temperature, the plates were immersed in a 50% Calcium Chloride solution at 110 °C for 90 min, were then immersed in ice water at 2.5 °C and finally in water with 1% methylene blue for 12 h to look for cracks, as shown in Fig. 3.

Fig. 3. Immersion of plates in methylene blue to look for cracks after heat treatment.

The impregnation of colloidal silica nanoparticles as shown in Fig. 4 was performed on the ceramic matrix composite material with a concentration of 0.5% and 1% [17]. The material is subjected to visual inspection at 1000X and 500X to differentiate the surface before and after applying nanofillers with 1% and 0.5% colloidal silica.

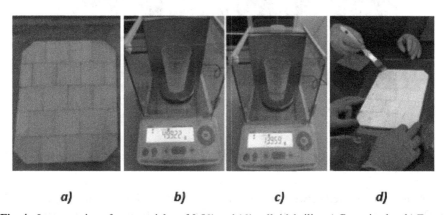

a)   b)   c)   d)

Fig. 4. Impregnation of nanoparticles of 0.5% and 1% colloidal silica a) Ceramic plate b) Epoxy resin c) Hardener d) Impregnation

In the bending test as shown in Fig. 5, the original ceramics measuring 25 x 50 x 10 were used as specimens, under the ASTM C-1291 standard. The universal testing machine with a 5-ton load cell was used with the lower support cylinders 46mm apart. The diameter of the piston applying the forces is 18mm with a travel speed of 1mm/min.

a)   b)

Fig. 5. a) Schematic and 3-point bending test on ballistic ceramics. Taken from Materials Science, applications and engineering (Figs. 3, 4, 5, 6) [18], and b) Ceramic specimens for flexural testing 0%, 1% and 0.5% of colloidal silica nanofillers dimensions 25x50x10.

The chemical composition of the ceramic was obtained using the RX fluorescence technique. For the generation of the ballistic plate, a polymeric matrix is manufactured with epoxy resin 2000 reinforced with Kevlar 49 and Dyneema fibers [18]. The configuration of the sheets of the ballistic plates is orthogonal with a balanced fabric as shown in Fig. 6. This configuration is used because in ballistic impact tests the results are acceptable with orthotropic behavior [19]. The material was cured with a vacuum autoclave, extracting the air trapped between the sheets. This procedure was performed to compact the sheets, reduce humidity and optimize the content of the matrix [20].

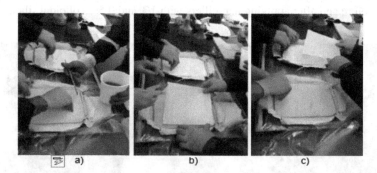

a)   b)   c)

Fig. 6. Lamination process a) resin application b) Kevlar sheets c) Dyneema sheets.

Weight is compared between original and reconstructed Kevlar ballistic plates, such as Dyneema. In addition to a bulk density test. Finally, the ballistic plate impact test was carried out in the ballistic tunnel, under the NIJ Standard – 0101.06 standards for level III protection plates, as represented in Fig. 7 and Fig. 8.

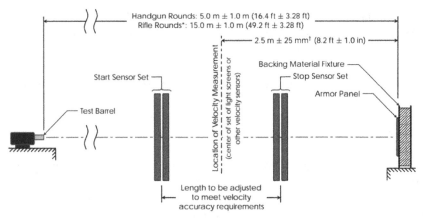

Fig. 7. Ballistic plate impact test. Taken from Ballistic Resistance of Body Armor NIJ Standard-0101.06 (Fig. 8) [16]

Fig. 8. a) Impact test on an original plate with the respective trauma and b) Impact test on a repowered plate with the respective trauma.

3   Results and Discussion

The characterization of the mechanical and physical properties of the components of the ballistic plate is to determine whether or not it is necessary to replace the respective piece. The tests were carried out with four samples K, N, C, and Q (5 specimens of each sample). The first two represent the Kevlar fibers (current and new respectively), C represents the ballistic ceramic and Q represents the ballistic ceramic for the analysis.

Table 5. Chemical analysis of ceramic (RX fluorescence)

Test tube	SiO_2 (%)	Al_2O_3 (%)	Fe_2O_3 (%)	TiO_2 (%)	CaO (%)	MgO (%)	NaO (%)	K_2O (%)	ZrO_2 (%)	HfO_2 (%)	V_2O_5 (%)
Q-3	2,58	89,04	0,22	0,04	0,59	1,69	1,02	0,15	4,53	0,09	0,05

The chemical analysis, as shown in Table 5, indicates a high content of Al2O3 with 89.04%. Another important component is ZrO2 with 4.53%. This value is significantly high compared the other elements identified in the analysis.

Table 6. Physical and mechanical characteristics of the components of the ballistic plate.

	K	N	C	C1	C2	RESIN
Stress (mpa)	318,44 ± 43,81	395,49 ± 122,08	–	–	–	313,02
Bend(mpa)	–	–	245,81 ± 9,08	245,80 ± 11,20	245,80 ± 7,81	238,03
Young´s module	10,42 ± 1,34	26,05 ± 9,85	17,68 ± 2,30	17,67 ± 1,26	17,64 ± 0,61	25,99
Strain	0,02 ± 0,00	0,01 ± 0,00	–	–	–	–
% strain	1,61 ± 0,11	0,77 ± 0,00	–	–	–	1,31
Absorption	–	–	0,004 ± 0,005	–	–	–
Density	–	–	–	–	–	–
Microscopy	–	–	–	Base	Improve	Improve
Cracked	–	–	No	–	–	–

Table 6 presents a summary table with the physical and mechanical properties of the level III ballistic plates once the different tests have been completed. Based on the ASTM D3039 standard, the base Kevlar 49 (K) sample has a tensile strength of 315.64 MPa compared to the N 400.39 MPa sample. If the two values were compared, it can be determined that the Kevlar 49 base has decreased its mechanical resistance characteristics to tension by 21.16%.

The study of the physical and ballistic impact characteristics of the ballistic plates that were subjected to the recovery of the soft part with laminates of composite materials reinforced with Kevlar or Dyneema fibers. For this, 7 sample configurations were made with 5 specimens in each one, as shown in Table 7, obtaining the results of Table 8 and Table 9.

Table 7. Ballistic plate samples.

Setting	Sample
Plates with kevlar 49 base	PB
Plates with kevlar 49 UD	PK
Kevlar with 0.5% nano fillers in the ceramic	PK1
Kevlar with 1% nano fillers in the ceramic	PK2
UD dyneema plates	PD
Dyneema with 0.5% nano fillers in the ceramic	PD1
Dyneema with 1% nano fillers in the ceramic	PD2

According to Table 8, PK2 would have a weight of 2296.00 gr, making it the heaviest of all. In volume displacement PB with 955.50 cm3, PD with the highest density value

Table 8. Physical characteristics of the ballistic plate.

	PB	PK	PK1	PK2	PD	PD1	PD2
Weigth (G)	2391,40 ± 19,47	2288,80 ± 9,09	2291,00 ± 2,35	2296,00 ± 1,22	2169,00 ± 2,74	2182,00 ± 1,58	2184,00 ± 0,71
Volumen (CM3)	955,50 ± 4,88	878,48 ± 4,08	890,18 ± 5,56	890,18 ± 6,54	818,03 ± 4,08	829,73 ± 4,08	835,58 ± 2,67
Density (G/CM3)	2,51 ± 0,01	2,61 ± 0,02	2,57 ± 0,02	2,58 ± 0,02	2,65 ± 0,02	2,63 ± 0,01	2,61 ± 0,01
Absorption %	2,912 ± 0,02	0,87 ± 0,00	0,87 ± 0,00	0,86 ± 0,00	0,91 ± 0,00	0,95 ± 0,00	0,95 ± 0,00
Thickness (MM)	1,96 ± 0,01	1,80 ± 0,01	1,83 ± 0,01	1,83 ± 0,01	1,68 ± 0,01	1,70 ± 0,01	1,71 ± 0,01

with 2.65 g/cm3, the plate with the greatest absorption is PB with 2.92% and the thickest would be PB with 1.96 mm.

Table 9. Ballistic properties of the different samples.

	Trauma (mm)			Diameter (mm)			Energy (J)
PB	21,67	±	1,57	78,97	±	4,94	3443,56
PK	19,50	±	0,40	64,04	±	2,64	3443,56
PK1	21,52	±	0,83	65,69	±	1,18	3443,56
PK2	22,24	±	1,12	68,62	±	0,65	3443,56
PD	20,02	±	0,58	64,36	±	1,68	3443,56
PD1	20,76	±	0,40	65,65	±	1,33	3443,56
PD2	21,91	±	0,62	67,67	±	1,22	3443,56

The results of the samples shown in Table 9 maintained a maximum of 22.24 mm about trauma, complying with what is required in the NIJ Standard.

4   Conclusions

After comparing the new Kevlar Fiber found in bulletproof vests and 5-year-old Kevlar Fibers also found in bulletproof vests, it was found that the tensile strength in the 5-year-old Kevalr fibers decreased by 21,16%, indicating that after 5 years of use they have degraded.

After performing the corresponding chemical procedures, it was determined that the rigid part was made up of a composite Al2O3 ceramic matrix material reinforced with Zr2O at 4,53% yielding a flexural strength of 24,88 MPa, and thanks to its physical characteristics of absorption, density, and cracking, this material has no impurities, pores, or cracks.

In the impact tests, the PB base sample, despite having finished its useful life, had a trauma of 20.66 mm which falls within the 44 mm trauma range established in the NIJ Standard 0101.06 Ballistic Resistance of Body Armor.

In the samples where the soft part was replaced by laminates of polymeric matrix composite materials reinforced with Kevlar 49 and Dyneema fibers, reusing the rigid part, represented by samples PK, PK1, PK2, PD, PD1, PD2 passed the NIJ Standard.

A weight reduction of up to 9.48% has been obtained, and one of the main improved characteristics is the percentage of water absorption of around 70.54% thus allowing the Kevlar 49 and Dyneema fibers not to come into contact with external agents thanks to the covered made out of polymeric matrix.

The application of nano-filled colloidal silica at 0.5% and 1% in the ceramic material improved the morphological appearance. Mchanically, it did not alter the ballistic behavior in the plate since, when carrying out the impact tests, it was possible to verify that internally the rigid part of the ballistic plate constituted by the ballistic ceramic had the same behavior as without the application of the nanofillers.

Acknowledgments. The authors would like to thank the support of Fuerza Aérea Ecuatoriana and Universidad de Fuerzas Armadas - ESPE (Projects Numbers 2016–002-ESPE-k-1).

References

1. Zahari, R., Regan, J., Ordys, A., Sultan, M., Yidris, N.: Ballistic impact analysis of double-layered metal plates. Mat. Sci. Eng. **405**(1), 012012 (2018)
2. Kosla, K., Kubiak, P., Fejdys, M., Olszewska, K., Landwjt, M., Chmal, E.: Preparation and impact resistance properties of hybrid silicone-ceramics composites. Appl. Sci. **10**(24), 9098 (2020)
3. Narayanan, A., Sundharesan, S., Saif, I.: Kevlar-based composite material and its applications in body armour: a short literature review. Mat. Sci. Eng. **987**, 012003 (2020)
4. Santos, F., Costa, F., Souza, M., Cassiano, L., Neves, S.: Composites with natural fibers and conventional materials applied in a hard armor: a comparison. Polymers **12**(9), 1920 (2020)
5. Gilson, L., Rabet, L., Imad, A., Coghe, F.: Experimental and numerical assessment of non-penetrating impacts on a composite protection and ballistic gelatine. Int. J. Impact Eng. **136**, 103417 (2020)
6. INEN, Norma Técnica Ecuatoriana 2939, 19 (2015)
7. Medvedovski, E.: Ballistic performance of armour ceramics: Influence of design and structure. Ceramics International (2010)
8. Gavín, Á.: Historias de Innovación: El descubrimiento del Kevlar. Zaragoza, p. 1, Jul (2017)
9. Ballistic, S.: Shandong sanda scientific and technological development limited corporation (1993). https://es.sandaballistic.com/
10. Joven, R.: Manufactura de Paneles de Kevlar a partir de procesos de termocurado. Experimental and numerical assessment of non-penetrating impacts on a composite protection and ballistic gelatine (2008)
11. Serra, N.: Cálculo y simulación de un blindaje multicapa en base a cerámica. Tucumán (2016)
12. Fernández, J.: Simulación numérica de ensayos balisticos sobre laminados de fibra de carbono y estudio de resistencia post-impacto. Carlos III de Madrid (2014)
13. Malaki, M., Hashemzadeh, Y., Karevan, M.: Effect of nano-silica on the mechanical properties of acrylic polyurethane coatings. Prog. Org. Coatings **101**, 477–485 (2016)
14. Haro, E.E., Odeshi, A.G., Szpunar, J.A.: The energy absorption behavior of hybrid composite laminates containing nano-fillers under ballistic impact. Int. J. Impact Eng. (2016)

15. Sánchez, L.: Análisis mecánico y fisicoquímico de un material compuesto de matriz termoestable y refuerzo de fibra de carbono: Comparativa de propiedades del material curado fuera y dentro de autoclave. Univ. Carlos III Masdrid (2011)
16. Hernandez, A.M.C., Buchely, M.F.: Dynamic characterization of roma plastilina no. 1 from drop test and inverse analysis. Int. J. Mech. Sci. **100**, 158–168 (2015)
17. Lee, J., Jin Lee, K., Jang, J.: Effect of silica nanofillers on isothermal crystallization of poly(vinyl alcohol): In-situ ATR-FTIR study. Polym. Test. **27**(3), 360–367 (2008)
18. Colman, A.: Compuesto. In: Bloomsbury Encyclopedia of Popular Music of the World (2017)
19. Ruiz, R.R., Galán, M.A.T. Carillo, J.G., Gamboa, R.A.: Evaluation of ultra high molecular weight polyethylene (UHMWPE) anisotropic configuration sample of Tensylon[TM], Dupont[TM] at medium velocity impact test. Mex. J. Mater. Sci. Eng., (2015)
20. Portocarrero Hermann, J., Maldonado, J., Serrano, C., Novoa, D., Yela, C.: Desarrollo de placas de protección balística en materiales compuestos con sistema multicapas para la reducción de peso y aumento de las propiedades balísticas. Rev. Colomb. Mater., (2013)

Technology Trends

A Blockchain-Based Model for OAuth Authorization via Third-Party Web Application

Julio C. Mendoza-Tello(✉) ⓘ and Nelson R. Baquero-Parra

Facultad de Ingeniería y Ciencias Aplicadas, Universidad Central del Ecuador, Quito, Ecuador
{jcmendoza,nrbaquero}@uce.edu.ec

Abstract. Authentication and authorization are critical factors for network security. In this context, three problems were identified. First, password fatigue, the difficulty of remembering a password when Internet service usage increases. Second, services centralization; that is, the dependence on a single entity for the operations management, which can infringe the privacy of users. Third, lack of service availability; it means, the permanent, or temporary suspension of the service. Denial-of-Service attacks denials cause delays in response times, and severe interruptions to centralized schemes. Faced with these challenges, this research proposes a blockchain-based model for OAuth authorization via third-party web application. For this, the versatilities that both technologies provide to solve the aforementioned issues. Then, it explains how together blockchain and OAuth 2.0 grant access to a web resource via a third-party web application. Consequently, a model is developed and addressed using smart contracts and web forms. To demonstrate the validity of our model, we propose a study case for a user to access a web resource using a third-party web application. Finally, conclusions and future work are described at the end of the paper.

Keywords: OAuth · Authorization · Authentication · Blockchain · Access token

1 Introduction

Identity management systems are constantly evolving to solve the problems related to authentication and authorization. A preliminary user and password authentication model allows the creation of user and access accounts. This model was a burden, not only for the user who must remember the password, but also for the user account manager. This causes a problem called password fatigue for the user. To solve this problem, a federated model was used to delegate authentication to a specific server, which processes all network activity using the SAML protocol (Security Assertion Markup Language)[1]. The federated model greatly alleviated the password fatigue problem. However, centralized services are vulnerable to a temporary system crash or failure. Centralized models had drawbacks related to big data management, which leads to a privacy issue (e.g., identity theft, phishing, data leakage).

With the advent of Web 2.0, several social media providers offered an alternative to the traditional scheme. It is a system that authorizes user access via third-party pages

© The Author(s), under exclusive license to Springer Nature Switzerland AG 2023
M. Botto-Tobar et al. (Eds.): ICAT 2022, CCIS 1755, pp. 441–454, 2023.
https://doi.org/10.1007/978-3-031-24985-3_32

using the social network account. Each provider offered its own access system; however, this caused an overhead for the deployment infrastructures. This led to the need to create a standard known as OAuth [2]. Despite this innovation, OAuth uses centralized management servers.

Internet is based on decentralized services. In this sense, it is not feasible to continue using centralized authorization and authentication systems. Faced with these challenges, Blockchain is a decentralized solution based on cryptographic algorithms that allow a distributed consensus, without the need for a third party, or supervisory authority. Blockchain establishes trust between unknown entities, through a cryptographic proof provided by the network, instead of third-party services. The immutability property of Blockchain guarantees non-repudiation, and data integrity. In this context, blockchain-based smart contracts are implemented to execute codes agreed by the network nodes, which contributes to the mitigation of man-in-the-middle attacks. With these considerations, this research proposes a blockchain-based model for OAuth authorization via third-party web application.

The sections of this paper are structured as follows. In section two, the methodology is pointed out. Section three describes the background related to basic concepts, related works, and materials used for research. With these considerations, the model is developed based on blockchain and OAuth 2.0 characteristics. Finally, conclusions and future research are presented in section five.

2   Methodology

This section briefly describes the methodology used during this research. Two technologies were addressed, namely: blockchain y OAuth 2.0. For this, three consecutive phases were carried out, namely: theory, practice, and conclusions.

With respect to the theoretical phase. A brief theoretical description of both technologies was addressed, as well as a review of related works.

With respect to the practical phase. Hardware and software required for model development were identified. In addition, the versatilities that both technologies provide to the model were identified. Then, it is described how both technologies can work together to grant access to web resources via third-party web application. Consequently, the prototype was developed using smart contracts and web forms.

With respect to the conclusions phase. Contributions, and future research work were addressed within this final phase.

3   Background

This section describes core concepts, related works, and materials used for research.

3.1   Core Concepts

Core concepts such as digital identity, blockchain, smart contracts, and OAuth were described within this section.

3.1.1 Digital Identity

Identity is a set of attributes that characterize an individual compared to others. Digital identity is the set of credentials that allows access to online services. It can include the following attributes: email address, password, full names, username, phone numbers, social network accounts, among others [3]. The digital identity is created manually through voluntary data entry, or automatically with machine learning algorithms. When a digital service collects data, it must ensure the privacy of the user, according to two premises, namely: (i) the data will only be used to provide the service offered, and (ii) the data will not be stored or delivered to third-party service.

3.1.2 Blockchain and Smart Contracts

Blockchain is a linked and ordered data structure of transaction blocks. Due to the decentralized nature, participants can approve or reject transactions. This functionality is provided by consensus mechanisms based on cryptographic algorithms, which validate the veracity of the operations, and guarantee the integrity of the whole scheme. In this way, blockchain removes the need for trusted third parties, and provides disruptive characteristics for society and e-commerce [4].

A blockchain has immutability property, which is guaranteed by two metadata located within the header of each block. (i) Previous block header hash, which is obtained by applying the SHA-256 function twice on the previous block header. Each subsequent block has a copy of this identifier hash within its header. In this way, each time a block is created, it is also linked to a previous block. (ii) Merkle tree, which is a mechanism that dual groups transactions using hash functions. Next, a timestamp function that provides a timestamp for these operations [5].

The cryptographic design ensures the integrity of the scheme because the tampering of a transaction affects the block, and this event is not a trivial task. If a previous block header hash changes, it is necessary to change the hash of the subsequent block, which implies the use of large amounts of processing, and calculation to be able to generate all the transactions in the same chronological order.

Blockchain is the underlying technology of cryptocurrencies. It provides a guarantee of anonymity, non-repudiation of behavior between participants, and prevents double-spend attacks. In addition, blockchain has a versatile structure to transport digital assets, such as smart contracts.

A smart contract is a set of self-executing instructions according to programming conditions, which represent the prior agreement between the participants of a transaction. In this context, a smart contract is implemented through the publication of a transaction (within the blockchain) and can be invoked by another smart contract, or by an external entity (e.g., a user application). The contract structure is defined by three fields: (i) program code based on Turing complete language, (ii) account balance to send and receive cryptocurrencies, and (iii) storage to read, write, modify, and delete data.

A blockchain-based smart contract guarantees compliance with established agreements without exception[6]. Due to the immutability feature, once it is implemented within the blockchain, the code cannot be altered. Figure 1 shows smart contracts interacts with the blockchain.

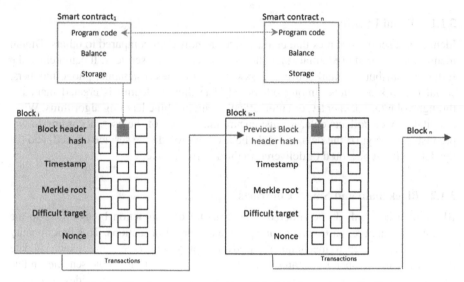

Fig. 1. How do a smart contract and blockchain work together?

3.1.3   OAuth 2.0

The OAuth 2.0 framework is used to solve the problem of authorization delegation; that is, the granting of access to resources via third party applications without sharing credentials [2]. OAuth 2.0-based schemes include the following entities: (i) A resource server that hosts an owner resource, (ii) a client that wants to access that resource, and (iii) an authorization server to generate the access tokens. In our research, blockchain is used to generate these tokens, rather than an authorization server.

Access tokens are granted to authorized clients by the resource owner. For additional security, a token is associated with a private key; in this way, only users who prove possession of this key can use the token.

3.2   Related Works

Previous research developed solutions based on blockchain and OAuth. A framework that combines blockchain technology with IoT for identity authentication was presented by Tian et al.[7]. An OAuth-based framework for IoT systems was proposed by Shieh et al. [8]. A blockchain-based authentication, and identity management scheme for mobile networks was developed by Xu et al. [9]. A blockchain-based decentralized identity management system for public transportation was developed by Stockburger et al. [10]. Blockchain-based digital identity management for smart city management was proposed by Asamoah et al. [11]. A blockchain-based self-sovereign identity model that complies with OAuth 2.0 was designed by Hong et al. [12]. OAuth-Based Authorization and Delegation for Smart Home was defined by Mahalle et al. [3].

Unlike previous studies, our research differs in four ways, namely: (a) the user and owner data of the web resource were not stored within the smart contract; in this context, the authentication was performed through the Ethereum wallet, (b) a smart contract was developed to register the URL of the web resource, (c) a smart contract issues single-use authorization tokens for a specific web resource, and (d) a software development kit (SDK) was coded to facilitate the adoption and reuse of our model for any third-party web application.

3.3 Materials

A computer with the following features was used: 1 TB HDD, 32 GB RAM, 10th generation Intel Core i7 processor, and Windows 10 OS. Regarding the software, runtime environments, frameworks, and languages were necessary for building and debugging the approach. Below is a brief description of these.

- Node.js. Open source, cross-platform environment for developing, and running Java Script-based server applications.
- Node Package Manager (npm). Default package management system for Node.js.
- Visual Studio Code. Multilanguage code editor for building and debugging web and cloud applications.
- Ganache. Personal Ethereum Blockchain to test, inspect and execute smart contracts.
- Metamask. Ethereum wallet installed as a plugin for web browsers. It allows the storage of ERC-20 tokens, the execution of transactions in the blockchain and interaction with smart contracts.
- Solidity. Object-oriented language used to code and implement smart contracts on blockchain.
- TypeScript. JavaScript-based language at the application level. Code written in TypeScript requires a transpilation process before Node.js or any browser can run it.
- Truffle. Development environment for building, linking, and managing smart contracts. It provides a console for running command statements, and direct interaction with contracts.
- React. Open-source JavaScript library for building single-page applications.
- Next.js. Open-source web development framework based on Node.js for React applications.
- Vite. Modern web application packager. Frontend build tool. It is highly extensible through JavaScript API
- TSDX. A zero-config CLI for developing TypeScript-based libraries. It allows packaging and distributing the library using npm.

4 Results

In this section, an approach for granting access to web resources using OAuth 2.0 and blockchain was proposed. Three activities were addressed, namely: (1) the identification of versatilities that both technologies provide to the model, (2) description of how to use blockchain and OAuth 2.0 to grant access to a web resource via a third-party web application, and (3) development using smart contracts and web forms.

4.1 Blockchain and OAuth 2.0 Versatilities Applied to the Model.

This research proposes the use of OAuth 2.0 and blockchain to grant access to web resources. Three versatilities are identified, namely.

First, authorization and authentication. The combination of OAuth 2.0 with blockchain allows access authorization to be linked to a token, without requiring the web resource owner to be online to provide consent. In addition, users use a cryptocurrency wallet to sign authorization transactions and access web resources. For this, blockchain issues authorization tokens without the need for a central authorization server. Consequently, a user can authenticate using a third-party web application, without sharing their credentials.

Second, immutability of previously recorded data and events. Blockchain is immutable; thus, the registration, authentication and authorization policies encoded within a smart contract are transparent and immutable. In this way, the non-repudiation of behavior and the strict compliance of the participating entities is guaranteed.

Third, decentralized nature. It is an inherent characteristic of blockchain based schemes. The use of blockchain implies that registration, authentication, and authorization services are protected against denial-of-service attacks. This is because any P2P node (with administrative capabilities) can restore system functions and service requests.

4.2 How Do Blockchain and OAuth 2.0 Work Together to Grant Access to a Web Resource via Third-Party Web Application?

In our research, OAuth 2.0 solves the delegation problem using Blockchain. For this, we propose a study case for a user to access a web resource using a third-party web application. In this line, it is necessary to define the resources and actors that interact in this process:

- Web resource. It is the resource that requires an access authorization.
- Resource server. It is the server that hosts the web resource.
- Web resource owner. An entity with the ability to grant access to a protected resource. For this, the owner registers the resource URL within the blockchain using OAuth 2.0.
- User. End user or client who wants to obtain an authorization to access a web resource.
- Third-party web application. Web forms or external user interfaces used by the user to access a resource. In our case study, the application was used for functionality testing.
- Blockchain. P2P distributed ledger used to record the web resource URL, and provides authorization tokens for access to the resource. Blockchain replaces the authorization server used by OAuth 2.0 schemes.

A model overview is represented by two general functionalities. First, web resource registration. The web resource owner registers the application URL within the blockchain. Blockchain issues an identification token for each application.

Second, authentication and authorization. Through a third-party web application, the user wants access to a blockchain-protected web resource. For this, the following steps are necessary:

1 User requests a blockchain token. For this, user authenticates to blockchain and requests authorization to access a web resource.
2 Blockchain issues the token and provides the authorization for the user to access through the third-party web application. It should be mentioned that this token is valid only to access a specific resource.
3 The third-party web application uses the blockchain token, and the user accesses the web resource, without the need to share their credentials.

4.3 Model Development and Test

Model development was addressed through three stages: (1) development of smart contracts, (2) SDK (software development kit) for authentication using blockchain, and (3) development of web forms for functionality testing. Figure 2 shows the stages addressed in model development.

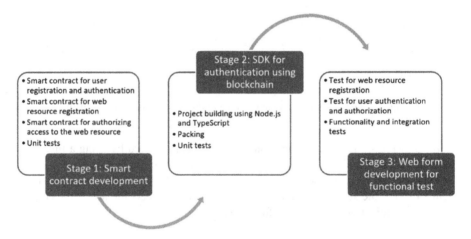

Fig. 2. Stages used for prototype development and testing

Stage 1: Smart Contract Development
Three smart contracts were developed to address the following main functionalities, namely: (i) user authentication, (i) web resource registration, and (ii) access authorization to web resource. In this context, Fig. 3 shows a layered overview for OAuth authorization based on blockchain.

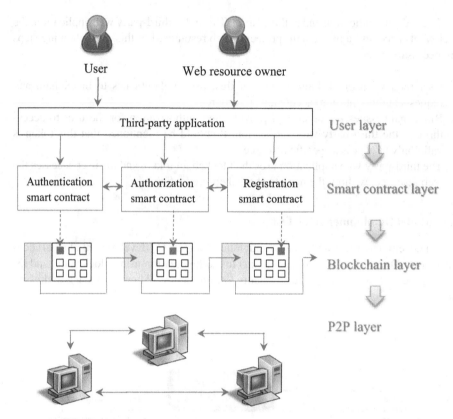

Fig. 3. A layered overview for OAuth authorization based on blockchain

(i) User registration and authentication. A user is registered by using a link token between the blockchain wallet and the web scheme. Through this token, the user can be authenticated in subsequent events, without the need to provide credentials again. Figure 4 shows the activity diagram for this functionality. In coding terms, the contract (named authentication. sol) has two functions:

- register_user(). It registers the user in the scheme through the blockchain wallet and generates a token for authentication.
- authenticate_user(). An authentication token links the web schema and the blockchain wallet. In this way, the user accesses the scheme, and an authorization process is executed transparently.

(ii) Web resource registration. This action is conducted by web resource owner. All tasks related to the registration of a web resource are encoded within the blockchain. Figure 5 shows the activity diagram for this functionality. For this, a contract is encoded to generate identification tokens for each web resource. In coding terms, the contract (called registration.sol) has two functions:

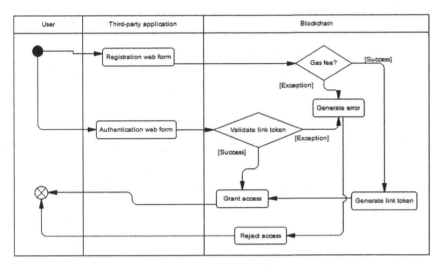

Fig. 4. Activity diagram for user registration and authentication

- generate_id_token(). The function generates unique tokens based on ERC721 specification.
- register_resource(). The function registers a web resource and receives two arguments: blockchain wallet address of the web resource owner, and web resource data (name, URL)

(iii) Application access authorization granted to the end user. The implementation of the OAuth 2.0 protocol was addressed. The particularity of this prototype lies in the absence of an authorization server to issue signed tokens. Therefore, the issuance and signature are carried out using the user wallet who wants to obtain authorization. Figure 6 shows the activity diagram for this functionality. In this line, the contract is coded to issue a link token between the user's wallet address and the web resource. In coding terms, the contract (called authorization.sol) has three main functions:

- link_user_web_resource (). After the registration of the web resource within the blockchain, it is necessary to implement an authentication flow using OAuth. The function generates unique tokens based on the ERC721 specification. In addition, the token must be generated only once, linking the web resource and the user's wallet address. If gas payment is successful, the scheme signs the token and authenticates the user.
- build_data_token(). The function saves the data inside the token using the ERC721 specification.
- sign_authorization_token(). The function enables token signing using the user's wallet.

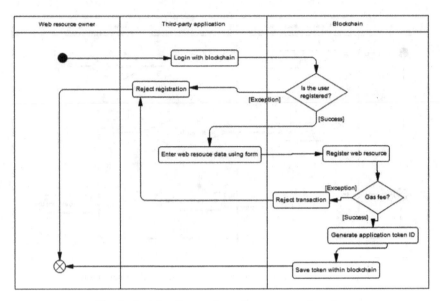

Fig. 5. Activity diagram for web resource registration

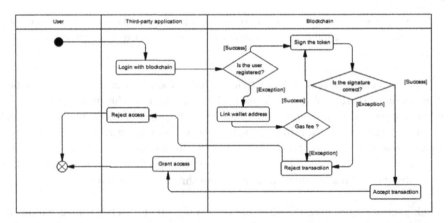

Fig. 6. Activity diagram for authorizing access to the web resource

Stage 2: SDK (Software Development Kit) for Authentication Using Blockchain
Once the functions necessary for the proper functioning of the system have been developed, it is ideal to pack all the functionality into a library that is easy to install and use. This activity was conducted through three consecutive steps:

1. Creating a project based on Node.js and TypeScript using the TSDX library. In this context, files are organized according to client and server functions.
2. Loading of configuration parameters. For the proper functioning of the SDK, the loading of the following parameters is necessary, namely: registration token identifier

of web resource, blockchain smart contract address, smart contract interface based on JSON format, and JSON-RPC server address.

3. Packaging. For a correct operation of the authentication process, it is necessary to encapsulate methods, functions, and attributes.

Stage 3: Web Form Development for Functionality Testing
Three main functionalities were developed for test, namely.

First, test for user registration. A page was designed to provide two forms of registration, namely:

- Via credentials. This registration is invoked when the "Sign up" button is clicked. The user registers the name, last name, email, and password (which are credentials that are stored using a database).
- Via blockchain wallet. This is functionality used to demonstrate the purpose of our research. A web form is developed to simulate a third-party web application. This form of registration is invoked when the button "Sign in with blockchain" is clicked. (Fig. 7). For this, the third-party application submits the user wallet address to the blockchain. In this line, registration smart contract links the wallet address with the web scheme. A gas payment must be executed to confirm the transaction. Next, an OAuth token is generated, signed, and validated for authentication purposes. In programming terms, the functions of the SDK are exported or abstracted into the button. In this way, blockchain solves the access delegation problem without the need for a registration server. Thus, the user does not need to share the credentials with third-party applications.

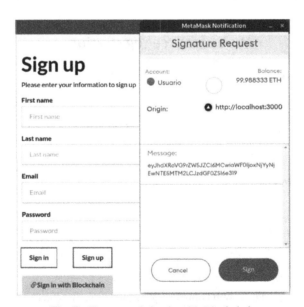

Fig. 7. Sing up and sign in with Blockchain

Second, test for web resource registration. A web form provides a communication interface between the web resource owner and the blockchain. In this context, web forms are created for the resource owner to register the web resource (Fig. 8). In coding terms, the functionality is as follows:

– Web resource_registration_form(). A resource owner registers web resource data using a web form. Then, the data is sent to the smart contract for registration within the blockchain.

Third, test for user authentication and authorization. A login page was designed to provide two forms of authentication, namely:

– Via credentials. This authentication is invoked when the "Sign in" button is clicked. The user accesses the application using email and password (which are credentials that was previously stored using a database).
– Via blockchain and OAuth 2.0. This is the authentication used to demonstrate the purpose of our research. A web form is developed to simulate a third-party web application. This authentication is invoked when the "Sign in with Blockchain" button is clicked (Fig. 9). For this, a user is authenticated using the blockchain wallet; in turn, the user is automatically authorized to use the web resource (which was previously registered by the owner of the resource). In programming terms, the functions of the SDK are exported, or abstracted into the button. In this way, blockchain solves the

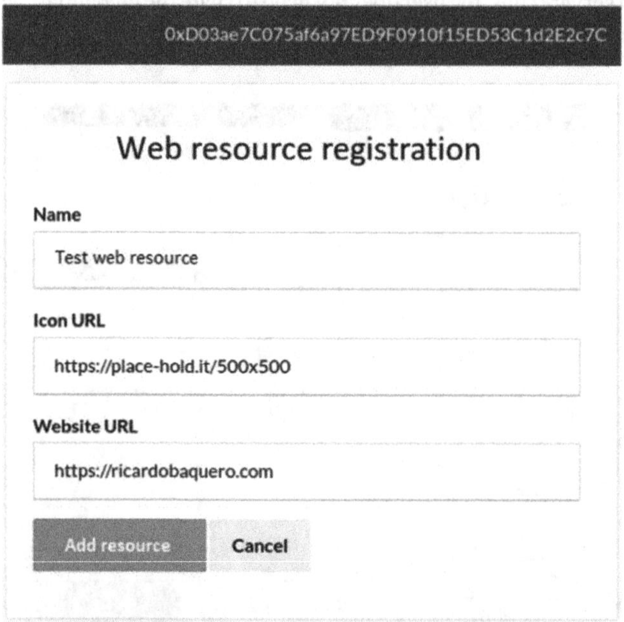

Fig. 8. Web Form for registering the web resource

access delegation problem without the need for an authorization server. Finally, the user does not need to share the credentials with third-party applications.

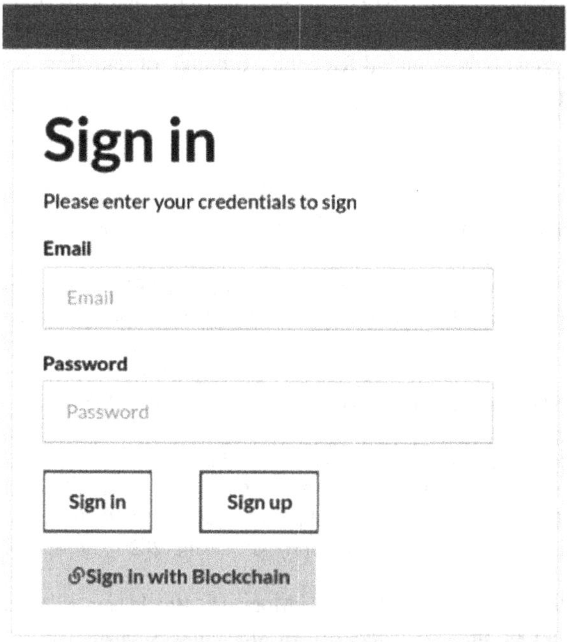

Fig. 9. Third-party web application for authentication using (a) credentials and (b) blockchain.

5   Conclusions

This research developed a blockchain-based approach to OAuth 2.0 authorization via a third-party web application. For this, a model for authorization and authentication was designed and coded using smart contracts. In this context, blockchain-based tokens were generated as proof of authorization. In this way, our approach removes the need for a central authorization server and provides the following contributions.

First, the model demonstrated the great potential that blockchain must solve the password fatigue problem. That is, users do not need to remember or maintain passwords because an Ethereum Wallet provides a valid authentication mechanism. In this context, the use of external authorization systems is not necessary, nor is the delivery of credentials to trusted third parties. It should be noted that no personal data of the user is recorded within the smart contract. Thus, the end user becomes the sole authority over their data and identity.

Second, the model reduced the amount of transactions for authentication and authorization. The only time the user interacts with the smart contracts is to get an authorization token.

Third, the packaging of our model inside an SDK. This ensures easy adoption and reuse of the model for any third-party web application.

Finally, the benefits of using blockchain and OAuth are evident to solve the problem of delegation of authorization. However, there are environments that demand higher security requirements. As future work, it is necessary to conduct research that combines our model with biometric-based authentication applications. In this way, the protection of a user's credentials is guaranteed for each exchange of data flow between platforms or unknown entities.

References

1. Wilson, Y., Hingnikar, A.: SAML 2.0. In: Hingnikar, A., Wilson, Y, (eds.) Solving identity management in modern applications, pp. 99–111. Apress (2019)
2. Siriwardena, P.: OAuth 2.0 Fundamentals. In: Advanced API Security. Apress (2020)
3. Mahalle, P.N., Shinde, G.R.: OAuth-Based authorization and delegation in smart home for the elderly using decentralized identifiers and verifiable credentials. In: Mahalle, P.N., Shinde, G.R., Dey, N., Hassanien, A.E. (eds.) Security Issues and Privacy Threats in Smart Ubiquitous Computing. SSDC, vol. 341, pp. 95–109. Springer, Singapore (2021). https://doi.org/10.1007/978-981-33-4996-4_6
4. Mendoza-Tello, J.C., Calderón-Hinojosa, X.: A blockchain-based approach to supporting reinsurance contracting. In: Botto-Tobar M., S. Gómez O., Rosero Miranda R., D.C.A. (eds) Advances in Emerging Trends and Technologies. ICAETT 2020. Advances in Intelligent Systems and Computing. pp. 252–263. Springer, Cham (2021). https://doi.org/10.1007/978-3-030-63665-4_20
5. Mendoza-Tello, J.C., Mendoza-Tello, T., Mora, H.: Blockchain as a healthcare insurance fraud detection tool. In: Visvizi, A., Lytras, M.D., and Aljohani, N.R. (eds.) Research and Innovation Forum 2020: Disruptive Technologies in Times of Change.Springer Proceedings in Complexity, p. 340. Springer, Cham (2020) https://doi.org/10.1007/978-3-030-62066-0_41
6. Mora, H., Mendoza-Tello, J.C., Varela-Guzmán, E.G., Szymanski, J.: Blockchain technologies to address smart city and society challenges. Comput. Human Behav. 122, (2021). https://doi.org/10.1016/j.chb.2021.106854
7. Tian, Z., Yan, B., Guo, Q., Huang, J., Du, Q.: Feasibility of identity authentication for IoT based on blockchain. Procedia Comput. Sci. **174**, 328–332 (2020). https://doi.org/10.1016/j.procs.2020.06.094
8. Shieh, M.-Z., Liu, J.-C., Kao, Y.-C., Tsai, S.-C., Lin, Y.-B.: OAuth-Based access control framework for IoT systems. In: Lin, Y.-B., Deng, D.-J. (eds.) SGIoT 2020. LNICSSITE, vol. 354, pp. 208–219. Springer, Cham (2021). https://doi.org/10.1007/978-3-030-69514-9_17
9. Xu, J., Xue, K., Tian, H., Hong, J., Wei, D.S.L., Hong, P.: An identity management and authentication scheme based on redactable blockchain for mobile networks. IEEE Trans. Veh. Technol. **69**, 6688–6698 (2020). https://doi.org/10.1109/TVT.2020.2986041
10. Stockburger, L., Kokosioulis, G., Mukkamala, A., Mukkamala, R.R., Avital, M.: Blockchain-enabled decentralized identity management: the case of self-sovereign identity in public transportation. Blockchain Res. Appl. **2**, 100014 (2021). https://doi.org/10.1016/j.bcra.2021.100014
11. Asamoah, K.O., et al.: Zero-Chain: a blockchain-based identity for digital city operating system. IEEE Internet Things J. **7**, 10336–10346 (2020). https://doi.org/10.1109/JIOT.2020.2986367
12. Hong, S., Kim, H.: Vaultpoint: a blockchain-based SSI model that complies with OAuth 2.0. Electron. 9, 1–20 (2020). https://doi.org/10.3390/electronics9081231

A Blockchain-Based Prototype to Support the Medical Prescription Control

Mario Morales-Morales, Julio C. Mendoza-Tello$^{(\boxtimes)}$ (iD), and Michael Ponce-Cevallos

Facultad de Ingeniería y Ciencias Aplicadas, Universidad Central del Ecuador, Quito, Ecuador
{mmoralesm,jcmendoza,mfponce}@uce.edu.ec

Abstract. Supervision of medical prescriptions involves challenges related to counterfeiting, self-medication, traceability, and fraud. In this process, three actors were identified, namely: doctor, patient, and pharmacist. These users require the information be integrated and immutable using a secure and reliable scheme. Faced with these issues, blockchain is a disruptive technology that provides trust between strangers without the need for third-party supervision. Thus, cryptographic algorithms are implemented to achieve a decentralized consensus on the transactional validity of the scheme. As a result, the objective of this research is to develop a prototype based on blockchain to support medical prescription control. To do this, a methodology is conducted through four essential steps, namely: requirements specification, process diagram, model development and application integration. Conclusions and future work are described at the end of the document.

Keywords: Blockchain · Smart contracts · Medical prescription

1 Introduction

In Ecuador, the population of cities reports self-medication practices between 37% and 94% [1]. In addition, the consumption of narcotics (such as heroin) is a national health problem, including 2.5% of high school graduates Ecuadorians report heroin consumption. Counterfeit medical prescriptions to satisfy the consumption of substances known as opioids [2]. These problems can largely be addressed through the control of medical prescriptions (which come from medical centers and hospitals). A medical prescription can be registered as a digital asset within a database. However, it is necessary that this prescription is not altered or falsified.

With these challenges, blockchain is a technology that guarantees the integrity, immutability, traceability, and security of digital assets, guaranteeing non-repudiation of behavior among its participants, without the need for third parties (which are exposed to corruption events)[3]. For this reason, this research proposes a blockchain-based model for the control of medical prescriptions.

The structure of the document is as follows. Section 2 explains the methodology addressed in the research. Briefly, Sect. 3 describes the concepts, software and hardware used. Section 4 explains the results obtained according to the phases defined by the methodology. Finally, conclusions and new research challenges are proposed at the end of the document (Sect. 5).

M. Botto-Tobar et al. (Eds.): ICAT 2022, CCIS 1755, pp. 455–465, 2023.
https://doi.org/10.1007/978-3-031-24985-3_33

2 Methodology

This research focuses on four main phases, namely: requirements specification, process diagram, model development, and application validation. Figure 1 shows a Research phases overview carried out.

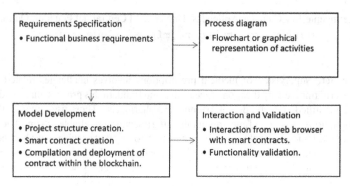

Fig. 1. Research phases overview

3 Materials and Background

Briefly, theoretical concepts, hardware and software are described.

3.1 Core Concepts

This investigation was addressed through three important concepts. First, Blockchain. It is a ledger based on decentralization principles and cryptographic techniques. In this context, blockchain is a disruptive technology because it changes the established paradigm in society; that is, instead of relying on a third party or control authority, this technology relies on the veracity of cryptographic proofs validated by the participating nodes of the network [4]. Furthermore, blockchain could transport any digital asset (such as cryptocurrencies and smart contracts) on top of its structure [5]. Blockchain is made up of a group of blocks linked sequentially through a header hash. In turn, each block is made up of a set of transactions, which are encrypted using a Merkle tree [6].

Second, smart contract. It represents a set of encodings that respond to predefined rules. A smart contract (implemented on the blockchain) inherits the property of immutability; that is, it cannot be altered. In this way, the scheme provides guarantee of compliance of the parties without the need for trusted third parties [7]. This research uses Solidity (as a programming language for smart contracts) because it provides a set of libraries, functions, modifiers, structures and inheritance, features that support high-level programming [8].

Third, decentralized consensus mechanism. It is a protocol that allows to obtain an agreement about the final version of the blockchain; that is, the sequential order of transactions or history of events. When a user makes a transaction, it is propagated and validated throughout the network. This research uses proof of work as a consensus mechanism[9].

3.2 Hardware and Software

A computer with the following features is used: 16 GB RAM, 8th generation Intel Core i7 processor, 1 TB HDD, 1 GB graphic card, and Windows 10 OS. In this line, the following software was used, namely.

- Node.js, a JavaScript-based environment used to run HTML 5.
- React.js, a JavaScript-based library used to create single page applications.
- Bootstrap, a set of tools used to design web interfaces based on HTML and CSS.
- IntelliJ Idea, an integrated development environment (IDE) used to program web applications and smart contracts.
- Truffle.js, a framework used for developing and deploying Ethereum-based smart contracts.
- Ganache, a personal Ethereum blockchain used to execute, deploy, and test transactions.
- Metamask, a cryptocurrency software installed over a web browser, and used to interact with the Ethereum blockchain.
- Web3.js, a library collection used to integrate Metamask, React and smart contract.

4 Experiments and Results

According to the methodology (Fig. 1), this research presents the results for each phase.

4.1 Requirements Specification

It is against this background that, two functional requirements were identified. First, user management. Requirements related to user authentication, role management and privileges were identified. To do this, it is necessary to execute the following activities, namely: (i) creation of a personalized access modifier through a wallet, (ii) definition of a connection between the web application and the digital wallet manager, (iii) creation of users (patient, doctor, pharmacist), and (iv) display of options menu according to user role.

Second, administration of medical prescriptions. Requirements related to the management of medical prescriptions provided by doctors were identified. To do this, it is necessary to carry out the following activities, namely: (v) coding of a friendly form to record prescription data, (vi) display of medical prescription history, and (vii) prescription download (pdf format).

4.2 Process Diagram Phase

According to the requirements, Fig. 2 shows the activities identified for our case study.

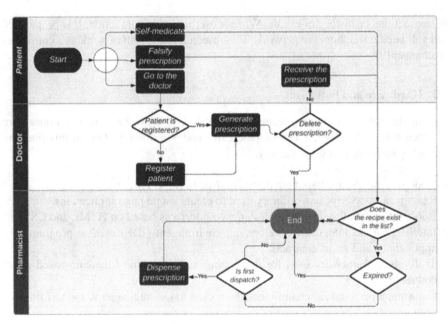

Fig. 2. Model flowchart.

4.3 Model Development Phase

Three activities were carried out for this phase. First, project structure creation. Figure 3 shows the directory tree of the React.js-based project. In this context, a connection to the blockchain is made using Truffle. Additionally, four folders and files were automatically created, namely:

– Contracts folder, which contains smart contracts.

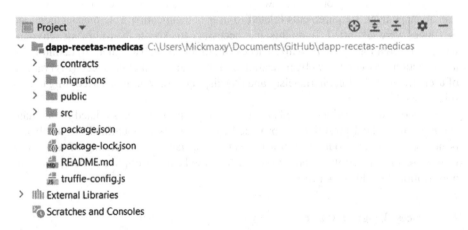

Fig. 3. Project directory tree

- Migrations folder, which contains JavaScript files that provide an interface between solidity-based coding and the web application,
- src and public folders, which store the source code of the web application.
- package.json, which contains the dependencies configuration
- truffle-config.js, which contains the necessary configuration to connect to the blockchain network.

Second, creation of the smart contract. Solidity language version 0.8 was used to code the smart contracts. This version incorporates a special feature known as ABI Encoder V2, which allows structures and variables to be embedded as function parameters. A smart contract was basically coded by three core elements:

- Five structures were defined (with their respective members), namely: doctor structure (professional license, names, surnames, specialty), patient structure (identification, names, surnames, email, cell phone), medicine structure (name, indication), pharmaceutical structure (identification, name), and medical prescription structure (identifier, doctor, patient, diagnosis, indications, medicines, date).
- Nine state variables were defined and permanently stored within the contract. It is important to highlight the use of a complex structure called mapping, which has a key with its corresponding value. The first variable is used to create a prescription, which was added to the prescription array (second state variable); the following variables verify the existence of a doctor or a pharmacist, and the total number of patients attended.
- Functions were defined to support business rules for registration, query, deletion of patients and prescriptions. Figure 4 shows a summary of the smart contract design.

Third, smart contract compilation and deployment. In this activity, a suitable environment is prepared for the implementation of the smart contract. Three configuration files stand out, namely:

- truffle-config.js, which contains the essential configurations to compile, and connect to the blockchain network.
- Migrations. Sol, which is a Truffle smart contract used for deployment.
- 1_initial_migrations.js, which monitors and ensures no duplicate migrations.

```
struct medicine { }
struct doctor { }
struct patient { }
struct pharmacist { }
struct prescription { }

Prescription private prescription;
Prescription[ ] private prescriptions;
mapping (address => Doctor) public doctors;
mapping (address => Patient) public patients;
mapping (address => bool) public associateDoctorAccount;
mapping (address => bool) public associatePharmacistAcoount;
mapping (address => Patient []) public patientsByDoctor;
mapping (address => uint) public patientsTotalByDoctor;
mapping (address => Pharmacist) public Pharmacists;

function admitPatient();
function admitPrescription();
function getPrescription();
function removePrescription();
function sentPrescription();
```

Fig. 4. Smart contract design

4.4 Interaction and Validation Phase

Two activities carried out for this phase. First, interaction with the smart contract. Metamask was used for asynchronous method creation and access to Web3 objects. In this way, user access from the web is safe and guaranteed. Figure 5 shows the wallet addresses of users connected to the blockchain using Metamask, for example: (1) it represents the address through which the smart contract was deployed, (2) it represents the wallet addresses of enabled medical users, and (3) it represents the address of the wallet of the pharmacy that distributes the medicine. Other addresses were assigned to patient wallets.

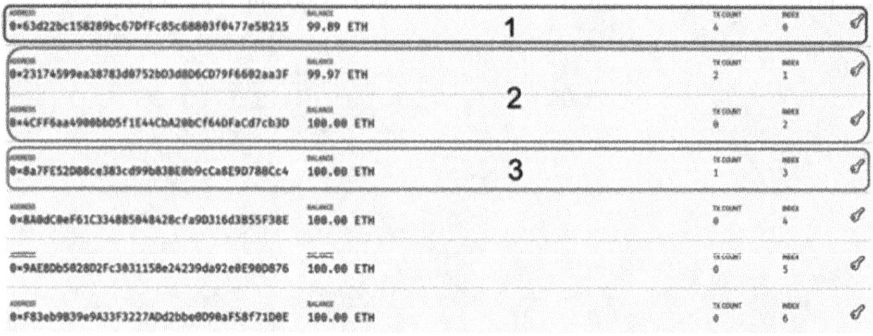

Fig. 5. User wallet addresses using the Ganache console.

Second, functionality validation. Three functionalities stand out, namely:

- Patient registration. In our application, a doctor registers patient information data within the system (Appendix A). For this, a medical user must authenticate. After user validation, the doctor will perform the following sequential steps, namely: registration of the requested data, and confirmation of the transaction by paying an amount of GAS for each registration action within the blockchain. Appendix A shows the transaction recorded within the blockchain using the TX DATA field.
- Preparation of medical prescriptions. Previously, both the medicine and the patient must be registered in the system. In our app, a doctor records a prescription (Appendix B). For this, the doctor will carry out three sequential steps, namely: patient selection, medicine selection and prescription generation. Appendix B shows the transaction recorded within the blockchain using the TX DATA field.
- Search for medical prescriptions. A registered recipe can be viewed. The doctor can download (pdf format) or delete the prescription. If the remove action is executed, the pharmacist cannot fill the prescription because it will disappear from the list. If the prescription was sent, the doctor will be able to view the prescription, but will not be able to delete it, the button will be automatically locked (Appendix C). It should be noted that the user will not have the option to delete a medical prescription. Appendix D shows the medical prescription (pdf format).

4.5 Previous Studies

Previous studies have developed blockchain-based models to support healthcare activities. A distributed architecture model to integrate health records was developed by Roehrs et al. [10]. The model addresses the unified view of health records, as well as access to updated data by patients and doctors. Furthermore, a review of the blockchain application for the health system was conducted by Cirstea et al. [11]. The review presents Blockchain technology as a tool for the decentralization of health care processes. Efficient and scalable health record management using Blockchain technology was also discussed by Mukherji et al. [12]. Finally, Misbhauddin et al. [13] propose an architecture to develop blockchain applications using IPFS (InterPlanetary File System); this allows physicians, lab technicians, and patients to manage medical records. Unlike previous studies, our research proposes a web prototype that supports the control of medical prescriptions to guarantee immutability, integrity, and security of digital assets.

5 Conclusions

5.1 Contributions

In our research, the case study is the control of medical prescriptions. For this, a model based on blockchain, and smart contract was developed. In that case, four phases were conducted, namely: requirements specifications, process diagram, model development, interaction, and validation. With these considerations, the main contribution is to provide a prototype that avoids self-medication and forgery of medical prescriptions. Thus, a decentralized, secure application focused on three main users (doctor, patient, and pharmacist) is provided.

5.2 Future Works

There are still many challenges to be solved. Blockchain adoption is in the early stages of development. In this context, it is necessary to define clear policies, and viable procedures that contribute to making visible the versatilities and benefits of this technology. One of these challenges is to achieve the integration of doctors and pharmacies to make a leap from the traditional prescription system to a blockchain-based ecosystem. As future work, it is suggested to extend and integrate the model to other requirements of the health area (such as: medical records, laboratory tests, and radiographs). Once this happens, it does not mean that the traditional systems will be replaced, rather they will work together; that is, both will be a complement to the other and will offer greater benefits to society.

Appendix A: Patient registration

See Fig. 6

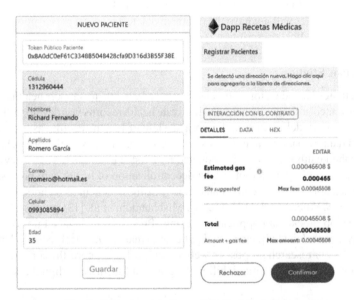

Fig. 6. Patient registration within the blockchain

Appendix B: Prescription registration

See Fig. 7

1312960444 - Richard Fernando Romero G...
Diagnóstico
Inflamación Lumbar
Seleccionar Medicamentos
Medicina Recetada Indicación Acción
1 VOLTAREN AEROSOL Solución para pulverización cutánea 11.60 mg 1, cada 6 horas Quitar
2 NAPROXENO PARACETAMOL GENAMERICA Comprimido 300 mg+275 mg 8, tomar 2 al día Quitar
Indicaciones Extras
Reposo y Ejercicios de estiramiento diarios
Fecha de Caducidad: 25/2/2022
Generar Receta
Dapp Recetas Médicas
Registrar Recetas
Account 2
0x0be...9A84
Se detectó una dirección nueva. Haga clic aquí para agregarla a la libreta de direcciones.
DETALLES DATA HEX
TIPO DE FUNCIÓN: Interacción Con El Contrato
DATOS HEXADECIMALES: 1988 BYTES

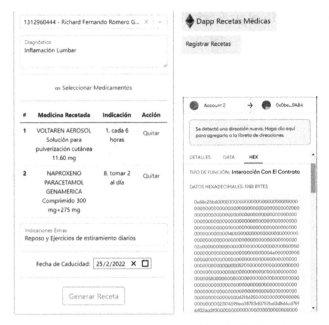

Fig. 7. Prescription registration within the blockchain

Appendix C: Search for medical prescriptions

See Fig. 8

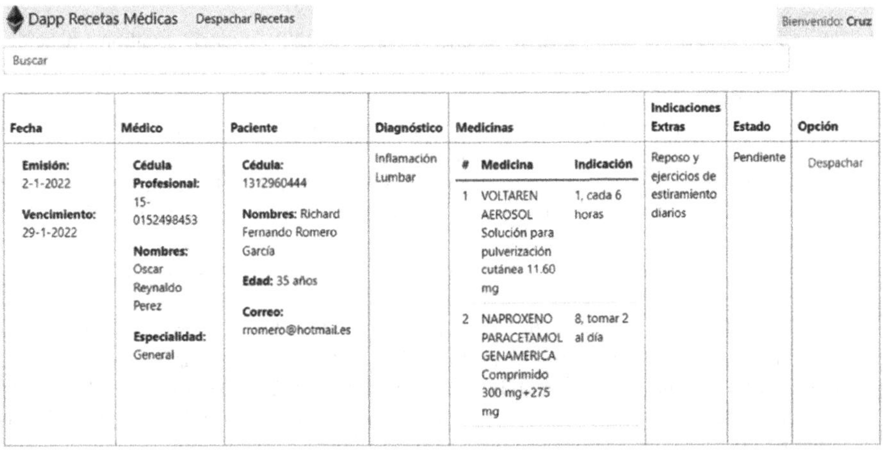

Dapp Recetas Médicas
Despachar Recetas
Bienvenido: Cruz
Buscar
Fecha
Médico
Paciente
Diagnóstico
Medicinas
Indicaciones Extras
Estado
Opción
Emisión: 2-1-2022
Vencimiento: 29-1-2022
Cédula Profesional: 15-0152498453
Nombres: Oscar Reynaldo Perez
Especialidad: General
Cédula: 1312960444
Nombres: Richard Fernando Romero García
Edad: 35 años
Correo: rromero@hotmail.es
Inflamación Lumbar
Medicina Indicación
1 VOLTAREN AEROSOL Solución para pulverización cutánea 11.60 mg 1, cada 6 horas
2 NAPROXENO PARACETAMOL GENAMERICA Comprimido 300 mg+275 mg 8, tomar 2 al día
Reposo y ejercicios de estiramiento diarios
Pendiente
Despachar

Fig. 8. Search for medical prescriptions

Appendix D: Medical prescription (PDF format)

See Fig. 9

Fig. 9. Medical prescription (PDF format)

References

1. Ponce-Zea, J.E., Ponce-Zea, D.M., Rivadeneira-Cando, J.D.: Prevalencia de automedicación: estudio exploratorio en la provincia de Manabí, Ecuador. Dominio las Ciencias. 5, 27 (2019). https://doi.org/10.23857/dc.v5i3.922
2. Escobar-Lema, A.E.: Factores de protección y éxito que aportan a corto plazo a la abstinencia en pacientes ecuatorianos adictos a opioides (2018)
3. Mendoza-Tello, J.C., Mendoza-Tello, T., Villacís-Ramón, J.: A Blockchain-Based Approach for Issuing Health Insurance Contracts and Claims. In: Botto-Tobar, M., S. Gómez, O., Rosero Miranda, R., Díaz Cadena, A., Montes León, S., Luna-Encalada, W. (ed.) Lecture Notes in Networks and Systems, pp. 250–260. Springer, Cham (2022) https://doi.org/10.1007/978-3-030-96147-3_20
4. Mendoza-Tello, J.C., Calderón-Hinojosa, X.: A blockchain-based approach to supporting reinsurance contracting. In: Botto-Tobar, M., S. Gómez O., Rosero Miranda, R., D.C.A. (ed.) Advances in Emerging Trends and Technologies. ICAETT 2020. Advances in Intelligent Systems and Computing, pp. 252–263. Springer, Cham (2021) https://doi.org/10.1007/978-3-030-63665-4_20
5. Sharma, P., Jindal, R., Borah, M.D.: A review of blockchain-based applications and challenges. Wireless Pers. Commun. **123**, 1201–1243 (2021). https://doi.org/10.1007/s11277-021-09176-7
6. Antonopoulos, A.: Mastering Bitcoin: Unlocking Digital Crypto-Currencies. O'Reilly Media Inc, Sebastopol, CA (2015)

7. Palma, L.M., Gomes, F.O., Vigil, M., Martina, J.E.: A transparent and privacy-aware approach using smart contracts for car insurance reward programs. In: Garg, D., Kumar, N.V.N., Shyamasundar, R.K. (eds.) ICISS 2019. LNCS, vol. 11952, pp. 3–20. Springer, Cham (2019). https://doi.org/10.1007/978-3-030-36945-3_1

8. Zheng, G., Gao, L., Huang, L., Guan, J.: Solidity advanced topics. In: Ethereum Smart Contract Development in Solidity, pp. 85–136. Springer, Singapore (2021). https://doi.org/10.1007/978-981-15-6218-1_4

9. Nakamoto, S.: Bitcoin: a peer-to-peer electronic cash system (2009)

10. Roehrs, A., da Costa, C.A., da Rosa Righi, R.: OmniPHR: a distributed architecture model to integrate personal health records. J. Biomed. Inform. **71**, 70–81 (2017). https://doi.org/10.1016/j.jbi.2017.05.012

11. Cirstea, A., Enescu, F.M., Bizon, N., Stirbu, C., Ionescu, V.M.: Blockchain technology applied in health the study of blockchain application in the health system (II). In: Proceedings of the 10th International Conference on Electronics, Computers and Artificial Intelligence, ECAI 2018, pp. 1–4. IEEE (2019)

12. Mukherji, A., Ganguli, N.: Efficient and scalable electronic health record management using permissioned blockchain technology. In: 4th International Conference on Electronics, Materials Engineering and Nano-Technology (IEMENTech) 2020. (2020). https://doi.org/10.1109/IEMENTech51367.2020.9270106

13. Misbhauddin, M., Alabdulatheam, A., Aloufi, M., Al-Hajji, H., Alghuwainem, A.: MedAccess: a scalable architecture for blockchain-based health record management. In: 2nd International Conference on Computer and Information Sciences, ICCIS 2020, pp. 1–5 (2020)

Identification System Based on Facial Recognition Services in the Cloud

Saul Obando[1], Darwin Alulema[1,2]([✉]), Rodrigo Silva[1], and Nicolás Padilla[2]

[1] Universidad de Las Fuerzas Armadas ESPE, Sangolquí, Ecuador
{smobando,doalulema,rsilva}@espe.edu.ec
[2] Applied Computing Group, University of Almería, Almería, Spain
npadilla@ual.es

Abstract. Currently, important approaches such as the Web of Things (WoT) have emerged, making web services such as those offered by cloud computing integrated with smart objects. This is how it is proposed to use facial recognition services for the implementation of a personal identification system. The proposal integrates sensors, storage services and APIs for face detection, identification and aggregation of people using the Microsoft Azure cloud through REST services. To verify the functioning of the system, the percentage of reliability of face recognition in the periods of day and night, performance and usability are evaluated.

Keywords: Cloud computing · Facial recognition · Cloud computing · REST

1 Introduction

Currently, most countries have a video surveillance service to monitor activities that may generate risky situations [1]. In this sense, the Web of Things (WoT) has facilitated the integration of new services such as image recognition in the cloud [2] with specific hardware. This integration provides processing power that sensors do not have. A type of image recognition is facial identification that allows several applications, one of the most notable is to carry out security controls in parks, hospitals, banks, means of transport to counteract crimes and emergencies.

The use of facial identification has several applications, one of the most notable is to carry out security controls in parks, hospitals, banks, means of transport to counteract crimes and emergencies. In China, for example, facial identification is used in the Beijing subway to separate groups of people based on security credits, for people with abnormal feedback, they capture the thousands of faces of passengers who will be subjected to additional controls. Likewise, the use of platforms as a service helps the proposal of the identification system since it reduces the complexity of the infrastructure, simplifies the code and allows each service to be managed independently to later relate them to facilitate the configuration and administration of the elements. of the system such as the image recognition and identification modules. In addition, the use of the platform as a service allows improving security and adjusting the computational resources required by the system.

This work proposes a personal identification system based on facial recognition services in the cloud, which has an interface that allows the user to train new images. The digital camera captures photos of the face. These are transmitted to the cloud service platform, in which face recognition is performed, which selects the facial characteristics and the identification module that will carry out the identification process. Compare the face of the person with the faces that were trained and presents a percentage of reliability for the identification of the person.

This article is structured with the following sections: (i) related works, where some of the works that follow the line of research are commented; (ii) system design, the FrontEnd, the BackEnd, and the hardware; (iii) implementation, deal with the specific details of the technologies used for the deployment of the system, (iv) tests and results, to validate the proposal, usability, load and operation tests are carried out, and (v) conclusions and future works that emerge from the investigation.

2   Related Works

The search for articles was done in IEEE Xplore, MDPI, ScienceDirect and Springer Link. Within the applications and fields of action of facial recognition, they have been implemented to maintain order, assist in security, health and education as mentioned in [8], which Deep Learning was implemented for facial recognition. [9], apply facial recognition to be used in security in homes and offices, [10] use recognition services for the identification of people's faces in hospitals or through the face for patients who, when detecting some type of fatigue that alerts medical personnel, in [11] it was implemented in intelligent security systems through facial recognition.

The devices that were used to carry out the processing or capture of photographs is very varied since it depends on the place where it is going to be implemented and what its purpose will be, as mentioned in [12] in which occupies a Raspberry Pi to perform the processing of information that comes from capturing faces through a mobile device, [13] occupies the same Raspberry Pi for image processing in addition to RFID technology that helps improve the registration of students, together with a webcam, [14] proposes a recognition system through a system of video surveillance cameras controlled from a computer which performs the recognition in conjunction with a server in the cloud, [15] performs the recognition through of video surveillance cameras connected to a DVR, from which the video recordings are extracted and subsequent recognition is made in the time that the motion sensors were activated.

In addition to the integration of devices and services as well as their programming, there are several software products or IoT frameworks that allow requests to be made to facial recognition services in the cloud, among which we can mention [17] that uses Node-RED to connect the cameras with character recognition APIs to establish surveillance and license plate monitoring, like [18] which, through Node-RED, controls the photo capture of a Raspberry Pi and makes requests to a facial recognition service in the cloud in Indoor test environments, [19] they use BLYNK as an IoT platform for Android and iOS devices and THINGSPEAK to establish a platform where it is deployed in a database of the age and gender of the people, statistically. In [20] they prefer to use libraries that facilitate facial recognition such as Open CV, TensorFlow for machine learning to develop the recognition system directly in programming languages such as Java or Python.

Finally, the selection of the cloud service platform was based on the quality of service offered by each one in various investigations and their results in the implementation of recognition systems. In [21] an analysis of the service platforms that perform recognition is carried out, in the study a facial verification simulation is carried out, in which 2000 pairs of facial images are selected from the data set. One thousand pairs of them contain faces with different identities, another 1000 pairs contain faces with the same identity. After receiving the service requests, the platform returns the similarity confidence between each pair of facial images. Trust determines that two faces belong to the same person. In which the results were that AWS has greater precision, along with Tencent and Azure, while the processing time latency was lower for Baidu and Microsoft Azure with 250 ms. In addition, the same procedure is carried out for OCR and video, from which it can be concluded that the Microsoft Azure cloud facial recognition service is one of the best due to its high accuracy and data processing capacity.

However, in other works, they carry out an approach to a certain QoS variable according to the recognition system developed in each study, of which we can highlight the work of [22], in which the transmission speed tests were obtained which for upload was 1,409 kbps while the download rate was 3,692 kbps for a CPU speed of 1GHz with 576 MB of RAM. In [23] it is analysed according to the response time to the recognition services and according to the size of the image, it evaluates the mobile phone whose CPU speed is 1.6GHz with 1GB of memory, in the best of cases. Cases for an image size of 50X50 allows energy savings of 66.7% and access latency by 54.3%, which confirms that using cloud recognition services can be viable and do not perform a great consumption of computational resources and energy in the implementation of these services.

3 Proposed Architecture

The first stage of the system includes the capture and transmission of images, which will be controlled by the microprocessor so that every so often, depending on the movement or proximity of people, the sensors activate the capture of images and these, in turn, are sent to the cloud service platform for face recognition to be performed. In this phase, facial characteristics are discriminated against, and the identification module compares the person's face with the faces that were trained in the system. The design of the block diagram of the identification system is indicated in Fig. 1. The Backend corresponds to the facial recognition services and the management service that allows entering the images for training. In addition, there is hardware made up of a microprocessor that controls the camera and the sensors that detect movement when a person passes in front of the camera. On the Frontend side is the interface that consumes the services and that allows the user to enter their session to manage the system.

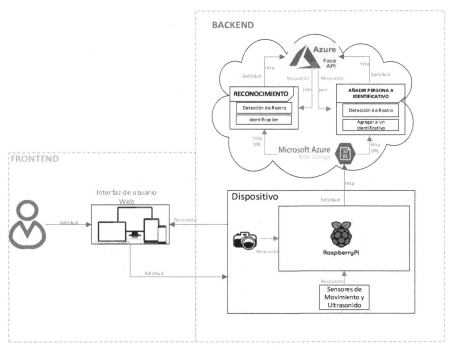

Fig. 1. Block diagram of the person identification system based on facial recognition services in the cloud.

4 System Implementation

The development of the recognition system is divided into 2 different processes which use the Recognition and Identification services: (a) Recognition of people, and (b) Adding people to an identifier.

For the development of the project, the services in the Azure cloud were used, such as the API Face and Azure Blob Storage, which will be used and implemented in the Node-RED software, for this, the Raspbian operating system must be previously installed together with the desktop and the Node-RED framework for the Raspberry Pi, for this the following steps must be followed.

Azure Blob Storage
First of all, you must select the option to create resources, locate yourself in the Storage category and select storage accounts, as indicated in Fig. 2.

Fig. 2. Create the Azure Container resource (taken from Microsoft Azure, 2021).

As a second step, the data that needs to be filled is displayed, such as giving the name of the resource group, name of the Storage Account, the Region in which the resource is going to be located and the performance that depends on the type of Account from Azure, finally, Review and Create must be selected, as indicated in Fig. 3.

Fig. 3. Azure Container resource specification configuration (taken from Microsoft Azure, 2021).

Once the account has been created, you must select the Containers option and select the name for the Blob, and then select the access keys that can be used to make requests to the Azure Blob Storage applications, as indicated in Fig. 4.

Fig. 4. Key generation for Azure Container (borrowed from Microsoft Azure, 2021)

Face API

First of all, a new resource must be created, located in the IA and Machine Learning category and select the Face option in Create, as indicated in Fig. 5.

Fig. 5. Creation of the Face API resource (taken from Microsoft Azure, 2021).

As a second step, the data that needs to be filled is displayed, such as giving the name of the resource group, name of the Storage Account, the Region in which the resource is going to be located and the performance that depends on the type of Storage Account. Azure, finally, Review and Create must be selected, as indicated in Fig. 6.

Finally, to use the resource in Node-RED, you must select Access keys, which will allow you to authenticate FACE API application requests through the generated key, as indicated in Fig. 7.

Fig. 6. Face API resource specification configuration (taken from Microsoft Azure, 2021).

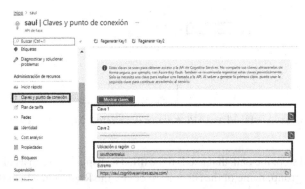

Fig. 7. Key generation for the Face API resource (taken from Microsoft Azure, 2021).

Electronic Circuit Design

The connection diagram of the electronic elements such as the sensors, the fan and the camera is directly connected to the raspberry pi as indicated in Fig. 8.

Web Interface

The design of the graphic environment was developed through the nodes of the node-red framework, in which the processes of recognizing people and adding a person can be carried out, as indicated in Fig. 9.

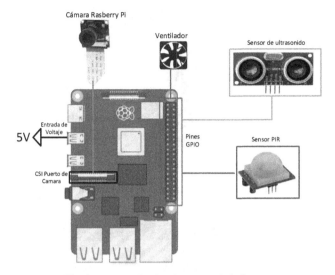

Fig. 8. Electronic circuit connection diagram

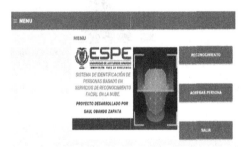

Fig. 9. Menu window.

When selecting the Recognition option, it will request the entry of the identification which denotes the group of people to which the client belongs and then a screen will be displayed in which the photograph of the person captured by the sensors and the information of the person recognized with a percentage of coincidence, as indicated in Fig. 10.

In the add person window, a form is presented in which you ask to register your name, surname, and identification to which you belong or create a new group, when you select accept, the person's face will be captured, then, a screen is presented with the face of the person who was captured when registering their data and the information with which they registered, as indicated in Fig. 11.

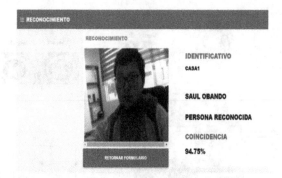

Fig. 10. Facial recognition process information window

Fig. 11. Add people process information window

Functionality test

In the performance test, the environment for the recognition of the people in the home is carried out during the day and night periods to analyse the accuracy of the system, for which the device will be installed on the home door. To verify the operation, the system will be submitted to the following simulation, for which four people from the household will be registered as belonging to an identifier called house 8, in which the accuracy of the recognition in the environment described above is compared, as indicated in Table 1.

Table 1. Tests of operation of the same identifier

User	Day		Evening	
	Precision	Condition	Precision	Condition
U1	98.06%	Recognized	94.12%	Recognized
U2	92.65%	Recognized	92.49%	Recognized
U3	95.54%	Recognized	84.16%	Recognized
U4	97.59%	Recognized	91.53%	Recognized
Average	**95.96%**		**90.58%**	

According to the results obtained from the system, it can be said that the precision value increases in the day 5% compared to the night period, however, both comply with the recognition, since they exceed the specified threshold of the 80% that allows to recognize or ignore the face of the person.

Usability testing

This type of test is intended to quantify the user's interaction experience with a device. For the preparation of the usability test, the SUS test will be used, which through a survey of 10 questions with 5 different response ratings according to the Likert Scale) (1 to 5), from 5 (strongly agree), up to 1 (strongly disagree).

The usability test will be carried out by 10 people, through which the evaluation of the developed application will be known. This SUS value should be expressed as a percentage. Table 2 shows the average and results of the usability tests.

Table 2. SUS score of surveyed users

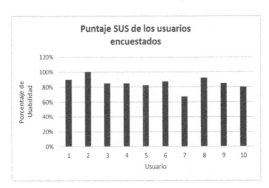

The average of the SUS scores of all the users surveyed is 85.5%, which indicates that the application is very favourable for users. It should be noted that the percentage could be improved if the client is instructed and guided in the web application. And device since the survey reflects that the client perceives inconsistencies and that he needs technical support.

5   Conclusion and Future Work

This document presented developed a facial identification system based on facial recognition services in the cloud. The system uses the services of Face API and Azure Blob Storage, from Microsoft Azure, which was integrated with the physical device through Node-RED. In addition, a hardware device was implemented that allows the capture of faces through a camera and motion and ultrasound sensors that allow the recognition of people, which are connected to the Raspberry Pi microcomputer. The following conclusions have been identified from this work:

- Through the performance tests, it was evaluated that the system works correctly in the periods of the day and at night, in which they presented an average value of the degree of the reliability of 95.96% and 90.58%, respectively.
- When carrying out the usability tests, the system obtained 85.5%, which is considered a good assessment to implement the recognition system, however, the type of users and the application must be considered. Which will be implemented.

The following lines of research emerge from the work: (a) Implement facial recognition through detection algorithms, which works alongside the facial recognition service in the cloud, which works in situations where the Internet is not available; (b) Add to the facial recognition system other sensors that help to specify the detection or another identification system such as biometrics, RFID, among others, that allows increasing the security and reliability of the systems, in addition to other systems that facilitate the registration of people to through virtual assistants; and (c) Implement security mechanisms through SSL certificates of authenticity and data encryption in the web application to improve user privacy.

References

1. Servicio integrado de seguridad ECU 911: Rendición de cuentas 2019. Diciembre 2019. [En línea]. shttps://www.ecu911.gob.ec/rendicion-de-cuentas-2019/
2. Rui y, J., Danpeng, S.: Architecture design of the internet of things based on cloud computing, pp. 1–4. IEEE (2015)
3. Smith y, M., Miller, S.: Correction to: the ethical application of biometric facial recognition technology. AI & Soc (2021)
4. Kendall Roundtree, A.: Testing Facial Recognition Software for Young Adults and Adolescents: An Integrative Review. In: Moallem, A. (ed.) HCII 2021. LNCS, vol. 12788, pp. 50–65. Springer, Cham (2021). https://doi.org/10.1007/978-3-030-77392-2_4
5. Sabharwal, T., Gupta, R.: Facial marks for enhancing facial recognition after plastic surgery. Int J Inf. Technol. **13**(1), 391–396 (2020). https://doi.org/10.1007/s41870-020-00566-x
6. Che, S., Kamphuis y, P., Kim, J.: A comparative analysis of attention to facial recognition payment between china and South Korea: a news analysis using latent Dirichlet allocation (2021)
7. Nemmaoui, S., Elhammani, S.: A new approach based on steganography to face facial recognition vulnerabilities against fake identities. In: Fakir, M., Baslam, M., El Ayachi, R. (eds.) CBI 2021. LNBIP, vol. 416, pp. 269–283. Springer, Cham (2021). https://doi.org/10.1007/978-3-030-76508-8_19
8. Belhouchette, K.: Facial recognition to identify emotions: an application of deep learning. In: Saeed, F., Mohammed, F., Al-Nahari, A. (eds.) IRICT 2020. LNDECT, vol. 72, pp. 496–504. Springer, Cham (2021). https://doi.org/10.1007/978-3-030-70713-2_46
9. Bharadwaj, G., Saini, S., Chauhan y, A., Kumar, P.: Automated surveillance security system using facial recognition for homes and offices. Springer, Singapore (2021). https://doi.org/10.1007/978-981-15-9509-7_13
10. Salhi: Face detection and tracking system with block matching, means if and camshaft algorithms and Kalman filter, vol. 18, pp. 139–145. IEEE (2017)
11. Libby, C., Ehrenfeld, J.: Facial recognition technology in 2021: masks, bias, and the future of healthcare. J. Med. Syst. **45**(4), 1–3 (2021). https://doi.org/10.1007/s10916-021-01723-w

12. Verma, R.K., Singh, P., Panigrahi, C.R., Pati, B.: ISS: intelligent security system using facial recognition. In: Panigrahi, C.R., Pati, B., Mohapatra, P., Buyya, R., Li, K.-C. (eds.) Progress in Advanced Computing and Intelligent Engineering. AISC, vol. 1198, pp. 96–101. Springer, Singapore (2021). https://doi.org/10.1007/978-981-15-6584-7_10

13. Ayad, M., Taher y, M., Salem, A.: Real-time mobile cloud computing: a case study in face recognition, pp. 73–78. IEEE (2014)

14. Masruroh, S., Fiade y, A., Julia, I.: NFC based mobile attendance system with facial authorization on raspberry pi and cloud server, pp. 1–6. IEEE (2018)

15. Mehedi, M., Ghulam, M., Hesham, A., Cheikhrouhou, O., Ibrahim y, S.M.: Deep learning-based intelligent face recognition in IoT-cloud environment, Computer Communications, pp. 215–222. IEEE (2020)

16. Yi, S., Jing, X., Zhu y, J., Cheng, H.: The model of face recognition in video surveillance based on cloud computing. In: Jin, D., Lin, S., (eds) Advances in Computer Science and Information Engineering. Advances in Intelligent and Soft Computing, pp. 105–111. Springer, Berlin, Heidelberg (2012). https://doi.org/10.1007/978-3-642-30126-1_18

17. Lee, H., Lee, Y.C., Hyuck y, H., Kang, S.: iEdge: an IoT-assisted edge computing framework. IEEE (2021)

18. Nazri, T., Gaafar y, T., Sajak, H.: IoT parking apps with car plate recognition for smart city using node-red. IEEE (2020)

19. Sabr, O., Kanakis y, T., Belton, J.: Identifying and tracking individuals in a smart indoor environment. IEEE (2019)

20. Mittal y, S., Singh, V.: Gender and age-based census system for metropolitan cities. IEEE (2020). https://doi.org/10.1109/ICRITO48877.2020.9198030

21. Subrahmanya, M., Srinivas y, Y., Rojee, J.: Insider threat detection with face recognition. IEEE (2017)

22. Srirama, S., Paniagua y, C., Flores, H.: Social group formation with mobile cloud services. SOCA, pp. 351–362 (2016)

23. Yunqui, Y., Liangliang y, X., Bastani, F.: Leveraging service clouds for power and QoS management for mobile devices. IEEE (2015)

24. Microsoft Azure, Conceptos del reconocimiento facial FACE (2019). [En línea]. https://docs.microsoft.com/es-es/azure/cognitive-services/face/concepts/face-recognition

ESPE-Chat: An Inclusive Application
for People with Hearing Impairment

Verónica Martínez-Cepeda(✉), Eduardo Benavides-Astudillo,
Luis Alberto Castillo-Salinas, Luis Ortiz-Delgado,
Jennifer Daniela Cadena-Oyasa, and Johnny Ismael Merino-Sangoluisa

Departamento de Ciencias de la Computación, Universidad de las Fuerzas Armadas
ESPE, Sede Santo Domingo de los Tsáchilas, Ecuador, Santo Domingo, Ecuador
{vimartinez1,debenavides,lacastillo12,laortiz9,jdcadena3,
jimerino}@espe.edu.ec

Abstract. This project is oriented to the development of a mobile application for people with hearing disabilities, carried out at the Universidad de las Fuerzas Armadas ESPE Sede Santo Domingo de los Tsáchilas. This application breaks the communication barrier between deaf and hearing people, through messages that are translated from text to audio and vice versa. The API used generates text in Spanish from messages sent in real time, a functionality that facilitates communication for people with hearing difficulties, who require visual support to access information, communicate and learn. The Agile SCRUM development methodology was used for the organization of work in blocks of time and the management of software development. In addition, open source development tools were used. Likert scale surveys were used, where the results obtained were that the development of the created mobile application has usability and inclusive accessibility. For the operation of the hybrid application (mobile and web), it is essential to have technological factors such as hardware and software, for its projection on screens of mobile devices with Android operating system or multiplatform computers with access to the web.

Keywords: Hearing disability · Ecuadorian sign language · Inclusive education · Inclusive web and mobile application

1 Introduction

As time has gone by, mankind has seen the need to incorporate a series of changes to facilitate the use of language, a series of changes to facilitate the use of language, and at the same time to evolve in communication. From an early age, man has the need to to transmit ideas, as well as emotions, in other words, communication has become one of the in other words, communication becomes

Supported by Universidad de las Fuerzas Armadas ESPE Sede Santo Domingo de los Tsáchilas.

one of the primordial foundations of human coexistence   [1]. For Therefore, being limited in this ability generates in the human being, isolation, as well as dissatisfaction, as well as the dissatisfaction of a full existence.

In Article 2, the Convention on the Rights of Persons with Disabilities mentions the following definition: "communication" shall include text languages, Braille, tactile communication, macrotypes, easily accessible multimedia devices, as well as written language, auditory systems, plain language, digitized speech media, and other augmentative or alternative modes, means and formats of communication, including easily accessible information and communications technology and communications technology. In addition, it is also mentioned that language shall mean both spoken language and sign language and other forms of nonverbal communication" [2]. On January 30, 2020, Coronavirus disease is declared as a health emergency. Coronavirus disease 2019 (COVID-19) was declared as a health emergency, which rapidly through several countries, easily affecting a large number of people [3]. As a result of COVID-19, including a series of changes in society, one of them being educational disruption. The United Nations Educational, Scientific and Cultural Organization [4], established the Global Coalition for Education to work on gender, connectivity and teachers [5]. However, this reality has been difficult for both students and teachers, as it involves adapting to a new educational system. The population is generally unaware of the use of sign language, since people commonly employ the use of writing and text messages, in addition to the service of interpreters. But even the evolution of technology has led to the implementation of features that allow communication between hearing and non-hearing people, such as the Google Meet application through video calls and the activation of subtitles or the "write by voice" tool within the Google Docs worksheet. These tools were used by teachers and students, as they facilitate communication with the deaf person, at the Universidad de las Fuerzas Armadas ESPE Sede Santo Domingo de los Tsáchilas. The chat type mobile application provides two benefits, the first one related to the translation of text messages to voice and the second one, achieves the translation of voice messages to text, with the objective of facilitating communication, student experience, development and inclusion of the student in his environment.

2   Background

At the Universidad de las Fuerzas Armadas ESPE Sede Santo Domingo de los Tsáchilas, in the Carrera en Tecnologías de la Información, there is a need for the presence of an interpreter to facilitate communication between the teacher and the student with hearing impairment. However, since March 2020 with the arrival of COVID-19, a pandemic that caused many changes worldwide, forced the mandatory closure of institutions, and as a result causes the implementation of virtual education from home, therefore, originates the development of the mobile application. [6]. Also, the use of certain technologies such as: voice dictation of Google documents, Google Meet, video calls and the activation of subtitles were very useful for communication with students who do not have disabilities and those who have hearing loss, when joining classes and continuing their learning from the virtual classrooms.

Education in the Covid-19 Pandemic:

The Organización de las Naciones Unidas para la Educación, la Ciencia y la Cultura (UNESCO) indicates that since February 2020, COVID-19 has had a major impact on education, resulting in school closures and affecting 54,037,980 students enrolled in preschool, primary, lower secondary and upper secondary education, figures taken as of January 26, 2022, from the La Organización de las Naciones Unidas para la Educación, la Ciencia y la Cultura (UNESCO) Institute for Statistics, as shown in Fig. 1, global monitoring of school closures.

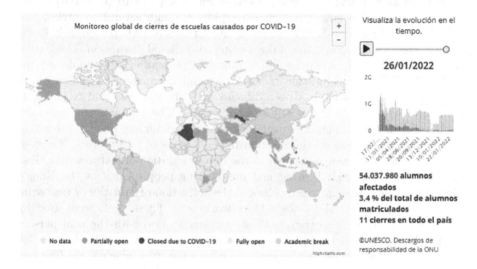

Fig. 1. Global monitoring of school closures by Covid-19. Note: Figure 1 represents the overall evolution of school closures caused by the Covid-19 pandemic.

As a consequence of the lack of connectivity and devices in certain students, multiple disadvantages become evident, such as the interruption of learning remotely. However, the ability to adapt to the situation prompted to take full advantage of technologies, partnerships and innovations for the benefit of students during this health crisis. In this way, UNESCO supports countries in their efforts to adapt their education systems to the new challenges. [4]. As can also be seen in 2, in Ecuador the number of students affected by school closures is 4'304,718, the same value corresponds to the preschool, primary and secondary levels.

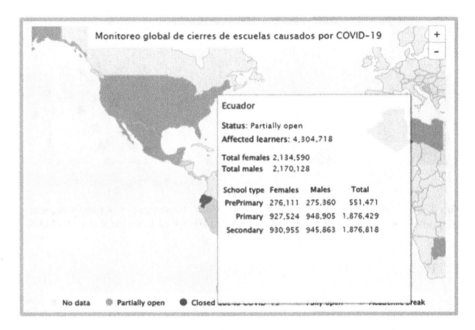

Fig. 2. Students affected by school closures in Ecuador. Note: Fig. 2 represents the global evolution of school closures caused by the COVID-19 pandemic in Ecuador.

Stefania Giannini, Assistant Director-General for Education at UNESCO, mentions in her foreword that "Higher education is no exception, although at this level digital technology has had the greatest impact in the last decades". [4]. The most vulnerable students are those who entered higher education under inconsistent conditions, becoming one of the main causes of dropout in higher education. However, students with disabilities may be affected, as they require specific support and teaching tools that are generally not available in distance education. [4].

Hearing Impairment in Ecuador:
CONADIS shows that, in January 2022, Ecuador registered a total of 471,205 people with disabilities nationwide, of which 215,156 (45.66%) have physical disabilities, 108.957 (23.11%) have intellectual disabilities, 66,538 (14.12%) have hearing disabilities, 54.397 (11.54%) have visual disabilities, and 26.157 (5.55%) have psychosocial disabilities, as shown in the Fig. 3 [7].

Fig. 3. Persons registered by type of disability. Note. Total number of people registered by type of disability from the Ministry of Public Health of Ecuador and CONADIS.

3 Related Works

The present research is searched in different repositories, where the project "Mobile application interpreter between visually impaired and hearing impaired people based on natural language processing techniques" was reflected. [8]. The same project uses speech recognition and text-to-speech technologies to serve as an interpreter for communication between the hearing impaired and the visually impaired. It is also evidenced in the project entitled "Digital product design as a support tool to improve communication for the hearing impaired". [9]. This project proposes the development of a mobile instant messaging application to improve communication between deaf and hearing people, as well as multimedia elements with animations in sign language.

4 Methodology

Scrum is called a process in which good practices are applied, which seek to optimize and increase productivity and improve the delivery of all functional products. The developers of the Scrum guide, Ken Schwaber and Jeff Sutherland, mention that Scrum is a framework that allows the development and maintenance of complex products. [10]. Moreover, thanks to its agile approach, it allows dividing a project, in this case software, into work cycles, by allowing the fulfillment of the respective deliverables in an iterative and incremental way. The Fig. 4, shows the Scrum process in the framework of this project, which is composed of work teams, events and Scrum artifacts. [10].

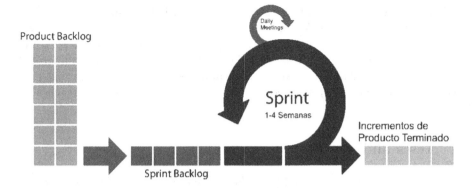

Product Backlog

Sprint
1-4 Semanas

Daily Meetings

Incrementos de Producto Terminado

Sprint Backlog

Fig. 4. Scrum process diagram

In order to meet the objectives of this research work, the inclusive mobile application of chat type was developed, in addition, the agile development methodology SCRUM is implemented, in order to meet the customer's need, in terms of short-term deliveries from the planning of activities (Planning), as well as the functions of the SCRUM team, communication between team members (meetings), in addition to the work cycles (Sprint) and communication with the customer. Therefore, in order to elaborate the requirements analysis it is important to be clear about the Scrum Team conformation and its main roles:

– Product Owner: Verónica Isabel Martínez Cepeda.
– Scrum Master: Verónica Isabel Martínez Cepeda.
– Development Team: Cadena Jennifer y Merino Johnny.

The development was carried out in 110 working days distributed in 5 Sprint, as shown in the following Table 1 :

Table 1. Table of distribution of working days by Sprint.

Workdays	Sprint 1	Sprint 2	Sprint 3	Sprint 4	Sprint 5
Start date	18/10/2021	15/11/2021	13/12/2021	10/1/2022	7/2/2022
End date	13/11/2021	11/12/2021	08/01/2022	05/02/2022	19/02/2022
Total days	24	24	24	24	14
Total	**110**				

The architecture is composed by the frontend, one of the technologies that compose it is Socket IO, this is used for sending and receiving messages in chats in real time. The APIs used for the translation of both text-to-audio and audio-text messages were avoided using those that are of payment, the API used for the translation of text-to-audio in the web version of the application is webkitspeechrecognition and for the mobile version is Ionic speech to text. The technologies used that make up the frontend development are Ionic, Angular and TypeScript, because it is a hybrid application the application has its web version, which means that it can be used from a web browser and mobile through the installer as its Apk for Android. The application makes a request that must pass through the internet so internet access is required, this request reaches the backend.

5   Tests and Results

In this project we developed ESPE-Chat, a mobile application for deaf people, implemented at the University of the Armed Forces ESPE Santo Domingo de los Tsáchilas. It was born from the Project of Linkage with Society of the Department of Computer Science called "Inclusive digital enlistment for rural and marginal urban parishes of the province of Santo Domingo de los Tsáchilas".

System Application:
Before starting it is necessary to install the application on the mobile device, with the following features:

– Cell phone with Android operating system, version 9 or later.
– 2GB of internal memory space.

Access Requirements:
Within it are: Internet connection, also it is necessary to have the application installed on your Android mobile device, as well as, in case of web access, through browsers such as Google or Mozilla, even through the mobile browser, through https://espechat.espe.edu.ec:8082/ also, to create your account it is necessary to have a valid email, as well as to enter the application it is necessary to have registered, and activated your account.

Application Description:
The application is composed of three major sections: Chats, Learn and Contacts. The first section, Chats appears on the main screen when you enter the application, chats management (send, forward and delete), account management (update) and contacts management (add and delete). As a second section, Learning is the section where you can spell the word, numbers, and certain special signs/characters; by returning on the screen the gif and images of each letter or number, also, to see the spelling it is necessary to slide the screen in case of entering a word or numeric digit. The last section is contacts, which allows adding contacts to the user's contact list, deleting contacts, as well as initiating or opening a chat.

– **Functional Testing:** Also referred to as Black Box Testing ("black-box testing") since the external behavior of the system is assessed.

- **Unit testing.** They are those that allow to guarantee that each component of the code provides the expected results, in these tests the developers observe the UI and the specification of a component, with exhaustive tests, so that, in an autonomous way before passing to another unit.
- **Unit tests from the web.** They are those that are responsible for the function of recording audio is checked that everything works correctly, long and short audios are recorded without any novelty. The error found in the mobile version does not occur. In the Fig. 5 shows the tests in the browser.

Fig. 5. Web browser testing of the ESPE-Chat application. Note: Audio recording from the web.

- **Unit Tests from the Mobile.** Its function is focused on recording from the mobile device, it is verified that it records long audios of more than one second without problems, however, it does generate an error when pressing the record button and releasing it immediately, if after this you want to record another audio, the send button is enabled again. When you exit the chat and try to record an audio of 10 s or more, the send button remains blocked. In the Fig. 6, shows the tests on the mobile device.
- **Smoke Testing.** These are performed to verify the most significant functionalities of the application, so that the most basic of the software is executed correctly with simple and fast tests. For further illustration, Fig. 7, shows the Smoke Testing.

The spelling option recognizes words with tilde, uppercase and lowercase letters, punctuation marks do not affect sign language, and if any character entered by the user is not available, the message "Not available" is issued. It is important to remember that even the correct use of punctuation marks is encouraged.

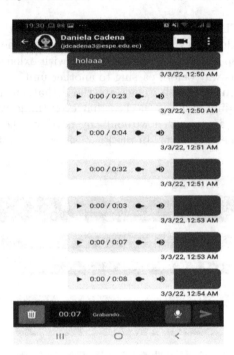

Fig. 6. Tests on the ESPE-Chat mobile device. Note: Audio recording from the mobile device.

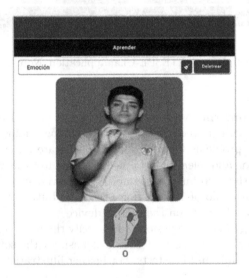

Fig. 7. Smoke test to the ESPE-Chat application. Note: Spelling section in Ecuadorian Sign Language.

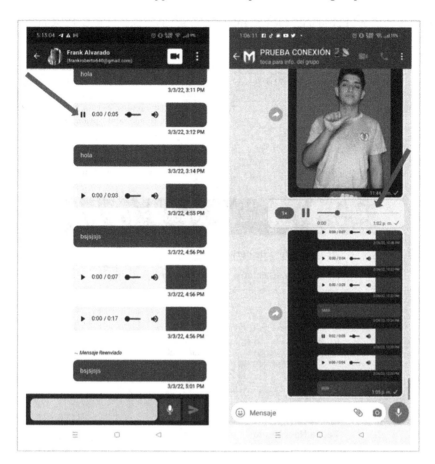

Fig. 8. Interaction of the components of the Chat section of the ESPE-Chat application.

- **System Testing.** It is the one that allows to evaluate how the different components of an application interact together in the complete and integrated system or application. In the Fig. 8, illustrates the interaction of the application components. It is determined that ESPE-Chat is not correctly coupled to the use of the speaker of the mobile device, for example, when reducing an audio in WhatsApp and playing another audio in Facebook, the latter application Facebook takes over the speaker and plays only the audio from Facebook.

  When playing an audio from WhatsApp or another social network and going to ESPE- Chat, it does not take over the speaker and plays the audio without pausing the WhatsApp audio, so that results in 2 instances of audio playback.
- **Sanity Testing.** This is a quick and basic test to determine if a particular application or component is behaving correctly. To illustrate in Fig. 9, the behavior of the components can be seen.

Table 2. Surveys to evaluate the design and user satisfaction of the ESPE-Chat application, on a Likert scale.

Surveys	Faculty	Students	Others	Results
Imago type survey ESPE-Chat	11,7 %	71,7 %	16,6%	Out of 60 surveys, 46.70% chose option 1
Interface design	29,6 %	63 %	7,4 %	Out of 54 surveys, option 3 won with 37% for light theme, and option2 won with 42.60% for dark theme
Satisfaction survey (UX y UI)	60 %	20 %	20 %	Of 20 questions, it is obtained that 74% are in Total Agreement, 20% are in Agreement, 5% neutral and 1% Disagree

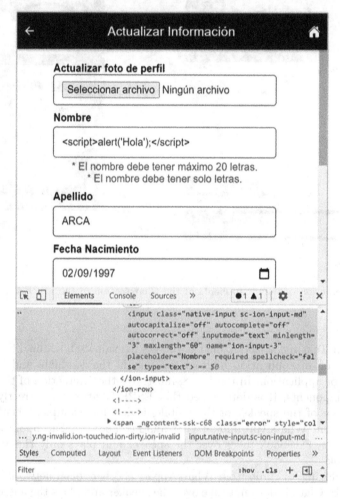

Fig. 9. Behavior of the components to update information. Note. XSS or Cross Site Scripting injection in the inputs to update information.

Finally, the results of the surveys where the Design and User Satisfaction of the ESPE-Chat application were evaluated, based on the Likert scale, are analyzed.

6   Conclusions

It is determined that the analysis of functional and non-functional requirements is the key point to improve communication through the conversion of audio to text, by means of instant messaging applications, through which communication facilities are provided between deaf and hearing people.

The biggest challenge of this project was to create an application that contains the Learn section, where it shows images and gifs of the alphabet, numbers and special characters for spelling in Ecuadorian Sign Language, which meets the approval of the Santo Domingo Association of the Deaf.

In addition, it was determined that the Scrum framework adapts to the needs for the agile development of the project, in the first phase the priority is the Learning section and Chat section to develop instant messaging communication from audio to text and vice versa with the use of free Apis, which facilitate communication between deaf and hearing people.

In the comparison made, it is determined that the transcription of audio to text between the two APIs, it is evident that the VOSK API showed 52% in the effectiveness of the number of words transcribed from speech to text, while the Google Cloud Speech To Text API maintains 49% effectiveness.

Based on the usability and inclusive web accessibility tests, it is verified that the application is directly accessible for the use of people with hearing disabilities, since, through audio transcriptions, communication between deaf and hearing people is improved.

References

1. Gómez, FSJ.: La comunicación. **20**, 5–6 12 (2016)
2. Unidas, N.: Convención sobre los derechos de las personas con discapacidad. Salus
3. Organización Panamericana de la Salud OPS. La oms caracteriza a covid-19 como una pandemia. 2020
4. UNESCO. Covid-19 y educación superior: De los efectos inmediatos al día después. 2020
5. UNESCO. Educación de la disrupción a la recuperación. 2021
6. del Rocío, F., Gordón, A.: Del aprendizaje en escenarios presenciales al aprendizaje virtual en tiempos de pandemia. Estudios pedagógicos (Valdivia) **46**(3), 213–223 (2020)
7. CONADIS. Estadísticas de discapacidad. ecuador. 2022
8. Vélez, E.S.C., Tasiguano, E.L.C.: Aplicación móvil intérprete entre personas con discapacidad visual y auditiva a partir de técnicas de procesamiento de lenguaje natural. B.S. thesis, LATACUNGA/UTC/2016, 2016

9. Cano, S.D.R.: El diseño de producto digital como una herramienta de apoyo para mejorar la comunicación de las personas con discapacidad auditiva. B.S. thesis, Universidad Técnica de Ambato. Facultad de Diseño y Arquitectura. Carrera de Diseño Gráfico Publicitario, 2021

10. Schwaber, K., Sutherland, J.: La guía de scrum tm. Recuperado de https://www.scrumguides.org/docs/scrumguide/v2017/2017-Scrum-Guide-Spanish-SouthAmerican.pdf, 2017

IoT for Energy Saving at Homes in Santo Domingo de Los Tsáchilas

Diego Salazar-Armijos[1]([⊠]) [ORCID], Verónica Martínez-Cepeda[1] [ORCID],
Luis Ortiz-Delgado[1] [ORCID], and Rodrigo Bastidas-Chalán[2] [ORCID]

[1] Departamento de Ciencias de la Computación, Universidad de las Fuerzas Armadas ESPE. Sede Santo Domingo, Vía Santo Domingo-Quevedo km 24, Santo Domingo de los Tsáchilas, Ecuador
`{drsalazar,vimartinez1,laortiz9}@espe.edu.ec`
[2] Departamento de Ciencias Exactas, Universidad de las Fuerzas Armadas ESPE. Sede Santo Domingo, Vía Santo Domingo-Quevedo km 24, Santo Domingo de los Tsáchilas, Ecuador
`rvbastidas@espe.edu.ec`

Abstract. Energy saving is very relevant worldwide. Lower energy consumption reduces: environmental pollution, costs generation, transmission and distribution of electrical energy. As a result, producing economic benefits for both countries and families that reduce their Energy. Home automation and the Internet of Things (IoT) are trends in several countries; They increasingly offer better services with the rise of Artificial Intelligence and its branches: Machine Learning and Deep Learning. This research aims to demonstrate that the automation of homes in the province of Santo Domingo de los Tsáchilas with IoT can reduce energy consumption and spending. The methodology used was experimentation, in a practical case applied to a model house that was automated for this purpose. The energy consumption in months before and after automation was taken as a reference. The results obtained showed that there can be significant energy savings, as long as there is an adequate programming of the devices, avoiding malfunctions and bad habits of the consumer.

Keywords: IoT · IoE · Energy saving · Embedded systems · Virtual assistants

1 Introduction

Energy saving is of great relevance worldwide. Lower energy consumption reduces environmental pollution and reduces the costs of generating, transmitting and distributing electrical energy. As a result, a great economic benefit is generated for nations, industries, organizations and families. According to statistics from the Ecuadorian electricity sector, from the Agency for the Regulation and Control of Energy and Non-Renewable Natural Resources, the demand for regulated electrical energy at the residential level in 2021 was 7,959.12 GWh. It accounts for 34.77% of residential energy consumption nationwide, being the sector with the highest consumption of electricity. [3]

The annual per capita consumption of electricity in the Province of Santo Domingo de los Tsáchilas is 1042.20 kWh/inhabitant. The electricity service coverage percentage in said province is 99.42%. The number of residential consumers in Santo Domingo is 148,775 users and the energy billed in the aforementioned province at the residential level was 207.10 GWh for the year 2021. [3].

In other aspects, the Internet of Things (IoT) consists of a set of electronic devices (things) interconnected with each other through computer networks. Devices are made up of sensors and actuators that exchange information. With this information they make decisions and interact with the physical world, considering this aspect as "intelligent". [14].

The authors state that home automation and IoT are a trend in several countries and that they are increasingly offering better services with the rise of Artificial Intelligence and its branches, Machine Learning and Deep Learning. According to Fernández, L. IoT and energy saving are correlated. They are dual terms because IoT has enabled more precise energy monitoring and control. IoT makes use of sensors and actuators to efficiently run devices and thus gain energy efficiency. [5].

The low level of awareness of citizens about climate change translates into the waste of electrical energy sources. The awareness of each individual is essential to reduce energy consumption in today's society. Our approach to energy reduction must be human-centered [10].

According to Benavides, et al. Among the strategies used by Ecuadorian families to save electricity is turning off the lights when leaving a room by 96.77%, as well as avoiding putting hot food containers in the refrigerator by 93.22% among other. [1]

Saving energy in homes becomes a complex task due to the constant intervention in its controls by the human factor. According to Lu, Ching-Hu [11], this behavior can be controlled by building a cyber-physical system, taking into account the benefits offered by IoT.

Nguyen and Aiello [13] found that user intervention can increase energy use and cost in buildings and homes by a third. In other words, if home automation only involves remote device management, there will surely be no benefits in terms of energy savings.

Humayun, M et al. [7], tell us that energy efficiency can be achieved in smart cities, buildings and homes. For this, a combination of sensors must be used in controlled devices with the information they send to the cloud. In addition to the above, the application of artificial intelligence algorithms is required to regulate its operation, automation and the on and off times.

For the purpose of this research we address "energy saving" globally. Internally we focus on "energy consumption". Consumption falls under the time in which the devices connected to the home automation systems are turned on and the nominal power of the interconnected devices; The relevant information will be the on and off statistics. In the local market, no devices were found with a statistical reporting system for energy consumption in home automation processes.

For example, a smart switch found in the local market provides the information shown in Fig. 1.

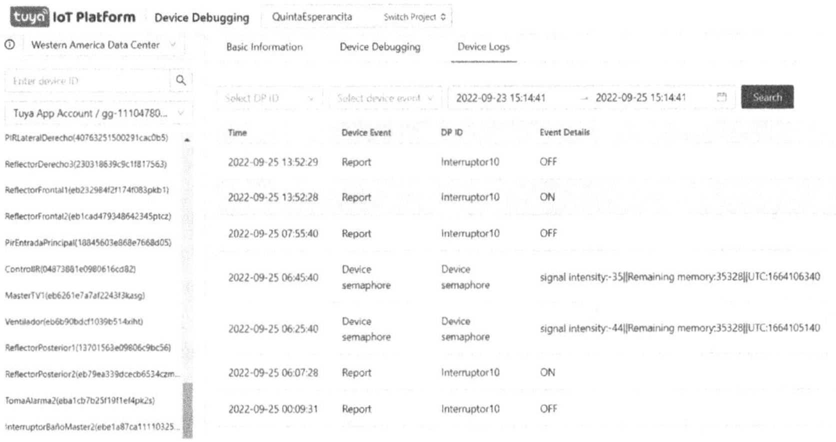

Fig. 1. Statistics of a smart switch compatible with Tuya Smart Life [8].

At the national level, there are no statistics on the use of home automation and IoT devices. Large commercial chains such as KIWY, Importadora el Rosado and Coral Hipermercados are currently offering and marketing IoT devices, mainly smart switches and light bulbs. Likewise, these products are offered to the public in local establishments such as: Novicompu, Computron and AlexTech. In the Facebook Marketplace we find several providers of IoT devices located mainly in the cities of Quito and Guayaquil. Product costs range from $8USD for smart light bulbs to $25USD for smart switches or plugs.

We see a significant difference in costs between normal devices and their smart counterparts. Regular bulbs cost $1USD versus $8USD for smart bulbs. Factor that could influence the decision of customers to automate their homes. An analysis of the cost-benefit ratio, as well as the return on investment, is required for customers to decide whether to automate their homes.

According to the Ecuadorian Ministry of Energy and Mines [12], the average rate per kWh is $0.092USD. To make up the difference of $7USD to buy a smart light bulb, a user would have to save an average of 76kWh, which would imply feasibility if a home automation campaign were implemented.

Currently there is very little or no statistical information on the use of home automation in Ecuador. It was necessary to resort to the source of information provided by Google Trends [9]. This feed shows the search trends for the terms, sentences, and phrases that users search for. The results are detailed in percentage form and can be filtered by region and sub-regions. The results considered the national context and its relationship with home automation and IoT trends in the province of Santo Domingo de los Tsáchilas. The results of the IoT usage trends are shown in Table 1.

Table 1. Search trends for IoT devices Ecuador.

Search item	Highest Trend Ecuador	Trend in Santo Domingo
Domotics	Guayas with 100 position 1	Not enough stats
Smart House	Not enough stats	Not enough stats
Alexa virtual assistants	Azuay with 100 position 1	59 place 14
Google Assistant	Tungurahua with 100 position 1	No trends shown
Siri assistant	Succumbs with 100 position	69 place 11
Smart spotlights	Not enough stats	Not enough stats
Smart switches	Not enough stats	Not enough stats
Wi-Fi spotlights	Not enough stats	Not enough stats
Wi-Fi switches	Not enough stats	Not enough stats
Tuya Smart	Only Pichincha	Not enough stats
Smart life	Not enough stats	Not enough stats
Smart devices	Not enough stats	Not enough stats
Smart tvs	Pastaza with 100 place 1	85 place 3
Surveillance cameras	Guayas with 100 position 1	Not enough stats
Smart camera	Guayas with 100 position 1	Not enough stats
Security cameras	Succumbs with 100 position 1	62 place 3
Smart sensors	Not enough stats	Not enough stats
Motion sensors	Not enough stats	Not enough stats
Smart alarm	Not enough stats	Not enough stats
Security alarm	Not enough stats	Not enough stats
Alarm system	Orellana with 100 place 1	75 place 7
Nexxt	Azuay with 100 position 1	Not enough stats
Smart air conditioner	Not enough stats	Not enough stats
Air-conditioning	Orellana with 100 place 1	46 place 9
Tank	Imbabura with 100 position 1	85 place 3
Smart plug or similar	Not enough stats	Not enough stats

Google Trends provides graphic information. Regarding the present investigation and to obtain the information in Table 1, each of the search terms was filtered. Work carried out with the Ecuador region filter and in the Spanish language, achieving the results shown in Figs. 2 and 3.

In the graphic information it can be seen that the term Alexa was the most searched for at Christmas time where it obtained its peaks. The largest number of searches of this type were carried out in the provinces of the Ecuadorian highlands. Google Trends allows you to compare search terms such as: Alexa, Siri, and Google Assistant, as shown in Fig. 4.

According to the results shown in Fig. 4, it can be inferred that the Alexa smart assistant is the most requested. Second Siri and third the Google Assistant. IoT devices are accessed and controlled by the aforementioned virtual assistants.

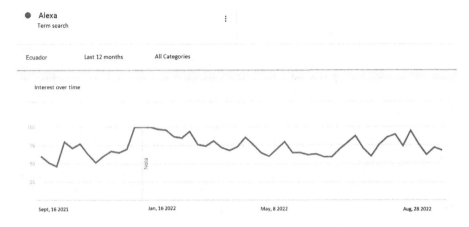

Fig. 2. Google Trends on the search term Alexa in points 0–100 [9].

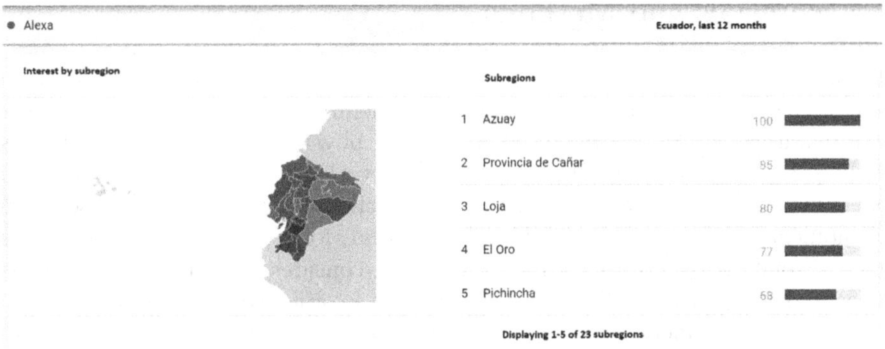

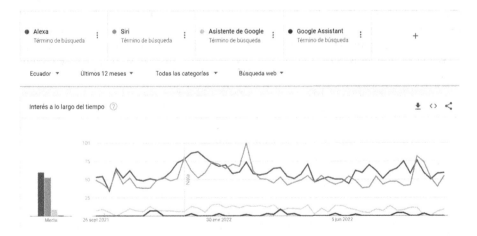

Fig. 3. Search trends related to Alexa by province according to Google Trends [9].

Fig. 4. Comparisons of smart assistant search terms in Trends [9].

Choosing one of them is important to select compatible IoT devices. Likewise, this information could be used for marketing purposes.

The previous results allow us to infer that the home automation and IoT market in Santo Domingo is still incipient. This implies that the average Ecuadorian family is not aware of the relevance of home automation and its benefits. To obtain significant energy savings, it is necessary to generate a certain degree of autonomy in IoT devices that frees up manual user interaction. The virtual assistants would be controlling the reduction of energy consumption.

This research aims to demonstrate that the automation of the average home in Santo Domingo and the use of IoT can reduce residential energy consumption. The epistemic approach with which the results are intended to be achieved is inductive empiricist and the level of depth of the research is descriptive. The results are derived from the information provided by the Alexa assistant and from energy measurements made by CNEL EP.

2   Materials and Methods

To meet the research objectives, the experimental method was used from an inductive empiricist epistemic approach. According to Padrón, J [6]. The inductive empiricist approach was used mainly by physicists of classical mechanics such as Newton. His style is based on the observation of a set of experiments and phenomena, inducing regular behavior by which laws linked to these observable phenomena are inferred. It should be noted that, for a physicist, the observable goes beyond the use of the senses and can be considered as that which can be measured or quantified. This type of approach is objective in nature.

For the experiment, electrical consumption measurements were made before and after automating the house with IoT devices. An average house was considered, with a family of 4 members, a typical case for the province of Santo Domingo de los Tsáchilas [2]. Critical automation points where user interaction is required were taken into account. The IoT devices used for the experiment were: lighting, televisions, switches, electrical outlets, etc., That is, those that allow connecting and disconnecting devices. Smart cameras and equipment such as refrigerators were not taken into account because they need a permanent connection.

The total number of IoT devices considered for automation was 45 devices, distributed as described in Table 2.

Table 2. Total of IoT devices and total load they control

Device types	Number of device	Total power or load connected to devices (W)
Smart reflectors	3	90
Smart lights	6	69
Smart Outlets	11	2167,85
Smart tv	3	480
Universal control	1	45
Smart Switches	17	190
Smart assistants	4	60
Total	45	3101, 85

Considering the installed power, it can be inferred that the control of the consumption of the loads connected to the IoT outlets must be those that are programmed in the most favorable way to influence energy consumption.

The technical specifications that are described in most IoT devices are listed below:

1. IPV4 Addressing
2. Wifi IEEE 802.11 N 2.4GHz not compatible with the 5GHz band except for Google and Alexa assistants that are compatible with both bands.
3. They work at 110/240 (V)
4. Frequency 50/60Hz
5. All devices are compatible with Alexa and Google, therefore they can be controlled by voice commands.
6. Most of the devices are compatible with the IoT provider Tuya Smart Life and with Nexxt Solution, both cases manage their own configurations and allow the creation of programs and automation routines between devices.
7. Google and Alexa allow devices from different brands, compatible with them, to be integrated through routines.
8. Smart spotlights are 9W RGB LED type and 30W reflectors.
9. The switches support a maximum current intensity of 15A for Nexxt outlets and 10A for Tuya brand switches, it should be noted that the capacity is sufficient to connect an iron, fans or water pumps, however, it is not suitable for use them with air compression systems.

The Nexxt Solutions outlets, for example, have the technical specifications shown in Fig. 5, it can be seen that these devices support a current of 15A inclusive.

Smart Wi-Fi wall power outlet
with USB port

Technical specifications

MPN	NHE-W100
Input	
Nominal voltage	110-240V
Frequency	50/60Hz
Amperage	15A
Rated power	Single outlet: 1500W
	Total: 2500W
Wireless frequency	IEEE 802.11N, 2.4GHz (not compatible with 5GHz Wi-Fi networks)
Output	
Nominal voltage	110-240V
Frequency	50/60Hz
USB port	5V/2.1A
Physical features	
Dimensions (LxWxH)	4.9x1.3x3.15in
Housing	Fire-retardant plastic
Color	White
Weight	6.34oz
Environment	
Operating temperature	-4°~16°F
Storage temperature	-4°~16°F
Relative humidity	95% non-condensing
Additional Information	
Installation requirements	Standard outlet wall-box and neutral wire
System requirements	• Mobile device running iOS 8.1 or higher, Android™ 5.0 or higher
	• Nexxt Home app
	• Existing Wi-Fi network
Certification	ETL, FCC
Warranty	Two years

* Not designed to be used with metal face plates, as it may interfere with the Wi-Fi signal

Fig. 5. Specifications of Nexxt solution smart outlets [15].

The phases of the experiment were divided into the following:

The monthly energy consumption was taken into account before installing the IoT devices. The automation of the home was carried out on July 16 and 17, 2022. The cutoff for billing is made on the 15th. The purpose of the investigation was to verify the differentiation of energy consumption and tariff before and after automation.

In this phase, the programming of the devices or automation scenes is not established to determine the user's incidence when controlling their devices remotely.

The energy consumption of the IoT devices was estimated, considering the power established on their nameplate, if any. For those that do not have a board, the average power of devices in standby similar to the existing ones and the energy consumption of the loads connected to IoT devices compatible with Alexa Power Panel are considered, as seen in Fig. 6.

To calculate the consumption of IoT devices, the average power without load has been considered. For example, in one of the mentioned devices, the average power without load is 0.29W according to the information of the standby mode of the TCL televisions [4]. That is, with the necessary power for the device

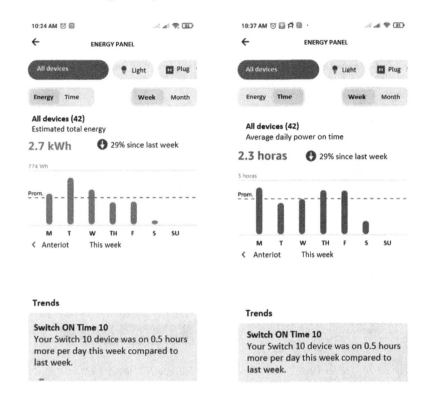

Fig. 6. Alexa power dashboard information.

to connect to the network and turn on the relays for the loads. The energy consumption calculation formula is as follows:

$$Device consumption = Power installed load(W) * time of use(h)/1000 \qquad (1)$$

IoT devices for 30 d of energy consumption is approximately 9,40kWh.

The devices with the highest power consumption were programmed and automated considering the statistics from the Alexa Assistant power panel, as shown in Fig. 7.

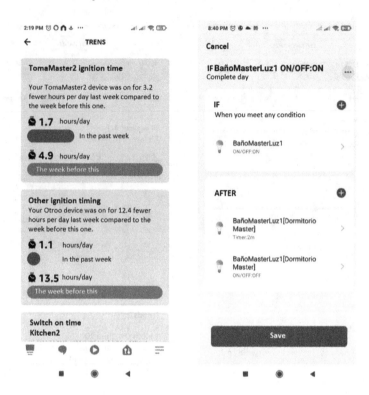

Fig. 7. Consumption trends by device according to Alexa energy panel.

To estimate the average daily consumption of the load connected to the aforementioned devices Alexa power panel stats were considered. The panel shows data and powers of the loads connected to the IoT devices. Alexa allows manual entry of electrical consumption loads as shown in Fig. 8.

According to data from the Alexa energy panel, the average monthly consumption of loads installed on IoT devices is 80kWh. Keep in mind that Alexa does not consider Smart Android TVs for compatibility reasons. In televisions, the average monthly consumption is 84kWh. Therefore, the electricity consumption for a period of 30 d would be 173.4 kWh. The permanent monthly consumption of the surveillance cameras and refrigerator is 122.45 kWh.

Fig. 8. Power connected to IoT devices and set in the Alexa power panel.

In order to compare if better results were obtained than for the previous cases. The energy consumption of the house was taken into account after the configurations, programming and automation of the devices.

3   Results and Discussions

According to the established phases, the following results were obtained: the energy consumption before the automation of the model house according to the consumption invoices of the authorized distributor of the CNEL EP service was 329 kWh. The measurement reflects the period between June 9 and July 12, 2022, with a total of 33 billed days, as shown in Fig. 9.

The aforementioned energy consumption does not include the set of IoT equipment and devices that could increase the energy consumption of the home once installed for home automation purposes.

The house was automated one weekend, specifically on July 16 and 17, 2022. Initially, the automation did not consider the programming of routines or the hours of use of the devices. In order to determine if the automation itself is decisive in saving energy and/or if it increased energy consumption when installing

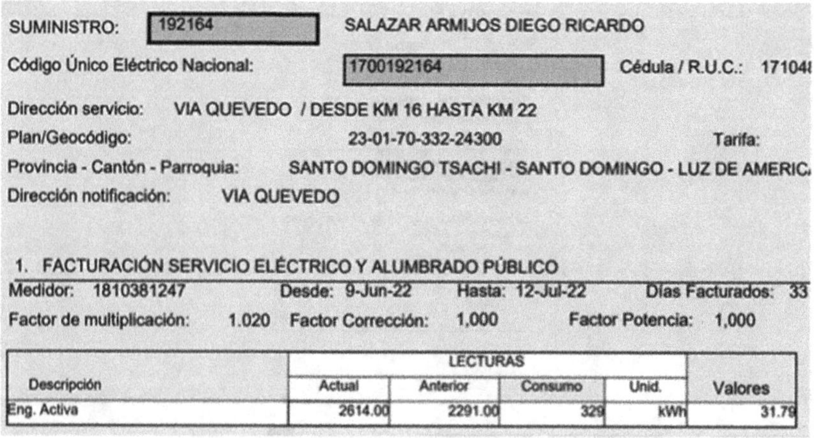

SUMINISTRO: 192164   SALAZAR ARMIJOS DIEGO RICARDO

Código Único Eléctrico Nacional: 1700192164   Cédula / R.U.C.:   171104{

Dirección servicio: VIA QUEVEDO / DESDE KM 16 HASTA KM 22
Plan/Geocódigo: 23-01-70-332-24300   Tarifa:
Provincia - Cantón - Parroquia: SANTO DOMINGO TSACHI - SANTO DOMINGO - LUZ DE AMERIC
Dirección notificación: VIA QUEVEDO

1. FACTURACIÓN SERVICIO ELÉCTRICO Y ALUMBRADO PÚBLICO

| Medidor: 1810381247 | | Desde: 9-Jun-22 | Hasta: 12-Jul-22 | | Días Facturados: 33 | |
| Factor de multiplicación: | 1.020 | Factor Corrección: 1,000 | | Factor Potencia: 1,000 | | |

Descripción	LECTURAS				Valores
	Actual	Anterior	Consumo	Unid.	
Eng. Activa	2614.00	2291.00	329	kWh	31.79

Fig. 9. Energy consumption measured by the company CNEL EP for the model house before automation.

new devices to the main energy load. The results of this phase comprise the energy consumption period between July 12 and August 13, 2022 with a total energy consumption of 207 kWh and a consumption time of 32 d as shown in Fig. 10.

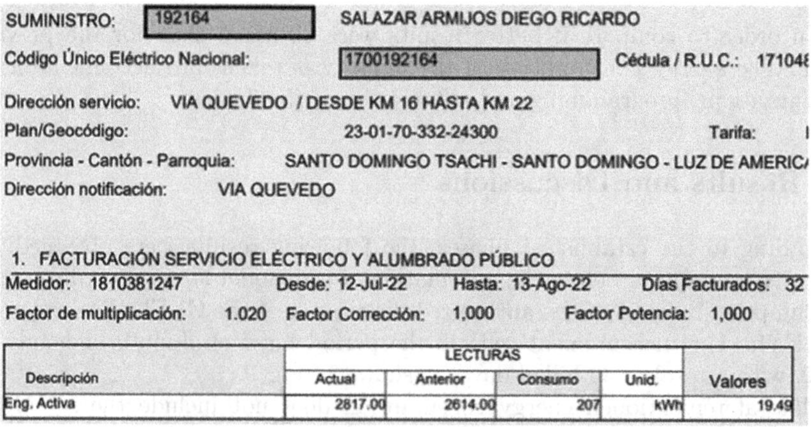

SUMINISTRO: 192164   SALAZAR ARMIJOS DIEGO RICARDO

Código Único Eléctrico Nacional: 1700192164   Cédula / R.U.C.:   171104{

Dirección servicio: VIA QUEVEDO / DESDE KM 16 HASTA KM 22
Plan/Geocódigo: 23-01-70-332-24300   Tarifa:
Provincia - Cantón - Parroquia: SANTO DOMINGO TSACHI - SANTO DOMINGO - LUZ DE AMERIC
Dirección notificación: VIA QUEVEDO

1. FACTURACIÓN SERVICIO ELÉCTRICO Y ALUMBRADO PÚBLICO

| Medidor: 1810381247 | | Desde: 12-Jul-22 | Hasta: 13-Ago-22 | | Días Facturados: 32 | |
| Factor de multiplicación: | 1.020 | Factor Corrección: 1,000 | | Factor Potencia: 1,000 | | |

Descripción	LECTURAS				Valores
	Actual	Anterior	Consumo	Unid.	
Eng. Activa	2817.00	2614.00	207	kWh	19.49

Fig. 10. Energy consumption of the model house once automated.

In this context, if the two phases are compared, the average daily energy consumption of the model house before automation is 9.97 kWh per day. In the second case, after deducting 2 d of energy for the start-up and 1 day for the configuration of the equipment, the average daily energy consumption of the home after automation is 7.14kWh. A substantial improvement in energy consumption can be observed. The fact of controlling devices remotely can be decisive. The user can control the devices from anywhere without having to manually disconnect the loads. There are other factors such as climate change and prolonged absences of household members, among others, that could influence the result. Therefore, a new evaluation of the energy consumption is required to establish that the energy consumption trend is maintained and even improved with the creation of automation scenes.

The energy consumption reflected in the CNEL electrical spreadsheet of the model house was 199kWh as shown in Fig. 11. This invoice reflects the consumption of the period between August 13 and September 9, 2022 for a period of 27 d. Already counting on the programming and automation of scenes.

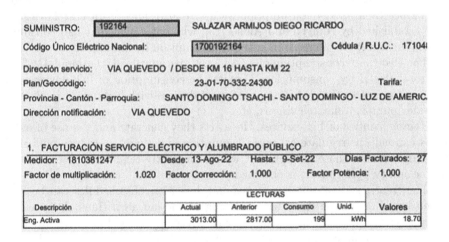

Fig. 11. Power consumption after scene creation and automation.

The estimated average daily consumption for this case is 7.37kWh. A regular trend of previous consumption is denoted. The programming of the devices considered the scenarios of lower consumption suggested by the Alexa energy panel. Despite the slight average increase, it can be inferred that energy savings can be improved if automatic scenes are generated and tuned for regulated control of devices. Following the three phases, the results shown in Table 3 are obtained.

The programming of the devices was adjusted to the suggestions of Alexa. An important point are the lights that for one reason or another remain on unnecessarily or the televisions that are left active for several hours at night.

Table 3. Summary of energy consumption per month per phase

Phases	Consumption (kWh)	Consumption of connected load IoT devices (kWh)
Before automation	329	194,31
After automation	207	79,55
After programming	199	80,34

4   Conclusions

It can be concluded that the automation of homes and residences through the IoT can reduce their energy consumption by up to 26%. This result correlates with that established by Nguyen and Aiello [13], who determine that bad consumer habits can affect the increase in energy consumption by one third.

The electricity consumption of IoT devices, without load, is around 4.25% of the total electricity consumption. Despite the consumption of IoT devices, the savings are greater than when we disconnect devices with high power loads such as water pumps, irons, televisions, etc.

Remote control of IoT devices, the alerts they generate and the use of assistants can help us regulate energy consumption and therefore reduce pollution. By programming those devices that we inadvertently tend to leave connected, better energy performance is obtained.

The creation of automation scenes and device on/off schedules can be fine-tuned based on sensor statistics and using prediction algorithms. Automating everything can also end up causing user inconvenience. An alternative would be to use artificial intelligence algorithms when predicting user behavior within the residential context.

The information provided by the Alexa energy panel is approximate and should be complemented with an analysis that better reflects reality. For example, fixed loads are set on the switches for the entire connection time. If these switches are connected to devices that have other sensors or whose load is not connected to the IoT device, it can cause errors in the calculation of power consumption.

The average consumption of the loads connected to the smart devices and that are registered through the Alexa Energy Panel, can help to program the devices for independent control of the devices of the users, which helps to save energy, however, the adjustments should consider an additional percentage to avoid inconvenience to users.

The results of the Alexa energy panel are close to the results of the energy distribution company CNEL EP, so it can be inferred that these devices can help verify energy consumption billing.

Google Home does not have a presentation panel like Alexa, providing a service that gives you added value. There are Google devices such as Android TVs that are not compatible with Alexa, which makes it difficult to control and measure energy consumption. In the context of the Province of Santo Domingo, applying IoT in residences would imply an approximate saving of 62.13GWh at the residential level.

References

1. Benavides, R., Guallasamin, K., Pilataxi, C., Murgueitio, M., Naranjo, L.: Módulo de información ambiental en hogares. Documento Técnico. Quito: Instituto Nacional de Estadística y Censos pp. 5–6 (2017)
2. de Estadísticas y Censos INEC, I.N.: ecuadorencifras.gob.ec (2010), https://www.ecuadorencifras.gob.ec/wp-content/plugins/download-monitor/download.php?id=337&force=
3. de Regulación y Control de Electricidad, A.: Estadística anual y multianual del sector eléctrico ecuatoriano (2021) (2021)
4. factoryreset.tv: Television TCL 55p615 specifications (2022). https://www.factoryreset.tv/specifications/tcl-55p615
5. Fernández Lagares, J., et al.: Tecnologías IoT para ahorro energético en edificios (2018)
6. Guillén, J.P.: Epistemología Evolucionista. GRIN Verlag, Una Visión Integral (2018)
7. Humayun, M., Alsaqer, M.S., Jhanjhi, N.: Energy optimization for smart cities using IoT. Appl. Artifi. Intell. 1–17 (2022)
8. Life, T.S.: Tuya IoT platform (2022). https://us.iot.tuya.com/
9. LLC, G.: Google trends (2022). https://trends.google.com/trends/?geo=US
10. Lovett, T., Gabe-Thomas, E., Natarajan, S., O'neill, E., Padget, J.: Just enough'sensing to enliten: a preliminary demonstration of sensing strategy for the energy literacy through an intelligent home energy advisor (enliten) project. In: Proceedings of the Fourth International Conference on Future Energy Systems, pp. 279–280 (2013)
11. Lu, C.H.: IoT-enabled adaptive context-aware and playful cyber-physical system for everyday energy savings. IEEE Trans. Human-Mach. Syst. **48**(4), 380–391 (2018)
12. de Energía y Minas, M.: Las tarifas de energí¿ía eléctrica no se incrementarán en el 2022 (2022). https://www.recursosyenergia.gob.ec/las-tarifas-de-energia-electrica-no-se-incrementaran-en-el-2022/
13. Nguyen, T.A., Aiello, M.: Energy intelligent buildings based on user activity: a survey. Energy buildings **56**, 244–257 (2013)
14. Serrano Hipólito, D., et al.: Control de consumo energético usando Internet of Things (2020)
15. solutions, N.: Nexxt home-tomacorrientes de pared (2022). https://nexxt-connectivity-frontend.s3.amazonaws.com/media/docs/SmartWallPowerOutlet_DS_SPA.pdf

Monitoring System Based on an IoT Platform for an AFPM Generator

Myriam Cumbajín[1] , Patricio Sánchez[1] , Oscar Ortiz[2] ,
and Carlos Gordón[2](✉)

[1] SISAu Research Center, Facultad de Ingeniería, Industria y Producción,
Universidad Tecnológica Indoamérica, UTI, 180103 Ambato, Ecuador
{myriamcumbajin,patriciosanchez}@uti.edu.ec
[2] GITED Research Group. Facultad de Ingeniería en Sistemas, Electrónica e
Industrial. Universidad Técnica de Ambato, UTA, 180207 Ambato, Ecuador
{oortiz4659,cd.gordon}@uta.edu.ec

Abstract. In the present work, a monitoring platform is made for an Axial Flow Permanent Magnet (AFPM) Generator without magnetic core, the objective is to permanently monitor the values that come from the generator, where the generator variables have been acquired through an open source development board called Arduino MEGA, which sends the data to a Raspberry PI, where they are displayed and stored so that they can be processed. The variables are displayed using the graphical node-red environment that offers a very eye-catching dashboard, which will be displayed on a 7 in. liquid-crystal display screen. All the data obtained is stored in a database that will allow its use for specific purposes. The monitoring platform has been built with the ability to monitor the speed of the rotors, the voltage and the current of a phase and thus be able to process the total power supplied by the generator. As a result, the monitoring system is a promise component for Pico Hydro power station to control the power all the time provided by the Axial Flow Permanent Magnet Generator.

Keywords: Internet of Things · Axial · Flow · Generator

1   Introduction

The Internet of Things (IoT) is a technology that has gained strength in various fields such as transportation, agriculture, energy, and smart buildings, there are even smart meters that can be directly connected to the electrical grid [1]. IoT devices can function as sensors [2] or actuators [3], which is why they are called as intelligent [4], which is why they have great ease of interaction with many devices. They are typically managed by a controller application, which provides the logic for data flow, processing, and decision making [5]. Communication technologies [6] and protocols [7] will be used and integrated to create efficient IoT infrastructures that regulate the exchange of information [8]. There are some issues related to managing large amounts of data [9], security [10] and privacy [11], and scalability [12]. Appropriate tools should be adopted to perform a preliminary assessment of new designed solutions, prior to actual deployment [13].

Previously developed works use these platforms for various reasons such as in agriculture in 2018, to monitor the moisture content of the soil, we have used an internally developed sensor. In the proposed network, the nickname IITH is used as a receiver and sensor node that provides low-power communication [14]. The implementation of an Internet of Things application has been developed that performs temperature and humidity detection through the DHT11 sensor on Raspberry Pi, and data transfer to the IBM (International Business Machine) Bluemix cloud [15]. A system is proposed that connects and controls most of the IoT devices connected by voice. As the number of cloud devices increases, the firmware needs to be updated more frequently. Node-Red is used, a visual wiring tool that helps connect devices with ease, resulting in quick and effortless connection setups [16]. In 2019, the proposed system uses Internet of Things technologies such as IBM Cloud, node-RED and MQTT (Message Queuing Telemetry Transport) to acquire, transmit and display different parameters. A microcontroller is used to acquire data from the sensors and then the data is sent to the WiFi (Wireless Fidelity) module. The data is then sent to an MQTT broker online [17]. A reliable, open source and low cost Supervisory and Data Acquisition (SCADA) control system is presented for the home control and monitoring system. The presented SCADA system consists of analog sensors, ESP32, Node-RED and Message Queue Telemetry Transport over local Wi-Fi to access and control devices remotely [18].

The monitoring platform has been manufactured with the ability to monitor the speed of the rotors, the voltage and the current of a phase, the generator variables have been acquired through an Arduino MEGA, which sends the data to a Raspberry PI, where they are displayed and stored so that they can be processed. The variables are displayed using the red node graphical environment offered by a very eye-catching control panel, which will be displayed on a 7-inch tft liquid-crystal display (LCD) screen. All the data obtained is stored in a database that will allow its use for specific purposes.

What is obtained in this document is comparable to many other applications that use analog and Node-RED sensors, but none of them had previously been applied to Pico Hydro power plants, which are those that are located only in strategic places or remote from the urban area.

The selection of components for the creation of the platform was made carefully and after an analysis of various options on the market, since each of these are essential for proper monitoring.

2   Component Selection

From the generator it has been decided to obtain the value of some of the variables that intervene in the power generation process, which are the generator's rotation speed, its voltage and current. To carry out the monitoring of the data obtained from the generator to later be compared with those obtained by simulation, it is necessary to use a device that allows this to be done, there are a good number of technological tools available in the local market that have the necessary requirements to carry it out.

To obtain and process data through the sensors, an Arduino MEGA, depicted in Fig. 1, will be used, which is a microcontroller board based on the ATmega2560. It consists of 54 digital IN/OUT pins, 16 analog inputs, 4 UARTs, 16 MHz speed, USB connection, and a power connector.

Fig. 1. Arduino MEGA with ATmega2560

In addition, due to the accessibility, capacity and price, the raspberry pi will be used, since it has the functionalities to meet the desired expectations, such as the visualization of the data.

Data Visualization. It is necessary to view the values obtained in real time so that while the generator is in operation there is a record of the values it is working for, for which various characteristics of LCD screens in the local market are analyzed. The display selected for viewing is the 7-inch touch LCD, which is shown in the Fig. 2. Because the size of this allows the visualization of all the variables to be very comfortable.

Voltage Measurement. To measure voltage, the characteristics of various sensors have been analyzed. The sensor based on the ZMPT101B transformer seems the most suitable option for voltage measurement, but the problem lies in its working frequency since at low generator speeds it will not be able to measure anything in addition to requiring a constant frequency to work well. So it has been chosen to rectify the current and through a voltage divider send

Fig. 2. Waveshare 7 in. LCD screen

the Arduino to an analog input and perform the necessary calculations for the voltage. The circuit diagram for making voltage measurements is shown in Fig. 3.

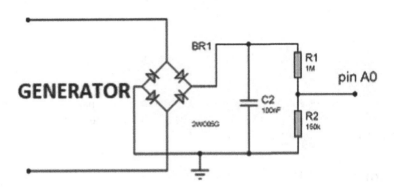

Fig. 3. Voltage Measurement Circuit Diagram

Current Measurement. A comparison of various current sensors has been made. The ACS712 sensor module, sketched in Fig. 4, is used. The device is made up of a Hall sensor circuit. The applied current flowing generates a magnetic field that is detected by the Hall integrated circuit and converted into a proportional voltage.

Measurement of Revolutions per Minute. There are several types of sensors that can be used to perform this function, however the sensor that will be used is a hall effect sensor, which allows to take advantage of the location of the magnets in the rotors to measure the revolutions in the Fig. 5 used hall effect sensor KY-003 shown.

Fig. 4. ACS712 Current Sensor

Fig. 5. KY-003 Magnetic Field Sensor

Since this will be located close enough when a magnet passes in north polarization, it will be read by the sensor and this data will be sent to a pin of the Arduino where the rpm will be processed.

3   Monitoring Platform Construction

A monitoring platform is developed to obtain the value of some of the variables involved in the power generation process in the axial flow permanent magnet generator, which are the generator rotation speed, voltage and the current of a generator phase. To carry out the monitoring of the data obtained from the generator to then be compared with those obtained by simulation, for which the following components will be used:

- Power supply. 5 [V], 12 [V].
- Raspberry PI.
- Arduino Mega.
- 7 in. LCD screen.
- Fan.
- ACS712 current sensor.
- Voltage Sensor.
- Hall effect sensor.

Power Supply, This is the one that will be used to power all the components that make up the monitoring system, 12 V to power the LCD display and the fan, the 5 V to power the Raspberry pi, the Arduino and the sensors, the diagram of the source used is observed in the Fig. 6.

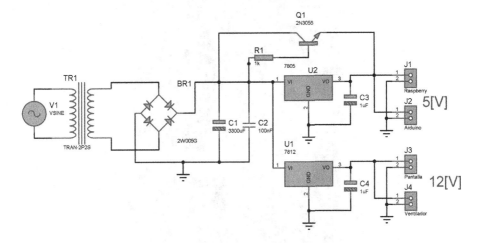

Fig. 6. Power supply diagram

Finally, in the Fig. 7 it is observed how this monitoring platform is constituted, which is inside a 2-line acrylic box.

Where:

1. Raspberry PI.
2. Power supply. 5 [V], 12 [V]
3. Arduino MEGA.
4. 7 in. LCD screen.
5. Fan.

3.1   Storage in the Database

This process consists of two stages as shown in the diagram of the Fig. 8. The data is acquired an through the communication the data is stored in the database.

The data acquisition stage is done by the Arduino MEGA board as depicted in Fig. 9, in which, the connection of this stage is shown in more detail, the measurement has been made to a single phase, with the data obtained the power per phase and the three-phase can be obtained.

On the Raspberry PI, the Raspberry PI (OS) operating system has been installed on the microSD card, to store the database, a manager of these has been installed, which is phpmyadmin, which will allow us to manage the database graphically. In addition, the treatment of the data obtained will be carried out in the node network, which is a programming tool to connect hardware

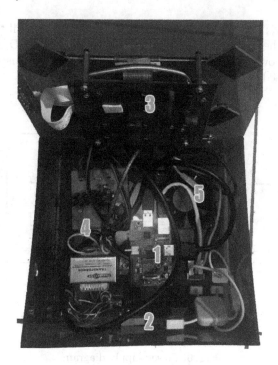

Fig. 7. Physical monitoring platform

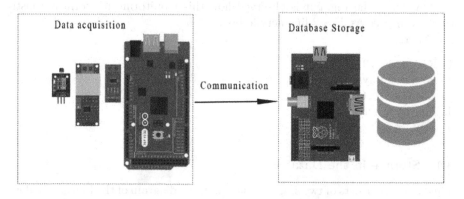

Fig. 8. Data communication scheme

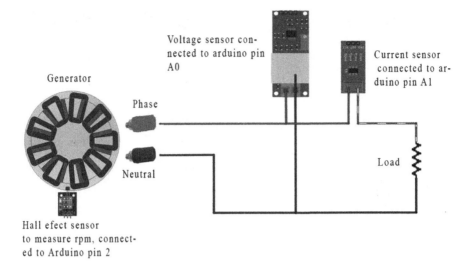

Fig. 9. Data acquisition scheme

devices, which also provides a browser-based editor that allows easy programming through node flows.

Enable Serial Port on Raspberry PI. To begin, the connection of the UART serial communication will be made in the raspberry GPIO14 (TxD) and GPIO15 (RxD) and in the respective ports of the Arduino MEGA board.

Consequently, it is enabled in the interfaces in Rasberry PI OS, the serial port is enabled and the device is restarted as depicted in the Fig. 10.

Node Network Programming for Data Visualization. Nodes are created for serial communication, visualization of the variables in Dashboard, the calculation of power and to save the data in a database as sketched in the Fig. 11.

Send to the Database. The sending to the Database is done through the node of the "Save in base" function, which means that JavaScript sends the variables to the database called generator, its code is shown in the Fig. 12.

4   Results

Then, you can see the monitoring screen of the node-red dashboard in the Fig. 13, which will be displayed on the LCD screen. The interface of the monitoring platform is very simple and attractive.

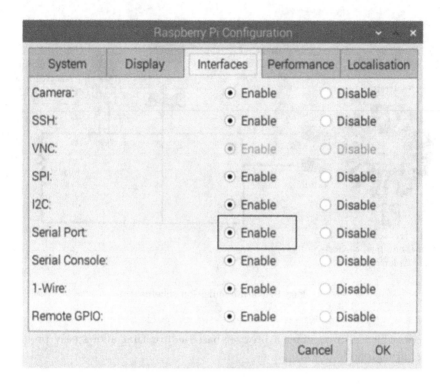

Fig. 10. Enable serial port on raspberry PI

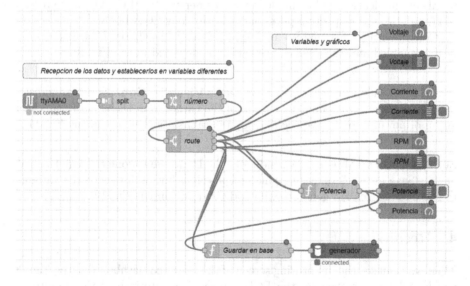

Fig. 11. Node flow for data display

```
 1  numero = msg.parts.index
 2
 3  if (numero===0)
 4▾ {
 5      volt = msg.payload;
 6▴ }
 7  if (numero==1)
 8▾ {
 9   corr = msg.payload;
10▴ }
11  if (numero==2)
12▾ {
13   rpm = msg.payload;
14▴ }
15   pot = msg.payload1;
16
17  msg.topic="INSERT INTO datos (ID,Voltaje,Corriente,Velocidad,Potencia)
18  msg.payload=['NULL',volt, corr, rpm, pot];
19  return msg;
```

Fig. 12. Node flow for data display and saving

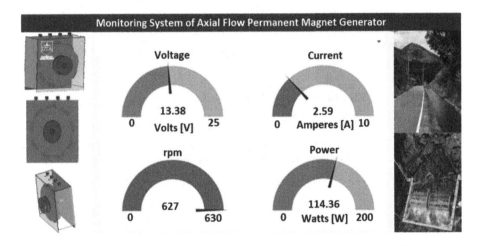

Fig. 13. Monitoring screen of AFPM generator

The data is saved in the database as shown in the Fig. 14, so that these can be used to analyze the data later.

		ID	Voltaje	Corriente	Velocidad	Potencia	1
Haga clic en la flecha desplegable para cambiar la visibilidad de la columna.			3.46	2.73	627	121.26	
Editar Copiar Borrar		42	13.36	2.73	627	120.36	
Editar Copiar Borrar		43	13.36	2.73	627	120.36	
Editar Copiar Borrar		30	13.28	2.73	627	119.64	
Editar Copiar Borrar		31	13.28	2.73	608	119.64	
Editar Copiar Borrar		36	13.36	2.69	627	118.6	
Editar Copiar Borrar		11	13.36	2.69	608	118.6	
Editar Copiar Borrar		35	13.36	2.69	627	118.6	
Editar Copiar Borrar		37	13.36	2.69	627	118.6	
Editar Copiar Borrar		32	13.15	2.73	608	118.47	
Editar Copiar Borrar		38	13.33	2.69	627	118.33	
Editar Copiar Borrar		46	13.46	2.66	608	118.15	
Editar Copiar Borrar		45	13.46	2.66	627	118.15	
Editar Copiar Borrar		19	13.3	2.69	608	118.06	
Editar Copiar Borrar		18	13.3	2.69	627	118.06	

Fig. 14. Data saved from the AFPM generator

Figure 15 shows a connection diagram of the devices used for monitoring, where all the components of the Axial Flow Permanent Magnet Generator are sketched.

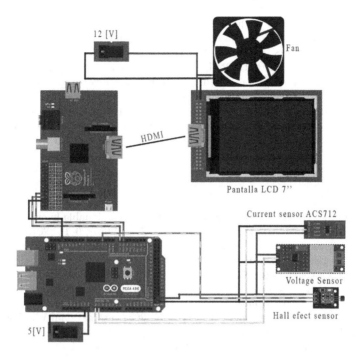

Fig. 15. Architecture of the monitoring system

5   Conclusions

The document presents the implementation of a Monitoring System Based on an IoT Platform, created by using the Raspberry PI 3 model B, ACS712 current sensor, rectification-based voltage sensor and a voltage divider, and the KY-003 hall effect sensor. The cloud application displays the data collected from the Raspberry PI and the sensors the current, voltage, power and rpm of the generator using Node-RED. With Node-RED The data on Node-RED is stored in a database on the local server. The collected data can be stored in a database created on some external database server. The real-time monitoring of physical assets, allows to determine the moment when a measurement is out of range, and thus perform the detection of early problems, previous investigations use this monitoring method, for operations similar to ours but not carried out for the maintenance management of Pico hydro power plants as is our case. Finally, the implemented system allows the continuous sensing of voltage, current and revolutions per minute, in order to provide data of a power generated by an Axial Flow Permanent Magnet Generator implemented in a Pico Hydro power station. Then, the data obtained will allow to control the generated power and take decisions when something is wrong at any time.

Acknowledgement. The authors thank the invaluable contribution of the Technological University Indoamerica, for his support in conducting the research project "ESTUDIO DE ALGORITMOS HIBRIDOS DE APRENDIZAJE AUTOMATICO PARA LA PREDICCION DE GENERACIÓN DE ENERGÍAS RENOVABLES", Project Code: 281.230.2022. Also, the authors thank the Technical University of Ambato and the "DirecciÓn de Investigación y Desarrollo" (DIDE) for their support in conducting this research, in the execution of the project "Captación de Energía Lim-pia de Baja Potencia para Alimentación de Dispositivos de Quinta Generación (5G)", approved by resolution "Nro. UTA-CONIN-2022-0015-R". Project code: SFFISEI 07.

References

1. Barnaghi, P., Sheth, A., Henson, C.: From data to actionable knowledge: big data challenges in the web of things. IEEE Intell. Syst. **28**(6), 6–11 (2013)
2. Rayes, A., Salam, S.: Internet of Things From Hype to Reality. Springer, Cham (2019). https://doi.org/10.1007/978-3-319-99516-8
3. Murata, S., Matsumoto, N., Yoshida, N.: IoT actuator networks based on inverse directed diffusion. J. Computations Model. **12**(3), 13–23 (2022)
4. Bekri, W., Layeb, T., Rihab, J.M.A.L., Fourati, L.C.: Intelligent IoT systems: security issues, attacks, and countermeasures. In: 2022 International Wireless Communications and Mobile Computing (IWCMC), pp. 231–236. IEEE (2022)
5. Proposal for a Low Cost Platform Based on the Internet of Things for Smart Agriculture. http://investigacion.utmachala.edu.ec/revistas/index.php/Cundos/article/view/462. Accessed 14 Nov 2022
6. Herrero, R.: Fundamentals of IoT Communication Technologies. TTE, Springer, Cham (2022). https://doi.org/10.1007/978-3-030-70080-5
7. Zrelli, A.: Hardware, software platforms, operating systems and routing protocols for Internet of Things applications. Wireless Pers. Commun. **122**(4), 3889–3912 (2022)
8. Gayathri, A., et al.: Cooperative and feedback based authentic routing protocol for energy efficient IoT systems. Concurrency Comput. Pract. Experience **34**(11), e6886 (2022)
9. Sreedevi, A.G., Harshitha, T.N., Sugumaran, V., Shankar, P.: Application of cognitive computing in healthcare, cybersecurity, big data and IoT: a literature review. Inf. Process. Manage. **59**(2), 102888 (2022)
10. Rondon, L.P., Babun, L., Aris, A., Akkaya, K., Uluagac, A.S.: Survey on enterprise Internet-of-Things systems (E-IoT): a security perspective. Ad Hoc Netw. **125**, 102728 (2022)
11. Giordano, G., Palomba, F., Ferrucci, F.: On the use of artificial intelligence to deal with privacy in IoT systems: a systematic literature review. J. Syst. Softw. **193**, 111475 (2022)
12. Honar, P.H., Rashid, M.A., Alam, F., Demidenko, S.: Experimental performance analysis of a scalable distributed hyperledger fabric for a large-scale IoT testbed. Sensors **22**(13), 4868 (2022)
13. Sicari, S., Rizzardi, A., Coen-Porisini, A.: Smart transport and logistics: a Node-RED implementation. Internet Technol. Lett. **2**(2), e88 (2019). https://doi.org/10.1002/itl2.88

14. Heble, S., Kumar, A., Prasad, K., Samirana, S., Rajalakshmi, P., Desai, U. B.: A low power IoT network for smart agriculture. In: IEEE World Forum on Internet of Things, WF-IoT 2018 - Proceedings 2018, vol. 2018–01, pp. 609–614, WF-IoT (2018)
15. Lekić, M., Gardašević, G.: IoT sensor integration to Node-RED platform. In: 2018 17th International Symposium on INFOTEH-JAHORINA, INFOTEH 2018 - Proceedings, vol. 2018-January, pp. 1–5, INFOTEH (2018)
16. Rajalakshmi, A., Shahnasser, H.: Internet of Things using Node-Red and alexa. In: 2017 17th International Symposium on Communications and Information Technologies, ISCIT 2017, vol. 2018–01, pp. 1–4, ISCIT (2017)
17. Mehmood, M., Ali, W., Ulasyar, A., Zad, H., Khattak, A., Imran, K.: A Low Cost Internet of Things (LCIoT) based system for monitoring and control of UPS system using Node-Red, CloudMQTT and IBM Bluemix. In: 1st International Conference on Electrical, Communication and Computer Engineering, ICECCE (2019)
18. Zare A., Iqbal, M.: Low-Cost ESP32, Raspberry Pi, Node-Red, and MQTT protocol based SCADA system. In: IEMTRONICS 2020 - International IOT, Electronics and Mechatronics Conference, IEMTRONICS (2020)

Cyber-Physical Systems in Education:
A New Approach to Continuous Improvement and Agile Learning

Fausto Robayo[1]([envelope]), Milton Román[1], Freddy Morales[3], Daniel Jerez[3],
and Ricardo Plasencia[2]

[1] Technical University of Ambato, Ambato, Ecuador
{frobayo2258,mn.roman}@uta.edu.ec
[2] University of the Armed Forces ESPE, Latacunga, Ecuador
arguanoluisa1@espe.edu.ec
[3] Espíritu Santo University, Guayaquil, Ecuador
jcjuniorcheo@gmail.com, djerez@uees.edu.ec

Abstract. The current changes have allowed technology and daily activities to intertwine in a better way, causing activities such as work or education to become virtual, in that aspect the implementation of specialized systems that allow a better management of the new modalities generated is a first level priority, in that aspect, the implementation of cyber-physical systems is an alternative, because they allow the integration of physical and virtual modules, in addition, to generate communication between all entities that manipulate or manipulate the system, in that context, The objective of this project is the implementation of mechanisms that allow the educational improvement, being one of the most worrying factors in Ecuador, for this reason the proposal presented is the implementation and testing of a cyber-physical system, applying Lean Startup and Design Thinking agile methodologies, destined to the interactivity between students, teachers and tutors, in order to improve the deficiencies produced by virtual education, generating environments and areas of study that allow to improve the intellectual capacities of the students, which will be evaluated by the users themselves through the use of tests and means of satisfaction that verify the quality of the system.

Keywords: Cyber-physical · Design thinking · Education · Environment · Lean startup · Students · Teachers · Virtual

1 Introduction

Cyber-physical systems (CPS) are the complex evolution of classical software systems. These systems integrate the traditional physical layer together with the new aspects of CPS [1, 2]. Enabling a wide range of applications in various fields such as academic, governmental, industrial, etc., significantly expanding the functionality and quality of the services [3], the technological-virtual fusion allows a better interaction between the user and the system, creating new realities in the technological management.

The CPS being a new type of digital technology, where, the combination of integrated and cyberspace components, are relevant in its construction, allowing to extend the functionality and quality in many commercial and informative domains [4, 5]. For this, the use of agile methodologies allows a better communication between the users and the CPS. Generating environments where the application of graphic methodologies such as Design Thinking (experimental and innovative learning methodology that immediately guarantees the development of competencies and growth for those who apply it) together with the activities proposed by the system produce a greater absorption of information [6].

In addition, the use of Lean Startup, a methodology much more focused on developing the customer, the market, the business model and obtaining validated learning [7]. in the development of the proposal, allowed speeding up development times, thanks to the creation of canvases and the generation of minimum viable products.

With the outbreak of COVID-19, in Ecuador, in the educational field, the virtual modality was implemented, being a country that does not have technology as a priority, it has been a serious blow, producing that 70% of students have difficulty in accessing online education. The lack of smart phones or Internet, the drop in income and the lack of training prevent the normal education of millions of children [8], and taking into account that the role of tutor is taken by the parents themselves, adding one more task to their morning activities, they do not allow the child to develop in a better way, since he/she does not have an appropriate guide [9], producing poor quality education and therefore underestimating online education, underestimating the importance of the application of systems and tools that help to improve academic activities.

In this context and with the vision of improving the quality of education in the country, the application of CPS is an alternative to the current virtual classes, where the generation of systems allows an approach and communication between teachers, students and legal representatives, allowing the application of agile methodologies such as Design Thinking [10], encouraging creativity through the implementation of virtual environments with key activities related to each subject of study, which awaken the interest of students.

The main objective is to demonstrate the feasibility of SCP in the educational environment through the analysis of an immersive system focused on the continuous improvement of the user, in order to promote the use of mechanisms that allow collective participation between student and teacher [11].

This research seeks the implementation of controlled hybrid systems in the educational environment, allowing children in a context of economic scarcity to have access to quality education, for this we took into account the current trends in the area of gamification, working with 3D models focused on capturing the attention of each adult and the use of routines in the handling of scripts, improving the interaction with the system, allowing in turn that while students participate in an activity, they are controlled by teachers and tutors in charge through their mobile devices or computers, creating a participatory education.

2 Background

2.1 Virtual Education

The current education gave a great change with the emergence of the pandemic, making it unintelligible without the use of new technologies. The school, as an educational agent, assumed the changes of society, in general, and of children, in particular, sharing this burden with the tutors of each student by becoming virtual, incorporating virtual classes as a means of teaching, where, Ecuador a growing country showed the lack of implementation of these media, not only in the implementation, but also in the management of each of the teachers in charge of teaching, leaving in sight the lack of training of the same [12].

Virtual education, also known as online education, develops the teaching-learning relationship virtually, whereby teachers and students must interact without the direct face-to-face relationship between teacher and student through a virtual classroom [13, 14]. The situation is similar in Ecuador, where 70% of students have difficulty in accessing online teaching in the Andean country. The lack of smartphones or Internet, the drop in income and the lack of training prevent the normal education of millions of children during the pandemic [15].

Even so, not everything is negative, the adaptation of students to new technologies has given way to a better distribution of their time, being the first step towards a better education, from that point, we seek to change the approach of the current teacher, focused on a task-based teaching to a teaching based on interactivity.

2.2 Smart Education

Currently, teaching methods are seeking a new approach, focused on improving the interaction between the teacher and the student, where intelligent learning allows to perceive through various audiovisual techniques, movement, expression and other factors applied in the education process, allowing to better impart knowledge [16, 17]. In such a way that it enables web accessibility for the students [18], an essential resource in human activity which, when carried out in the best way, broadens capabilities by being a means of expanding knowledge.

2.3 Design Thinking

In these times where technology has changed, is changing, and will continue to change, we must create a link between matching people's needs with what is technologically possible, aligned with a feasible strategy that can be converted into value for each client [19]. This is where Design Thinking puts developers in the customer's shoes, allowing development teams to create empathy with the user before development begins. Empathy is the core of Design Thinking and does not require expertise in the field that the customer resides in, rather it requires critical thinking [20].

As a methodology that can not only be applied in the development environment, but expands to other areas, it allows the developer, project leaders and stakeholders to expand their base idea into an infinite set of possibilities.

2.4 Lean Startup

The lean startup method is a methodology based on "validated learning", i.e., verifying hypotheses little by little before having the final product (the definitive startup) and starting to scale the business [21]. The idea is to define and shorten the development cycles, launching different proposals for a period of time and obtaining valuable feedback from our potential customers or users, with which to improve the next final version of the product.

The application of Lean Startup, allowed to improve development times and ensured a constant workflow, thanks to the creation of Canvas boards and the implementation of combined tools of agile methodologies, allowing the rapid implementation of the system.

3 Structure of the Environment

The design of the applied software schematizes the connection and interaction between the main users and the main application, allowing to observe the communication between each of the actors, where the principles of cyber-physical systems were taken into account as shown in Fig. 1, where, (a) the process starts with the sending of tasks and activities from the school to a server where it can be reviewed by teachers, (b) with the assigned tasks the teachers will have the permissions to access these activities and manage the students that enter as well as the development of the same, while the tutor or parent will receive direct notifications to the linked device, on the part of the students, they will have the ability to perform tasks and be in communication with each of the teachers, allowing them to have a direct contact with the subject to be studied.

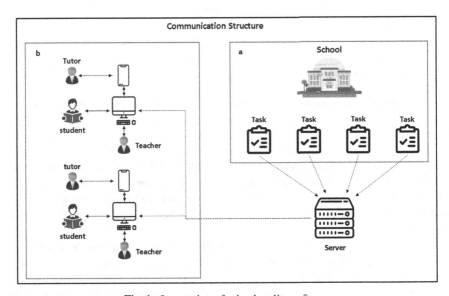

Fig. 1. Integration of mixed reality software

The proposed design allows to generate a technological stack focused on the co-communication of each one of the actors, where making use of new technological means allows a better communication, therefore, better interaction between the user and the system, In such a way that the user can carry out a process which at the moment of execution will call a series of multitasks or routines that will work internally, allowing to improve the precision by generating parallel work between the action and the moment to be executed, emulating processes similar to those of real life without affecting the performance of the application, as shown in Fig. 2.

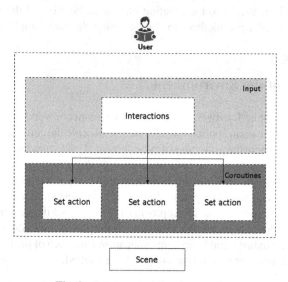

Fig. 2. Subprocess and task execution

4   System Development

The development of the system was focused on generating the greatest interaction between each of the users with the system. Through the use of agile methodologies Desig Thinking (used in the process of creating environments by applying user experience concepts) and Lean Starup (in charge of managing all task organization flows) a constant and iterative flow was managed, which allowed the creation and quick modification of both scenarios and scripts, also allowed to divide into groups the management of tasks, separating development and design tasks with those focused on issues of server connection, where infrastructure was used as code, facilitating the deployment of the application.

The development process begins with the creation of a modular style architecture, which allows specifying each of the modules with which the system interacts for its operation, as shown in Fig. 3.

The architecture of the application consists of four modules, (i) Modules: responsible for controlling the scripts, routines and actions of the actors in the process of interaction

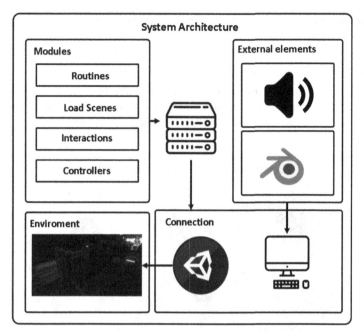

Fig. 3. System architecture

of the system, in addition, there is the necessary coding to perform the connection of the system, (ii) External elements: this module has each model designed, in addition to the sounds created for the realization of the environment within the application, (iii) Connection: this module is responsible for linking each of the elements for the proper functioning of the application, (iv) Scene: represents the execution of the application.

4.1 System Construction

The development process of the system consists of five modules, from the creation of each one of the elements, the construction of the application and its testing stage.

Construction Modeling of elements: For this section we proceeded to the design of models and bases similar to known games of today, generating a recovery that allows to develop the skills of the users tested in the first instance, using the Blender modeling tool [22], which will allow to clean and improve the performance of each element.

Model integration: For this stage, the models were added to the Unity development environment [23], where we proceeded to the generation of the path and the sections corresponding to the activities to be performed.

Codification of actions and controllers: With the developed environment we proceeded to the generation of scripts in Visual Studio [24], destined to be each one of the actions to be developed within the virtual environment, in addition we made the corresponding connections with the databases destined to send and receive information of each activity.

Configuration of communication services: For the communication between applications we configured the Unity connect services [25], which allow to quickly manage the connection between different users, allowing to have a control of each of the participants and reducing the development times of a traditional cloud.

Environment and Communication Functional Tests: The testing stage was carried out by preparing in a room of the educational unit a total of 30 users, including students and teachers, who were subjected to a short introduction (See Fig. 4).

Fig. 4. Tests applied to students

5   Results and Discussion

This section presents the results obtained in the development and implementation of the Cyberphysical System. These results are divided into two stages, (i) Interaction with the system, which details the functionality of the developed application through the main attractions of the virtual environment and (ii) Validation of the application, which analyzes the results obtained from the manipulation of the system by a group of users.

5.1   System Interaction

To access the virtual environment, it is necessary to take into account the specifications that the mobile device must meet, such as 6GB of RAM, Android version 10 or higher and 450MB of available space. Next, the teacher in charge will send the application to the student for installation. Once the user accesses the application, he/she must click on the "Login" button to start the interaction. The application is designed to work with children between the ages of 7 and 12 (1) The application has an adaptation area for the user/visitor to explore and adapt to the functionalities and mechanics implemented in the environment. Once familiarized with the environment, (2) The student and the teacher will be able to carry out the activities proposed, obtaining recognitions through the tour, applying gamification principles in teaching. (3) Finally, the results can be obtained, which can be reviewed by both the teacher and the student's tutor (See Fig. 5).

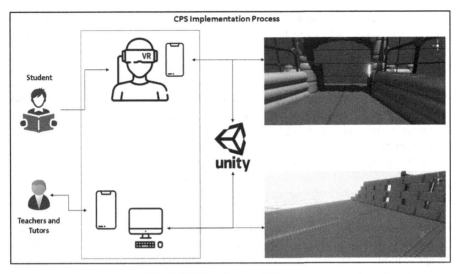

Fig. 5. CPS implementation process

The environments designed for the realization of the test seek to emulate those similar to the games present today, in order to give users an environment according to their current expectations, for this several rooms were designed in which students can interact a) Labyrinth: allows the student to move through the environment in search of the exit, asking different questions to advance, b) environment area: allows users to adapt to the systems, c) recreation area: allows users to perform various activities that motivate the physical work of the body, d) world area: allows users to present three-dimensional elements, for better absorption of knowledge (See Fig. 6).

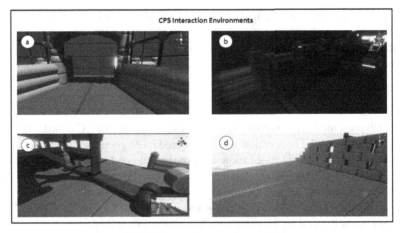

Fig. 6. Interaction environments

The connection model seeks to reduce response times between user and system, combining video game modeling techniques with programming by routines, we obtained an adequate execution time management for each action, where the execution of a function only happened if it was used, and the same case for each of the textures and models, applying mesh only in case of interaction, allowing an adequate use of memory and avoiding memory overloads in order to allow the system to be deployed on mobile devices such as PC. Finally, for the management of the application the respective configurations were made, applying tools of the IDE development, looking for the correct ergonomics in the location of each control where the user's comments were taken into account to create a better experience.

5.2 Validation

Experimental Results. Using the convenience sampling technique, 30 users, including teachers and students, were selected as respondents. After a brief general introduction to the application, each user uses the devices that already have the application. The participants begin to have a pleasant experience in the realization of the academic activities. The test session ranges from 20 to 30 min. At the end of the test in each of the educational environments, users are asked to perform an aptitude test.

To give consistency to the aptitude test, a reliability analysis was first performed using Cronbach's alpha, which yielded a value of 0.8016, indicating that the measurement items were positively correlated, therefore they are reliable constructs.

The formula applied was, by means of the variance of the items:

$$\alpha = \frac{k}{k-1}[1 - \frac{\sum V_i}{V_t}] \tag{1}$$

α : Cronbach's alpha. k : Number of items. V_i : Varriance of each item. V_t : Variance of the total.

Next, the aptitude test was applied, designed to analyze the effects of the learning process and the levels of educational absorption, based on the interaction with each recreational activity. The results show that the general opinions of the users were as follows:

- The students' learning of general knowledge showed a moderate improvement ($X^- = 3.6$, SD $= 1.00$).
- The path presented in the virtual environment was satisfactory ($X^- = 4.0$, SD $= 0.90$).
- The usefulness of the application was considered quite good ($X^- = 4.5$, SD $= 0.49$).
- The "enjoyability" of the application was considered good ($X^- = 4.1$, SD $= 0.79$).
- The exposed contents were of great help to spread the teaching in the educational unit ($X^- = 4$, SD $= 0.70$).
- The application helps students' learning and adaptation ($X^- = 4.22$, SD $= 0.59$).
- The application met their expectations ($X^- = 4.02$, SD $= 0.62$).

Additionally, SUS (System Usability Scale) was applied to measure the usability of the application. It has a questionnaire of 10 questions with five options. The results are tabulated and the usability score is calculated, with 100 as the maximum value and 0 as the minimum. If the value is above 80, the application has a high degree of usability for students/teachers, while if the value is below 68, it is considered to be below average.

The results shown in Table 1 detail the calculations made and it can be considered that the application is easy to use, since the average usability of the system is 85.02.

Table 1. Application usability evaluation

Evaluated parameters	Average	Weight	SUS Final Score
1. I think I would like to use the Designed System frequently	4,20	x-1	3,20
2. I have found the Designed System to be unnecessarily complex	1,12	5-x	3,88
3. I think the Designed System is easy to use	3,54	x-1	2,54
4. I think that I would need the support of a technician to be able to use the Designed System	1,22	5-x	3,78
5. I felt that the different functions of Sistema Diseñado were well integrated	4,69	x-1	3,69
6. I felt that there was too much inconsistency in Sistema Diseñado	1,10	5-x	3,90
7. I would imagine that most teachers and students would learn to use the Designed System very well	4,33	x-1	3,33
8. I found Sistema Diseñado to be very cumbersome (uncomfortable) to use	2,80	5-x	2,20
9. I felt very confident using Sistema Diseñado	4,70	x-1	3,70
10. I had to learn a lot of things before I started using Sistema Diseñado	1,20	5-x	3,80
Total Amount Sus Score			34,02 85,19

The results obtained show that the application of the system was successful, demonstrating that regardless of the social factor of the users, systems of this style will have great acceptance, as long as usability measures and the environment in which they work are taken into account, even so if we take into account the results of usability, the satisfaction obtained and the social environment, we can note the rapid adaptation and enjoyment of the system at the time of its use.

6 Conclusion and Future Work

In this project, advanced learning techniques were applied, in addition we sought the implementation of development methodologies in the process of learning in-teaching as is the Design Thinking, methodology that allows adaptability to any work environment, allowing to adapt it to any field, demonstrating that the paradigm established in education can be changed by one focused on trial, error and learning, also used connection tool as was the case of Unity Connect, which allowed the interconnection between the application and users, allowing to improve communication between teachers and students. This allowed each of the students who participated in the tests to interact more freely, demonstrating that improving the teaching processes means a better quality of education. Finally, we must take into account that the tested users belonged to an Andean group, who were not accustomed to the use of technology, Even so, their adaptation to the environment and the success of the tests demonstrates that the attitude changes when the method is good, in addition to the fact that the teachers were facilitated the interaction with their students and took into account the lack of training that is lacking in the country in the technological area.

The objective of this project in the future is to implement processes in the improvement of teaching at the country level, allowing a better connection between the present entities and changing the paradigms established by the current society, for which it is planned to expand the system and improve it, taking the interaction to more realistic levels, applying gamification techniques in the established teaching processes, in addition, it is planned to improve the proposed interfaces, changing the current environment for a local network so that each environment launched into production is fully functional without the need for internet, making use of old computer equipment as base servers.

References

1. Rehman, C.A.A.V.G.S.U.: Security requirements engineering: a framework for cyber-physical systems. IEEE, Islamabad (2019)
2. Khelil, A. A. A. A.: A security qualification matrix to efficiently measure security in cyber-physical systems. IEEE (2020)
3. Craggs, B., Rashid, A.: Smart cyber-physical systems: beyond usable security to security ergonomics by design, Buenos Aires: IEEE (2017)
4. Andreas, A., Abdelmajid, K.: A semantic model-based security engineering framework for cyber-physical systems. Guangzhou: IEEE (2021)
5. Rehman, S.U., Allgaier, C., Gruhn, V.: Security requirements engineering: a framework for cyber-physical systems. Islamabad: IEEE (2019)
6. OVTT, Metodologías ágiles de design thinking
7. Smith, A.: Diferencias entre Design Thinking, Lean Startup, Tentulogo (2022). https://tentulogo.com/diferencias-design-thinking-lean-startup-design-sprint-agile-scrum-kanban/
8. Constante, S.: Ecuador: la educación online desde casa es imposible e injusta, Quito, Pichincha: El País (2020)
9. Garcia, P.: 10 Estrategias para aprender cualquier cosa más rápido ¡Así funciona tu cerebro! (2016)
10. Maida, E.G., Paciencia, J.: Metodologías de Desarrollo de Software (2015)
11. Muñoz, I., Metodologias agiles para la innovaion educativa (2020)
12. unir, "¿Cómo introducir las TICs en Educación Infantil?," unir, 28 01 2022.https://www.unir.net/educacion/revista/tic-educacion-infantil/
13. Zavala, S.: El Telégrafo (2020). https://www.eltelegrafo.com.ec/noticias/columnistas/15/la-educacion-virtual

14. Romero, J.M.: Product-based learning adaptation to an online autonomous work strategy in restriction conditions by Covid-19. IEEE (2021). https://ieeexplore.ieee.org/document/938 1164

15. Constante, S.: El País (2020). https://elpais.com/elpais/2020/06/12/planeta_futuro/159195 5314_376413.html

16. Chaczko, Z., Chan, C.Y., Carrion, L.: Haptic middleware based software architecture for smart learning. IEEE, 16 07 2015. https://ieeexplore.ieee.org/document/7287029

17. Plasencia, R., Herrera, G.: Dissemination of cultural heritage: design and Implementation of a VR environment for the preservation of art and culture in Pujilí – Ecuador. IEEE (2022). https://ieeexplore.ieee.org/document/9726824

18. Campoverde, M., Luján, S.: Empirical studies on web accessibility of educational websites: a systematic literature review. IEEE (2020). https://ieeexplore.ieee.org/document/9092982

19. Campos, M.: TACTIC (2017). https://tactic-center.com/desarrollo-web/design-thinking/?loc ale=es

20. eserp, "QUÉ ES EL DESIGN THINKING Y SUS FASES," (2021). https://es.eserp.com/art iculos/que-es-el-design-thinking-y-sus-fases/

21. Alcalde, J.C.: Economipedia (2021). https://economipedia.com/definiciones/metodo-lean-sta rtup.html

22. Blender (2022). https://www.blender.org/

23. UNITY, "Unity," (2022). https://unity.com/es

24. Microsoft, "Visual Studio," (2022). https://visualstudio.microsoft.com/es/

25. Unity, "Arquitectura, Ingeniería y Construcción," (2022). https://unity.com/es/solutions/arc hitecture-engineering-construction

Open-Source Platform for Development of Taximeters: Adjustment Software

Héctor Mauricio Yépez Ponce[1] (ID), Darío Fernando Yépez Ponce[1,2](✉) (ID),
Edison Andrés Proaño Lapuerta[2] (ID), Carlos Enrique Mosquera Bone[2] (ID),
and Marcia Lizeth Alarcón Angulo[3] (ID)

[1] Ardutech.Ec, Otavalo 100450, Ecuador
dfyepez@utn.edu.ec
[2] Instituto Superior Tecnológico Luis Tello, Esmeraldas 080150, Ecuador
[3] Unidad Educativa Diocesana San Luis, Otavalo 100450, Ecuador

Abstract. In Ecuador, in order to change the configuration parameters of a taximeter, the vehicle owner must go to a metrological unit authorized by the national transit agency; there they proceed to completely disconnect the taximeter from the vehicle and connect it through a data cable (USB or RS232) to the instrument that performs the configuration, causing inconvenience to the owner and aesthetic damage to the means of transport. To facilitate the configuration process, a graphical interface was developed in Python that communicates wirelessly with an Arduino MEGA2560 board through the ESP8266 module. The Arduino board is in charge of processing all the measurable and non-measurable variables that allow the taximeter to operate. The interface allows to visualize and modify the data in a comfortable, fast and intuitive way without having to disassemble the taximeter from the vehicle. The platform was designed based on the INEN standard and the taximeter developed has an electronic paper screen on which the user can see the changes being made in the interface. In this way, an alternative open-source method was obtained in both hardware and software that differs from the traditional ones to adjust the parameters of the taximeters.

Keywords: Open-source interface · Taximeter with Python · Wireless Software adjustments

1 Introduction

The taximeter is a measuring and control instrument installed in public transportation service vehicles that gradually indicates the value to be paid by the user [1]. The use of the taximeter became mandatory in Ecuador in 1982, but for several years there were inconsistencies that prevented its application [2]. Finally, in 2013 the National Transit Agency (ANT) resolved the mandatory use of the taximeter in all cities of the country [3]. With the rapid urban construction, cabs have become an indispensable means of transportation in people's lives [4]. Currently, in the city of Ibarra there are approximately 1000 conventional cabs and 400 executive cabs [5]. The implemented taximeters have mainly two disadvantages: they have a high acquisition cost and must be constantly calibrated due to firmware misconfigurations and technical failures in the hardware. As a result, most cab users denounce irregularities in the billing of the taximeter, causing the customer not to receive a fair fare [5].

The main objective of this project was to develop a free software platform that allows adjusting taximeter fares wirelessly, thus solving the problem of having to remove the taximeter from the vehicle when software changes or calibration is needed. With the development of the platform, it was possible to configure the parameters of the taximeter wirelessly through a graphical interface, it also provides security to the user because the developed interface generates a report of the day, time and name of the person who made the changes, with this the ANT can have better control to prevent cab owners from making changes in unauthorized places.

The document is structured as follows: Sect. 2 presents the state of the art. Section 3 presents the methodology used for the development of the open-source platform, while Sect. 4 presents the results achieved. The discussion is presented in Sect. 5 and finally, Sect. 6 presents the conclusions.

2 State of the Art

In 2013, the ANT resolved the mandatory use of taximeters in vehicles providing public transport services in all cities in the country, whether under the conventional or executive mode. The Instituto Ecuatoriano de Normalización (INEN) is responsible for issuing certificates of approval of the model after verification of performance tests and compliance with regulations.

According to the INEN standard in [3], it establishes that the taximeter must be equipped with a user interface that allows the exchange of information between a human user and the taximeter; the same that must allow visualizing and configuring the following parameters:

- General information (Owner information).
- Verification marks (Constant k, taximeter serial number, vehicle identification, revision date, actual date and time).
- Tariff Information: The parameters of the tariffs presented in [3].

2.1 Commercial Taximeters in Ecuador

ANT in [6], describes the different models of taximeters approved in the country with their respective suppliers, control and safety.

Taximeters vary in functionality according to the manufacturer, however; the communication used for parameter configuration and firmware update are similar (wired).

Taximeter S700. It is Manufactured by the Company Centrodyne, Has 16 Standard Rates that Perform an Automatic Change, Programmable Speed Limit, Three Levels of Security Password and Communication with the Computer is via Bluetooth, USB or RS232 [7].

Taximeter M1 Plus. It is in the Form of a Rear-View Mirror of the Digitax Brand, Communication is Through Two RS232 Serial Ports at Any Baud Rate from 300 to 115200 and Uses the COMMTAX2 Protocol that Allows Remote Administration of the Taximeter, Chip Card Reading and Printer Functions Described in [8].

Taximeter Optronic TX-10. Device 100% Designed and Built in Ecuador by the Company Electrónica Industrial Optronic. It is Multi-rate, that is, It Can Operate with Different Rates Depending on the Time and Date of the day. The Communication is by TTL Serial, RS232 or RS485 and Can Be Connected to Various Peripherals Such as Printer and GPS [9].

Tango XP Taximeter. This Taximeter Has Six Independent Fares and Flexible Software that Can Be Modified According to Changes in Current Regulations and Ordinances. To Make Changes to the Configuration Software It is Necessary to Have a JTAG Module that Allows Communication with the Computer Through a COM Port [10].

2.2 Graphical Interface

An interface must allow intercommunication between the hardware and software of a device in a friendly way, i.e., the interface talks to the user, but not verbally, but through the graphic elements that compose it [11].

In [12] it is stated that the development of an interface is a multidisciplinary work that must be carried out between engineers, psychologists, sociologists, graphic designers, among others; in order to achieve a final product that is easy to understand, aesthetically pleasing, satisfies the user's needs and meets the required functionalities.

A user interface must take into account the physical and mental capabilities of the people who are going to use the software, for this reason [13], ensures that at least the following aspects should be considered during the process:

- User analysis: understand the tasks the user performs, identify and establish requirements.
- System prototyping: develop several prototypes of the system and expose them to the users, who can then guide the evolution of the interface.
- Evaluation of the interface: this activity will allow gathering information about the users' actual experiences with the interface.

Finally, the usability of a product will depend on the following aspects: effectiveness, efficiency, security, easy to learn and easy to remember [12].

3 Methodology

3.1 General System Structure

The general scheme of the system can be seen in Fig. 1, which shows in general terms the elements involved in the process of sending and receiving data between the taximeter and the graphic interface.

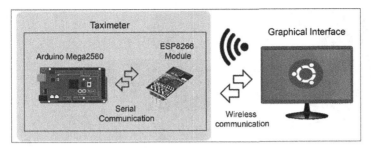

Fig. 1. General scheme of the system.

3.2 Evolutionary Development Model (Spiral)

For the development of the open-source platform, the evolutionary (spiral) development model proposed by Barry Boehm in 1986 was used. By applying the spiral model, the software is developed in a series of evolutionary deliveries. Each of the activities in the framework represents a segment of the spiral path, and each repetitive cycle brings the software to maturity [14]. A schematic of the Spiral model is shown in Fig. 2.

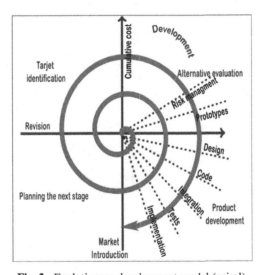

Fig. 2. Evolutionary development model (spiral).

3.3 Flowchart of Interface Operation

The flow diagram in Fig. 3 represents the sequence of activities that must be performed to configure the taximeter parameters from the graphical interface developed. For this purpose, the beginning of the process, the decision points, the data input and the end of the process are shown.

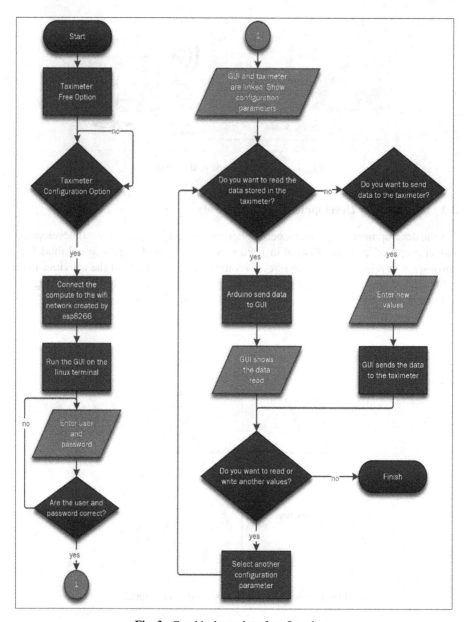

Fig. 3. Graphical user interface flowchart.

3.4 Development of the Adjustment Software

The adjustment software was developed on the open-source Ubuntu operating system, which is an easy to use, secure, stable and free Linux distribution that can be easily downloaded from the Internet [15]. The programming language for user interface development is Python, which is an interpreted, interactive, object-oriented general-purpose programming language that uses high-level data structures and a simple syntax [16].

The design of the graphical interface developed takes into account the characteristics shown in [17].

- Simple: only the necessary elements were placed, avoiding their saturation.
- Clear: the information is organized and easy to locate.
- Flexible: it is clear and can be easily understood, it uses formats that are compatible with other platforms.
- Consistent: it presents a similarity of design between the tabs or chapters of the program.
- Intuitive: allows the user to interact safely without having to guess at functions.
- Coherent: the graphics, colors and other elements are in accordance with the type of information to be transmitted.

The design of the developed graphical interface that meets the criteria described above is shown in Fig. 4.

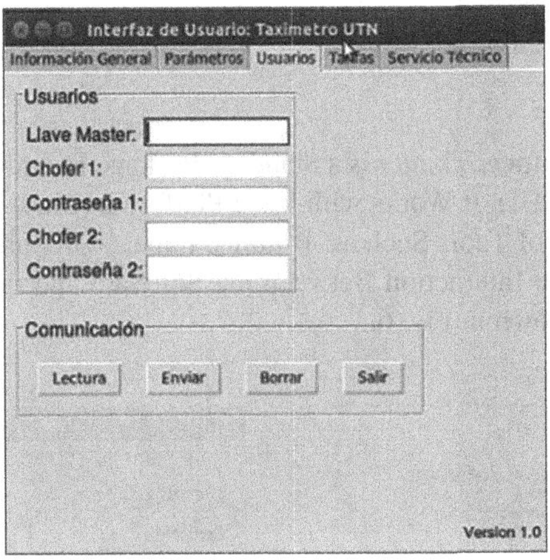

Fig. 4. Graphical user interface.

The configuration software integrates a verification system that allows access to the user interface only to authorized personnel who are registered in the database (see Fig. 5). This allows the interface to generate an auditable file that includes an event counter that which will increase each time an intervention is made on any of the taximeter parameters. Furthermore, it specifies the date, time and the person who made the intervention. This can be viewed in more detail in the date and time settings window.

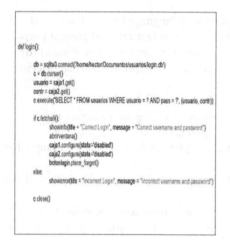
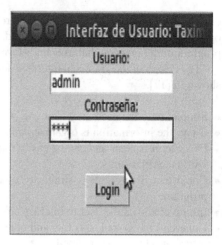

Fig. 5. Access window for authorized personnel with its source code.

The open-source platform is composed of three subsystems which are:

- Graphical user interface.
- Date and time configuration.
- Data transfer.

Graphical User Interface. Tkinter is a Standard Package Included in Python for Creating User Interfaces (GUI), It Works with Most Platforms (Linux OSX, Windows) [18]. Tkinter Has a Variety of Tools Such as: Buttons, Labels, Graphics, Text, Windows and Tabs that Facilitate the Interaction Between the Software and the User. The Code and User Interface Are Shown in Fig. 6.

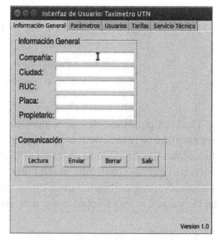

Fig. 6. Main window of GUI with its source code.

Date and Time Configuration. For This, the Packages Datetime [19], Calendar [20] and for Manipulating Time Expressions [21] Must Be Used. The Configuration of the Time and Date Can Be Done in Two Ways, the First One is Taking as Reference the Computer Time and the Second One is Entering Through the Text Boxes the Desired Time and Date (See Fig. 7).

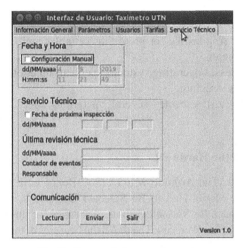

Fig. 7. Date and time configuration.

Data Transfer. The Data Transfer from the Computer to the Arduino MEGA2560 Board is Done via Wi-Fi Through the ESP8266 Module (See Fig. 8).

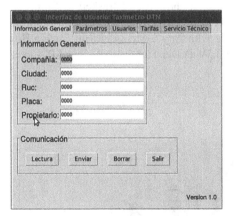

Fig. 8. Data transfer.

The data transfer is done through the TCP/IP protocol using the Python socket module [22]. This type of communication requires a server socket (ESP8266) and a client socket (Computer), which when connected will allow the writing and reading of parameters between them. The communication is successful when the IP address and port number between sender and receiver are correctly linked.

The number of bytes for sending and receiving data will depend on the size of the microcontroller buffer, that is why it was decided to dispatch the data in parts, thus achieving an orderly reading and writing without errors, avoiding the loss of information during transmission. Finally, three additional modules were used in the design of the adjustment software:

- sys module [23], is responsible for providing variables and functionalities, directly related to the interpreter.
- os module [24], accesses operating system-dependent functionalities, mainly manipulating the directory structure.
- Threading module [25], executes several operations simultaneously in the same process space.

3.5 Development of the Hardware

Arduino MEGA2560. The Arduino MEGA2560 Board is in Charge of Processing the Information, This Model Had to Be Selected Because It Requires Considerable EEPROM Memory Space for Variable Storage, Libraries for the SD Card, RTC and e-paper Monochrome Display Were also Used. All the Features of the Arduino MEGA2560 Board Are Described in [26].

RTC. The RTC DS3231 Module, Which is Connected to the Arduino Board, is Responsible for Determining the Different Fares Configured in the Taximeter.

E-paper Monochrome Display. E-Paper Technology (See Fig. 9) is a Technology that Allows the Creation of Graphic Displays with Virtually Zero Power Consumption. The Display Only Draws Power When It is Refreshed and Once Refreshed, It Continues to Display the Image or Graphics Indefinitely with Virtually no Power Consumption. It Works with an SPI Bus so It is Compatible with Any System that Has Such a Bus: Arduino, Raspberry, Feather Etc. It Needs a 3.3V Power Supply as Well as SPI Levels at the Same Voltage [27].

Fig. 9. 2.9-inch E-Ink display module.

4 Results

The source codes and the video of the operation of the open-software platform are available in the following repository https://github.com/hectorm1995/Taximeter-code.

The development of this graphical interface guarantees the user the reading and writing of information in a simple way, the interface consists of three windows and the actions they perform are:

- Control that the login is performed by authorized persons by means of a username and password.
- To visualize the parameters with which the taximeter is working at that moment, these data are stored in the EEPROM memory of the microcontroller.
- Send the new configuration values.

The ANT agent in the city of Ibarra that interacted with the open-source platform followed the following process:

- Energized the ESP8266 module and the Arduino board.
- Connected the computer to the wireless network created by the ESP8266 Wi-Fi module.
- He put the taximeter in configuration mode, for which he previously selected the option that was found free.
- Entered the user and verification password.

Once the user and password have been entered correctly, proceed to enter the following information:

- Main data of the owner and the vehicle.
- Values for the calculation of the rates.
- The rates set by the municipality according to the ordinance.
- The date of the next inspection.

Subsequently, the data was sent to the taximeter as shown in Fig. 10.

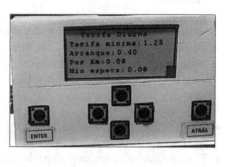

Fig. 10. Tariff values sent from the GUI are displayed on the taximeter display.

The process is completed by indicating the number of times the device has been modified and the name of the person who modified the values through the interface (see Fig. 11).

Fig.11. Registration of the person responsible for making changes in the adjustment software.

5 Discussion

The developed open-source platform communicates wirelessly with the taximeter unlike the taximeters developed by [8–10], which must be disassembled and connected to the computer by means of a cable with TTL Serial, RS232, RS485 or JTAG communication.

The configuration interface of taximeters from [7–10] use licensed software, the control units must cancel annually to the manufacturers; while the open-source platform developed no licensing costs must be cancelled. That is, the control units would make a single payment for the configuration interface.

The taximeter developed by [7], is able to communicate with the interface via wireless communication with an average range of 10 m in a straight line, on the other hand the open-source platform with the developed device in a straight line can communicate at a distance of 30 m. Similarly, Bluetooth communication allows sending data serially, i.e., one after the other, while the ESP8266 module sends all the platform data in a single chain.

The open-source platform developed, unlike those created by [7–10], generates a counter that indicates the number of times it has been configured and the name of the person who performed it, thus allowing better control of who manipulates the device.

6 Conclusions

In this work, a free software platform was developed that allows to configure the relevant data of a taximeter such as: general information of the owner and the vehicle, check marks for the calculation of cost among them the impulses per kilometer made by the car, adjustment of tariffs and finally updating the time and date. The changes are carried out through an interface developed in Ubuntu.

An algorithm was developed that performs the configurations wirelessly through the ESP8266 module that was configured as a server using the TCP/IP protocol, allowing the system to exchange information between the computer that contains the graphic interface and the Arduino Mega2560 board in charge of executing the entire process when the taximeter is in operation.

The interface was made using the Tkinter module which is the standard interface of the Python programming language, this module allowed to create an application that interacts friendly with the user without forgetting the security measures that avoid accidental changes of the parameters.

All the functionality of the computer system can be evidenced by the taximeter screen which displays the user's settings through the graphical interface and the taximeter is ready to enter the working mode.

References

1. Resolución N020-DIR-2013-ANT.: Reglamento de aplicación para la homologación, instalación y uso del taxímetro en el servicio de transporte comercial en taxis convencionales y ejecutivos. Quito, Ecuador (2013)
2. Cuasapaz, M.: Construcción e implementación de un prototipo de un taxímetro digital con impresora facturadora utilizando tecnología GPS y el desarrollo de un firmware en un microcontrolador. Tesis Pregrado, Escuela Politécnica Nacional, Quito, Ecuador (2013)
3. NTE INEN 2663:2013.: Taxímetros. Requisitos metrológicos y técnicos, procedimientos de ensayo. Quito, Ecuador (2013)
4. Wu, B., An, A.: FPGA design and implementation of taximeter anti -fraud system. In: IEEE Youth Academic Annual Conference of Chinese Association of Automation, pp. 654–659 (2018)
5. Morales, C.: Diseño, construcción e implementación de un taxímetro con almacenamiento de viajes mediante GPS en el vehículo Chevrolet corsa wind 1.4. Tesis Pregrado, Universidad Técnica del Norte, Ibarra, Ecuador (2016)

6. Agencia Nacional de Tránsito. https://www.ant.gob.ec/index.php/descargable/file/6007-direcciones-deempresas-distribuidoras-autorizadas-por-la-ant-al-19–12–2018. Accessed 06 Mar 2019
7. Centrodyne Inc. http://www.centrodyne.com/es/products/taximeters/s700. Accessed 06 Mar 2019
8. Digitax Automotive Electronics. http://www.digitax.com/products/Taximetro-M1.html. Accessed 06 Mar 2019
9. Optronic, http://optroniconline.com/category/taximetros. Accessed 06 Mar 2019
10. Ful-Mar S.A.: http://www.ful-mar.com.ar/productos/relojes.html. Accessed 06 Mar 2019
11. Martínez, Y., Córdoba, C.: Diseño de Interfaz de Usuario para Creación de Sistemas Multimedia para Apoyar el Desarrollo del Lenguaje. In: Tecnología y Diseño, vol. 9, pp. 39- 55 (2018)
12. Preece, J., Rogers, Y., Sharp, H.: Interaction Design: beyond human-computer interaction. G. Crockett, Ed. Estados Unidos de Amrica, John Wiley y Sons, Inc (2002)
13. Sommerville, I.: Ingeniería del Software. 7 th edn, Madrid, Pearson Educación. S.A., pp. 344- 346 (2005)
14. Zumba, J., León, C.: Evolución de las metodologías y modelos utilizados en el desarrollo de software. INNOVA Res. J. 3(10), 20–33 (2018)
15. Luna, L.: El diseño de interfaz gráfica de usuario para publicaciones digitales. In: Revista UNAM, vol. 5, no. 7, pp. 7–12 (2004).14
16. Al Housani, B., Mutrib, B., Jaradi, H.: The linux review-ubuntu desktop edition version 8.10. In: International Conference on the Current Trends in Information Technology (CTIT), Dubai, pp. 1–6 (2009)
17. Sanner, M.: Python: a programming language for software integration and development. J. Molecular Graph. Model. November (1998)
18. Python, Graphical User Interfaces with Tk. https://docs.python.org/3/library/tk.html. Accessed 06 Mar 2019
19. Python, datetime Basic date and time types. https://docs.python.org/3/library/datetime.html. Accessed 06 Mar 2019
20. Python, calendar general calendar-related functions. https://docs.python.org/3/library/calendar.html#modulecalendar. Accessed 06 Mar 2019
21. Python, time Time access and conversions. https://docs.python.org/3/library/time.html#module-time. Accessed 06 Mar 2019
22. Python, socket Low-level networking interface. https://docs.python.org/3/library/socket.html. Accessed 06 Mar 2019
23. Python, sys System-specific parameters and functions. https://docs.python.org/3/library/sys.html. Accessed 06 Mar 2019
24. Python, OS Miscellaneous operating system interfaces. https://docs.python.org/3/library/os.html. Accessed 06 Mar 2019
25. Python, threading Thread-based parallelism. https://docs.python.org/3/library/threading.html. Accessed 06 Mar 2019
26. Arduino, ARDUINO MEGA 2560 REV3. https://store.arduino.cc/usa/mega-2560-r3. Accessed 06 Mar 2019
27. Waveshare, 296x128, 2.9inch E-Ink display module. https://www.waveshare.com/2.9inch-e-paper-module.htm. Accessed 06 Mar 2019

XiMent: Multiplatform Cognitive Training System Based on Multimedia Technologies and Reminiscence Methodology for the Population of Older Adults with Mild Cognitive Impairment

Edison Richard Simbaña, Juan Carlos Velasco[⊠], Ximena López Chico, and Patricio Navas Moya

Universidad de Las Fuerzas Armadas ESPE, Sangolquí, Ecuador
{ersimbana2,jcvelasco3,xrlopez,mpnavas}@espe.edu.ec

Abstract. The application of memory stimulation programs in the aging stage is a term that emphasizes mental health and favors the maintenance or decrease of mild cognitive impairment. Over time, the methodologies used to apply traditional therapeutic exercises have become repetitive, monotonous and tedious therapies in older adults. The rehabilitation process of older adults with cognitive impairment requires multisensory stimulation involving games and multimedia materials that bring dynamism to the treatment, preventing patients from losing interest and motivation during the treatment. Mild cognitive impairment is a geriatric syndrome that affects the cognitive area of attention, learning, thinking and language, which tends to cause depression and feelings of uselessness in the elderly, however, older adults are one of the fundamental pillars of society, and it is essential to provide care and security to this population.

Keywords: Technology · Older adult · Mild cognitive impairment · Reminiscence

1 Introduction

One of the most prominent alterations faced by society in old age is depression and mild cognitive impairment. Mild cognitive impairment is understood as a process of loss of cognitive capacity in which biological, psychological and social factors are involved [1].

This condition present in older adults includes memory loss, difficulty in complet-ing activities, tasks, following instructions, and problem solving [2]. The older adult population with mild cognitive impairment is at greater risk for depression and feelings of worthlessness due to their inability to adapt in society [3]. In recent years, technological advances have made possible the development of treatments focused on methodolo-gies that motivate the patient during the rehabilitation process. Among these treatments is the multisensory approach, which allows the patient to receive sensory, tactile and

M. Botto-Tobar et al. (Eds.): ICAT 2022, CCIS 1755, pp. 545–558, 2023.
https://doi.org/10.1007/978-3-031-24985-3_40

visual stimuli, becoming a powerful tool for the treatment of cognitive stimulation [4]. Therapies using the multisensory approach show promising results in older adults [5]. However, in the country there is a lack of technological support tools in the geriatric area. This fact causes that the community of older adults with cognitive impairment does not receive proper rehabilitation [1].

The research proposes the development of a multiplatform system that supports the daily activities of patients with mild cognitive impairment. The development of multisensory therapy aims to perform intellectual activities to exercise memory, attention, calculation and interaction with video games that stimulate them at this stage of rehabilitation [6].

The project allows to adequately conclude the phases of software development, demonstrating the importance of technology to solve problems for the benefit of society in the stage of older adulthood [7]. For the development of the application, the research focused on the compilation and analysis of the bibliography of scientific publications, geriatrics books, and a field research work in a geriatric center where important results were obtained in the development of the interactive multisensory system based on the therapeutic program of Reminiscence [8].

2 Methodology

The multiplatform cognitive training system is composed of a web application that follows the progress of cognitive stimulation of the elderly, and a video game where the elderly can interact and play at any time. This video game is a perfect combination between the Reminiscence methodology and technologies that avoid distractions or lack of interest of elderly patients with mild cognitive impairment [9].

The methodologies used to improve the patient's well-being and quality of life are oriented to develop comprehensive intervention programs that include cognitive, behavioral, affective and physiological strategies. Using these strategies for the stimulation of memory and executive function in the older adult with this pathology, improve the problems related to memory loss or other loss of cognitive ability such as language, visual and spatial perception [10].

2.1 Mild Cognitive Impairment

According to the Spanish Association of Geriatrics, mild cognitive impairment is a clinical syndrome characterized by the loss of mental functions of memory, orienta-tion, calculation, visual recognition, judgment and personality [11]. Mild cognitive impairment is a weakness associated with difficulty remembering important events, solving problems, understanding instructions, and making decisions [12]. The older adult with mild cognitive impairment presents several social challenges, which include depressive state due to the decline in mental abilities associated with aging [13].

It is assumed that the constant expectation of failure experienced by older adults with mild cognitive impairment is associated with serious emotional consequences, such as depression. Where it is often accompanied by symptoms of psychomotor retardation, and includes loss of interest in performing usual activities. Along with aging, the physiological and psychological functions of older adults tend to weaken; in particular, the sensory organs and the nervous system involved in psychological activities undergo degenerative changes [10].

2.2 Technology and Digital Media in Geriatric Therapies

As society ages, there are changes in cognitive performance, with frequent neurological alterations in the areas of attention, memory, language, visuospatial ability and intelligence [14].

Among the effective non-pharmacological treatments for mild cognitive impairment, emphasis is placed on cognitive stimulation by means of new information and communication technologies, which make it possible to prolong life in a natural environment with greater security, and to reduce the feeling of isolation or rejection by society among older adults [15]. According to experts in Geriatrics, the continued use of everyday technology contributes positively against cognitive impairment, allowing to work varied cognitive processes such as reaction speed, response inhibition or avoid-ance of distractions [3]. Studies on "non-universal" design and development of tools that meet the needs of people with functional diversity and elderly people with mild cogni-tive impairment are very limited. The main problem in any kind of software applica-tions, including a geriatric assistive technology, is usability [15].

2.3 Multiplatform Application: Therapeutic Environment

In therapies, technological tools allow detecting possible cognitive impairment and propose personalized exercise sessions for the older adult to work on different areas and improve cognitive performance. The multiplatform application has become an essential support to exercise the mind constantly, stimulating attention and maintaining healthy habits of patients with mild cognitive impairment [16]. The development of multiplatform applications in the therapeutic environment is able to adapt to the environment of the older adult, allowing adaptation to the assigned activities and to develop in an environment with greater comfort [17].

The features and functionality of multiplatform environments serve as therapy for older adults suffering from this disorder, as they expose subjects to environmental adaptation, sensory stimuli, such as visual impressions and sounds, through the use of a tablet or cell phone [8].

2.4 Multisensory Reminiscence Therapy

The most effective psychosocial intervention for the older adult with mild cognitive impairment is Reminiscence therapy. Its approach is to recall events of the patient's personal history by stimulating memories with personal meaning and favoring their interrelation, reinforcing the self-esteem and the entity of the older adult [14].

Figure 1 shows the first step of the therapy, where the focus is on working the orientation and attention area of the older adult, through the fluid and accurate acquisition of

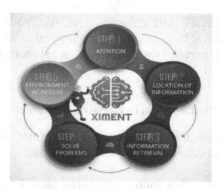

Fig. 1. Cognitive stimulation computational therapy

information. Then, it establishes the visual modality, where the patient should work on the area of information recognition and concepts in an orderly manner. The third step consists of the older adult focusing on the activity and retrieving the information after a short or long period of time. In this step the patient will have the ability to record, consolidate and recall previously stored information. In the fourth step, the older adult with mild cognitive impairment will be able to solve problems by acquiring a variety of information, which will enable him/her to form thoughts and ideas in an orderly and logical manner. In the last step, the patient will be able to develop mental manipulation of the position of objects, and will be able to adapt to modifications in daily activities that are presented.

2.5 Reminiscence Methodology for Videogames

Neuroscience studies indicate that the regular use of video games yields positive re-sults in skills such as memory, reaction speed and problem solving [11].

The Reminiscence methodology for video games aims to recall events in the per-sonal history of older adults with mild cognitive impairment through multisensory stimulation. Its multisensory structure allows older adults to work motor and visuospatial areas that favor neurodevelopmental rehabilitation. In turn, through the use of multisensory tools, the patient is provided, a space of comfort, in order to develop, at their own pace, their belonging and identity through memories [18]. To be characterized as a computational rehabilitation methodology, four main modules are established, where the area of atten-tion, orientation, recognition and memory are worked. Authors such as Williams and Dritschel (1988) argue that overgeneralized memories result from deficiencies in the encoding and retrieval processes due to a hypersensitivity to the emotional aspects of situations and a reduced use of positive stimuli in retrieval [8]. Taking into account the above explanations, reminiscence is pro-posed as a strategy to promote a style of remem-bering everyday episodes through multimedia therapy. The Reminiscence methodology aims to use easy and dynamic user interface designs, which occupy colors and resources in large size to help high-light important therapeutic content [14]. It also aims to provide the patient with a comfortable working environment, therefore, the orientation module is implemented. This module makes use of various multimedia instructions and settings in order to maintain order and concentration in the rehabilitation activities.

The third module of this methodology refers to the use of multimedia tools as responsible for facilitating and enhancing the recognition of information. This is due to the use of different ludic and recreational elements, which at the same time individu-alize the transmission of the content, allowing a greater depth in the therapy of the patient with mild cognitive impairment. Finally, in the memory module, recreational computer resources are used for therapeutic purposes to increase cognitive reserve and stimulate mental activity [6].

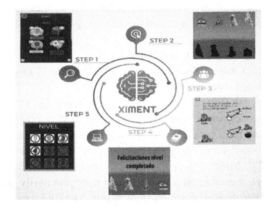

Fig. 2. XiMent-multisensory methodology of reminiscence

Figure 2 shows the XiMent video game using the Reminiscence methodology for video games. This multisensory therapy is used for the rehabilitation of mild cognitive impairment in older adults. In the first stage of the videogame, a dynamic menu is displayed that promotes colors and resources suitable for rehabilitation, such as attention, memory, calculation and executive function games. Subsequently, in the second stage, the patient will make use of multimedia resources (images and sounds) to perform the assigned activities. In the third stage, a help section (support) is presented in order to grasp the instructions of the game and move forward with their therapy. The objective of the fourth stage is to take care of the patient's mental health, congratulating his effort and recognizing his achievements. The last section refers to the adaptation of the video game to the patient. It visualizes the levels of progress that the patient has within the multisensory environment.

3 Implementation

3.1 Game Engine

XiMent is a multiplatform application that focuses on the development of 2D geriatric games, created for mobile phones and computers. In addition, it has a large catalog of libraries that allow its use for free [19]. The architecture of the multiplatform video game was built in Unity 2D, by means of creative tools for the development of quality environments [20]. The Unity graphics engine presents an efficiency to the requirements of older adults with cognitive impairment. The Unity game engine uses the C# programming language, because it provides special support for making multiplatform video games in planned times [21]. The development of web application support for the mild cognitive impairment specialist focused on using the PHP framework Laravel [22]. The use of Laravel allowed a highly functional development environment, with modules according to the patient's needs [23].

Computational therapy focuses on supporting the therapist through a web page, developed in Angular, which is a framework for web applications developed in TypeScript, open source, maintained by Google [24]. The security mechanism was elaborated with JWT (JSON Web Token), a standard that allows to encode in Base64 the patients' information.

The database system of patients with mild cognitive impairment was implemented in MySql, which is a relational database management system developed under dual license, where it has a structured data collection [25].

The following figure (Fig. 3) shows the development process of the multisensory therapy, assisted by a web application that will be administered by a specialist, and will evaluate the progress of the patient with mild cognitive impairment during its rehabilitation [26]. And a video game where the elderly with this condition can improve their cognitive aspects [27]. Multisensory therapy focuses on supporting patients with mild cognitive impairment, therefore, through physical tests previously performed, the specialist can help in their rehabilitation through multimedia tools, such as sound, images and instructions within an environment suitable to their condition [28]. Thanks to the

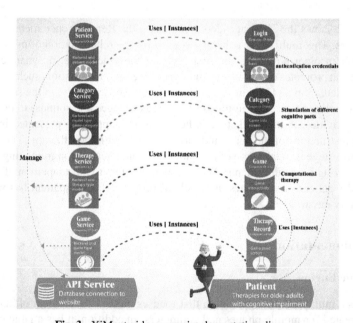

Fig. 3. XiMent video game implementation diagram

information stored in the database, the specialist will be able to visualize in a certain time the progress of the patients, it is suggested which aspects to reinforce. The execution of this project is done through multimedia tools and character controller functionalities for a realistic effect within the video game [26]. The project aims to be a virtual support and monitoring tool for older adults with mild cognitive impairment.

3.2 Multiplatform Application Environment

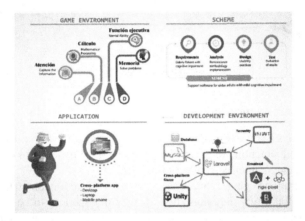

Fig. 4. Environment diagram

Figure 4 shows the development process of multisensory therapy, assisted by a web application that will be administered by a specialist, and will evaluate the progress of the patient with mild cognitive impairment during rehabilitation. And a video game where the elderly with this condition can improve their cognitive aspects.

4 Games

4.1 Cognitive Area Attention

The following figure (Fig. 5) proposes a space designed to work on the cognitive area of attention, implementing the games 'Jump and Join'. In the first instance, both games present an interface with instructions.

In the 'Jump' game, the objective is for the older adult to recognize the word presented on the screen and the images on the sides of the screen, once this process is completed, the patient must select one of the dates for the character to go to the image chosen, generating an animation of a jump. The objective of the 'Join' game is for the older adult to recognize the figures presented on the screen and to relate them to the name of the two pictures at the other end of the screen. Both games are based on reinforcing the cognitive area of attention as well as observation and coordination. The games have 5 sessions which are presented as the patient progresses through the therapy and a time and score statistic is kept.

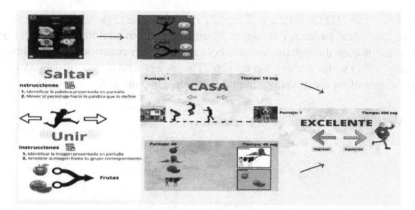

Fig. 5. Cognitive area attention games

4.2 Cognitive Area Attention Games

The following figure (Fig. 6) proposes a space designed to work on the cognitive area of calculation, implementing the games 'Operations and Advance'. In the first instance, both games present an interface with instructions.

In the 'Operations' game, the objective is to reinforce mathematical calculation in older adults, for which they must first identify the operator to be performed, then perform the mathematical operation and choose the correct option among the three options presented. The objective of the 'Advance' game is for the older adult to recognize what is presented on the screen, which can be a mathematical operation or a figure, at the bottom of the screen there are two options that the older adult must select, for each correct answer the patient gets, the dummy at the bottom moves forward, the session ends when the dummy reaches the goal.

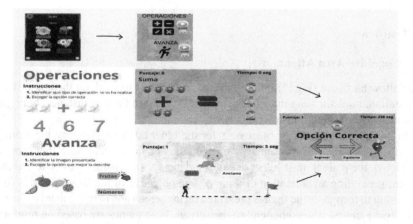

Fig. 6. Cognitive area calculation games

4.3   Cognitive Area Memory

The following figure (Fig. 7) proposes a space designed to work on the cognitive memory area, implementing the games 'Find the Pair and Match'. In the first instance, both games present an interface with instructions.

In the 'Find the Pair' game, the older adult works on memory by having to review and memorize the cards that belong to a group and have a similar pair. The patient must select a card, it will turn and will present on its front side an image that the patient must memorize, after 3 s it will turn over and the patient must find its similar pair, once the pair is found, these cards are eliminated from the screen, the session ends when all the pairs are found. The 'Match' game has the objective of reinforcing the memory of the older adult by presenting a question on the screen and three answer options, who must choose the appropriate option. The games have 5 sessions which are presented as the patient progresses through the therapy and a time and score statistic is kept.

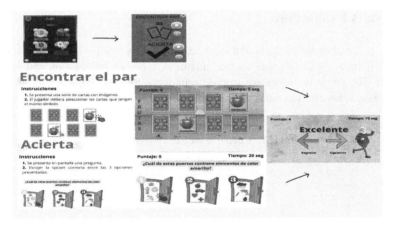

Fig. 7. Cognitive area memory games, Juegos area cognitiva memoria

4.4   Área Cognitiva Función Ejecutiva

Figure 8 shows a space designed to work on the cognitive area of executive function, implementing the games 'Target Shooting and Fit'. The objective in both games is for the older adult to reinforce his executive action of observing and coordinating.

In the game 'Target Shooting' the patient must identify the word presented on the screen and select the correct answer from the two possible options. In the 'Fit' game, the patient must use the arrows to move the ball through the maze to reach the goal at the other end of the maze.

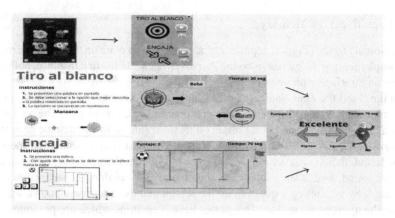

Fig. 8. Cognitive area executive function games

5   Results Evaluation

For data processing, an analysis of 5 therapeutic sessions was performed. Each session works different cognitive areas such as attention, memory, calculation and executive function. The cognitive areas are worked separately, and are implemented through 2 mini-games. Where the patient is studied the time it takes to solve the problems presented.

Table 1. Cognitive area assessment results

Patient – Session	Attention	Memory	Calculation	Executive Function
P1 -S1	596	389	499	625
P1-S2	688	497	1230	916
P1-S3	805	218	635	390
P1-S4	479	585	667	994
P1-S5	758	235	648	1034
P2-S1	530	201	768	492
P2-S2	610	557	1046	879
P2-S3	718	373	684	1021
P2-S4	430	426	1019	648
P2-S5	735	530	1384	991
P3-S1	778	562	1237	774
P3-S2	593	390	591	955
P3-S3	475	496	992	893

(*continued*)

Table 1. (*continued*)

Patient – Session	Attention	Memory	Calculation	Executive Function
P3-S4	836	501	1349	761
P3-S5	770	248	503	658
P4-S1	617	265	652	1061
P4-S2	727	475	1163	918
P4-S3	545	346	767	706
P4-S4	389	526	924	702
P4-S5	655	541	1006	401
P5-S1	758	420	587	988
P5-S2	816	204	576	938
P5-S3	474	529	1290	777
P5-S4	568	456	576	909
P5-S5	637	500	548	666

In Table 1. The study of 5 adults with mild cognitive impairment. Which were subjects of 5 sessions monitored for a significant time. For the realization and implementation of computational therapy, studies were conducted over a month. Monthly results of the 5 sessions were obtained for each patient. And evidence of adaptation to the computational environment of 2% and an improvement of 3% in cognitive geriatric rehabilitation was found.

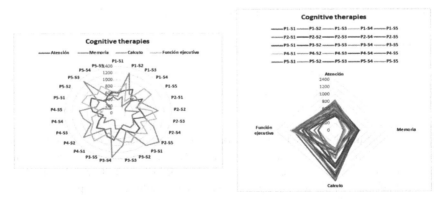

Fig. 9. Graphic representation of the evaluation of cognitive areas

Figure 9 graphically represents the results of each patient from the initial and final perspective of rehabilitation. During the time between sessions, it was determined that there was no continuous existence in the data statistics, due to extreme emotional cases presented by the patient. Varying from a positive state (better adaptation to the environment) to a negative state (rejection by the application). As for the geriatric results found, through the use of computer technologies, the patient was able to completely conclude his therapy.

6 Discussion

Cognitive impairment in older adults is strongly influenced by environmental and social factors, so it cannot be managed only with a clinical-pharmacological approach. Being a multifactorial pathology, it requires the management of public health policies that evaluate the patient. The XiMent software, through the Reminiscence Methodology, fosters a great opportunity to integrate technology into the lives of elderly people with mild cognitive impairment. This neuropsychological rehabilitation tool has been positively evaluated by elderly patients and the specialists in charge of their treatment. Its impact was positive, due to the implementation of the Reminiscence methodology for video games. This methodology provides applicability and effectiveness in cognitive functions such as attention, language, memory and executive-spatial functions. This methodology focuses on supporting cognitive therapy, therefore, social and friendly environments are used to capture the attention of elderly people with mild cognitive impairment.

7 Future Work

For future work, analyze the methodology in other research areas, focusing on neurodegenerative diseases in the elderly, and it is also suggested to apply the methodology in people with early dementia. Improve the application by increasing the number of cognitive areas and sessions to obtain more accurately in which area the older adult has greater difficulty and focus therapy in those areas. It is proposed to add virtual reality to the application by creating scenarios that resemble the patient's daily life and observe the possible results in the rehabilitation of the elderly patient.

8 Conclusions

Through the Ximent application, it is visualized that the Reminiscence methodology provides an improvement in the rehabilitation of the patient with mild cognitive impairment. Following the implementation of the application, the respective tests were conducted to obtain results based on the cognitive therapy sessions, which involve activities that speed up memory and help the brain and cognitive functions of the affected person, so that their memories are not lost quickly. The application pro-motes a close communication between the specialist and the patient in order to have a better control in a dynamic and friendly way, using multiplatform technology. The application is composed of five modules, which work in the areas of attention, orientation, recognition, memory and adaptation to the environment. This computational therapy allows patients to improve their cognitive abilities so that they can reduce memory loss over the years. It is deduced that computational therapies contribute positively in the field of geriatrics and psychology, helping in the treatment of the elderly with cognitive impairment resulting in confidence and motivation to the elderly.

References

1. Buenaño Barrionuevo, L.A.: Deterioro cognitivo, depresión y estrés asociados con enfermedades crónicas en adultos mayores, Cuenca 2014, p. 8, 2 de octubre de (2019)
2. Parada Peña, K., Rodríguez Morera, M., Otoya Chaves, F., Loaiza Quirós, K., León Quirós, Y.S.: Síndromes geriátricos: caídas, incontinencia y deterioro cognitivo, p. 10, 15 de diciembre de (2020)
3. Williams, S.E., Ford, J.H., Kensinger, Y.E.A.: The power of negative and positive episodic memories, Cogn. Affect. Behav. Neurosci., jun. (2022). https://doi.org/10.3758/s13415-022-01013-z
4. Lee, L.-P., Har, A.W.-Y., Ngai, C.-H., Lai, D.W.L., Lam, B.Y.-H. Chan, Y.C.C.-H.: Audiovisual integrative training for augmenting cognitive- motor functions in older adults with mild cognitive impairment, BMC Geriatr. **20**(1), 64 (2020). https://doi.org/10.1186/s12877-020-1465-8
5. Ge, S., Zhu, Z., Wu, B., McConnell, Y.E.S.: Technology-based cognitive training and rehabilitation interventions for individuals with mild cognitive impairment: a systematic review, BMC Geriatr. **18**(1), Art. no. 1, Sep. (2018). https://doi.org/10.1186/s12877-018-0893-1
6. Xu, J., Wang, B.: Efficacy of VR-based reminiscence therapy in improving autobiographical memory for Chinese patients with AD. In: Rebelo, F., Soares, M. (eds.) AHFE 2020. AISC, vol. 1203, pp. 339–349. Springer, Cham (2020). https://doi.org/10.1007/978-3-030-51038-1_47
7. Astell, A., Alm, N., Dye, R., Gowans, G., Vaughan, P., Ellis, M.: Digital video games for older adults with cognitive impairment. In: Miesenberger, K., Fels, D., Archambault, D., Peñáz, P., Zagler, W. (eds.) ICCHP 2014. LNCS, vol. 8547, pp. 264–271. Springer, Cham (2014). https://doi.org/10.1007/978-3-319-08596-8_42
8. Tsao, Y.-C., Shu, C.-C., Lan, Y.T.-S.: Development of a reminiscence therapy system for the elderly using the integration of virtual reality and augmented reality, Sustainability **11**(17), Art. no. 17 (2019). https://doi.org/10.3390/su11174792
9. Cheng, C., Fan, W., Liu, C., Liu, Y., Liu, X.: Reminiscence therapy–based care program relieves post-stroke cognitive impairment, anxiety, and depression in acute ischemic stroke patients: a randomized, controlled study. Irish J. Med. Sci. (1971) **190**(1), 345–355 (2020). https://doi.org/10.1007/s11845-020-02273-9
10. Kurth, F., Cherbuin, N., Luders, E.: Aging mindfully to minimize cognitive decline. J. Cogn. Enhancement **1**(2), 108–114 (2017). https://doi.org/10.1007/s41465-017-0027-2
11. Buzzi, M.C., Buzzi, M., Perrone, E., Senette, C.: Personalized technology-enhanced training for people with cognitive impairment. Univ. Access Inf. Soc. **18**(4), 891–907 (2018). https://doi.org/10.1007/s10209-018-0619-3
12. Monika, Kumar, S., Gupta, Y.A.: Relationship between cognitive impairment and postural stability in the elderly population. Sport Sci. Health (2022). https://doi.org/10.1007/s11332-022-00913-4
13. Singh, P., Govil, D., Kumar, V., Kumar, J.: Cognitive impairment and quality of life among elderly in India. Appl. Res. Qual. Life **12**(4), 963–979 (2016). https://doi.org/10.1007/s11482-016-9499-y
14. Li, A., Liu, Y.: Reminiscence therapy serves as an optional nursing care strategy in attenuating cognitive impairment, anxiety, and depression in acute ischemic stroke patients. Irish J. Med. Sci. (1971) **191**(2), 877–884 (2021). https://doi.org/10.1007/s11845-021-02600-8
15. Borrego, G., Morán, A.L., Meza, V., Orihuela-Espina, F., Sucar, L.E.: Key factors that influence the UX of a dual-player game for the cognitive stimulation and motor rehabilitation of older adults. Univ. Access Inf. Soc. **20**(4), 767–783 (2020). https://doi.org/10.1007/s10209-020-00746-3

16. Martini, L., et al.: GOAL (Games for Olders Active Life): a web-application for cognitive impairment tele-rehabilitation, pp. 177–182. Singapore (2019)
17. Shouse, G., Danilov, A.V., Artz, A.: CAR T-cell therapy in the older person: indications and risks. Curr. Oncol. Rep. **24**, 1–11 (2022). https://doi.org/10.1007/s11912-022-01272-6
18. Mahendran, R., et al.: Art therapy and music reminiscence activity in the prevention of cognitive decline: study protocol for a randomized controlled trial. Trials, **18**(1), 324 (2017). https://doi.org/10.1186/s13063-017-2080-7
19. Martins, R., Notargiacomo, P.: Evaluation of leap motion controller effectiveness on 2D game environments using usability heuristics. Multimedia Tools Appl. **80**(4), 5539–5557 (2020). https://doi.org/10.1007/s11042-020-09696-7
20. González García, C., Núñez-Valdez, E.R., Moreno-Ger, P., González Crespo, R., Pelayo G-Bustelo, B.C., Cueva Lovelle, J.M.: Agile development of multiplatform educational video games using a domain-specific language. Univ. Access Inf. Soc. **18**(3), 599–614 (2019). https://doi.org/10.1007/s10209-019-00681-y
21. Chover, M., Marín, C., Rebollo, C., Remolar, I.: A game engine designed to simplify 2D video game development. Multimedia Tools Appl. **79**(17–18), 12307–12328 (2019). https://doi.org/10.1007/s11042-019-08433-z
22. Soltani, M., Hermans, F., Bäck, T.: The significance of bug report elements. Empir. Softw. Eng. **25**(6), 5255–5294 (2020). https://doi.org/10.1007/s10664-020-09882-z
23. Bessghaier, N., Ouni, A., Mkaouer, M.W.: A longitudinal exploratory study on code smells in server side web applications. Software Qual. J. **29**(4), 901–941 (2021). https://doi.org/10.1007/s11219-021-09567-w
24. Pano, A., Graziotin, D., Abrahamsson, P.: Factors and actors leading to the adoption of a JavaScript framework. Empir. Softw. Eng. **23**(6), 3503–3534 (2018). https://doi.org/10.1007/s10664-018-9613-x
25. Malik, H., Shakshuki, E.M.: Performance evaluation of counter selection techniques to detect discontinuity in large-scale-systems. J. Ambient. Intell. Humaniz. Comput. **9**(1), 43–59 (2017). https://doi.org/10.1007/s12652-017-0525-1
26. Pérez-Quichimbo, S.-M., Navas-Moya, M.-P., Montes-León, S.-R., Sambachi-Chilig, P.-A., Barrera-Quimbita, E.-D.: Therapy using serious games to improve phonological awareness in children with functional dyslexia. In: Botto-Tobar, M., Montes León, S., Torres-Carrión, P., Zambrano Vizuete, M., Durakovic, B. (eds.) ICAT 2021. CCIS, vol. 1535, pp. 121–134. Springer, Cham (2022). https://doi.org/10.1007/978-3-031-03884-6_9
27. Plasencia, R., Herrera, G., Navas-Moya, P., López-Chico, X.: Virtualization of a multisensory environment for the treatment of stress in children with autism through interactive simulation. In: Botto-Tobar, M., Montes León, S., Camacho, O., Chávez, D., Torres-Carrión, P., Zambrano Vizuete, M. (eds.) ICAT 2020. CCIS, vol. 1388, pp. 417–429. Springer, Cham (2021). https://doi.org/10.1007/978-3-030-71503-8_32
28. Navas-Moya, P., Viteri-Arias, S., Casa-Guayta, C., Navas-Mayorga, C.-E.: Periodontopathies prevention in children through the digitalization of play activities. In: Guarda, T., Portela, F., Santos, M.F. (eds.) ARTIIS 2021. CCIS, vol. 1485, pp. 536–546. Springer, Cham (2021). https://doi.org/10.1007/978-3-030-90241-4_41

A Dataset for Analysis of Quality Code and Toxic Comments

Jaime Sayago-Heredia[1]([✉]), Gustavo Chango Sailema[1], Ricardo Pérez-Castillo[2], and Mario Piattini[3]

[1] Pontificia Universidad Católica del Ecuador, Sede Esmeraldas, Espejo y Subida a Santa Cruz Casilla 08-01-0065, Esmeraldas, Ecuador
{jaime.sayago,wilson.chango}@pucese.edu.ec
[2] Facultad de Ciencias Sociales de Talavera de la Reina, University of Castilla-La Mancha, Avenida Real Fábrica de Seda S/N 45600, Talavera de La Reina, Spain
ricardo.pdelcastillo@uclm.es
[3] Information Technology and Systems Institute, University of Castilla-La Mancha, Paseo de La Universidad, 4, 13071 Ciudad Real, Spain
mario.piattini@uclm.es

Abstract. Software development has an important human aspect, so it is known that the feelings of developers have a significant impact on software development and could affect the quality, productivity and performance of developers. In this study, we have begun the process of finding, understanding and relating these affects to software quality. We propose a quality code and sentiments dataset, a clean set of commits, code quality and toxic sentiments of 19 projects obtained from GitHub. The dataset extracts messages from the commits present in GitHub along with quality metrics from SonarQube. Using this information, we run machine learning techniques with the ML.Net tool to identify toxic developer sentiments in commits that could affect code quality. We analyzed 218K commits from the 19 selected projects. The analysis of the projects took 120 days. We also describe the process of building the tool and retrieving the data. The dataset will be used to further investigate in depth the factors that affect developers' emotions and whether these factors are related to code quality in the life cycle of a software project. In addition, code quality will be estimated as a function of developer sentiments.

Keywords: Sentiments analysis · Toxic comment classification · GitHub · SonarQube · Commits · Software quality · Software Engineering

1 Introduction

Research in the field of software engineering has increasingly applied techniques and methods from other research areas [1], such as sentiment analysis [2–5]. Software development has an important human-side. Hence, developer's feelings could have a significant impact on various aspects related to software development, such as quality, performance, etc. Nowadays, software development projects depend on a large number

M. Botto-Tobar et al. (Eds.): ICAT 2022, CCIS 1755, pp. 559–574, 2023.
https://doi.org/10.1007/978-3-031-24985-3_41

of programmers who collaborate with each other in their efforts to develop a software system [6]. These efforts to build and maintain a software project are continuous and sometimes also stressful for developers, which becomes a difficult problem to solve [7]. Research community are concerned that these feelings could lead (or at least contribute) to a buggy code and consequently poor quality software [5, 8, 9].

Developers usually cope with various problems every day and have to find a solution that require high levels of technical knowledge. For developers, these obstacles to successfully complete the development of a software project can be exhausting and stressful [7]. That fact, therefore, impacts on developers' ability to self-regulate their feelings and understanding [10], e.g. *commit messages* have a lot of negative feelings [11]. These messages contain an emotional expression (negative or toxic), which could either influence the quality of the code, or be a reflection of the fact that the quality of the code also influences the negative feelings of the developers. Therefore, there is a need to analyse, understand and relate developers' negative feelings and code quality, an important and understudied field of research. We have developed a research tool (classifier) to extract toxic comments from commit messages. Toxic language can be present in different places online (Facebook, YouTube and others), they are also present in commit messages software projects on GitHub. Toxic can manifest itself in multiple ways, in the case of software development, through messages corroborating the lack of help for a bug together with name calling, insults or threats. This tool obtains toxic comments from commit messages of the selected projects from GitHub and jointly extracts the code quality metrics corresponding to commit messages of the software projects. Our work makes a main contribution, verifying that toxic of messages can be identified through Natural Language Processing (NLP) techniques and obtaining a corpus of data with negative sentiments and toxic comments. Future research we will explore how code quality can affect developers' emotions. This paper allows us to expand our research possibilities and areas involved in sentiment analysis that we will explore in next future.

1.1 Related Work

Code quality is important for software projects. The attempt to measure software quality has led to the proposal of several metrics [1]. Previous research focused on developer, has demonstrated that emotions of software developers can affect task quality, productivity, creativity, group relatedness, and job satisfaction, among other [2].

Lesiuk [3] presented the study on the emotional impact of music on the performance of software developers. Khan et al. [4] came up with analysis of software developers' emotions and its impact on debugging performance. Guzmán et al. [5] proposed a sentiment analysis approach for discussions in mailing lists and web-based software collaboration tools. Ding et al. [6] conducted an entity-level sentiment analysis by creating a dataset and a *SentiSW* tool. SentiSW is an entity-level sentiment analysis tool that consists of sentiment classification and entity recognition and classifies problematic comments with significantly higher accuracy than other tools.

Ding et al. [6] performed sentiment analysis at the entity level by creating a dataset and a SentiSW tool, an entity-level sentiment analysis tool that consists of sentiment classification and entity recognition and can classify problem comments with significantly higher accuracy than existing tools. Murgia et al. [7] analysed whether development artifacts and issue reports, contain any emotional information about software development with which they verified an automatic tool for emotion extraction in software development artifacts; furthermore, they investigated if humans cannot determine any emotion from a software artifact, neither can a tool.

Cheruvelli and Da Silva [8] applied a sentiment analysis tool to issue tracking comments and observe how scores varied for issues with no reopening's, with one reopening, and with many reopening's and suggest that negative sentiment correlates with reopening issues, although the effect size appears to be quite small. These analyses focused on searching and finding emotions through tools that have not been created for the context of software engineering and therefore encounter some discrepancies in terms of their effectiveness, which may affect the results obtained, calling into question the validity of such results. This need for specific dataset-oriented analysis tools for software engineering has been recognized by some authors [9–11].

Additionally, there were several efforts to estimate software quality focus on source code measurement [12]. Static analysis tools measure low to high level quality metrics (code smells, architecture decays), or provide the means to execute such measurements [13]. Authors [13–15] focused on analysing sentiments and its impact on code quality through tasks and code quality metrics (refactoring, code cloning, commits) using different software engineering artefacts.

Analysing previous works, our research is focused to proposes a tool that obtains sentiments from commit messages and correlates them with quality metrics obtained from static analysis tools. This tool allows to extract the dataset, which will allow in depth analysis of the correlation with a case study.

2 Methods and Tools

This section provides technical details on how the developed tools gathers data set.

2.1 Classification Toxic Model

The context of the classification to be carried out to obtain the level of toxicity of developers' comments should be focused on software engineering as this is our area of study. The training data for study is acceptable. The developed tool extracts the toxicity of commit messages with natural language processing (NLP) classification techniques suggested by state-of-the-art review [16–18]. Tool uses Microsoft's ML.NET library, which allows developers to build complex machine learning pipelines. Pipelines are often composed of multiple transformation steps that feature and transform the raw input data [19]. The task used to train the model is binary classification. During the model training process, the model generator trains independent models with different options and binary classification algorithms to find the best performing model for the dataset [20]. Time required for model training is proportional to the amount of data. At the end of training the model the output will contain the algorithm that uses the model with the best performance on the input data. In our case it is the L-BFGS (Limited Broydon-Fletcher-Goldfarb-Shanno) algorithm which is a quasi-Newton optimization method of functions with a large number of parameters or of a high complexity [21]. It is a method that makes limited use of memory, using it optimally and in fewer algorithms for the same problem. L-BFGS allows obtaining the minimum of a function; it only needs the function and its gradient, but not the Hessian matrix, therefore, it is able to solve functions without restrictions in its parameters [22]. The result of the model generated using the L-BFGS algorithm is satisfactory with a percentage rate of 78.03%.

Binary classification will assign a score 0 (no negative sentiment) and 1 (negative sentiment) that are accumulated and allow to obtain a ranking of quantity and percentages of negative sentiment in each relay of the project. The tool also uses the SonarQube API to obtain the metrics that will be used to analyse the code quality. The tool extracts the project dataset (GitHub) and the metrics (SonarQube) and generates the corresponding analysis and statistics for each of the projects.

2.1.1 Code Repositories (GitHub)

Systems store project data, e.g., issue control systems and version control systems, are known as software repositories [23]. Software repositories are virtual spaces where development teams generate collaborative artifacts from the activities of a development process [24]. Software repositories contain large amount of software historical data can include valuable information on the source code, defects, and other issues like new features [25]. Moreover, we can extract many types of data from repositories, study them, and can make changes according to their need [26]. To meet the main objective, which is to correlate GitHub metrics with code quality. Initially, we extracted with the tools the complete information of the commit messages of each project. Then, we identified from the extracted corpus different GitHub metrics such as commits, commits per day, committers, changes per commit, which are grouped in the release of the project, that is, these messages are grouped by the version or distribution of the developed software project.

2.1.2 SonarQube

SonarQube [27] is one of the most common open-source static code analysis tools for static quality analysis. It can be executed on premise or with the free cloud-based service on sonarcloud.io. SonarQube calculates several metrics such as number of lines of code and code complexity and verifies the code's compliance against a specific set of "coding rules". In case the analysed source code violates a coding rule or if a metric is outside a predefined threshold (also named "quality gate"), SonarQube generates an "issue" [28]. The time needed to remove these issues (remediation effort) is used to calculate the remediation cost and the Technical Debt. Each rule is classified as being related to Reliability, Maintainability, or Security of the code. Reliability rules, also named "bugs", create TD issues that "represent something wrong in the code" and that will soon be reflected in a bug. Maintainability rules or"code smells" are considered as"maintainability-related issues" in the code that decrease code readability and modifiability [29]. It is important to note that the term"code smells" adopted in SonarQube does not refer to the commonly known code smells defined [30] but to a different set of rules. SonarQube claims that zero false-positive issues are expected from the Reliability and Maintainability rules, while Security issues may contain some false-positives. SonarQube also classifies these rules into five severity levels: Blocker, Critical, Major, Minor, and Info.

2.2   Implementation Details

Tool is a web application specifically built for the data extracted from GitHub and Sonar-Qube. Figure 1, describes functionality of the tool that integrates and extracts commit messages from the GitHub API which is the largest online platform and contains more than 3.4 million users [31] and metrics from the SonarQube API which is the most widely used tool on the market for code quality analysis [28]). We use for its development.Net Visual Studio, C#, HTML5 and the ML.NET library that allows developers to build complex machine learning and LNP artifacts [19]. First step is prepared dataset to be used for sentiment analysis. It is important to understand the dataset. The sentiment calculated from the commit message consists of a toxicity index, the numeric value of the sentiment provides a quantification. It is important determine and understand the words to understand the context of the sentence. When using the different words, we must differentiate the context from the software engineering to extract the correct sentiment values from the message. The tool uses different algorithms and trains separate models to find best performing model for dataset [20]. Tool extracts sentiment toxic from *commit messages* from project (GitHub) and metrics (SonarQube), result generates graphs with statistical analysis, dashboard by project and a dataset for each project.

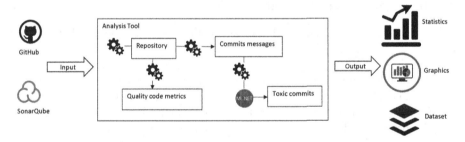

Fig. 1. Overview of tool functionality.

In Fig. 2, we can see the tool in production, in the statistics option various analyses of the project selected for the pilot study are described. From the unit of measurement, which is the project releases, we obtain the number of commits per author, the most used words, the total number of negative sentiments of the commits and the non-negative sentiments. Negative sentiments are represented by negative or toxic words, these words carry in their context insults, threats, hatred, or other words containing negativity. We observe in the tool, a distribution of the negative sentiments of the commits and a classification by author. In sonar-statistics option, the graphs presented correlate the negative commits of the project and the SonarQube quality metrics (classes, complexity, issues, bugs, etc.), taking as a unit the releases of the project. From this information a dataset is generated and can be exported to different formats. And the last option commits show a percentage distribution of the negative sentiments of the commits in the project that can be listed by author.

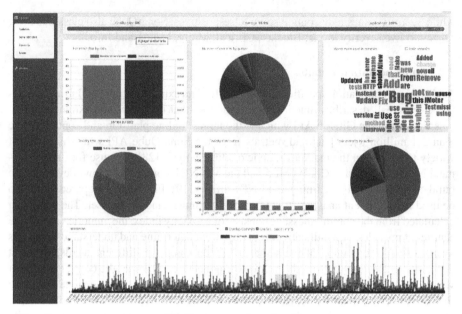

Fig. 2. A screenshot of tool.

2.3   Dataset Schema and Production

Figure 3 presents the schema of the dataset entities. It is composed of two linked databases.

- Relational database (SqlServer), in Fig. 3. we identify their respective relationships and fields of each entity and normalisation. *Repository* table contains the information referring to the software projects with their respective repository header fields. *Commit* table contains the different data concerning the commit messages together with their toxicity level. *Metrics* table contains the quality values of SonarQube. *UserRepository* and *User* tables correspond to the security module of the tool. These entities are for the tool's own management and administration.
- NoSQL database (MongoDB), in Fig. 3. we observe it is used to extract the large amount of data from the Api's of GitHub and SonarQube, it is more convenient to be a NoSQL DB based on BSON. Collections are not normalised by the amount of data that can be repeated. *CommitsByProject* collection represents the repository and the respective documents such as commit, author, committer, commitAuthor and toxicity. *AnalysesByProject* collection represents the information of each release extracted of repository. *IssuesByProject* collection contains the data of issues of extracted repository. *MeasureHistoryByProject* collection represents the information about the software quality metrics of each release of repository.

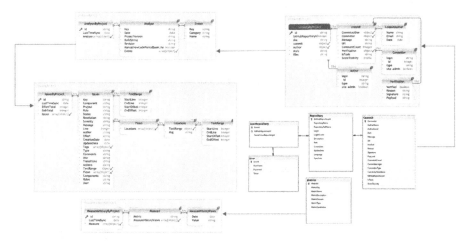

Fig. 3. Diagram of database of tool

3 Results and Discussions

In this section, we present the results of data extraction from the tool described in the previous section and its possible uses.

3.1 Project Selection for Data Set

The software projects were obtained from the search performed on the software repository GitHub, which is the largest online platform and contain more than 3.4 million users [31]. This significant number of projects can contribute to our research, although it can be detrimental when selecting software projects that are irrelevant, so it is necessary to define both selection and exclusion criteria to filter those results. Inclusion and exclusion practices and strategies are valuable in several researches concerning software engineering [32]. The following inclusion criteria were defined:

- The software project is in production.
- The metrics and reports are accessible from the SonarQube platform.
- The team of developers of the software project must meet an average value of developers (5) which is an average value obtained from the pilot review of the software repositories. In addition, we applied other criteria based on the research of [27]:
- More than 10 releases
- More than 5000 commits,
- More than 1000 classes,
- More than 100000 lines of code.

Exclusion criteria are the English language must be used by the development team in commit messages, incomplete software and projects that are on the SonarQube platform but with low or no activity i.e., without any recent analysis or releases.

Table 1. Open-source projects included in data set.

Id	GitHub Org.	GitHub project	SonarQube project	Description	Lang	LoC	Releases	From	To
P1	Eclipse	Eclipse/kitalpha	Kitalpha	Kitalpha is an environment to develop and execute MBE (Model-Based Engineering) workbenches for description of systems in system, software and hardware engineering	Java	150k	28	5/8/2020	13/9/2021
P2	Apache	Apache/incubator-hop	apache_incubator-hop	The hop documentation project consists of multiple types of documentation. Each with their own purpose	Java	100k	24	16/11/2020	26/10/2021
P3	Eclipse	Eclipse/capella	eclipse_capella	Capella is an open-source model-based systems engineering tool that provides methodological guidance, intuitive model editing, and viewing capabilities for Systems, Software and Hardware Architects	Java	343k	29	11/9/2020	13/9/2021

(continued)

Table 1. (*continued*)

Id	GitHub Org.	GitHub project	SonarQube project	Description	Lang	LoC	Releases	From	To
P4	Constellation	Constellation-app/constellation	Constellation-app_constellation	Constellation is a graph-focused data visualisation and interactive analysis application enabling data access, federation and manipulation capabilities across large and complex data sets	Java, CSS XML, Python HTML	214k	40	22/7/2020	26/10/2021
P5	Amazon Web Services	aws/aws-sdk-java-v2	aws_aws-sdk-java-v2	The Amazon Web Services SDK for Java provides Java APIs for building software on AWS' cost-effective, scalable, and reliable infrastructure products	Java, XML	145k	111	12/5/2021	26/10/2021
P6	Primefaces	Primefaces/primefaces	org.primefaces:primefaces	PrimeFaces is one of the most popular UI libraries in Java EE Ecosystem and widely used by software companies, world renowned brands, banks, financial institutions, insurance companies, universities and more	Java, XML	96k	20	14/1/2019	26/10/2021

(*continued*)

Table 1. (*continued*)

Id	GitHub Org.	GitHub project	SonarQube project	Description	Lang	LoC	Releases	From	To
P7	Apache	Apache/openmeetings	apache_openmeetings	Parent project for all OpenMeetings Maven modules. Required to hold general settings	Java	103k	10	11/7/2019	25/10/2021
P8	OpenWIS	OpenWIS/openwis	OpenWIS_openwis	OpenWIS is an implementation of WMO Information System (WIS) and aims to perform the three functions required by the WIS, i.e. GISC, DCPC and NC	XML, Java PL/SQL, JavaScript	380k	11	15/8/2019	5/8/2021
P9	AcademySoftwareFoundation	AcademySoftwareFoundation/openexr	AcademySoftwareFoundation_openexr	OpenEXR provides the specification and reference implementation of the EXR file format, the professional-grade image storage format of the motion picture industry	C, C++	214k	22	28/03/2020	25/10/2021
P10	Silverpeas	Silverpeas/Silverpeas-Components	Silverpeas_Silverpeas -Components	The different applications that are deployed in standard in Silverpeas	Java, JSP CSS, XML JavaScript	164k	102	1/9/2020	10/10/2021

(continued)

Table 1. (*continued*)

Id	GitHub Org.	GitHub project	SonarQube project	Description	Lang	LoC	Releases	From	To
P11	Apache	Jmeter	JMeter	Designed to load test functional behaviour and measure performance	Java	115	8	5/10/2019	26/10/2021
P12									
P13	Monicahq	Monica	Monica	Personal CRM (Customer Relationship Management)	PHP, JavaScript, CSS	48k	39	17/4/2018	26/10/2021
P14	Apache	Apache/iotdb	apache_incubator-iotdb	This is the top level project that builds, packages the tsfile, iotdb engine, jdbc, and integration libs	Java	201k	4	28/6/2020	22/9/2021
P15	Simgrid	Simgrid	simgrid_simgrid	Framework for the simulation of distributed applications (Clouds, HPC, Grids, IoT, etc.)	C++	91	6	2/2/2020	26/10/2021
P16	Apache	sling-org-apache-sling-app-cms	apache_sling-org-apache-sling-app-cms	Apache Sling is a Web framework designed to create content-centric, java-based applications	Java	10	11	2019-05-29	2020-03-08

(*continued*)

Table 1. (*continued*)

Id	GitHub Org.	GitHub project	SonarQube project	Description	Lang	LoC	Releases	From	To
P17	Apache	Sling-org-apache -sling-scripting-jsp	apache_sling-org-apache-sling-scripting-jsp	Support for JSP scripting in Apache Sling	Java	27	7	2019-09-26	2020-03-01
P18	Apache	sling-org-apache-sling-scripting -sightly-compiler	apache_sling-org-apache-sling -scripting-sightly-compiler	The Apache Sling scripting HTLM compiler	Java	7	17	2019-06-03	2020-03-09
P19	SonarSource	Sonarqube	org.sonarsource sonarqube:sonarqube	A tool for continuous inspection of code quality	Java	296	14	14/10/2019	21/9/2021

3.2 How to Leverage the Dataset

Dataset raw (Table 1) is collected from two sources: GitHub (an online version control system) and SonarQube. It consists of two linked databases, one relational (SqlServer) and one NoSql (MongoDB), see in detail in Sect. 2.3.

Research quality assurance we considered the following processes to ensure quality:

- We conducted a pilot case study to evaluate the constructed tool and the draft case study design. The P8 study was evaluated in the research. We applied the constructed tool, data mining along with analyses to obtain the preliminary results [33].
- A comprehensive follow-up of the case study protocol along with the data obtained from the 19 projects is also carried out.

The clean data set is available to the research community to ensure reproducibility of the multi-case study. The dataset obtained from the data extraction and cleaning can be consulted at the following link https://zenodo.org/record/6421855#.Yk777SjMLDc.

3.3 Threats to Validity

This study has a scope on GitHub commit messages and toxic comments that could affect code quality. We do not consider other elements that are part of the software repository such as pull requests, branches, mailing lists or formal project documentation. Moreover, the tool could improve toxic calculation if we modify the training set. The next step of improvement is to use a larger training set, which allows us to increase the accuracy of obtaining toxicity along with a larger number of projects. Finally, the validation of our study could be improved by using other data sources.

4 Conclusions

In this paper, we present the dataset for the analysis of the toxicity and code quality of a software project in its life cycle. It is a dataset extracted and cleaned, obtaining a total of 19 projects analyzed from the tool built (Sect. 2), which extracts sentiments from the commit messages (GitHub) from each release of the project and quality metrics from SonarQube. This data can be included and used in industry and research. We describe the process of building the tools we use to collect the data.

The dataset for analysis of quality code and toxic comments is available as a spreadsheet file to facilitate data queries. The creation of the dataset took 120 days due to the search for projects that meet the inclusion criteria imposed in this study. The results will allow researchers to conduct several studies on a clean dataset, compare their results and concentrate more on their research objectives rather than data collection. There is a mature and extensive field corresponding to sentiment analysis in software engineering [34], which allows analyzing and understanding the relationship between sentiment and code quality in the software project. Future work will be oriented to replicate it with a larger number of software projects and additional variables using different approaches, in order to obtain a deeper analysis, understanding and relationship of the factors affecting developers' emotions and, in turn, code quality in the life cycle of a software project.

Consequently, used to design measures and models that help identify the factors affecting developers and code quality and decrease the number of projects with toxicity levels and negative feelings.

Acknowledgements. This work is part of the SMOQUIN (PID2019-104791RB-I00) projects funded by the Spanish Ministry of Science and Innovation and ERDF.

References

1. Al Mamun, M.A., Berger, C., Hansson, J.: Correlations of software code metrics: an empirical study. In: ACM International Conference Proceeding Series Part F, vol. 1319, pp. 255–266 (2017). https://doi.org/10.1145/3143434.3143445
2. Votano, J., Parham, M., Hall, L.: Understanding affect in the workspace via social media. In: CSCW '13 Proceedings of 2013 Conference on Computer Supported Cooperative Work, pp. 303–315 (2013)
3. Lesiuk, T.: The effect of music listening on work performance. Psychol. Music **33**, 173–191 (2005). https://doi.org/10.1177/0305735605050650
4. Khan, I.A., Brinkman, W.P., Hierons, R.M.: Do moods affect programmers' debug performance? Cogn. Technol. Work **13**, 245–258 (2011). https://doi.org/10.1007/s10111-010-0164-1
5. Guzman, E., Azócar, D., Li, Y.: Sentiment analysis of commit comments in GitHub: an empirical study. In: 11th Working Conference on Mining Software Repositories MSR 2014 – Proceedings, pp. 352–355 (2014). https://doi.org/10.1145/2597073.2597118
6. Ding, J., Sun, H., Wang, X., Liu, X.: Entity-level sentiment analysis of issue comments. In: Proceedings of International Conference on Software Engineering, pp. 7–13 (2018). https://doi.org/10.1145/3194932.3194935
7. Murgia, A., Tourani, P., Adams, B., Ortu, M.: Do developers feel emotions? An exploratory analysis of emotions in software artifacts. In: 11th Working Conference on Mining Software Repositories MSR 2014 – Proceedings, pp. 262–271 (2014). https://doi.org/10.1145/2597073.2597086
8. Cheruvelil, J., Da Silva, B.C.: Developers' sentiment and issue reopening. In: Proceedings - 2019 IEEE/ACM 4th International Workshop on Emotion Awareness in Software Engineering, SEmotion 2019, pp. 29–33 (2019). https://doi.org/10.1109/SEmotion.2019.00013
9. Lin, B., Zampetti, F., Bavota, G., et al.: Sentiment Analysis for Software Engineering: How Far Can We Go. DlAcmOrg, pp. 94–104 (2018)
10. Jongeling, R., Sarkar, P., Datta, S., Serebrenik, A.: On negative results when using sentiment analysis tools for software engineering research. Empir. Softw. Eng. **22**(5), 2543–2584 (2017). https://doi.org/10.1007/s10664-016-9493-x
11. Howard, M.J., Gupta, S., Pollock, L., Vijay-Shanker, K.: Automatically mining software-based, semantically-similar words from comment-code mappings. In: IEEE International Working Conference on Mining Software Repositories, pp. 377–386 (2013). https://doi.org/10.1109/MSR.2013.6624052
12. Le Goues, C., Weimer, W.: Measuring code quality to improve specification mining. IEEE Trans. Softw. Eng. **38**, 175–190 (2012). https://doi.org/10.1109/TSE.2011.5
13. Behnamghader, P., Alfayez, R., Srisopha, K., Boehm, B.: Towards better understanding of software quality evolution through commit-impact analysis. In: Proceedings - 2017 IEEE INTERNATIONAL CONFERENCE on Software Quality, Reliability and Security, QRS 2017, pp. 251–262 (2017). https://doi.org/10.1109/QRS.2017.36

14. Singh, N., Singh, P.: How do code refactoring activities impact software developers' sentiments? - An empirical investigation into GitHub commits. In: Proceedings - Asia-Pacific Software Engineering Conference, APSEC 2017–Decem, pp. 648–653 (2018). https://doi.org/10.1109/APSEC.2017.79

15. Bharti, S., Singh, H.: Investigating developers' sentiments associated with software cloning practices. In: Luhach, A.K., Singh, D., Hsiung, P.-A., Hawari, K.B.G., Lingras, P., Singh, P.K. (eds.) ICAICR 2018. CCIS, vol. 955, pp. 397–406. Springer, Singapore (2019). https://doi.org/10.1007/978-981-13-3140-4_36

16. Saeed, H.H., Shahzad, K., Kamiran, F.: Overlapping toxic sentiment classification using deep neural architectures. In: IEEE International Conference on Data Mining Workshops, ICDMW 2018–November, pp. 1361–1366 (2019). https://doi.org/10.1109/ICDMW.2018.00193

17. Tare, P.: Toxic comment detection and classification. In: 31st Conference on Neural Information Processing Systems (NIPS 2017), pp. 1–6 (2017)

18. Geet, A., Illina, I., Fohr, D., et al.: Towards non-toxic landscapes: automatic toxic comment detection using DNN. In: Second Workshop on Trolling, Aggression and Cyber-bullying (LREC, 2020) (2020)

19. Ahmed, Z., Amizadeh, S., Bilenko, M., et al.: Machine learning at Microsoft with ML.NET. arXiv 2448-2458 (2019)

20. Sistema, I., Pomoću, P.: Net ML Development of recommender systems using ML.NET (2019)

21. Bollapragada, R., Mudigere, D., Nocedal, J., et al.: A progressive batching L-BFGS method for machine learning. In: 35th International Conference on Machine Learning, ICML 2018, vol. 2, pp. 989–1013 (2018)

22. Berahas, A.S., Takáč, M.: A robust multi-batch L-BFGS method for machine learning*. Optim. Methods Softw. 35, 191–219 (2020). https://doi.org/10.1080/10556788.2019.1658107

23. Falessi, D., Reichel, A.: Towards an open-source tool for measuring and visualizing the interest of technical debt. In: 2015 IEEE 7th International Working Managing Technical Debt, MTD 2015 – Proceedings, pp. 1–8 (2015). https://doi.org/10.1109/MTD.2015.7332618

24. GüemesPeña, D., LópezNozal, C., MarticorenaSánchez, R., Maudes-Raedo, J.: Emerging topics in mining software repositories. Progr. Artif. Intell. 7(3), 237–247 (2018). https://doi.org/10.1007/s13748-018-0147-7

25. De Farias, M.A.F., Colaço, M., Mendonça, M., et al.: A systematic mapping study on mining software repositories. In: Proceedings of ACM Symposium on Applied Computing, 04–08–April, pp. 1472–1479 (2016). https://doi.org/10.1145/2851613.2851786

26. Siddiqui, T., Ahmad, A.: Data mining tools and techniques for mining software repositories: a systematic review. In: Aggarwal, V.B., Bhatnagar, V., Mishra, D.K. (eds.) Big Data Analytics. AISC, vol. 654, pp. 717–726. Springer, Singapore (2018). https://doi.org/10.1007/978-981-10-6620-7_70

27. Lenarduzzi, V., Saarimäki, N., Taibi, D.: The technical debt dataset. In: ACM International Conference Proceeding, pp. 2–11 (2019). https://doi.org/10.1145/3345629.3345630

28. Lenarduzzi, V., Lomio, F., Huttunen, H., Taibi, D.: Are SonarQube rules inducing bugs? In: SANER 2020 – Proceedings of 2020 IEEE 27th International Conference on Software Analysis, Evolution and Reengineering, pp. 501–511 (2020). https://doi.org/10.1109/SANER48275.2020.9054821

29. Marcilio, D., Bonifacio, R., Monteiro, E., et al.: Are static analysis violations really fixed? A closer look at realistic usage of SonarQube. In: IEEE International Conference on Program Comprehension, May 2019, pp. 209–219 (2019). https://doi.org/10.1109/ICPC.2019.00040

30. Palomba, F., Panichella, A., Zaidman, A., et al.: The scent of a smell: an extensive comparison between textual and structural smells. IEEE Trans. Softw. Eng. 44, 977–1000 (2018). https://doi.org/10.1109/TSE.2017.2752171

31. Li, L., Goethals, F., Baesens, B., Snoeck, M.: Predicting software revision outcomes on GitHub using structural holes theory. Comput. Netw. **114**, 114–124 (2017). https://doi.org/10.1016/j.comnet.2016.08.024

32. Petersen, K., Gencel, C.: Worldviews, research methods, and their relationship to validity in empirical software engineering research. In: Proceedings - Joint Conference of the 23rd International Workshop on Software Measurement and the 8th International Conference on Software Process and Product Measurement, IWSM-MENSURA 2013, pp. 81–89 (2013). https://doi.org/10.1109/IWSM-Mensura.2013.22

33. Sayago-Heredia, J., Chango, G., Pérez-Castillo, R., Piattini, M.: Exploring the impact of toxic comments in code quality. In: Proceedings of the 17th International Conference on Evaluation of Novel Approaches to Software Engineering (ENASE 2022), pp. 335–343. SCITEPRESS – Science and Technology Publications (2022)

34. Mäntylä, M.V., Graziotin, D., Kuutila, M.: The evolution of sentiment analysis. Comput. Rev. **27**, 16–32 (2018)

Model-Driven Engineering Applied to User Interfaces. A Systematic Literature Review

Lenin Erazo-Garzón[1]([⊠]), Steveen Suquisupa[1], Alexandra Bermeo[1],
and Priscila Cedillo[2]

[1] Universidad del Azuay, Av. 24 de Mayo 7-77, Cuenca, Ecuador
{lerazo,alexbermeo}@uazuay.edu.ec, ssuquisupa@es.uazuay.edu.ec
[2] Universidad de Cuenca, Av. 12 de Abril, Cuenca, Ecuador
priscila.cedillo@ucuenca.edu.ec

Abstract. The complexity and dynamism of modern systems have made software development a task that requires a lot of time and effort since traditional methods and tools focus on the implementation domain instead of the problem. The implementation and maintenance of software user interfaces have been no exception. Model-Driven Engineering (MDE) emerges as a potential approach to increase the level of abstraction, improve the management of the complexity and evolution of the system, and ultimately maximize the productivity of software development projects. Therefore, this paper presents a systematic literature review to understand the state of the art on model-driven user interface engineering by following the Kitchenham's guidelines. This study aims to answer the following research questions: i) How is MDE used to build and maintain software user interfaces? and ii) How is the research addressed in studies related to using MDE to build and maintain software user interfaces? First, 1708 primary studies were collected from multiple research sources. Then, applying inclusion and exclusion criteria, 51 articles on relevant MDE proposals focused on software user interfaces were selected. Finally, quantitative and qualitative methods based on extraction criteria were applied to answer the proposed research questions, determine the advantages and disadvantages of the existing proposals, and identify the challenges, gaps, and research opportunities.

Keywords: Model-Driven Engineering (MDE) · Model-Driven Development (MDD) · Models@run.time · Systematic review · User interface (UI)

1 Introduction

The increasing complexity of modern systems is one of the main challenges for software development [1, 2]. Particularly, those systems operate in highly distributed scenarios, in which the heterogeneity of devices, computing platforms, and user profiles predominates; for example, screen size and resolution, storage capacity, bandwidth, operating systems, knowledge, experience, and capabilities of users, among others [3, 4]. In addition, modern systems are characterized by their ubiquity, looking for the permanent adaptation of user requirements based on their mobility and context [4, 5].

M. Botto-Tobar et al. (Eds.): ICAT 2022, CCIS 1755, pp. 575–591, 2023.
https://doi.org/10.1007/978-3-031-24985-3_42

The User Interface (UI) is the border between man and machine; therefore, it is responsible for ensuring that the user experience is satisfactory [1]. However, the UI is one of the aspects most affected by the growing complexity of systems. As a result, Its development and maintenance activities require more effort, time, and resources [6, 7]. In addition, about half the budget is invested in UI implementation tasks [8]. Therefore, it becomes essential to have software engineering methods and tools to facilitate and speed up the tasks of implementing and maintaining the UI requirements [1].

Model-Driven Engineering (MDE) emerges as an appropriate approach to abstracting the complexity of systems and improving their evolution [6]. MDE proposes the use of domain models as first-class citizen artifacts for the development or operation of systems [9]. Those models describe the system from different viewpoints or perspectives (e.g., architecture, behavior, UI), considering different abstraction levels [10]. In particular, the models can be used to capture the common characteristics of the UI and, through transformations, produce multiple implementations adjusted to the heterogeneity of the technological platforms, the context, or the users' needs [11]. Also, those models are used to reason about the state and behavior of the system at runtime in order to adjust its UI [12]. Thus, MDE provides important benefits to increase developers' productivity and reduce the system maintenance related to the UI.

In the literature, several systematic reviews [13–18] can be found that address, in general, the state of knowledge of MDE or that study other system perspectives different from the user interface. Hence, there is no an updated systematic review oriented to model-driven user interface engineering that evidences its particular state in order to understand aspects, such as the types of platforms and solutions to which the existing proposals are oriented, the models, languages, and tools they use, the empirical evaluation methods they apply, among others.

Consequently, this paper presents a systematic literature review to understand the state of the art on the use of MDE to support the development of software applications' UI, for which the guidelines of Kitchenham et al. [19] have been followed. This study aims to answer the following research questions: i) How is MDE used to build and maintain software user interfaces? and ii) How is the research addressed in studies related to using MDE to build and maintain software user interfaces? First, 1708 primary studies were automatically retrieved from multiple research sources. Then, applying inclusion and exclusion criteria, 51 articles on MDE proposals focused on the software user interface were selected. In addition, a quality assessment of the selected studies was carried out to classify them according to their scientific relevance. Finally, quantitative and qualitative methods based on extraction criteria were applied to answer the proposed research questions.

The structure of this paper is as follows: Sect. 2 presents a review of the related work. Section 3 describes the methodology and protocol used in the systematic review. Section 4 includes a discussion of the results of the systematic review, highlighting the strengths, weaknesses, gaps, and challenges of using MDE to support software user interfaces. Finally, Sect. 5 presents the conclusions and lines of future work.

2 Related Work

This section presents a bibliographic review of the leading systematic and mapping literature reviews that aims to show the technological state of MDE.

Gottardi and Braga [13] present a systematic mapping to identify the technological and application domains in which MDE is successful as well as the challenges in applying this methodology to general-purpose development processes. Similarly, Bucchiarone et al. [14] present a discussion about the significant challenges and research initiatives for the MDE scientific community. Regarding the application of models at runtime, Bencomo et al. [15] analyze the state of the art of this line of research. For this, a taxonomy is used to compare the main research approaches and results in the area during the last decade and identify the corresponding research gaps and challenges.

In other more specific work, Shamsujjoha et al. [16] research what Model-Driven Development (MDD) techniques and methodologies have been used to support the development of mobile apps and how those techniques have been employed, identifying key benefits, limitations, gaps, and potential future research. Likewise, in their systematic review, Tufail et al. [17] present an analysis of the MDD tools that have been proposed for mobile applications. Finally, Ordonez et al. [18] present a systematic review of MDD and software accessibility, including the review of accessibility standards and a qualitative evaluation of the existing proposals.

In conclusion, it can be determined that the existing systematic reviews and mappings on MDE do not deepen their study from the viewpoint of user interfaces. Therefore, this article aims to help researchers fill this information limitation and identify research gaps, challenges, and opportunities in this field to support future studies.

3 Research Methods

This systematic literature review is aligned with the guidelines of Kitchenham et al. [19, 20] to ensure a reliable, replicable, and auditable process. This methodology comprises three stages: i) planning the review, to identify the objectives and validate the review protocol; ii) conducting the review, to perform the previously defined protocol; and iii) disseminating the review, to prepare a report with the results of the review.

3.1 Planning the Review

Research Question. The overall objective of this systematic literature review is to understand the state of technological knowledge on Model-Driven User Interface Engineering. The proposed research questions are:

RQ1. How is MDE used to build and maintain software user interfaces?
RQ2. How is the research addressed in studies related to using MDE to build and maintain software user interface?

Data Sources and Search Strategy. The information sources selected for the automatic search of primary studies were Scopus and Google Scholar indexers. For the manual search, the most significant conferences, journals, and book chapters dealing with MDE oriented to software user interfaces were selected. In addition, the snowball technique was applied to find additional relevant articles. The search was conducted from 2000, when Model-Driven Engineering reached relevance since around this date, the interest of researchers increased with the launch of the Model-Driven Architecture (MDA) initiative of the Object Management Group (OMG). Table 1 presents the search string used, which was applied to the article metadata: title, abstract, and keywords.

Table 1. Automatic search string.

Concept	Connector	Synonyms and Acronyms
User interface	AND	UI, GUI
Model-driven engineering	OR	MDE, based-model
Model-driven development	OR	MDD
Model-driven architecture		MDA
Domain-specific language	OR	DSL, DSML
Metamodel	OR	Meta-model
Model at runtime	OR	Runtime model, models@runtime, models@run.time
Search string:	*(user interface OR ui OR gui) AND (model-driven OR based-model OR mde OR mdd OR mda OR domain-specific language OR dsl OR dsml OR metamodel OR meta-model OR model at runtime OR runtime model OR models@runtime OR models@run.time)*	

Selection of Primary Studies. The primary studies obtained from the automatic and manual search were evaluated and selected by four researchers based on the title, abstract, and keywords. Discrepancies in the selection of studies were resolved by consensus, after reviewing the complete paper.

Primary studies meeting any of the following inclusion criteria were included:

IC1. Primary studies that address paradigms, approaches, methods, or techniques of MDE to design and build software user interfaces.
IC2. Primary studies that propose tools or applications based on MDE to design and build software user interfaces.

Primary studies that met at least one of the following exclusion criteria were excluded:

EC1. Editorials, prologues, opinions, interviews, news, or posters.
EC2. Duplicate studies in different sources.
EC3. Short articles with less than four pages.
EC4. Articles written in a language other than English.

EC5. Gray literature, thesis, and introduction papers.

Quality Assessment of Primary Studies. A checklist of three questions was established to assess the quality of the selected studies (see Table 2). Each question was evaluated using a scale from 0 to 1. The scores obtained in the three questions were added to determine the total score for each article. The quality assessment was used only to classify the studies according to scientific relevance, and to have an adequate synthesis in the presentation of the results.

Table 2. Quality checklist.

No	Question	Answer and score
QAQ1	How many citations does the primary study have?	More than 10 citations, very relevant (1) Between 1 and 10 citations, relevant (0.5) No cited, irrelevant (0)
QAQ2	Has the primary study been published in relevant journals or conferences?	Very relevant (1), Relevant (0.5), Irrelevant (0)
QAQ3	Does the study present an empirical evaluation of the proposed solution?	Yes (1), No (0)

Data Extraction Strategy. A data extraction form was used to facilitate and standardize the collection and systematization of information from the articles, as well as to answer the research questions initially proposed (see Table 3).

Methods of Analysis and Synthesis. Two methods were used for the analysis and synthesis of the information collected: i) quantitative, based on the construction different types of graphs to represent the frequency of responses for each extraction criterion or combination of extraction criteria; and ii) qualitative, description of the most relevant proposals, identifying strengths, weaknesses, and research opportunities.

3.2 Conducting the Review

This subsection describes the process of collecting, selecting and assessing the quality of the primary studies, using the inclusion, exclusion, and quality criteria defined in the review protocol. Although the automatic search was carried out using indexers, Fig. 1 shows the results obtained in each activity of this process, classified according to the main computer digital libraries. A brief description of each activity of the process is given below:

1. *Automatic search.* The search string was adapted and executed in each indexer, collecting 1708 primary studies for further analysis.

Table 3. Data extraction form.

	RQ1. How is MDE used to build and maintain software user interfaces?	
EC1	Paradigm type	[Model-Driven Development, models@run.time]
EC2	Platform type	[Web Application, Mobile Application, Desktop Application, Does not specify]
EC3	Type of solution developed	[Methodology, Framework, Architecture, Middleware, Metamodel, Domain Specific Language (DSL), Transformations, Other]
EC4	Modeling and serialization language used	[MOF, ECORE, UML, IFML, OCL, XML, XMI, RDF, RDFS, OWL, JSON, Other]
EC5	Development tool used to build the DSL	[Sirius, Eugenia, EMF (Eclipse Model Framework), MetaEdit +, DSL Tools, Xtext, Other]
EC6	Development tool used to support transformations	[ATL, ACCELEO, QVT, VIATRA, M2T, MofScript, Other]
EC7	Programming language in which the UI artifacts are generated	[Java, JavaScript, Python, C + +, C#, ASP.NET, Objective-C, HTML, Other)
EC8	Operating system on which the generated UI artifacts run	[Windows, Android, iOS, Windows Phone, Other]
	RQ2. How is the research addressed in studies related to using MDE to build and maintain software user interfaces?	
EC9	Validation type	[Proof of Concept, Survey, Case Study, Experiment, None]
EC10	Study type	[New, Extension]
EC11	Approach scope	[Industry, Academy]

2. *First selection.* The titles, abstracts and keywords of the retrieved studies were evaluated according to the inclusion and exclusion criteria in order to determine their relevance to the research topic. As a result, 56 studies were selected.

3. *Second selection.* In this activity, discrepancies and doubts about the selection of some articles were resolved by consensus among all the participant researchers once the complete article had been reviewed. As a result, the repository was reduced to 42 studies. In turn, a manual search for articles was performed; and the snowball technique was applied to the selected articles, including 9 additional studies, having a total of 51 definitive studies.

4. *Quality Assessment.* As a final activity, the selected primary studies were ranked, according to their level of scientific rigor and relevance.

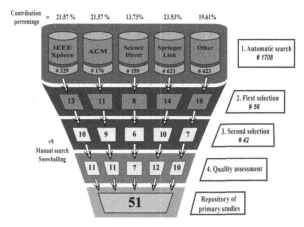

Fig. 1. Conducting the systematic review.

4   Results and Discussion

As a result of the execution of the systematic review, 51 primary studies on MDE proposals oriented to the UI have been selected. Figure 2 presents the distribution of the studies by year. It can be seen that starting in 2005, articles on MDE applied to the UI began to be published, with the highest publication years being 2010, 2013, and 2015 with 9, 7, and 6 articles, respectively. However, several years can also be seen with a low number of publications, which leads to think that it is a line of research that does not have a permanent interest on the part of researchers, especially as of 2015, there is a considerable decrease in publications. According to the type of publication, 32 studies have been published in conferences, followed by 17 studies in journals; and, finally, 2 studies are book chapters.

Regarding the evaluation of the quality of the studies (see Fig. 3), the QAQ1 question has achieved very satisfactory results, with 27 studies scored as very relevant (more than 10 citations), 22 studies as relevant (between 1 and 10 citations), and barely 2 studies as irrelevant (not cited). Similarly, the QAQ2 question presents a favorable assessment,

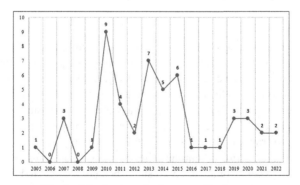

Fig. 2. Distribution of primary studies by year.

with 25 and 13 studies published in very relevant and relevant journals or conferences, respectively. Finally, the QAQ3 question shows a significant number of studies (15) that have not been subject to an empirical evaluation. In addition, of the 36 studies that include an assessment of their proposed solution, many studies (13) apply only a proof of concept. Consequently, the lack of evaluation or the type of evaluation used is the main threat to most of the proposed solutions' validity, reliability, and generalization.

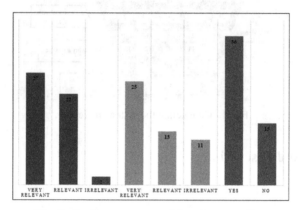

Fig. 3. Quality assessment of the primary studies.

RQ1. How is MDE used to design and build software user interfaces?

EC1: Paradigm type. This extraction criterion aims to determine the extent to which researchers use the MDD and models@run.time paradigms to support software UI development and operation, respectively. In this sense, of the 51 studies, 36 (70.59%) apply the models only at design time to increase the abstraction and automation of the UI artifact development process [1, 4, 6, 8, 10, 11, 21–50], while only 15 (29.41%) cover the use of runtime models [12, 51–64]. Therefore, an important research opportunity is to extend the use of runtime models to maintain a two-way causal relationship between the model and the operating system. In this way. Thus, it would be possible to have more robust and autonomous solutions that analyze the models at runtime to support the adaptation of the UI according to the behavior of the operating environment of the system.

Among the most relevant studies on MDD is Bouchelligua et al. [45], which propose a model-based approach for adaptive UI generation through parameterized transformations from an abstract interface to a concrete interface. These transformation parameters are determined according to the context of the use of the application. In turn, Bendaly et al. [4] present a generic approach that takes as inputs an accessibility context model of a given user and the UI model in order to provide as output the adapted UI model. Regarding models@run.time, Criado et al. [62] present a proposal to auto-adapt the component-based UI structure at runtime using dynamic model transformation since the rules that describe its behavior are not pre-established but are selected from a repository according to the context of operation.

EC2: Platform Type. This criterion aims to know the kind of platforms to which model-driven UI engineering proposals are oriented. Table 4 shows a uniform contribution of proposals for the different platforms; that is, 45.10% of studies are focused on the web, followed by 39.22% on desktop, and 33.33% on mobile. Among the most important studies, Sottet et al. [46] propose a variability management approach integrated into a web UI rapid prototyping process, which involves the combination of MDE and Software Product Lines; while Diep et al. [42] build an integrated development environment based on platform-independent UI models in order to create UIs for mobile applications on three different platforms: Android, iOS and Windows Phone.

Table 4. Frequency of platform type to which the MDE proposals are oriented.

Platform type	Relevant studies	Frequency
Web application	[1, 11, 23, 25, 27, 29, 31, 34, 35, 37, 46–48, 51–53, 55–58, 61, 62]	23
Mobile application	[4, 6, 10, 11, 21, 26, 27, 29, 33, 35, 42, 49–51, 57, 60, 63]	17
Desktop application	[4, 11, 22, 24, 27, 28, 38, 40, 43–45, 48, 49, 54, 57, 59–61, 63, 64]	20
Does not specify	[12, 30, 32, 36, 39, 41]	6

A noteworthy aspect is the existence of some multi-platform proposals, which shows the concern of researchers to create solutions that abstract the heterogeneity of platforms and allow, from the same high-level model, to generate UI artifacts for various types of platforms. A clear example is MANTRA [11], an approach based on abstract UI models to generate implementation code for different UI platforms (web, mobile, desktop). Furthermore, in recent years, notable proposals have appeared on MDE to support the construction of dashboards and infographics, especially in domains such as IoT and smart city [23, 50, 51].

EC3: Type of Solution Developed. The metamodels represent the type of solution that is mainly included in the studies (66.67%). However, a smaller number of studies (45.10%) go a step further to propose a DSL tool. A remarkable aspect is that 78.26% of the proposed DSLs have high-level graphical notation. In turn, there is also a significant number of transformation engine proposals (66.67%) that achieve the automation of models by translating them into code. Particularly, 54.90% of the proposals include model-to-model transformations, while 35.29% model-to-text transformations; existing studies that combine both types of transformations (see Table 5).

Regarding methodological solutions, the review found an important group of studies (54.90%) that describe in detail the proposed process to design platform-independent domain models and transform them into concrete UI artifacts. Similarly, for architectural solutions, there are several studies (39.22%) aligned with the Model-Driven Architecture

(MDA) proposed by the Object Management Group (OMG), extending and customizing this architecture to the UI domain. In turn, to a lesser extent, frameworks (27.45%) based on models have been proposed as an integral solution to automate the construction and evolution of UIs. Finally, there is a minimum of middleware-type solutions (3.92%) mainly focused on using runtime models to adapt the UI according to the operating environment (see Table 5).

In short, further research is required to take advantage of existing metamodels by building DSLs with a notation (concrete syntax) that provides an easy-to-understand and easy-to-use modeling interface for developers and domain experts. Likewise, consistent with the recommendation of the previous criterion, it is necessary to deepen the investigation of middleware based on runtime models.

Table 5. Frequency of solution type proposed.

Solution type	Relevant studies	Frequency
Methodology	[4, 10–12, 24, 25, 30–35, 37–39, 43–49, 51, 55, 56, 60–62]	28
Framework	[6, 21, 23, 30, 33, 34, 40, 46, 51–54, 58, 59]	14
Architecture	[6, 10, 11, 23, 26, 29–33, 37, 38, 42, 45, 48, 51, 54, 62–64]	20
Middleware	[55, 59]	2
Metamodel	[1, 4, 6, 10–12, 21–24, 26–29, 31–36, 38, 41, 45, 47, 49–51, 55–57, 61–64]	34
DSL	[6, 8, 10, 11, 21, 23, 24, 26, 27, 29, 33, 35, 37, 38, 43, 44, 48, 50, 51, 54, 57, 63, 64]	23
Transformations	[1, 4, 6, 8, 10–12, 21–24, 26, 28, 29, 33–35, 37, 38, 41–43, 45, 47–49, 51, 55–57, 60–63]	34

A complete study is the one proposed in [10], the authors present a comprehensive MDD solution to build graphical user interfaces from declarative models. The solution comprises a method called CIAT-GUI and a set of artifacts and tools that support this method, such as metamodels, graphical DSL, and automatic generators of the concrete user interface. The study also presents the solution's architecture and its relationship with MDA levels. Figure 4 shows a bubble chart where the extraction criteria EC1, EC2, and EC3 are related, showing the extent to which the MDE paradigms have been applied by type of platform and type of proposed solution.

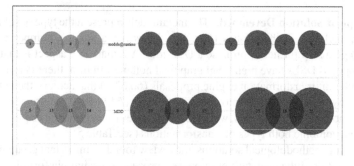

Fig. 4. MDE paradigms by platform type and solution type.

EC4: Modeling and Serialization Language Used. Among the leading modeling and serialization languages used by MDE proposals for UI, ordered according to their recurrence level, are: *XML* [10, 11, 21–24, 28, 33, 34, 41, 42, 44, 47–49, 57–60], *UML* [6, 10, 11, 22, 26, 28, 29, 33, 35, 38, 43, 48, 58], *ECORE - XMI* [1, 4, 8, 11, 21–24, 28, 29, 35, 50, 64], *MOF* [10, 23, 24, 28, 29, 33, 38, 41, 47, 58], *IFML* [25, 27, 31, 46], *OCL* [56, 62], *OWL* [32, 58], *KERMETA* [34, 45], *GOPPRR* [48, 50], and *JSON* [24].

EC5: Development Tool Used to Build the DSL. The most used tool by researchers to build DSLs is *EMF (Eclipse Model Framework)* [10, 11, 23, 24, 29, 51, 62, 64], followed well below by *Sirius* [21, 23], *MetaEdit+* [48, 50], *Xtext* [26, 29], and *Papyrus* [6].

EC6: Development Tool Used to Support Transformations. According to this criterion, the preferred tool of the researchers to build the transformations is *ATL* [1, 10–12, 22, 23, 35, 41, 62]. Then, other tools are used to a lesser extent, such as *ACCELEO* [1, 21, 23, 28], *M2T* [8, 33, 51], *XTEND* [26, 29], *XPAND* [35], and *MofScript* [10].

EC7: Programming Language in Which the UI Artifacts are Generated. The results of this criterion demonstrate that the studied approaches generate the code of the target UI artifacts in a variety of languages; however, *Java* [1, 4, 6, 10, 11, 21, 26, 28, 29, 35, 37, 38, 41, 48, 51, 53, 55, 59–62, 64], *HTML* [4, 11, 23, 24, 29, 37, 46, 47, 51, 52, 57, 58], and *JavaScript* [6, 23, 24, 27, 42, 51, 52, 57] are the most commonly used; while far below *Python* [24, 54], *C++* [44, 59], *C#* [11, 29], *Objective-C* [29], *XAML* [29, 38], *ASP.NET* [23] are used.

EC8: Operating System on Which the Generated UI Artifacts Run. Similarly, this criterion demonstrates the concern of researchers to create solutions for multiple platforms. In this sense, ordered according to their level of recurrence, the review has evidenced studies that generate UI artifacts to run on operating systems: *Windows* [4, 11, 22, 27, 28, 38, 40, 43–45, 48, 49, 54, 57, 59–61, 63, 64], *Android* [4, 6, 11, 21, 26, 27, 29, 33, 35, 42, 49, 51, 63], and *iOS* [6, 27, 29, 33, 35, 42, 57], preferably. Finally, a small group of studies generate solutions for: *Windows Phone* [29, 35, 42], and *BlackBerry OS* [35].

RQ2. How is the research addressed in studies related to using MDE to design and build software user interfaces?

EC9: Validation type. An essential aspect of the review of the selected studies was to define the type of validation that each of them performed on the respective research. The results show that the papers that carried out a case study represent 31.37%, while the proof of concept and experiment with 25.49% and 15.69%, respectively, and finally, the survey reaches only 1.96%. On the other hand, the papers that have not used any evaluation represent 29.41% (see Table 6). In summary, the studies that do not include an empirical evaluation and those that simply use a proof of concept represent more than half of the studies (54.90%), being the main limitation of this area of research. Hence, researchers should use more rigorous evaluation methods to determine the validity of the results. Figure 5 presents a bubble chart that contrasts the type of evaluation performed by the type of MDE solution proposed.

Table 6. Frequency of validation types.

Validation type	Relevant studies	Frequency
Proof of concept	[11, 12, 21, 26, 28, 29, 33, 41, 44, 46, 47, 60, 61]	13
Survey	[51]	1
Case study	[1, 6, 8, 10, 27, 34–36, 40, 45, 50, 51, 54, 56, 57, 63]	16
Experiments	[4, 23, 37, 42, 48, 51, 53, 62]	8
None	[22, 24, 25, 30–32, 38, 39, 43, 49, 52, 55, 58, 59, 64]	15

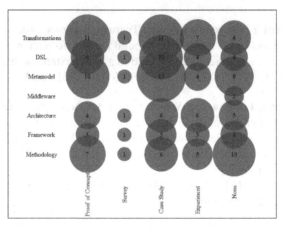

Fig. 5. Type of validation performed by type of MDE solution proposed.

Among the research papers to be highlighted in this section, firstly, the authors of [51] used a combination of evaluation types, consisting of a case study, a family of experiments, and a survey, in order to test the scalability, usability, and understandability of a smart city KPIs assessment modeling framework. In another study, Brambilla et al. [27] implemented three real industrial case studies to demonstrate the feasibility of their model-based approach to front-end and user interface design for IoT systems. Finally, the study presented by [10] presented a case study to evaluate the perception of software engineers from a pharmaceutical company about the usefulness of the proposed model-based user interface design method and tools.

EC10: Study type. It was found that 72.55% are new studies that have not presented a previous phase [1, 4, 6, 10, 12, 21, 24, 26–34, 36–38, 42, 44, 45, 47–50, 53–57, 59–64], while 27.45% correspond to research papers that are an extension of past research [8, 11, 22, 23, 25, 35, 39–41, 43, 46, 51, 52, 58].

EC11: Approach Scope. The results of this criterion show that 76.47% represent the research papers developed in an academic environment [1, 4, 6, 10–12, 21–26, 29–33, 36, 37, 40, 42–51, 53–56, 58, 59, 62–64], while only 23.53% were carried out with the participation of the industry [8, 27, 28, 34, 35, 38, 39, 41, 52, 57, 60, 61].

5 Conclusions and Future Work

The UI (front-end) is one of the fundamental components of the software to guarantee a satisfactory user experience. However, due to the intrinsic complexity and uncertainty of modern systems and the demands of multiple stakeholders, emerging methods, such as MDE, are required to improve the quality of the development and operation of software user interfaces. This work covers the need for an updated systematic literature review on Model-Driven Engineering applied to UIs that gives an overview of the current state and orientation for future research. The main conclusions and findings of the research questions are detailed below:

RQ1. Among the strengths of this field of research is the existence of an important group of multi-platform MDE proposals that combine methodologies, architectures, meta-models, DSLs, and transformation engines. Also, in recent years, studies have appeared focused on constructing dashboards. However, studies have concentrated fundamentally on design time; therefore, a significant research challenge is to delve into the use of runtime models to promote the UI's autonomous adaptation. One way to operationalize this requirement would be to propose model-based middleware at runtime. Likewise, it is necessary to take advantage of several proposed metamodels to complement them with a high-level visual DSL tool.

RQ2. The main concern is the large number of studies that have not been empirically evaluated or have applied a proof of concept. Hence, new studies should be promoted that contemplate more rigorous types of evaluation to validate the existing proposals, seeking a greater industry participation.

In future work, it is proposed to build a middleware based on runtime models to support the adaptation of UIs on multiple platforms, considering the strengths of the analyzed studies.

Acknowledgements. This study is part of the research project "Methodology and infrastructure based on models at runtime for the construction and operation of self-aware Internet of Things systems." Therefore, we thank LIDI - Universidad del Azuay for its support.

References

1. Zeferino, N.V., Vilain, P.: A model-driven approach for generating interfaces from user interaction diagrams. In: 16th International Conference on Information Integration and Web-based Applications and Services, pp. 474–478 (2014)
2. France, R., Rumpe, B.: Model-driven development of complex software: a research roadmap. In: Future of Software Engineering, pp. 37–54 (2007)
3. Mitrović, N., Bobed, C., Mena, E.: Dynamic user interface architecture for mobile applications based on mobile agents. In: Ciuciu, I., et al. (eds.) OTM 2016. LNCS, vol. 10034, pp. 282–292. Springer, Cham (2017). https://doi.org/10.1007/978-3-319-55961-2_29
4. Bendaly, H.Y., Zouhaier, L., Ben, A.L.: Model driven approach for adapting user interfaces to the context of accessibility: case of visually impaired users. J. Multimodal User Interfaces **13**(4), 293–320 (2019)

5. López-Jaquero, V., Vanderdonckt, J., Montero, F., González, P.: Towards an extended model of user interface adaptation: the Isatine framework. In: International Conference on Engineering for Human-Computer Interaction, pp. 374–392 (2008)
6. Khan, M., et al.: A retargetable model-driven framework for the development of mobile user interfaces. J. Circuits Syst. Comput. **31**(01), 2250018 (2022)
7. Zhang, L., Qu, Q.X., Chao, W.Y., Duffy, V.G.: Investigating the combination of adaptive uis and adaptable UIs for improving usability and user performance of complex UIs. Int. J. Hum.-Comput. Interact. **36**(1), 82–94 (2020)
8. Frey, A.G., Sottet, J.S., Vagner, A.: Towards a multi-stakeholder user interface engineering approach with adaptive modelling environments. In: Symposium on Engineering Interactive Computing Systems, pp. 33–38 (2014)
9. Erazo-Garzón, L., Priscilla, C., Gustavo, R., Moyano, J.: A domain-specific language for modeling IoT system architectures that support monitoring. IEEE Access **10**, 61639–61665 (2022)
10. Molina, A.I., et al.: CIAT-GUI: a MDE-compliant environment for developing graphical user interfaces of information systems. Adv. Eng. Softw. **52**, 10–29 (2012)
11. Botterweck, G.: A model-driven approach to the engineering of multiple user interfaces. In: International Conference on Model Driven Engineering Languages and Systems, pp. 106–115 (2006)
12. Criado, J., et al.: A model-driven approach to graphical user interface runtime adaptation. In: International Conference on Model Driven Engineering Languages and Systems, pp. 49–59 (2010)
13. Gottardi, T., Vaccare Braga, R.T.: Understanding the successes and challenges of model-driven software engineering-a comprehensive systematic mapping. In: XLIV Latin American Computer Conference (CLEI), pp. 129–13 (2018)
14. Bucchiarone, A., et al.: Grand challenges in model-driven engineering: an analysis of the state of the research. Softw. Syst. Model. **19**(1), 5–13 (2020)
15. Bencomo, N., Götz, S., Song, H.: Models@run.time: a guided tour of the state of the art and research challenges. Softw. Syst. Model. **18**(5), 3049–3082 (2019)
16. Shamsujjoha, M., Grundy, J., Li, L., Khalajzadeh, H., Lu, Q.: Developing mobile applications via model driven development: a systematic literature review. Inf. Softw. Technol. **140**, 106693 (2021)
17. Tufail, H., Azam, F., Anwar, M.W., Qasim, I.: Model-driven development of mobile applications: a systematic literature review. In: 9th Annual Information Technology, Electronics and Mobile Communication Conference, pp. 1165–1171 (2019)
18. Ordoñez, K., Hilera, J., Cueva, S.: Model-driven development of accessible software: a systematic literature review. Univers. Access Inf. Soc. **21**, 295–324 (2022)
19. Kitchenham, B., Charters, S.: Guidelines for performing systematic literature reviews in software engineering, vol. 5. Ver. 2.3 EBSE Technical report (2007)
20. Erazo-Garzón, L., Erraez, J., Cedillo, P., Illescas-Peña L.: Quality assessment approaches for ambient assisted living systems: a systematic review. In: International Conference on Applied Technologies, vol. 1193, pp. 421–439 (2019)
21. Ali, A., Rashid, M., Azam, F., Rasheed, Y., Anwar, M.W.: A model-driven framework for android supporting cross-platform GUI development. In: 4th National Computing Colleges Conference, pp. 1–6 (2021)
22. Thomas, M., Mihaela, I., Andrianjaka, R.M., Germain, D.W., Sorin, I.: Metamodel based approach to generate user interface mockup from UML class diagram. Procedia Comput. Sci. **184**, 779–784 (2021)
23. Rojas, E., Bastidas, V., Cabrera, C.: Cities-board: a framework to automate the development of smart cities dashboards. Internet Things J. **7**(10), 10128–10136 (2020)

24. Vázquez-Ingelmo, A., García-Peñalvo, F.J., Therón, R., Conde, M.Á.: Representing data visualization goals and tasks through meta-modeling to tailor information dashboards. Appl. Sci. **10**(7), 2306 (2020)
25. Kai, C.R., Liu, X.: IFML-based web application modeling. Procedia Comput. Sci. **166**, 129–133 (2020)
26. Sabraoui, A., et al.: MDD approach for mobile applications based on DSL. In: International Conference of Computer Science and Renewable Energies, pp. 1–6 (2019)
27. Brambilla, M., Umuhoza, E., Acerbis, R.: Model-driven development of user interfaces for IoT systems via domain-specific components and patterns. J. Internet Serv. Appl. **8**(1), 1–21 (2017)
28. Roubi, S., Erramdani, M., Mbarki, S.: Generating graphical user interfaces based on model driven engineering. Int. Rev. Comput. Softw. **10**(5), 520–528 (2015)
29. Lachgar, M., Abdali, A.: Generating android graphical user interfaces using an MDA approach. In: 3rd International Colloquium in Information Science and Technology, pp. 80–85 (2014),
30. Zouhaier, L., et al.: A model driven approach for improving the generation of accessible user interfaces. In: 10th International Joint Conference on Software Technologies, pp. 1–6 (2015)
31. Da Costa, S.L., Graciano Neto, V.V., De Oliveira, J.L.: A user interface stereotype to build web portals. In: 9th Latin American Web Congress, pp. 10–18 (2014)
32. Zouhaier, L., Hlaoui, Y.B., Ben Ayed, L.J.: Generating accessible multimodal user interfaces using MDA-based adaptation approach. In: 38th Annual Computer Software and Applications Conference, pp. 535–540 (2014)
33. Schuler, A., Franz, B.: Rule-based generation of mobile user interfaces. In: 10th International Conference on Information Technology: New Generations, pp. 267–272 (2013)
34. Ben Ammar, L., Mahfoudhi, A.: Usability driven model transformation. In: 6th International Conference on Human System Interactions, pp. 110–116 (2013)
35. Sabraoui, A., El Koutbi, M., Khriss, I.: A MDA-based model-driven approach to generate GUI for mobile applications. Int. Rev. Comput. Softw. **8**(3), 844–852 (2013)
36. Frey, A.G., Céret, E., Dupuy-Chessa, S., Calvary, G.: QUIMERA: a quality metamodel to improve design rationale. In: 3rd Symposium on Engineering Interactive Computing Systems, pp. 265–270 (2011)
37. Shirogane, J., Mukaeda, H., Iwata, H., Fukazawa, Y.: GUI prototype generation based on an MDA process. In. International Conference on Information Systems, pp. 478–482 (2010)
38. da Cruz, A.M.R., Faria, J.P.: A metamodel-based approach for automatic user interface generation. In: Petriu, D.C., Rouquette, N., Haugen, Ø. (eds.) MODELS 2010. LNCS, vol. 6394, pp. 256–270. Springer, Heidelberg (2010). https://doi.org/10.1007/978-3-642-16145-2_18
39. Raneburger, D.: Interactive model driven graphical user interface generation. In: 2nd Symposium on Engineering Interactive Computing Systems, pp. 321–324 (2010)
40. Ahmed, S., Ashraf, G.: Model-based user interface engineering with design patterns. J. Syst. Softw. **80**(8), 1408–1422 (2007)
41. Ian Bull, R., Favre, J.M.: Visualization in the context of model driven engineering. In: MDDAUI@MoDELS (2005)
42. Diep, C.K., Tran, Q.N., Tran, M.T.: Online model-driven IDE to design GUIs for cross-platform mobile applications. In: 4th Symposium on Information and Communication Technology, pp. 294–300 (2013)
43. Raneburger, D., et al.: Optimized GUI generation for small screens. In: Hussmann, H., Meixner, G., Zuehlke, D. (eds.) Model-Driven Development of Advanced User Interfaces, SCI, vol. 340, pp. 107–122, Springer, Heidelberg (2011). https://doi.org/10.1007/978-3-642-14562-9_6

44. Frey, A.G., Calvary, G., Dupuy-Chessa, S.: Xplain: an editor for building self-explanatory user interfaces by model-driven engineering. In: 2nd Symposium on Engineering Interactive Computing Systems, pp. 41–46 (2010)

45. Bouchelligua, W., Mahfoudhi, A., Benammar, L., Rebai, S., Abed, M.: An MDE approach for user interface adaptation to the context of use. In: Bernhaupt, R., Forbrig, P., Gulliksen, J., Lárusdóttir, M. (eds.) HCSE 2010. LNCS, vol. 6409, pp. 62–78. Springer, Heidelberg (2010). https://doi.org/10.1007/978-3-642-16488-0_6

46. Sottet, J.-S., Vagner, A., Frey, A.G.: Model transformation configuration and variability management for user interface design. In: Desfray, P., Filipe, J., Hammoudi, S., Pires, L.F. (eds.) MODELSWARD 2015. CCIS, vol. 580, pp. 390–404. Springer, Cham (2015). https://doi.org/10.1007/978-3-319-27869-8_23

47. Miñón, R., Moreno, L., Martínez, P., Abascal, J.: An approach to the integration of accessibility requirements into a user interface development method. Sci. Comput. Program. **86**, 58–73 (2014)

48. Gibbs, I., Dascalu, S., Harris, F.C.: A separation-based UI architecture with a DSL for role specialization. J. Syst. Softw. **101**, 69–85 (2015)

49. Aquino, N., Vanderdonckt, J., Pastor O.: transformation templates: adding flexibility to model-driven engineering of user interfaces. In: Symposium on Applied Computing, pp. 1195–1202 (2010)

50. De Morais, C.M., Kelner, J., Sadok, D., Lynn, T.: SiMoNa: a proof-of-concept domain specific modeling language for IoT infographics. In: Symposium on Visual Languages and Human-Centric Computing, pp. 199–203 (2018)

51. De Sanctis, M., Iovino, L., Rossi, M.T., Wimmer, M.: MIKADO: a smart city KPIs assessment modeling framework. Softw. Syst. Model **21**(1), 281–309 (2022)

52. Bezerra, J.D.H., De Souza C.T.: A model-based approach to generate reactive and customizable user interfaces for the web of things. In: 25th Brazillian Symposium on Multimedia and the Web, pp. 57–60 (2019)

53. García, A., et al.: Model-based self-explanatory uis for free, but are they valuable? In: IFIP Conf. on Human-Computer Interaction, pp. 144–161 (2013)

54. Akiki, P.A., Bandara, A.K., Yu, Y.: Cedar studio: an IDE supporting adaptive model-driven user interfaces for enterprise applications. In: 5th Symposium on Engineering Interactive Computing Systems, pp. 139–144 (2013)

55. Criado, J., et al.: Adapting component-based user interfaces at runtime using observers. In: 16th Jornadas de Ingeniería del Software y Bases de Datos, pp. 707–712 (2011)

56. Iribarne, L., Padilla, N., Criado, J., Vicente-Chicote, C.: An interaction meta-model for cooperative component-based user interfaces. In: Meersman, R., Dillon, T., Herrero, P. (eds.) OTM 2010. LNCS, vol. 6428, pp. 259–268. Springer, Heidelberg (2010). https://doi.org/10.1007/978-3-642-16961-8_44

57. Paterno, F., Santoro, C., Spano, L.D.: MARIA: a universal, declarative, multiple abstraction-level language for service-oriented applications in ubiquitous environments. ACM Trans. Comput.-Hum. Interact. **16**(4), 1–30 (2009)

58. Kapłański, P., et al.: Automated reasoning based user interface. Expert Syst. Appl. **71**, 125–137 (2017)

59. Coutaz, J., Balme, L., Alvaro, X., Calvary, G., Demeure, A., Sottet, J.-S.: An MDE-SOA approach to support plastic user interfaces in ambient spaces. In: Stephanidis, C. (ed.) UAHCI 2007. LNCS, vol. 4555, pp. 63–72. Springer, Heidelberg (2007). https://doi.org/10.1007/978-3-540-73281-5_7

60. Khaddam, I., Mezhoudi, N., Vanderdonckt, J.: Adapt-first: a MDE transformation approach for supporting user interface adaptation. In: 2nd World Symposium on Web Applications and Networking, pp. 1–9 (2015)

61. Criado, J., et al.: An MDE approach for runtime monitoring and adapting component-based systems: application to WIMP user interface architectures. In: 38th Euromicro Conference on Software Engineering and Advanced Applications, pp. 150–157 (2012)
62. Criado, J., et al.: Toward the adaptation of component-based architectures by model transformation: behind smart user interfaces. Softw. Pract. Exp. **45**(12), 1677–1718 (2015)
63. Roscher, D., et al.: Dynamic distribution and layouting of model-based user interfaces. In: Hussmann, H., Meixner, G., Zuehlke, D. (eds.) Model-Driven Development of Advanced User Interfaces, SCI, vol. 340, pp. 171–197, Springer, Heidelberg (2011). https://doi.org/10.1007/978-3-642-14562-9_9
64. Lehmann, G., Blumendorf, M., Albayrak, S.: Development of context-adaptive applications on the basis of runtime user interface models. In: 2nd Symposium on Engineering Interactive Computing Systems, pp. 309–314 (2010)

A Model Based on Attitudinal Factors Which Impact the Development of Technical Projects as Undergraduate Work

Shirley Coque[1]([✉]) [ID], Vanessa Jurado[2] [ID], and Guillermo Pizarro[3] [ID]

[1] Universidad de Especialidades Espíritu Santo, Samborondón, Ecuador
scoque@uees.edu.ec
[2] Escuela Superior Politécnica del Litoral, Guayaquil, Ecuador
[3] Universidad Politécnica Salesiana, Guayaquil, Ecuador

Abstract. The degree works are considered as the most difficult step in obtaining a university degree, its development involves a great dedication and effort that determine the success or failure of it. A very frequent problem in its elaboration is the commitment that students have with their degree process, this process contemplates several points of view that affect the progression of the same, this due to the appearance of factors that affect the development of the project. The objective of this study is a model of attitudinal factors to evaluate themselves impact on the elaboration of technical projects for undergraduate work. The methodological approach applied is descriptive with a quantitative research method. A survey was applied as an evaluation instrument to 41 individuals who have been part of a degree process. The results obtained to show a model of global dependency factor such as: Tutorial organization and involvement, Individual students' attitude to-wards the tutorial process, Overall performance of the degree work, Overall satisfaction which denotes a contingency plan in case of problems arising during the development of the tutorial process.

Keywords: Degree works · Reliability analysis model · Attitudinal factors · Evaluation tool · Dependency factor

1 Introduction

Frequently degree works have been a difficult and complex step for students when they try to finish their careers. The degree works demand a huge dedication, motivation and effort, which determine the personal factors [1] that the student should put into practice at the moment of the elaboration of the titular process to have an impact on succeeding or failing.

The degree works are often presented as one of the most difficult and complex steps that the student can choose for the completion of his university degree. Such work requires a great deal of dedication, motivation and effort, which determine the personal factors [1] that the student must put into practice at the time of the elaboration of the degree process, influencing this as a factor of success or failure.

© The Author(s), under exclusive license to Springer Nature Switzerland AG 2023
M. Botto-Tobar et al. (Eds.): ICAT 2022, CCIS 1755, pp. 592–603, 2023.
https://doi.org/10.1007/978-3-031-24985-3_43

The demand for compliance with these measures leads in many cases to the abandonment of the degree work due to the low level of interest in its development, since the degree work is seen as one more requirement for the academic culmination of the student and not as an opportunity to develop the competencies necessary for the work environment [2].

One of the factors that have the greatest impact are the so-called attitudinal factors, which are related to motivation, commitment, concentration capacity and will [3] on the part of the students in the development of the degree work. These factors generate in the students a series of favorable and unfavorable feelings that can affect the performance of the work, including the quality of life of the student himself.

Attitudinal factors play a vitally important role in the development of technical projects, which is linked to the achievement of personal goals and goals, serving as a stimulus to carry out all the necessary activities and tasks proposed for its completion. At the same time, attitudinal factors affect the level of management in which the degree work is carried out, being these the optimal indicators for the general performance of the work and obtaining as a result the desired levels of satisfaction.

A very frequent problem in the moment of the elaboration of the degree works is the commitment that the students have with their degree process, this process contemplates several points of view that affect the progression of this one, this due to the appearance of factors that have repercussions in the development of the project.

The purpose of this work is to identify and understand the factors that influence the elaboration of degree projects, as well as to understand the personal difficulties that the student goes through when elaborating the degree project and the importance of establishing the relationship between the factors found and the dependence of these factors.

2   Materials and Methods

The proposal for the development of the present work was detailed in a logical order of use of materials and methods as shown in Fig. 1.

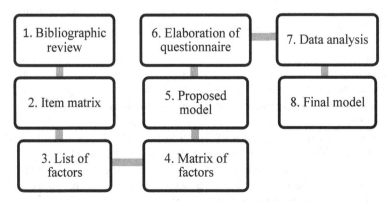

Fig. 1. Logical order of the development proposal.

2.1 Definition of the Proposal

1. A bibliographic review was made of several studies carried out previously that address the problem of degree projects, especially those that correspond to undergraduate programs in technical projects.
2. A matrix of academic articles was designed, identifying the factors of greatest incidence and the relevant findings by the author.
3. A list of relevant factors was defined for each academic article, and a list of factors per article was identified, grouping them into categories of the same type.
4. A matrix of "Affected by" and "Affecting" factors was developed, indicating which factors influence others (Affecting) and which are influenced (Affected by), which have an impact on the performance of the degree work.
5. Based on the matrix, the first model for the analysis of the incidence of attitudinal factors was developed.
6. Elaboration of a questionnaire to carry out the reliability analysis of the attitudinal factors, for the questionnaire was proposed the development of two sections: the first (Section A) section referring to informative data and of interest of the respondent and the second section (Section B) related to the evaluation scale of the proposed model.
7. Analysis of the data under the IBM SPSS Statistics tool, with which the correlation of data could be checked under a reliability or Cronbach's analysis.
8. Elaboration of the new proposed model under the reliability of the analysis tool.

2.2 Attitudinal Factors that Affect the Titling Process

This section presents the attitudinal factors used to generate the model. This model was developed to identify and analyze the degree of incidence between factors and how they affect the development of technical projects. This leads to exposing which are the hindering and facilitating factors of this correlation [4], identifying the problem referred to the desertion of degree works [5], identifying the potential success factors in the development of degree works [6] and the development of a final adoption model.

The incidence analysis model is based on a set of factors of an attitudinal nature. The explanation of each proposed factor is detailed below:

- Poor communication between teacher and student (PC), describes the poor relationship between tutor and student in the development of activities that denote effort, the poor communication of those involved in the development of the degree work leads to the generation of disagreements that can chain stumbles and major failures in the development.
- Non-existence of research groups (NG), referring to the degree of inclusion of the participants within an adequate space to generate development proposals.
- Very little time devoted by tutors (LT), understood as the little follow-up given to the thesis work of the thesis students, has an impact on an institutional determinant related to the general performance of the work.
- Lack of support from tutors to thesis students (LS), scarce participation and collaboration in the work of the thesis holder.

- Individual attitude of students towards the tutorial process (IA), personal determinants that play an important role in the performance and effort of the degree work, associated with motivation and self-efficacy for the generation of cognitive competencies [7].
- Overall performance of the degree work (OP), final determinant of the success or failure factor existing in the degree work.
- Tutorial organization and involvement (OT), detailed planning in the elaboration of the degree works, schedule of activities to be developed and fulfilled within the established time.
- Global Satisfaction (GS), related to the success factor, leads to the total fulfillment of the requirements established in the incumbent job.

2.3 Analysis of Attitudinal Factors

Table 1 shows the interrelationship between the factors of greatest incidence in the development of technical projects; indicating whether the factor affects or is affected by another. The symbol ($\downarrow$) indicates that the factor influences another, the symbol ($\uparrow$) indicates that the factor is influenced or affected by another.

Table 1. Relationship between attitudinal factors

Factors[1]	PC	NG	LT	LS	IA	OP	OT	GS
PC				$\downarrow$			$\downarrow$	
NG						$\downarrow$	$\downarrow$	
LT						$\downarrow$	$\downarrow$	
LS						$\downarrow$		
IA						$\downarrow$		$\downarrow$
OP	$\uparrow$	$\uparrow$	$\uparrow$	$\uparrow$	$\uparrow$			$\downarrow$
OT	$\uparrow$	$\uparrow$	$\uparrow$	$\uparrow$		$\downarrow$		
GS					$\uparrow$	$\uparrow$		

[1] Attitudinal factors

2.4 Proposed Model

Based on the analysis of the model and the interrelation of the factors that comprise it, the first development proposal was generated as shown in Fig. 2.

For each factor of the proposed model, a set of statements was elaborated that establish their relationship with respect to the level of incidence with the attitudinal factors; these statements are shown in Table 2.

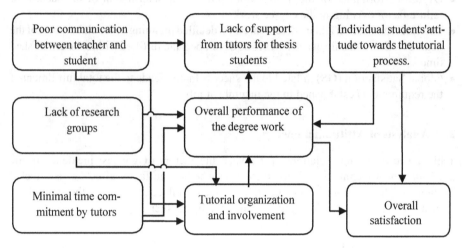

Fig. 2. First resulting model based on the degree of incidence of attitudinal factors.

2.5   Evaluation of the Model

For the evaluation of the model, an evaluation instrument was designed in the form of a questionnaire, which contains two sections: general information about the respondent and the scale of relationships of the attitudinal factors model. The first section contains the academic information of the participants, age, sex, business sector where they work, work department and position held. The second section contains the set of statements shown in Table 2. For each statement, the participant had to indicate his or her level of agreement or disagreement, using a 5-point ordinal scale ranging from Strongly Disagree (1) to Strongly Agree (5).

For this study, female and male students graduated from the Universidad Politécnica Salesiana Sede Guayaquil who have completed the degree option process within the periods 2013 to 2020 participated. The invitation was sent by e-mail with a period of one month for its completion.

Table 2. Assertions associated with each factor of the proposed model.

Poor communication between teacher and student (PC)

- The poor communication between teacher and student has an impact on the overall performanceof the degree work.

Lack of research groups (NG)

- Existing research groups to support and assist students in generating degree work are to a largeextent the main drivers for optimal performance.

Minimal time commitment by tutors (LT)

- It is necessary that tutors dedicate more time to their thesis students in the elaboration of the different stages of development of the degree work.
- It is feasible to adapt the degree schedule to the interests and needs of the thesis students.

Lack of support from tutors to thesis students (LS)

- The lack of support from tutors to thesis students implies, to a certain extent, a low general performance of the degree work and therefore an undesired level of satisfaction.

Individual student attitude towards the tutorial process (IA)

- A good (individual) attitude on the part of the student towards the tutorial process satisfies to a large extent the expected performance of the degree work and thus a desired overall level of satisfaction.
- Implementing institutional devices such as: organizational strategies, superficial learning, self-efficacy and intrinsic motivation, will favor the academic integration of thesis students with the degree process.
- The thesis students voluntarily accept the processes established for the development of the degree work.

Overall performance of the degree work (OP)

- A correct implementation of development strategies leads to expected performance.

Tutorial organization and involvement (OT)

- A correct tutorial organization satisfies (globally) the overall performance of the degree work.
- The tutoring sessions help students to adapt their expectations to the reality of the degree program.
- The degree work is very often presented as a collaborative work with the directors or tutors of the different research areas. They are the ones who plan the development and elaboration of the thesis in many cases. But in many cases, it is often the thesis students who propose the topic and receive unequal support from the supervisors of the thesis. Can good planning and tutorial organization on both sides solve this problem?
- The response to the expectation and organization of the tutorial system is adapted to the interestsof the participants.

Overall satisfaction (GS)

- The desired level of satisfaction meets the objectives proposed for the solution of the problem.

---

3 Results and Discussion

The questionnaire was answered by 41 graduated students belonging to the Systems Engineering branch between November 18, 2020 and December 3, 2020; mostly male

(63.4%) and with ages ranging from 18 to 46 years old, predominantly between 26 to 35 years old (75.6%).

3.1 Resulting Reliability Analysis of the Evaluation Instrument

IBM SPSS Statistics software was used for data analysis and Cronbach's Alpha analysis was used to check the reliability of the model. With the help of the tool the reliability of the instrument was checked, giving a result of 0.949 with all the statements established given the descriptor factors of the model.

The scale for data analysis was defined as the Attitudinal Factors Scale, which contains the number of items representing the first 12 statements associated with each attitudinal factor as shown in Table 2. The statistics of the items comprise the mean and standard deviation of the evaluation made on the 41 individuals surveyed as shown in Table 3.

Table 3. Item statistics.

Item	*Media*	*Standard deviation*
@1. Poor teacher-student communication affects overall work performance	4,17	1,302
@2. The lack of support from tutors to thesis students implies, to a certain extent, a low general performance of the degree work and therefore an undesired level of satisfaction	3,76	1,241
@3. A correct tutorial organization satisfies (globally) the overall performance of the degree work	4,37	1,135
@4. Existing research groups to support and assist students in generating degree work are to a large extent the main drivers for optimal performance. Would their non-existence affect this assertion?	3,61	1,093
@5. It is necessary that tutors dedicate more time to their thesis students in the elaboration of the different stages of development of the degree work	4,07	1,191
@6. A good (individual) attitude on the part of the student towards the tutorial process satisfies to a great extent the expected performance of the degree work and thus a desired overall level of satisfaction	4,22	1,294
@7. The tutoring sessions help students adapt their expectations to the reality of the degree program	4,22	1,129
@8. It is feasible to adapt the degree schedule to the interests and needs of the thesis students	3,73	1,265

(continued)

Table 3. (*continued*)

Item	Media	Standard deviation
@9. Implementing institutional devices such as: organizational strategies, superficial learning, self-efficacy and intrinsic motivation, will favor the academic integration of thesis students with the degree process	4,10	1,114
@10. The degree work is very often presented as a collaborative work with the directors or tutors of the different research areas. They are the ones who plan the development and elaboration of the thesis in many cases. But in many cases, it is often the thesis students who propose the topic and receive unequal support from the supervisors of the thesis. Can this problem be solved by good planning and tutorial organization on both sides?	4,12	1,166
@11. The thesis students voluntarily accept the processes established for the development of the degree work	3,61	1,222
@12. The response to the expectation and organization of the tutorial system is adapted to the interests of the thesis students	3,32	0,986

3.2 Matrices Resulting from Inter-element Correlation

Tables 3 and 4 detail the matrices resulting from the inter-item correlation, while Table 4 shows the values of the Cronbach's alpha coefficients and their respective evaluation if the item is discarded (Table 5).

Table 4. Inter-element Correlation Matrix {@1–6}

	@1	@2	@3	@4	@5	@6
@1	**1,000**	0,707	0,718	0,558	0,701	0,838
@2	0,707	**1,000**	0,686	0,518	0,554	0,626
@3	0,718	0,686	**1,000**	0,662	0,738	0,778
@4	0,558	0,518	0,662	**1,000**	0,618	0,504
@5	0,701	0,554	0,738	0,618	**1,000**	0,686
@6	0,838	0,626	0,778	0,504	0,686	**1,000**
@7	0,671	0,592	0,833	0,638	0,638	0,719
@8	0,544	0,515	0,662	0,555	0,826	0,495
@9	0,730	0,597	0,822	0,587	0,654	0,661
@10	0,793	0,695	0,778	0,588	0,731	0,777
@11	0,577	0,414	0,538	0,407	0,724	0,482
@12	0,444	0,433	0,408	0,489	0,320	0,473

Table 5. Inter-element Correlation Matrix {@7–12}

	@7	@8	@9	@10	@11	@12
@1	0,671	0,544	0,730	0,793	0,577	0,444
@2	0,592	0,515	0,597	0,695	0,414	0,433
@3	0,833	0,662	0,822	0,778	0,538	0,408
@4	0,638	0,555	0,587	0,588	0,407	0,489
@5	0,638	0,826	0,654	0,731	0,724	0,320
@6	0,838	0,495	0,661	0,777	0,482	0,473
@7	**1,000**	0,515	0,758	0,738	0,480	0,475
@8	0,515	**1,000**	0,604	0,582	0,706	0,350
@9	0,758	0,604	**1,000**	0,722	0,616	0,518
@10	0,738	0,582	0,722	**1,000**	0,560	0,466
@11	0,480	0,706	0,616	0,560	**1,000**	0,437
@12	0,475	0,350	0,518	0,466	0,437	**1,000**

Table 6. Total-element statistics

	Correlation element-total correlation corrected	Cronbach's alpha if the element is removed
@1	0,833	0,943
@2	0,714	0,947
@3	0,874	0,942
@4	0,685	0,947
@5	0,825	0,943
@6	0,801	0,944
@7	0,800	0,944
@8	0,717	0,947
@9	0,827	0,943
@10	0,851	0,942
@11	0,667	0,948
@12	0,531	0,952

The application of the instrument on the 41 individuals provided a satisfactory result with a high rate of consistency of the proposed statements as shown in Table 6.

As can be seen in Table 6, the item with a significant improvement in Cronbach's alpha if it were to be eliminated is @12, which is related to the Tutorial Organization and Involvement (OT) factor, showing an increase of 0.003 from the original result of 0.949.

Nevertheless, the (OT) factor according to Table 1 has a significant level of dependence for the model, as it relates several primary factors to itself, which in turn are key indices of the Overall Degree Work Performance (OP) factor.

3.3 Model Resulting from the Assessment

It can be evidenced that the Tutorial Organization and Involvement (OT) and the General Performance of the degree work (OP) are key factors in the development of the model. This indicates that individuals must establish an optimal level of organization before starting the development of their degree work, a detailed planning of the activities to be performed is necessary. In the case of problems related to the lack of communication, dedication and commitment on the part of the individuals involved, it is necessary to define a schedule of work times that allows a record to be kept ensuring the progression of the work.

The model proposed in Fig. 3 describes Tutorial Organization and Involvement (OT) as a new global factor, which encompasses the factors related to scarcity, lack of support, non- existence and negligible dedication to the tenure process.

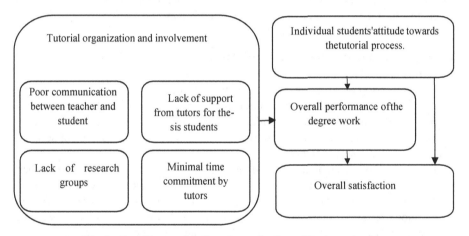

Fig. 3. Resulting model given the evaluation of its dependencies.

3.4 Resulting Final Model

In (OT) the most frequent problems related to the development of a titration process converge, that is why a complementary factor was defined to group all these problems and unify them as a new one, as shown in Fig. 4.

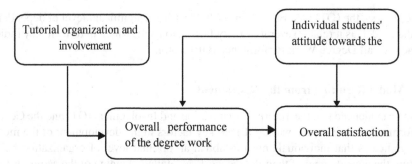

Fig. 4. Final model resulting from the convergence of the factors implicit in OT, denoted as the global dependence factor.

Factors that converge in the factor of tutorial organization and involvement have been unified, in Fig. 4 shows the final model which has a significant improvement according to the Cronbach analysis showed in Table 6. The cluster factors are: The poor communication between teacher and student, Lack of support from tutors to thesis students, Non-existence of research groups, Insignificant dedication of time by tutors, factors that have been named by authors cited in this paper.

4   Conclusions and Recommendations

The initial proposal of this study is based on the development of an analysis model that allows indicating the incidence of attitudinal factors that affect the development of a technical project as undergraduate work, as can be seen in Fig. 2, the model presents 8 related factors, which were measured by means of a reliability measurement software with an estimated result of 0.949.

The analysis of the elements showed that the Tutorial organization and involvement factor is a factor of little relevance in the model; however, it has a very strong relational incidence between factors to be eliminated as shown in Table 1, for that reason, Tutorial organization and involvement factor was considered to define it as a global dependency factor and to group within it the factors: Poor communication between teacher and student, Lack of support from tutors to thesis students, Lack of research groups, Minimal time commitment by tutors, to the achievement of an important improvement with respect to the initial model proposed.

Two key factors in this process are performance and satisfaction, which are factors that determine success or failure within the established parameters of the work. The individual student's attitude is deeply rooted with personal [2] and motivational determinants [8], while the tutorial organization encompasses the problems that can be gendered during the process.

References

1. Vargas, G.M.G.: Factores asociados al rendimiento académico en estudiantes universitarios, una reflexión desde la calidad de la educación superior pública. Revista educación **31**(1), 43–63 (2007)
2. de Universidades, C.: Indicadores en la Universidad: Información y decisiones. MEC, Madrid (1999)
3. Garrote Rojas, D., Garrote Rojas, C., Jiménez Fernández, S.: Factores influyentes en motivación y estrategias de aprendizaje en los alumnos de grado (2016)
4. Carlino, P.: Desafíos para hacer una tesis de posgrado y dispositivos institucionales que favorecerían su completamiento. Segundo encuentro nacional y primero internacional sobre lectura y escritura en educación superior (2008)
5. Contreras, K., Caballero, C., Palacio, J., Pérez, A.M.: Factores asociados al fracaso académico en estudiantes universitarios de Barranquilla (Colombia). Psicología desde el Caribe **22**, 110–135 (2008)
6. Gallego, M.G., Cáceres, J.H.: Identificación de factores que permitan potencializar el éxito de proyectos de desarrollo de software. Scientia et technica **20**(1), 70–80 (2015)
7. Colmenares, M.: Correlation among academic performance and achievement motivation: elements for discussion and reflection. REDHECS-REVISTA ELECTRONICA DE HUMANIDADES EDUCACION Y COMUNICACION SOCIAL, vol. 5, no. 3 (2008)
8. Torrecilla Sánchez, E.M., Rodríguez-Conde, M.J., Herrera García, M.E., Martín Izard, J.F.: Evaluación de calidad de un proceso de tutoría universitaria: la perspectiva del estudiante de nuevo ingreso en educación (2013)

Author Index

Printed in the United States
by Baker & Taylor Publisher Services